# STONEWALL JACKSON

*The last portrait of Stonewall Jackson, taken at Moss Neck.*

Reproduced from the Collections of the National Archives

LENOIR CHAMBERS

•

# STONEWALL JACKSON

Volume Two

*SEVEN DAYS I*
*to*
*THE LAST MARCH*

WILLIAM MORROW & CO. — New York
1959

Second Printing, November, 1959

Grateful acknowledgment is made to Rosemary Carr Benét and to Brandt
& Brandt for permission to quote from *John Brown's Body*, by Stephen
Vincent Benét, published by Rinehart & Company, Inc., copyright 1927,
1928 by Stephen Vincent Benét, copyright renewed 1955, 1956 by Rosemary Carr Benét.

Published simultaneously in the Dominion of Canada by George J.
McLeod Limited, Toronto.
Printed in the United States of America.

Library of Congress Catalog Card Number 59-14841

# CONTENTS

v

# MAPS

(*by James MacDonald*)

# STONEWALL
# JACKSON

# 24 | SEVEN DAYS I

*"Never take counsel of your fears."*

McClellan's advance up the Peninsula between the James and the York Rivers to within sight of Richmond was the most imaginative large-scale movement of the war in Virginia. His leading division, embarking at Alexandria on March 17, sailed down the Potomac and through the lower Chesapeake Bay to Fort Monroe near the tip of the Peninsula. McClellan himself arrived there on April 2. By his own account he was promised 155,000 men but found 135,000 to start with. In his successive reckonings during many weeks of unhappiness he reported that number as dropping to 92,000. In gloomy moments he cut another 17,000 to 18,000 for noncombatant necessities.[1]

Correspondence between Fort Monroe and Washington argued numbers and re-enforcements at length, with President Lincoln taking a hand, and never with any agreement. Numbers concerned McClellan because of both his native caution in the field and his inaccurate intelligence service, headed then by the civilian detective Allan Pinkerton, who concealed his status from most of the army under the name of Maj. E. J. Allen. His reports of Confederate strength were always high and sometimes fantastic. Before Jackson's arrival he credited Lee with 180,000[2] men, whereas the number was hardly above 65,000. Manpower was never McClellan's major problem.

The Federal army moved out from its Fort Monroe camps early in April, but at the sight of Yorktown defenses McClellan halted. Although a determined assault had a good chance of succeeding, he

3

went into deliberate siege operations. It was May 4 before Johnston, who had shifted from the Manassas area to meet this Peninsula threat, pulled back. The two forces clashed the next day in a sharp fight at Williamsburg, awkwardly conducted on both sides, and the Confederates withdrew again. Jackson on that day was moving into the McDowell operation west of Staunton.

Spring rains made all movements difficult and discouraged Mc-Clellan as he followed slowly. Because he expected to gain Mc-Dowell's corps of 40,000, he edged more to the northern, or York River, side of the Peninsula. This led to the establishment of depots above West Point, at White House Landing on the Pamunkey, which supply ships could reach.

From White House the Richmond and York River Railroad ran toward Richmond, a distance of about 30 miles. McClellan supplemented the rail line with a wagon line. He preferred from the start the James River side of the Peninsula for his depots (it was safe after the destruction of the *Merrimac* on May 11), but the prospect of McDowell's reaching out a hand from the north was controlling.

On May 31 McClellan arrived at the Chickahominy, the looks of which he did not like. That sluggish stream rises some 15 miles to the northwest of Richmond, flows dankly and diagonally across the city's eastern front and empties into the James 40 miles below. Some 40 feet wide normally, but variable in width, and fringed with heavy growths of trees along most of its channel, it is bordered in many places by marshland. Heavy rains cause a swift rise and a broad overflow, flooding the bridges or destroying them, and leaving a blanket of water on the bottom lands. The region was thought by upland people to be unhealthful. Small farms were scattered among the tangles of woods, but the roads were poor and after rains or in winter were virtually impossible for wagons to traverse. McClellan's bleak spirits that wet spring had their origin in the physical scene as well as in the doubts that slowed him in the presence of an enemy.[3]

By May 24 Johnston had withdrawn all his forces to the right bank of the Chickahominy. On the 31st, when the prospect of Mc-Dowell's re-enforcement seemed to him strong, he struck at Mc-Clellan in the battle which the Confederates called Seven Pines and the Federals Fair Oaks. For two days the armies maneuvered in confusion, but fought bitterly and bloodily when they collided,

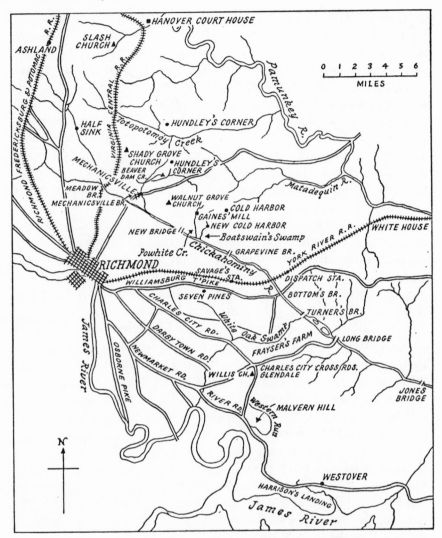

RICHMOND AND THE CHICKAHOMINY REGION.

without material change in their positions. Johnston suffered severe
wounds, and Maj. Gen. Gustavus W. Smith had to struggle with the
second day's fighting. The real change, and the most significant out-
come of the battle, was that General Lee, still military adviser to
President Davis, was appointed commander of the army.

This was not the Lee of later established confidence. He had man-

aged his difficult and delicate duties with the President with tact
and a sound sense of strategy, but it was not heroic work and did
not reach public attention. Nor had his earlier operations in the
lower South or the campaign in western Virginia resulted in a popular reputation. Lee seemed at that time a solid man but not a brilliant one, and he had been unlucky. Those who worked with him
intimately or saw the play of his mind had different opinions, as
Jackson had. But Lee had yet to win public approval. When he set
the army to digging fortifications before Richmond he offended
many Southerners still bemused by a romantic concept of war. Nevertheless, his firm hand exercised a new control almost from the first
day of his command.

Lee decided quickly, having little confidence in his ability to keep
the superior Federal artillery from battering Richmond, to attack
McClellan and drive him down the Peninsula. McClellan had extended his right far to the north to reach out toward a supposedly
oncoming McDowell who would have to be supplied from the White
House Landing depots. ("Herein," McClellan argued in later years,
"lay the failure of the campaign. . . ." [4]) His left advanced over
the Chickahominy, but because that stream flowed diagonally across
his front, his right remained on the left bank. The sluggish waters
cut his army in two, and gave Lee the stimulus for his plan.

Something more Lee needed to know. On June 12 he sent Stuart
with 1,200 cavalrymen—the cream of the army's mounted force—on
a long, swinging reconnaissance to the north, to the east, to the rear
of McClellan's right flank. Stuart was to find out where, and on
what, McClellan's right rested and whether it could be turned;
what was the condition of the terrain between the Chickahominy
and the Pamunkey, and whether it was good enough for Jackson's
force to advance in the direction and by the route Lee had in mind;
and whether the lines of supply ran back to the White House Landing.

This was a mission that stirred the souls of Stuart and his young
men. He carried it out with superb spirit and boldness. The deeper
he circled, and the more he overran the small and feeble contingents
he encountered, the more alluring the prospect grew. In the last
analysis Stuart thought it safer—and assuredly more dramatic—to
keep right ahead than to retrace his steps. With a touch of luck here
and there, and with ingenuity, endurance, and courage, he swung

all around the circle, and came home in a triumph that entranced the whole Confederacy.

Stuart brought back the information that McClellan's right hung in the air, wide open to encirclement. The terrain was adequate for advancing infantry. The lines of supply still ran to White House Landing—he had cut them, though he could not remain.

This was precious information. It gave Lee the lacking essentials. But it may have given McClellan a lesson too. He could not overlook the weakness of his right flank or the danger to his supply lines. Although he knew the virtues of basing on the James—where the line of communications was assured and there was no flank danger— rather than on the Pamunkey and the York, he must have thought more and more about the advisability of changing. This Lee did not realize, and the fact that he didn't realize it grew increasingly important.

What Lee did know was the necessity of bringing Jackson to Richmond to lead the attack he was planning.

The probability that the Army of the Valley might have to come to the aid of the army defending Richmond had been understood in the capital since McClellan's advance grew into a serious threat— at least since April. Subsequent developments of the Valley operations, with their brake on McClellan by holding back his re-enforcements, had placed any such plan in abeyance. Jackson's thinking led him to the conclusion—as his sending Boteler to Richmond from Halltown on May 30 showed—that if he had 40,000 men instead of 15,000 to 17,000, he could carry the war into Pennsylvania. Lee and Davis considered this request, and Davis reported to Jackson, in his letter of June 4, that it was not feasible.

Lee had been attracted to the idea. He wrote to the President the next day that "after much reflection, I think if it was possible to reinforce Jackson strongly, it would change the character of the war. This can be done," Lee continued, "only by the troops in Georgia, S. C. and N. C. Jackson could in that event cross Maryland into Penn. It would call all the enemy from our Southern Coast and liberate those states. If these states will give up their troops I think it can be done." [5]

This strong endorsement of Jackson's idea—"it would change the character of the war"—does not appear to have had any influence on the President, and it may not have come to Jackson's knowledge.

There is no record that Lee communicated it to him or that Jackson referred to it. But Lee did scratch hard for more men to help Jackson, as did Secretary Randolph. The latter suggested that some Georgia regiments just coming up from the south in Brig. Gen. A. R. Lawton's brigade ("I wish they were mine," Lee commented [6]) might be available. Lee agreed that with a North Carolina battalion they would enable Jackson to fill his ranks, although "he ought to have more, or these will not materially aid him. His plan is to march to Front Royal and crush Shields. It is his only course, and as he is a good soldier, I expect him to do it." [7]

Lee had also directed Harman, the quartermaster in Staunton, to collect all troops in that neighborhood, "magnify their number, and march down the Valley" to Jackson. "It will shake Shields and make him pause," Lee added. [8]

This was on June 5, after Jackson had extricated himself from the Federal trap and was in Harrisonburg on his retreat to the south. Two days later, after hearing of the death of Ashby, Lee told Randolph on June 7 (as we have already seen) that "we must aid a gallant man if we perish." He requested Randolph to send the Georgia regiments to Jackson. But when Jackson reported in his letter of June 6, while waiting for Frémont or Shields to come within hitting distance, that he did not see that he could do much more than drill his men, Lee thought that re-enforcements would be lost on him.

Then came Cross Keys on June 8 and Port Republic on June 9. When word of these engagements reached Richmond, Lee assumed that Jackson, if re-enforced, could resume the offensive and perhaps smash Frémont or Shields or both. Lee wrote him on June 11 that re-enforcements were coming "at the expense of weakening this army." Lawton was already on his way with six regiments from Georgia. Now Brig. Gen. W. H. C. Whiting—Jackson's old friend at West Point, who had aided the green cadet in his early struggles with mathematics—had been ordered to pick eight regiments and set out for the Valley immediately, adding, with Lawton, perhaps 7,000 men to the Army of the Valley. One of the brigades Whiting took with him was commanded by Brig. Gen. John B. Hood, the big Kentuckian who had become a Texan and was already in personal physique and leadership a marked officer.

In this same letter of June 11 Lee returned to the plan of Jackson's coming to Richmond. The object of the re-enforcements, he told Jackson, "is to enable you to crush the forces opposed to you." But in the next sentence Lee said: "Leave your enfeebled troops to watch the country and guard the passes covered by your cavalry and artillery, and with your main body, including Ewell's division and Lawton's and Whiting's commands, move rapidly to Ashland by rail or otherwise, as you may find most advantageous, and sweep down between the Chickahominy and Pamunkey, cutting up the enemy's communications &c., while this army attacks General Mc-Clellan in front." [9] He asked Jackson, if practicable, to precede his troops so that Lee could confer with him and arrange simultaneous attacks.

This was the main feature in the plan Lee had devised for dealing with McClellan and later sought to carry out. When his letter reached Jackson is not clear, but apparently not by the 13th. Jackson had already written Johnston on the 6th that he could reach the Virginia Central Railroad at Mechum's River Depot in two days. He had read Lee's letter of the 8th with its request that "should there be nothing requiring your attention in the valley . . . to prevent your leaving it for a few days, and you can make arrangements to deceive the enemy and impress him with the idea of your presence, please let me know, that you may unite at the decisive moment with the army near Richmond. Make your arrangements accordingly"—which to Jackson must have sounded like an order—"but should an opportunity occur for striking the enemy a successful blow, do not let it escape you." [10] Jackson, nevertheless, had not given up the idea that with 40,000 men he could strike far north into enemy territory.

Now, June 13, the day after he moved the army from Brown's Gap to the Mount Meridian camps, Jackson sent Boteler on a second mission to Richmond to deliver a reply to Lee's letter of the 8th, which had reached him only that day. In his letter Jackson reported that Shields was 10 miles north of Luray two days earlier, Frémont was at Mount Jackson the day before he was writing, and Munford's cavalry was patrolling 12 miles north of Harrisonburg. Then the vital statement: "So circumstances greatly favor my moving to Richmond in accordance with your plan."

Jackson added two statements which must have encouraged Lee further: (1) "You can halt the re-enforcements coming here if you

so desire, without interfering with my plans provided the movement to Richmond takes place"; and (2) "my opinion is that we
should not attempt another march down the valley to Winchester
until we are in a condition under the blessing of Providence to hold
the country." [11]

A major blow northward was another matter, and its possibilities
still stirred Jackson. In a rare revelation of his thinking Jackson told
Boteler [12] that with 40,000 men he would move northward swiftly
and secretly on the eastern side of the Blue Ridge—outside the
Valley—until beyond Banks' force, now in Winchester. He would
turn then to the nearest gap, cross the Blue Ridge fast, pour down
on Banks' rear, and destroy him. Then, with the road open, he
would turn north by Williamsport into Maryland and into Pennsylvania. Boteler must take this plan to Richmond, urge its adoption,
and ask for the necessary troops.

Boteler set out immediately, and the following evening, June 14,
he was in Richmond. It was after office hours, but he saw the War
Secretary at his residence. Randolph referred him to the President,
and Boteler went to the White House. Davis told him to see Lee,
and though it was growing late, Boteler procured a horse and rode to
Lee's headquarters. He found the General still up. As Boteler delivered his message Lee listened "with the kindly courtesy which so
eminently characterized his intercourse with every one." [13]

Then Lee began to ask questions. Didn't Boteler think Jackson
had better "come down here first and help me drive these trouble-
some people away from before Richmond?" Boteler said he was
not competent to answer that question, but Lee pressed him; "I'd
like to know your opinion."

"Well, if I have to answer at all," Boteler replied, "it must be in
the negative."

"Why so?" Lee asked.

"Because," Boteler answered, "if you bring our Valley boys down
here at this season among the pestilential swamps of the Chickahominy the change from their pure mountain air to this miasmic
atmosphere will kill them off faster than the Federals have been
doing."

Lee swept that aside and asked if Boteler had any other reason.
Yes, Boteler said: "Jackson has been doing so well with an independent command that it seems a pity not to let him have his own way,

and then, too, bringing him here, General, will be—to use a homely phrase—putting all your eggs in one basket."

Lee laughed at that. "I see that you appreciate General Jackson as highly as I myself do, and it is because of my appreciation of him that I wish to have him here." He asked Boteler many questions about the Army of the Valley, about its battles, about the Valley's crops, and then late at night he told Boteler to come to see him before he left—"I may have a communication to send by you to General Jackson." [14]

Obviously Lee did not think as well of Jackson's northern invasion plan on the 14th as he had on the 5th. He may have realized better, perhaps after talking further with Davis, the difficulties of stripping Georgia and the Carolinas of troops. He certainly had no doubt of the importance of Jackson's written message. That letter he sent to Davis with an endorsement: "I think the sooner Jackson can move this way the better—The first object now is to defeat McClellan. The enemy in the Valley seem at a pause—We may strike them here before they are ready there to move up the valley. They will naturally be cautious and we must be secret & quick. Will you ask the Sec. to make arrangements for moving Jackson down if you agree with me, as soon as his troops are refreshed a little. They must rest in the journy [*sic*]. . . ." Davis added a "Views concurred in" endorsement. [15]

The letter that went to Jackson on the 16th assumed that time was too short for Jackson to engage his enemies in the Valley and then come to the defense of Richmond. Besides, Frémont and Shields seemed already shaken and disorganized. "If this is so, the sooner you unite with this army the better," Lee told Jackson. [16]

There was strong warning about secrecy. "The country is full of spies, and our plans are immediately carried to the enemy," Lee wrote. He wished Jackson to spread the idea among his troops that they were maneuvering against the enemy in their front. Troops left in the Valley should be disposed so as to deceive the enemy. "To be efficacious, the movement must be secret." He had said as much on the 11th, and he repeated it with great emphasis. He told Jackson also that "I should like to have the advantage of your views and be able to confer with you. Will meet you at some point on your approach to the Chickahominy." [17]

Jackson went immediately into action. Lee had made no effort to conceal the dispatch of Lawton's and later Whiting's commands toward the Valley. Though he sought to have the Richmond newspapers keep silent about the movement of Whiting's men, perhaps not to overdo public talk of the movement, he did not try to conceal, and even seemed to display, the passage of the troops, apparently in the confidence that spies would carry the news to Washington and that Stanton and Lincoln would be concerned once more about what a re-enforced Jackson in the Valley might do.[18]

Jackson knew how to play this game. He saw to it that captured Federal officers, who would soon be exchanged, caught glimpses of the re-enforcements coming in, knowing the officers would carry the news to Washington. Munford on outpost duty in Harrisonburg carried the deception further. When a Federal major and a surgeon came under a flag of truce to discuss the release of wounded soldiers, Munford asked them to wait in an adjoining room while he sent their request back to Jackson. The waiting visitors heard an orderly arrive at Munford's room and report that he came from Jackson. When Munford asked for news, the orderly burst out with tales of re-enforcements.

"The road from Staunton this way is chock-full of soldiers, cannon, and wagons, coming to re-enforce Jackson in his march down the Valley," he said. "There is General Whiting, General Hood, General Lawton, and General I-Don't-know-who. I never saw so many soldiers and cannon together in my life. People say there are thirty thousand of them." [19]

All this poured through the thin walls into the next room, and the eager Federal ears absorbed it with excitement. When Munford reported eventually that Jackson would not agree to their proposal, the Federal negotiators returned to Frémont carrying the tall tales. As they did so Munford's kinsman, William Gilmer, returned to his role of trooper after playing this amateur drama of deception in which he pretended to be the orderly.

Jackson instructed Munford on the 13th to cut all communications "between us and the enemy." He directed him to impress on bearers of a flag of truce "an idea of a heavy advance on our part, and let them return under such impression." [20] After Lee directed Jackson on the 16th to deceive the enemy and "be careful to guard from friends and foes" his purpose to leave the Valley, Jackson was back at Munford again: "Do all you can," he directed on the 17th, "to cut off communication across the lines between us and the enemy. Also let there be as little communication as practicable between your command and that of the infantry. Let your couriers be men you can trust, and caution them against carrying news forward, as it may thereby reach the enemy." [21]

Later that day Jackson told Munford that citizens who drove their cattle to the Confederate side of the lines would have to remain a few days. He wanted to talk with Munford and asked for a meeting at Mount Sydney that night. "I will be on my horse at the north end of the town, so you need not inquire after me," Jackson wrote him. "I do not desire it to be known that I am absent from this point." [22]

To his own officers Jackson said nothing. He welcomed Whiting on the 17th with a friendly note as soon as that officer reached Staunton, directed him to move his command to Mount Crawford, and asked him to come to his headquarters. But when Whiting came, Jackson told him to turn around and march back to Staunton.

Whiting, once away from the General's presence, exploded. "I believe Jackson hasn't any more sense than my horse," he exclaimed. When he received orders a little later to march to Gordonsville, and nothing more, he thought this was too much. "Didn't I tell you he was a fool, and doesn't this prove it?" he asked in fury. "Why, I just came through Gordonsville day before yesterday." [23]

Late on June 17 Jackson left for Staunton, and the troops began to move at the same time. The major movement of the army began on Wednesday the 18th toward Brown's Gap and Mechum River Station, about 25 miles distant. Ewell, second in command, had orders to go to Charlottesville, which, with Whiting's orders for Gordonsville, established the initial direction but not the destination. At Gordonsville one road continued northward, another turned eastward toward Richmond. Whiting and Lawton, starting from Staunton, marched directly eastward through Waynesboro toward Rockfish Gap. March discipline was stricter than ever before. Not only did cavalry screen the advance and block all lateral roads, it also followed the rear to pick up stragglers. [24]

Jackson attended to numerous details in Staunton, chiefly with his quartermasters, and with Jed Hotchkiss rode into Waynesboro at 5 P.M. and climbed the hills to the top of the Blue Ridge at Rockfish Gap. They reached it after night when Whiting's and Lawton's

men were camped for miles up the slopes. Their campfires (Hotchkiss thought) made "a very fine sight." The two spent a long time
looking for the General's wagons, and Hotchkiss finally reported:
"General, I fear we will not find our wagons tonight," only to have
Jackson turn on him with earnestness. "Never," he said, "never take
counsel of your fears."

Next day (the 19th), after they had dropped down to Mechum
River, Jackson called Dabney to his room, locked the door, and told
him that he was going to Richmond to see Lee.[25] The army, he told
Dabney, must push through to Richmond to join in a major operation against McClellan. During his absence Dabney must direct the
movement. He should follow the railroad, with Ewell in the lead.
Secrecy must be maintained, and the General wrote out a series of
precautions for Dabney to observe about it. Then he had his trunk
put on a train, and shook hands all around without telling anybody
else anything, "saying good-bye as earnestly as if he was off to
Europe." [26]

The young bucks of the staff left behind looked at each other
with puzzled eyes. "What the devil is he up to now?" one of them
asked. In Charlottesville an inquisitive fellow, inexperienced in
asking questions of the General, blurted out: "General, where *are*
you going?"

"Can you keep a secret? Yes? Ah, so can I," was the answer.[27]

Ewell knew nothing beyond his Charlottesville destination. When
he and Dabney dined that night, he fretted about his ignorance
of what was happening, as he had when perched on the Blue Ridge
in early May.

"Here, now," Ewell complained, "the General has gone off on
the railroad without intrusting to me, his senior major general, any
order, or any hint whither we are going; but Harman, his quartermaster, enjoys his full confidence, I suppose, for I hear that he is
telling the troops that we are going to Richmond to fight McClellan."

Dabney, with the secret locked in his own head, tried to reassure
Ewell of Jackson's regard for him. "As for Major Harman," he continued, "he has not heard a word more than others. If he thinks we
are going to Richmond, it is only his surmise, which I suppose every
intelligent private is making." [28]

The orders for secrecy and strict guarding of lines of communication went down to all ranks. Jackson saw one of Hood's Texans quit

the line of march to make for a cherry tree and asked where he was going.

"I don't know," the soldier replied.

"What is your command?"

"I don't know."

"What state are you from?"

"I don't know."

When the General asked another soldier for an explanation, the answer was: "Old Stonewall and General Hood gave orders yesterday that we were not to know anything until after the next fight." *

Jackson's transportation plan went into effect at Mechum's River Station. He could muster only about 200 cars on the Virginia Central, far from enough to carry his approximately 18,500 men. To make the most of these, he directed army stores, artillery (apparently only in part), and baggage to be loaded on freight cars. The passenger cars and some others he directed to pick up the rear brigades, transport them for a while, return for the brigades then in the rear, and repeat the process. The wagon train, the cavalry, and part of the artillery marched, the infantry marched and rode by turns.[29]

The June weather was good, and the columns wound down through the Albemarle country with early summer ablaze, the men stirring up the red dust of the Virginia Piedmont.[30] Marching and riding, they passed through Charlottesville, saw the two sycamore trees that people said Jefferson planted at the gateposts of Shadwell, where he was born,[31] and headed northward toward Gordonsville.

To the younger half of the staff—the "genial" Boswell,† the "impulsive" Ned Willis, the "witty, droll, and handsome" Crutchfield, the "always pleasant, ever faithful" McGuire, the "best-beloved" Pendleton—it was almost like a holiday. Through Albemarle and Louisa they found the lighted parlors with bright girls and merry music, "seeking new Desdemonas at the close of every day," and rather glad that Major Dabney was busy with official duties, "for

---

* Later during the march toward Richmond, when Jackson left Frederickshall long before dawn to confer with Lee, his own outpost held him up (Jackson being unwilling himself at first to tell who he was) for identification. The captain of the picket did identify him ultimately. Jackson ordered both to say nothing of his passage, and continued to ride.

† This was Lieut. (later Capt.) James Keith Boswell, Jackson's engineer officer, a young Virginian from Fauquier County who was highly regarded at headquarters and was especially intimate with Hotchkiss and Douglas. He was killed in the volley (May 2, 1863) that wounded Jackson.

he was too old, and too reverend, and too unelastic to fit in such a crowd." [32]

Back in Richmond, Boteler, completing his work in the capital, went again on the night of the 18th to see Lee. Referring to their earlier conversation, Lee told him that the movement to the north proposed by Jackson would have to be postponed "for reasons which I have already communicated to him, and of which you will soon be apprised." He gave Boteler a letter for Jackson and suggested that he had better stop in Charlottesville and wait for orders there.

This seemed strange to Boteler, but he asked no questions. Next day, Thursday, June 19, he left for Charlottesville and arrived about noon. The town was in a fever of excitement, with a cordon of pickets posted around, preventing all movement from the place. People told him that at least a dozen trains of empty cars had passed through hours before to the Valley.

"Presently," Boteler remembered, "the scream of an engine announced an approaching train, and as it came thundering up to the station I saw, as I expected, it was filled with troops, who not only fully occupied the interior of the cars, but likewise their roofs, and, in fact, seemed to cover them over like clusters of bees. . . . I recognized Jackson, who was seated in a postal car next to the tender, and who, as I approached, said in his quick, sententious way:

" 'Glad to see you, jump in!', at the same time extending his hand to assist me in clambering up at the side door.

" 'Got a pencil?' he asked.

" 'Yes,' I replied.

" 'Paper?'

" 'Yes.'

" 'Then sit down, please, and write as I shall dictate to you.' "

The orders poured out. On reaching Gordonsville telegraph to Dabney in Charlottesville to telegraph in his turn to Brig. Gen. B. H. Robertson to send the Second Cavalry (Munford) to the vicinity of Port Republic to await orders, and reply when it would be there. Telegraph Crutchfield to forward a battery of artillery to Lawton. Organize a corps of signalmen, with six to ten additional men, and have their flags made. Tell Harman to have eighteen additional battle flags for infantry made at once.*

---

* Harman wrote his brother in Staunton on the 20th from Charlottesville: "I want battle flags very much. Can you have some made. . . . Try and have the battle flags made, as the General wants them." (Hotchkiss Papers, J. A. Harman letters.)

At Gordonsville, Boteler tumbled off the train to send these messages to Dabney, then approximating the position of Jackson's chief of staff. The next day (June 20) Jackson ran into a rumor in Gordonsville that a large Federal force was on the Rapidan 16 miles distant. His own force was now stretched out for many miles as the march-ride-march-ride movement continued. He held some troops, including part of Lawton's brigade, in Gordonsville, while he sent a private citizen—a local dignitary who was well acquainted with the Rapidan region—to investigate the reported threat to his flank. That amateur scout returned the next day with assurance that the Rapidan was clear. The better part of two days had been lost by Jackson, though not by the troops still coming up from Charlottesville.

To control their movements Jackson had called in Boteler again on the 20th, directed him to go to Charlottesville to see the Virginia Central superintendent there in order to have the troops advance in his chosen order. Whiting's division was to come first, followed by the remainder of Lawton's brigade and Jackson's old division (now Winder's). All were directed to go on to Louisa Court House, some 14 miles east of Gordonsville, except Lawton's units, which would unite in Gordonsville with the remainder of the brigades.

Jackson added details about loading the cars, handling baggage, keeping the trains in motion at night to catch up with troops carried ahead in cars, and numerous minutiae of a complicated movement. "Let there be no delay in having the above complied with," Boteler's notebook with Jackson's orders showed. Especially did Boteler emphasize this among his instructions: "The General requests that the cars continue to run constantly and carefully until tomorrow midnight, as he does not wish them to run on Sunday." [33]

Boteler doubled back to Charlottesville to carry out these orders, spent the night there, and returned to Gordonsville on the 21st. There Jackson gave him a new batch of instructions about moving Lawton's men on to Louisa, sending back empty trains for that purpose, and then sending them back again for Ewell's troops. Boteler was to telegraph Jackson in Frederickshall as the trains arrived. Jackson was watching the movement intently. Though he directed the troops to march so as not to be distressed—"say some fifteen miles per day"—he wanted no lagging. But he would not move on Sunday.

On Sunday, June 22, accordingly, the whole movement ground
to a halt. Jackson had ridden by train the previous evening to Frederickshall, accompanied by Dabney, and found quarters at the
Nathaniel Harris home. Whiting and Hood were there too.[34] Jackson attended a religious service in Hood's brigade during the afternoon, but did no military work that day except to summon Dabney's
brother, C. W. Dabney, a lawyer of Hanover, who knew the countryside, to be his guide in a part of Virginia which the General did not
know at all.

The advance units of the army now in the Frederickshall neighborhood, some 50 miles from Richmond, were far from where the
left flank of Lee's army confronted Brig. Gen. Fitz-John Porter's
Fifth Corps of McClellan's army on the left bank of the Chickahominy. Jackson's men, enjoying the day of rest, the better because
of the heavy rain as they passed through Louisa, were still puzzled
about where they were going. When they turned eastward at Gordonsville, one series of possibilities died—in spite of a talkative
Presbyterian minister who told one of the Valley soldiers there, "as
a profound secret, not to be breathed to a mortal man, that we
would move at daybreak on Culpeper Court House to intercept a
column of the enemy coming across the mountains . . . he had it
from General Jackson himself." [35] But they could still turn north
for Fredericksburg, and many men thought they would.

The army was now five days out of its camps at Weyer's Cave,
but some of it had been held up by the false rumor in Gordonsville,
and all of it was stretched out at ease on this Sunday. The distance
from the Valley camps was 80 to 85 miles. The army had marched
four days, or in some units less. At the specified rate of "some fifteen
miles per day," it could not have covered the distance, but the railroad pickup arrangement had helped. The men had been subjected
to the hardship that any such march entails, but there is no evidence
to show severe or exhausting strain. The Valley veterans had known
much worse.

Unless Jackson had a bad night on the 21st–22nd, he does not
appear to have been under more physical hardship than on many
previous occasions. Nor does he appear to have considered the
pressure to speed the movement so great that he could not rest on
this Sunday. Lee's letter of ten days ago had directed him to "move
rapidly to Ashland by rail or otherwise," and he had moved well,

perhaps even "rapidly," thus far, though he was still approximately 32 to 34 miles from Ashland, his rear units much farther. Now he had something else on his mind.

An hour past midnight on the night of June 22nd–23rd Jackson set out on a 52-mile ride to Lee's headquarters in the Dabb house on the Nine Mile Road east of Richmond. The evening before, Mrs. Harris had asked him whether he wished breakfast. His policy of secrecy held, and he told her to have it at the usual time. But when she was ready, there was no Jackson. She inquired of the General's servant, Jim Lewis. He was surprised that anyone should think the General was waiting for a civilian breakfast. The General, he told her, had left at 1 A.M. and "I spec' by this time he's whipping Banks in the Valley." [36]

"By this time" Jackson—riding hard with Charles Harris, Harman, and an unidentified guide—was covering the long miles toward Richmond through the night and day hours, taking relays of horses and punishing them severely, but punishing himself more.[37] He was traveling incognito, still maintaining the secrecy that had characterized the entire movement, with a pass from General Whiting for "one officer," unidentified.

Fourteen hours later, about 3 o'clock in the afternoon of June 23, Jackson drew up to Lee's headquarters. Travel-worn, tired, undemonstrative, and a little formal in these surroundings, he swung off his horse and looked around the headquarters of a superior officer he admired greatly but knew little from personal contact.

Gen. D. H. Hill saw Jackson thus a little later and noted how tired he looked.[38] Jackson had not wished to interrupt Lee when he heard the army commander was busy, and had waited outside. Now Hill and Jackson went in together for Lee's greeting. Jackson refused food but accepted a glass of milk. Presently Longstreet and A. P. Hill came in—Longstreet broad and strong of body, assured and confident, basking now in the reputation gained at Seven Pines that was not to be modified for years, possessed of a solid foundation of military knowledge and capable on occasion of blunt talk; the younger Hill slender and seemingly frail, with a touch of neat elegance in his uniform and appearance and of eagerness and suppressed excitement in his manner, sensitive and proud and insistent on his rights, and capable of bold and dramatic action.

Jackson knew them both, most recently from association with

Longstreet at Manassas and with Hill (a member of his West Point class until health forced him back a year) in the Valley before Manassas.

If Jackson looked at them questioningly, it was they who were the more curious. All men turned and stared at Jackson now, trying to penetrate the surface of that personality that seemed colorless in repose yet obviously—from the record—must be dynamic in action. Whether he knew it is uncertain, but Jackson stood on a pinnacle, and there was none beside him. The pinnacle seemed higher because he had appeared, a little while ago, unlikely to loom so high. Though he was not a man to encourage questioning, the others must have tried to draw him out. He was both hero and curiosity, and the combination was puzzling.

Jackson had arrived on the eve, almost literally, of Lee's first attack on McClellan. To the generals who would direct the attack, now gathered in the Dabb house, Lee reviewed, and for Jackson outlined, his plan of operation. His two other division commanders —Benjamin Huger and John Bankhead Magruder, Jackson's old Mexican War superior and friend ("Prince John" of the days of '48), both of whom had retreated all the way up the Peninsula—would have holding duties on the right wing, quite different from the plan of action on the left, and were not present.

The heart of Lee's plan was maneuver, and the chief actor in the maneuver was Jackson. By frontal attack Lee could not get at Porter's 30,000 men in the Federal Fifth Corps on McClellan's right flank without crossing the Chickahominy and attacking the defenses behind it, all thoroughly prepared and probably well served.

The manner in which Porter's men had handled Brig. Gen. L. O'B. Branch's force—much smaller, it is true—at Hanover Court House in May had shown their quality. A. P. Hill's division was now opposite the Meadow Bridges, D. H. Hill's and Longstreet's were opposite the Mechanicsville Bridge lower down the river. If they forced their way across these bridges, they would run into stronger lines slightly to the east, certainly along Beaver Dam Creek, a smaller north-south stream which emptied into the Chickahominy and was admirably adapted, as the Confederates themselves had noted on their retreat up the Peninsula, for defense. Still farther down the Chickahominy was New Bridge, even better adapted for crossing and, for that reason, probably better defended.

Lee's purpose was to avoid any struggle, which undoubtedly would be difficult and costly, over the crossing. Therefore, he planned the vigorous, timely, and, he hoped, unexpected thrust of Jackson's command of 18,500 men around the upper reaches of the Chickahominy, around Porter's right flank and deep into his rear, and around the headwaters of Beaver Dam Creek. He hoped to maneuver, primarily through Jackson's movements, so that Porter would abandon his position in order to avoid encirclement and disaster.

On paper it was an excellent plan. Since it was designed to employ some 56,000 of Lee's approximately 83,500 men (including the commands of Longstreet and the two Hills), against Porter's 30,000, it would leave only about 27,000 men under Huger and Magruder in front of the remainder of McClellan's army—say, 55,000 men—that had already crossed the Chickahominy to the south. Davis had expressed concern to Lee about the danger there. What was to prevent McClellan—while Lee was engaged in his maneuver on his left flank—from surging forward against Richmond on the Confederate right flank?

The question was important. Lee answered it in part by pointing to the resistance he expected from Huger and Magruder and the time created thereby for re-enforcements to be brought from the James and more from his own left wing. He answered the question in greater part by his knowledge of the character and probable reactions and movements of McClellan. That officer Lee could not depict as likely to throw his entire left flank forward in a determined, decisive assault on Richmond.

In that respect Lee's judgment was sound. But his plan had weaknesses for any army that had never fought a large offensive battle, had never worked together as a unit, and would not be united until the day of battle. The requirement that widely separated divisional movements must be precisely timed and the inadequacies of staff resources—then meagerly developed—for battlefield control raised serious questions.

Since Jackson would be directed to cross the Virginia Central Railroad seven miles north of the Meadow Bridges, before he began to turn southeastward, it was necessary to make special liaison arrangements with him. For that purpose Branch's brigade of A. P. Hill's division was to take position at Half Sink on the Chickahominy,

between five and six miles north of the Meadow Bridges. When
Jackson began his movement at 3 A.M. on the day of battle, he would
communicate with Branch, and Branch would communicate with
A. P. Hill. Then Branch would cross the Chickahominy at Half Sink
and turn sharply southward, following the left bank of the river.
As his brigade proceeded toward the Meadow Bridges he would
catch the defenders there in the flank and enable A. P. Hill to cross
the easier.

When A. P. Hill was across, he would turn southeast and advance
on Mechanicsville, which seemed to offer no serious obstacle to his
division. From Mechanicsville he would continue southeastward so
as to uncover the Mechanicsville bridge and to make it easier for
D. H. Hill and Longstreet, waiting there now, to cross.

A. P. Hill's direction would continue to be southeastward and thus
parallel to the Chickahominy, but somewhat to the east of it.

D. H. Hill, when he had crossed the Mechanicsville bridge would
go to the support of Jackson, still farther to the east. To do so he
would have to cross the track of A. P. Hill.

Longstreet, when he had crossed the Mechanicsville bridge, would
turn southeastward immediately, moving parallel to the river also
but closer to it than A. P. Hill, whom he would support.

This was a complex succession of moves. When they were executed, the four divisions, in echelon, with Longstreet nearest the
Chickahominy, then A. P. Hill, then D. H. Hill, and then Jackson,
with Stuart's cavalry still farther to the left, protecting the flank,
would sweep down the left side of the river along a broad front.
Their objects would be to cut McClellan's wagon route to White
House, to cut his railroad line to the depot there, and to force him
back (it was hoped) on the larger left wing, but with the river between the two. With perfect performance the result might be brilliant. To expect perfection, however, was asking a great deal of the
kind of army Lee commanded.

All this Lee sketched for the four generals. To Jackson every
detail was new. His sole information was from Lee's letter of June
11 telling him in general terms that he would attack McClellan's
right wing from between the Chickahominy and the Pamunkey.
But now Lee left the room, saying that he wished the four generals
to talk over procedures. This was an unusual and unwise move.
Nothing was more important at the moment than thorough and un-

questioned agreement about all parts of a complicated operation.

What followed among the four generals is vague. None of them left a satisfactory record. Longstreet, by his own later summary,[39] asked Jackson when he could arrive at a position from which to launch the first move.

The night of the 24th, Jackson is reported to have replied [40]—an answer that is difficult to understand. The night of the 24th was hardly more than 24 hours ahead. Jackson was 40 to 50 miles from his forces. He could not know how far they had marched that day, and did not know their condition for a march on the 24th, which he could have calculated as of the order of 25 or 26 miles for his advance units, more for others. Longstreet suggested an additional day, and Jackson agreed.

D. H. Hill's account [41] has Longstreet saying to Jackson: "As you have the longest march to make, and are likely to meet opposition, you had better fix the time for the attack to begin." Whereupon, Hill reported later, Jackson said: "Daylight of the 26th," meaning that he would be in place on the night of the 25th.

That was a day later than Longstreet reported that Jackson proposed. Even then, by Hill's account, Longstreet pointed out to Jackson that "you will encounter Federal cavalry and roads blocked by felled timber, if nothing more formidable; ought you not to give yourself more time?" But the night of the 25th, with the attack to start on the 26th, was the decision.

In view of the subsequent importance of timing in the engagement, even though that could not have been entirely foreseen, it was an unfortunate decision for Lee to leave to others. Jackson was coming down from the Valley with an exceptionally high name for swift marching. But he was coming into a different region, terrain, and climate, about which he knew nothing; and his movements would launch the whole operation. He needed advice and guidance, and he would take it better from Lee, for whom he had a frank admiration, than from others.

The conference broke up "about nightfall," [42] shortly after 7 o'clock. How long Jackson stayed for food or other needs, or what else he did, is not clear. He faced another night ride of nearly 40 miles and a second consecutive night's loss of sleep. Rain was falling, and the roads, bad enough at best, were now soft and slippery. Though he probably completed the trip in less than the 14 hours required for reaching Lee, this long, black, soggy ride in the wet and mud could not have been easy. It was a weary man who reached Beaver Dam Station on the railroad on the morning of the 24th.°

The leading units were just getting under way, moving sluggishly in the rain, without knowledge of their goal, without zest, without leadership. When Jackson had left the troops at 1 A.M. on the 23rd in Frederickshall, Dabney was nominally in charge of the movement, with no assigned responsibility for General Ewell, the second-ranking officer, or for many others of higher rank than Dabney. No one besides Dabney knew officially that the army was joining Lee, although many had guessed right. Now Dabney, worn out with the exertions and hardships forced on a person with a sedentary background, had reached the limit of his strength the day before. He was forced to his bed, ill with intestinal troubles. He could provide no stimulus.[43]

The march of the 23rd from Frederickshall to Beaver Dam for the front units, though far from good, had not been drastically behind the pace of recent marching. The distance was 12 or 13 miles. The rear elements, however, were 15 miles behind in the rain and the red mud of Louisa County. Other difficulties were mounting. The roads were more puzzling to pick out for an army that was badly served with maps and often had no maps at all. The farther the army advanced, the more destroyed bridges it encountered. But the prime deficiency was the lack of effective leadership.

In that respect conditions did not improve materially on the 24th. Dabney was knocked out completely. Jackson was in such a state of exhaustion that on a day described somewhat mysteriously in the meager records, or not at all, the most conspicuous report coming down the years is that he sought rest in the Henry Carter house, read a novel for a time—an extraordinary, an almost unheard-of, thing for him to do—and went to sleep.[44] Members of his staff found him there, and Douglas thought him "not a very refreshing or creditable sight. . . . His wet and muddy uniform was being dried by the fire and the appearance of his ponderous boots indicated that he might have been wading all night through mud and mire." [45]

Jackson did not yet have Lee's battle order. He had in his head

° The railroad station of that name between Frederickshall and Ashland and the creek of the same name toward which Jackson would march on the eastern side of the Chickahominy are some 30 miles apart.

the details explained verbally at the Dabb house conference and a memorandum which read:

Maj Gen Jackson to be in position on Wednesday night [June 25] on the Hanover Ct. Ho. road, or near that road, about half way between Half Sink Bridge, and Hanover Ct. Ho. He will communicate to Maj Gen A. P. Hill, through Brig Gen Branch at Half Sink Bridge his position.

Gen Jackson will commence his movement, precisely at 3 o'clock Thursday morning, and the moment he moves, send messengers to Gen Branch in duplicate, to inform Gen Branch, who will immediately move himself.

Gen Jackson to move from his position down the second road from Chickahominy, parallel to the first road, and near to it. Major Gen A. P. Hill, as soon as the movement of Jackson or Branch is shown on the other side of the Chickahominy, will push his columns across the Chickahominy at Meadow Bridge, turn to the right and move on Mechanicsville. Maj Gen Jackson will endeavor to come into the Mechanicsville Turnpike in rear of Mechanicsville.

Maj Gen Jackson and Hill will unite here, and taking different roads bear down toward Coal [sic] Harbor, and on to the York R.R. Maj Gen Longstreet to support Maj Gen A. P. Hill, and Maj Gen D. H. Hill to support Maj Gen Jackson. If practicable, it will be best for the supporting columns to take different roads from, but near to the main columns.[46]

On this morning of Tuesday, June 24, Jackson in Beaver Dam could have calculated (if he had an adequate map, which is by no means certain) that his army had approximately 25 miles to march on the 24th and 25th if it was to reach the jumping-off position half-way between Half Sink and Hanover Court House. If he was to jump off at 3 A.M. on the 26th, his men should get to sleep as soon as possible and have as much rest as possible the previous day. They would need time to cook rations, of which they would probably carry three days' supply. Twenty-five miles was a long day's march, not impossible, but in the circumstances not desirable. Since he had two days to cover 25 miles, Jackson apparently thought the rate at which he had been moving should be sufficient.

Yet the army was so stretched out that it would have to be closed up if it was to deliver its full weight at a target. Much time appears to have been spent closing the columns.[47] Marching conditions were deteriorating. Dabney was critical later of young and inexperienced officers not capable of keeping the men up to a long and continuing movement. On the other hand, others—notably Douglas—were critical of Dabney for being "not equal to the occasion." [48] If Jackson had been himself instead of a thoroughly exhausted man, deprived of sleep for two nights (Jackson, who of all men needed sleep), he would have done more than read a novel and take a nap in the Henry Carter house.

Late that night, possibly near midnight, Jackson received by courier the battle order for the 26th—General Orders, No. 75, Headquarters, Army of Northern Virginia—which bore the date of the 24th. The first paragraph read as follows:

General Jackson's command will proceed tomorrow [the 25th] from Ashland toward the Slash Church and encamp at some convenient point west of the Central Railroad. Branch's brigade, of A. P. Hill's division, will also tomorrow evening take position on the Chickahominy near Half-Sink. At 3 o'clock Thursday morning, 26th instant, General Jackson will advance on the road leading to Pole Green Church, communicating his march to General Branch, who will immediately cross the Chickahominy and take the road leading to Mechanicsville. As soon as the movement of these columns are discovered, General A. P. Hill, with the rest of his division, will cross the Chickahominy near Meadow Bridge and move direct upon Mechanicsville. To aid his advance, the heavy batteries on the Chickahominy will at the proper time open upon the batteries at Mechanicsville. The enemy being driven from Mechanicsville and the passage across the bridge opened, General Longstreet, with his division and that of General D. H. Hill, will cross the Chickahominy at or near that point, General D. H. Hill moving to the support of General Jackson and General Longstreet supporting General A. P. Hill. The four divisions, keeping in communication with each other and moving *en échelon* on separate roads, if practicable, the left division in advance, with skirmishers and sharpshooters extending their front, will sweep down the Chickahominy and endeavor to drive the enemy from his position above New Bridge, General Jackson bearing well to the left, turning Beaver Dam Creek and taking the direction toward Cold Harbor. They will then press forward toward the York River Railroad, closing upon the enemy's rear and forcing him down the Chickahominy. Any advance of the enemy toward Richmond will be prevented by vigorously following his rear and crippling and arresting his progress. [49]

The second paragraph dealt with Huger's and Magruder's responsibilities on the right, and the third with cavalry operations in that direction. In the fourth paragraph Lee directed Stuart to cross the Chickahominy on the 25th and take position "to the left of

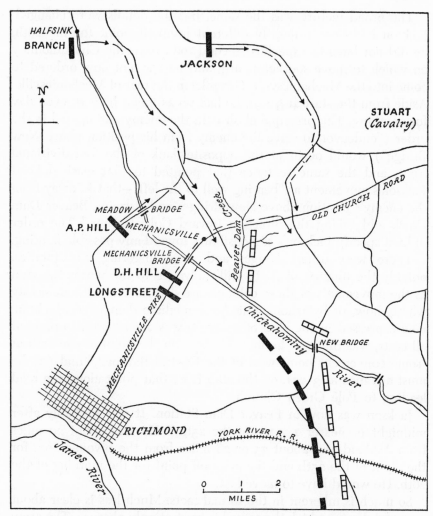

LEE'S PLAN FOR THE MOVEMENTS OF JACKSON, BRANCH,
A. P. HILL, AND LONGSTREET ON JUNE 26, 1862.

General Jackson's line of march. The main body will be held in
reserve. . . . General Stuart will keep General Jackson informed
of the movements of the enemy on his left and will co-operate with
him in his advance."

The fifth paragraph placed troops on the distant right flank, and
the sixth described arrangements for rations (three days, cooked),
ambulances, ordnance trains, and other troop and train movements.

The broad picture was the same, but the details were changed. Jackson had now a slightly different jump-off point for the 26th, he did not have the specified second road from the Chickahominy on which to move southeastward, and he was not now ordered to come into the Mechanicsville Turnpike in the rear of Mechanicsville. Aside from the start at 3 A.M. he had no assigned hour or even day for anything. The principal clash with the enemy anticipated in the order ("endeavor to drive the enemy from his position above New Bridge") would occur at the opposite flank of the four-divisional front; and the same sentence that pointed to that clash defined Jackson's movement as "bearing well to the left"—that is, away from the enemy's position above New Bridge—and "turning Beaver Dam Creek and taking the direction toward Cold Harbor." The order did not specify Jackson's responsibility toward any possible fighting.

There were other changes and some lingering uncertainties, notably the hinging of A. P. Hill's advance to the words "as soon as the movements of these columns are discovered" without saying where, how, or by whom. But the immediate demand on Jackson, now expressed in the kind of order he was accustomed to obey at all costs, was that (1) he must encamp on the night of the 25th at "some convenient point west of the Central Railroad," and (2) he must advance at 3 A.M. on the 26th from that point along the road leading to Pole Green Church.

Jackson was now in Beaver Dam Station. It was probably after midnight or nearer 1 A.M. on the 25th.[50] He was about 20 miles from Ashland and about 25 or 26 miles from the bivouac area for the night of the 25th and the jump-off point for the morning of the 26th. He would have to move fast.

So much is inherent in the formal facts. Much less is clear about a second day on which the record is frustratingly obscure. The army was better closed up, thanks to the efforts of the rear units on the 24th. But it was a bad day. Jackson's formal report, written eight months later, does not attempt to explain, nor did anyone else on the spot. Dabney, writing later, blamed "the indolence and carelessness of julep-drinking officers" for delays in starting.[51] He said supply wagons were often out of place, breakfasts were slow, and the cooking of rations added to the delays.

Handicaps developed during the day. Mud bogged down the marchers. All streams were high. More bridges were down, some by enemy action, some by floods. Though Maj. Jasper Whiting had come to help in guiding,[52] along with Major Dabney's brother, the army was still a stranger in a strange land, confused at every crossroad and forced into detours. But if these were factors of genuine importance, as most of them were, including lack of preparation for the problems the army was encountering—bridge repair, for instance—there was also evidence of deterioration in the commands, nowhere more conspicuously than at the top.

Jackson was an increasingly exhausted man. Though he indulged in that strange afternoon nap on the 24th, he could not have had a full night's sleep following it. Lee's battle order did not reach him until a late night hour. It demanded careful examination, much thought, and probably nighttime action. The one certainty is that for the march problems of the 25th, which seem appreciable but not insuperable, he did not have the power to find the solutions. On the basis of his whole career, such a failure would have to be attributed to other factors than those in the situation itself—to such a factor as his own physical condition.

The long day of struggle on the 25th dragged to its close when the leading units were just approaching Ashland, a march of 19 miles by ruled line, two or three more as the men walked. It was still more, before they could reach Ashland, for units to the rear. This was good marching, but not good enough; and it left Jackson—that precisionist in obeying orders!—with no one ever knew what thoughts tearing at his sense of responsibility. He had to decide now whether to let a tired army drop to the ground and try to drive it at top speed on the morrow; or whether to drive it now through the darkness to its rendezvous with General Orders, No. 75 five or six miles farther, and to arouse it on the morrow after little sleep for another march and perhaps major action.

The Jackson of another day and of a different physical condition would not have hesitated. An order was an order. If he was short of his goal, somehow he would get there. But the Jackson of this moment let the army halt. The men flopped, ate, slept, and thought of what might come.

For their General it was a night of constant activity. A message from Lee reached him. It suggested that he move eastward from the Virginia Central Railroad by two roads. Possibilities of that kind occurred to Ewell and Whiting late in the night. They went to Jackson after midnight to inquire whether such arrangements could be made. Jackson pondered the question and said he would let them know later. As the two officers walked away, Ewell said to Whiting: "Don't you know why Old Jack would not decide at once? He is going to pray over it first."

Later, when Ewell returned for the sword he had left, he found Jackson on his knees.[53]

It was a night for work as well as prayer. Jackson had a report that cavalry pickets south of Ashland had engaged in running clashes with Federal cavalrymen who were cutting telegraph lines. He forwarded that information to Lee with a notation of his own presence. Thereby he told Lee that the prospect of starting the battle movements on time on the 26th was already destroyed. He conferred with senior and staff officers, discussed routes, and checked on arrangements for rations. Still concerned about not having completed his march on the 25th, he set the hour of departure next day for 2:30 A.M.

One pleasure Jackson did find that night of the 25th. Sometime between darkness and dawn a visitor was announced—in strode Jeb Stuart.[54] That sight lighted his eyes! He had not seen Jeb since early in the spring. Now both men were famous, and in some measure for the same spirit and qualities. (The Richmond *Whig* had said just that in its first hallelujah over Stuart's ride around McClellan.[55]) Jackson and Stuart liked and admired each other, the serious Puritan and the sparkling Cavalier, and they would welcome association any time.

Stuart had trotted out of Richmond on the 25th with 2,000 cavalrymen and his three-gun horse artillery, the latter under a strikingly youthful, handsome, bold, and skillful artillery officer, Capt. John Pelham from Alabama, who had left West Point just before graduation the year before to join the Confederate forces. Stuart ran into Jackson's army at Ashland after dark, swung behind the first contingents in order to place himself on its left as ordered, and went into bivouac. He had known of Lee's general plan since his raid on June 13–15, had scouted the country for Jackson (in effect), and gave him now all the information he had.[56] Whatever he may have thought of Jackson's not being where his orders specified, he was renewing an old relationship that delighted both officers.

A night that wore on thus was not a night for sleeping. Jackson must have been thinking much about the work ahead. Dabney had no doubt of his attitude toward it. "His ardent soul," said he, was "on fire with the grandeur of the operations before him, and with delight in their boldness and wisdom." But the work and worries of the moment, Dabney continued, "forbade rest or sleep for him on this important night. He deliberately devoted the whole of it to the review of his preparations, and to prayer." [57] Even if he sought some sleep, the late night work and the early rising precluded any possibility of long rest.

The results were disastrous. For the fourth straight night Jackson lost either the whole or the larger part of his sleep. Innately strong though his body was and capable of standing up under strain, as shown at every other period of his military career without exception, the overburdening to which he was subjecting himself now was much too great not to have important and—almost it might be said—controlling effects on his physical capacity, his energy, his grip on himself, and his judgment. The Jackson that faced the critical 26th of June was not the normal Jackson.

Another officer was looking hard to the next day. McClellan believed on June 20 that Jackson was receiving re-enforcements from Richmond.[58] On the 24th he thought Jackson was at Gordonsville but could not fathom his purposes.[59] On the next day a deserter came into Federal lines and said Jackson had left Gordonsville on the 21st for Frederickshall for the purpose of attacking McClellan's rear on the 28th. The story alarmed McClellan, and he reported it to Stanton with a request for all information about Jackson. Stanton replied on the 25th with candor that "we have no definite information as to the numbers or position of Jackson's force." But he showered McClellan with rumors.[60]

General Rufus King, Jr., then at Falmouth, had turned in a deserter's statement that nine days earlier Jackson had 40,000 men; location not indicated. "Some reports" put Jackson at Gordonsville with 10,000; other reports put him at Port Republic, Harrisonburg, and Luray. Frémont, then at Middletown in the Valley, reported the day before rumors that western Virginia was threatened. Gen. B. F. Kelley had Jackson advancing on New Creek, where Frémont had his depots, but Stanton discounted this theory. Banks' most recent report from the Valley said the enemy's pickets were strong at Luray. McDowell, then at Manassas, did not have "any accurate information."

A letter had come in from Gordonsville informing the War Department that as soon as McClellan attacked Richmond, Jackson would attack Washington and Baltimore, but Stanton thought this a blind. He had so many reports on hand that he suspected the enemy was practicing deliberate deception. He was beginning to suspect that Jackson's real movement was toward Richmond. In conclusion Stanton wrote that the report of McClellan's deserter might be another blind, but it could not safely be disregarded.

McClellan cut through this mass of misinformation with a good estimate, helped along by fresh reports from some Negroes who drifted in from upcountry. "I incline to think that Jackson will attack my right and rear," he informed Stanton on the 25th at 6:15 P.M. (just about the time Jackson was arriving at Ashland). But, McClellan-like, he had to exaggerate numbers out of all reason. He had heard from contrabands that Beauregard had arrived at Richmond with strong re-enforcements, though Beauregard was nowhere near, and that Lee now had 200,000 men.

"I shall have to contend against vastly superior odds if these reports be true," he lamented, but "I will do all that a general can do with the splendid army I have the honor to command, and if it is destroyed by overwhelming numbers at least die with it and share its fate." In that gloomy event, McClellan took care to add, "the responsibility cannot be thrown on my shoulders; it must rest where it belongs." [61] These were unhappy days for correspondence between Washington and the Peninsula.

McClellan went ahead, on the 25th, with a minor operation on his left front (on the right bank of the Chickahominy) designed to straighten out his lines and get in position for a later advance. Heintzelman's corps and a few other troops were engaged in this strictly limited affair. But it included artillery fire and a sharp clash of skirmish lines, and it gave Lee a bad few hours before he could be certain that it had no relation to his operations of the next day.

On this June 26, when Jackson had advanced his starting time to 2:30 A.M., the early hours disclose a worse and a more inexplicable beginning even than the indifferent marching of the 23rd, 24th, and 25th. What happened between 2:30 and 9 A.M. is difficult to discover.

From Ashland to the Virginia Central Railroad is five to six miles. At the rate of one mile in 25 minutes, with a ten-minute rest in each hour, the troops should have reached the railroad in three hours or less. But Jackson required six and a half hours from 2:30 A.M. to reach the railroad. Despite all efforts the army did not move until after sunrise [62] at 5 A.M. Drinking water was short at the start, and many men had to scour the countryside for wells to fill their canteens before setting out.[63] There are suggestions of lack of rations.[64] In such respects as maps and guides, which he had to procure himself, Jackson did not receive the co-operation to which he was entitled.

He was moving into enemy country, it is true, and caution was mandatory. Whiting, whose division was in the lead, had Hood's Texans in the advance guard, with skirmishers deployed in front of all [65]—not a formation for speed. Alarms could halt the column or parts of it, as one alarm did when word reached Dabney that Federal troops were seen off to the left. Being far from Jackson at the moment, he halted the troops about him on his own responsibility, sent out a regiment to reconnoiter, and lost time.[66] Much that day was different from marching at full stride along a macadamized turn-pike through Valley country with which everyone was familiar, untroubled by the enemy—or even with the enemy on his tail.

The head of the column reached the Central Railroad at 9 A.M.[67] Jackson sent a message to Branch immediately so that officer could start his movement southeastward toward the Meadow Bridges. (Jackson's later report put the hour at 10 o'clock, which may refer to the passage of the army over the railroad.) He was six hours behind. He still had miles to march, and the loss of so much time early in the day meant that he would arrive at his objective probably so late as to destroy for effective purposes the whole day.

No sign of this situation appeared in Jackson's behavior. He was in good humor when he passed Henry Clay's birthplace in the Slash country south of Hanover Court House. He pointed it out to those near him, and talked about that statesman, whose speeches he had been reading a dozen years ago.[68] The men were marching in drier country now, and before midday they were covered with dust. Stuart and his engineer officer, Capt. William W. Blackford, came upon them thus, and Blackford was "thrilled to see the spirit of these men, evinced in their every movement, and the lightness with which they stepped, in spite of the tremendous march they had made." [69]

Jackson and Stuart rode over to one side for consultation as the troops marched by. When the men from the Valley realized who it was that was sitting there beside their General on a splendid mount, in smart Confederate gray uniform, a cocked felt hat with a sweeping black plume, and high cavalry boots, the cheers rolled along the long lines that marched past. Stuart's ride around McClellan was on everyone's lips these days.

The contrast with Jackson was striking. "Now a man whose fame was known to the civilized world," at thirty-eight years of age he was, wrote Blackford, "a little over medium height, of compact muscular build, with dark hair, and eyes that lit up on occasions with great expression, though he did not often indulge in conversation. . . . General Jackson was careless about his dress and equipments, and, though always clean, his clothes looked as if they formed no part of his thoughts . . . he was mounted upon a dun cob of rather sorry appearance, though substantial in build, and was dressed in a threadbare, faded, semi-military suit, with a disreputable old Virginia Military Institute cap drawn down over his eyes. . . ." [70]

This was early in the afternoon near Dr. Shelton's. Jackson had encountered Federal cavalry scouts just beyond the railroad, but they scattered. Ewell turned south less than a mile beyond and marched toward Shady Grove Church. Jackson, who did follow the two-road suggestions, continued two-thirds of a mile farther, then turned south, aiming now for Pole Green Church on a road that roughly paralleled Ewell's. They had no adventures before Jackson met again with Stuart, who had been ranging to the north and east without encountering large forces. The road swung to the southeast now, and in the distance Totopotomy Creek cut across it.

Stuart sent a force ahead to secure the bridge. He had a scrimmage with Federal cavalry there, and when Whiting came up the bridge was in flames and some of the enemy were blocking the road on the opposite side. Capt. James Reilly's guns shelled woods and road ahead until Hood's skirmishers and some of the cavalry made their way across and drove off the enemy. Detachments from Stuart and Whiting rebuilt the bridge, and the troops continued toward Pole Green Church with the loss of an hour. [71]

This was between 3:30 and 4 in the afternoon in an area where Jackson should have been at 9:30 to 10 in the morning or earlier. At about the same hour Ewell, marching steadily a little to the west, discovered Branch's force plodding along a road still farther to the west which verged for a time close to his own. Then the road veered away and Ewell and Branch swung apart without exchanging important information and without notifying anyone. When Ewell reached Shady Grove Church, he turned directly eastward toward Hundley's Corner. Jackson, having passed Pole Green Church after the delay at the creek, had to slow his pace because of felled trees across the road, but he was waiting when Ewell came up.

It was about 5 o'clock, and the sun was still high. Jackson had marched some 16 miles, Ewell a little more. Jackson had advanced "on the road leading to Pole Green Church," as ordered. He had notified Branch, as ordered. He was near the headwaters of Beaver Dam, and he could have argued that in effect he had turned it, as ordered. He had kept his line of march bearing well to the left, as ordered; and he had taken the direction toward Cold Harbor, as ordered also. He had heard nothing from Lee; nothing from A. P. Hill, who was to move on Mechanicsville when Jackson's and Branch's columns had been "discovered"; and nothing from D. H. Hill, who was ordered to come to his support. Nor had any of these heard a word from him. He was singularly alone on the edge of a developing battle involving 160,000 men and possibly the fate of the campaign, and just conceivably of the war; and he might have been back in the Valley for all the immediate effect he was having. It seemed plain enough that his presence on this spot was not known to Porter or, if known, was not such a threat as to cause Porter to retreat.

Jackson's orders gave him no directions for these circumstances. He pondered the problem and was noticeably troubled by it.[72] But his decision was firm. He had carried out his orders and in the absence of additional orders he would hold his ground.

One thing he did hear. By 4 o'clock, as the army slogged southward, the summer afternoon was broken by the sound of firing from the Mechanicsville direction. The sound mounted in intensity. Jackson called it later "the rapid continuous discharge of cannon, announcing the engagement of General A. P. Hill with the extreme right of the enemy." [73] Whiting described it as "a furious cannonade" and thought it indicated a "severe battle." [74] Trimble heard distinctly volleys of artillery and musketry and thought that "we should have marched to support General Hill that evening." [75]

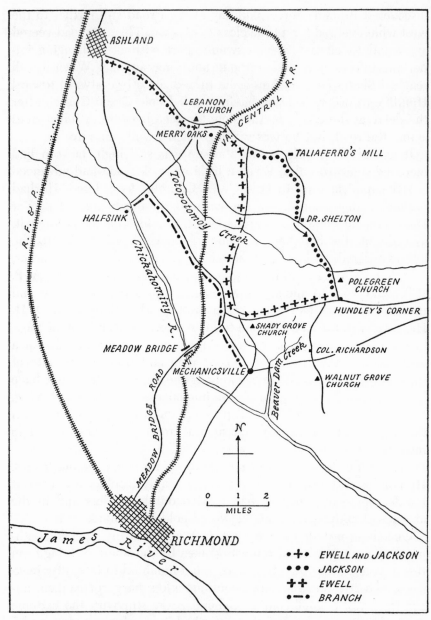

JACKSON'S, EWELL'S, AND BRANCH'S MARCHES ON JUNE
26, 1862.

It was A. P. Hill, locked in combat with Porter. Hill, looking back on that day later, said bluntly: "It was expected that General Jackson would be in the position assigned to him by early dawn, and all my preparations were made with the view of moving early." A young division commander and conscious of his responsibility, Hill waited with rising impatience all morning. No word from Jackson. No word from Branch. No guidance from Lee. At 3 o'clock he could stand the strain no longer. "I determined," he described his own feeling later, "to cross [the Chickahominy] at once rather than hazard the failure of the whole plan by longer deferring it." [76]

Hill made the crossing easily and pushed through Mechanicsville without major trouble. But in the fields stretching toward Beaver Dam Creek his division came under the cool, deliberate artillery fire from Porter's formidable position behind the creek—and the results were murderous.

"Expecting every minute to hear Jackson's guns on my left and in the rear of the enemy," Hill wrote of this dark moment, "I forebore" to attack frontally.[77] That would be unbearably costly. But in open country, with no cover except on the banks of the creek, he was under continual artillery fire from behind Beaver Dam, from gun positions he could not locate. Lee sent him a message not to assail the main Federal position, still hoping with Hill that Jackson would strike at Porter's right and rear at any moment.[78]

Later Lee came up, shocked by Hill's independent action and at the tragic loss that ensued. President Davis, who could not easily resist a battlefield, appeared too and began to issue orders. When D. H. Hill's division arrived, having crossed the Chickahominy after A. P. Hill's advance had cleared the Mechanicsville bridges, Lee and A. P. Hill—seeking now to make the best of a bad situation —tried to turn Porter's left. They sent forward A. P. Hill's right brigade, under Brig. Gen. W. Dorsey Pender, and D. H. Hill's leading brigade, under Brig. Gen. R. S. Ripley.

But Porter smashed them with relentless musketry and artillery fire as they struggled to cross the creek and penetrate his defenses, and they fell back with disastrous casualties, especially among officers who were leading green troops by personal example.[79] Artillery fire kept up along the lines after darkness, and although all infantry action was over by 9 o'clock, sporadic shooting continued. It was late before silence, save for the terrible cries of the wounded, fell on the dead.

The total Confederate casualties of the day were between 1,350 and "nearly 2,000," and for Porter 361.[80] No troops except A. P. Hill's division and Ripley's brigade of D. H. Hill's were in action, not many more than 14,000 out of the 55,000 that Lee planned to throw against McClellan's right flank. They had engaged Porter's 25,000 under precisely the conditions Lee had sought to avoid. This first battle of Lee's with the Army of Northern Virginia was—or when quiet finally took possession, it seemed to be—a day of complete failure.

The major responsibility of A. P. Hill for the attack is unmistakable. He was under orders to cross the Chickahominy and advance on Mechanicsville "as soon as the movements" of Jackson and Branch "are discovered," but not before. He crossed at 3 P.M. without a word from either Jackson or Branch. He knew that Jackson had been ordered to start at 3 A.M. from "some convenient point west of the Central Railroad," thereby touching off Branch's advance. Lee's General Orders, No. 75, were loosely written, but not on the point at issue. Hill had no authority for advancing and ran counter to Lee's orders when he did so. If Lee was at this time at Ravenswood Farm, overlooking the river valley,[81] Hill was hardly more than two miles distant and could have communicated with him prior to advancing. He did not.

Jackson's reasons for not advancing at 3 A.M. on the 26th, from the starting point designed by Lee, are inherent in the record of his ineffective marching on the 23rd, 24th, and 25th. His unwillingness to march on Sunday the 22nd was a factor too. A 15-mile advance then would have counted much in the end.

The reasons for this ineffective marching are inherent in the record too. They include poor roads, rain and mud, destroyed bridges, supply deficiencies, lack of maps, and poor organization which did not bring into play the abilities of senior officers. They include the enemy—from rumors, to roadblocks, to open clashes. But the question remains as to whether all these combined would have been sufficient to delay Jackson's Army of the Valley as much as they did if Jackson had shown the energy and ingenuity of other marching operations, if he had managed to communicate from his own command capacity the power that had driven these men before.

The logic of the record is plain. This was a period of ineffective leadership by Jackson. This was also a period of unparalleled physical depletion in Jackson because of the loss on four consecutive nights of all or nearly all his sleep. Whether at this time Jackson was a sick man in the clinical sense is not indicated (he was sick in that sense before the campaign ended), but there is no question about the state into which lack of sleep had lowered him. In this condition he was a general with less of the personal leadership that counted for much in 1862, less of the strength he shared habitually with others, less of the tight control he exercised normally, and less of the inner resources to rise above handicaps—as he did many times before and afterward—in what history has recognized, not inaccurately, as "Stonewall Jackson's way." He was a victim of exhaustion.

Other questions arise. Could Jackson, starting from Ashland, have done more on the 26th? For an army that was ordered to march at 2:30 A.M., the arrival at the Central Railroad at 9 A.M., for an advance of five to six miles, is inexplicable. The records give no clear reason. It seems probable that the principal reason was the general deterioration that had set in during recent days, stemming in the main from Jackson's physical condition, the lack of any capable officer designated to take up the slack, and the consequent weakening of control. Beyond the railroad the army, despite enemy obstacles, marched moderately well. But should Jackson have bivouacked at Hundley's Corner? Or should he have marched farther? Did he obey the order to turn Beaver Dam Creek? When he heard the artillery fire, should he have rushed to the sound of guns?

Consideration of these questions must take some additional factors into account. Lee's map was inaccurate in its depiction of the relationship of Pole Green Church to roads farther south, in its locating of Hundley's Corner, and in its tracing the course of Beaver Dam Creek.[82] It is probable, therefore, that Lee thought Jackson's presence "on the road leading to Pole Green Church" in the vicinity of Hundley's Corner (beyond Pole Green Church) would constitute more of a passage around the headwaters of Beaver Dam Creek than it did and so would be a worse threat to Porter. Porter's own account of the day indicates that he did not know, while engaged with A. P. Hill, where Jackson was except vaguely, and did not know until later in the night that Jackson had reached Hundley's Corner.[83] When Porter and McClellan did find out, they retreated.

More important, it appears that what Lee expected of Jackson and what Jackson thought Lee expected of him were quite different. The battle order set no time for the accomplishment of any of the objectives it outlined. Whether Lee communicated verbally any schedule during the Dabb house conference on the 23rd is not known. Jackson did not see Lee on the 24th, 25th, or 26th, or hear from him except briefly at Ashland about advancing by two roads. That Lee expected Jackson's advance to be such a threat to Porter as to force his retirement without any large-scale engagement is plain from Lee's own report and from the comment of officers close to him who knew the purposes of his plan.

Jackson's report suggests a different understanding.[84] He did not regard it as part of his obligation to pass far beyond Beaver Dam Creek on the 26th, nor did his written orders specify that he should. He said in his formal report that "in pursuance of instructions from the commanding general, I took up the line of march for Cold Harbor on the 26th." As to the 27th, he said: "Continuing to carry out the plan of the commanding general, I inclined to the left and advanced on Cold Harbor." The emphasis on Cold Harbor is clear and significant. The memorandum about the operation, which he had before the order, contained the same emphasis. Jackson appears to have thought that Lee had ordered him to move toward that goal rather than fight at Mechanicsville or at any other specific spot.

There is additional evidence that Jackson's officers, as well as Jackson himself, thought their responsibility on the 26th was to get into position for events on the 27th. The reports of twenty-nine of these officers [85] on "the battles around Richmond," some written a few days after the campaign, others seven months later, almost invariably begin with the operations of the 27th and ignore the 26th as if it were not one of the Seven Days of battling in front of Richmond. Whiting and Ewell mention the marching on the 26th, and Ewell and Bradley Johnson refer to the skirmishing at Hundley's Corner that evening. All the others assume—with the exception of Trimble, who wanted to plunge ahead to where A. P. Hill was engaged—that the fighting aspects of the campaign, at least so far as they were concerned, were to start on the 27th. Most of them so reported before Jackson wrote his own report of a day on which he seemed to assume that he had done all that duty required of him.

That was also the understanding of Boteler. He had been establishing a line of couriers for Jackson between Louisa and Charlottesville, and he left Louisa Court House on horseback on the morning of the 25th. The next morning he reached Ashland and had a substantial meal with Governor Letcher. "The same evening, June 26th," Boteler's story continues, "I rejoined General Jackson near Hundley's Corner, where we laid on our arms that night, vainly trying to sleep amid the angry mutterings of the coming storm of battle, which next day"—June 27—"burst upon us and raged with such unexampled violence for seven successive days around the city of Richmond." [86] (Jackson appears to have lost more sleep during this night—the fifth such night.)

The inference from Boteler, as from nearly all of Jackson's officers and from the words of Jackson's own report, is that the Army of the Valley was not under orders to attack on the 26th and that it met its requirements by reaching Hundley's Corner. Boteler goes further than the others in the bluntness of his words that the fighting "for seven successive days around the city of Richmond" did not begin until the 27th. That is not what A. P. Hill thought when he wrote later: "It was never contemplated that my division alone should have sustained the shock of this battle" of Mechanicsville on the 26th.[87] It is not what Lee thought. But in so far as his own responsibility was concerned it may well have been—by a reasonable interpretation of Lee's orders—what Jackson thought.

Actually the fat was in the fire long before 5 o'clock in the afternoon, and it is by no means certain that Jackson could have pulled it out late in the day. But although technically his attitude was correct, much might have been different had Jackson been in his correct position the night before, had he begun the day's march when ordered and carried it through effectively, and thus had arrived on Porter's flank at, say, 11 A.M. instead of 5 P.M. The events of the 27th would prove the gravity of this error.

# 25 | SEVEN DAYS II

*"Let us . . . see if tomorrow
we cannot do something."*

During the night of June 26–27 the soundness of Lee's basic battle plan became evident. McClellan had been with Porter during the heavy fighting on the 26th. They had heard through cavalry outposts of Jackson's approach to Porter's right rear, but they did not know his exact position. The skirmishing near Hundley's Corner during the late afternoon and the night of the 26th must have made it clear. McClellan went back to his headquarters at 1 A.M., telling Porter that he would send word later whether to stick it out or fall back. At 3 A.M. Porter received the order to retire. Not A. P. Hill's attack in front on the 26th but Jackson's presence on the right-rear was the decisive factor.

On the morning of the 27th, about dawn (near 4:30 A.M.), Hill felt out the enemy behind Beaver Dam Creek again. Porter had left a skeleton force there with few guns. His men carried out their role so well that Hill's artillery fired for two hours before the fragility of the line ahead was disclosed. Hill pushed right ahead then, rebuilt the bridge at Ellerson's Mill, and advanced eastward. His advance permitted Longstreet to follow, in accordance with Lee's plan (General Orders, No. 75), and enabled D. H. Hill to move, on a line a little to the north, toward his assigned position in support of Jackson.

How much rest Jackson had during the night is difficult to determine. The skirmishing at Hundley's Corner probably interfered

with sleep again. The day's start was not brilliant. Winder was on
the move by 5 A.M.,[1] but not all other units were. Nor did any of
them discover that from about 3 A.M. until well after daylight Porter
was withdrawing more than 25,000 men, with guns, wagons, and
all his equipment, across Jackson's front at a distance of not more
than three miles. A vigorous advance after dawn might have caught
the tail of this parade.

Jackson moved southward—"early in the morning," he said—with
Ewell's division in the lead. His force crossed the upper waters of
Beaver Dam Creek, observed Federal troops to the west, and noted
—as did the enemy force—D. H. Hill's men coming in from the
same direction. That was enough for the Federals, and Jackson
continued three miles to Walnut Grove Church, where he waited
for A. P. Hill to come up.

Someone else came up: General Lee himself. The two had not
seen each other since the Dabb house conference on May 23. It was
the first time some of Lee's staff officers had ever seen this officer
who had come down from the Valley with the highest reputation
of all Confederate generals. For their part, members of Jackson's
slim staff who were with him stared at Lee with curiosity.

What these two said to each other is conjectural. The scene remains—Lee sitting on a cedar stump and Jackson standing in front
of him, battered cap in his hand, the two talking quietly and earnestly [2]—but that is all. That they were talking of the day's operations can be taken for granted. Lee had sent Maj. Walter H. Taylor
of his staff earlier that morning with instructions, and Taylor had
seen Ewell. There should have been no lack this day of understanding between the army commander and Jackson, who, now that D. H.
Hill was coming under his direction, commanded the larger part of
the Army of Northern Virginia on the left bank of the Chickahominy.

While the two were there A. P. Hill's force filed by, looking, Dabney thought,[3] remarkably fit after the rough experience of the day
before. Hill was still searching for the line to which Porter had
fallen back. Jackson, who would be on A. P. Hill's left for the contemplated sweep down the Chickahominy, moved in the same direction but by a road farther to the east. D. H. Hill had pushed on
ahead of him. Jackson's movement was to him a continuation of the
plan of Lee, and the direction may well have seemed to both Lee
and Jackson more important than ever. They knew that Porter—

who was McClellan's right wing—was in retreat. They assumed that McClellan still relied on his lines of communication via the York River Railroad and the highway with his Pamunkey base at White House Landing. They were coming closer with every move to cutting these lines. They must have talked about the best role that Jackson could play in operations which would start from A. P. Hill's and Longstreet's pressure on Porter's new position.

A. P. Hill, with a South Carolina brigade under Maxcy Gregg in the lead, pressed on to New Cold Harbor and found the enemy about noon. Porter had lined up behind a sluggish stream called Boatswain's Swamp, which curved from the northeast to the southwest and then straightened out, north and south, to reach the Chickahominy. Within this semicircle, behind the banks with their belts of timber and tangled underbrush on each side, Porter's corps, now re-enforced by Brig. Gen. Henry W. Slocum's division to about 35,000 men,[4] occupied a position of exceptional strength. The rising ground behind the stream permitted successive lines of infantry, one above the other, to have the same field of fire, and the undulating plateau behind provided shelter for artillery.

Gregg had plunged ahead, passing Gaines' Mill at Powhite Creek and pushing back skirmishers with what A. P. Hill was to call "the handsomest charge in line I have seen during the war." [5] But when Gregg sent back word that he had come upon the enemy's main line, Hill halted him. He brought up other forces, the brigades of Branch, Pender, Archer, Anderson, and Field, organized the attack, and at 2:30 P.M. hurled it at the enemy.

Two hours of hard fighting followed, with A. P. Hill, as on the day before, carrying all of it. Brigade after brigade ran forward across the open fields toward the stream, the men falling in great numbers as they did so. They stormed into the trees and even into the water, and, in a few instances, struggled up the opposite bank. Brig. Gens. George W. Morell and George Sykes—the latter the officer who had behaved admirably at Manassas—were defending this sector coolly and resolutely. To such force as Hill commanded their position was impregnable, but Hill hammered it desperately before he gave up.

This was a beginning so similar to the fighting of the day before that it seemed Hill was pursued by an evil genius. Once again Lee had not been able to bring his full strength to simultaneous attack. Lee wrote later in his formal report that "the arrival of Jackson on our left was momentarily expected, and it was supposed that his approach would cause the extension of the enemy's line in that direction. Under this impression, Longstreet"—who was on A. P. Hill's right—"was held back until this movement should commence." [6]

Where was Jackson, and why did he not attack? For guides he had found men in a cavalry company who had grown up nearby and knew the country. To them, in his laconic way, Jackson gave the goal of Cold Harbor and nothing else. They had a choice of two roads, a direct route that led to Gaines' Mill and turned east to Cold Harbor, and a longer route, farther to the east. They chose the direct road. A mile and a half down it the sound of artillery ahead grew increasingly loud. Jackson asked the guide where the firing came from.

"Over Gaines' Mill way."

"Did this road lead to Gaines' Mill?"

"Yes."

"But I do not wish to go to Gaines' Mill. I wish to go to Cold Harbor, leaving that place on the right."

"Then the left-hand road was the one which should have been taken; and had you let me know what you desired, I could have directed you aright at first." [7]

The column had to reverse itself, had to march back to Walnut Grove, and had to lose more than an hour, perhaps nearly two hours. The staff fumed, but Jackson took it calmly. "No," he said, when someone suggested the loss was irreparable, "let us trust that the providence of our God will so over-rule it that no mischief will result."

Dabney, who had been among those upset, even thought no harm resulted because D. H. Hill had just reached the junction point near Cold Harbor when Jackson eventually arrived. But there was not yet pressure on Porter's arc of defense to aid the heavily engaged A. P. Hill far over to the right of Jackson and D. H. Hill.

The latter began to investigate the enemy in front of him. But a battery which Jackson ordered forward was overwhelmed by counterfire, and Jackson ordered D. H. Hill to pull back into sheltering woods. There they waited. Jackson's explanation, in his formal report, was in these words:

Soon after General A. P. Hill became engaged, and being unacquainted with the ground, and apprehensive, from what appeared to be the respective positions of the Confederate and Federal forces engaged, that if I then pressed forward our troops would be mistaken for the enemy and be fired into, and hoping that Generals A. P. Hill and Longstreet would soon drive the Federals toward me, I directed General D. H. Hill to move his division to the left of the road, so as to leave between him and the wood on the right of the road an open space, across which I hoped the enemy would be driven. Thus arranged, it was in our power to distinguish friend from foe in case the enemy should be driven as expected.[8]

This is a labored explanation. Earlier in the day Gregg of A. P. Hill's division had come under artillery fire from Jackson, as Jackson almost surely learned. The Confederate lines as they were beginning to shape up around Porter's position presented a concave semicircle to the foe; so that an advance from Jackson's area might come under fire from A. P. Hill. Jackson's staff believed long afterward that he held his ground, and restrained D. H. Hill, because Lee had given him verbal orders earlier in the day to do so.[9] Lee had the opportunity at Walnut Grove. He had expected originally that Porter would retreat in the direction of Jackson's position. That way ran the line of communication with White House. But Lee's report indicates his expectation that Jackson would attack. The important fact is that he did not.

Eventually Lee ordered Longstreet on A. P. Hill's right to make a diversion. When Longstreet began to do so, he saw that the situation in front of Hill was bad, and judged that he himself should attack in earnest, this in spite of the fact that he thought he was in a position from which the enemy wished him to attack.[10]

Jackson, convinced now that A. P. Hill and Longstreet could not drive the enemy across his front where his enfilading fire would be deadly, began to rally his resources with something of his normal energy and determination. He ordered D. H. Hill, now occupying the left of the entire Confederate line, to drive ahead. He called on Ewell's division, still in the lead of his own force, to swing into line on D. H. Hill's right.

As the Louisiana Tigers of Taylor's old brigade marched by, Maj. Roberdeau Wheat, the soldier of fortune, rode up to Jackson with a plea that the General keep out of danger. The giant Falstaffian Wheat, as unlike Jackson as any man who shared Valley days and nights with him, had developed an unusual affection for his commander.

"General, we are about to get into a hot fight and it is likely many of us may be killed. I want to ask you for myself and my Louisianians not to expose yourself so unnecessarily. . . . What will become of us, down here in these swamps, if anything happens to you . . . ?"

Jackson, listening closely, took Wheat's hand and promised to do his best. But, "Major, you will be in greater danger than I, and I hope you will not get hurt. Each of us has his duty to perform, regardless of consequences. We must perform it and trust in Providence."

Before the day was over, Wheat was mortally wounded. Even then he asked about the General and, his days of adventure running out fast, repeated a prayer he had learned as a boy from his mother.[11]

Jackson, turning from Wheat, and looking around for a messenger, saw his quartermaster, Maj. John A. Harman, who had left his post in the rear. He ordered Harman to instruct Lawton, Whiting, and Winder, who were waiting behind Ewell, to move forward in succession fast toward the right into the area between Ewell and A. P. Hill. It was now between 3 and 4 o'clock. There was no room for maneuver. This would be direct and brutal.

D. H. Hill, already touching the enemy, came into action first and was heavily engaged for the remainder of the day. He discovered, as all other commanders on this flank did, the difficulties of placing, without maps and often without guides, large forces into line in country badly cut up by woods, copses, underbrush, and swampy ground. Some of his regiments were squeezed out and forced to the rear, others lost their way and arrived at unexpected places. The fighting was bitter, and the losses were costly.

Ewell's division came up next, moved off to the right, and encountered Major Taylor of Lee's staff and, in a few minutes, Lee himself. They placed the division in the gap between D. H. Hill and A. P. Hill, though not in immediate contact with either. Lee, very active on the field of battle, told Ewell to send back word for Whiting, Lawton, and Winder to come fast.

Ewell's brigades moved into thick woods and came under hot fire. They met many men falling back and saw regiments marching out "in such good order," Trimble thought, "as showed they had fallen back without hard fighting." They encountered warnings from skulkers: "You need not go in. We are whipped. You can't do anything."

Trimble's men shouldered them aside—"Get out of our way; we will show you how to do it!" [12]—and kept boring into the deadly fire. They had the fight of their lives for the next hour, and they paid a grievous price.

Lawton, Whiting, and Winder were slower in arriving, through no fault of their own. Dabney heard Jackson give Harman the message that called them into action. Something about the incident caught his eye. Harman, effective quartermaster that he was, had no experience on the battlefield and had never delivered an order of this kind in these circumstances. Did he grasp it all? Could he make it clear to Lawton, Whiting, and Winder? Jackson had told him:

"The troops are standing at ease along our line of march. Ride back rapidly along the line and tell the commanders to advance instantly *en échelon* from the left. Each brigade is to follow as a guide the right regiment of the brigade on the left, and to keep within supporting distance. Tell the commanders that if this formation fails at any point, to form line of battle and to move to the front, pressing to the sound of the heaviest firing and attack the enemy vigorously wherever found. As to artillery, each commander must use his discretion. If the ground will at all permit, tell them to take in their field batteries and use them. If not, post them in the rear." [13]

When Dabney, still troubled, saw that the commanders in the rear did not respond instantly to this message (which might better have been written out), he could stand the strain no longer. On his own initiative, he rode to Whiting, asked what orders he had received, and had his fears confirmed. Harman had delivered a message which, when Whiting took it apart, seemed to direct him to hold his ground.[14] Dabney had a difficult time convincing him of the error. Eventually Whiting, followed by Winder and Lawton, moved out to the right.

They ran immediately into the confusions of the terrain, the battle, and the heavy smoke which had settled down like a blanket on this hot day. Whiting swung out to the right beyond Ewell and came up behind the tattered remnants of A. P. Hill's brigades as they lay suffering under artillery fire. The aides of several generals claimed

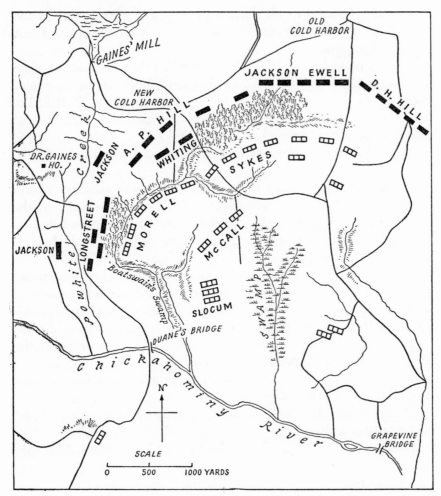

GAINES' MILL—THE FINAL LINEUP OF FORCES.

his assistance, but Lee appeared, and Whiting took directions from
him. Many men were leaving the field in disorder,[15] and Whiting's
arrival could not have been more timely.

Lawton, with 3,500 men, all Georgians, came up from the rear
supposedly to swing even farther to the right. But when he heard
that Ewell was in distress, he went to his aid at the double-quick,
saw a gap in the line where two regiments had just moved out, and
promptly moved into the dense timber and the miry ground. "I met

with Major-General Ewell, then hotly engaged, who, as he saw this
long line advancing under fire, waved his sword and cried out,
'Hurrah for Georgia!' " [16]

Winder moved to the right, following Whiting, lost control of his
regiments (as many another did that day), and eventually placed
most of the brigade in the area between Ewell and A. P. Hill. But
the Second and Fifth Virginia of Jackson's old brigade kept going
to the right, passed behind A. P. Hill, and came up on Longstreet's
right flank, virtually the last troops on the line toward the Chickahominy.

These movements, plus the delay of Harman's mistake, took a
long time. But there were compensating factors. As units of the
Army of the Valley began to edge into position beside the troops of
the two Hills and of Longstreet, the eyes of weary and half-shocked
men opened in surprise and with a new light.

"Jackson's men!" "The Valley men are here!" [17] They passed the
word from man to man, from company to company, and from regiment to regiment. Rumors they might have heard. Here was evidence in the flesh of the arrival of Stonewall. This was new hope!

When all his troops were on their way, Jackson rode along the
road from Cold Harbor toward New Cold Harbor. He was sucking
a lemon. Lee met him in the road, the second time these two had
come face to face that day.

"Ah, General," Lee said, "I am very glad to see you. I had hoped
to be with you before."

Jackson bowed. "That fire is heavy," Lee continued. "Do you
think your men can stand it?"

Jackson pondered this a moment, seeming to listen to the guns.
Then he spoke. "They can stand almost anything! They can stand
that!" [18]

His spirits were rising as the day's climax came nearer. Bradley
Johnson, seeing him earlier in the afternoon, saw his lips clamped
closer than ever, and the blaze of his eye betraying his excitement.
He sat straighter than usual in his saddle, his head raised up as if
to catch every sound. When he gave an order to Bradley Johnson
he called him by name: "Johnson, make your men shoot like they
are shooting at a mark, slow and low, hit them here and here," and
he thrust his forefinger at the Colonel's waist. It was the first and
last time Johnson heard Jackson call anyone by name alone. [19]

Dabney saw him later in the afternoon when all his troops had been ordered forward for action. Riding restlessly to and fro, he issued his orders with a voice that rang. Cheek and brow were blazing red, and his eyes, under the old drab cap, made men quail. He sent for Stuart, suggested a cavalry charge, and called that off as soon as he had suggested it. He could not understand why all the brigades, still struggling to get into position, had not leaped into the attack. The shadows were lengthening. He turned with a sudden move to waiting couriers and sent them galloping to all commanders. "Tell them," he ordered, "tell them this affair must hang in suspense no longer. Sweep the field with the bayonet!" Jackson—at this moment—was himself again.[20]

D. H. Hill, on the extreme left of the line, was coming close to carrying out these orders. He could reach around the Federal flank if he could smash a battery that guarded it. When Col. Alfred Iverson's Twentieth North Carolina rushed at the guns and captured and held them for a precious ten minutes before losing them again, Hill thrust his division forward across a 400-yard open field in a mad drive that broke the end of the Federal line. Hill thought it the first and decisive cracking of the front.[21] But Porter, now feeling the pressure all along the line, thought the break came near his left front where, he said, he least expected it.[22]

This was the heroic climax of the day. Whiting, coming up from near the rear of Jackson's troops, had struggled through woods and swampy ground and lost his way, before he came out behind A. P. Hill's spent and dispirited troops. He had two brigades, Hood's Texas Brigade with the First, Fourth, and Fifth Texas Regiments and the Eighteenth Georgia, with Hampton's Legion from South Carolina attached, and Col. E. M. Law's brigade of the Sixth North Carolina, the Fourth Alabama, and the Second and Eleventh Mississippi.

"Can you break his line?" Lee asked the broad-shouldered Hood as he pointed to Porter's position.

"I will try," Hood said.[23]

He strode to the front of his brigade, Law to his. They marched to the front, through men leaving the field in every direction, past woods where other men lay in safe cover from which they would never again stir. Now they were out in the open under full fire from the guns behind the water. Carrying their rifles at the trail and never firing, they changed into double-time and bowed their heads to the murderous fire.

Steadily, relentlessly, almost mechanically they rolled forward, men falling with every step but nobody faltering. On, and on, and on, and on. Now they were in the thickets. Now they were charging into the ravine with a wild yell. Now they were climbing up the slopes. Now they were within 20 yards. Now their yells rose to a fierce crescendo of fury—and now the defenders could stand it no longer. They broke and fled.

Only then did the Texans and the Mississippians raise their rifles and pour volley after volley into retreating masses. Then on again, and now the guns began to fall into their hands until they could count 14 of them, and now a whole regiment was caught and surrendered. This was the beginning of the end.

But behind Hood's and Law's proud remnants lay a long line of young men, all passion spent—broken with wounds and writhing in pain or lying very still, a thousand of them hit in the few minutes of a charge that the Army of Northern Virginia and its commander never forgot. Jackson followed this trail the next day in wonder and admiration. "These men," he said, "are soldiers indeed!" [24]

Lee had ordered a general forward movement about the time that Jackson gave the same order to his units. From north to south, from D. H. Hill to Longstreet, the troops along the crescent line, struggling forward all together now, crushed defenses they could not break piecemeal.

In the twilight Porter drew off unit after unit swiftly and with mounting losses but without panic. He lost 22 guns in the darkness, and he left behind 894 dead and 2,836 missing, which, with 3,107 wounded, raised his casualties to 6,837. He might have suffered more as he struggled southward through the night across the Chickahominy bridges, burning them after him, to the right bank on the route toward the James, but for Confederate weariness and confusion after an exhausting and confusing day.

Lee's units were scattered and mixed, and knowledge of the country (close though it was to Richmond) was meager. At one point Jackson, riding out in front of his troops with a few staff officers, blundered into the presence of 15 or 20 Federal troops. He recovered before they did and immediately launched a personal offensive. Riding confidently toward them, he called out a demand that they surrender—and they did. A little later, when Elzey's brigade of Ewell's division was moving into action, it encountered the prisoners headed toward the rear. A tall fellow at the head of the party cried out, in a loud voice and with an oath: "Gentlemen, we had the honor of being captured by Stonewall Jackson himself!" [25]

The Confederate command was still bemused, after the battle, by the assumption that McClellan would retreat, when he did, toward White House, the Pamunkey, and the York. Stuart's 2,000 cavalrymen, who might have ripped some of Porter's retreating columns to pieces even in the darkness, were far to the left watching a line that McClellan had in fact abandoned.

McClellan had abandoned something else. He had given up all hope of capturing Richmond or winning the Peninsula campaign. However disjointed and unco-ordinated the Confederate movements were during the Gaines' Mill fighting (as during the Mechanicsville fighting of the day before), and however heavy were Lee's losses (which probably exceeded Porter's and may have reached above 8,000), June 27 marked the collapse of McClellan's last lingering confidence in himself. The day-long battering of Porter, the clear knowledge that Jackson had joined Lee with a greatly exaggerated force (the news of which had now swept through both armies), and the retreat of the Federal right wing, all combined to cast the Federal commander into black despair.

McClellan called a meeting of his corps commanders that night: Brig. Gens. E. V. Sumner of the Second Corps, S. P. Heintzelman of the Third, Erasmus D. Keyes of the Fourth, Porter of the Fifth, and W. B. Franklin of the Sixth. To them he announced his plan to retreat to the James and began the preparation of orders to that effect. The distance was 16 miles from the Grapevine Bridge across the Chickahominy by a straight line and less for units to the south and east. But the roads were winding, unmarked, poorly mapped, and impossible for fast marching. Lying squarely in the path loomed the barrier of White Oak Swamp.

This spread out east and west some seven miles from the vicinity of Seven Pines to the Chickahominy, and at points was four miles across for a retreating army, with varying water depths and difficulties. Chiefly a stream but partly a morass, at its heart it had to be bridged, and the bridge was a bottleneck of critical dangers. McClellan had to transport more than 75,000 men across this swamp, plus all the artillery of the army, plus all the baggage train—hardly less than 3,000 vehicles, perhaps 5,000.[26] It was a tremendous undertaking. It was an enormous opportunity for a pursuing army if it was informed and aggressive.

By 1 A.M. on the 28th McClellan placed orders in Keyes' hands directing the movement and requiring Keyes to pass across the bridge before daylight and then to go into defense position to protect the four corps that followed. Porter would be next. Sumner, Heintzelman, and Franklin would follow. Keyes could not keep up with that schedule because the bridge had to be repaired, but he had part of his corps across two hours after daylight. Thereafter the movement continued fast.

This was the kind of movement McClellan could organize. But for the rest his heart had failed. Shortly after midnight, following Porter's long battle and retreat, he wrote to the Secretary of War that extraordinary letter—an almost unprecedented expression from a field commander to the War Department—which spoke of sacrifice and honor and hopeless odds against him and the bad treatment he had received, all in a tone that would have resulted in most generals' recall immediately. He closed with these words:

As it is, the Government must not and cannot hold me responsible for the result. I feel too earnestly tonight. I have seen too many dead and wounded comrades to feel otherwise than that the Government has not sustained this army. If you do not do so now the game is lost.

If I save this army now, I tell you plainly that I owe no thanks to you or to any other persons in Washington.

You have done your best to sacrifice this army.

A telegraph operator in Washington and the military supervisor of telegraphs took it upon themselves to delete the last two sentences in the copy going to Stanton.[27] But the campaign to capture Richmond had been jarred on the 26th and broken on the 27th—in the mind of the commander. Hereafter it would be a campaign to save the Federal army.

In this fundamental respect the fighting of the 27th at Gaines' Mill takes on great importance. It was handled with intelligence and tenacity by Porter and his officers and men. It was handled, in its organization and control, with uncertainty and ineffectiveness by Lee and his commanders for the greater part of the day. The Army of Northern Virginia was still a group of divisions rather than an army. It was not lacking in bravery. "There was more individual gallantry displayed upon this field than any I have ever seen," Longstreet thought.[28] But it was lacking in unity and co-ordination, and control from the top.

Eventually, although not until just before night, Lee managed to bring all his force to bear on the enemy, and since he had under his immediate hand more than 50,000 men to Porter's 35,000, and most of them were full of drive, he could step up the pressure beyond Porter's endurance.

Finally, after long travail, Jackson had managed to thrust his entire force forward, directing some of it closely, making other parts available for Lee's personal utilization, and opening the way for much local initiative. The arrival of this strength enabled Lee to carry out his plan. In the late afternoon hours Jackson regained something of the organizing and directing force, the energy and the relentless spirit that characterized his earlier operations. The attacking force employed little artillery. It was lavish in its human expenditure. But it broke McClellan's spirit, and it sealed the safety of Richmond.

Yet these results were not entirely discernible at Lee's headquarters. The care of the wounded and the burial of the dead demanded action, and the collection of lost units and men began with daylight on Saturday, June 28. Jackson advanced from the left wing and Longstreet from the right, looking for the enemy. Longstreet sent a staff officer, Maj. G. Moxley Sorrel, over to establish locations and co-operation with Jackson if need be, and Sorrel found the General "brisk enough." He thought Jackson was "cheerful and pleasant." "Explain, Major, to General Longstreet, where I am and how my troops are lying, and say, with my compliments, I am ready to obey any orders he may send me," he told Sorrel.[29]

Though the ground was covered with the debris of an army—half-burned wagons, half-spoiled food, weapons of all kinds, axes, picks and shovels, blankets and overcoats half buried in the mud, later collected for weeks by the army and by the countryside—no Federal troops in effective strength remained on the left bank, or north side, of the Chickahominy.

Lee could not tell, in a country largely covered with woods, whether the retreat was toward White House and the line of the York, or down the center of the Peninsula by routes McClellan had used in advancing, or southward toward the James. For Lee had committed the military sin of losing contact with a retreating enemy. A great deal that happened later in the campaign might have been avoided if through cavalry or fresh infantry Lee had kept in hot pursuit of Porter's withdrawal from his crescent lines along Boatswain's Creek near Gaines' Mill.

In the effort to find out in which direction McClellan had disappeared, Lee directed Jackson to send Ewell's division down the left (north) bank of the Chickahominy to Dispatch Station on the Richmond and York Railroad, and sent Stuart toward the White House base at the head of the York River. The two cut telegraph lines and tore up track. In the White House vicinity Stuart found buildings in flames, or already destroyed, and his men reveled in the abandoned food and supplies of the deserted base. Clearly the Federal forces were not using that line of retreat.

The 28th wore on without definite information for Lee to act on. While his whole left wing, now the striking force of his army, waited in its tracks for twenty-four hours, Porter's corps, following Keyes', pushed on during the day for the White Oak Swamp Bridge, and passed over it during the afternoon and night of the 28th.[30] It was not until night that the evidence of McClellan's southward retreat toward the James became clear to Lee. Even then he kept in mind the possibility that McClellan would turn eastward later and retreat overland down the Peninsula.

Early on the 29th Lee was ready with plans. They directed Jackson to march southward across the Grapevine Bridge, which he would have to rebuild after the Federals had destroyed it, and then down the right (south) bank of the Chickahominy. In Lee's words he "was directed to pursue the enemy on the road he had taken." [31] In Dabney's postwar recollection, Jackson's duty, once he had crossed the river, was "to march east-ward by the Savage Station Road, parallel to and not far from the Chickahominy; to guard all the northward so as to prevent any attack, thus forming a line of protection on that side for the movement of Lee's other columns south of him; and not to leave that east-bound road until he had passed the extreme northern flank of McClellan's force and gotten in rear of the Federals." [32]

The direction would be toward Magruder's force and eventually White Oak Swamp. Magruder was to advance by the Williamsburg

Road and hit the retreating army before it reached White Oak Swamp—though nearly two-fifths of the Federal army had already done so. Huger, who had shared Magruder's responsibilities on Lee's right wing, was ordered to pursue by the Charles City Road, slightly to the south of Magruder's route, and to join the attack. Together they had 25,000 fresh men. If they slashed hard into the flank of the retreating forces, they ought to be capable of damaging and delaying the movement while other elements of Lee's army came up.

Longstreet and Hill were ordered to cross the Chickahominy higher up at New Bridge and to swing farther south and west to the Darbytown Road, roughly parallel to the Charles City Road. They would have to march across the rear of Magruder and Huger. Then they were to turn into the more easterly Long Bridge Road for a wide end run to Lee's right that would enable them (it was hoped) to block the line of Federal retreat to the James. From the south side of that river Maj. Gen. Theophilus H. Holmes, with much peacetime experience but little under fire, had been ordered to join the encircling movement with his 6,000 men.

On paper these divisions amounted to an impressive force against an army in full retreat, carrying an enormous baggage train along poor roads and across a narrow bridge over a swamp stream. But, as in preceding operations, Lee's army was widely separated, marching over different routes and out of central control, during movements which depended for success on the nice fitting-together of all the parts—a very difficult task, and in the end too much to ask of it.

June 29 was a Sunday. Jackson could do nothing until he had rebuilt the Grapevine Bridge. Dabney wrote later that Jackson set him to that responsibility—an unusual choice for such an engineering duty.[33] A rough-and-ready railroad constructor attached to Jackson's command as chief of pioneers, Capt. C. R. Mason, may have had a hand in the work. He was known for his blunt language and scorn for professionals. The story ran that Jackson called him in when the work was going badly (Dabney said the men at his own disposal were "shilly-shally"[34]) and told him plans and specifications were coming from the engineers. "Never mind pictures, General!" Mason broke in. "If you will send me men enough who will wade in the water and tote poles, I will have the bridge ready by the time the engineers can prepare pictures."[35]

But D. H. Hill recorded in his report, with a show of firm responsibility, that "my pioneer corps, under Captain [William Proctor] Smith, of the Engineers, repaired Grapevine Bridge on the 29th and we crossed over at 3 o'clock that night." [36]

Soldiers remembered the hard work. Heavy poles had to be cut, dragged, hauled, and lifted into place, with little equipment, for the long corduroy approach as well as the passage over the stream. "While six of us were carrying a log on the bridge with hand-sticks," Private Casler recalled, "General Jackson was standing on the bridge, with his back toward us, directly in the way. As we were turning to one side to pass around him, he noticed us and, quickly stepping to one side, said 'Oh! come on, never mind me,' as if he were somebody of small importance." [37]

Magruder, meantime, reached on the 29th the retreating enemy's covering force near Savage Station. He looked to the right for reenforcement from Huger and to the left from Jackson, who, he had understood, was to support him. To Jackson, Magruder sent a staff officer, Maj. Henry Bryan, to inquire as to Jackson's progress. Bryan returned shortly, bringing Jackson's engineer, Lieut. J. K. Boswell, with him. Boswell reported that Jackson had to build the bridge but that it should be finished in two hours. The time of this report is not clear. [38]

Finally, after much delay, Magruder launched his attack with two brigades and some additional regiments. He kept the effort going for two hours, but it did not seriously embarrass the Federal troops guarding the flank of the line of retreat. He had too few troops for the formidable force facing him.

At some time during the day—again an impossible hour to determine—Lee's staff officer, Maj. Walter H. Taylor, carrying a message to Magruder, learned that when Magruder was reaching out for aid before the battle, one of his division commanders, Brig. Gen. D. R. Jones, reported hearing from Jackson, then about three miles away across the river. Jones told Magruder that "I had hoped Jackson would have co-operated with me on my left, but he sends me word that he cannot, as he has other important duty to perform." [39]

Puzzled by the "other important duty," Taylor carried the word of it back to Lee; and Lee added a postscript to a message he was sending Magruder: "I learn from Major Taylor that you are under the impression that General Jackson has been ordered not to support you. On the contrary, he has been directed to do so and to push the pursuit vigorously." [40]

The "other important duty" phrase seemed suspicious in later years to some persons who thought Jackson was not himself during the Seven Days. When it was added to the report from Boswell that the bridge would be finished in about two hours (from an unknown point in time), it suggested to such persons the possibility that the bridge was in fact completed, but that Jackson, on this Sunday, decided to give the day over to religious worship or contemplation, although Magruder was fighting three miles away and McClellan's army was slipping out of Lee's grasp.

No evidence supports this remarkable suggestion. The rebuilding stretched out longer than expected. Winder reported, for instance (as did others), that his brigade was ordered up for passage but, the bridge not being ready, returned to bivouac. [41] Abundant evidence shows that Jackson spent much effort to have the bridge repaired, driving his men until 11 o'clock Sunday night to do so. Evidence of another kind indicates that, though Jackson was driving to set up the bridge again, he was obeying orders by staying where he was.

For on this day Lee sent to Stuart, then still in the White House vicinity, behind Jackson (to the north and east of him), this message through his Assistant Adjutant General, Colonel Chilton:

Gen'l Stuart

The Gen'l Comd'g requests that you will watch the Chickahominy as far as Forge Bridge, ascertain if any attempts will be made in that direction by the enemy, advising Gen'l Jackson, who will resist their passage untill reinforced. If you find that they have passed down below where they cannot cross, leave a force to watch movements which may be made, & recross yourself to this side for further operations. I am Sir Resply

                    yr obdt sert
                    R H Chilton
                    AAG

Hdqrs Charles City Road
June 29

Stuart, after taking note of these orders, sent the message on to Jackson. The hour at which Lee sent the message to Stuart is unknown, as is the hour when Stuart received it. But it reached Jackson about 3 P.M. He read it and then wrote across the margin of the message, before sending it back to Stuart, these words:

3 h. 5 m. P.M. Genl. Ewell will remain near Dispatch Station & myself near my present position. T.J.J.*

Lee, it would appear, had received new indications that McClellan's retreating columns might turn eastward from their southeasterly direction toward the James and head for the Chickahominy and an overland retreat down the Peninsula. Or Lee was acting cautiously to reassure himself on his original thinking that McClellan might choose this eastward route—a possibility that had bothered him all of the 28th.

The orders were, in any event, clear and specific. Stuart followed them exactly. He had sent the First Virginia Cavalry down the Chickahominy to lower crossings on the 29th. On the 30th he reached Forge Bridge, 13 miles from his start, and several miles farther from Grapevine Bridge, at 11 A.M. Stuart found Federal troops at Forge Bridge and at Long Bridge, six miles upstream, though how many he could not tell. He spent the whole day trying to find out, acting normally and intelligently in response to the Chilton message from Lee.[42]

Jackson, following the same orders with the same exactness, re-

---

* The importance of Colonel Chilton's message to Stuart was stressed by Frank E. Vandiver in *Mighty Stonewall*, pp. 312 and 520. He pointed out that the message, the original of which is in the Stuart Collection, Henry E. Huntington Library, had escaped notice by earlier students of the Seven Days, especially students of the confused and half-hidden events of June 29. Its direct order to Jackson to resist the passage of Federal troops if they attempted to cross the Chickahominy from the right bank to the left bank is one which he would be expected to obey without question—as he said, in effect, he would. He could not have crossed the Chickahominy with troops in any event, and therefore could not have aided Magruder at Savage Station. On the evidence of the Chilton order, Lee did not contemplate his doing so even if the bridge had been rebuilt.

The seeming conflict between Lee's assurance to Magruder that Jackson "has been directed" to "support you . . . and to push the pursuit vigorously," and Lee's order through Chilton for Jackson to resist any attempt by McClellan to cross the Chickahominy, which led Jackson to say he would remain on the left bank of the river, appears to arise out of the different hours when they were issued. The order which at 3:05 P.M. Jackson said he would obey appears to have been based on information which Lee did not have when he sent to Jackson—probably early in the morning—his orders for the day. It is less easy to reconcile Lee's order by Chilton with Lee's statement (*O.R.*, XI, pt. 2, 680) that "the report sent to General Magruder by General Jones that General Jackson had informed the latter he could not co-operate with him, having been ordered on other duty, originated in some mistake. . . ." The nature of the mistake is not clear.

mained "near my present position," as he had announced he would. He had the "important duty" of rebuilding the Grapevine Bridge as originally directed, and the additional and precise "important duty" of resisting the passage of the Chickahominy if Stuart discovered that any parts of McClellan's army were turning in that direction. Stuart found no such shift of direction. On the contrary, he discovered much evidence that the Federal retreat was continuing in its original southeasterly direction across and beyond White Oak Swamp toward the slopes of Malvern Hill and, beyond that, toward the sharp drop to the level of the James.[43]

Late in the afternoon Jackson did cross the unfinished bridge, picking his way across its timbers with his staff, and inspected the country. They reached the Trent house nearby, where McClellan had his headquarters earlier, and marveled at its appointments and, with more reason for concern, at the remnants of the headquarters telegraphic equipment.[44] They had nothing comparable. But they were back on the northern side before Magruder began his attack late in the afternoon. "The sound of combat," Dabney thought, "kindled again in Jackson's heart the fire of battle, and as he lay down under the open sky for a short repose, he gave orders that everything should be ready to move in pursuit at the earliest dawn."[45]

At midnight a rainstorm drenched Jackson. After futile attempts to find shelter he decided to ride on to Magruder's headquarters to consult about movements. He reached Magruder at 3:30 A.M. and found that officer still up.[46] The troops were on the march before he arrived there. They had set out at 2:30 A.M., with D. H. Hill in the lead, and presently Hill discovered Jackson drying his uniform at a campfire. Jackson was in a bad humor this morning of Monday, June 30. The night before he had told Munford of the cavalry to meet him at a crossroads at daylight. Munford and his horsemen suffered from the storm just as Jackson did. They scattered to find shelter from its downpour. When the night began to turn gray Munford could locate only 50 of his men, and doing so took time. He reached the crossroads to find Jackson sitting his horse with visible impatience.

"Colonel, my orders to you were to be here at sunrise," Jackson said.

Munford began his explanation, piled the details of distress one on another, and said that circumstances had conspired against him.

"Yes, sir," the cutting voice came back. "But, Colonel, I ordered you to be here at sunrise."

Jackson relented enough to direct Munford to drive in enemy pickets when they appeared, and Munford set out with his handful. From the rear other cavalrymen came riding up from time to time, and Jackson sent word to Munford that his men were straggling badly. Back Munford rode and began his explanations again. But Jackson would have none of them. "Yes, sir," he said. "But I ordered you to be here at sunrise, and I have been waiting for you for a quarter of an hour."

Munford surrendered at that.[47] He sent back an adjutant to collect stragglers and bring them up in a body and himself marched ahead looking for pickets on whom to take out his feelings.

Hill, leading the main body, kept going right through Magruder's headquarters. Jackson's men were still curiosities to the remainder of the army, and remarks and cheers greeted them this morning. "No wonder they march so; the men carry no baggage," said a soldier by the road about troops who had discarded knapsacks. When F Company of the Twenty-first Virginia came by and its captain showed a naked sword, "See there," came the comment from the inspecting troops, "the officers don't even carry scabbards for their swords."[48] The route was by the Williamsburg Road. The objective was the White Oak Swamp. But progress was slow.

Lee was up early this calm and cloudless morning. He rode first to see how Magruder had fared in yesterday's fight at Savage Station, and there met Jackson.

Jackson rode up on his sorrel horse. Robert Stiles, a young Yale graduate from New York who had gone south two years earlier and become a Southern soldier, stared at this General he had never seen but about whom he had heard much.

"Jackson and the little sorrel stopped in the middle of the road, probably not 50 feet off," Stiles wrote later. "He sat stark and stiff in the saddle. Horse and rider appeared worn down to the lowest point of flesh consistent with effective service." Hair, skin, eyes, and clothes all seemed one neutral tint to Stiles, "and his badges of rank so dulled and tarnished as to be scarcely perceptible. The 'mangy little cadet cap' was pulled so low in front that the visor just cut the glint of his eyeballs."

This was a battlefield not yet cleaned up. The dead lay round about. Jackson looked over the scene, then turned his attention to the road—"the ideal of concentration, imperturbable, resistless. . . ."

Lee rode up, dismounted gracefully, handed his bridle reins to an orderly, drew his gauntlet from his right hand, and turned toward Jackson, who was flinging himself from Little Sorrel. The two generals greeted each other warmly and, standing face to face, began serious talk.

No one was close enough to hear, and the circling officers and couriers could only seek to interpret each move, gesture, expression. They saw Jackson talking in a jerky, impetuous way. He began to draw a line on the ground with the toe of his right boot. The silence of the watchers was profound. They saw two swift lines at an angle —two sides of a triangle. Jackson hesitated, looking at Lee's face, then looking at the ground, talking earnestly, and then drawing slowly a third line that would connect the other two—slowly, earnestly, questioningly. Then, the triangle complete, he lifted his foot sharply and brought it down emphatically, saying, "We've got him," and immediately signaled for his horse, mounted him, and was gone.[49]

But the advance continued to move slowly. Long lines of white tents loomed ahead, and Hill's men gaped at an abandoned Federal hospital with 2,500 wounded and sick men and many nurses and attendants. Other prisoners drifted in from the woods or were routed out by the circling cavalry, until Hill had accumulated 1,000 of them and had to detach two regiments to send them to the rear. An officer muttered something about the amount of food required to feed all those prisoners. "It is cheaper to feed them than to fight them,"[50] Jackson, ever the realist, countered.

He had to wait while this work was being done, and he sat down by the road to write to Anna.

> Near White Oak Swamp Bridge.
> An ever-kind Providence has greatly blessed our efforts and given us great reason for thankfulness in having defended Richmond. Today the enemy is retreating down the Chickahominy towards the James River. Many prisoners are falling into our hands. General D. H. Hill and I are together. I had a wet bed last night, as the rain fell in torrents. I got up about midnight, and haven't seen much rest since. I do trust that our

God will soon bless us with an honorable peace, and permit us to be together at home again to the enjoyment of domestic happiness.

You must give fifty dollars for church purposes, and more should you be disposed. Keep an account of the amount, as we must give at least one tenth of our income. I would like very much to see my darling, but hope that God will enable me to remain at the post of duty until, in His own good time, He blesses us with independence. This going home has injured the army immensely.[51]

It was noon before the main body began to reach the darkly shadowed waters of White Oak Swamp, where another Federal hospital with 500 sick had been left.[52] The stream itself was normally from 10 to 20 feet wide, narrower in dry weather, a broad bog after rains, but with many variations as the ground rose or flattened out. The banks and adjoining areas were miry now from last night's rain. The underbrush was thick. To Jackson's left a forest of pines offered concealment, but his right was more open. Across the stream the situation was reversed. Looking to his left on the other side, Jackson could see open country, with three Federal batteries on lines of rising ground, and infantry beyond, and in the far distance wagons pulling away. But to his right he could see only the June foliage of thick trees.

Crutchfield, the artillery chief, had reached the area early and had studied it systematically. He discovered that if he could place his guns along the top of a ravine that cut cross his right before the stream he would have a clear range in front of the Confederate left. Jackson saw the point, and Crutchfield set artillerymen to work cutting a road through trees to the site. Still unseen, he gathered 23 guns, hauled them behind the crest and loaded them. At about 1:45 P.M. he opened fire with all guns on the unsuspecting enemy.[53]

The effect seemed sufficient. After a few shots in reply the Federal batteries, save for guns knocked out, scrambled back out of sight. Jackson ordered a battery down near the bridge to clear the woods opposite of sharpshooters. Turning to Munford, he told him to cross the stream with his cavalry. He himself followed, splashing through the water with Hill and several of his staff, including McGuire.

They had a clear view of the bridge, a crudely built structure of untrimmed poles only a few feet above the dark water. Now the poles were partly burned, partly hanging disjointedly in the stream.

Early this morning the last of McClellan's army had poured across this bridge, the stragglers jamming it at daylight so tightly that for a time they could not move.[54] But beyond its bedraggled ruins the woods were full of hidden life, and still farther to the rear, on the Confederate right, the enemy was waiting.

As the reconnoiterers pushed ahead the crash of unexpected guns brought them to a surprised stop. Although Crutchfield had cleared the open Federal right, the Federal left behind its protecting trees was firing furiously with grape and canister. Jackson and Hill, and the staff officers, turned and rode back—"rapidly," said Hill.[55] Munford kept on downstream under sheltering trees until he was out of range. The battery near the bank had to be ordered back. It was under the fire of guns so placed that they could not be reached by Crutchfield. The whole situation would require thought.

Lee's plan for the 30th had rested on the assumption that, while Jackson was following in its tracks, McClellan's army would be marching across the front of the remainder of his army. He had called in Maj. Gen. T. H. Holmes with 6,000 men from the south side of the James River to be the extreme right of the Confederate movement, almost under the shadow of Malvern Hill, toward which the Federal troops seemed to be aiming. Holmes was ordered to attack when his advance down the New Market Road located the enemy.

Lee directed Magruder to pull back from Savage Station and to circle around by the Darbytown Road so as to come up behind Longstreet and A. P. Hill. These two Lee kept moving down the Darbytown Road to the Long Bridge Road with the goal of attacking when they encountered the enemy. Huger was ordered to move down the Charles City Road, to the left of Longstreet and A. P. Hill.

The anticipated line of attack, left to right, against the Federal flank would be Huger, Longstreet-Hill, with Magruder in support, and Holmes. If they could co-ordinate their movements and strike simultaneously, with pressure against the flank while Jackson stormed at the rear, they should severely damage, if not destroy, as much of McClellan's army as had not already slipped beyond reach. But once more success depended largely on precise timing of separated movements far from central control.

Nothing developed as planned. The Federal retreat, despite McClellan's leaving its direction chiefly to his corps commanders, moved steadily, even swiftly, and in good control. Huger's advance slowed

in thick woods where Federal troops had cut down trees in his path
and he had to cut them to pieces to get through—a strange affair
of ax men. Holmes discovered Federal trains moving across Malvern
Hill. It was a tempting target, but when he opened fire his guns
were overwhelmed by massive counter-battery fire and his further
movements were discouraged. Longstreet and Hill marched as directed and came up to the Federal line where the Charles City, Long
Bridge, and Quaker Roads met at Riddell's Shop on ground marked
both by Frayser's Farm and Glendale.

By this time, between 3 and 4 o'clock, Lee had counted on battlefield co-operation from Holmes, Huger, and Jackson, whereas, in
effective steps, he had none. But by this time the Federals were
slipping out of his grasp. He resolved to attack with what he had,
Longstreet and A. P. Hill's 20,000 men.

The battle of Frayser's Farm (or Glendale) that followed was a
hard-driving though disjointed attack by Longstreet. It broke
through the Federal skirmishers, cut into the main line with much
hand-to-hand fighting, captured or destroyed guns, and achieved
with bitter effort an initial tactical victory.

That was not enough. The Federal forces were too large. Longstreet, with Hill following later, penetrated and battered them, but
he did not break them; and in the end he had trouble holding his
ground. As at Mechanicsville, Gaines' Mill, and Savage Station, part
of Lee's army fought the battle while the remainder, though within
sound of the guns, did not. Nearly 50,000 Confederate troops were
within a few miles, most of them under three miles, and yet did
not participate directly.

When the battle died away about 9 o'clock that night, Lee's plan
had failed. McClellan, almost within the trap again and again and
again, had escaped finally. Now Lee could only follow him. "Had
all our troops been at Frayser's Farm," D. H. Hill said later, "there
would have been no Malvern Hill" [56]—and he was right.

Throughout this afternoon of June 30 Jackson had been held up
by the destroyed bridge across White Oak Swamp (he who so often
had held up his enemies by burning bridges) and by the Federal
sharpshooters and guns on the other side. When his first attempt to
cross in a rush, after the initial artillery salvos, had failed, Jackson
ordered Winder and D. H. Hill to take shelter in the pine forest on
the left, kept his artillery firing in the effort to silence the Federal

guns, and ordered working parties to repair the bridge. But the latter came under the fire of Federal skirmishers, suffered losses, and could not be held to the work.[57] Artillery fire continued for the remainder of the afternoon from both sides, but without clear vision

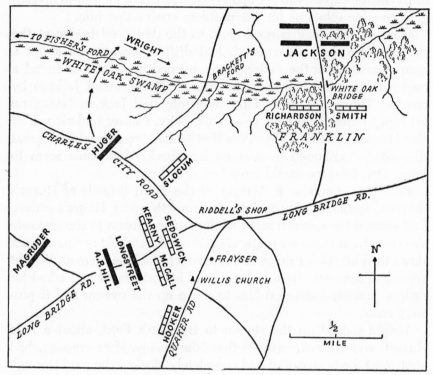

JACKSON AT WHITE OAK SWAMP.

or material effect even though one Federal battery expended 1,600 rounds. Jackson's second attempt of the day failed.

The third attempt of the day should obviously be searches for other ways to cross the swamp stream. Strangely enough, there is no firsthand evidence that Jackson attempted anything of the kind. Henderson said that he did ("Having ascertained . . . that every road was obstructed, and that there was no means of carrying his artillery over the creek, or favorable ground on which his infantry could act, Jackson gave up all hope of aiding Longstreet . . ."[58]), but the basis for this statement is not clear. What does seem clear is that while other officers on their own initiative were striking along the swamp stream for crossings, in two instances reporting possibilities that impressed them, Jackson showed increasingly less interest in the reports and appeared progressively overcome by exhaustion or physical incapacity to act upon their findings or himself to investigate possible solutions for the problem confronting him.

Munford, who had crossed close to the destroyed bridge at the time Jackson and Hill crossed, had drifted downstream about a quarter-mile when the Federal guns opened up. There he found a cow path that led him over the swamp. He informed Jackson by courier. Thirty-nine years later he wrote that Jackson "made no attempt to cross where we re-crossed. Why, I never understood." [59] But Munford also said elsewhere that he had "re-crossed with great difficulty," [60] although he was on horseback. The words seem to imply that infantry would have had a bad time.

Brig. Gen. Ambrose R. Wright, of the Third Brigade of Huger's division, reconnoitering in brigade strength under Huger's orders, had crossed the upper reaches of the swamp stream in the opposite direction from Jackson's route. He traversed its whole northern bank down to White Oak Bridge, and reported to Jackson there at, Wright recorded, 2:30 P.M. He told Jackson of his movement and asked for orders. Jackson instructed him to move up the swamp and if possible cross.

Wright moved up the stream to Brackett's Ford, about a mile distant, and there discovered that "the enemy, after crossing, had destroyed the bridge, and had completely blocked the road through the swamp by felling trees in and across it." He scouted further and "was enabled to make a good reconnaissance of the enemy's position and force." Heavy batteries of field artillery, posted on a range of hills commanding the open field which extended from the swamp, "could be used with terrible effect."

After further discouraging information from two prisoners, Wright abandoned hope of crossing there. He marched higher upstream, found a cow trail called Fisher's Ford three miles farther (four from White Oak Bridge), and crossed there.[61] But he does not appear to have informed Jackson.

The Wright evidence on Brackett's Ford runs counter to that of Maj. Gen. W. B. Franklin, commander of the Sixth Corps. McClel-

lan directed him to defend the swamp crossing. Although he had
two divisions and three brigades, some 22,000 men, Franklin was
much disturbed by the meager defense of Brackett's Ford, "where I
knew we were very weak."

Jackson, Franklin wrote twenty-odd years afterwards, "ought to
have known of the existence of Brackett's Ford, only one mile above
White Oak Bridge, and ought to have discovered the weakness of
our defense at that point. He had troops enough to have attacked
the ford and the bridge with forces at both points exceeding ours
at the bridge, and the two attacks, to say the least, would have embarrassed us exceedingly." In that event, Franklin said, the result
at Frayser's Farm might have been different—"in fact, it is likely
we should have been defeated that day. . . ." [62]

The inescapable fact, whatever the merit of these contradictory
reports about Brackett's Ford, is that Jackson did not investigate
the area at all.

Brig. Gen. Wade Hampton, the South Carolina planter turned
officer, submitted in the last year of his life an even more critical
report. After the first failure at the bridge, his brigade lay in the pine
forest to the left of the road, but General Hampton, with two aides,
went scouting. Above the bridge—how far is not clear—he found an
area where the swamp was comparatively open, the ground "not
at all boggy," the stream "very shallow, with a clear sandy bottom,
not more than 10 or 15 feet wide." He crossed. Presently he saw a
Federal line facing in the direction of an attack that might come
from below the ford, but not facing where he had crossed. He recrossed and reported the situation to Jackson.

Could he build a bridge? Jackson asked. Hampton thought he
could for infantry, but not for artillery without disclosing the operation. Build it, Jackson directed him.

Hampton set to work and built a rough bridge. Then "on my
return to our side of the swamp, I found Gen. Jackson seated on a
fallen pine alongside of the road that led down to the ford, and
seating myself by him, I reported the completion of the bridge and
the exposed position of the enemy. He drew his cap down over his
eyes which were closed, and after listening to me for some minutes,
he rose without speaking. . . ." That, and nothing more. [63]

Jackson himself reported formally eight months later, after noting
the maintenance of artillery fire until dark, that "a heavy cannonad-

ing in front announced the engagement of General Longstreet at
Frazier's [Frayser's] farm and made me eager to press forward; but
the marshy character of the soil, the destruction of the bridge over
the marsh and creek, and the strong position of the enemy for defending the passage prevented my advancing until the following
morning." [64]

The difficulties were apparent to all. Not apparent then were the
reasons why the General who had achieved great things by energy,
imagination, and resourcefulness in the face of difficulties seemed
unaware of the need for these qualities now—seemed unaware of
the need to cross the swamp in any way he could find and to press
with all speed and force to the aid of Longstreet and Hill in their
desperate struggle only three miles away. It was not that Jackson
did not know. Longstreet sent an officer, Maj. J. W. Fairfax, to see
Jackson during the afternoon. The purpose is not known, but Fairfax surely gave full information about Longstreet. Yet, on this hot
June afternoon, Jackson seemed interested only in going to sleep.

Winder sent his aide, McHenry Howard, to see what was causing
the delay. Howard found Jackson's staff and learned that the General was lying asleep under a tree. He looked around: "The trees
were large and not close together here and through them could be
seen the road descending over open ground, curving to the left in
doing so, to where it appeared to cross a stream. . . . At intervals
a shell came from across the stream but not falling or passing near
us. . . . With the exception of this slow firing everything seemed
to be quiet, and it looked to me as if on our side we were waiting
for Jackson to wake up. . . ." [65]

When Jackson did wake up, it was only to sit quietly, as though
drained of energy and incapable of action, with a seeming indiffer-
ence to the life about him or the men he had led who were waiting
behind him, or the army ahead that was waiting for him. He watched
the day end, listlessly and in great weariness. That night at supper,
while eating with his staff, he nodded at the table with a biscuit
in his mouth. [66] Rousing himself from this surrender to exhaustion,
he turned to his staff and said: "Now, gentlemen, let us at once to
bed, and rise with the dawn, and see if tomorrow we cannot *do
something.*" [67]

The confession is unmistakable. Jackson knew that he had failed
to overcome the difficulties, serious though they were, that blocked

his path to co-operation with his commander. He knew, on this last day of Lee's created opportunity to hit full sail at the Federal army in flight, that he had not risen to the achievement men expected of him or the achievement he owed himself.

Two weeks later, when Crutchfield, McGuire, and Pendleton were discussing the question of why Jackson had not managed to go to Longstreet's aid (the question every student of the campaign or of Jackson has had to ponder ever since), he came into the room and overheard his young friends. "If General Lee had wanted me, he could have sent for me," he said curtly.[68]

It is the only comment he is known to have made on the subject. The comment has some point. Lee could have maintained liaison better than he did. So could Jackson. At his best he would have informed Lee of inability to force the passage of the swamp, if in fact he was unable to do so at the main bridge, or at Brackett's Ford, or at a combination of both, or at the ford Hampton discovered, or perhaps by the trail Munford found. Lee and Jackson were not more than forty minutes apart by courier.[69]

Whether Jackson could have shifted troops by any other route than the swamp passage is uncertain. The roads were clogged,[70] and the time element would have been serious. But any such possibility would depend, in the first instance, on the very qualities of energy, resourcefulness, and determination which Jackson did not exhibit this day. The underlying fact is not so much the possibilities of methods and routes. It is Jackson's seeming inability from midday on to take any positive action of importance whatsoever.

This fundamental fact is so contradictory to Jackson's record before and after the campaign that it encouraged hypotheses of almost fantastic nature at complete variance with Jackson's character.[71] Serious debate may be held over Jackson's explanation that a crossing at the main bridge was not possible, as it was defended on July 1—a belief that McGuire also entertained—or that his orders restricted him to the main bridge crossing and forbade (for one who obeyed orders literally and expected others to do so) attempts elsewhere, as McGuire and Henderson argued; or that he was unaccustomed to commanding so many troops and, presumably, did not know what to do with them, although on this point his record on the 25th and 26th would provide more evidence than anything on the 30th.

The gossip of the day, which lingered over the years, went further. It included theories that Jackson did not like his subordinate position and therefore would not co-operate; that he felt his troops had already done more than their share of hard fighting, and that others should bear the burden now; and that, accordingly, he would not commit his infantry to operations where casualties were likely to be heavy.[72]

There is no creditable evidence to sustain these theories and a great deal of evidence to indicate their grave injustice to Jackson and their departures from the known facts. Jackson's willingness and eagerness to join Lee and his high opinion of Lee as a commander, and of Lee's plans for the week's operations, have already been indicated and are well known. Jackson's conviction in favor of aggressive operations and his determination to press for victory had been shown on numerous battlefields and would be shown on many more. It is grimly ironical to suggest that such a commander, whose flaming zeal and aggressiveness had already been attested by Federal as well as by Confederate commanders, could be seriously thought of as deliberately withholding his troops from the fighting for such reasons. No specific evidence that he did so has ever been cited.

If this gossip were soundly based, Jackson would have been guilty of conduct so gravely reprehensible that Lee would have been justified in removing him from command, if not in instituting more severe disciplinary action. Jackson would have been deliberately refraining from doing his duty in front of the enemy. For such an officer the regulations and traditions of every army provide condign punishment.

Even if there was not at hand specific explanatory evidence to sweep away such a suggestion, Jackson's character from his boyhood to his death would stand as a stone wall against gossip of this kind. The overwhelming testimony of those who knew him, together with the record of his entire life, establishes that it would have been impossible for this man to countenance such behavior. His personal characteristics included traits which, on occasion, could make men uncomfortable, particularly if they had fallen short of their duty. But it was not in him to give less than its due to constituted authority, or to sulk on the battlefield, or deliberately to refrain from doing his best in the presence of the enemy.

What, then, is the explanation of Jackson's six-day record which suggested at least awkwardness and delay in co-operation: in the march toward Ashland; in the slow approach on the 26th and the decision not to join the battle at Mechanicsville, the guns of which he could hear; in the uncertain movements and the waiting on the morning of the 27th when the fighting near Gaines' Mill was rising in intensity; in the long wait on the 29th at the Grapevine Bridge, which others expected, justifiably or not, to be rebuilt before 11 o'clock that night; and in the seeming loss of spirit on the afternoon of the 30th before a swamp-crossing problem which the Federal commander on the opposite side thought Jackson could have solved with a little energy?

Some of the minor but not inconsiderable reasons have already been indicated. It is possible that Jackson did not feel at home with 18,000 men, which grew to some 27,500 when D. H. Hill came under his command. He had never before commanded more than 14,000. It is certain that liaison between the army command and the Jackson command was seriously defective. This was Lee's first major operation, and his staff resources were meager. The whole army suffered from an extraordinary lack of maps and from ignorance of the country, none more so than Jackson, who was accustomed to exactly opposite conditions. The Army of Northern Virginia was facing, moreover, some very tough fighting men who had developed important skills, notably in artillery, and were fighting now against destruction itself.

But of Jackson personally there is little doubt about the primary handicap. It was exhaustion and illness.

The exhaustion resulted from lack of sleep that began before the battles started. The fourteen-hour horseback ride from Fredericks-hall to Lee's headquarters east of Richmond, starting at 1 A.M. on June 23, and the return ride to Beaver Dam (almost as far) during the night of June 23–24, deprived Jackson of two nights' sleep before the Seven Days began. He never regained it. Instead, he lost more and more sleep as the operation developed.

On the night of June 24–25 he received Lee's operation order (General Orders, No. 75) after midnight [73] and must have examined it carefully and made his own disposition for obedience at dawn or shortly after. He was busy all night of the 25th–26th with orders and prayers. On the 26th–27th he bivouacked at Hundley's Corner

and lost sleep because of the heavy skirmishing nearby and for reasons which Boteler recounted. On the night of the 27th–28th he
was up after midnight conferring with Stuart. He may have had full
sleep on the 28th–29th, after the army's delay when McClellan's
direction of the retreat was obscure. But the next night—the 29th–
30th—he was drenched by rain shortly after midnight, slept no more,
and arrived at Magruder's headquarters at 3:30 A.M.

Throughout these eight days Jackson was up every morning at
or before dawn, which during this period varied from shortly before
4:30 A.M. to shortly after it. He shared with the remainder of the
army the strains of the daytime operations, which were extremely
heavy, and he had his own large responsibilities in addition. Except
for the afternoon nap on the 24th, after his return from Lee's headquarters at the Dabb house, and again at the White Oak Swamp, he
is not known to have slept during the daylight hours. Although he
was described by others as "brisk" or normal on several mornings,
the loss of sleep was so great that it must have affected seriously one
who was a notoriously heavy sleeper and was unusually dependent
on sleep.

Dabney, who was especially close to Jackson during the Seven
Days, wrote that "this temporary eclipse" at White Oak Swamp "of
Jackson's genius was probably to be explained by physical causes." [74]
More informally and vividly he elaborated on this idea after the
war:

Nobody could blame Jackson for being done out that day. Remember
he had had a hard time since leaving Beaver Dam; not a wink of sleep
the night at Ashland; not a regular meal after leaving Hundley's Corner
Friday morning. Our headquarters wagon and servants all in the rear;
no mess chest, no cook; no regular rations drawn; no mess tables set,
Friday, Saturday, Sunday, Monday, nor Tuesday. Very little sleep Sunday
night, which from 1 o'clock on was spent on horseback. I suppose he had
neither breakfast nor dinner Monday. . . . He must have been a man
of iron indeed, had not body, brain, and animal spirits, felt the depressing
effects . . . he appeared to me to have less of his usual push and decision. . . .[75]

He "appeared" much worse. The General who went to sleep at
the supper table on the 30th, a biscuit between his teeth, was an
exhausted and badly depleted man, far below his normal physical
strength. This condition, not the gossip of deliberate refusal to do

his duty—a completely unsustained suggestion of great injustice—
was undoubtedly part of the explanation of his lack of energy at
White Oak Swamp and probably was a factor in earlier operations.

The second factor demands consideration as an addition to exhaustion or a part of it. Jackson wrote to Anna shortly after July 1
and referred briefly to what Anna called "his varied experiences in
this memorable week." He told of arriving at White Oak Swamp
and finding the bridge destroyed; of the operations there (skimmed
over) and of "many prisoners" who "really appear gratified at the
idea of being taken"; of the Malvern Hill battle of July 1, chiefly
to praise D. H. Hill; and of his location, when the letter was written,
at a point three miles north of the James River and 25 miles below
Richmond.

All the circumstances show that he was writing about the Seven
Days. It is for this reason that the following sentence has special
significance: *"During the past week I have not been well, have
suffered from fever and debility, but through the blessing of an
ever-kind Providence I am much better today."* [76]

The nature of the fever and the debility is not described. The
debility may be the effects of—or virtually the same as—the exhaustion from which Jackson was known to be suffering. His own statement adds to other evidence that he was not normal physically, and
in a way which would limit his energy, resourcefulness, imagination,
and driving power on the battlefield.

The "fever" is impossible to estimate accurately as a factor in
Jackson's record during the Seven Days. But this was the first time
since Jackson left Lexington that he told of being sick. Although
scarcely a letter between his departure from Mexico City in 1848
and his departure from the Virginia Military Institute in 1861 failed
to refer to physical ailments, scarcely a letter during the war mentioned such ailments, nor does the comment of men who knew him
indicate that he had any. Nor did the subsequent ten months and
few days of his life show any problem of health. So far as is known,
he did not lose a day from military duty because of sickness.

These words—"during the past week I have not been well, have
suffered from fever and debility"—are the only known evidence of
sickness during his war career, and they refer to his condition during
the week of the Seven Days when friends as well as critics were
sometimes puzzled by his behavior, especially at White Oak Swamp.

That Jackson was a sick man as well as an exhausted man thus appears to be definite. How much fever he had, what it indicated, how long it continued, are not disclosed from any known record. Nor was his physical condition apparent to all men who saw him. In particular, Dr. McGuire, whose opinion commands respect, said he never saw Jackson "more active and energetic than during the engagement" at the swamp. This is apparently a reference to the morning activities when the artillery caught the Federal troops by surprise and Jackson crossed and recrossed the stream. It could hardly refer to the afternoon when he slept. He slept the sleep of exhaustion and perhaps the sleep of a sick man, certainly of a man who had been sick during the week and could hardly have been expected to be himself during these operations.

Whether Jackson should have informed Lee—himself now near the breaking point from the strain of the operations [77]—cannot even be estimated without more information of Jackson's condition. The fact of Jackson's physical impairment rises clearly, however, over any supposition of unwillingness to co-operate or of deliberate and ignoble refusal to join battle—an extraordinary allegation to make against the strongest and most persistent advocate and exemplar of bold offensive action in the whole army.

By Tuesday morning, July 1, White Oak Swamp had been stripped clean of defenders and Jackson could build the bridge at leisure and cross it undisturbed. With Whiting in the lead, the Jackson force marched two to three miles southward to the road center at Riddell's Shop, where Longstreet and A. P. Hill had fought their stubborn engagement the day before. Magruder had moved in during the night to replace their weary survivors. He, too, had waked this morning to find the enemy gone.

Lee, full of disappointment that McClellan's army had slipped out of his grasp, met his commanders early in the morning, and after sending for Huger to come up—the whole army would be united then—directed the pursuit southward. Jackson took the lead, telling Magruder that his troops were fresher.[78] They started southward past Willis Church on a road called both the Willis Church Road and the Quaker Road. There was another Quaker Road farther to the west, and Magruder found himself shortly on this Quaker Road and marched away from, not toward, the real goal. It was one more example of the bad maps, or no maps, and the deep ignorance of the country that handicapped all Confederate operations.

The real goal was Malvern Hill. A mile wide and a mile and a half in length, it rose 150 feet at the highest point of its plateaulike top. Turkey Run flowed by its western side where the drop was almost perpendicular, Western Run along its eastern side where the slope was more gradual, as it was to the north where the Confederates were approaching. The Crew house to the west and the Binford house to the east, farm homes with outbuildings, gardens, and cultivated fields, and the Malvern house well to the south, overhanging the James, gave a pleasant aspect to the hilltop. But the hill's dominance over the surrounding country, the convex front it thrust out to the north, its swells and slopes for the protection of defenders, gave it a superb military value. The approaches multiplied its defensive strength. Junglelike woods and underbrush and swampy streams made it difficult for infantry to force through to the base, and almost impossible for artillery. Once arrived there, attackers faced bare slopes 400 to 800 yards long, now completely at the mercy of Federal guns massed hub to hub on top, and to infantry concentrated there. Behind it the Federal gunboats in the James could fire over the hill into the back area of an attacking army.

The Confederate commanders were singularly ignorant of the ground. Lee did not know it at all in a military sense. One of those who did know it was the Rev. L. W. Allen of Magruder's staff. He described the terrain to D. H. Hill in such a way that Hill repeated it to Lee and suggested: "If General McClellan is there in force, we had better leave him alone." Longstreet overheard this and laughed. "Don't get scared, now that we have got him whipped," he said.[79]

Longstreet could be blunt in such circumstances. Like many others that day, he did not yet know the difficulty of moving infantry to the point of attack, the far greater problem of hauling guns through the jungle, or the massive power of Col. Henry J. Hunt's 100 pieces of Federal reserve artillery, including siege guns, on the hilltop in addition to brigade and divisional guns, a total of perhaps 350, admirably placed and served,[80] or, finally, those naked slopes across which attacking infantry would have to march into the cannons' mouths.

Jackson, leading Lee's army toward this ominous powerhouse, swung off to his left through the trees to circle part way around the

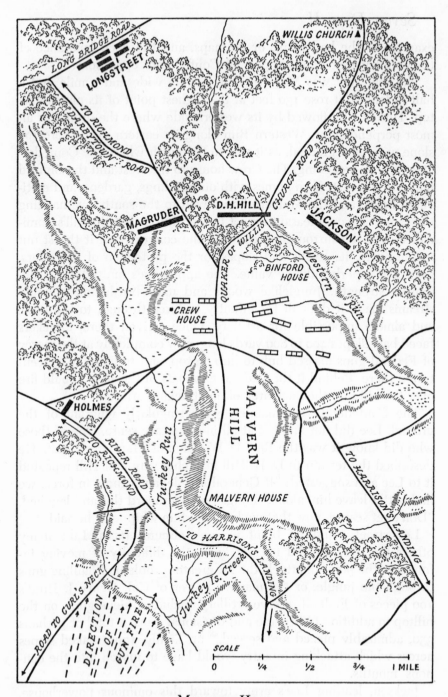

MALVERN HILL.

Federal right. D. H. Hill's division straddled the Willis Church (Quaker) Road. Magruder was to continue the line to the right, but, as he was still lost on the other Quaker Road, two of Huger's brigades, Wright's and L. A. Armistead's, came into line next to Hill. Magruder eventually extended the line around to the right. Part of Huger's force and all of Longstreet's and A. P. Hill's were in reserve. Jackson held Winder and most of Ewell in support.

Longstreet, directed by Lee to reconnoiter the right of the line, came back with the report that if 60 guns could be placed partly on an elevation on the right and partly in an open field in Jackson's area on the left, they could crisscross semi-enfilading fire on the hill with promising results. Lee approved.

Putting the plan into execution was another matter. Federal guns were already punishing all movements. The only road was under direct fire. The dense woods were such a formidable barrier that not many guns could be dragged through them. All of D. H. Hill's guns had been sent to the rear because he had no ammunition. The army had a reserve of 100 guns under General Pendleton, the Lexington rector with the West Point background. He spent the morning looking for Lee to find out his orders and looking for artillery positions. He found neither. "To remain near by, therefore, and await events and orders, in readiness for whatever service might be called for, was all that I could do," he reported of a day of remarkable futility. He added that "no occasion was presented for bringing up the reserve artillery . . . it seemed that not one-half of the division batteries were brought into action." [81]

The few batteries that did get into action fired boldly at the hilltop before most of them were smothered by return fire. Nevertheless, the plan remained the same: when Brig. Gen. L. A. Armistead, who was so placed that he could observe the effect of the artillery fire, was satisfied that the Federal lines were broken, he was to charge with a yell, whereupon all others were to do the same.

Lee realized by 2:30 P.M., after an hour's one-sided artillery engagement, that the plan was not working well. Taking Longstreet with him,[82] he rode to the left to see if a turning movement was possible, for which Longstreet and A. P. Hill would be available. Just at this time Whiting on Jackson's left noticed a shift of troops on the hill. He thought the Federals were retreating, and so reported. In a few minutes word came from the right wing that Armistead had driven in skirmishers and seemed to be progressing. Lee assumed that the battle had changed color. He sent word to Magruder to "press forward with your whole command and follow up Armistead's successes." [83]

Magruder could gather together, given time, 15,000 men of his own and Huger's divisions, but the brigades were scattered. Only William Mahone's and Wright's brigades, 2,500 strong, both of Huger's division, plunged forward on the right and Armistead to their left.

The Federal defenders had not retreated, though Sumner had shifted ground. The effectiveness of the meager Confederate artillery fire is suggestive of what it might have accomplished had its idle guns come into play. Armistead's earlier successes were minor. Now his men came into a heightened and sustained storm of artillery fire that ripped their lines. They kept on advancing with romantic ardor, but men fell in great numbers, dead on the spot or bent in anguish. When they could stand no more, they rolled behind protecting ground swells and into ravines on the right. They had reached within 300 yards of the Federal guns, but their number condemned them to be a forlorn hope from the start.

To their left, near the center of the encircling line, D. H. Hill, observing the punishment of the Confederate batteries, sent a note to Jackson to say that "the firing from our batteries was of the most farcical character." [84] But Jackson repeated the order from Lee for a general advance at the signal of shouting from Armistead's men.

At about 5:30, while Hill was conferring with his brigade commanders, they heard shouting on their right followed by musketry, and Hill turned his men loose. They advanced across the open field. The Federal guns, shifting from the target of the hardly more than 3,500 men in Armistead's, Wright's, and Mahone's brigades, concentrated on the more than 10,000 men of Hill's division, bare and unprotected as they marched to destruction.

The long lines staggered under blistering fire. They tried to pierce the left of Phil Kearny's division, thrust at one side of Couch's division and then at the other, and fell back in disorder. [85] Re-forming, they came on again; and again Hunt's artillery cut them to pieces, killing their officers in great numbers and tearing their ranks apart. "It was not war," Hill said later of Magruder's attack on his right; "it was murder." [86] He could have said it of his own division.

Finally Hill asked Jackson for re-enforcements. Jackson ordered up Winder's division and part of Ewell's. But darkness was beginning to fall now, the thick woods were worse barriers than ever, and no re-enforcements arrived in time. Hill fought for nearly two hours alone.

The final drama of the ghastly day rose now to its crescendo on the right. There Magruder, finally bringing up his other brigades and Huger's, sent them up the hill to aid the pinned-down Armistead, Wright, and Mahone. "I never saw anything more grandly heroic," D. H. Hill wrote of the attack of the men of McLaws, G. T. Anderson, Semmes, Toombs, Barksdale, Cobb, Kershaw, and Ransom (of Holmes' division).[87]

The weight of eight brigades, delivered hard after Hill's attack, fell heavily on the defenders and shook them. Ransom pushed to within twenty yards of a battery. But from the hilltop regiment after regiment rose with its volleys to add to the guns. The lines crumbled, lost contact, broke in confusion, and could only seek shelter from the merciless rain of steel or fall back down the hill.

The day was done—a tragic day of ignorance and mismanagement, all the way from the hasty decision to attack a formidable position without knowledge of the terrain to the inadequate artillery preparation, the insufficient utilization of the army's strength, and the absence of control of the units that did attack. McClellan's powerful artillery cut them to pieces one by one.

None of Jackson's two-division reserve went into action, nor did Longstreet's division, nor A. P. Hill's. All of the reserve artillery remained in reserve. Stuart's cavalry was absent. Of the infantry alone, 15 brigades (ten from Magruder, Huger, and Holmes, and five from D. H. Hill) charged up Malvern Hill, while 24 brigades (six of Longstreet's, six of A. P. Hill's, ten of Jackson's—of which four were Ewell's, two were Whiting's, and four were Winder's and Lawton's—and two of Holmes') waited as spectators.

Against these Porter had on Malvern Hill the divisions of Morell, Sykes, and McCall (now commanded by Seymour) of his own Fifth Corps, Couch's division from the Fourth Corps, and two brigades from Heintzelman's Third Corps and one brigade from Sumner's Second Corps, a total of 15 infantry brigades, supported by the remainder of Sumner's and Heintzelman's Corps—virtually the whole of McClellan's army. Porter had full time to organize in his superb defensive position. He had all the Federal artillery, well placed and ably directed, in contrast to an attacking force that was badly served by its own artillery. Most of the Confederate casualties resulted from artillery fire. Only in the reckless courage of the assault did the Confederates match the effective Federal defense.

Hindsight has suggested—as some foresight, like D. H. Hill's, did suggest—that Malvern Hill should not have been attacked head-on. It might have been enveloped from the Confederate left, by Jackson, who led the advance to the left. Lee was on the point of that decision when misinterpreted information turned him aside. His regret at the end of the day was profound. Probably he had been influenced by the disappointments of earlier days when the quarry had slipped away. Now when the quarry turned to fight, it was tempting—when the strength of the position was not understood—to leap in for the kill. But it was a costly mistake.

Jackson had no part in the major mistake. Precisely what orders he was under is difficult to determine. If Lee's order for units to advance when Armistead let go with a shout applied to the whole of Jackson's force, instead of only to D. H. Hill's division of his force, then he would have something to answer for. Hill's report reflected bitterness that others did not attack when he did. He did not mention Jackson, but in view of his distress on the field Jackson's waiting to strengthen him until Hill did ask for re-enforcements (to which Jackson responded promptly, although the re-enforcements did not reach Hill in time to be effective) needs explanation.

It is not clear that Lee's order had the purpose of bringing all units into the assault. Jackson in his report referred to Lee's order "that at a given signal there should be a general advance of the whole line," [88] and Hill's report mentioned that Armistead's shout "was to be the signal for a general advance, and all the troops were then to rush forward with fixed bayonets." [89] The signal did not apply, however, to Longstreet and A. P. Hill, in support, and apparently it did not apply to troops Jackson was holding in support.

More to the point is the fact that Lee was in contact with Jackson during the battle. Jackson had his headquarters on the Willis Church Road at a pair of gateposts near the residence of C. W. Smith, and Lee's headquarters were nearby. [90] They were together when word reached Jackson of the punishment one of his batteries was undergoing, and they discussed briefly what to do. Although

Lee moved about the field, he does not appear to have tried to reach Jackson with additional orders to attack or to have been disappointed that only Hill's division of the Jackson force stormed the hill.

Yet Malvern Hill was a battle on which Jackson exercised curiously little influence. He seemed to be of it but not in it, to be doing what was asked of him but only when it was asked, and no more. He seemed to remain apart from it as though not at ease in his relationship to it. It was the first battle in which Jackson participated under Lee's eye, and the events suggest that Jackson and Lee, who had established quickly a happy understanding in correspondence, may not yet have established the personal understanding which later was exemplified in remarkable degree.

In other respects Jackson presented a striking contrast to his exhaustion the day before at White Oak Swamp. He helped personally in pulling a gun of Capt. James Reilly's North Carolina battery through the woods.[91] He accompanied Hill on a reconnaissance of the forbidding slope up which Hill subsequently advanced.[92] When the fiery Trimble was all for throwing his brigade against the Federal defenses after Hill had fallen back, Jackson restrained him with grim comment about Hill's experience with an entire division and "I guess you had better not try, sir." [93] When a message came that a battery was in bad shape, Jackson left Lee's side, despite Lee's protest, and set out with Pendleton and Douglas to remedy the situation. They came under artillery fire, had a shower of dirt from a shell thrown over them, and yet, with Jackson leading, persisted on their course, the young men erect and unhappy, Jackson apparently unaware of danger. A member of Lee's staff followed them at a gallop and said quickly: "General, General Lee presents his compliments and directs you to return at once." They returned.[94]

Late in the day Stuart sent Blackford of his staff with a message. In the darkness and confusion it was no easy assignment, and Blackford, asking questions, came upon a wounded soldier and inquired where Jackson was. "Do you hear that 'ar firing? Well, that's where you will always find Old Jack," was the reply.[95]

Blackford reported briefly of Stuart's experiences at the White House base of the Federals, now abandoned by McClellan.

"That's good, that's good," Jackson said in his characteristic words. "Changing his base, is he?" He chuckled. By this time McClellan's change-of-base policy had become a byword among the soldiers.

When they saw a rabbit in flight, some soldier was likely to say he was "changing his base." [96]

Jackson asked Blackford to spend the night and peppered him with questions about Stuart's adventures. It was a night of extraordinary confusion. Attacking units had left a heavy proportion of their ranks on the field, in death or in the agony of their wounds; and all night long the cries of youngsters in torture made the night hideous. The remnants that survived were scattered in the woods. Re-enforcements coming up often lost their way. Few officers or men knew where other units were or where they themselves stood. The army was perilously like a mob.

Competent officers were so shocked by the disorder around them that they feared an attack by McClellan which they saw no chance of resisting. Jackson went to sleep on a pallet which his Jim had prepared for him, with Dabney nearby. About 1 A.M. Ewell and Hill sought out the bivouac, woke Jackson, and pressed upon him their fears. Jackson listened and asked some questions.

"General Ewell," he said suddenly, "where is Taylor's brigade?"— for which Jackson had a special feeling.

"General, practically it is nowhere," Ewell told him.

Squatting on Jackson's pallet, they talked more, their heads together and looking (Dabney thought) like frogs. Finally Ewell could stand it no longer. He blurted out: "If McClellan knows what he is doing, he will take the aggressive in the morning, and I tell you we are in no condition to meet it."

"Oh, no," Jackson said immediately. "McClellan will clear out in the morning." [97]

Jackson was right. When July 2 dawned in a thick mist that was as wet as rain, the Federal forces, except for a thin screen, were plodding down the back slopes of Malvern Hill along the eight miles that led to Harrison's Landing, hard by the great house of Westover, and the sheltering guns of the Federal fleet.

Back on the battlefield Jackson, up early, put working parties to the grisly task of collecting the dead. He did it with such furious zeal, trotting to and fro on his horse, issuing his sharp commands, and pushing the men too fast for them to rifle the pockets of the slain (they cursed him for this behind his back), that Blackford, who had volunteered to act as his aide, was puzzled almost beyond containing himself.

He watched Jackson drive his men as they laid out the bodies in rows, from a dozen to 40 or 50, covered them completely with blankets and oilcloths, piled their muskets and accouterments in gullies for concealment, and then picked up "every scrap of clothing and caps, and every scrap of human flesh scattered around, such as legs and arms, etc. etc." (Artillery casualties were terribly mutilated.)

Blackford remembered talks of the General's eccentricity and even unsoundness of mind. When nothing remained of the scattered dead except dark stains on the ground, and Jackson "had swept his dust in piles, like a good housewife, and the floor looked clean though the piles were still there," Blackford put the question to Jackson: "Why?"

"I am going to attack here presently, as soon as the fog rises," Jackson told him, "and it won't do to march the troops over their own dead, you know; that's what I am doing it for." [98]

When it became clear that the Federal forces had left, the General directed the men to build fires, cook rations, and dry their soaking clothes, now saturated with the rain that had begun to fall heavily. He himself went with McGuire to the Poindexter house to see Lee. But he had already made up his mind about the proper course. It was to pursue the enemy with full strength and immediately.

Lee was trying to obtain information of Federal movements and to lay out the army's course. Longstreet was there, and other officers. President Davis came in. McGuire pointed him out to Jackson, and the General immediately stiffened like a corporal at attention, not a muscle moving. Lee, surprised to see Davis, looked around to be sure that he knew everyone, noticed no sign of recognition of Jackson, and turned back to the President. "Why, President, don't you know Stonewall Jackson? This is our Stonewall Jackson," he said.

Davis came forward immediately, as warm in his prepared greeting as he had been in actual greeting of others. But at the sight of Jackson, frozen like a ramrod, he halted after a step. Immediately Jackson brought his hand up to his head in formal military salute. Now Davis froze for a second. Then he bowed to the violently saluting Jackson and turned to others in the room.[99]

This was the first time Jackson had seen the President since the Romney campaign and the intervention of Secretary Benjamin at the President's direction. What had happened then he still remembered, and perhaps he remembered promotions he did not approve, or additional grievances.

The experience drove Jackson into deeper silence. He sat in a corner, listened to reports that told of almost impassable roads and deep mud everywhere, growing worse under the continuing downpour, and said nothing unless asked a direct question. But he did not like what he was hearing. Davis caught Jackson saying once, "They have not all got away if we go immediately after them." [100] But to Lee the idea seemed impracticable, and it was so decided. Jackson's troubled face told of his disappointment. He was all for going hard after the enemy.

The next day, July 3, the rain eased, and Stuart located the enemy along the James, behind the ridge called Evelington Heights, with streams on both sides and gunboats in the river. Longstreet led Lee's advance in pursuit. But the Willis Church (Quaker) Road southward was so cut up by the passage of McClellan's army through the rain that Lee turned Longstreet back for some three miles in order to pursue by roads farther to the east.

Jackson, behind him, repeated the maneuver. It was horrible marching, and he made only three miles through the mire. He went to bed in a farmhouse east of Willis Church, furious at the delay.

"Now, gentlemen," he said to the staff that night, "Jim will have breakfast for you punctually at dawn. I expect you to be up, to eat immediately, and be in the saddle without delay. We must burn no more daylight." [101]

But the staff was exhausted. At dawn (July 4) the General stomped downstairs, found Dabney up and waiting for him, but nobody else.

"Major," the words crackled, "how is it that this staff never will be punctual?"

"I am in time. I cannot control the others," Dabney replied.

The General, furious now, turned to Jim. "Put that food back into the chest, have that chest on the wagon, and that wagon moving in two minutes," he ordered.

Dabney suggested that the General had better eat, but the General was in no humor for food. He went to Ewell's headquarters, found that officer in bed, and exploded once more. Turning to

Douglas, who had stumbled in a few minutes before, he sent him to put Ewell's division in motion.

Eventually Jackson, Longstreet, and A. P. Hill came up to McClellan's defenses on Evelington Heights. Stuart had ridden up the Heights the day before and found them undefended, so demoralized had McClellan's army been after Malvern Hill, the march in the rain, and the weariness of the whole campaign.

Stuart could overlook half of the Federal army. He hauled up a single gun and began to blaze away—a futile piece of bravado that spurred the Federals into driving him off the Heights and occupying it themselves. Had Stuart waited for Longstreet, the occupation of Evelington might have been a formidable, even decisive, advantage. Now Longstreet, A. P. Hill, Jackson, and D. R. Jones (just ordered up by Lee) were in battle array at the foot, preparing to attack.

Jackson did not like the prospect and insisted to Longstreet that he wait until Lee arrived. Lee did not like the prospect either, once he had surveyed it, and he decided not to throw his army again at a prepared and heavily defended position. He drew back.

That was the finish. The campaign had ended. It had cost Lee 20,141 casualties, 5,590 of them on the slopes and under the guns of Malvern Hill, against 15,849 for McClellan. Of the Confederate casualties the dead numbered 3,286, the wounded were 15,909, and the missing were 946.[102] McClellan's dead and wounded were only half as many, 1,734 and 8,062, respectively; but his missing were six times as numerous—6,053.[103]

Lee's disappointment was extreme. "Under ordinary circumstances the Federal Army should have been destroyed," he wrote in his report. "Regret that more was not accomplished," he conceded, "gives way to gratification to the Sovereign Ruler of the Universe for the results achieved," [104] but the mood of judgment was grim.

Jackson, whatever his thinking about the Seven Days, expressed no such regrets. "Undying gratitude is due to God for this great victory," he concluded, "by which despondency increased in the North, hope brightened in the South, and the capital of Virginia and of the Confederacy was saved." [105]

The achievement was greater than that. Lee might grieve—justifiably—at opportunities lost and thrown away, for which many men bore the responsibility. But the major Federal campaign of the first

seven months of 1862, made with superior numbers and a more
powerful force in every respect, had been hurled back in failure,
most emphatically in the mind of its commander. More than two
years would pass before the danger grew so imminent again. Though
the price in blood was cruelly high, the strategic victory was unmistakable and decisive.

# 26 | CEDAR RUN

*"Your General will lead you. . . ."*

Jackson—after a few days of rest—came out of the Seven Days himself again: disturbed that the army was sitting on its haunches while there was work to be done, restless to be about it, imaginative in devising ways and means of making his views known, and watchful over the needs of his troops.

His command formed part of the lines that circled Harrison's Landing until July 8, constantly ready for battle. On that day the troops began to move back. A mile and a half to their rear they came to a creek, and the General halted for several hours and ordered the men to bathe—they needed to.[1] The troops spent the night at White Oak Swamp, of grim memories, then moved on to the Morris farm neighborhood on the Mechanicsville road to the northeast of Richmond.[2]

Not since April 29 in the Valley, after Kernstown, had the Valley troops spent four consecutive days in one camp. To a man, including their General, they disliked the lowlands beside the James: disliked the water, missed the sight of the mountains, longed for upland air.[3]

The General fumed at the delay. Before leaving the lines around McClellan he sent for Boteler and to him exploded. "Do you know that we are losing valuable time here?" he demanded.

"How so?" Boteler asked.

"Why, by repeating the blunder we made after the battle of Manassas, in allowing the enemy leisure to recover from his defeat and ourselves to suffer from inaction. Yes"—his voice rising in emo-

89

tion—"we are wasting precious time and energies in this malarious region that can be much better employed elsewhere, and I want to talk with you about it."

The General elaborated. McClellan's army was thoroughly beaten, he said. It would have to be re-enforced and reorganized before it could be effective. So far as it was concerned, the safety of Richmond was assured. (On July 1 McClellan asked Lincoln for 50,000 re-enforcements. On July 3 he raised the figure to 100,000. By the 24th he had reduced this figure to 30,000, and when the issue arose as to whether he should remain on the Peninsula or withdraw, he thought that with 20,000 more troops he could capture Richmond.) The time was thus ripe, Jackson continued, for the northward movement about which he had talked with Boteler in the Valley.

This, Jackson said, he wished Boteler to tell the President. When he did, Boteler must say that the proposal did not represent self-seeking on Jackson's part. He would be willing to follow any designated commander.

"What is the use of my going to Mr. Davis?" Boteler asked. "He'll probably refer me again to General Lee. So why don't you yourself speak to General Lee upon the subject?"

"I have already done so," Jackson replied.

"Well, what does he say?" Boteler asked in turn.

"He says nothing," Jackson said. But he added quietly: "Don't think I complain of his silence. He doubtless has good reasons for it."

Boteler, probing for more information, asked another question: "Then you don't think that General Lee is slow in making up his mind?"

"Slow!" Jackson exclaimed. "By no means, Colonel. On the contrary, his perception is as quick and unerring as his judgment is infallible. But with the great responsibilities resting on him, he is perfectly right in withholding a hasty expression of his opinions and purposes."

After a pause Jackson said: "So great is my confidence in General Lee that I am willing to follow him blindfolded. But I fear he is unable to give me a definite answer now because of influence at Richmond where, perhaps, the matter has been mentioned by him and may be under consideration. I therefore want you to see the President and urge the importance of prompt action."

Next morning Jackson suggested to Boteler that since the President would like exact information about the enemy he had better go along with Whiting and himself on a personal reconnaissance they were making. The three rode toward the Federal outposts, tied their horses in woods, and crept, on a hot morning, across an open field behind a fence overgrown with bushes, watching Federal pickets that were plainly visible. They reached a knoll that permitted a fine view of the Federal camp, and the officers surveyed the scene with glasses.

A balloon began to rise—"Professor" Lowe * at work again—and to Boteler it seemed to hover almost over their heads. The three left, and that afternoon Boteler rode 25 miles, "the hottest and most exhausting [ride] I've ever had before or since," to Richmond.

The next day Boteler saw the President and "said all that was necessary upon the object of my interview." It was the third time he had acted as Jackson's personal emissary to urge vigorous military action in the Northern States.[4] Nothing happened.

But Jackson's strong feeling on this subject did not change.

Just as the Seven Days fighting was beginning, on June 26, the War Department in Washington united the Mountain Department (Frémont), the Shenandoah Department (Banks), and the Rappahannock Department (McDowell) into the Army of Virginia with orders to demonstrate toward Gordonsville and Charlottesville in the hope of drawing off some of Lee's forces. Maj. Gen. John Pope, who had commanded the army corps called "The Army of the Mississippi" with success [5] in the West and had a reputation as a breezy and optimistic officer in the old army, came in to command it. Frémont, an older man, resigned in a huff, and Franz Sigel succeeded him with the First Corps. Banks and McDowell had the Second and Third, respectively.

Pope had, before July ran out, 56,000 men in the field, though they were widely scattered from the Valley to the Rappahannock, and virtually no Confederate forces opposed him. He was a bombastic officer who celebrated his taking command with a proclamation that contained the following sentiments: "I come to you from the West where we have always seen the backs of our enemies; from

---

* Thaddeus S. C. Lowe was a balloonist whose scouting of Confederate areas and troops in a succession of balloons drew derision from both sides at first, but later was recognized as a valuable service. He was called "the most shot-at man" in the war. The Confederates tried to duplicate his work and produced a balloon of silk, much of it from women's clothes, but it was not a success.

an army whose business it has been to seek the adversary and beat
him when he was found; whose policy has been attack and not defense. . . . I desire you to dismiss from your mind certain phrases,
which I am sorry to find so much in vogue amongst you. I hear constantly of 'taking strong positions and holding them,' of 'lines of retreat,' and of 'bases of supplies.' Let us discard such ideas. . . .
Let us study the probable lines of retreat of our opponents, and
leave our own to take care of themselves. Let us look before us,
and not behind . . . disaster and shame lurk in the rear. . . ." [6]

The report spread through the Army of Northern Virginia, already
amused at these words, that Pope had dated this proclamation
"Headquarters in the Saddle" (though he had not). The Confederate ranks, where soldiers liked few things better than to put boastful officers in their places, crackled with jokes about generals who
put their headquarters where their hindquarters ought to be. But
what followed changed their guffaws into anger.

In quick succession Pope issued a series of harsh orders. One
order was for his troops to subsist upon the country, taking supplies
where they found them and offering vouchers payable at the end of
the war if those presenting them could show they had been "loyal
citizens of the United States" since accepting the vouchers. [7]

A second order provided that if a railroad, highway, or telegraph
line was damaged by guerrillas, citizens within five miles should
turn out *en masse* to repair the damage and pay the cost; that if a
soldier or "legitimate follower of the army" was fired at from a
house, the house should be razed and the occupants made prisoners,
and if such an incident occurred "distant from settlement," the
people within five miles would be held accountable and should be
levied on for indemnity, and if anyone was caught in such acts, he
should be shot on the spot. [8]

A third provided that all citizens within the army's lines or in its
rear should be required to take an oath of allegiance to the United
States and, if they would not, should be escorted southward beyond
the picket lines, and, if they returned, should be shot. [9]

From Lee down, the whole army muttered angrily about these
orders, the more particularly since McClellan had gone to unusual
lengths to preserve private property and protect civilians. To Jackson the first boastful proclamation was bad enough. He had heard

Stuart speak well of Col. L. S. Baker's First North Carolina Cavalry, in which one of the captains was Rufus Barringer, who had married Anna's sister, Eugenia Morrison; and he asked Stuart to have Barringer, whom he did not know well, come to see him. Barringer spent the night with Jackson, and the two had a long talk. The only report of that talk is by Barringer. In substance it follows.

Jackson, disturbed by Pope's attitude, reminded Barringer that before the war he had thought Federal invaders ought to be treated in the spirit of "the black flag"—"no quarter to violators of our homes and firesides!" Such a policy, of which the Bible furnished examples, would have been in the end humanitarian and merciful, Jackson explained, and would have brought the North "to its senses." Other policies, however, had been adopted, and Jackson had accepted them. Now he was troubled about how the South could wage the war most effectively.

This line of reasoning (as reported by Barringer) brought Jackson back to his familiar theme. He thought it impossible to defend all coasts, all cities, and all areas. He would concentrate on a few strong interior camps, well fortified, and two, four, or more light movable columns, built around cavalry and field artillery, capable of fast, long-range marching. He would hurl these flying columns at invaders. But especially he would hurl them deep into the Northern States, against cities and "teeming regions"—perhaps hundreds of miles away, from Pennsylvania to Ohio to Kansas. He would avoid "regular battles," would subsist his troops on Northern people, would levy on cities, and would hold leaders as hostages.

This kind of war, Jackson thought (as Barringer remembered him), best suited Southern temperament—"the dash and daring of the Southern soldier . . . the horsemanship of the Southern boy, and the personal courage. . . ." He had been much impressed by Stuart's ride around McClellan. He had talked to Lee of these ideas, Jackson said, and had the promise—no time indicated—of organizing such a column as he had in mind. If he did, he wanted Barringer as his quartermaster general. Harman was excellent in many ways, he said, but lacked command and troop-handling ability.

"All this may come to naught," Jackson said more than once (by this account). "General Lee will do just what the situation requires."

Barringer left the next morning and did not see Jackson again until the night of Antietam (when he said Jackson mentioned the conversation), and heard no more of the idea.*

For the most part the twelve days after Malvern Hill were a period of rest for Jackson. Riding one day with Douglas near the picket lines, then firing spitefully about Harrison's Landing, Jackson

---

* The Barringer report covers thirteen pages in Chapter 16 of Mrs. Jackson's *Life and Letters of General Thomas J. Jackson*, Harper & Brothers, New York, 1892. Substantially the same volume was published in 1895 under the title *Memoirs of Stonewall Jackson* by the Prentice Press, Courier-Journal Job Printing Company, Louisville, Kentucky, with some additional sketches of Jackson and tributes by officers, and other added detail after the main narrative; but this volume does not contain Chapter 16 of the original *Life and Letters*.

Of the Barringer report Henderson said (Vol. II, 202, footnote): "In Mrs. Jackson's Memoirs of her husband a letter is quoted from her brother-in-law, giving the substance of a conversation with General Jackson on the conduct of the war. This letter I have not felt justified in quoting. In the first place, it lacks corroboration; in the second place, it contains a very incomplete statement of a large strategical question; in the third place, the opinions put in Jackson's mouth are not only contradictory, but altogether at variance with his practice; and, lastly, it attributes certain ideas to the General—raising 'the black flag,' etc.—which his confidential staff officers declare he never for a moment entertained."

Hotchkiss advised Mrs. Jackson to leave "the Barringer stuff" out of her book. (Hotchkiss Papers, Box 12, Letter of Hotchkiss to McGuire, June 15, 1898.)

No important corroboration has been found for the "black-flag" views which Barringer attributed to Jackson, and they are undoubtedly at variance with his practice. The flying-column idea, however, is not an illogical expansion in principle of Jackson's well-known advocacy of carrying the war into Northern States.

Other difficulties of time and place cloud the Barringer report. In Mrs. Jackson's *Life and Letters* Barringer said that he received on July 14 a note which Stuart wrote to Baker, Barringer's commanding officer, on July 6, asking that Barringer be sent to Jackson, and that the conversation took place on the night of the 14th. The date of July 6 is puzzling because the note also includes a request from Stuart to Baker: "Please forward a report of operations of your cavalry from 26th June to 10th July as soon as possible," thereby suggesting that the note was written after July 10.

The date of July 14 is puzzling because Jackson was ordered on the 13th to move to Louisa and left Richmond on the 16th (Worsham, 107). Both Mrs. Jackson in introducing the Barringer report and Barringer in the body of the report indicate that Jackson was concerned about Pope's harsh orders. Yet the boastful proclamation of Pope is dated July 14, one of the offensive orders is dated July 18, a following one is dated July 10 but with a question mark after the date by the editors of the *Official Records*, and the third is dated July 23.

That Barringer, a respected man, had a talk with Jackson which dealt with some aspects of the subject mentioned, does not seem in doubt. Writing long after the event, Barringer may have been confused as to Jackson's references to Pope's orders, at least two of which, and possibly all of which, Jackson could not have known about on the 14th. Barringer may have been confused as to other details, or as to the exact meaning or emphasis which Jackson intended. It is not surprising, however, to read a report that the General who wished to pursue the retreating enemy after First Manassas as well as Malvern Hill, and sent Boteler three times to plead with high authority in Richmond for more aggressive action in Northern States, expressed a belief in such policies in an intimate moment to his brother-in-law.

saw blackberries and must have some. The two left their horses, and, with Jackson in the lead, pushed among the bushes until they came between the lines, Douglas conscious that the bullets were as plentiful as the berries, Jackson seemingly unaware of anything but the berries. So Douglas thought.

But Jackson, a berry in his fingers, turned to Douglas with a question. In what part of the body would Douglas prefer to be shot if he had a choice? Douglas suggested a preference for being shot in his clothes, but handed the General two especially luscious berries and said anywhere except in the face or in his joints. Jackson continued the subject by saying he had a prejudice against being shot in the back, so much so, indeed, that he often found himself turning his face toward the firing.

*Crack!* went a minié ball. It splintered a sapling, and the horses snorted. Jackson muttered something about not getting the horses killed, and they left. Douglas breathed easier.[10]

But when Jackson found the picket lines of Gen. Robert Toombs' brigade with both flanks hanging in the air, he rode straight to Toombs' headquarters. The day was hot, and that Georgia dignitary was stretched out in the shade. Jackson questioned him sharply, and, when Toombs protested that the pickets were all right, directed him to go at once, in person, and correct the mistake.[11]

That same afternoon Jackson stretched out at his headquarters for a nap, then roused himself, and asked if anyone had a novel—an unusual request from him. The wagons were far back near Mechanicsville, and the staff could find nothing, until Hugh McGuire in Thomas L. Rosser's cavalry gave him a yellowback, "sensational and full of wood cuts." Would it do?

The General went to work as if the book were a duty. His features sometimes relaxed, but his eyes did not leave the pages of large print, and he said not a word. Then he returned it with thanks. It was a long time since he had read a novel, he said—and it would be a long time, he added, before he read another.[12]

On the 8th, when they all moved back toward Richmond, the General and the staff brought up the rear. It grew late, and the General, riding Little Sorrel, was tired and sleepy. He nodded and swayed through the night ride. The staff watched in fascination, but he always righted himself. So they moved through the camp-fires, the roasting corn, and the immense humanity of the army.

One of the men from a fence corner, watching that awkward figure swaying on horseback, jumped to his feet, and came forward.
"I say, old fellow, where the devil did you get your liquor?"

The General straightened up at that, shook his head, and looked
around.

"Dr. McGuire, did you speak to me? Captain Pendleton, did you?
Somebody did"—and he reined in Little Sorrel.

For the first time the soldier had a good look at him. "Good God!
It's Old Jack!" And with the words he turned, jumped the fence,
crashed into the darkness, and was gone.

When McGuire explained the situation, the General, said Douglas,
was much amused. Halting, he got off his horse, stretched out beside
the fence, slept half an hour, and said he felt better.[13]

Another day when Jackson rode in a hurry across a farmer's
plowed field, the owner intercepted him and let go, verbally, with
all his guns. What was he riding across a plowed field for? Didn't
he have better sense? What was his name?

"Jackson," the General said.

"Jackson? Jackson? What Jackson?"

The General began to explain, and the light broke.

"You are Stonewall Jackson?" A sweep of his hat, a bow. "General
Jackson," he said, "ride over my whole field. Do whatever you like
with it." *

One day a package came. The General and Jim, unpacking it,
discovered a present from an admiring woman. It was a strange-
looking straw hat. Straw hats of curious sizes and shapes were tried
out in several units that summer. The Sixteenth New York Regiment
found out that straw hats were easily seen and attracted bullets,[14]
and therefore got rid of hats fast. Jackson tried on his present and
looked at himself in a mirror. "Under its transformation," Douglas
remembered, "our General, never any Apollo, became a caricature."
The General handed the hat to Jim, who received it "with mock
gravity and carried it off daintily."[15] That was the end of the straw
hat.

* Mrs. Jackson, 303.
  But Douglas tells the story differently. (Douglas, 118.) He has the farmer giving
in no inch. Startled but firm, he told the General he was setting a bad example
which his troops would follow. The next day the General pointed out the field to
others and said: "There I received the severest lecture I ever had, and it will make
me more careful hereafter."

During his stay near Richmond, Jackson went into the city on Sunday, July 13, to hear the noted Presbyterian ministerial orator, the Rev. Dr. Moses Drury Hoge. He slipped into the church unknown and unnoticed, and by some accounts was never recognized.[16] But Douglas testified that he, McGuire, and Pendleton accompanied the General, and that by the end of the service many in the congregation realized that the officer in the side pew was the national hero. They crowded around him, and the three staff officers were pushed aside. When they rescued the General, they had still to encounter outside the church a woman (who evidently knew Jackson, said Douglas). She walked down the street with him, having taken him by the arm, while the young men waited by their horses for fifteen minutes before he returned.[17] In Dabney's and Mrs. Jackson's accounts Jackson visited a mother whose son had been killed.

McGuire added to the tales of the day that when Jackson settled himself in church he went to sleep soon after the service began and slept through the greater part of it. "A man who can go to sleep under Dr. Hoge's preaching can go to sleep anywhere on the face of the earth," McGuire thought.[18]

Dr. Hoge preached later in the day at the Stonewall Brigade's camp, and the next day Jackson wrote to Anna of both services, and added: "It is a great comfort to have the privilege of spending a quiet Sabbath within the walls of a house dedicated to the service of God. . . . People are very kind to me. How God, our God, does shower blessings upon me, an unworthy sinner!" [19]

He gave Dr. Hoge an unusual pass:

> Headquarters, Valley District,
> near Richmond.
> Permit the bearer, the Rev. Moses D. Hoge, to pass at pleasure from Richmond to any part of my command.
> T. J. Jackson, Major-General.[20]

All of Lee's army waited this July, watching McClellan in his beachhead on the James and recovering from the strain of the Seven Days. Lee put many men to work on fortifications. He himself had two major responsibilities. The first was the reorganization of his army after the Seven Days had disclosed its strength and weakness. The second was the attempt to foresee the movements of McClellan,

who still had more men than Lee; of Pope to the north, who was
threatening in actions as well as words; and of a 10,000-man force
at Fort Monroe under Maj. Gen. A. E. Burnside which had come up
from the North Carolina coast when McClellan's fortunes were at
their lowest, as well as an unknown force at Fredericksburg.

In the army reorganization Magruder, who had already been assigned to the Trans-Mississippi Department, cut his ties with the
Army of Northern Virginia. Holmes, with a mediocre record, went to
the same region. Huger, ineffective in the Seven Days, was made
inspector of artillery and ordnance. D. H. Hill, who had done well,
took Holmes' place and ceased to be a part of Jackson's command,
to which he had been temporarily attached during the Seven Days.
A. P. Hill's impetuosity counted against him, but he was aggressive
and fought hard. Longstreet stood highest on the record.

About Jackson, whose over-all performance was below earlier
achievements and Lee's expectations, Lee uttered no word of criticism but possibly was puzzled. Jackson lost Whiting's Division to
D. H. Hill's new command, and only Ewell remained beside the old
Jackson division, to which Lawton's brigade had been added. This
was only some 11,000 men, though the Valley Army was itself again,
whereas Jackson had swung down on McClellan's right wing with
(including D. H. Hill) some 28,000. In the broad division of the
army into Longstreet and Jackson commands (not yet designated
corps) Longstreet had all the rest.*

Ewell remained loyal to Jackson. Some officers in Ewell's division
entertained the idea of separation and went to the War Department
with the suggestion. When Ewell heard about it he was deeply
disturbed and went in person to see Cooper, the Adjutant General,

* Freeman, in *R. E. Lee*, II, 248, points out that "Jackson fought the Seven Days
with fourteen brigades; in the reorganization, he was allotted seven. Longstreet had
carried six brigades across the Chickahominy; he soon had twenty-eight . . . the
disproportion in the size of Longstreet's and Jackson's commands must reflect, to some
extent, Lee's belief at the time regarding the comparative willingness of the two men
to co-operate." It should be added that D. H. Hill with five brigades had been
only temporarily attached to Jackson and that A. P. Hill with six brigades was placed
under Jackson's command before July was out. When Longstreet was ordered August
13 to the Gordonsville area to join Jackson, he carried ten brigades.

Some officers, it is true, looked askance at the light casualties in Jackson's command, proportionately, wondering if this was evidence that these units had not borne
their share of the campaign's hard fighting. The ratio of Jackson's casualties of
6,721 to the army's total of 20,168, as enumerated by Alexander, was considerably
less than the ratio of his command to the army.

to protest against being separated from Jackson. Cooper told him that no such move was in contemplation.[21] Nor was it later. Ewell remained a part of Jackson's command thereafter.

Jackson lost Dabney. That theologian-turned-staff-officer was worn out during the Seven Days, suffering cruelly from lack of food and sleep and succumbing to sickness which did not respond to treatment. He needed badly to rest, and Jackson had to let him go. "It was with tearful eyes that I consented to our separation," Jackson told Anna.[22] No one had worked more industriously than Dabney. He had mind and character, and the General liked to have him nearby. He was never able to come back.

Lincoln and Stanton had more reorganizing to do than the establishment of Pope's Army of Virginia. They called for 300,000 volunteers, and on July 11 they ordered Maj. Gen. H. W. Halleck from the West to be general in chief. Halleck arrived at Washington on the 23rd and went the next day to see McClellan at Harrison's Landing to appraise the situation there. His judgment was that McClellan must withdraw, but as usual McClellan needed time to move. He resisted the decision strongly, and it was not until August 14 that he began moving.

Pope was more impetuous. He struck southward from the Washington and Manassas area, and on July 12 Lee had word that he had occupied Culpeper. That called for action. At Culpeper he was getting close to the Central Railroad at Gordonsville. On July 13 Lee ordered Jackson with Ewell to move to Louisa and, if practicable, to Gordonsville.*

---

* Charles Minor Blackford, then a captain commanding Company B, Second Virginia Cavalry, reported in *Letters from Lee's Army,* Charles Scribner's Sons, New York, 1947, under a date of July 13, that "I am sure General Jackson got orders or arranged to move tonight when in town. I was invited by Col. A. S. Pendleton, his adjutant [who was not a colonel until later] to go with General Jackson and his staff into town this morning. . . . We went first to the Governor's mansion and there, I suppose by appointment, we met General Lee. The two generals went into the house. . . . They were there only a short time; then the two generals and Gov. Letcher came out on the front steps. . . . The two then rode around to Jefferson Davis' house where some other generals met them and I suppose they had a council of war—certainly a lunch." The staff, meanwhile, was dismissed for an hour.

Blackford went elsewhere for luncheon, then returned, and his narrative continues: "I went back to the President's house where I found the staff officers assembling in front . . . soon the different generals, Longstreet and others, came out, but the particular two were kept to the last and then Lee, Jackson and President Davis came out together, a very distinguished trio, and stood talking on the steps . . . they shook hands cordially in telling each other good-by, but our observant eyes satisfied us that both Lee and Davis bade Jackson farewell in a manner that indicated they

"This new General claims your attention," someone remarked to Jackson as he set out.

"And, please God, he shall have it," Jackson replied.[23]

The Valley Army moved by rail, going into Richmond for entraining on the Richmond, Fredericksburg and Potomac, then changing to the Virginia Central, and riding to Louisa. The movement began on July 16 and continued to the 18th. Jackson himself was at Beaver Dam on the 17th and at Frederickshall on the 18th, doubling back on the footprints he had left when he came out of the Valley. At Frederickshall he was in the home of the Nat Harrises, whence he had set out on the post-midnight ride for Lee's headquarters on June 23.[24]

Learning in Louisa that Pope had not occupied Gordonsville, Jackson pushed swiftly on and arrived there on the 19th. He had cut across Pope's path to the railroad. But with only 11,000 to 12,000 men he was in no position to resist if Pope brought together the 47,000 men under his field command. Jackson wrote hurriedly for re-enforcements.

The region brought the Valley Army, including its commander, immediate re-enforcement of spirit. They were in the rolling Piedmont again. The hills rose and fell, the streams sparkled among them, the air seemed to mountain men to have a superb quality, and far

would not see him again for a while,—or in other words that he had been ordered to move. The opinion was confirmed by the manner in which he rejoined his staff. He got on his old sorrel horse, which his courier was holding for him, and without saying a word to anyone, in a deep brown and abstracted study started in a gallop towards the Mechanicsville Pike, which we soon reached." His camp was near that road.

The conference so vividly described does not appear to be recorded by others or to be reported in major biographies of those who, Blackford said, participated. A question arises as to the date. Jackson wrote Anna on July 14 that he had heard Dr. Hoge preach in his church in Richmond on Sunday, July 13, and that night in camp to soldiers. Douglas reported that McGuire, Pendleton, and he accompanied the General to church in Richmond on that Sunday, and Douglas and McGuire described incidents of the experience in some detail. Neither mentioned the General's going to Governor Letcher's or President Davis', although these were distinctly unusual events. A conference with Davis such as that described by Blackford was unusual indeed, and, aside from its military importance, would be thought of as attracting comment from McGuire, who wrote piquantly of the stiff formality of the meeting only eleven days earlier between Davis and Jackson at Lee's headquarters after Malvern Hill. If Jackson attended Sunday morning service at Dr. Hoge's church on the 13th, as he said he did, and as Dabney, McGuire, and Douglas said he did, it is difficult to see how the Letcher and Davis conferences could have been held that morning. Douglas reported that Jackson visited Richmond once at night (in addition to the Sunday visit) on official business.

to the west the Blue Ridge could be seen on a clear day. The General, staying with a Presbyterian minister, the Rev. D. B. Ewing, and later with Mr. Ewing's mother-in-law, Mrs. Barbour, wrote to Anna that "my tent opens upon the Blue Ridge in the distance." [25] He found the Ewing children pleasant, spent much time with them, and so won the heart of one of the young girls that she asked for a brass button from his coat—and she got it. [26]

Although Jackson now remained in the same neighborhood for nineteen days, the volume of demands on his time led him to tell Anna after a week of it that "I am just overburdened with work, and I hope you will not think hard at receiving only very short letters from your loving husband . . . people keep coming to my tent"— but he broke off there. "A Christian should never complain," he said. "The apostle Paul said, 'I glory in tribulations!' What a bright example for others!" [27]

Lee hesitated long before sending re-enforcements to Jackson. He carried on a spirited correspondence with Jackson, writing on July 23, 25, 26, 27, August 4, 7, and 8, nearly always in response to letters from Jackson which have not been found.

Re-enforcements, Lee wrote on the 26th, are a "difficult question." He was sorry Jackson felt himself so weak, and he hoped returning stragglers would swell the ranks. A Louisiana brigade and a battery would definitely be sent to him, and, Lee hoped, a division later. He himself had to watch McClellan.

By the next day (in answer to Jackson's letter of the 26th), he promised to send A. P. Hill's division and the Second Louisiana brigade—in all, 18,000; and he thought Jackson's command must already number as many (though Jackson had only 11,000 or a little more with him). "What has become of them? I heard they were coming to you from the Valley." Advice followed: "Do not let your troops run down if it can possibly be avoided by attention to their wants, and comforts, &c., by their respective commanders. This will require your personal attention; also consideration and preparation in your movements." [28]

What Lee had in mind is not clear. Jackson drove his men relentlessly on the march and in battle, but he had no name for mistreatment or hardship in normal circumstances.

But Lee was plain enough about Pope. "I want Pope to be suppressed," he told Jackson. "The course indicated in his orders, if the newspapers report them correctly, cannot be permitted and will lead to retaliation. You had better notify him [Pope] at the first opportunity." [29]

Lee was especially angry at the report of Brig. Gen. Adolph von Steinwehr's holding five citizens of Luray as hostages in the event any of his soldiers were shot by guerrillas. "The order of Steinwehr must be disavowed," Lee wrote, "or you must hold the first captains from his army in retaliation. They will not be exchanged." [30]

Lee turned to a more delicate subject. He wrote: "A. P. Hill you will, I think, find a good officer, with whom you can consult, and by advising with your division commanders as to your movements much trouble will be saved you in arranging details, as they can act more intelligently." And then, as if to explain such suggestions—unusual from Lee to Jackson—he added: "I wish to save you trouble from my increasing your command." [31] He wished also, and primarily, to tell Jackson that he should keep his higher officers informed of what he was doing. But if he suggested—as an army commander certainly had a right to suggest to the equivalent of a corps commander—two respects in which he should improve, neither related directly to those questions of Jackson's conduct during the Seven Days which had caused most surprise and criticism. The letter does not appear to have changed Jackson's ways.

Hill received the order to join Jackson on July 27. He moved by rail, and by August 2 was on hand, bringing with him such a large train of wagons that Lee tried to retain some of them and warned Jackson about them.

While Jackson waited for re-enforcements his command moved from Gordonsville to Liberty Mills on the Rapidan and then to Mechanicsville, not far from Louisa [32] (good foraging country). The headquarters men were gathering, as they always did on the eve of big events. Hotchkiss, off on a mapping trip, received word from Jackson to report. When he returned, he thought Jackson and his troops too looked the worse for their Chickahominy experiences.

A smooth-faced, handsome young cavalry lieutenant, with a quiet manner and a steady eye, passed through with a letter of introduction from Stuart to Jackson which characterized him as "bold, daring, intelligent, and discreet." He was John S. Mosby, later the partisan par excellence, and he was on his way to scout beyond the enemy's lines in the Fredericksburg region. Mosby's letter from

Stuart included an inquiry as to whether Jackson had received a copy of Napoleon's *Maxims of War* which Stuart had sent recently.*

Capt. R. E. Wilbourn came in as a signal officer on a hot Saturday (and would remain long). The General heard Mr. Ewing preach on the 20th on "the goodness and severity of God," and Hotchkiss again thought he looked jaded.

Monday, when headquarters tents were shifted to a spot four miles from Gordonsville on the road toward Madison Court House, the hillsides were full of blackberries, and the troops were out in droves, the General among them. Boteler showed up again on the 24th, the day Lawton's Georgia brigade arrived.

On August 3 the General heard the Rev. Dr. Joseph C. Stiles preach to the Georgians from the text "Show thyself a man." Hotchkiss thought him eloquent and noted that "his voice thrilled like a trumpet." He knew that perspiration rolled down the preacher's face. When he prayed against the sin of straggling he showed an appreciation of current military problems.[33]

Another of Jackson's military problems was his cavalry. They had a new commander now, recently promoted Brig. Gen. Beverley H. Robertson, a Virginian and a West Pointer. Administratively and in discipline the cavalry had presented problems from the days of Ashby's command. Part of it had remained in the Valley, the Seventh and Twelfth Virginia and the Seventeenth Virginia Battalion. The Second Virginia under Munford and the Sixth under Flournoy had been with Jackson. Now, as the Valley horsemen rode into Gordonsville, all these units united in the Laurel Brigade, and Davis named Robertson to command it.

Jackson did not like Robertson, nor did most of the horsemen. He was strict and precise, whereas they had grown up on loose and adventurous ways. Eventually Jackson complained to Lee of Robertson, asking that Col. W. E. Jones (known as "Grumble" Jones) be named in his place. "That subject," Lee replied on August 7, "is not so easily arranged. . . ." He feared the judgment of Robertson "may be hasty."[34] To Jackson's dissatisfaction Robertson remained. Jones went to the Seventh.

Another problem was the old, unhappy issue of Jackson's arrest of Brig. Gen. Richard B. Garnett after he withdrew from Kerns-

* Freeman said (*LL.*, II, 2) that when he examined this book in the Confederate Museum in Richmond in 1907 he could not see that it had ever been opened.

town. Garnett, firm in his belief that he had acted wisely, and bitter at the severity of Jackson's judgment (especially Jackson's statement that "if he is given charge of a good brigade, it would become a bad one"), insisted on a court-martial. Lee sought to avoid that clash. He had suspended Garnett's arrest before the Seven Days and assigned him temporarily to D. H. Hill. A court was ordered to sit after the Seven Days, but Jackson's order to go to Gordonsville delayed action then.

Now, in the brief interval near Gordonsville, the courts-martial piled up on Jackson so that he had trouble finding officers for a trial of Colonel Conner for his actions at Front Royal.[35] In connection with another court-martial he sent out a circular to say that no sentence of flogging would be approved.[36] Eventually, on August 6, the Garnett court-martial opened at Ewell's headquarters. The day before, Sandie Pendleton, who expected to testify, wrote to his mother that the most important witness for Jackson, Frank Jones, had died from wounds received near Richmond and that "the case will most probably go by default in favor of Garnett."[37]

The testimony and examinations, moving in icy courtesy, disclosed sharp disagreement between Jackson and Garnett on the events at Kernstown. It produced a powerful attack on Jackson by Garnett for Jackson's not informing him of battle plans. Garnett said that, though second in command, he was kept in as profound ignorance of Jackson's intentions "as the humblest private in his army."[38] But once again the decision was held up.

For in the midst of the trial word reached Jackson on August 7 that only part of Pope's command was at Culpeper. This was the target for which he had been looking ever since he left Richmond: a semi-isolated force which he could strike without encountering superior numbers—as always he sought to do. He suspended the court at once and ordered an immediate advance. Lee had written him on August 5[39] warning against attacks on the enemy's strong points and advising him instead to turn his position, but leaving the decision about moving to his discretion. Before the 7th ended Jackson had his whole force on the move toward Orange and the Rapidan crossings on the route toward Culpeper.

Winder was sick that day, but when he heard of the advance he was determined, sick or not, to command his division in battle, if there was to be a battle. He told his aide, McHenry Howard, to ask Jackson if a battle was impending, and if so, where and when, so that he could be there. Howard reminded Winder that Jackson did not like such questions. But Winder was adamant.

Howard, still unwillingly, went to Jackson's quarters at the Jones house, near the foot of Haxall's Mountain. When he entered the General's room he found Jackson on his knees packing an old-fashioned carpetbag, his side face to the young officer. He kept on packing.

"General, General Winder sent me to say that he is too sick to go with the command," Howard said to the figure on the floor.

"General Winder sick? I am sorry for that," Jackson interrupted in a voice that Howard thought was "curt" and slightly "miffed."

"Yes, sir," Howard continued, "and the medical director has told him he must not go with the brigade. But he sent me to ask you if there will be a battle, and if so, when, and he would be up, and which way the army is going."

Howard waited for the blow to fall on his head. But Jackson, still kneeling, said nothing for a few moments, his head turned slightly away. Then his mouth widened a little with what Howard thought of as "one of his diffident smiles," and Howard relaxed.

"Say to General Winder that I am truly sorry he is sick"—then a slight pause—"that there will be a battle but not tomorrow, and I hope he will be up. Tell him the army will march to Barnett's Ford —and he can learn its further direction there." [40]

Although August 7 was a steaming hot day, and orders for the start were not given until well into the day, all units pressed forward, covering an average of some eight miles to the vicinity of Orange. This would mean a 20-mile march on the 8th, severe but not impossible. Jackson himself reached Orange, where he spent part of the night on a stile in the streets, but eventually he and his staff found lodging in the Willis home. [41]

The orders went out that night for the march next day, the 8th. Ewell was to lead, Hill to move next, and Winder's division to follow. [42] Fast marching was essential if Jackson was to place his army in position by the night of the 8th to assault Pope's advance guard, now known to be some six or seven miles on the near side of Culpeper. It was a risky move at best, striking, as Jackson was, at what was assumed to be a smaller force but one that almost surely was supported not many miles away by much larger forces. Secrecy and fast movement were important.

For these reasons Jackson had not been happy about the operations of his cavalry. A day or so earlier, when he was in a good humor, being amused at McGuire's eating a Bermuda onion, he had asked Robertson where the enemy was. Pope had been pushing his own cavalry hard and had strengthened its command by bringing in Brig. Gen. John Buford to replace Brig. Gen. John P. Hatch, who had seemed sluggish on two raids. Brig. Gen. George D. Bayard was his other commander, a vigorous cavalryman.

When Robertson heard Jackson's question, he replied, "I really do not know." All the glee dropped out of Jackson's face. He turned away, black as a thundercloud, and—said McGuire, who was present —telegraphed Lee for Stuart's services.[43]

Before morning on the 8th Jackson changed the marching orders, sending Ewell toward the Rapidan by a route higher up leading to Liberty Mills which would still bring his division to Barnett's Ford. Hill had no information about this change of orders.[44] At dawn on the 8th he had his division in the streets of Orange, ready to follow Ewell. When a column marched by he assumed it to be Ewell's, and one or two brigades had passed before he learned that this was Winder's division and that Ewell had moved out by another route.

Hill waited for Winder to pass, then found that Winder's wagon train was following his marching men, and waited for it to pass too. Jackson came up about this time, angry at the delay, talked to Hill, and ordered Winder to push on. But the road was clogged with wagons, and at Barnett's Ford the convergence of Ewell's men coming in from their route and Winder's men jammed the ford. Besides, the weather had grown ferociously hot, and men were falling out of ranks.

Eventually some of the advance troops made as much as eight miles, but those in the rear covered scarcely two. A worse beginning for an advance in which speed was a primary consideration would be hard to imagine.

Jackson's gloom was heavy. "I am not making much progress," he reported to Lee early on the 9th. The enemy was threatening his wagon train—another black mark against Robertson; the heat was oppressive; and the mix-up had slowed down the pace tragically.

"Hill's division is too large," Jackson continued, and he promised to reduce it. Meantime, "today I do not expect much more except to close up and clear the country around the train of the enemy's cavalry. I fear that the expedition will, in consequence of my tardy movements, be productive of but little good." *

On the 9th progress was much better. Ewell had the lead along the Culpeper road following Robertson's cavalry, which had thrown back Bayard's men from the crossing. Winder, commanding the division that was still called Jackson's, followed. Hill, up before daylight this morning, caught up with Lawton's and Taliaferro's brigades just as they set out. Federal cavalry could still be seen to the left, and Hill detached Gregg's brigade to guard the trains, to which Jackson assigned Lawton's brigade. The 1,200 wagons were cumbersome.

The long column stretched out for seven miles on the road to Culpeper, plodding through the dust and heat of the rolling country, the Blue Ridge visible in the haze to the west. The countryside was heavily wooded but cut up by fields of wheat and corn, and an occasional small stream ran across the road and splashed eastward to the Rapidan. As the troops advanced they saw in the distance a sharp rise on their right. Out of the undulating plain it rose to the proportions of a minor mountain called Cedar Mountain because of the two-forked stream that flowed around its northern base. It was also called Slaughter's Mountain from the family of that name that lived below the eastern face.

Ahead the road split, one fork turning northwestward to climb higher to Madison Court House, the other stretching out northeast-ward toward Culpeper. Half a mile ahead Federal cavalry, no longer retreating, topped a ridge. Ewell hauled up artillery and near noon opened fire. Immediately artillery fired back.

This looked like serious action. Jackson, his eyes on Slaughter's

---

* O.R., XII, pt. 2, 215.

Jackson must be blamed for poor staff work in not informing Hill of the change in plans, for not arranging better for the trains, and for permitting the jam at Barnett's Ford. Jackson charged that Hill's men were late in their bivouacs on the 8th, and he appears to have thought that Hill should have followed Ewell when Ewell's route was changed, presumably without further orders. But Hill was slow to find out his mistake in assuming Winder's division to be Ewell's. Jackson pointed out that he himself was about three-quarters of a mile from Orange, and seemed to imply that Hill, if in doubt, could have found out faster what the situation was. Some of Jackson's staff thought Hill did not show much energy. See O.R., XII, pt. 2, 214, 216 for the statements of Jackson and Hill; also Freeman—LL, II, 12 for additional details of the argument.

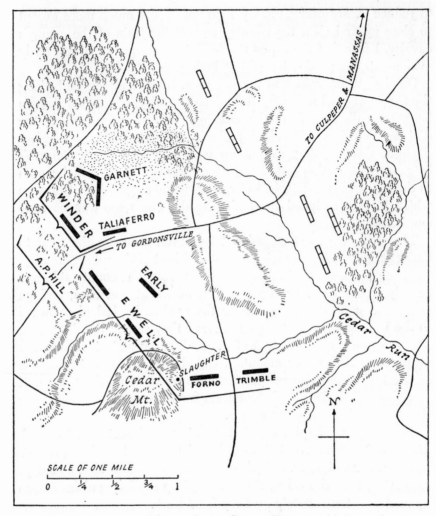

THE LINES AT CEDAR RUN.

Mountain a mile and a half to the right, the dominant natural feature on the landscape, ordered Ewell to swing to the right of the
road and to anchor his right flank on the mountain. In turn Ewell
directed his leading brigade to the area adjoining the road. This
was Elzey's old brigade, now commanded by Brig. Gen. Jubal A.
Early, just back to active duty after a wound at Williamsburg in
May. A West Pointer of the class of 1837, nine years ahead of Jackson, Early had resigned early from the army, practiced law in Vir-

ginia, and acquired a legal reputation. The war brought him back. A tall, thin, long-bearded officer, severely stooped, who looked older than he was and could be strict and severe, he was just coming into his own.

The other two brigades of his division Ewell sent all the way to the mountain: Trimble's brigade and the Louisiana regiments formerly commanded by Taylor, now called Hays' brigade but commanded at the moment by Col. Henry Forno. Ewell himself stationed the guns of Latimer's battery and part of Johnson's battery under Lieutenant Terry on the lower slopes of the mountain so that they had a long field of fire.

Less attention appears to have been paid to the left. This was assigned to Winder. That officer, fighting off his illness, placed the Third Brigade (W. B. Taliaferro) in the area adjoining the road and sent the Second Brigade, formerly Campbell's but now commanded by Lieut. Col. Thomas S. Garnett, farther to the left. The First Brigade (the Stonewall), now under Col. Charles A. Ronald, was in reserve. The batteries of Poague, Carpenter, and Caskie were in front of the infantry near the road.

Taliaferro's Third Brigade, as it was lined up parallel to the road and facing it, seemed almost to reflect an assumption that all the Federal forces were on the right of the road. When Garnett carried his brigade to the extreme left, he was under orders from Winder to avoid enemy batteries then in plain view by moving leftward through thick woods in which he could not be seen.

The original plan was that at the point where the woods ended— assumed to be beyond the Federal guns—Garnett was to charge the nearest Federal battery by a flank movement while Winder's artillery played upon it. But when Garnett reached the end of the woods, he saw that he would have to charge across an open field swept by the fire of a formidable force of infantry which he could now discern and a long line of Federal cavalry behind a fence. He halted immediately, sent an officer to report the situation to Winder, and received an order in reply to hold his ground.[45]

Garnett stationed his men along the edge of the woods. They looked across a brush field and fields of corn and wheat in shock with heavy woods some 300 yards in the distance. The Twenty-first Virginia Regiment was nearest Taliaferro's brigade, and the Forty-eighth Virginia was on its left. The line of woods curved back to the left at this point, and the Forty-eighth curved back with it. The Forty-second Virginia and then the First Virginia Battalion at the far edge of the flank were almost at right angle to the Twenty-first. The brigade presented a convex front to the enemy. Where the First Battalion waited at the extreme left, the woods were "so dense," said Maj. John Seddon, its commander, "that no other portion of our brigade could be seen from our position." [46] It may well have seemed a lonely position.

Hill's division, still on the march in the rear, was marked for reserve duty. Jackson would have some 20,000 infantry when all units were up, though hardly more than half as many without Hill; and he was well served by artillery. He was confident the force ahead of him was smaller.

It was. To support Bayard's tired horsemen Pope had sent at first a brigade (Brig. Gen. Samuel W. Crawford's) and followed with other units of the Second Corps. The commanding officer was Jackson's old Valley antagonist, Banks. He placed the division of Brig. Gen. Alpheus S. Williams on the right of the Culpeper road, opposite Winder's division, and Brig. Gen. Christopher C. Augur's division on the left, opposite Ewell.

Banks had no more than 8,000 men, his corps being depleted at the time. But Ricketts' division of the Third Corps was a bare four miles behind him with more than 10,000 men. Sigel had been ordered to hurry in from Sperryville with 14,000 men of the First Corps, and King's division of McDowell's corps, another 10,000, was ordered to come from the east. The three would make 34,000; with Banks, 42,000. Sigel lost his way, however, and King was not close enough for use.

Pope gave Banks orders which led to sharp disagreement later. Col. Louis Marshall (a nephew of Lee, who was much upset because Marshall was with the "miscreant Pope" [47]) delivered the orders verbally, but Banks told him immediately to dictate them to a staff officer. Banks insisted ever afterward that the orders directed him to "attack him [Jackson] immediately as he approaches." Pope insisted that he intended Banks to act defensively. Banks may have been the more eager, after humiliating experiences in the Valley, to catch Jackson at a disadvantage and obtain revenge when, as the Federal commanders believed, he was merely reconnoitering. Banks rarely, if ever, shrank from fighting, and although Jackson added once, "and he generally gets licked," Jackson had more respect for him than did some others. There was no doubt about Banks' aggressiveness this day, but a question remains of his wisdom.[48]

Ewell and Winder required nearly two hours to straighten out their lines, and it was close to 2 o'clock when Garnett's men on the far left heard firing to the right of the Culpeper road. Sandie Pendleton had given Early orders from Jackson to advance, supported by Winder when the latter was ready.

When the word came from Winder, Early began his maneuver. Designed for a flank attack on guns in front of him, it carried him behind a friendly slope to the left of the road, then back to the right. He pushed in enemy skirmishers, drove off some cavalry, and mounted to the top of a low ridge overlooking the valley of Cedar Run and the slope that rose beyond. As soon as he came into sight, three batteries across the valley opened on him vigorously. He fell back behind his own ridge and sent for artillery. If rough work was coming, Early did not like the look of the gap on his right, between his own brigade and the Trimble-Forno force on the flank, and he asked for a brigade to fill it. At the same time Early noticed Federal troops moving to the left, and he sent word of it to Winder—too late as it turned out.

Guns came up quickly from Capt. William D. Brown's and Capt. William F. Dement's batteries. They began a searching fire that was taken up along the line, left and right of the Culpeper road. It continued for two hours without decisive results. But it led to a grave loss on the left.

There General Winder, still an ill man and suffering from the heat, but a conscientious officer, had stripped off his coat the better to direct in person the fire of Poague's guns of the Rockbridge Artillery. A constant stream of enemy shells was crashing through the trees and bursting close by. Winder in his shirt sleeves saw that the guns opposite were changing position, and turned and shouted an order. In the furious noise nobody could hear it. Young Edward A. Moore, of the Rockbridge, being nearest, walked toward him to ask what he had said. Winder put his hand to his mouth to shout the order again. As he did so a shell tore through his side and uplifted arm, wounding him severely. He fell back and, said young Moore, "lay quivering on the ground." [49] A few hours later he was dead.

It was a grave loss both at the moment and in the long future.

Taliaferro had to take over the division without knowledge of Jackson's plans (there is no evidence that Winder knew much more), and although Taliaferro was not to blame for what followed, he was a new hand in control at a bad time.

Jackson and Taliaferro quickly had the news of Winder's wounding, and both went immediately to the scene. Jackson, unmistakably alert now to the dangers on the left, told Garnett of the Second Brigade to look well to his left flank [50] and to report at once to Taliaferro for re-enforcements. Garnett sent out officers to establish contact with Taliaferro.

The latter sensed the danger too. Almost immediately after assuming command he rode out to the Second Brigade's position to familiarize himself with it and reconnoitered the enemy's position from the wheat field in front of the First Battalion. He saw no enemy troops in front but noted blue uniforms partly concealed by undulations of the ground on the right. [51]

Before Garnett could make arrangements about re-enforcements, or Taliaferro had returned from his reconnaissance, the blow began to fall. It hit first at Early. About 5 o'clock skirmishers appeared along his front. When some artillery pieces of Capt. W. J. Pegram and Lieut. W. B. Hardy shifted from Winder's area to Early's, thereby rumbling dangerously close to Federal troops they could not see, Early sent forward his brigade at the double-quick to save them. [52] Federal troops on the point of attacking struck back, and his whole front blazed into action.

Jackson was watching this situation closely. Lieut. Col. R. Lindsay Walker, commanding the artillery in Hill's division, rode furiously into the melee to extricate his batteries. His roaring voice, hurling profanity now in the excitement of great effort, rolled over the field. Jackson came up on his horse, and Walker, who knew the General's views on swearing, cut his words instantly. But in the heat of this struggle the General understood.

"That's right, Colonel; give it to them," he shouted. [53]

Fortunately the re-enforcement Early had asked for came up— D. H. Hill's leading brigade, commanded by Brig. Gen. Edward L. Thomas. Early used it to pin down his right and steady that half of his line. It held under stiff attack. But as he turned back to his left he found it crumbling.

Banks was going all-out for a victory over Jackson. After the two hours of bombardment and the strengthening of his own right wing, he attacked at 5:45 against the dangling Confederate left with a well-organized frontal assault, effectively concealed and quickly delivered. Some 1,500 men of Crawford's brigade broke out of the woods that lapped around two sides of the First Virginia Battalion and the Forty-second Virginia Regiment. They ran across the open fields, firing as they came.

Seddon's men in the First Battalion, so isolated that they could see none of their comrades, fired as the enemy came within 150 yards, but saw little result. They fired two more scattering volleys and still could discover no effect. By this time the overlapping lines were close to their front and had closed in on their left flank. The battalion broke and ran in confusion. "Being on the extreme left of the brigade," Seddon reported later in sadness, "we were the first to see the flank movement of the enemy." [54]

The Forty-second saw it almost as soon and fired with coolness and rapidity, remaining in good order for half an hour.[55] But Maj. Henry Lane, the commanding officer, was fatally wounded early in the engagement, and the enemy flanked the regiment on the right as well as the left, and began to come into its rear. It fell back, fighting with the bayonet as it did so, and losing many officers and men as prisoners.

The Forty-eighth Regiment at the curve of the line fought against attacks on both its fronts, but "finding the enemy had got in our rear, almost entirely surrounding us, we were ordered to make our way out. . . ." [56]

The Twenty-first Regiment, still farther to the right, resisted "in high spirits" under Lieut. Col. R. H. Cunningham (who, like Winder, was sick that day), "all seeming eager for the engagement." When "another regiment of them emerged from a cornfield and arrayed themselves in line of battle to our left oblique," it seemed to heighten the ardor of the men, "who fought with all the gallantry and energy that could have been desired." But "suddenly and without any warning whatever a murderous fire was poured upon us from the rear, at least a brigade of the enemy having passed through the woods and reached within 20 or 30 paces of us. We had supposed that our rear was protected; why it was not is not for me to say."

Capt. W. A. Witcher succeeded to the command when "our gallant and beloved leader, Lieutenant Colonel Cunningham, fell mortally wounded," and "the adjutant was taken by the enemy, though afterward escaped; the sergeant-major was shot down; the flag-bearer was shot dead; a corporal of the guard, seizing the colors, shared the same fate, and a private who next raised them fell, wounded in three places." [57]

A Yankee sergeant, Private Worsham remembered, stepped out of nowhere and "actually took hold of one of the men of our regiment and pulled him out of ranks, and started toward the rear with his prisoner. One of our men, who was in the act of capping his gun, raised it to his shoulder, fired, and the sergeant fell dead not ten feet away. By this time the road was full of Yankees, and there was such a fight as was not witnessed during the war; guns, bayonets, swords, pistols, fence rails, rocks, etc., were used all along the line. I have heard of a 'hell spot' in some battles, this surely was one." [58]

The whole left wing was collapsing regiment by regiment. In Taliaferro's old brigade next in line, commanded now by another officer of the same name, Col. Alexander G. Taliaferro, two Alabama regiments facing combat for the first time, the Forty-seventh and the Forty-eighth, began to break. Here, because of the way the lines ran, the brigade came under fire from two directions. Part of the Thirty-seventh Virginia gave way, and the whole regiment had to be pulled back. With their flank open and raw, the next two, the Tenth and the Twenty-third, were recalled, and the entire brigade had melted away.

The contagion jumped the Culpeper road and spread into Early's left regiments. They could see the confusion and flight to their left, and the opening of their flank. They began to drift to the rear. Only the stanchness of Early's right, especially the Twelfth Georgia Regiment, parts of the Fifty-second and Fifty-eighth Virginia, and Thomas' fresh brigade, kept the anchor deep and firm. [59] But the crisis was grave, and it was threatening to grow worse.

Into this chaos Jackson stormed on his horse, his sword held high, the first and last time he ever raised it in battle, and his head bare so that all men could see his face. His voice cut through the noise like a knife: "Rally, brave men, and press forward!" "Your General will lead you—Jackson will lead you!" "Follow me!" [60]

Jackson's presence, his manner, his words, even his sword, had quick effect. He saw immediately that Winder's guns could be saved only by swift action. The word went up, and back they came at a

gallop. But he knew that the great task was halting the backward
flow, steadying the uncertain men, and making military units out
of disintegrated groups.

He had plenty of help. Officers all over the field were working
furiously to stem the flight, reorganize the regiments, and strike
back at the enemy. Many units had fallen back under orders, not
in panic; many men, once they fought off fright, were ashamed and
full of anger and wanted to vent it. The retreat, though plain to see,
was not deep and only in small degree was outright flight. The First
Brigade, reserve for the division, would surely come up at any
moment. Hill's big division, which had already sent its leading
brigade to Early's aid, could not be far behind. Still, it was a touch-
and-go affair of desperately fought minor combats all over the left
front, full of dangers for anyone within reach.

In the midst of these furies General Taliaferro caught Jackson's
bridle rein. "This is no place for you," he said. "You should go back.
You must go back immediately."

Jackson stared at him for a moment, nodded his head, said, "Good,
good," in the old way, and turned his horse's head out of the mad-
house.[61]

Ronald brought the First Brigade up, the Second, Fourth, Fifth,
Twenty-seventh, and Thirty-third Virginia Regiments which had
followed Jackson in the Valley. They advanced to the left of the
ground where the Second Brigade had broken and fallen back, with
the Twenty-seventh on the extreme right and the Thirty-third next
to it. Then they went forward in good spirit, though with both flanks
wide open. Driving through woods, they came under artillery fire,
pushed on to the open field, and halted to obtain orders from General
Taliaferro. He sent them forward again. They advanced into the
open, saw the enemy coming at them 300 yards away, poured in
volley after volley, and charged, Ronald at their head.[62] They drove
the enemy back into the woods.

"We had severe fighting for a short time, when the enemy broke,"
Private Casler remembered. "An officer came dashing down between
the lines to rally them and was riddled with bullets. He was a lieutenant colonel, I know, for I took particular notice of his shoulder
straps a few minutes afterward; they were such beautiful ones,
with silver leaf." [63]

But at this moment the enormity of its isolated position penetrated

the brigade. The right flank in particular was completely undefended
against firing that was coming all the way from the right of the
Culpeper road. The Twenty-seventh caught the brunt of these attacks, suffered from the cross firing, and began to drop back into
the woods. Its men scattered and could not be united again that
day, though detached groups made themselves useful.[64]

Ronald ordered a change of front to meet these attacks from the
right—a difficult move in combat and made now only with some
delay and confusion. The brigade direction was now at right angle
to its original direction. The Fourth fell back momentarily to re-form
after this move, as did the Thirty-third for 100 yards; but they recovered and joined the others in renewed advance.

Jackson, in the rear where Taliaferro had urged him to go, saw
and understood the movements, and recognized the need. He turned
to Hill. Branch's brigade had come up next after Thomas. Jackson
found it ready and waiting. He told Branch his left "was beaten and
broken, and the enemy was turning him and he wished me to advance."

Branch had sat in the Congress of the United States and had a flair
for oratory. He turned to his men with an exhortation that threatened
to spread into a speech. Jackson cut in curtly: "Push forward, General; push forward!" [65]

Branch went forward immediately along the Culpeper road, then
turned sharply left and plunged into woods. "I had not gone 100
yards through the woods before we met the celebrated Stonewall
Brigade, utterly routed and fleeing as fast as they could"—a reference to the Twenty-seventh, not to the other four regiments. Branch
let the men through, waited steadily for their pursuers, and met
them with crashing volleys.

The enemy reeled under this fire, and Branch moved ahead relentlessly, his lines straight, the whole brigade like a phalanx. The
Stonewall fell in on its left. The Third Brigade, relieved of pressure
now, re-formed and began to push forward again. Archer and Pender
brought their fresh brigades up from Hill's division, found Branch
engaged with the enemy, who had rallied again, and aided in pushing him back once more.

Branch, going ahead with great steadiness and determination,
came out into an open field, found no enemy, and halted in doubt
as to his next move. "Just at that moment," he wrote in his journal,

"General Jackson came riding up from my rear alone. I reported my brigade as being solid and asked for orders. My men recognized him and raised a terrific shout as he rode along the line with his hat off. He evidently knew how to appreciate a brigade that had gone through a hot battle and was then following the retreating enemy without having broken its line of battle, and remained with me directing my movements until the pursuit ceased." [66]

One last gesture of Banks' cavalry caught the eye of the whole field. Bayard ordered the First Pennsylvania's first battalion under Maj. Richard I. Falls to charge through the Confederate lines at a point where Bayard thought they were forming for a charge against Federal batteries. Falls led 164 cavalrymen down the road at a rapid gait until he had reached within 50 yards of the lines, gave the command "Charge!" in the old traditional style, and thundered at top speed against overwhelming odds and overwhelming fire from Taliaferro's and Branch's brigades.

It was another "charge of the light brigade." Falls rode back with 71 men [67] and no visible results on a battle that had already been decided. For the flood was mounting now all along the line. Ewell, who survived attacks on his front, found his counterattack blocked by a millpond and by artillery fire from guns on his own side to the left. He managed eventually to halt that fire, and pushed ahead from the right, Trimble in the lead. Early had shot away nearly all his ammunition and thought his men were exhausted, but Hill urged him to join the general advance.[68] Jackson, determined to make the most of the occasion now, put Hill's division in the lead and plunged forward in the darkness after Banks' retreating force.[69] At every advance his men were picking up discarded weapons and supplies, but Jackson was aiming for larger goals. He wanted to reach Culpeper before morning.

The main force advanced more than a mile and a half. But the darkness confused the units. Federal resistance began to stiffen. When Pegram's battery, supported by Field's brigade, opened fire on the fleeing Federals, it did much damage at first, but shortly drew such sharp counter-battery fire as to silence it. Jackson's most reliable scout, a man named Farrow, reported that the enemy was banked up only a few hundred yards ahead. Grumble Jones' cavalrymen, coming in from Madison, picked up a prisoner who said Sigel's corps had arrived.

Jackson called a halt.[70] He pulled back his advanced troops to the lines along Cedar Run and Slaughter's solid mountain. Thoroughly exhausted after a long, hot, and difficult day—it was now nearly 11 o'clock—he rode back with his staff. They inquired at one farmhouse after another for shelter, but every house was converted to hospital use and was full of wounded men. When the General saw a plot of grass in the darkness, he swung off his horse under the trees, spread a cloak, and lay face down. Did he want food? "No, I want rest; nothing but rest," and he closed his eyes.[71]

Everywhere around him the fighting men—except the wounded, whose moans and cries filled the night, fading often here and there into silence—did the same. A weary army slept.

They were all up at daylight watching for what might come from ahead. Jackson's first concern was the greatly enlarged Federal force in front of him. The possibility existed that Pope had now, with Ricketts and Sigel, as many fresh troops as Jackson had all together (in fact he did). When Stuart rode in during the morning, Jackson put him immediately in command of the cavalry and asked for a reconnaissance of Pope's strength and movements. The resulting information led to a decision against renewing the action, but Jackson thought that the army, posted as it was, could stand off any enemy attack. The two armies held their ground.[72]

The gruesome housekeeping of a day after a battle occupied the army all day. The wounded were sent back (Hotchkiss, riding over the field while mapping it, heard "the most amazing shrieks and groans"), the dead were buried, and the captured equipment and supplies, including 5,300 rifles, were sorted out. A heavy rain broke the afternoon heat.

The losses had been chiefly on the left. In all, 223 men were killed, 1,060 were wounded, and 31 were missing, a total of 1,314. Banks' casualties were 314 killed, 1,445 wounded, and 622 missing—total, 2,381.

Jackson's severest loss was Winder. He paid a full tribute in his formal report of the battle. "It is difficult within the proper reserve of an official report," Jackson wrote, "to do justice to the merits of this accomplished officer. Urged by the medical officer to take no part in the movements of the day because of the enfeebled state of his health, his ardent patriotism and military pride could bear no such restraint. Richly endowed with those qualities of mind and person which fit an officer for command and which attract the admiration and excite the enthusiasm of troops, he was rapidly rising to the front rank of his profession. His loss has been severely felt." [73]

Winder could be severe in discipline. Casler told later that some men of the First Brigade who had been punished by Winder for straggling ("bucked" all day, Casler said: that is, tied while sitting, with legs drawn up, bound hands placed over and below the knees, and a stick inserted under the knees and above the hands to hold the victim in an awkward and painful position), had determined to kill him in the next battle. [74] But officers admired him and were confident, like Jackson, that he was destined for larger responsibilities.

On the 11th, with Jackson still watching to see what the superior forces ahead of him would do, Pope sent in a flag of truce for removing the dead and wounded. Jackson put Early in charge of the field. All day long the soldiers of both armies mingled in their grisly duties. Stuart sat down with old comrades in the Union forces and chatted. Early on his horse caught the imagination of Federal soldiers. But Jackson, estimating the situation, decided it was imprudent to remain so close to some 40,000 of the enemy (King's division of McDowell's corps had now joined Pope). If he retreated far enough, he thought he might lure the enemy to follow him recklessly. That night he marched back all the way to Gordonsville, not stopping at the natural barrier of the Rapidan. Pope followed slowly to the Rapidan and planned to go farther. But Halleck in Washington guessed Jackson's purpose. He telegraphed Pope: "Beware of a snare. Feigned retreats are secesh tactics." [75]

Jackson's ultimate purpose was still far to the north. Even as he was pulling back from Cedar Run he directed Hotchkiss to start immediately on maps of all the country up to the Potomac. The next day (August 13) he pushed Hotchkiss again. "Do not be afraid of making too many," he said. The General questioned his map maker almost daily on this subject. [76]

Jackson reported early on the 11th to Lee that "God blessed our arms with another victory." He thought the force opposite him in battle consisted of Banks', McDowell's, and Sigel's commands, an overestimate; and he noted "the loss of some of our best officers and men," though the number was smaller than the enemy's losses.

To Anna he wrote that "our God again crowned our arms with

victory . . . all glory to God for his unnumbered blessings." He
continued:

The thought that there are so many of God's people praying for His
blessing upon the army, which, in His providence, is with me, greatly
strengthens me. If God be with us, who can be against us? That he will
still be with us, and give us victory after victory, until our independence
shall be established, and that He will make our nation that people whose
God is the Lord, is my earnest and oft-repeated prayer. Whilst we attach
so much importance to being free from temporal bondage, we must attach far more to being free from the bondage of sin.

But he could not forget Winder. "I can hardly think of [his] fall
. . . without tearful eyes," he told Anna.[77]
Lee gave him a warm reply:

I congratulate you most heartily on the victory which God has granted
you over our enemies at Cedar Run [Hotchkiss had suggested that name
to Jackson, who used it [78]]. The country owes you and your brave officers
and soldiers a deep debt of gratitude. I hope your victory is but the pre-
cursor of others over our foe in that quarter, which will entirely break
up and scatter his army.[79]

On the other side the felicitations to Pope and Banks were almost
as warm. Pope was in an embarrassing situation. He had not wished
Banks to attack, but he liked the vigor with which Banks fought.
By the 14th Halleck was convinced that Banks had won a "hard
earned but brilliant success against vastly superior numbers" and
that his men had "covered themselves with glory, and Cedar Mountain will be known in history as one of the great battle-fields of the
war." Pope forwarded this praise to the army while saying—with a
curious choice of words—that he was "delighted and astonished at
the gallant and intrepid conduct . . . of the Second Corps." [80]

These contradictory interpretations in the North and the South
reflected confusions as to the nature of the battle. On the one hand,
Banks met an advancing Jackson, held him off with half as many
men, caught his left wing by surprise and smashed it back, and
eventually saw Jackson retreat to his starting place. This would be
an achievement even though Banks' losses were nearly twice Jackson's—40 per cent more men and nearly a third of his force.

The more accurate point of view takes in a broader background
and a larger purpose. Pope's forces, not all collected, were twice as

large as Jackson's. They were pushing southward at the same time that they were concentrating. Jackson could not fight them all and did not wait to do so. His purpose was to catch a detached force in a vulnerable position and to halt the advance. In this view his design was excellent. But the ineffective march of August 8 cost a day and enabled re-enforcements (Ricketts and Sigel) to save Banks following a battle in which, after all, Banks was driven from the field—a battle which, probably, Banks should not have fought by himself, certainly not the way he did.

After the battle and facing 40,000 men with half as many, Jackson waited two days before he withdrew from a clear and present danger, still hoping, however, to tempt Pope into following him far enough for another opportunity to arise to catch an isolated part of Pope's army and turn upon it.[81] That hope was not fulfilled. But Pope's southward advance was definitely checked. Banks' corps was so badly punished, moreover, that two weeks later, on August 25, Pope complained to Halleck, when he needed troops badly, that it was still "very weak" and "much demoralized," and that it "must be left somewhere in the rear to be set up again." [82] That, in itself, was an important achievement.

The issue of the left wing remains. A curious fact about this blow, which to Confederate commanders seemed to produce a "critical" situation—a word several of them used—is that Federal officers did not give it such high rating. Pope's reports indicate no belief that Jackson's left wing was in serious trouble or that Banks was rolling up his line. Banks was injured shortly after the battle when his horse fell, and made no formal report at the time.

Williams, who commanded the Federal right, reported successes in the attack, as did Crawford, whose brigade was a principal element of the assault force. But neither made large claims, or assumed a victory was possible, or lamented a lost opportunity. Both stressed losses as heavily as gains. Gordon, whose brigade supported Crawford, stressed his losses and showed no belief of important success. Regimental commanders like Col. George L. Andrews of the Second Massachusetts and Col. Silas Colgrove of the Twenty-seventh Indiana, which spearheaded part of the attack, stressed their losses even more. All these reports record quick rallying and re-enforcing of the Confederate left.[83] The Federal assault may have burned itself out sooner than those who had felt its fire realized.

This would not alter Jackson's responsibility as army commander for a dangling flank or for the demonstrated inability in this instance of the left wing to deal adequately with the assault when it did come. If Seddon did all that he could, as he appears to have done, then the line of responsibility would run from brigade commander to division commander to army commander, or from Garnett to Winder to Jackson. Each would bear some blame, but Jackson, as army commander must in the last analysis, be responsible even if all others failed to be sufficiently careful. There is no question about Jackson's personal role in restoring the broken left. His energy, judgment, and courage then were unmistakable, and thus he personally influenced the victory as much as—probably more than—he did on any other field.

In its relation to other events the battle influenced Lee decisively. There was no longer any question that Pope had a more formidable force than Jackson or that Pope was receiving re-enforcements and shortly would receive more. For Lee now knew that the 10,000 men under Burnside, who had come up from the North Carolina coast when McClellan's pleas for more men were driving Halleck to look for aid in every direction, had already left Fort Monroe for Aquia on the Potomac and had gone thence to Fredericksburg.[84] McClellan had received (after strange and long negotiations between Halleck and McClellan) definite orders on August 3 to follow Burnside.[85] He continued to debate the issue and, on Malvern Hill, demonstrated impressively enough to bring Lee in person to appraise what was going on.[86] Although McClellan's troops were strung out along the Peninsula as they marched overland to Fort Monroe, McClellan was heading northward now. Every day would bring him nearer the force in front of Jackson. It would swell with his arrival to seven times Jackson's strength.

The time had arrived when Lee, hitherto watching intently the McClellan force on one side and the Pope force on the other, could make his move. Pope was now indisputably the target. Lee must re-enforce Jackson to the hilt. He must himself move to the Rapidan region and take command. He must do so while Pope could be got at and attacked with a chance of success—before McClellan came to Pope's aid and created through the junction of Pope, McClellan, and Burnside an army of 150,000 men. That meant a race between Lee and the Federal re-enforcements, and it might be close.

Lee acted with superb energy. On August 13 he ordered Long-street with ten brigades to Gordonsville.[87] On the same day he ordered Stuart to find out whether Burnside had joined Pope and, if he had, to leave part of his cavalry to protect the Central Railroad and move the major part to Gordonsville. Simultaneously Lee ordered Hood's division with two brigades (Whiting's and his own) to Hanover Junction, where he could guard the railroad and also be nearer Gordonsville.[88]

By the next day (August 14) Hood was ordered to move straight to Gordonsville. Lee asked Secretary of War Walker to order R. H. Anderson's division from Drewry's Bluff on the south bank of the James to Gordonsville. He himself wrote to Longstreet about the desirability of hitting Pope from the right or the left (Lee favored the right, but wished more information) and of having Stuart sweep around his flank and cut his communications. He had arranged to leave for Gordonsville the following day. Meantime, "let me know where I shall find you. I should like, if convenient, to see Jackson, too." [89]

Lee left Richmond by train at 4 A.M. on August 15 and went immediately into conference with Longstreet and Jackson that afternoon. The campaign which Jackson had begun at Cedar Run was expanding now to large and historic proportions.

# 27 || SECOND MANASSAS

*"Who could not conquer
with such troops as these!"*

Lee's decision was to hit Pope at the very first moment,
front and rear, and with every ounce of weight that could be thrown
against him. Pope had crept up to the Rapidan after the fight on
Cedar Run. His left flank was near Raccoon Ford, his center near
the recent battlefield, and his right along the Robertson River, a
small tributary of the Rapidan. These dispositions placed all his
troops in the great V formed by the confluence of the Rapidan and
the Rappahannock Rivers, near Fredericksburg, and their widening
courses stretching back westward and northwestward toward the
mountains. Behind Pope flowed the Rappahannock. All his lines of
communication ran across it, and he himself, if forced to retreat,
would have to cross it.

To Lee and his generals this situation presented an extraordinary
opportunity. If they could assemble sufficient troops in front of
Pope to smash him hard, and if simultaneously they could cut his
lines of communication in the rear, they would have him in a trap.

For the first necessity Lee was now bringing up every man he
could find. He urged the War Department on August 16 and later
to send all possible units of the Richmond garrison. For the second
necessity Lee counted on Stuart to circle Pope's flank, in the style
now becoming Stuart's own, and destroy the bridge at Rappahannock Station where the Orange and Alexandria Railroad crossed
the river—Pope's principal line of communication and retreat. If
everything developed perfectly—strength in front, secrecy, quick

action before re-enforcements built up Pope, exact timing—the results might be spectacular.

Strength began arriving, though not as much or as fast as Lee had hoped. Anderson's division was delayed, and Longstreet had moved out of the Richmond area with such haste that he was short of bread and had to organize his supply system before he could do anything else.[1] Secrecy no one could be sure of, but a solitary eminence called Clark's Mountain, which rose out of the Piedmont much as Cedar Mountain did, furnished a barrier to Federal vision northeast of Orange. Behind its flanks many thousand soldiers could hide. Its top was a superb observation tower with a range over virtually the whole of Pope's sprawling army.

The cavalry for Stuart's raid was another matter. Much of it was farther east toward Fredericksburg, where it had been peering into Federal movements there. Stuart came into Orange by train on August 17. Brig. Gen. Fitzhugh Lee's brigade of Stuart's force had moved from Hanover to Beaver Dam on the 16th and had been ordered to march to Raccoon Ford on the 17th. When it came up, the attack could be launched: Stuart to swing around Pope's right, Lee with Longstreet and Jackson to smash his left flank, all movements to fit together on the 18th. Jackson may have urged, and almost surely suggested, crossing the Rapidan on the 16th and storming Pope's left flank on the 17th (it would have been like him if he had), but the army was not ready.[2]

As events turned out, the cavalry wasn't even on hand. Stuart rode out from Orange on the 17th to the hamlet of Verdiersville, on Fitzhugh Lee's route to Raccoon Ford, to join his brigade as it came up, and slept that night on the porch of a friendly house. Early on the 18th, while waiting impatiently, Stuart heard horsemen a few hundred yards off and sent officers to guide Fitzhugh Lee (as he thought it must be).[3]

In the morning mist a shout, then pistol shots, then pounding hooves, broke through the air. Stuart's officers came racing back. Yankees! Yonder! Flee!

Stuart ran for his horse, scrambled into the saddle, dug spurs into flanks, and raced across country. His staff did likewise, each for himself, the enemy in mad pursuit among the trees, through brush, and dramatically down the road. There Stuart's big-boned Prussian aide, Lieut. Heros von Borcke,* pressed hard by Federal horsemen, was galloping furiously, only a few lengths in the lead.

Most of them escaped. But not Stuart's Assistant Adjutant General, Maj. Norman Fitzhugh, whom Stuart had sent down the road to reconnoiter. And not Stuart's coat and hat with the fine feather which he adored and his men marked him by. This humiliating loss of face he might (and subsequently did) compensate for. But Fitzhugh carried documents. One of them described the plan of Lee's attack. It went straight to Pope.

That General was receiving warnings from other sources—from a spy in his employ, from a report by Maj. Gen. Jesse L. Reno that correctly estimated the situation, and possibly from his own reasoning. But the document on Fitzhugh was official and confirmatory. Its loss shook Stuart into sharp criticism of Fitzhugh Lee, who, with no word as to the route or time of his march, had gone a roundabout way to Louisa, where his trains were, to build up his rations. Toombs, whose Georgians were supposed to protect against such an irruption across Raccoon Ford as that of Col. F. T. Broadhead's First Michigan Cavalry, which put Stuart to flight, was placed under arrest.[4]

Pope saw the light. He began pulling his trains out of the V on the 18th. When Lee, who had to postpone the attack to the 20th, climbed Clark's Mountain with Longstreet on the 19th, glasses in hand, they could oversee all the region over which they hoped next day to sweep, and most of the Federal army which they hoped to roll up, capture, or destroy. But what they saw was the dust of withdrawing columns, the long lines of infantry that plodded northward toward the Rappahannock, and the abandoned camps from which Pope was moving as fast as he could. The game was up. The prey had discovered the trap and fled. Lee had to organize a pursuit, not launch an attack.

For this purpose Jackson's three divisions of the poised left wing had thinner ranks than he liked, but the men were in good shape and cheerful. He himself had been cheerful enough on the 17th when he

---

* Von Borcke, a high-spirited, romantic officer, had come to aid the Confederacy at the start of the Seven Days, bringing letters of introduction to governmental officials. They sent him to Stuart, who received him well and attached him to his staff. Well trained in Prussia, he adapted himself quickly to military methods in Virginia, added a rich boyish joviality to Stuart's headquarters, and—with his size, his accent, and his unaffected fondness for display—became a well-known and well-liked figure, about whom tales and legends grew. His *Memoirs of the Confederate War,* in two volumes, tell of his adventures.

and Hotchkiss went on a fine warm day to Sunday morning services with one of W. B. Taliaferro's brigades on the slope of Clark's Mountain. He discussed with Hotchkiss what he considered "the right sort of man." The General thought it was one who was always striving to do his duty and was never satisfied if anything could be done better.[5]

Doing his own duty, as he saw it, could require a firm application of law. Eight or ten men of Jackson's old division, worn by hard work and weary of the war, had deserted. Three of them had been caught. A court-martial tried and convicted them, and the sentence was death. On the day before the wing crossed the Rapidan the whole division was mustered out to witness the executions. Led by bands playing the dead march, the columns marched solemnly through woods, came out into an open field, and lined up in formal array. They stared ahead at three blindfolded men, kneeling in front of open graves. A platoon of twelve or fifteen men, half their rifles loaded, half loaded only with blank cartridges, stood in painful solemnity, waited for the order "Fire!" and cracked out the volley. Then the whole division marched close by so that all men might see the lifeless bodies.[6]

Desertion was on Jackson's mind, and he felt the need of convincing action. A little later Stuart captured two men who had gone over to the Federal ranks. For men fully identified and convicted, as these two were, the normal punishment was death before a firing squad. The bodies were hung to a limb on a roadside and left there for all men to see.[7]

The General and his staff had quarters at the Crenshaw farm on Mountain Run, six miles from Orange, and there they left wagons, tents, and other impedimenta behind when at 3 A.M. on the 20th they marched north. The day started badly when Jackson found that A. P. Hill's men were not on the move at an hour when he thought they should have been, and Jackson put a staff officer with each division to see that marching orders were obeyed. He put another black mark on Hill's record that would lead to worse trouble later.[8]

With Longstreet crossing the Rapidan by Raccoon Ford, Jackson by Somerville's, the 50,000 infantry and 4,500 cavalry advanced without opposition. The order of march placed Jackson's wing of the army (his old division now under W. B. Taliaferro, and Ewell's and A. P. Hill's divisions) on the left. He pushed ahead steadily, straight north, in the Stevensburg direction south of a railroad station named Brandy that cavalrymen would remember. He made 20 miles that day. By night all of Lee's army was leaning on the Rappahannock across which Pope waited—Sigel's corps farthest upstream, Banks' corps near the railroad that ran across the river at right angles, McDowell's corps farther southeast, and Reno's division on the southern flank. Twenty miles farther down the river Fitz John Porter's corps, fresh from the transports that brought it from the Peninsula, was stretching its land legs to join Pope. The Federal bank of the river stood higher and overlooked the Confederate side most of the length of the stream. Pope would not retreat farther. He was certain to grow stronger, and he could wait for the inevitable attack.

When Lee found Pope waiting for him on the 21st, he debated whether to swing right or left, and decided that the hunting was better upstream. Jackson had that flank and led the march, with Hill, Ewell, and Taliaferro in column. Longstreet followed, close to Jackson's rear so that Pope would have no temptation to cross the river himself and cut the Confederate line. Robertson's cavalry brigade preceded all.

They were searching for an unguarded ford. But Pope could see the movement, and on his side of the river he marched with it. So when Robertson crossed above Beverly Ford (as did Stuart), Federal cavalrymen were waiting. There was racing to and fro, and shooting, and a few prisoners, but the prospects did not look promising. Robertson and Stuart withdrew and left the guns on each side to continue the feeling-out.[9]

On the 22nd Jackson's three divisions, Ewell leading now, kept marching upstream. They crossed a tributary, Hazel Run, at Wellford's mill and left Trimble's brigade to guard the crossing of the wagons. Federal troops were moving with them, step by step. Near noon Federal raiders even crossed the river and surprised part of the train, but they were driven off without booty. Nearer 4 P.M. Trimble had real trouble. The enemy crossed the river and attacked him while the train was crossing Hazel Run. A sharp fight followed, in which Hood, leading Longstreet's wing, came up to aid Trimble. Together they drove the enemy back across the river.[10]

Meantime, Jackson's main force ascended the Rappahannock to

Freeman's Ford, found it well guarded, and continued to a point opposite Fauquier White Sulphur Springs. The bridge was destroyed, and other signs of the enemy were visible, but the way was open at the moment, and Jackson sent the Thirteenth Georgia of Lawton's brigade and Brown's and Dement's batteries over immediately to occupy the white cottages of this resort. A mile below the Springs a dilapidated mill dam presented another opportunity. The crossing was difficult, but Early's whole brigade scrambled over.

The time was late in the afternoon, rain was falling, and the river was rising. Early tried to establish communications with the Georgia regiment higher upstream, but in the darkness Early's officer, Maj. A. L. Pitzer, feeling his way north, was captured by six Federal cavalrymen. (Pitzer, although disarmed, convinced the six cavalrymen later that they were all surrounded by Confederate troops and induced them to surrender to him, and subsequently brought them in as prisoners.[11]) Early held off further efforts during the night. The rain increased to a downpour. By morning the Rappahannock was in flood, and Early was cut off.[12]

Early kept his nerve. A messenger got through to the Georgia regiment. Another swam the river and informed Jackson of the situation. Early united with the Georgians, though disappointed that no more of Lawton's brigade was by his side. He went into a defensive position, hidden by woods and assured of artillery support from the other side of the river. Jackson was working furiously on a new bridge. He joined the engineers of Hill's division, became quickly a wet and mud-covered General, encouraged men hauling heavy timbers through waist-deep water, and saw the structure rise swiftly.[13] But it was touch and go on the morning of the 23rd with Federal troops all around Early's position and the whole of Pope's right wing coming up to join them.

By afternoon the swift rise of the Rappahannock was followed by a swift drop. Jackson sent the remainder of Lawton's brigade across. Some of Robertson's cavalry and artillery joined Early from much higher up the river, and later in the day, when the Federals attacked, Early beat them back. After two nights and a day of wet and anxious adventures, both brigades recrossed the river. But the solution of the problem of circling Pope had not been found. In starts and jerks, with minor clashes and frequent artillery fire, the two

armies moved up the river opposite each other, matching step for
step as though engaged in a gigantic military minuet. Time was
running out.

Jackson's patience was running out too. His quarters during the
days of worrying about Early were in a yellow farmhouse opposite
the resort. "A very nice paling fence" encircled the house. The General sent down word that although a worm-fence at some distance
was available for campfires, nobody should touch this paling fence.

Brig. Gen. Maxcy Gregg's brigade camped in the area. The rain
poured down, and the five South Carolina regiments that made up
the brigade (First South Carolina, Provisional Army, and First South
Carolina Rifles, and Twelfth, Thirteenth, and Fourteenth South
Carolina Regiments) had a bad time. One of the colonels, Edward
McCrady, Jr., of the First (Provisional), who thought himself lucky
to find shelter in an outhouse, heard some noise at the sacred fence
during the night and tried to stop it but was told men from other
regiments were responsible.

The next morning Jackson rode through the yard of the farmhouse and looked at what was left of the paling fence. In McCrady's
words:

A few minutes afterward [I] was ordered to report to General Gregg,
with whom I found the other four commanding officers of regiments of
the brigade, and was told that General Jackson had ordered us all under
arrest. We were released upon arrangement with the owner of the farm
to pay for the damage done. Five regimental commanders—and I always
believed, but never actually knew, our brigadier himself—all arrested for
a few palings of an ornamental fence taken under such circumstances!
And then to be told that there was no discipline in our army! [14]

A Georgia colonel would have agreed. Two days later, the General, out of humor with the quartermasters and the commissary officers because provisions were not coming up in time, told the
colonel that "field officers were intended to be useful as well as
ornamental." [15]

Stuart, restless under these conditions and looking with a cavalryman's spirit far to Pope's rear, suggested to Lee that he should
circle to the left and reach with the torch the wooden bridge at
Catlett's Station on the Orange and Alexandria Railroad which
Pope relied on for supplies. On the 22nd Lee gave the word. Stuart
set out with some 1,500 men. They passed through Jeffersonton,

crossed the Rappahannock at Waterloo Bridge and Hart's Mill below it, and reached Warrenton untouched in the afternoon. Stuart swooped down on Catlett's.

But the rain that isolated Early drenched the cavalrymen, slowed their march, darkened the night ("The darkest night I ever knew," Stuart said), and soaked the trestle they wanted to burn. Guided by a Negro whom he had known elsewhere, now discovered providentially this black, wet night, Stuart sent Col. W. H. F. Lee's regiment splashing and stumbling into the quarters of Pope's surprised staff and captured officers and men. Rosser cut the railroad, and Captain Blackford tackled the bridge. But burning its heavy, saturated timbers was impossible. Blackford procured a few axes and set his men to chopping. This was rough work in the dark against increasing enemy fire from the other side. Fuming, Stuart was forced to give up his chief objective.[16]

The haul on Pope's headquarters was richer. The booty that had been scooped up contained not only Pope's greatcoat that would restore the face Stuart lost at Verdiersville with his plume: it contained also numerous official documents. They left no doubt that the goal of destroying Pope before he could be re-enforced by McClellan's army as it returned from the Peninsula was now becoming a matter of a few—a very few—days. Two of McClellan's corps (the Third and Fifth) and Reynolds' Pennsylvania Reserves were reported to be within two days' marching. It appeared likely that the Second, Fourth, and Sixth Corps, with other troops, including 7,000 from western Virginia in the Kanawha region, would unite with Pope in five more days. Within a week his force of approximately 50,000 would probably grow to 130,000.[17] The campaign had reached a crisis.

Lee acted with characteristic energy and extraordinary—almost unparalleled—boldness. He went into conference with Jackson on the 24th.[18] The only reports of that conference are by McGuire and Douglas. McGuire said that "Jackson—for him—was very much excited, drawing with the toe of his boot a map in the sand, and gesticulating in a much more earnest way than he was in the habit of doing. General Lee was simply listening, and after Jackson had got through, he nodded his head, as if acceding to some proposal." McGuire believed, "from what occurred afterward, that Jackson suggested the movement as it was made," but he added, "I have no further proof than the incident I have just mentioned." [19]

Douglas' report is altogether different. A council of war, he said, was held on the afternoon of the 24th, though none of those reported present ever told of attending it. He described it thus: "A table was placed almost in the middle of a field, with not even a tree within hearing. General Lee sat at the table on which was spread a map. General Longstreet sat on his right, General Stuart on his left, and General Jackson stood opposite him; these four and no more. A group of staff officers were lounging on the grass of an adjacent knoll. The consultation was a brief one. As it closed I was called by General Jackson and I heard the only sentence of that consultation that I ever heard reported. It was uttered by the secretive Jackson and it was 'I will be moving within an hour.'" [20] (He didn't start out until the next morning.)

It is impossible to reconcile these two reports. No other evidence has been found to confirm either report, and Douglas seems likely to have confused the scene with another. Lee, in his formal campaign report, said: "In pursuance of the plan of operations determined upon, Jackson was directed. . . ." [21] Jackson's formal statement six months later was: "Pursuing the instructions of the commanding general, I left Jeffersonton. . . ." [22]

In Hotchkiss' diary on March 4, 1863, written when the army was in winter quarters and men were reflecting on the past year's work, an entry tells of Hotchkiss' visit that day to Stuart, and of a conversation they had about the August, 1862, operation. It continues in these words: "He [Stuart] said General Jackson was entitled to all the credit for the movement round the enemy and General Lee had, very reluctantly, consented to it. He spoke of the great results it had. . . ."

Again, in the entry for March 6, 1863, Hotchkiss reported visiting Stuart again, and this time quoted Stuart thus: "He says General Lee came to us at Gordonsville with rather a low estimate of Jackson's ability," but now, in March, 1863, wished he had many Jacksons, and further: "Lee asked him [Stuart] if he did not think it was very hazardous for General Jackson to attempt to go round the enemy when we crossed the Rappahannock in August."

It is possible that both generals thought of the plan, or that others did. It had a precedent of a sort in the original idea of Stuart's circling Pope, when the Federal army lay between the Rapidan and the Rappahannock, in order to destroy the bridge at Rappahannock Station, and another precedent of a sort in Stuart's raid on Catlett's Station. In the end, and probably from the beginning, both Lee and Jackson understood the necessity for quick and even desperate action if they were to deal adequately with Pope. Perhaps both saw a great opportunity. Both were willing to take the risk. But Lee carried the responsibility, and Jackson made no claim of having induced Lee to accept such an idea from him.

The plan that emerged was for splitting a numerically inferior army in two, in the presence of the enemy and in contact with him, and sending nearly half of it on a 50-mile encircling movement around Pope's right, deep in his rear, and squarely across his line of communications. Jackson was to carry his whole wing—Ewell's, A. P. Hill's, and Taliaferro's (the old Jackson) divisions, with Stuart's cavalry joining him—and he was to go all the way to the line that ran between Pope and Washington. He would necessarily go on foot, for this was in 1862, but in principle the plan conceived of Jackson's 23,000 infantry and some 4,000 cavalry as somewhat comparable to parachute troops of ninety years later. Their long, circling march would, in effect, drop them behind the enemy in order to convert a static front into a fluid one. In this way, Lee hoped, the opportunity would come, through the enemy's mistakes or his own ingenuity, to accomplish more than he could by frontal attack on the lines along the Rappahannock.

Such a concept violated outright the major principle of concentration and subjected each separate wing to multiplied risks. Jackson might be caught en route by superior forces (though he could retreat toward the Valley) or might be overwhelmed when in Pope's rear by the superior forces that could be gathered quickly there. Lee might be broken while he stood with hardly more than 32,000 men after Jackson departed, though Lee did not intend that Longstreet's wing linger on the Rappahannock. It would hold that line long enough for Jackson to get away, and would demonstrate so vigorously there that Pope would not know that only little more than half as many troops were on his front. But Longstreet would follow soon to join Jackson. He would do so in time, Lee hoped, to unite all his strength in the major battle that was inevitable—the battle that Lee was taking fearful risks to force Pope to join in circumstances, as Lee also hoped, in which he could catch Pope off balance or otherwise at a disadvantage.

Years later, when men still marveled at the risk of such a movement, Lee dismissed their head-shaking with these words: "Such criticism is obvious, but the disparity . . . between the contending forces rendered the risks unavoidable." [23] His calm postwar words do not lessen the hazards he set up. Nor can they suggest the stir of excitement that seized those committed to this great gamble or the importance in such an adventure of the style in which Jackson would carry out his mission.

Jackson went into immediate action. Not knowing the country intimately, he sent at 3 P.M. on the 24th for his chief engineer, Capt. J. K. Boswell, who did know, and instructed him in Jeffersonton to select (in Boswell's words) "the most direct and covered route to Manassas." Boswell recommended a route that ran through Amissville, Henson's Mill, Orleans, Salem (the modern Marshall), Thoroughfare Gap, and Gainesville. Jackson approved it. He told Boswell to select guards (whom Boswell obtained from Capt. John A. Adams' company of the Sixth Virginia Cavalry) and lead the front division in person at dawn the next morning.[24]

To his three divisions Jackson sent marching orders that Sunday afternoon for dawn on August 25. They would leave behind their quartermasters and commissaries, with forage and subsistence stores —the canvas-covered wagons parked in the Jeffersonton region. Only a few ambulances and a limited ordnance train would roll with the marching men, though a herd of cattle was ordered for the march.[25] Even the men's knapsacks would be left behind. Three days' rations would be cooked and carried in haversacks and pockets.

The orders for action—there were none for destination—sent an electric shock through the whole left wing. Veterans of the Valley knew immediately that something big was in preparation, that Old Jack was on the prowl again, and that he would drive them furiously and lead them to unforeseeable adventures. That night "there was so much disturbance, as marching orders had been issued, that we did not rest much," Hotchkiss wrote in his diary.

The three Jackson divisions had to break loose from the line along the Rappahannock and pull back in preparation for the morrow's work. Longstreet had to bring some of his troops into line, and all had to be done neatly and without any indication to the enemy

across the river of what was going on. Longstreet would have to
make a bold pretense the next day, like Magruder below Richmond,
to keep Pope's men occupied.

There was so much disturbance, and so much strain on the commissary that attempts to provide three days' cooked rations broke
down. At dawn on the 25th, when there could be no further delay
for any reason, numerous men were still clutching half-baked biscuits and raw dough [26] and were still carrying raw beef without the
salt that could preserve it through hot days of marching. If these
deficiencies seemed a grim joke then to soldiers in a hurry, the price
would be heavy later.

Ewell's division lay farthest west, and Boswell went to its front.
Hill came next, and Taliaferro followed. Dawn came up on a clear,
cool August morning that would be hot later. Now in this pleasantly
rolling country, dustless and green from the hard rains of recent
days, with the Blue Ridge visible off to the west, it was a time for
young men to be on the march. Not a man among them, not an officer among them save Boswell and the General, knew where they
were going, but they followed in high spirits and with the excitement of anticipation, chattering as they set out and damning the
hurry that lost them rations.

Jackson found a moment that morning to write to Anna, though
only a few lines. "The enemy has taken a position, or rather several
positions, on the Fauquier side of the Rappahannock," he told her;
but he had nothing to say to Anna about what he was setting out to
do. His thoughts and feelings were another matter. "I have only
time to tell you," he wrote, "how much I love my little pet dove." [27]

Waterloo Bridge up the Rappahannock, the one bridge in all that
country, seemed the natural objective. But the lead veered farther
westward, and the men raised their heads. Where to? The Valley?
What was up? They strode into tiny Amissville, seven miles from
the start, sweating now under the drive of their pace and the mounting sun.

The road began to turn into a northerly direction. That meant
crossing the Rappahannock somewhere. It had split into Carter's
Run, which flowed far from their route, and Hedgeman's River,
which they would encounter soon. They came into its lush valley at
Henson's Mill, splashed thigh-deep through the cold water,[28] and

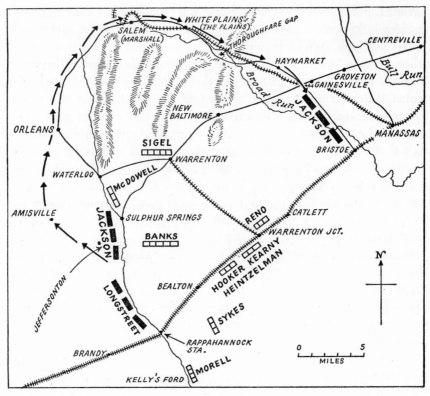

JACKSON'S MARCH AROUND POPE'S RIGHT, AUGUST 25–26,
1862.

kept right on going. Munford's cavalrymen were picketing every converging road until the army passed.

Boswell's knowledge of the country came into play now. He guided Forno's Louisiana brigade (formerly Hays'), which was leading Ewell's division, off the highway, across fields, over ditches and fences, and through a patch of woods, seeking the short cuts and trying to keep the cover that Jackson had ordered. Then Boswell received new orders for himself from Jackson. He took part of the Black Horse Cavalry (Capt. Robert Randolph) and a company of the Second Virginia Cavalry (Capt. W. W. Tebbs), and pushed on fast toward Orleans, Thumb Run Church, and Salem, reaching Salem about 4 P.M. They saw none of the enemy. The way was clear.

Later Munford came up with the Second Cavalry, and they camped at Salem.

The way was clear of the enemy, but the long lines of infantry had other troubles. Morning cool gave way to midday heat. In August it could be blistering. The early zest for talk had ended, and the ranks strained forward silently. Bad shoes—the bane of the Confederate infantry—began to take their toll, and men limped, and some of them hauled off shoes altogether and kept their pace barefooted. Food was a problem. Men who had managed to prepare three days' cooked rations had eaten—like all soldiers—as much of it at the start as they could cram into their throats. Those who lost out at the start with uncooked dough and unsalted beef looked to the green corn in the fields and the apples on the trees, and foraged as they advanced.

Wherever Old Jack was, the word was always: "Close up, men! Close up!" Even if he was at the head or the tail of the column, his officers had caught his insistent doctrine: "Close up, men! Close up!" The miles fell behind their shoulders, but nobody showed mercy. Keep going! It must be something big! Old Jack! Close up, men! Close up!

So along the winding roads, farther and farther, deeper and deeper into the north, more and more remote from the Rappahannock and Pope's guns and Longstreet's divisions behind them, heading somewhere if sore feet and bent backs and hot sweat and weary muscles could keep them at this everlasting march. Old Jack! What did he have up his sleeve?

Orleans came up near midday and dropped behind them, and still they slogged on. The way ran upland a little here, the hills were sharper, and every step was now more of an effort. All through the long summer afternoon they mounted steadily in a direction that seemed to carry them toward the Valley, might carry them straight north to nobody knew where, and still left them free to turn this way or that. Only Old Jack knew. "Close up, men! Close up!"

Late in the afternoon the long column—weary and stripped of many stragglers now—began to reach up to Salem. A mile to its south the advance guard, looking ahead, saw a great stone protruding from the bank that rose a little above their road, and beside it an officer standing. His head was uncovered, and the sun that was setting behind the Blue Ridge shone full on the tanned face and light brown beard. The dirt of the road and the dust that had come up with heat of the day covered his uniform. He was one of them— he was Old Jack! He was leading them God knew where, on a great adventure—God knew what—and there he was!

The strained faces in the ranks began to break into grins. The broad hats came off, and men began to wave them. A voice raised, and another, and a yipping yell broke out from a bold spirit, and another, and the sound rolled down the line and formed into a steady volume of cheering.

The General raised his arm immediately. This wouldn't do. The noise would reverberate across the countryside that might conceal the ears and eyes of a Federal cavalryman. Some officer understood the gesture, and "No cheering!" ran down the ranks.

So they marched by in silence, their arms waving wildly, their dirty faces a long panorama of grins, and their spirits a little raised by the sight of the General. He was taking an informal review at the end of a day of great marching, at the end of a solid 25 miles from their start on the Rappahannock, and he was as much impressed as they were. He turned to a staff officer and exclaimed: "Who could not conquer with such troops as these!" [29]

They slept where they sank by the road, in grotesque positions through the warm summer night, sometimes without food, drugged with exhaustion and too dead to the world to reflect that still nobody knew where they were going or what lay ahead.

Tuesday, August 26, came up in the predawn darkness of another warm day, and the army began to rub its muscles and stir into life again. The bread and meat came out for those who had it, the apples of the orchards for others. The ranks began to form in the gray of morning, and the army was on the march again.

Northward the column headed along the mile that led to Salem (more for the body and tail of the stretched-out column). The road ran straight into the hamlet, swung off to the northwest on the route that would lead to the Valley but turned abruptly right and eastward to go toward Manassas. A guide stood at the intersection. He pointed eastward. Ewell's division, Forno's brigade still leading, swung sharply toward the sun that was rising over all the country behind Pope's army.

Eastward! Behind Pope! So this was the plan, this the reason for yesterday's long march. They were going for Pope's rear. They were already behind a line drawn to extend his flank. They would have to eat up the miles to reach all the way down to his direct line of communication with Washington, to the railroad, and to the heart of the enemy country. But they were on their way!

They were on their way, simultaneously, out of the last semblance of Pope's vision or knowledge of their purpose. Though Jackson had tried to keep the march of the 25th under cover, Federal eyes had followed it with an appraisal of its progress and strength that was as remarkable for its accuracy in these respects as for the complete lack of understanding of where the movement was going or what it signified.

A Federal signal station in the hills east of Waterloo Bridge had caught sight of the moving men, and especially the regimental colors, as early as 7:15 A.M. At 8:45 A.M. a report was ready that the column of infantry and artillery was still passing on the road between Jeffersonton and Amissville. At 9:45 another report cited batteries, a few wagons, and six to eight regiments moving rapidly and well closed up. At 10:30 more details were on the way. By noon Pope informed Halleck in Washington that 20,000 men were on the march—a shrewd count—and that McDowell's corps had been alerted.[30]

The surface facts were good enough; the interpretation was completely wrong. For Pope assumed that the movement was toward Luray or Front Royal in the Valley, that it was covering the flank of the main body of the Confederate army (Longstreet's wing was showing that day an aggressive and even a vindictive spirit on the Rappahannock),[31] that it was anything but a blow aimed at his vital lines of communication. Pope's headquarters could understand a Confederate foray toward the Valley and, since Lee's strength was regularly overestimated, the movement of 20,000 men might not seem unusual. The essential boldness of Lee's dividing his army in the presence of the enemy, and sending nearly half of it on a march of more than 50 miles to the rear of superior forces confronting him, was too much to assume. The very daring of the plan was, in remarkable degree, its protection.

Pope was concerned about pushing forward a reconnaissance in force at Waterloo Bridge to see what was across the Rappahannock there. Other reports came in during the 26th of movements on the same route along which men marched on the 25th (this was Long-street's wing following the footsteps of Jackson), but nobody who would enlighten Pope knew that Jackson in force had turned east-ward at Salem. Despite a hint or two in inquiry and report,[32] no-body of importance took seriously the possibility that he would. Pope's summary of the situation, sent to Porter at 7 P.M. August 26, shows clearly that he had no idea that Jackson was within less than an hour of bringing down the whole world about his ears.[33]

To this point Jackson had arrived by a march of heroic propor-tions, admirable in any circumstances, doubly admirable for an army that was not in the best condition after five days' operations on the Rappahannock and since then had lacked food and sleep and had endured the long march of the 25th.

Men looked east out of Salem to low-mountain country, through which the road ran close to the Manassas Gap Railroad. Five miles ahead they reached White Plains [34] at a crossroads at the southern end of Fishback Ridge, with Pignut Mountain off to their right front, both isolated offshoots of the Blue Ridge. Beyond White Plains the Bull Run Mountains lay squarely across their path, split by Thoroughfare Gap straight ahead. There a well-placed division might hold up an army a long time. Munford rode forward with cavalry, and back came good news. The gap was undefended, the road was clear.

They climbed its gradual slopes with slower and slower steps. The column began to stretch out. Although the constant commands of "Close up! Close up!" could be heard up and down the line, the officers did not enforce marching standards beyond reason. The urgency of the march kept the troops moving relentlessly, but men weak from hunger, men with blistered feet and sometimes bare and bleeding feet, men who had lost heart and soul, dropped off. The rear guards, exercising a discretion beyond the usual require-ments, let the disabled men lag, with warnings to catch up at night. Men running into the fields to tear green corn from stalks lost their places in the shuffling column and could not catch up, but they too kept on moving.[35]

More than any other major march Jackson commanded, this one lost something of its normal military formality without thereby los-ing its steady forward movement. Contrary to standard practices, the column did not stop for regular rests—the ten minutes out of

every hour that Jackson enforced. Nobody stopped to eat. Men ate
as they strode along if they had food, or they did without.[36] To
Stuart's staff officer, Blackford, who had joined Jackson with a
message and remained, "it was like each man was walking the distance alone, stopping to rest a moment or drink, within certain
wide limits," but moving ahead at a pace which, if kept up for
twelve hours, averaged about three miles an hour. He was impressed
by "the spirit of the men, their unbounded confidence in their
leader, and their perfect faith in the success of the expedition." The
only dread Blackford detected was "a dread with each one that he
would give out and not be there to see the fun." [37]

So they dug into the rocky and narrow confines of the Gap, blessed
its coolness in the middle of another hot day, and lengthened their
strides as the road fell downward and the mountains receded behind
them. In four miles they reached the hamlet of Haymarket, and in
another two they came to Gainesville; and now they stood astride
the turnpike from Alexandria to Warrenton. At the two villages
Munford picked up 12 to 15 Federal cavalrymen on outpost duty.
They were completely ignorant of the movement which was pouring
down on them. The main highway at Gainesville was bare of any
others of the enemy. The last, long miles lay ahead.

Stuart joined them here with Fitzhugh Lee's and Robertson's
brigades.[38] They had pulled away from the Rappahannock at 2 A.M.
on the 26th, followed Jackson's trail part of the way, cut the corners
of his route, and now came jingling by, old friends and welcome
allies. Jackson set them to guarding his right, and the whole force
felt better to have them on hand.

At Gainesville the road forked, one road reaching on to Manassas
Junction, the other turning a little to the right and leading to Bristoe
Station on the Orange and Alexandria, seven miles south of Manassas
Junction. Jackson followed the latter road. He could cut the railroad
at either destination, but Bristoe was a little closer and was weakly
defended, and there the railroad crossed Broad Run, which ran
tumbling down from Thoroughfare Gap. To destroy that bridge
would be more effective than anything he could do at Manassas
Junction, which, after Bristoe, he could seize at leisure. The major
danger was to the south, where Pope pondered what next to do
during an afternoon when he had lost Jackson completely and was

thinking—characteristically and erroneously—of his front and not his rear.

Up and down the column Jackson had ridden all day. He knew the volume of straggling, but he knew also the indefatigable drive that kept the spent men tramping ahead. He knew that the head of the column was coming within striking distance of the slight Federal forces at Bristoe, and that he would have to give time for the remainder to close up. There was nothing to do but wait.

He found a farmhouse by the roadside, sat down in a cane-bottomed armchair tilted against the wall and immediately went to sleep. The staff stretched out on the floor. Sandie Pendleton lay down in the hall inside the front door to receive dispatches or attend to other business, and he too went to sleep. Blackford, the visitor, lay down on the parlor floor and was just beginning to doze when an officer came up to the front door and talked briefly with Pendleton. (The General, taking no risks of his own making about this march, had ordered a guard to be placed by every leading brigade at every fork in the road to direct the following brigade.)

Pendleton listened for a few minutes, turned, walked to the sleeping General, laid his hand on his shoulder, and said: "General, General ——— [Blackford, who told the story, wouldn't tell the name] failed to put a picket at the crossroads and the following brigade took the wrong road."

The General opened his eyes when Pendleton touched him. He listened without moving his body. Then he answered: "Put him under arrest and prefer charges," and in a moment he was gently snoring again.[39]

About sunset, when Ewell's division limped into sight of Bristoe, Munford carried a hundred of his horsemen undetected within a hundred yards of the station. Then he went forward at a gallop. Forno's Louisiana infantry followed. A company of Federal infantry and another of cavalry guarded the minor depot. Most of the cavalry raced away. The infantry took refuge in a hotel and opened fire from the windows, but surrendered. "What sort of a man is your Stonewall Jackson?" one of them asked. "Are his soldiers made of gutta-percha, or do they run on wheels?"[40]

Before Munford and Forno had swept in, they had heard a train passing by. They had hardly taken possession when another came up from the south. Men dashed to the rails to try to tear them loose.

Others threw ties on the tracks. But Train No. 6, with an engine named "Secretary," and with an engineer who damned the torpedoes and went ahead, dashed through the station, scattering the few ties on the track. Riddled with bullets but still chugging, "Secretary" fled with the word to the north.

That wouldn't do. Officers and men went to work in earnest, removed a stretch of track, and waited. An engine and twenty empties rattled in, crashed off the rails, and plunged down an embankment to the roars of the spectators. Soon another train came up, hit the same trap, and smashed full force into the wreckage. Eventually one more train approached from the south. But this one had a suspicious engineer. He saw trouble ahead, stopped, backed up, and was away before he could be caught.

The word would go in both directions now but with a bad estimate of the situation. "Secretary" reported that 500 cavalrymen had fired upon it at Bristoe, and Federal authorities assumed that Stuart was raiding again. The great fact, the overwhelmingly successful achievement, was that 20,000 infantry had marched 51 to 54 miles in two days and were now astride Pope's main railroad reliance 13 miles in his rear. Their presence was a mystery, their strength unknown, and their succeeding moves beyond the guessing of anyone who had, in the middle of the night, to deal with this inexplicable menace.

Bristoe was no prize in itself. But Jackson learned there that Manassas Junction was. It was a major depot. He must have it, and he must have it this night. He looked around at three divisions of men as exhausted as any he had seen. When Trimble offered his services—Trimble, who once told Jackson that "before this war is over I intend to be a major general or a corpse" [41]—Jackson accepted.

With two regiments of weary men, the Twenty-first North Carolina (Lieut. Col. Saunders Fulton) and the Twenty-first Georgia (Maj. Thomas C. Glover), Trimble set out.[42] Jackson later sent Stuart, senior to Trimble, to take command of the expedition.[43] (Trimble did not know that, and the two quarreled bitterly in their reports about who did the work and deserved the credit.)

About midnight both infantry and cavalry reached the outskirts of the Junction, ran into the picket fire of an alerted garrison, but stormed the defenses through intense darkness with minor loss, capturing eight pieces of artillery and 300 prisoners. Trimble kept

his regiments under arms all night. Re-enforcements reached him
at dawn. The rest of the army, officers and men (save necessary
pickets and sentries), slept the sleep of complete exhaustion, isolated in enemy country but, for the moment at least, safe.

Next morning, August 27, Jackson moved Hill's and Taliaferro's
divisions to the Junction, leaving most of Ewell's division at Bristoe.
En route, a mile from the Junction, a regiment of Federal cavalry
appeared, but Colonel Baylor drove it off. Soon after the troops
reached the Junction long-range artillery began dropping shells
from the north, but this battery was driven off too.[44] How that was
done is not quite certain, for the Junction had now become the
scene of one of the historic orgies of the war.

At that railroad junction the Federal command had established a
supply base—"vast in quantity and of great value," in Jackson's
words [45]—designed to provide not only for Pope's army but for Mc-
Clellan's as well when it came up.

Warehouses held, among an immense variety of other foods, 2,000
barrels of flour, 2,000 barrels of salt pork, 1,000 barrels of corned
beef, and 50,000 pounds of bacon. Two trains of freight cars, re-
portedly half a mile long each, were jammed with other goods of
every description and much ordnance, including two newly developed 3-inch bronze rifled guns, distinctive in the sound of their
shells, which the Confederates had admired on the Peninsula. Huge
pyramids of shot and shell stood in long, ominous rows. A large
assortment of sutlers had set up for business, so that the Junction,
in addition to being a base for staples and ordnance, was a gigantic
bazaar for young men with money in their pockets. Now it had all
fallen into the hands of the hungriest, dirtiest, most ragged, and
most omnivorous troops in eastern America.

Trimble tried to keep the captured supplies inviolate, knowing
Jackson's normal care about public property. But though he posted
guards, he couldn't command sympathy. The cavalry began to sneak
in and out of the lines. When Taliaferro's division marched in shortly
after dawn, it was put to guard duty too, but aside from some of
the higher-echelon officers nobody had his heart in this kind of duty,
and perhaps the officers themselves didn't. When Hill's division
followed about 10 A.M. the looting began in earnest.

The men had to have rations. Some of them hadn't eaten anything to speak of for two days, and what they would have done

without the food now in their possession is difficult to say. But when systematic supplying of rations began, it was hard—in a supply center with everything from calomel to McClellan saddles—to keep men from breaking into other boxes. Besides, with such a choice, men had trouble making up their minds.

Said John H. Worsham, one of the Old F men, of Richmond (F Company, Twenty-first Regiment, Second Brigade, Taliaferro's division):

The first thing brought to us was a barrel of cakes; next, a bag of hams. We secured a camp kettle, made a fire, and put a ham on to boil; and we had hardly gotten it underway before a barrel of sugar and coffee, the Yanks had it mixed, and a bag of beans were sent to us. After a consultation, we decided to empty the ham out of the kettle, as we could take that along raw, and in its place put the beans on the fire, as they were something we were fond of and had not had for a long time. About the time they commenced to get warm, a bag of potatoes was brought us;—over the kettle goes, and the potatoes take the place of the beans. We now think our kettle is all right, as potatoes cook in a short time, but here comes a package of desiccated vegetables, and the kettle is again emptied, and the vegetables are placed on the fire, as soup is so good. We were also given a barrel of syrup. This was a liberal and varied bill of fare for our company, which was small then.[46]

Jackson had some idea of holding the goods for Lee's arrival,[47] but when pressure from the enemy increased during the morning, and calculations showed that Lee with Longstreet's wing could not arrive for another day or so, he determined to utilize every article he could—"rations and other articles which they [the troops] could properly make subservient to their use," in the official prose of Jackson's report—and destroy the remainder so it would not fall back into Federal hands.

For a time the delicacies and elegancies of the sutlers' stores were reserved for officers, but the irrepressible Private Casler and his crew had ways of dealing with such problems. "We would form in a solid mass around the [sutlers'] tents and commence pushing one another towards the center until the guard, who was not very particular about it, would give way, and then we would make the good things fly for a short time, until some officer would ride up with more guards and disperse us."

Weary of this, Private Casler led a raid on a commissary building full to the eaves. He rummaged among the coffee, sugar, and molasses, and found a barrel of whiskey. Because canteens were full of molasses, this was temporarily embarrassing; but "we soon found an old funnel . . . and while one would hold his hand over the bottom another would draw it full," and "in this way it was passed around" until officers broke up that game too.[48]

Medical supplies in a freight car seemed less exciting to the Casler command until Casler discovered that the medical stores in boxes included bottles of brandy and whiskey. When Private Casler left that freight car, ordered out by medical officers trying to locate and preserve morphine and chloroform (precious articles then), he carried four brandy bottles under his jacket. He broke one when he jammed in a door, and reached his company of the Thirty-third Virginia with three, "where I divided two of them with my Captain and the company, keeping one for myself." [49]

Jackson fought hard to keep liquor out of the troops' hands, ordering barrels to be poured out and setting special guards over others until he could dispose of it. (Men knelt on the ground and scooped up the liquor with their hands or drank it as it flowed.[50]) He was firm against taking blue uniforms, although no one knew better how much the men needed new uniforms of some kind; and he kept the big base bakery working full blast, with prisoners on duty there, because he needed the bread. Shoes were fair loot, and many a lean and hairy fighter turned up in elegant underwear and with fine linen handkerchiefs.

They turned up, in fact, with almost everything: potted ham, lobster, tongue, candy, cakes, nuts, oranges, lemons, pickles, catsup, mustard (one man took nothing but French mustard and traded it for other food for the next ten days), cigars, soap, toothbrushes, cheese, sardines, shirts, blankets, spurs, cavalry boots, lager beer, Rhine wine, and champagne.[51]

The problem of knowing what to try to carry, each for himself, was enormous, and no two men decided it alike. Infantrymen grumbled because cavalry could carry more on horseback and artillerymen in their vehicles. Not since they put on uniforms had the men known anything like this, and never as long as any of them lived did they forget the special flavor of this day. What a day! What a day!

It was not all a day of looting, and for some troops there was no chance at all. By 8 P.M. on the 26th, "Secretary" having spread the news of Confederates at Bristoe, Pope ordered Heintzelman, whose corps was at Warrenton Junction south of Bristoe, to send a regiment to the scene by train. Heintzelman did so early on the 27th, but when the regiment saw the strength of the Confederate force it turned around and went back where it came from.

At 9:30 P.M. on the same day Halleck in Washington ordered Col. Herman Haupt, in charge of transportation, to collect from any available troops as many as he could send by train southward to protect the Bull Run bridge. Haupt roused Brig. Gen. W. S. Hancock, who was in command of Franklin's Sixth Corps, recently arrived from the Peninsula, and Hancock sent Brig. Gen. G. W. Taylor with a brigade of four New Jersey regiments, followed by the Eleventh and Twelfth Ohio under Col. E. Parker Scammon on a train. Taylor thought (as did all others at that time) that the force ahead of him was small. His regiments boldly crossed the Bull Run bridge on the morning of the 27th and advanced toward Manassas Junction, "with great spirit and determination and under a leader worthy of a better cause," Jackson thought.[52]

Poague's battery had gone north to deal with the long-range gun that was plopping occasional shells toward the Junction, and Jackson went with it. He saw the glint of Taylor's bayonets and puzzled over whose troops these were. When the blue uniforms became unmistakable, Poague opened fire. Carpenter's battery joined him, and most of Hill's brigade came up. The shells tore Taylor's ranks so badly that Jackson, watching carefully, did an unusual thing. He ordered a halt to the firing and rode forward toward the enemy. Waving a white handkerchief, he cried out a demand for surrender. But all he got was a blaze of fire in return—a narrow escape. Thereupon he turned loose his guns.[53]

There could be only one result. Taylor's brigade was ripped so badly by rifle and artillery, of which it had none, that it broke. Taylor was mortally wounded, and the whole force withdrew about 11 A.M. Scammon held on in the rear until the afternoon before withdrawing. Jackson does not appear to have forced the issue. The common verdict was that if Taylor had been permitted to continue his audacious advance, his whole force could have been captured or destroyed.[54] But the artillery was in a hurry—men wanted to get back to the fleshpots of the Junction.

Meantime, south of the Junction at Bristoe Station, Ewell was

coming under attack. In the afternoon the enemy began to arrive
in force. It was the division (re-enforced) of Maj. Gen. Joseph
Hooker, about 5,500 strong. Ewell held it off for a time with artillery
fire, but when his flanks were threatened he obeyed Jackson's direction to fall back on the Junction if hard pressed. This required neat
maneuvering for brigades actually engaged with the enemy, but
Ewell, with the assistance of Early, managed it with skill and minor
loss, and the whole force dropped back to Jackson's main body.
Hooker, whose ammunition was down to five rounds per man, did
not advance beyond Broad Run. Boswell destroyed the bridge.

Jackson stood, nevertheless, in extreme danger. The moment
Pope learned that the force in his rear was not a few hundred raiding cavalrymen but 20,000 men under Jackson, his concern with the
Rappahannock line was ended. He must turn back to take care of
his logistical necessities in a rear which he had professed to ignore.
He must turn back for his own safety. If Jackson was there, Lee
might be able to join him. The two together, blocking his communications and standing between him and re-enforcements arriving
from McClellan's debarking troops on the Potomac, would have
him in a critical position. On the other hand, if Pope could about-
face rapidly enough to catch Jackson before Lee arrived, he ought
to be able to smash that small force to bits and avenge the insult
to his rear. Pope made up his mind quickly. He broke loose from
the Rappahannock on the 27th and moved northward.

Lee himself was now on the march. He had sent Longstreet's
right wing in motion on the afternoon of the 26th (when Jackson
was swinging down from Thoroughfare Gap to Bristoe), leaving
only Richard H. Anderson's division on the Rappahannock. By night
Longstreet, following Jackson's route, had reached Orleans. On the
27th he pushed on to Salem and then, after a hot and thirsty march,
to White Plains, which some of the units did not reach until 2 A.M.
Jackson was reaching them with couriers, and he knew they were
coming. But he did not know when.

What Jackson did know by the evening of the 27th was that
Manassas Junction was untenable. Pope was moving 54,500 men
northeastward to the Gainesville–Manassas Junction line. The corps
of McDowell and Sigel, and Reynolds' division, about 40,000 men,
were ordered to march on Gainesville. The divisions of Reno and
Kearny moved parallel on the right, toward Greenwich. Hooker's

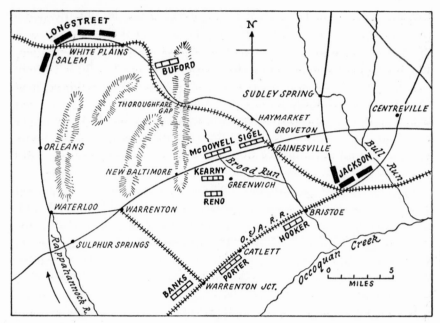

JACKSON AT MANASSAS JUNCTION, EVENING OF AUGUST 27, 1862.

division, as we have seen, was moving parallel and still farther to the right, on the railroad toward Bristoe and ultimately the Junction; and Porter's corps was directed to follow him. Banks guarded the trains in the rear.

The weight of the force was with McDowell and Sigel, and their destination, Gainesville, would place them directly between Jackson and the Lee-Longstreet wing and roughly halfway between the two. Since Pope's army was double the number of either Jackson's or Longstreet's wing, its position should enable it to hold Jackson and Longstreet apart and crush either at will.

But the perfection of this countermaneuver rested on the supposition that Jackson would turn directly to join Lee or would remain conveniently at Manassas Junction while Pope moved between him and Lee. Jackson did neither. Entirely from his own mind, with no order or word of advice from Lee, and without consultation with anyone, Jackson developed now the strategy which, in its different kind of excellence, matched the excellence of his great march of

the 25th and 26th. He sought (1) a location on the enemy's flank
so as to evade his full blow and yet be able to strike effectively if
necessary; (2) a location within reach of Longstreet's advance; and
(3) a location from which, if Longstreet was barred, he could aid
in removing the barrier or, if necessary, withdraw and unite with
Longstreet behind the Bull Run Mountains.[55]

Since Pope's units were advancing now by the line of the railroad
and along the Warrenton–Alexandria turnpike, Jackson determined
to cross the line of advance ahead of Pope, move beyond the turnpike, and there, in a position adaptable for both defense and offense,
hover on the flank of the advancing columns. The low ridge that
ran back of Groveton and the woods to the north met these specifications. Hidden there beside the main highway, he could watch the
ebb and flow of Pope's troops. He would be nearer Longstreet. He
could stand off a stiff attack on that slope, and if his situation grew
critical, he could fall back westward through the Bull Run Mountains at Aldie Gap, north of Thoroughfare.

On the night of the 27th Jackson set fire to the supplies which
his troops could not carry on their backs or in their stomachs. As the
conflagration lit up the Manassas plain for miles around, Taliaferro
set out, soon after night fell, on the road toward Sudley Mill, on
the upper Bull Run, near the ford that McDowell had used for his
sweeping flank movement at First Manassas. His troops marched
nine miles on a starlit night through a ground haze and found a
secluded area among the trees early in the morning.[56]

They marched with ghosts. The route took them directly across
the main Confederate battlefield of First Manassas. The Henry Hill
—where a brigade first came into its own and a commander first
caught the eye of the world—rose above them on the right. The
Second, Fourth, Fifth, Twenty-seventh, and Thirty-third Virginia
Regiments, striding now past the birthplace of their fame, could
not have included many men this August night who had lived
through the hot July day of the year before and all subsequent days.
But the First Brigade knew its origins. Federal troops had crept up
this road to threaten their left flank. Off to their left stretched the
ground where the South Carolina regiments, and then Kirby Smith
and Elzey, and finally Early, had struck so effectively. Ahead of
them—they would cross it soon—ran the Warrenton–Alexandria
turnpike. The Stone House sat where the roads met, and beyond

it rose Matthews Hill, where Evans and Bartow and Bee had first halted the flank movement, and in the distance along the road they were following stood all the Sudleys—the Mill, the Church, and the Ford.

Weeds and briers had taken possession of the decaying winter quarters, their roofs tumbled down now and their side walls sagging. But Col. Campbell Brown, of Ewell's division, when he crossed the battle area later that night, found a box of star candles among the lingering debris near Mitchell's Ford and put them to good use later when the surgeons amputated Ewell's leg. All the moving Confederates this night marched through and beyond their old lines and into old Yankee land north of the turnpike, behind Groveton and on to Sudley Church.

Hill, setting out nearer 11 P.M., headed toward Centreville. He had no specified orders beyond following the guide Jackson sent him, and some men believed later that the guide did not himself know where to go and had not been directed to Centreville. If that was so, the god of battles was on Jackson's side.

Ewell had more difficulty getting away. Trimble's brigade was strangely missing, and Ewell spent hours scouting for it. He did not move out until long past midnight. Early's division, meantime, waiting north of Manassas, had grown weary of all this delay and went into bivouac again. When the remainder of the division came along, "we saw them just at dawn," Campbell Brown remembered, "sleeping in a little valley on the side of the road, every man covered with his [captured] white tent looking as picturesque as Scott describes the Welshmen before 'La Gorde Doloreuse' in 'The Betrothed.' . . . As we moved off the magazines were fired, and the successive explosions were loud enough to wake all stragglers and start them after us." [57]

Ewell didn't know where to go. Moving uncertainly toward Centreville, he found Trimble, who had followed Hill. In the morning both divisions were ordered to retrace their steps from four to seven miles. In hot irritation they moved southward on the turnpike to the Stone Bridge which First Manassas veterans remembered, and the Sudley road. There they turned right and joined Taliaferro behind Groveton. They had marched 14 miles, with some confusion,[58] but they had marched completely out of Pope's sight or beyond the reach of his guesses.

That general, after his quick and sound decision to move on Gainesville, thrusting the weight of his force between Jackson and the hills to which Jackson lifted up his eyes for help, changed his mind on the evening of the 27th. He believed then that Jackson was tied down to the Manassas fortifications and would fight it out there. In a drastic revision of orders Pope directed all his army to swing east and concentrate on Manassas.[59] So consumed was he by the dream of catching Jackson at last that he virtually ignored the possibility—in his rear again—of Lee's and Longstreet's coming through Thoroughfare Gap. This, in the classic simplicity of Alexander's words, was "the order which cost Pope his campaign." [60]

For even as Pope was issuing this order for his troops to swing eastward, Jackson was sliding with his troops northward and a little westward across the line of advance which Pope had abandoned. In effect they passed one another, with Jackson running like a half-back in American football who reverses his field. So it came about that, whereas Pope rubbed his hands in glee on the 27th in the expectation that in Manassas "we shall bag the whole crowd," [61] he arrived at noon on the 28th at a smoldering, desolated, and abandoned Manassas with no idea where Jackson had gone.

When word came in later of Hill's appearance near Centreville, and also of a raid by Stuart farther along the railroad at Burke, only 12 miles from Alexandria, Pope leaped at the supposition that he had found Jackson once again. He sent Sigel, Kearny, and Reno in that direction.[62] That, too, was wrong, for Hill and Ewell had retraced the steps of their wanderings toward Centreville during the night of the 27th, and their men were now stretched out at ease, and completely out of sight or knowledge, in the region around Sudley Mill and Catharpin Run.

Jackson had acted with dispatch, but he did not know the exact nature of the Federal moves. When he received indications early on the 28th from a captured order that the Federals were moving northward, he sent word to Hill, in the Centreville area, to hold the line of Bull Run against the advancing enemy. By the time that order reached him, Hill had a captured order of his own that showed no Federal advance to the north but rather the swing eastward toward Manassas which Pope in fact had ordered. Hill, always a man of courage, decided to disregard Jackson's order because he had later information.[63] He continued toward the Sudley road and the

Stone House as originally directed. He was right, and, although no record of his reporting to Jackson is known, the very silence suggests that Jackson recognized the virtue of Hill's decision.

About noon Jackson assumed from another captured order (the cavalry were active this day) that a Federal column was moving by the turnpike from the Gainesville area toward the Sudley road. This time he determined to meet it. He roused Taliaferro and Ewell and sent them through the woods, well back from the turnpike, southward for two and a half miles to a commanding position near Brawner's house. But then he learned that the Federal movement was not northward but toward Manassas. He waited.[64]

Bradley Johnson of Taliaferro's Second Brigade, farther south than any other troops save the restless cavalry, saw troops leaving the turnpike in the Manassas direction and fired on them. A sharp clash threatened and, had it developed, might have uncovered all of Taliaferro's and Ewell's divisions in the woods along the turnpike. But Johnson, when his flank was threatened, fell back, and the Federals did not follow him. The long afternoon dragged on.

(This day at 3 P.M. Longstreet reached Thoroughfare Gap and found it occupied. Although Pope had paid little attention to it, McDowell had ordered Ricketts' division to guard it, and Buford's cavalry were all over the country east of the Gap. Longstreet prepared to attack headlong, but sought other passages across Bull Run Mountains too. He sent Hood with two brigades up a discovered path on the left, and Cadmus Wilcox three miles still farther left to Hopewell Gap. Then he waited for the morning.)

In the woods Jackson pondered. Satisfied now that Pope's movement was toward Manassas, he asked himself what that meant in terms of the grand strategy of the operation on which he was engaged. He himself seemed relatively safe where he lay. But what if Pope joined McClellan's oncoming re-enforcements? What if the result of the maneuvers was to confront Lee's army when united with a united Federal army of twice its size or more? Lee could not stand that disparity. The major purpose of hitting Pope a devastating blow while he was still relatively weak would be lost. The long flank march, the breaking of the communication line, the jarring of Pope from the Rappahannock and his move to the north, the neat side-stepping by which he himself had faded from Pope's sight, these were all well enough. But Pope was still loose, gaining strength, and becoming increasingly dangerous—and was almost within arm's reach. Jackson had not completed his purpose, and the sands were running out.

So he reckoned if he appraised the situation correctly as the sun began to sink on this August afternoon. His men lay packed like herring in a barrel in the woods, between the long rows of stacked arms, lounging at ease, gossiping, laughing, playing cards, amply supplied with cooked rations, restricted as to fire or music which might give away their position, but talking so much that the woods sounded like the hum of a beehive—"all the careless merriment of troops confident in themselves, their cause, and their leader." [65]

Jackson had been restless all day, riding about alone, cross as a bear, his expression one of suppressed energy that reminded Blackford of an explosive missile, "an unlucky spark applied to which would blow you skyhigh." Then a courier came galloping in, his horse jaded, with a message from Lee. It told Jackson that Lee was at Thoroughfare Gap and would cross in the morning.

"Where is the man who brought this dispatch?" Jackson demanded. "I must shake hands with him." He knew now that Lee and Longstreet would be with him the next day. That news colored his calculations. Still, the region was quiet, the enemy was not in sight, and he would wait.

Blackford, enjoying himself hugely this day, learned that buttermilk was to be had at a farmhouse half a mile distant and went with several others. They found it, drank all they could, and Blackford filled his canteen. When he came back, he offered it to Jackson, who was very fond of buttermilk; and the General tilted back his head and took a long drink. Others consumed the rest just as Ewell came up and asked what they were drinking.

"Buttermilk? For God's sake, give me some!" he exclaimed.

Blackford told him it was all gone, but more could be had if Ewell sent his orderly to the farmhouse. So Blackford and four or five others made a second journey. This time they saw five horses hitched outside the door. Enemy! Blackford posted two men at the rear and charged. Five men came tumbling out; four surrendered, and the fifth ran under fire.

From a hundred yards off the fire was returned smartly, and now Blackford, filling canteens with buttermilk and sweeping hot corn cakes, butter, eggs, and fried ham into haversacks, beat a retreat—

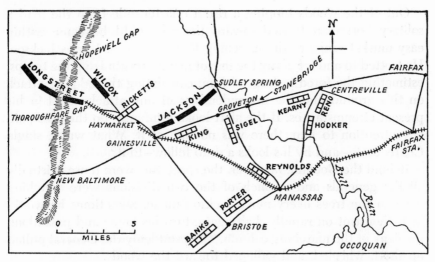

JACKSON'S POSITION AT GROVETON ON THE EVENING OF
AUGUST 28, 1862.

under fire until he put his prisoners in the rear. Ewell got his buttermilk, and Jackson knew now that the enemy was near and presently
knew that the enemy was in force and that Blackford had been
playing with his advanced flank guard.

For now in the sunset glow a full division appeared on the turnpike, marching in superb stride northward, trim and built for business, but completely unaware that Jackson with two divisions hung
on its flank and was peering at it through the woods with thousands
of eyes. This was Rufus King's division of McDowell's corps, originally ordered to Manassas but caught en route with a change of
orders that sent it, when Pope thought Jackson had gone north,
toward Centreville. John P. Hatch's brigade was in front, John
Gibbon's came next, Abner Doubleday's followed, and M. R. Patrick
brought up the rear. A mile or more separated the brigades. King,
who had fallen out sick that day, was not present.

Hatch had deployed some of his men to reconnoiter the very
ground over which the eyes of Jackson's two divisions were peering,[66]
but though they saw a few Confederates in the distance (and were
probably involved in the affair of the buttermilk), they discovered
nothing to disturb the continuance of the march. Hatch's brigade
moved on.

Out of the woods topping a rise a quarter-mile from the road a solitary horseman trotted toward the pike until he came within easy musket range of the marching Federal troops. It was Jackson. He trotted to and fro along the line of march, scrutinizing the troops, estimating the force in front of him, calculating the odds of attack on this ground and the imponderables of any attack at all in his present circumstances. If the alert-looking infantry on the pike paid any attention to him, there was no sign of it. What was a single Confederate—and by his looks a drab fellow—to it?

Behind the General, however, the spectators were tense. Virtually all the generals and colonels of the two divisions were watching through the trees every move Jackson made. Sometimes he would halt, then trot on rapidly, halt again, turn his horse and pass along the flank of the marching column. Then suddenly the General pulled up short, wheeled, and galloped toward the woods.

"Here he comes, by God!" several of them exclaimed. Jackson rode up to the assembled group "as calm as a May morning and, touching his hat in military salute, said in as soft a voice as if he had been talking to a friend in ordinary conversation, 'Bring out your men, gentlemen!'"

The calm scene changed instantly into a fury of action. Every officer raced back to his units where men had been watching them with as keen interest as they watched the General. "From the woods arose a hoarse roar like that from cages of wild beasts at the scent of blood." Orders rang out, men scrambled into line, stacked arms were broken, battle flags rose to the sunset, and columns began winding out of the trees.[67]

Ahead of them, off to the left, a battery crashed through the underbrush into the open, unlimbering at top speed, and began to fire on the marching troops. Far down to the rear, beyond the limits of the brigade now on the pike, another battery came out and went into action. Instantly the Federal troops dropped to the ground and sought cover by the road. This was Gibbon's Black Hat Brigade, with the Second, Sixth, and Seventh Wisconsin, and the Nineteenth Indiana, never in action before, but long trained and full of pride and vigor.[68]

Gibbon had no idea enemy infantry was within miles, and assumed that cavalry batteries were annoying him. He ordered out Capt. J. B. Campbell's battery, and another from Hatch up ahead came into action. They fired so effectively that the Confederate batteries (Capt. E. V. Garber and Capt. George W. Wooding) had to change position. Gibbon then sent the Sixth Wisconsin across the field to complete the job.

The virgin troops advanced in schoolbook style, topped a ridge in the field, and encountered immediately the fire of massed and hitherto-invisible infantry. Oho! This was different! Gibbon sent the Nineteenth Indiana, and then both his other regiments, and was committed now up to the hilt. In front to Hatch and back to Doubleday and Patrick he hurried pleas for aid. Doubleday sent up the Fifty-sixth Pennsylvania and the Seventy-sixth New York, and later the Ninety-fifth New York to support Campbell's battery.

Gibbon got nothing from Hatch or Patrick. For the most part he fought his fight alone. He had some 2,800 to 3,000 men, and he faced parts of two divisions. But the operations on the Rappahannock, the strain of the march of the 25th–26th, the fighting on the 27th had depleted Jackson's units to extremely low levels, especially the Stonewall Brigade, and his men in action numbered perhaps 4,500.[69]

It was the strangest battle of Jackson's career. He advanced Taliaferro's division on the right, parts of Ewell's on the left. The extreme right was held by Col. A. G. Taliaferro's brigade, with the Stonewall now under Baylor to its left, and then Stafford's Louisiana brigade under Brig. Gen. William E. Starke. Lawton's brigade of Ewell's division stood next, and Trimble was on the extreme left. The brigades of Early, Forno, and Johnson did not participate, and Hill's division had remained near Sudley.

Across the slope the brigades marched toward Gibbon's Westerners until the long lines confronted each other at hardly more than a hundred yards, erect and blazing away.

There was no maneuvering to speak of. Jackson sent units on a flanking movement to the right, but the men ran into a ravine, lost their direction in the growing darkness, and arrived nowhere. There was no cover of importance: one farmhouse, an orchard, a few bushes, a few swells and depressions in the terrain. There was no artillery fire of effectiveness after the early exchanges until near the end Stuart's young artilleryman, Capt. John Pelham, got in some blows from the right flank. The lines were too close together. There was no material re-enforcement of either side, although two other brigades of King's division were ahead and behind Gibbon, and although Jackson might have called up his unused brigades and even Hill. With Doubleday's two regiments added, the original forces stood up at short range and murdered each other, standing up to death with incredible bravery as if this were a normal condition of life.

Taliaferro recorded in his formal report:

Twice our lines were advanced until we had reached a farm-house and orchard on the right of our lines and were within about 80 yards of a greatly superior force of the enemy. Here one of the most terrific conflicts that can be conceived of occurred. Our troops held the farm-house and one edge of the orchard, while the enemy held the orchard and inclosure next to the turnpike. To our left there was no cover, and our men stood in the field without shelter of any kind. The enemy, although reenforced, never once attempted to advance upon our position, but withstood with great determination the terrible fire which our lines poured upon them. For two hours and a half, without an instant's cessation of the most deadly discharges of musketry, round shot, and shell, both lines stood unmoved, neither advancing and neither broken nor yielding, until at last, about 9 o'clock at night, the enemy slowly and sullenly fell back and yielded the field to our victorious troops.[70]

The losses were grave. Ewell, the most valuable of all Jackson's officers, went down with a shot through his knee that forced amputation by McGuire and ten months' absence from the field. General Taliaferro suffered a lesser wound. Gibbon lost, in killed or wounded, seven of his twelve field officers and more than a third of his entire force. His Second Wisconsin left behind 298 of the 500 men it took into action. The Confederate losses are impossible to deduce from reports that covered the whole campaign, but, in the Stonewall Brigade, Colonel Neff of the Thirty-third and Colonel Botts of the Second were killed, and Colonel Grigsby of the Twenty-seventh was wounded. The Second went in with 140 men and lost 48; the Fourth with about 180 and lost 76; and the Twenty-seventh with 65 and lost 28.[71]

What did it mean? Jackson's explanation of his attack, which Lee repeated, said merely that "as his [King's] column appeared to be moving by, with his flank exposed, I determined to attack at once." [72] It was a powerful temptation, although in the end the approximate standoff and heavy losses made it look less attractive. But Jackson was hardly exposing his entire wing to the far more powerful forces of Pope merely for the values of smashing a passing brigade or division. He knew that attacking these troops would give away his own presence and draw Pope's army on him. He attacked in spite of that certainty.

He attacked, it seems reasonable to conclude, because of that certainty. Jackson knew, on the one hand, that Lee and Longstreet would arrive on the morrow and, on the other, that, by the direction of King's movement, Pope might even yet be moving his whole force north of Bull Run, into a stronger defensive position and nearer to McClellan's re-enforcements. *That* he must prevent or the whole campaign would fail of its purpose. He forced Pope to turn upon him, gambling that he could hold off Pope until Longstreet was by his side and Lee would command a united army again.

So while King's division retreated through the night toward Manassas, Jackson pulled in the remnants of Taliaferro's and Ewell's divisions (now commanded by Starke and Lawton) and united them with Hill's waiting men in the position he had chosen to fight off the blows that were sure to come.

The position extended from the Sudley Springs southwesterly toward the Warrenton pike. An unfinished railroad line presented here a series of cuts and fills, ranging from eight to fifteen feet, so that defensive infantry might line up on top of the cuts and lie behind the fills. The front of about 3,000 yards faced open land on its left where Hill's division formed in two lines, though underbrush restricted the defenders' view. Then a strip of woods 200 to 600 yards broad protruded almost to the line in the left center and permitted an advance under cover. Lawton with two brigades of Ewell's division held the center, and then Jackson's old division under Starke looked out on an open field of fire. Farther to the right the ground was more loosely held, but on the right flank Jackson placed Early and Forno to pin it down. He had about 18,000 infantry.

Behind the railroad line the ground rose and was wooded, and Jackson's forty guns had effective positions for firing. Stuart had cavalry on both flanks. It was a strong position, and if Jackson must retreat, his route would be toward the advancing Longstreet. He planned a waiting, defensive engagement and directed division commanders not to advance far and to avoid a general battle.[73]

Pope, who was out of touch with his commanders and with events themselves, misinterpreted the action of the 28th to mean that King's division had intercepted Jackson in retreat and that his retreat continued. He dreamed of crushing Jackson between a force built up from King's and Ricketts' divisions on the west, under McDowell, and his remaining corps on the east. But King and Ricketts had withdrawn toward Manassas, McDowell had moved in the same direction, and there were no troops west of Jackson save Federal cavalry and the advancing Longstreet.

Pope succeeded, however, in hurrying Sigel's First Corps from its bivouac near the Henry Hill under orders to attack Jackson vigorously at dawn on the 29th. Sigel had his artillery in action soon after daybreak and lined up Schurz's and Robert C. Schenck's divisions, Milroy's independent brigade, and Reynolds' division of McDowell's corps for an assault all along the line. It broke down under artillery and musketry fire but continued spasmodically until after 10 o'clock.

After Reno's Ninth Corps and Kearny's division of Heintzelman's Third Corps arrived on the field at a moment which Sigel called "critical, when the enemy had almost outflanked us on both wings, and was preparing a new attack against our center," the Federal attacks began to take on more force and purpose. They aimed especially at Hill's left flank. There, advancing under cover of the woods before debouching for the assault, they pierced Hill's front lines. But Hill called in Branch from his reserve and cleared the lines. Although Sigel had substantially as many men to begin with as Jackson had, and was now greatly re-enforced, his blows came piecemeal, and they lacked real vigor.

Federal troops were troubling Jackson in the rear as well as in the front. Some of them reached the woods where his train was parked. Stuart discovered them there. He ordered cavalry to the area, and young Pelham—"always at the right place at the right time," said Stuart—unlimbered his battery and cleared part of the woods. Stuart directed his aide, von Borcke, to ride fast to Jackson with the news, meantime sending any troops he saw to the area.

Von Borcke encountered Hill and gave him the word, then galloped on toward Jackson. He found him sitting by a caisson writing a dispatch in the midst of smoke where an occasional shell would crash close enough to scatter dust on his manuscript so that, von Borcke thought, like one of Napoleon's generals under similar circumstances, the General needed no sand to dry his ink. He delivered his message and told the General this was a hot spot.

"I am very much obliged to you, Major, for the orders you have given," he told the Prussian. "Hill will take care of the enemy in our rear. I know what they are. There cannot be more than two brigades of them. As for my position here, I believe we have been together in hotter places before." He went on writing.[74]

Pope reached the field after noon, and set about organizing a new attack, aided now by the arrival of Hooker's division. The artillery on Hill's far left held off Kearny, who had to advance over open ground, and the real danger came from Reno and Hooker on Hill's center and right. (Sigel had been used up and was out of action for the day.) Hooker's fresh troops attacked with great spirit against the brigades of Charles W. Field and E. L. Thomas, crossed the railroad line in their front, and engaged in severe hand-to-hand fighting. But again Hill threw in re-enforcements at the right moment, Pender's brigade this time, and swept the enemy out. Pender's enthusiasm carried him so far in pursuit that he came under heavy artillery fire and was hurt before he reached safety again.

Taking advantage of this confusion, a solitary brigade of Hooker's division hitherto in reserve—commanded by Brig. Gen. Cuvier Grover and consisting of three Massachusetts regiments, one from New Hampshire, and one from Pennsylvania—threw itself into the attack with exceptional determination. It swept over Hill's first line in a short, sharp, hand-to-hand struggle, reeled under the fire from the second line, then blasted ahead, penetrated that one too, and stood quivering in its triumph. At this moment Forno's Louisiana brigade and a Georgia regiment from Lawton's hit Grover's men head-on. It was too much. Grover fell back, panting, as Hill's line re-formed once more. In 20 minutes he left 486 men on the field, but he had written a name that nobody on the field forgot.[75]

Once again Hill had found in a desperate moment the additional force to throw in the face of the enemy, and this time above all others he was blessed by exact planning and exact movements. Jackson had shifted Forno's brigade from the far right flank where he had placed it with Early at the start of the day. Jackson could shift it because now the strategic event of the day had taken place: Longstreet had arrived, and Lee commanded a united army.

This was the development for which Jackson and his whole wing waited. The General had ridden out with McGuire the night before, a mile or so, in the direction of Thoroughfare Gap; and he had swung off his horse and put his ear to the ground listening for the beat of Longstreet's march. "I shall never forget the sad look of the man that night," McGuire remembered, "as he gazed toward Thoroughfare Gap, wishing for Longstreet to come." [76]

On the morning of the 29th the General sent Stuart out with a cavalry regiment to connect with Longstreet. Stuart moved about 9 o'clock, saw the dust of the marching troops a few miles ahead, and rode up to Lee and his staff ahead of the column. That was a warm greeting! Lee, Longstreet, and Stuart turned aside at a grassy plot and sat before Stuart's map as he explained the situation, the column marching by all the while. The infantry halted for Stuart to cut through so as to place his cavalry on the extreme right of the line that would now be greatly extended. Then the march renewed, and Hood in the lead reached Gainesville and turned left toward the sound of firing. Jackson came up shortly and spoke to Hood. The time was about 10:30 A.M.[77] He reported briefly to Lee later.

Hood hitched on to Jackson's right, where Early and Forno were stationed, and the whole of Longstreet's wing gradually moved into line, not extended straight from Jackson's but with the two lines forming an obtuse angle. There was little action on this front, and with Longstreet's 32,000 men Jackson could pull out Early and Forno and dispatch them to the center and left where the tides had beaten heaviest all day and now in the afternoon were making up for the worst blows of all.

Lee and Longstreet were reconnoitering the ground in front of them, and Lee was trying to estimate the drama into which he had come in the midst of its action and as it approached its climax. He wished to join battle immediately, but Longstreet thought the ground not favorable and pleaded for delay, and finally won it. Their presence brought a long, rolling cheer down the ranks of Jackson's worn and weary men. Far to the left the meaning came in the counterattack of Forno's just-arrived Louisiana men who, in a moment of crisis, saved the left flank from impending disaster.

There the all-day blows had taken their toll of men and ammunition. Gregg's brigade at the far flank was cooped up on a rocky knoll separated by a gap of 125 yards from Thomas' brigade. Federal en-

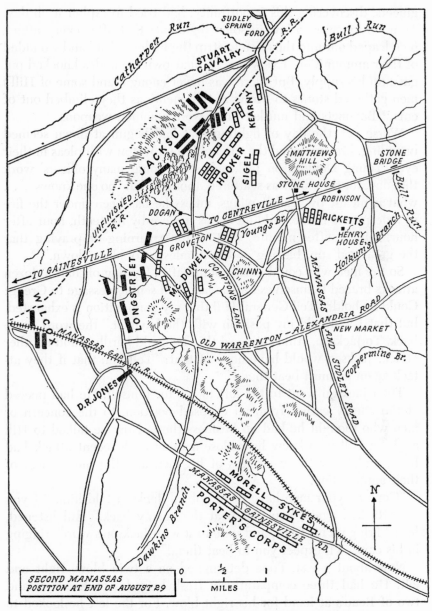

JACKSON AND LONGSTREET AT SECOND MANASSAS ON THE
EVENING OF AUGUST 29, 1862.

gineers, discovering this opportunity, had tried to exploit it all day.
Ammunition was so low in some regiments that after every attack
men leaped out into the open to strip the Federal dead and wounded
of their ammunition. Every one of their own comrades knocked out
gave up his supply. But there was never enough, and some of Hill's
men gathered stones to throw at the enemy as they climbed out of
cuts.[78] Bayonets and musket butts were common weapons.

Worse yet, the day of fighting that had begun at dawn seemed
unending. Men watched the sun behind Groveton with pleas in their
eyes. Young Douglas on Jackson's staff, doing many officers' work
that day, for the staff was scattered, thought that "no one knows . . .
what is meant by 'leaden wings' unless he has been under the fire
of a desperate battle, holding on, as it were by his teeth, hour after
hour, minute after minute, waiting for a turning or praying that
the great red sun, blazing and motionless, would go down." [79]

So the men who could hardly stand after fighting off half a dozen
attacks braced themselves for the last. Hill sent a message to Gregg:
Could he hold? "Tell General Hill that my ammunition is exhausted,
but that I will hold my position with the bayonet," the word came
back. To Jackson, Hill sent word that he could hardly stand another
attack. Jackson would have none of that: "Tell him that if they attack again he must beat them!" [80]

Then Jackson went to the left to see for himself. He had peered
at the enemy earlier from an exposed position, to the concern of
men who thought he had no business there. Now he talked to Hill
again—a Hill who knew how close a thing each recent attack had
been, and knew the weariness of his men and the meagerness of
their ammunition.

"General, your men have done nobly," Jackson told him. "If you
are attacked again, you will beat the enemy back." Hill listened,
heard firing on his front, and rode to it with Jackson's words ringing
in his ears: "I'll expect you to beat them!" [81]

Now about 3 P.M. Pope determined on a twin blow, right and
left. He had three comparatively fresh brigades of Kearny's and
two of Reno's at hand for his right blow. For the left he looked to
McDowell, who had been bringing King's and Ricketts' divisions
back from Manassas, and to Porter's 10,000 men, who had not yet
come under fire. Pope still believed he could crush Jackson's left
flank, and he remained unaware, difficult though it is to believe it,

that Longstreet had reached the battlefield. Porter, he thought, could roll up Jackson's right flank.

The inability of Porter to do so, and the resulting confusions and misunderstandings, led to Pope's charges against Porter, the court-martial and conviction of Porter, and in the postwar years his vindication. But the blow that Pope delivered against Hill's front was the heaviest and most threatening of this long day.

Gregg's brigade had just come out of an ordeal. In the interval between its right and Thomas' left the railroad cut was deep. The enemy got into the cut at a point farther to the right, crawled to the deep section, concentrated a formidable force there, and broke out with a rush toward the gap in the lines. The South Carolina regiments on guard for Gregg were caught by surprise. The attack reached into the interval, carried deep to the rear, and isolated the whole of Gregg's command. But the Fourteenth South Carolina in reserve and the Forty-ninth Georgia of Thomas stormed into the assailants, and gradually the men who had been pushed back re-asserted themselves. The fighting raged up to the cut, with firing at ten paces' distance, and heavy losses. Then it was over, the enemy was thrust out, and the line restored. "But none doubted," Lieut. Col. Edward McCrady, Jr., of the First South Carolina, recorded, "that the great struggle was still to come." [82]

It came with a furious rush in the faces of defenders now count-ing every shot and resorting frequently to stones for the bullets they did not possess.

Thus McCrady remembered the desperate hours:

Our men fell fast around us. . . . They pressed on, crossed the cut, and slowly compelled us, step by step, to yield the long-coveted position. Here again our men fought the enemy at a few yards. . . . This was a most critical moment. . . . The enemy had by this time driven us back some 300 yards from the railroad cut and were possessors of most of the long-contested field. . . . It was now about 5 o'clock in the afternoon. Our regiment had lost half of its officers carried into action and nearly half of the men, our ammunition, too, was exhausted, and with the rest of the brigade we were thoroughly worn out.[83]

This was the moment when Early, after shifting from the right flank, roared into the conflict with his brigade and the Eighth Louisiana of Lawton's division. They were fresh and spirited, and they came across an open field in the face of Kearny's breathless advance, and smashed it full in the front. They beat it back through woods to the railroad cut and forced it out into the open again. Then, on orders from Hill, they halted. "As soon as I could arrest the advance of my brigade," said Early, "I moved it back to the railroad." Behind him lay Gregg's completely worn South Carolinians, lying with their bayonets extended to be ready if once more they had to fight.

It was the end. The artillery kept up fire, but no more did the tides of infantry that had beat on the position all day flow back. Far off on the southern flank, where Hood's guns had helped Jackson, King's division came up late in the day from Manassas, but Hood was making a reconnaissance in force for Longstreet, and King's men walked straight into an advancing Hood. A sharp fight forced King back, and the day was over.

Not a man among all that were left of Jackson's wing failed to rejoice that it was. In holding off Sigel, Milroy, Reynolds, Hooker, Kearny, and Reno they had stood up against some 37,000 men, double their number.[84] They had done it because Pope never did bring his full strength to bear at once, because they had professional skill to utilize their own strength to the utmost, and because they were imbued with some of their commanding general's determination and benefited from his deft handling of all the resources he had. But it was a long and weary and bitter day of suffering and death.

Trimble was down with a wound. So were Forno and Field, brigadiers of Lawton's and Hill's divisions. The losses among younger officers were cruel, and Hill's division had suffered heavily. For Jackson there was a more intimate loss. William C. Preston, an eighteen-year-old son of his old Lexington friend, Col. J. T. L. Preston, had come recently from the Virginia Military Institute, and Jackson asked him—he had known Willie Preston from boyhood—to remain at headquarters for a few days before joining his company, the Liberty Hall Volunteers. The young man had an excellent background, pleasant manners and bearing, and the staff became unusually attached to him. The General intended in time to make him an aide. He joined his company just before the heavy fighting.

That night McGuire mentioned to Jackson many of the wounded and told something about their condition, "and presently, calling by name the lad we all loved, told him that he was mortally wounded."

The news hit hard. The General's cook, Jim, rolled on the ground in his grief. According to McGuire, "The General's face was a study. The muscles were twitching convulsively and his eyes were all aglow. He gripped me by the shoulder till it hurt me and in a savage, threatening manner asked why I had left the boy. In a few seconds he recovered himself and turned and walked off into the woods alone. He soon came back, however, and I continued my report of the wounded and the dead."

They were sitting by the fire drinking coffee out of their tin cups when McGuire said: "We have won this battle by the hardest kind of fighting."

Jackson answered him gently and softly: "No, no, we have won it by the blessing of Almighty God." [85]

But Pope, who had punished them severely (while taking much punishment himself), could not be convinced on the 30th of anything but a Confederate retreat. He had for justification the facts that Hood, after beating back King's division on the evening of the 29th, had himself retired to his original position, for prudence overnight and because it was a good position; and that Jackson on the other flank, after the final clearing of the railroad grade of all enemies, had pulled back a short distance into woods, for such reasons as Hood's and perhaps to deceive the enemy. When Pope's early morning skirmishers found the fighting ground at the two flanks bare of defenders, and few men or guns were to be seen anywhere (they were all concealed), he jumped to conclusions.

"The news just reaches me from the front that the enemy is retreating toward the mountains," he informed Halleck early on the 30th.[86] Then he drew up his orders: "The following forces will be immediately thrown forward and in pursuit of the enemy and press him vigorously during the whole day. Major General McDowell is assigned to the command of the pursuit. . . ."

The last thing Lee was thinking of was retreat. He had surrendered unhappily to Longstreet's views against attacking on the afternoon of the 29th. Hood and Wilcox brought him further reports of unfavorable conditions for attack. He reconciled himself to waiting till the morning of the 30th to see if Pope would renew his attacks, but he thought also, if Pope did not initiate action, of enveloping Pope's right flank on the 31st.[87] Each side feared on the 30th that the other might get away.

Pope had about 65,000 men on the field [88] and the prospect of re-enforcements of more than 40,000 from the corps of Sumner and Franklin and the divisions of Cox and Sturgis [89]—a probability that suggests he should have dug in defensively until he expanded his numbers, as he would have. Lee's approximate 52,000 (17,000 with Jackson, 32,000 with Longstreet, and the cavalry) would be re-enforced eventually by troops hurrying up from Richmond: the divisions of D. H. Hill, McLaws, and Walker, Hampton's cavalry, and Pendleton's reserve arti"ery—in sum about 20,500. But that was all. The future lay in Federal hands, if the Federal command had the wit to exploit it.

When Pope was slow in starting on the morning of the 30th, the Confederate leaders did much reconnoitering and conferring. Jackson and members of his staff rode to the right, and Jackson talked with Baylor, then in command of the Stonewall Brigade. They watched Federal troops shifting in the far distance. Occasional guns had been firing since 8 o'clock, but in no apparent pattern. Jackson told Baylor that it looked like no fight today, "but keep your men in line and ready for action." [90] The Stonewall was down to pitifully small strength. In its five regiments no regimental officer higher than a captain was left.[91]

Jackson went to see Lee and found Longstreet there. Presently Stuart arrived, and the four conferred. When they broke up, Jackson rode back to his wing and went down to the extreme front for a look there. The sun was steaming hot now, the grass all around was burned to a yellow crisp, and sometimes it would catch fire from bursting shells; and sometimes the grass fires would reach the dead, burn their clothes off [92] and scorch their flesh.

Federal movements were plain enough, though difficult to interpret. Once when a battery reached a threatening spot, Jackson ordered the Rockbridge Artillery to drive it away. Poague's men hurried into action and in a few minutes had four guns firing. In five or six rounds they drove the Federal guns off the ridge. Jackson, watching intently, rode up to the battery. "That was handsomely done, very handsomely done," he said.[93] But the day dragged past noon without any real action. Jackson rode to the rear, dismounted, and rested on a rail fence.

Then, like an explosion in the hot sky, the Federal guns began furious fire, and 12,000 Federal infantry [94] came surging across the

Manassas fields straight for Jackson's front. Pope had spent the morning organizing. Disregarding Longstreet's wing entirely (as he had done on the previous day), he directed Porter's hitherto-unused corps, stiffened by King's division now under Hatch, to drive at Jackson's center and right. The thirty-seven assaulting regiments had a front of about a mile and a quarter and were backed by nine batteries—in all, one of the most formidable assaulting forces of the entire war. Porter had Sykes' division on the left, Butterfield's in the center, and Hatch's on the right.

The formations within the assaulting divisions varied, but the effect was to provide much depth to the attack. Swarms of skirmishers flitted ahead.[95]

By hitting at the center and right of Jackson's force, Porter gained better advantage from the stretches of woods that grew almost to the railroad grade. The storming forces reached the open, in many places so close to their goal that—with their depth—they had great penetrating power.

Desperate fighting followed all along the front. The Federal guns behind the assault, and the Confederate batteries behind the railroad grade, fired at top speed. The start of the assault brought Jackson's brigades pouring out of the woods of their concealment to their old defenses along the cuts and fills—to The Deep Cut and The Dump of bloody memory. This was no army in retreat! But the staggering blasts of the first volleys from the old defenses only halted the huge Federal phalanx. It strode relentlessly forward, full of fight under the afternoon sun. It swelled up to the railroad grade, lapped over it at point after point, and threatened to move endlessly onward.

"As one line was repulsed another took its place and pressed forward . . . by force of numbers and fury of assault," Jackson recalled this attack.[96]

"I saw a Federal flag hold its position for half an hour within ten yards of a flag of one of the regiments in the cut and go down six or eight times, and after the fight 100 dead were lying 20 yards from the cut, some of them within two feet of it. Lieut. Lewis Randolph, of the battalion, killed one with a stone, and I saw him after the fight with his skull fractured"—so Bradley Johnson of Jackson's old Second Brigade remembered the scene.[97]

"It was one continuous roar from right to left" to Private Casler.

"The enemy would form in the woods and come up the slope as regular as if on drill, and we would pour volley after volley into them as they came; but they would still advance until within a few yards of us, when they would break and fall back to the woods, where they would rally and come again." [98]

The assault spread eventually to Jackson's left flank. Heintzelman's corps was assigned to this flank, with Kearny's division on the extreme right next to Bull Run and two brigades of Ricketts' division to his left, tying up with Hatch. Kearny's men went forward in good spirit against a supposedly bare flank and ran into trouble. "We were sent forward to pursue the enemy, who was said to be retreating. We found the enemy, but did not see them retreat," reported one of Kearny's regimental commanders.[99] Gregg's, Thomas', and J. J. Archer's brigades held them off for a time, but Kearny's men ripped their way through the front line. Then out of his reserve Hill sent Pender and Field's brigade (now under Col. J. M. Brockenbrough) to throw them back, and the division counterattacked.

Jackson had no illusions about his right and center. He must have help. He sent word to Lee, to Longstreet too, asking for re-enforcements immediately. Lee directed Longstreet to send a division. But Longstreet, whose whole wing had been watching the massive attacks on Jackson, had a quicker remedy. At the lock where the two wings joined in their jaws-agape relationship, a ridge presented an ideal spot for artillery to sweep enfilading fire along Jackson's front. The ridge was a quarter-mile long, and it commanded a field of fire of 2,000 yards. There Col. Stephen D. Lee, commanding Lee's light artillery battalion, after consulting Hood, had placed his 18 guns early on the 30th. Now Longstreet, near this spot, weighing the best way to relieve Jackson and knowing that a division of infantry would require an hour and a half to reach him,[100] concentrated additionally on artillery. He ordered up three batteries attached to his divisions, 12 guns in all.

Thus, 30 pieces began enfilading Pope's assault lines in addition to the head-on fire of Jackson's guns on the ridge behind his infantry. The gunners could not touch the forward waves that were already in contact with the defense and in some instances had broken through. They concentrated on the later waves. The effect was immense.

In ten minutes the guns had thrown into confusion the middle and rear of the assault. In thirty minutes it was broken up. By this time Jackson brought his own reserves into action to take care of the early arrivals. Stripped of re-enforcements and left high and dry, the assault brigades fell back from their own successes, recrossed the cuts and fills, came into the open ground again, and retreated to the woods. The guns had scored one of the most brilliant artillery feats of the war.

They had done more. What Jackson thought at this moment of delivery is not a matter of formal record. His divisions had endured much. But Lee and Longstreet simultaneously and separately leaped to the offensive. Lee hurried an order to Longstreet. Now is the moment! Sweep forward with everything! It reached Longstreet just after he had given this precise order, on his own, and had set it in motion.[101]

Now along the long line of the army's right wing the bugles ran out, the flags lifted in the afternoon light, and the brigades stormed out of their lines. Wilcox's men on the left next to Jackson's right, Hood's Texas regiments nearer the center with Evans' regiments right behind them, James L. Kemper's entire division to their right, and David R. Jones' on the extreme right, with Anderson in reserve until later when he formed the right flank of the attack—all came out simultaneously with a high yell and a long, twisting, surging line of attack that looked in the distance toward that exact Henry Hill where Jackson had stood a year before.

The left wing of Jackson was slower to jump to the attack. It had been pounded for two days, most of it for three days, and was worn and thinned. It had fought almost to exhaustion this day, and only now had escaped an attack that might have devoured it. Longstreet complained that by delaying its advance it caused some Federal guns to catch his own troops in the flank. But in time Hill and Lawton and Starke moved down from the railroad grade until the great counterassault ran in a semicircle more than four miles long from the Bull Run at Sudley Springs across the Warrenton turnpike and south of the Henry Hill almost to New Market. Lee was attacking with a large part of his 50,000 available men. He was attacking mainly on his right, where Longstreet was now pressing forward, against a flank from which Pope had drawn much strength to concentrate on his own attack against Jackson.

Longstreet's wing, with Hood's Texans leaping forward, ate up the distance across the uneven fields. Then they ran into hard knots of defense. Units became separated. Two brigades wandered over to Jackson's area and stayed with him. The speed and ardor of the assault wore down the men making it. But with increasing halts and jerks the line overran Warren's brigade on its hill near the Dogan house, swept along the Chinn house area and Bald Hill, and fought forward to the approach of Henry Hill. Half a dozen Federal units had established a Gibraltar on top, and the fighting there and on the slopes toward the Stone Bridge was severe.

Farther north the Porter remnants formed pockets of resistance between Groveton and Sudley, and fighting ran along the Warrenton turnpike as the darkness began to fall. Hill's pursuit of Kearny carried faster than Jackson's other divisions, with Branch, Thomas, Archer, and Pender pushing on through varying resistance to Bull Run. Federal stragglers clogged the route where the Sudley–Manassas road crossed the turnpike and suggested a demoralization that did not extend through most units. But the rain falling in the growing darkness concealed a Federal army that, with only temporary islands of defense, was headed toward the old Centreville lines and would keep on moving with increasing demoralization. By nighttime it had retreated a mile and a half everywhere, and it continued to fall back. By midnight McDowell and Porter marched off the Henry Hill, crossed the Stone Bridge, and headed north.

Jackson came back at last and almost stumbled over a soldier trying to climb up the railroad grade where lately the furies had raged. He asked the man if he was wounded.

"Yes, General, but have we whipped them?"

With that the General got off his horse and asked which regiment he belonged to.

"The Fourth Virginia, your old brigade, General," the soldier replied. "I have been wounded four times, but never before as bad as this," he added, and then: "I hope I will soon be able to follow you again."

The wound in the thigh was deep and ugly. Jackson asked some of his staff to carry the soldier to a more comfortable spot, sent out a search for Dr. McGuire, and called up an ambulance to take the wounded man to a hospital. Sobs shook the soldier now, and he could not speak. But Jackson, with a hand on his head, told him:

"You are worthy of the old brigade and I hope, with God's blessing, you will soon be well enough to return to it." [102]

The pursuit—as at First Manassas and at Malvern Hill—lacked genius. Darkness and rain were hard to overcome. Bull Run was swollen, and by the 31st the Stone Bridge had been destroyed. The universal weariness and the heavy casualties in Jackson's wing held back his units. Pope still had a larger number of men, and there was little of the panic of July a year ago. But his was an army in retreat which, if hit just right, might have broken badly.

Stuart sent men out early on the 31st toward Centreville but had trouble locating the enemy. Lee and Jackson reconnoitered, and Lee determined to push Jackson to the left in the effort to turn Pope's right flank and force him out of the Centreville defenses. Longstreet remained on the battlefield, clearing up there, then followed. The route took Jackson by the Sudley Ford and on toward the Little Creek turnpike that came in from Winchester and Aldie and led to Fairfax Court House and on to Alexandria. He moved after a late start through rain along a muddy country road. The advance reached ten miles on this Sunday, and the General set up headquarters at a small house near Pleasant Valley.

The first day of September found him on the turnpike, with some of Stuart's cavalry in front. They reached forward to the Chantilly estate and to Ox Hill beyond. Hotchkiss, who had been drawing maps for Jackson in the rear regions, joined him during the morning, and the General demanded new and more maps from him. The soldiers were almost famished, the wagons not being able to keep up, and were suffering from thirst. Hotchkiss thought them "very bad, stealing everything stealable they could lay their hands on, after trying to buy it." He had a hard time keeping them out of the house where he was drawing more maps for his insatiable General. [103]

By noon the Federals had discovered them, and Pope sent Reno's corps, led by Brig. Gen. I. I. Stevens' division, to block the way. Jackson threw Hill out to the right, Lawton in the center, and Starke on the left, all on the right of the turnpike. His artillery was on the left. Late in the afternoon the two forces clashed in a torrent of rain. They fought backward and forward with accompanying lightning and thunder without major tactical result, and broke off in the drenched darkness where they first hit each other.

At one depressing moment in the deluge a brigadier in Jackson's command, never really identified in the memory of the repeaters of the day's best story, sent word to the General that the rain had soaked his ammunition and he would have to withdraw. "Hold your ground," the General sent word back. "The enemy's ammunition is just as wet as yours." [104]

The Federal interception stopped Jackson's advance, although at the cost of Generals Kearny and Stevens, much-admired officers who might have gone higher. When Jackson heard of Kearny's death in front of the Confederate line into which he had blundered in the rainy darkness, he directed that the body be brought with all the General's belongings to his headquarters.[105] The next morning Lee sent the body to Pope in an ambulance under a flag of truce.

Both sides lost heavily. Longstreet reached the field when the fighting died away and thought, and in his blunt way said to Jackson, that his men seemed to be pretty well dispersed. "Yes, but I hope it will prove a victory," Jackson replied. Tactically it was a standoff. Strategically it had a demoralizing effect on Pope. The next day, September 2, he pulled back to the fortifications of Washington.

The campaign was over. "Well, John, we are whipped again, I am afraid," Lincoln had said to young John Hay, his secretary, on the last night of Second Manassas, and a little later he told General Meigs, in a moment of depression: "Chase says we can't raise any more money; Pope is licked and McClellan has the diarrhoea. What shall I do? The bottom is out of the tub, the bottom is out of the tub!" [106]

For Lee it was a brilliant achievement. When added to the operations below Richmond, to which it was integrally related, the campaign was a classical demonstration of utilizing forces on interior lines against two major armies, each of which was larger than his own. He had thrown McClellan back from an advance that carried the Federals within sight of the spires of Richmond. He had turned upon the advancing Pope and thrown him back to the forts along the Potomac. He had learned so much from the mistakes of the Seven Days that his handling of the army against Pope was in comparison a model of control. It was marked by the extraordinary gamble of dividing his force while in contact with the enemy, but the plan had worked successfully. Hardly one of the mistakes on the

Chickahominy, of which there were many, was duplicated on the Rapidan, the Rappahannock, and Bull Run. Lee was blessed by Pope's confusion once Jackson's startling movement threw him into a series of mistaken assumptions, and was greatly aided by the eyes and ears of the cavalry of Stuart, but he had established in six weeks a command capacity that won universal respect.

These things were done at a cost conspicuously lower than Pope had paid. From Rapidan to the forts of Washington the Army of Northern Virginia had lost 1,468 men killed, 7,563 wounded, and 81 missing—the latter a significantly low figure that tells much about which army was dominating the scene. The total is 9,112 against Pope's over-all casualties of 14,462. Though Pope's 1,747 deaths and 8,452 wounded numbered more than Lee's, the greatest difference was in the missing. There Pope's figure was 4,263 against Lee's 81. Lee gained 30 pieces of artillery, more than 20,000 small arms, and collected or destroyed a vast amount of supplies.[107]

For Jackson the six weeks of late July and August were a record of such effectiveness in all major respects, such a return to the sparkling performances of the Valley campaign, that he rose high above the unhappy memories of the Peninsula. The Cedar Run operation had been spotty in the slow march out of Orange toward Culpeper and in the collapse of his left wing. But in other respects he had shown intelligence, energy, rallying power, and increasing control of new units. In design Cedar Run was a shrewd stroke. In execution Jackson overcame a bad half-hour, made his other estimates correctly, and was thinking far ahead, and imaginatively, at every stage.

The failure to catch Pope in the V between the Rapidan and the Rappahannock was not his fault and might have been avoided if his advice for fast action could have been followed. He moved up the Rapidan at a good pace, feeling swiftly for weakness and seeking to exploit every opportunity. When the big moment came, to which he may well have contributed significantly in planning as well as execution, he seized it swiftly and exploited it to the limit. The 54-mile march of August 25 and 26 in the great semicircle that deposited 20,000 infantry directly in Pope's rear was as successful in performance as it was bold in design.

From that moment, when every decision was his own and each one presented numerous alternatives that might have led to disaster,

Jackson was so conspicuously right in all major moves that an occasional tangle and a possible questionable act or so served chiefly to suggest that the commanding general and the army were human beings.

This was the old Jackson touch. Beside the grim ruggedness of the battles of August 28, 29, 30, and September 1, where men endured to the death in the Stonewall spirit, must be set the genius of movements made repeatedly just beyond the reach of superior forces with such precision in timing and sureness in direction as to deceive and confuse his encircling enemies. Pope had unusual energy and some unusually competent corps and division commanders. He had shown field talent early in the campaign. But Pope was dazzled and made to look awkward and foolish by a foe who was always within reach and yet never was really touched until he himself determined, lest his larger enemies get away, to jolt them into understanding where he was. It was an exhibition of military genius.

It was also a notable exhibition of military co-operation. The relations between Lee and Jackson in the Seven Days had been marred by lack of communications between the army commander and the corps commander and the absence of understanding to compensate. Jackson began the new campaign as part of the army. He was a commander on his own from July 16 to August 15, from the time he arrived at Gordonsville until after he fought at Cedar Run. He was again a part of the army from August 15 to August 25, when he set out on the great march. He was on his own from August 25 to August 29, when Lee came up to him with Longstreet's wing. Thereafter he was a part of the army until well into the Maryland campaign.

This was a swiftly alternating series of relationships. But Jackson was now much more at home in the army, and Lee worked with him more smoothly. Away from the army Jackson was still the lieutenant who, while carrying on his own activities (in this campaign with extraordinary skill), yet held to the strategy and purposes of the army at every moment and made his movements serve the larger design. The relationship was rare. It was also secure. From now on there would never be any lack of understanding or of easy, friendly adaptation to changing events, no presumption by Jackson but no lack of respect by either man. The Lee-Jackson concept—an intimately co-operative partnership of two remarkably different men—was now free to rise to assured and continued development, conspicuously in the Maryland campaign that lay ahead.

On the night of the fight at Chantilly, Jackson wrote to Anna in the mood of a man who had been through great danger and was grateful.

We were engaged with the enemy at and near Manassas Junction Tuesday and Wednesday [August 26 and 27], and again near the battlefield of Manassas on Thursday, Friday, and Saturday; in all of which God gave us the victory. May He ever be with us, and we ever be His devoted people, is my earnest prayer. It greatly encourages me to feel that so many of God's people are praying for that part of our force under my command. The Lord has answered their prayers; He has again placed us across Bull Run; and I pray that He will make our arms entirely successful, and that all the glory will be given to His holy name, and none of it to man. God has blessed and preserved me through his great mercy. . . .[108]

It was nearly eight months before he completed his formal report on this campaign, but the mood was the same:

For these great and signal victories our sincere and humble thanks are due unto Almighty God. We should in all things acknowledge the hand of Him who reigns in heaven and rules among the armies of men. In view of the arduous labor and great privations the troops were called to endure and the isolated and perilous position the command occupied while engaged with greatly superior numbers of the enemy we can but express the grateful conviction of our mind that God was with us and gave to us the victory, and unto His holy name be the praise.[109]

# 28 || MARYLAND

*"History records few examples
of greater fortitude and endurance. . . ."*

Lee made up his mind quickly. He could not attack
120,000 men or more (when all of McClellan's army united with
Pope's) in fixed defenses. Nor could he wait complacently on their
front until they reorganized to envelop him. The region was stripped
of food and forage, and his lines of communication with Richmond
had lengthened. He considered turning east, south, west, but he saw
objections to all these. North lay Maryland. There he could obtain
supplies from rich and productive districts untouched as yet by
war. There the Federal forces would have to follow him, relieving
Virginia of their presence; and a moving enemy was always potentially one who might be caught in an awkward movement and
smashed. Lee might thus break up any plan of further Federal offenses before winter halted the fighting. He and Davis in Richmond
hoped that military success in Maryland would stimulate recruiting
and encourage Marylanders to show in larger and more formal ways
the sympathy for the Confederacy which many individual Marylanders and some groups had shown.

Lee looked farther north. After seizing Harper's Ferry and moving the army to Hagerstown, he could effectually destroy the Baltimore and Ohio's east-west connection. If he could march then to
Harrisburg, Pennsylvania, destroy the long bridge of the Pennsylvania Railroad over the Susquehanna nearby, there would remain
only one east-west connection by the Great Lakes, and "after that

I can turn my attention to Philadelphia, Baltimore, or Washington, as may seem best for our interests." [1]

Disadvantages and dangers were inherent in such operations. Lee counted heavily on McClellan's slowness in the field, but the condition of his own army worried him. It had never recovered from the Seven Days, in physical condition or in clothing and equipment, before he threw it into the Manassas campaign. Jackson's wing in particular had undergone a second "seven days" (August 26–September 1). Many units had no cooked rations from August 25 until September 4.[2] The marches had been fast and long, the fighting had been severe, the losses heavy. Clothing had worn out until whole brigades looked like scarecrows. Shoes were a worse deficiency. The number of barefoot men mounted into the thousands. Straggling, because of all these factors, had reached fantastic proportions. Twenty thousand re-enforcements had come in with D. H. Hill, McLaws, Walker, Hampton, and Pendleton, but Lee estimated 8,000 to 10,000 stragglers were strung out from Bull Run to Rapidan Station, and other counts ran higher. He had few more than 50,000 men at hand now—perhaps 53,000 to 55,000. The *élan* of the survivors was superb, but materially they needed everything.

Maryland would be amazed at the ragged appearance of these soldiers, but so was Virginia. When the Fifty-fifth Virginia passed through Leesburg a woman watching from her home stared at these men and then instinctively threw up her hands and, with tears in her eyes, exclaimed: "The Lord bless your dirty, ragged souls!" [3]

The line of communication would be a problem. Lee could count (he calculated) on local supplies to a large extent, but not entirely. His ammunition and much else would have to come from Richmond. If the line of supply ran east of the Blue Ridge it would be subject to Federal cavalry raids. The Valley was the safer route, but the longer one. The wagon train was depleted and much of it in bad shape; and it would be subjected now to a greater strain than it had ever known. Until Harper's Ferry with 9,000 troops and Martinsburg with 2,000, and other areas at the foot of the Valley, were captured and cleared, the wagon train could not even start moving along the Valley route. The firm and quickly determined decision was, nevertheless, forward.

The decision met Jackson's complete approval. He had shown many times his advocacy of aggressive action into enemy territory.

"I am cordially with you," he wrote to a friend, "in favor of carrying the war north of the Potomac." [4] In consultation with Lee he advised a route into Maryland that would run into the Valley, pass through or near Winchester, where Federal forces would have to be cleaned out, and across the Potomac at or near Harper's Ferry. But Lee thought this line would take him too far from McClellan and might not induce McClellan to go into Maryland too—a major reason for Lee's going there. [5] He decided to cross the Potomac lower down.

On September 3 Jackson's wing, with D. H. Hill's division in the lead, and only the cavalry ahead, marched north and west in fine weather toward Dranesville—by the Ox Road, the Lawyers Road, and Thornton Station, a concealed route. The advance passed across the Dranesville battleground and the men bivouacked a mile beyond. Stuart went on to Vienna. [6] Cavalry crossed into the Valley and occupied Winchester.

The next day, September 4, after an early start, Jackson pushed on to Leesburg and beyond it, at the Big Spring, for the night. The route ran past the Ball's Bluff battlefield. The men sensed that the goal was Maryland and were excited. The weather was excellent: cool at night, warm in the day. But an old problem broke out in a new form this day, and it had long and serious repercussions.

Jackson's orders on the night of the 3rd specified the starting hour for the march of the 4th. When he rode up and down the line early on the 4th, A. P. Hill's division had not started at the designated time. Jackson asked one of Hill's brigade commanders, Gregg, why his brigade was not on the move. He received what he thought was an unsatisfactory reply, namely, that the men were filling their canteens, and eventually, when the canteens were full, Jackson ordered the brigade into movement. Memories of old troubles with A. P. Hill's division came back. Jackson kept his eye on it. There was too much straggling, he thought. At the end of the hour, when orders called for a halt, the division continued its march. In person Jackson ordered the leading brigade, Thomas', to halt. Hill came back, furious, and demanded of Thomas by whose order he had halted.

"I halted because General Jackson ordered me to do so," Thomas told him.

With that Hill turned to Jackson, drew his sword, and presented its hilt to the General. "If you take command of my troops in my presence, take my sword also," he said.

"Put up your sword and consider yourself in arrest," Jackson replied to him.[7]

Four days later, on September 7, Hill having formally requested of Jackson a copy of the charges against him, Jackson's acting-Assistant Adjutant General, Maj. E. F. Paxton (a Lexington friend who became a voluntary aide on July 25 and A.A.A.G. on August 8), replied for Jackson that "should the interests of the service require your case to be brought before a court martial a copy of the charges and specifications will be furnished in accordance with army regulation. In the meantime you will remain with your division." [8] That held the issues in abeyance for the time being, but the bitterness was serious. Hill was not ready to let the matter drop.

Jackson, looking ahead, had called in on the 4th Bradley Johnson, a Marylander, well acquainted with the country across the Potomac, and asked many questions about the topography, resources, and political conditions in Maryland. Johnson warned the General that a large part of the people were ardent Unionists, whereas Confederate sympathizers, although numerous in nearby Maryland, had been under military influence and could not be expected to provide material aid unless they had the assurance of a continuing occupation. The General was impressed by Johnson's information and took him that night to see Lee, who was making his headquarters in Leesburg.

Lee put Johnson through a rigorous examination, especially about the banks of the Potomac between Loudoun County in Virginia and Frederick County in Maryland, and about the Harper's Ferry and Williamsport area. The talk lasted several hours. Jackson, said Johnson, "sat bolt upright asleep." [9]

He was awake enough the next morning, September 5, when he led the army to White's Ford, near Edwards' Ferry, just below Ball's Bluff, about 11 miles south of Frederick. Here the river spreads out to half a mile in width with a pebbly bottom and a depth (then) of two or three feet.[10] Oaks hung over the water with thick vines tumbling down from them, wild flowers lined the banks, a graceful green island lay to the south, and the scene was pleasant. Beyond lay Maryland.

The soldiers were in great good humor. The weather had turned mild under the September sun, and a historic moment was at hand. Jackson, on a cream-colored horse (Sorrel was temporarily missing), rode to the left of the advance. The Tenth Virginia Regiment, of the Third Brigade in Jackson's old division, was in the lead, marching in a column of fours, preceded by a band and with a Virginia flag raised high.[11] At the water military formality gave way to human arrangements. The men stripped off their trousers or rolled them high, and, with shoes hanging from their shoulders and with muskets and powder held aloft, waded in. Jokes were running along the loose column, and laughter, and some attempts at singing.

When the band reached the Maryland shore, it went to work in earnest on "Maryland, My Maryland!" and now the singing swelled into a fine roar, and the high scream of the rebel yells sounded across the water. Jackson splashed into the water, pulled off his hat, and sat his horse [12] as the whole column took up the song and pressed forward toward the high banks on the far side. Marylanders among the men led in an enthusiasm that now stirred the whole scene. This was new. This was adventurous. This was full of possibilities. "Maryland, My Maryland!"

The head of the column spread out quickly on the exciting soil. Contingents marched off to the canal that paralleled the river. Federal pickets could be seen on distant hilltops, but there was no firing. More important at the moment was a boat loaded with melons bound for the Washington market, found in a lock in the canal— "which our men bought," wrote Hotchkiss in his diary. Behind them the long, long line of soldiers kept on wading into the river, kept on crossing it, kept on scrambling up the banks with high yells and jerky singing. Thus for two days as the invasion of the North—if Maryland turned out to be part of the North—began.

There was another hero of the crossing, and he did not remain unheard. At some stage the ford was completely blocked by a confused mass of wagons whose drivers could not control their mules and were winding themselves into a thicker and tighter mass seemingly beyond all unraveling. When Jackson saw the situation, he turned to his quartermaster, the former stagecoach manager, John A. Harman, big of frame, big of voice, and in the judgment of the army a superb man at swearing, particularly at mules. This was a crisis. Imboden recorded the scene:

Harman dashed in among the wagoners, kicking mules, and apparently inextricable mass of wagons, and, in the voice of a stentor, poured out a volume of oaths that would have excited the admiration of the most scientific mule-driver. The effect was electrical. The drivers were frightened and swore as best they could, but far below the Major's standard. The mules caught the inspiration from a chorus of familiar words, and all at once made a break for the Maryland shore, and in five minutes the ford was cleared.

Jackson witnessed and heard it all. Harman rode back to join him, expecting a lecture, and, touching his hat, said:

"The ford is clear, General! There's only one language that will make mules understand on a hot day that they must get out of the water."

The General smiled and said: "Thank you, Major." . . .[13]

Some Marylanders appeared, surprised but friendly, and invitations began to reach the staff. Jackson was more interested at the moment in a field of corn he saw ahead. He ordered its purchase, and had the corn distributed to the men and the stalks to the horses. He bought fence rails and ordered a day's rations cooked—the ubiquitous green corn—and kept ready for dawn on the 6th.[14] They camped near Three Springs south of Frederick, with the General sleeping in the open.

A gift of the day was a big gray mare for the General, more suitable for artillery than for the saddle, some of his staff thought, but welcome while Sorrel was still missing. Next morning the General tried his new mount, but she balked. When he put a spur to her she reared up, fell backward to the ground, and carried the General with her. He was stunned and bruised by the hard fall, and he lay for half an hour before moving. He was not able to continue in command and placed D. H. Hill in charge while he resorted to an ambulance.

Lee was in trouble too. On August 31, while he was standing by his mount Traveler, shouts about Federal cavalry reported nearby caused the horse to start. Lee reached for the bridle, tripped over the long rubber overalls he was wearing in the rain, and pitched forward. He put out both hands to break the fall, and his weight fell on them. A small bone was broken in one hand, and the other hand was sprained; and since he could not hold his reins, he had to ride in an ambulance.

By September 6 Jackson had his wing in the region of Frederick. Starke's division (the old Jackson command) marched through the town, not accompanied by the injured Jackson, and the old Jones brigade under Bradley Johnson was posted in the town as a provost guard. Lawton and A. P. Hill were in position near the railroad bridge over the Monocacy River, in the direction of Washington. Lee, Jackson, and Longstreet pitched their tents close together in Best's Grove. The army paused, looked at Maryland, and in turn was stared at by cautious Marylanders who could hardly believe their eyes as they looked at these strange men. A private in Kemper's division remembered the occasion as follows:

For six days not a morsel of bread or meat had gone into our stomachs. Our menu [had] consisted of apples and corn. We toasted, we burned, we stewed, we boiled, we roasted these two together, and singly, until there was not a man whose form had not caved in, and who had not a bad attack of diarrhoea. Our underclothes were foul and hanging in strips, our socks were worn out, half the men were barefoot, and many were lame and were sent to the rear; others, of sterner stuff, hobbled along and managed to keep up while gangs from every company went off into the surrounding country looking for food, and did not rejoin their commands until weeks after. Many became ill from exposure and starvation, and were left on the road. The ambulances were full, and the whole route was marked with a sick, lame, limping lot, that straggled to farmhouses that lined the way and who, in all cases, succored and cared for them. But we fared better in the rich fields of Maryland.[15]

There the reception was, in the main, quiet and reserved. Country people lined the roads, following every step of these ragged rebels, the first they had seen, giving liberally of food for the first to arrive, but reserving judgment in other respects. They were amazed by the army they saw. In the words of a woman of Frederick:

I wish, my dear Minnie you could have witnessed the transit of the Rebel army through our streets. . . . I could scarcely believe my eyes; was this body of men moving so smoothly along, with no order, their guns carried in every fashion, no two dressed alike, their officers hardly distinguishable from the privates—were these, I asked in amazement, were these dirty, lank, ugly specimens of humanity, with shocks of hair sticking through holes in their hats, and dust thick on their dirty faces, the men that had coped and encountered successfully, and driven back again and again our splendid legions with their fine discipline, their martial show and colour, their solid battalions keeping such perfect time to the inspiring bands of music?

And then, too, I wish you could see how they behaved—a crowd of boys on a holiday don't seem happier. They are on the broad grin all the time. Oh! They are so dirty! I don't think the Potomac River could wash them clean; and ragged—there is not a scarecrow in our corn-fields that would not scorn to exchange clothes with them; and so tattered!— there isn't a decently dressed soldier in their whole army. I saw some strikingly handsome faces though; or, rather they would have been so if they could have had a good scrubbing.

They were very polite, I must confess, and always asked for a drink of water or anything else, and never think of coming inside of a door without an invitation. Many of them were bare-footed. Indeed I felt sorry for the poor, misguided wretches, for some were limping along so painfully, trying to keep up with their comrades. . . .[16]

It was the era of the graybacks—the army lice—and

every evening in Maryland . . . hundreds [of soldiers] could be seen, sitting on the roads or fields, half denuded with clothes in laps busily cracking, between two thumb-nails, these creeping nuisances . . . the men would boil their clothes for hours—next day these confounded things would be at work as lively as ever . . . many used to place their under-raiment, during the night, in the bottom of some stream and put a large stone to keep them down; in the morning they would hastily dry them and get a temporary relief. . . .[17]

Inside Frederick, as the soldiers began to sift in, despite orders, the buying began in a rush. Some stores would not sell; many did.[18] Quartermasters managed to buy 1,000 pairs of shoes (and 250 pairs later in Williamsport and 400 pairs in Hagerstown), only a small fraction of the number needed. Jackson's policing of the town was strict. When word came that some soldiers, identified only as for-eign-looking, had been discourteous in a store, the General ordered a Louisiana brigade, to which he thought the offenders might be-long, to march through the streets so that they might be identified. Starke protested the order and directed the brigade not to march, and was placed under arrest,[19] but the dispute was healed.

The general officers attracted intense interest, and many Mary-landers visited the tents in Best's Grove for a sight of them, espe-cially Lee and Jackson. These two, with their injuries and much work to do, kept to their tents for the most part, although when Douglas' mother and a group of friends came, both Lee and Jack-son greeted them. Jackson said little, "but that little was of his kind," Douglas thought. He urged Mrs. Douglas to spend the day with her son. Later, when Jackson was going to Lee's tent, two Baltimore girls jumped out of a carriage, "rushed up to him, one took his hand, the other threw her arms around him, and talked with the wildest enthusiasm, both at the same time, until he seemed miserable." When they drove away "happy and delighted," Jackson "stood for a moment cap in hand, bowing, speechless, paralyzed, and . . . he did not venture out again until late in the evening." [20]

Nor did the General go to church in the morning of the next day, Sunday, September 7, but that night he asked Douglas and Anna's brother, Lieut. Joseph G. Morrison, who had joined the staff as an aide before Cedar Run, to go with him to church in Frederick. Before they set out, the General still in an ambulance, the young officers on horses, he asked Douglas if he had obtained a pass. Douglas suggested there was no need. But the General insisted, referring him to one of Lee's orders, and presently Douglas came back with this:

> Hd. Qrs. Valley District
> Sept. 7. 1862
>
> Guards and Pickets
>   Pass Maj. Genl. T. J. Jackson and two staff officers and attendants to Frederick to church, to return tonight.
>                                 By Command of
>                                 Major Genl. Jackson
>                                 E. F. Paxton
>                                 A. A. Genl.[21]

There was no service that night in the Presbyterian Church, and Douglas led the party to the German Reformed Church, where Dr. Daniel Zacharias was the minister. This was Jackson's first sight of Frederick, and he liked it immediately. When he wrote to Anna the next day, he told her:

> The town appears to be a charming place, neat and beautiful. The ladies and gentlemen were sitting in front of the doors, and all looked so comfortable, and I may say elegant, according to my ideas, and their enjoyment looked so genuine, that my heart was in sympathy with the surroundings. If such scenes could only surround me in Lexington, how my heart would, under a smiling Providence, rejoice! [22]

In the church General Jackson and the two officers sat in a rear pew. Jackson described "the building [as] beautiful. The pews are arranged in a circular form, so that every person faces the pulpit."

He thought the minister "a gifted one," but "I was not quite near enough to hear all the sermon, and I regret to say fell asleep; but had I been near enough to hear would probably not have been so unfortunate." [23] As it was, he didn't hear Dr. Zacharias pray for the President of the United States, "but if he had," Douglas recorded, "I've no doubt he would have joined in it heartily." In Douglas' recollection, "his head sunk upon his breast, his cap dropped from his hands to the floor, the prayers of the congregation did not disturb him and only the choir and the deep-toned organ awakened him." [24]

Maryland, as a whole, was cautious and watchful. When the army marched through Frederick, "the streets were generally well filled with citizens, and the balconies and porches too, but there was positively no enthusiasm, no cheers, no waving handkerchiefs and flags—instead, a death-like silence—some houses were closed tight, as if public calamity had taken place; there were many friendly people in windows and doors, but they seemed afraid to make any manifestation of their feelings—only smiling covertly." [25] Recruits were few, signs of formal action were lacking, and even the supply of food, which by the look of the countryside should have been plentiful, was difficult to maintain.

Lee's proclamation on the 8th recited the hardships under which he thought the people of Maryland were living and announced that the army "is prepared to assist you with the power of its arms in regaining the rights of which you have been despoiled." It asserted that "we know no enemies among you, and will protect all, of every opinion. It is for you to decide your destiny freely . . . this army will respect your choice, whatever it may be. . . ." But this temperate and dignified utterance had no visible effect. There was no revolution or promise of one. Lee looked to further military movements, as he had planned from the first.

He was under no pressure from the Federal army. In travail of spirit Lincoln had decided on September 2 that Pope would have to go and that McClellan would command the two united armies, and on the 5th the decision became effective, despite much opposition in the Cabinet and the country. Lincoln himself thought McClellan had acted badly in not strengthening Pope more effectively. ("He wanted him to fail.") But he thought "we must use what tools we have. There is no man in the Army who can man these fortifications [of Washington] and lick these troops into shape as well as he." [26] So McClellan it was again, and Lee knew that he and his army would not have to hurry.

But the supply line from Richmond to the Valley, and from the Valley into Maryland, was a necessity. That meant capturing Harper's Ferry, from which Lee had estimated the Federal command would withdraw by this time. McClellan favored withdrawal, but Halleck overruled him. Lee had discussed the problem with Longstreet, and, according to the latter, had "proposed" that Longstreet should surround the garrison and capture it. [27] But Longstreet thought then that the men needed rest, and he opposed dividing the army in enemy territory.

On the 9th Lee called Jackson to his tent and discussed the problem with him. With his knowledge of the Valley and his experience in Harper's Ferry, Jackson was obviously the officer for the operation, and he looked forward to it eagerly. He spoke to Lee about his long neglect of friends there. Lee picked up the jocular remark and carried it further. Jackson had "some friends" in the Valley who, he feared, would not be glad to see him. [28]

While they were talking Longstreet came to Lee's tent, inquired for Lee, and was invited inside. The subject was reviewed, but Longstreet did not press his opposition further beyond suggesting that if a move was made against Harper's Ferry, the whole army should make it. [29] But that view did not prevail. The decision was to move, and to move immediately.

Since Lee wished to penetrate deeper into western Maryland, where his line of communication would be more direct, where supplies (he hoped) would be more bountiful, and McClellan would be drawn farther from his base, the orders would cover the whole army. The operation against Harper's Ferry would have to be three-pronged, in order to surround that punch bowl in the hills, and the army would be divided into at least four—and, as events turned out, five—parts. This extraordinary boldness rested squarely on the assumption that McClellan would be McClellan.

Special Orders, No. 191, was therefore an involved document. To capture Harper's Ferry and its garrison too the logical plan was to occupy with artillery the two major eminences confronting it, Loudoun Heights across the Shenandoah and Maryland Heights across the Potomac from Harper's Ferry, and to occupy simultaneously Bolivar Heights in the rear (west). The well-justified hope was that artillery on Loudoun and Maryland Heights, as well as in the rear, would render Harper's Ferry untenable and that retreat routes would be blocked. Lee's orders, made after consulting Jackson, called for:

1. John G. Walker's division of Longstreet's wing to cross the Potomac at Cheek's Ford, below Harper's Ferry, ascend the right bank to Lovettsville, take possession of Loudoun Heights, if practicable, by the morning of Friday, September 12; and, as far as practicable, to co-operate with Jackson and McLaws, "and intercept retreat of the enemy."

2. Lafayette McLaws, with his own division and that of R. H. Anderson, both of Longstreet's wing, to advance on the Hagerstown road as far as Middletown, then take the route toward Harper's Ferry, "and by Friday morning [the 12th] possess himself of the Maryland Heights and endeavor to capture the enemy at Harper's Ferry and vicinity."

3. Jackson's wing, minus D. H. Hill's division, to move beyond Middletown, "with such portion as he may select, take the route toward Sharpsburg, cross the Potomac at the most convenient point, and by Friday morning [the 12th] take possession of the Baltimore and Ohio Railroad, capture such of them as may be at Martinsburg, and intercept such as may attempt to escape from Harper's Ferry."

This was much the longest march of the three. When Jackson lengthened it by making a wider sweep to Williamsport, the distance grew to 62 miles. He required, with interruptions, three and a half days, averaging just under 18 miles a day. McLaws (who commanded Anderson) was designated to "endeavor to capture the enemy." Both he and Walker would come under Jackson's command at Harper's Ferry, but not before.

For the remainder of the army, Lee's plans in Order No. 191 were for Longstreet to move with his other two divisions (Jones' and Evans') to Boonsboro, and for D. H. Hill to form the rear guard. The trains and the reserve artillery were divided between them. Stuart was to send squadrons of cavalry for Jackson, McLaws, and Longstreet. His greatest responsibility was to keep McClellan's moves under strict observance. Once Harper's Ferry was captured, Jackson, McLaws, Anderson, and Walker would return to the Boonsboro or Hagerstown area and unite with Longstreet and Hill.[30]

Actually, when Lee heard that a force was gathering in Pennsylvania to the north, he sent Longstreet on to Hagerstown, 13 miles to

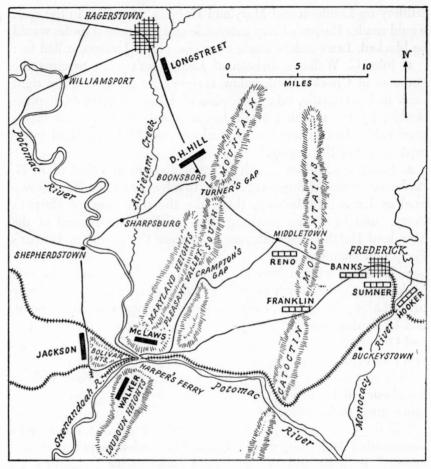

THE DIVISION OF LEE'S ARMY FOR THE CAPTURE OF
HARPER'S FERRY.

the northwest of Boonsboro. The threat did not amount to anything,
but the 13 miles did.

A document such as Special Orders, No. 191, outlining this division of Lee's army, was designed to present to the Confederate
commanders a clear picture of the purposes and itinerary of all major
elements of the army for the next several days, or until the capture
of Harper's Ferry and the uniting of the army. If it fell into anyone
else's hand, it would be invaluable. It was not only a schedule of
movements but of movements that dismantled the army as a single
unit and set up four scattered contingents.

The importance of Special Orders, No. 191, was so apparent to Jackson, that when he received it on September 9, and thought it his duty to send a copy to D. H. Hill, who was attached to his command but would not be with him, he did not entrust the copying to anyone else. He himself wrote out Hill's copy with his own pen, and sent it to Hill, who received and preserved it.[31] Longstreet had the same feeling. He memorized his copy of the order and "chewed it up."

Jackson, able to ride once more, was up at 3 A.M. on September 10. Accompanied by a few members of his staff, Douglas among them, and a light cavalry escort from the Black Horse Troop, which he had attached to his headquarters as guides and couriers (this proud troop from the Loudoun and lower Valley area had been Joseph E. Johnston's bodyguard on the Peninsula prior to his wounding at Seven Pines), he rode into Frederick from his camp in Best's Grove. He was not with the infantry, which followed a different route along the streets of the town, because he wished to see the Presbyterian minister, Dr. John B. Ross.

Jackson had known Dr. Ross in Lexington, but had missed him on the only other occasion he had entered Frederick: Sunday night when he rode in an ambulance to the German Reformed Church. In the early dawn there was no sign of activity at the manse adjacent to the Presbyterian Church, and Jackson did not attempt to wake Dr. Ross. Instead, he left a note for him. Then, with the accompanying horsemen, but no other troops, he rode by Mill Street—"The Mill Alley," it was generally called—out of town and eventually to the head of the infantry column.

Early as it was, many inhabitants of Frederick were up. By asking conspicuously for maps of Pennsylvania, Jackson had caused a report to start that he was moving in that direction. The town understood that some movement was being made, and it was buzzing with the departure of the troops. A girl of about eleven or twelve years stood in a doorway, a flag of the United States in her hand and a younger girl by her side. She was waving the flag and saying: "Hurrah for the Stars and Stripes! Down with the Stars and Bars!" The marching soldiers were amused and joked about the girls. A one-legged man who had followed the army on horseback—General Early thought he had been drinking—said something of an uncomplimentary nature about the girls, and Early shooed him away. Nothing happened.

In the western part of town, as troops were marching by an alley, a woman, whom Early described as "coarse and dirty," appeared suddenly at the mouth of the alley with a United States flag (much soiled, said Early) in her hand. Hays' Louisiana brigade was passing and an Irish soldier cracked out something about a "dom'd old dirty rag," and the woman fled.[32] There may well have been other incidents during the occupation and the day of departure.

On another street from that used by the marching troops, about three hundred yards from the route taken by their General and the men on horseback with him, stood the house—in Patrick Street near the Town Creek Bridge—in which Barbara Frietchie lived. She was then beyond her ninetieth year. She was in feeble health, and by some persons who knew her she was thought to be incapable of waving a flag at a window. Jackson did not pass her house, although it is possible some troops did.[33] She did not see him. There was no incident involving Jackson like that which the poet John Greenleaf Whittier described in the stirring lines that swept the Northern States as few other American war poems have ever done and became a permanent part of American literature:

> Up rose old Barbara Frietchie then,
> Bowed with her fourscore years and ten;
> Bravest of all in Frederick town,
> She took up the flag the men hauled down:
> In her attic window the staff she set,
> To show one heart was loyal yet.
> Up the street came the rebel tread,
> Stonewall Jackson riding ahead.
> Under his slouched hat, left and right
> He glanced: the old flag met his sight.
> "Halt!"—the dust-brown ranks stood fast.
> "Fire!"—out blazed the rifle blast;
> It shivered the window, pane and sash;
> It rent the banner with seam and gash.
> Quick, as it fell from the broken staff,
> Dame Barbara snatched the silken scarf:
> She leaned far out on the window-sill,
> And shook it forth with a royal will.
> "Shoot, if you must, this old gray head,
> But spare your country's flag," she said.
> A shade of sadness, a blush of shame,

Over the face of the leader came;
The nobler nature within him stirred
To life at that woman's deed and word:
"Who touches a hair of yon gray head
Dies like a dog! March on!" he said.

As wartime balladry this is superb. Whittier believed the story when he heard it from a Washington novelist. He said it had been published in the press. Twenty years after the war he was "still constrained [in his own words] to believe that it had foundation in fact." Earlier he said: "If there was no such occurrence, so much the worse for Frederick City." His words, like those of the poem, are proof of the emotions that grip men in war.

Men who knew the circumstances in Frederick and who knew Jackson were vigorous in their denials from the publication of the poem in the *Atlantic Monthly* in October, 1863, but the slow influence of time was necessary to establish broadly—as it was established long ago—that no such incident occurred.

"Imaginative art is seldom anchored in precise fact," one of Whittier's biographers wrote correctly; and "a popular ballad cannot be delicate in its shading," wrote another. But it is at least ironical that the actions ascribed to Jackson on that day are actions which no other general officer in the Confederate armies would be more incapable of taking.*

* Valerius Ebert, nephew of Mrs. Frietchie and administrator of her estate after she died on December 18, 1862, and Mrs. Handschue, niece and adopted daughter of Mrs. Frietchie, and "other relatives," denied that Mrs. Frietchie saw Jackson or waved a flag at Confederate troops or was present at any shooting episode. See George O. Seilheimer in the Philadelphia *Times*, July 21, 1886, reprinted in *B. & L.* II, 618.

Mrs. Handschue's daughter, Mrs. Abbott, is quoted by Seilheimer as saying that Mrs. Frietchie stood on her porch, leaning on her cane, when Federal troops marched by her house two days later on September 12; that Mrs. Frietchie waved her hand at them, and they cheered her; that her cousin, Harriet Yoner, said, "Auntie ought to have a flag to wave" and that the family flag was obtained from the family Bible, and Mrs. Frietchie waved it at the Federal troops.

Douglas (Douglas, 151–152) said that he was with Jackson every minute in Frederick; that Mrs. Frietchie did not see Jackson and that Jackson did not see her, and "nothing like the patriotic incident so graphically described by Mr. Whittier in his poem ever occurred." Douglas suggested that "the real sentiments of the old lady had a flavor of disloyalty," the only one to make that suggestion.

The Ebert denial appeared in a letter to the Baltimore *Sun*, written August 27, 1874. It is reprinted in *S.H.S.P.*, XXVII, 287, in a letter by W. Gordon McCabe, dated January 27, 1900, to the *Sun* protesting against some other statements about Barbara Frietchie. He included the Ebert statement to support his case.

Gen. Bradley T. Johnson, in an address on October 23, 1884, reprinted in *S.H.S.P.*,

On this September day, hot and dusty in the country around Frederick, the Army of Northern Virginia, divided now into four parts—shortly to be five and, if Stuart's cavalry to the east of Frederick is counted, six—set out on the complex series of movements outlined in Special Orders, No. 191.

McClellan, who had been moving up from the Washington forts at the rate of six miles a day, was still 12 miles or more east of Frederick. He was overestimating in the old Peninsula style the forces confronting him. On September 9 he reported to Halleck that Jackson and Longstreet had 110,000 men near Frederick.[34] On the 10th he noted reports of enemy strength varying from 80,000 to 150,000.[35] On the 11th he made the figure "120,000 men or more." [36] But his slow advance constituted a major element in the diverse picture that was now developing to the southwest of Frederick, where the Potomac flowed, and to the west. There the low ridge of the Catoctin Mountains, the higher ridge of the South Mountain, a creek called Antietam, and the Potomac itself, in changed direction, all ran north and south. Men were moving day by day, unit by unit, in all directions, but in designed patterns and toward climaxes seen and unseen.

On Wednesday, September 10, Jackson, with three divisions

XII, 503, includes an outline of streets in Frederick to show that Jackson's movements with his staff, including the visit to the Presbyterian parsonage, did not take him past the Frietchie house and that Mrs. Frietchie did not see him. General Johnson was born in Frederick and lived there until May, 1861, when he joined the Confederate forces. "I had known Barbara Frietchie all my life," he said. "I knew where she lived as well as I knew the town clock."

The two Whittier biographers quoted are John A. Pollard (*John Greenleaf Whittier, Friend of Man;* Houghton Mifflin Company, Boston, 1949) and George Rice Carpenter (*John Greenleaf Whittier* in the "American Men of Letters" series, Houghton Mifflin Company, Boston, 1903). Neither of these biographers attempted to establish any historical basis for the poem, and both thought that the question was not important. Pollard said: "All the controversy over the question [of "the literal accuracy of all the facts of the story"] simply slid off the obvious truth that imaginative art is seldom anchored in precise fact." Carpenter said: "The alleged facts on which 'Barbara Frietchie' was founded have been somewhat hotly discussed; but it is clear that Whittier was guiltless of distorting in any way the incident as it was reported to him, and that, furthermore, whether the supposed incident actually occurred or not is of no importance." It is not necessary to dispute this point of view of the poet in order to note that it would be important to students of Jackson if Jackson had behaved as the ballad portrays him as behaving.

Pollard, Seilheimer, and others report that Whittier first heard the story which he set forth in his poem from Emma D. E. N. Southworth, of Washington. The quoted Whittier comment is from Pollard. *B. & L.,* II, 619, contains Whittier's defense in his letter of June 10, 1886, to the *Century Magazine.*

totaling about 11,500 men (Ewell's under Lawton; his own under the returned John R. Jones; and A. P. Hill's under Branch while Hill was in arrest), led the advance westward on the National Road through the Catoctins and on to Middletown. The General and his staff and escort rode half a mile in front. Lieut. George G. Junkin, Jr., the aide who was captured at Kernstown, reported during the day after escaping from a Federal prison. Two pretty girls, with red-white-and-blue ribbons in their hair and small United States flags, came to the curb in Middletown and waved at the General. He bowed, lifted his dusty cap to the girls, and, turning to the staff, remarked: "We evidently have no friends in this town." [37]

The column climbed Turner's Gap in the South Mountain and dropped down its slopes to Boonsboro, 14 miles this day, longer for units camped east of Frederick. The General stopped at the home of John Murdock,[38] a mile from the village. Headquarters tents were set up across the road. The soldiers camped in the fields. Douglas and Col. S. Bassett French, of Governor Letcher's staff, now acting as a volunteer aide to the General, rode into Boonsboro, and French went to a hotel.

Out of nowhere a Federal cavalry contingent appeared. Douglas reached his horse in a rush. He fled in desperate galloping, escaped by a narrow margin, and lost his hat with a bullet hole through it. When he topped a hill on his flight, he saw the General walking alone beside the road, leading his horse and swinging his cap.

The General knew trouble when he saw it. He mounted fast, wheeled to the rear, and raced away, for all the world like a cavalry lieutenant in an affair of outposts.

A few headquarters cavalrymen came up, including Lieut. A. D. Payne of the Black Horse Troop. With Douglas reversing his course, they drove the Federals away. In the windup Douglas recovered his hat and in mock heroics presented the General with the gloves Jackson had dropped as he scurried out of danger; and Colonel French came back from the hotel cellar into which he had dived.[39] It was Jackson's narrowest escape since Port Republic.

Walker with his division of some 3,400 men was at the mouth of the Monocacy on the 9th trying to destroy the aqueduct of the Chesapeake and Ohio Canal. The masonry defied his inadequate tools. When Special Orders, No. 191, reached him, he turned to Cheek's Ford, as directed. It was within range of Federal guns, and he crossed the Potomac at Point of Rocks on the night of the 10th.

McLaws, with four brigades in his own division and six in Anderson's, or about 8,000 men all told,[40] set out on the march of 20 miles between the camps near Frederick and the foot of Maryland Heights. The column reached a point east of Brownsville Gap in the South Mountain Ridge, about a mile and a quarter south of Crampton's Gap, and bivouacked there.

Longstreet, following earlier movements of the day along the National Road, climbed through Turner's Gap and camped beyond it. When word reached Lee of a military threat from Pennsylvania, he directed Longstreet with his two remaining divisions (D. R. Jones' and Evans') to march next day northwestward to Hagerstown to be in better position in the event the threat developed.

D. H. Hill, forming the army's rear guard and protecting much of the baggage train, followed Longstreet toward Turner's Gap and Boonsboro.

Jackson decided during the night of Thursday, September 11, not to turn southwestward toward Sharpsburg and thence in a direct line to Martinsburg, but to continue in a westerly direction toward Williamsport before advancing from the north on Martinsburg. This was a more sweeping and longer movement. Special Orders, No. 191, did not specifically provide for it. But it is probable that Lee, who had discussed the operation with Jackson, gave him verbal discretion.*

Jackson moved fast toward Williamsport. He captured a Federal picket there, crossed the Potomac at Light's Ford with a band playing and the men singing "Carry Me Back to Ol' Virginny," and marched past the battlefield of Falling Waters and camped in the rain at Hammond's Mill, a mile and a half north of Mountain Depot on the Baltimore and Ohio. There they heard the evening gun at Martinsburg, seven miles away.[41] It was the last such gun they could have heard for some time, for Brig. Gen. Julius White, in command of the Federal garrison in Martinsburg, having learned of the ap-

* William Allan's report of Lee's views on the Maryland campaign, as set forth in a conversation on February 15, 1868 (see Freeman–LL, II, 721), contains the following with reference to the Harper's Ferry operation: "The orders [Special Orders, No. 191] named the points to be reached by the divisions concentrating at Harper's Ferry, and indicated the purpose, but this had all been fully *explained* to Jackson verbally, and no one could imagine that the order did not contemplate just what Jackson did."

proach of Jackson, marched out that night and headed for Harper's
Ferry with 2,000 men—thereby jumping from the frying pan into
the fire. The effectiveness of Jackson's sweeping movement was now
becoming apparent. The column marched 20 miles this day.

A. P. Hill, restless under arrest at the prospect of action at Harper's
Ferry, asked Douglas to approach Jackson on his behalf. He would
like to command his division in battle, and thereafter would revert
to his present condition. Jackson, who had no doubt about Hill's
command capacity in battle, agreed, and an order on the 11th restored him to the command Branch was holding.

Walker remained in the camp on the Virginia side of the Potomac
below Harper's Ferry all of the 11th. He reported his men exhausted
after two nights' and days' marching.

McLaws crossed Brownsville Gap, entered the Pleasant Valley
beyond it, and reached Elk Ridge, the southern part of which is
Maryland Heights.

Longstreet moved to Hagerstown, and Lee rode with him. They
found no development of the Pennsylvania threat. They did find a
warmer reception than in Frederick. The residents "threw wide
their hospitable doors and filled their houses with soldiers, feeding
the hungry and clothing the naked. . . . I saw a citizen," Alexander
Hunter continued, "take the shoes off his feet and give them to a
limping, barefoot soldier." [42] But a woman sang "The Star-Spangled
Banner" to Lee as he was riding by. He lifted his hat to her, and
then gave orders that no one should disturb her. [43]

D. H. Hill remained at Boonsboro.

Friday, September 12, was the day when Lee hoped all elements
of the Harper's Ferry operation would be in place for the kill. None
was. Jackson moved southward on Martinsburg, with Hill's division
taking the main Williamsport–Martinsburg road and Jones and
Lawton swinging farther west so as to approach the goal from two
directions. Jackson sent cavalry still farther south. They all marched
into an ecstatic Martinsburg, and the General was back in his
beloved Valley again.

He went to the Everett House to work, [44] locked himself in a parlor,
and wrote steadily despite the crowd that gathered in the hotel and
outside it. Men and women called him at the windows and through
the doors. Children rattled the closed shutters. Boys broke the
shutters at one window, and faces pressed against the pane to peer

at the famous man. He gave up. When a courier took his dispatch, he directed him: "Now admit the ladies."

They almost overwhelmed him. "Blushing, bowing, almost speechless, he stood in the midst of this remarkable scene, saying, 'Thank you, thank you, you're very kind.' " [45] Children were all around him. A little girl, attracted by his brass buttons, asked him for one. He cut it off and gave it to her. Then everyone wanted buttons, and before he could escape his coat tails were almost bare. An older girl asked for his autograph in her album, and he wrote his name there. Everyone wanted autographs, and he took sheets of foolscap and wrote "T. J. Jackson," and distributed the signatures.

A woman asked for a lock of hair—but there he set up his own stone wall.

"Really, ladies, this is the first time I was ever surrounded by the enemy," he told them. Outside, some people began to pluck hairs from the mane and tail of his horse (Sorrel was still missing) until a staff officer put an end to that. The hero of the Valley was at home again, and he and the Valley were delighted.

Hill pushed his division six miles beyond Martinsburg toward Harper's Ferry, and the army bivouacked on that side of Martinsburg, most of it on the Opequon. Quartermaster, commissary, and ordnance stores fell into their hands. Hotchkiss bought a hat in Martinsburg for the General, and another for himself.[46] The rain on the previous night had settled the dust, and the day was pleasant. The over-all advance was 16 miles.

Walker, coming out of the camp far to the south where he had spent the 11th, moved up the right bank of the Potomac and camped at Hillsborough.

McLaws, appraising the problem of driving Federal defenders off precipitous Maryland Heights, sent Kershaw's brigade, supported by Barksdale's, up the ridge at Solomon's Gap, four miles north of Maryland Heights, with orders to advance along the top of the heavily wooded ridge. This was rough work that took time. McLaws, with the remainder of his two divisions, moved southward in the Pleasant Valley toward the Potomac and reached the river by nightfall.

Longstreet remained at Hagerstown. There Lee learned from Stuart that McClellan's army (about 87,000 men) was advancing on Frederick. Stuart had succeeded in picketing roads so successfully that McClellan's cavalry could not penetrate them for information, but Stuart could not hold off McClellan's massive force. Hampton's brigade, fencing with the Federal advance guards, pulled out of Frederick just ahead of the arrival about noon of the Twelfth Army Corps. Before the day was out Lee knew about it. He was concerned at not hearing more about the Harper's Ferry operation. McClellan in Frederick was beginning to be a threat to McLaws on Maryland Heights.

On Saturday, September 13, the pieces began to fall into place around Harper's Ferry. Jackson, seemingly not worried about being a day behind schedule (he had marched well, and co-ordination rather than speed was the need in the contemplated operation), moved southeastward until he reached the Charlestown–Halltown road. By 11 A.M. his advance guard saw enemy forces drawn up in defenses on Bolivar Heights. Familiar scenes these! Jackson stood where he had stood last May when he was demonstrating against Harper's Ferry's defenders. Now he sent Hotchkiss and two engineer officers, First Lieut. Thomas T. L. Snead and Second Lieut. W. G. Williamson, to Loudoun Heights. Hotchkiss was to establish a signaling system with flags, the other two to aid Walker in placing artillery.

Walker reached the foot of the Blue Ridge during the day and climbed to the top by night. No Federal troops had been placed there. Jackson's mission established contact with him. But Jackson could not establish contact with Maryland Heights.

McLaws' attacking forces, Kershaw and Barksdale, working southward on the spine of Elk Ridge on the 12th, had covered most of the distance toward Maryland Heights but not the last long mile of organized defense. On the 13th they stormed ahead through thick undergrowth and along steep slopes where the defenders had used boulders and felled trees for barriers and had artillery as well as 2,000 men. By 10:30 Kershaw and Barksdale had cleared the most formidable defenses. By 4:30 P.M. they had the whole of Maryland Heights.[47]

Walker and McLaws still faced the problem of hauling up artillery. McLaws heard this day heavy cannonading to the east and northeast, but could not determine its exact meaning or the meaning of reports from cavalry scouts of enemy troop movements to the north—to his rear.

Lee, still in Hagerstown, grew increasingly worried about dangers to McLaws' rear from McClellan's continued advance, and sent warnings twice, especially warning McLaws to watch the road from Frederick, which McClellan had reached the day before. At night Lee had more ominous news. Stuart reported that Federal troops had driven him back from the Catoctins, on the Frederick–Boonsboro road, and were continuing to advance toward Turner's Gap.

Lee immediately ordered D. H. Hill, then at Boonsboro three miles west of the Gap, to defend it. Lee turned then to Longstreet and ordered him to march next morning from Hagerstown to Turner's Gap to join Hill's defense. Longstreet demurred. He argued that to march 13 miles and then plunge into a defense that threatened to be desperate work would be asking too much of him. He proposed withdrawal to Sharpsburg.[48]

But Lee held to his plan. Greatly puzzled by the evidence of surprising action from McClellan, he saw the threat to McLaws if McClellan forced a way through the South Mountain ridge, and could catch McLaws between his own forces and the Potomac.

What was McClellan doing? Why had he abandoned his slow and almost aimless pace for this new driving spirit?

The answer lay in a big envelope containing three cigars, wrapped in a manuscript, lying in an open field outside Frederick where lately D. H. Hill's division had camped. Two men of the Twenty-seventh Indiana Infantry, which had marched from the east into Frederick on the morning of the 13th, found the envelope—Private Barton W. Mitchell and First Sgt. John McKnight Bloss. They were lolling in their new camp area, stretched out on the grass, waiting in the immemorial way of soldiers for the next order. Mitchell picked up the envelope, looked with delight at the cigars, and turned eventually to the paper around them. It was Special Orders, No. 191, from "Headquarters, Army of Northern Virginia," signed by "R. H. Chilton, Assist. Adj.-Gen." and addressed to "Maj. Gen. D. H. Hill, Commanding Division."[49]

What followed is wholly to the credit of McClellan's army. The two men carried the paper immediately to Captain Kopp of Company E. It went swiftly to Col. Silas Colgrove, and from him to the headquarters of Brig. Gen. A. S. Williams, division commander, where the Assistant Adjutant General was Col. S. E. Pittman. It went from him, at a gallop, to McClellan's headquarters. Pittman knew Chilton well and identified the handwriting. Within an hour—fast moving from private to army commander—Special Orders, No. 191, was in McClellan's hands.[*]

When McClellan looked at the document he saw a blueprint of Lee's whole campaign, and knew that Lee's army was scattered and wide open to destruction by an opponent who was as near as McClellan was, as powerful as McClellan's resources were, and as well armed with information as McClellan now was. The gods of war were smiling on him now.

[*] The history of the copy of Special Orders, No. 191, which the two Federal soldiers found in the open field outside Frederick, on paper wrapped around three cigars, remains a mystery to this day. Two official copies designed for D. H. Hill are known to have existed. One was sent to him from Lee's headquarters. The other was sent to him by Jackson, and this one Hill preserved. It is in existence today, in Jackson's handwriting, in the North Carolina Historical Commission's collection.

Of the copy sent by Lee's headquarters, these assertions are on record: Hill said that he never saw it and that it did not reach his headquarters. Hill's Assistant Adjutant General, Maj. J. W. Ratchford, made an affidavit after the war saying that he did not see it and that it did not reach Hill's divisional headquarters. (*B. & L.*, II, 570.)

Lee's Assistant Adjutant General, Col. R. H. Chilton, said that couriers carrying such orders were required to obtain receipts for them and that if a receipt for Special Orders, No. 191, had not been obtained at Hill's headquarters, a failure of that kind would have been noted in Lee's headquarters. (Freeman—*LL*, II, 722.)

The status of D. H. Hill's division led to the sending of two copies of the order. Hill had been placed under Jackson for the advance into Maryland, and no previous orders had detached him. The order for the Harper's Ferry operation did not list him with Jackson, and it has been suggested that Jackson's sending a copy of the order to Hill was his way of notifying Hill of his detachment from Jackson's wing. For instance, William Allan's memorandum of a conversation with Lee on February 15, 1868, as printed in Freeman—*LL*, II, 720 ff., contains this report of Lee's words: "He [Lee] had the orders sent from his own headquarters to Hill, as the latter was now under his immediate command, and it was perfectly proper for Gen. Jackson to do so too, to inform Hill that he was no longer under his [Jackson's] orders." Hill said, "I went into Maryland under Jackson's command. I was under his command when Lee's order was issued. It was proper that I should receive that order through Jackson and not through Lee. . . ." (*B. & L.*, II, 570.)

Hill argued in the postwar years that the lost order was actually helpful to Lee, principally because it indicated to McClellan that South Mountain was defended by Longstreet as well as Hill and therefore made McClellan cautious and slowed him there. Lee thought the information a great aid to McClellan and expressed the belief after the war that otherwise he would have met McClellan under more favorable circumstances and defeated him. (Freeman—*LL*, II, 717, 718.)

The full text of the order contains ten numbered paragraphs. The first forbade officers and men of Lee's army to visit "Fredericktown" except on business. The second related to the route for sick soldiers, and others unable to walk, to use when going back to Culpeper. It is only with the third paragraph that the vital parts of the order come to light: "The army will resume its march tomorrow . . ." and thereafter with the detailed movements.

Neither the copy that Jackson sent to Hill in his handwriting nor the copy that reached McClellan included the first two paragraphs.

McClellan bubbled with excitement. "Here is a paper with which, if I cannot whip Bobbie Lee, I will be willing to go home," McClellan told General Gibbon that afternoon. "Tomorrow we will pitch into his center, and if you people will only do two good, hard days' marching, I will put Lee in a position he will find it hard to get out of." [50]

*Tomorrow!* If the document was genuine, its possessor should have been on the move within the hour. McClellan had the game in his hand now, but he must play his cards fast and right. Already the news was going to Lee almost as quickly as it had gone to McClellan. A Marylander in Frederick learned on the 13th of McClellan's possession of Lee's order—in what should have been a piece of great good luck for the Confederates—and rode furiously that evening to Stuart's headquarters with the news. Stuart passed it on to Lee, who may have received it as early as 10 P.M. on the 13th. [51] He sent grave warning to McLaws about the danger at his rear at that hour.

But there was little more that Lee could do. He had already ordered D. H. Hill to defend the passage of South Mountain and Longstreet to rally to Hill's aid. All his other divisions were in the Harper's Ferry operation, which he hoped was nearing its climax. He could not break it off now. McClellan did not know these conditions. But he did know that three days had passed already since Lee had split his army into segments. If he was to take advantage of this unparalleled opportunity to thrust between the segments and bite them off as he chose, he must act swiftly—he must act immediately.

By Sunday, September 14, Jackson's primary concerns were to coordinate the artillery and his infantry advance. He had now taken complete charge of this three-part operation and was assuming that his infantry, not McLaws', would capture Harper's Ferry. As senior officer he would be in command. As a practical officer in the field he did not hesitate to shift plans to meet shifting conditions; and his doing so was understood and accepted by Lee and by the generals co-operating with him.

Jackson's signal officer, Capt. J. L. Bartlett, operating on the first hill south of Halltown, had not been able to reach McLaws. A message by courier from Jackson, dated 7:20 A.M. on the 14th, noted that Jackson had heard from McLaws the day before and informed him that Walker occupied Loudoun Heights. "I desire you to move forward until you get complete possession of the Maryland Heights," Jackson told him.

After details about battery emplacements and enemy positions, Jackson continued:

So soon as you get your batteries all planted, let me know, as I desire, after yourself, Walker, and myself have our batteries ready to open, to send a flag of truce, for the purpose of getting out the non-combatants, should the commanding officer refuse to surrender. Should we have to attack, let the work be done thoroughly; fire on the houses when necessary. The citizens can keep out of harm's way from your artillery. Demolish the place if it is occupied by the enemy, and does not surrender. . . . The position in front of me is a strong one, and I desire to remain quiet, and let you and Walker draw attention from Furnace Hill [west of Bolivar Heights], so that I may have an opportunity of getting possession of the hill without much loss.[52]

No evidence has come to light that Jackson did send in such a flag of truce, probably because of difficulties that developed during the day.[53] Walker began at daylight to drag guns to the top of Loudoun Heights. By 8:30 A.M. (he reported later) he had three Parrotts and two rifles there. At 10 A.M. Bartlett received by flag the message: "Walker has his six rifle pieces in position. Shall he wait for McLaws?" "Wait," Jackson replied.

McLaws had to cut a road to the top of Maryland Heights, and it was 2 P.M. before he could complete that difficult task. Jackson, meantime, sent a long message by flag signals to Walker and McLaws during this Sunday morning:

If you can, establish batteries to drive the enemy to the hill west of Bolivar and on which Barbour's house is, and any other position where he may be damaged by your artillery, and let me know when you are ready to open the batteries, and give me any suggestions by which you can operate against the enemy. Cut the telegraph line below the Potomac if it is not already done. Keep a good lookout against a Federal advance from below. Similar instructions will be sent to General Walker. I do not desire any of the batteries to open until all are ready on both sides of the river, except you should find it necessary, of which you must judge for yourself. I will let you know when to open all the batteries.[54]

Messages of such length, and one of greater length embodying the formal orders for the day, plus shorter messages back and forth,

placed a strain on a signaling system that lacked large experience.
Jackson's operational report notes that "before the necessary orders
were thus transmitted the day was far advanced." [55] But McLaws'
troubles in hauling his artillery up the heights and getting it in position were clearly an important factor during a day when Jackson
was restless under delays he could not control.

Actually, in the methodical design of taking Harper's Ferry by
positional, almost siegelike warfare which Lee and Jackson had
adopted, this Sunday was a distinctively successful day. Walker had
been chafing most of the morning, the more so because he heard
artillery fire from the South Mountain direction. He suspected a
serious enemy advance there, and so notified Jackson, who could
not imagine McClellan had turned aggressive. So great was Walker's
concern that, by his own testimony, he determined to force the issue.
He maneuvered two regiments on Loudoun so that they would be
seen from Harper's Ferry. They drew fire, and Walker immediately
replied. That was about 1 P.M.[56] Jackson's guns west of Bolivar
Heights began shortly afterward, and McLaws' quickly after they
were in position about 2 P.M.

Though the Loudoun and Maryland guns could not reach all the
way to the Federal troops on Bolivar Heights facing Jackson's forces,
they held the town of Harper's Ferry under heavy fire, knocked out
several artillery pieces, and shook the morale of the Federal forces.
Jackson, meantime, sent his ground troops forward and by the end
of the day he had the main enemy defense line reeling.

He did so by ordering Hill on the afternoon of the 14th to move
along the left bank of the Shenandoah and turn the enemy's left.
Lawton moved in support of him, Jones demonstrated at the opposite end of the line, with Grigsby's brigade (the old Stonewall
Brigade) and a battery. Grigsby seized a well-placed hill and occupied it with Poague's and Carpenter's batteries. They used it to
great advantage.

Hill headed off to his right toward the Shenandoah. He sent
Pender, Archer, and Brockenbrough's brigades to a hill at that end
of the enemy line, advanced Branch and Gregg along the river, and
directed them, after night fell, to continue their advance across
ravines along the flank of Bolivar Heights. They crept forward until
they reached the rear of the enemy line.

Crutchfield, the artillery commander, crossed 10 guns over the

Shenandoah to its right bank and placed them, in a shrewd move, so that they would enfilade the enemy lines on the heights.[57]

By morning Jackson had the situation in his hand and needed only dawn to spring the trap that he had elaborately set. He was aware of no pressure of time and directed—unlike any other engagement—an almost cautious, stey-by-step series of moves based on complete appreciation of the terrain and a purpose to make it serve his ends.

At every other point where Lee's scattered segments were in action this September Sunday was a day of defeat and grave concern. McClellan was now moving with a new spirit. After pushing Stuart's cavalry back through the Catoctin pass, he kept on westward with 70,000 men toward the main pass through the South Mountain ridge—Turner's Gap. Hill had only two of his five brigades on the ridge when the advanced Federal division, Jacob Cox's, of Reno's corps, worked its way up the rough slopes and began battering the few Confederate defenders. Cox bent back Samuel Garland's brigade, killed Garland on the field, and then mysteriously halted.

No. 191 was, in this instance, a deceptive document. It led McClellan to believe that Longstreet as well as Hill had been left at Boonsboro and was now on the ridge in front—three divisions instead of one. McClellan, with his lavish estimates of enemy strength, would not go all-out for the pass until he had more of his own strength up. He had an impressive amount.

"The marching columns," Hill reported later, "extended back far as eye could see in the distance. . . . It was a grand and glorious spectacle, and it was impossible to look at it without admiration. I had never seen so tremendous an army before. . . ."

When Reno's Ninth Corps came into the hills, north as well as south of the gap, the fighting was heavy. Longstreet, footing it for 13 hot miles from Hagerstown, began to arrive about 3 P.M. and sent his men straight into action, brigade by brigade. But there could be only one result here. Hill and Longstreet still held at night to some of the high points, but they knew—and told Lee—that McClellan could pour through the gap in the morning. If McClellan had pushed hard, he would have forced the gap and, said D. H. Hill, could have "captured Lee's trains and artillery and interposed between Jackson and Longstreet before noon on that 14th of September." Lee ordered a night retreat to Sharpsburg.[58]

Farther south the story was the same. McLaws, already concerned with his objectives of bombarding Harper's Ferry, assaulting it with his forces (as Lee had directed), and preventing Federal escapes across the Potomac, had sent the brigades of Paul Semmes and William Mahone back to Brownsville Gap by which the McLaws command had crossed the South Mountain ridge. Semmes learned that Crampton's Gap, nearly two miles farther north, was a more serious danger point, and sent three regiments and a battery. Stuart, coming south from Turner's Gap, also saw the danger at Crampton's Gap, left the Laurel Brigade there, and, when he joined McLaws, warned him of the situation. McLaws sent more troops to the gaps behind him.

But McLaws had too many irons in the fire to guard against the 18,000 men that Franklin pushed toward Crampton's Gap. By late afternoon the Federal forces had stormed the hills and were in complete possession. McLaws hurried more troops back from Maryland Heights, five miles away, almost stripping his strength there. He drew up a defense line across the Pleasant Valley to try to prevent Franklin from rolling southward toward the Potomac and the relief of its defenders. But Franklin was bemused, like McClellan, by his estimates of the strength opposite him, and had not been instructed to plunge ahead. Once he had the pass, he waited.[59] It was fatal to his main opportunity.

The action at Turner's Gap had left no doubt in Lee's mind as to the necessary action. "The day has gone against us," he wrote to McLaws at 8 P.M., "and this army will go to Sharpsburg and cross the river"—the Potomac. "It is necessary for you to abandon your position tonight. Send your trains not required on the road to cross the river. . . ."[60] No other word from Lee during the campaign shows such depression.

Yet just as he was sending this gloomy communication to McLaws, with its plan for leaving Maryland entirely, Jackson was sending word to Lee that materially altered the commanding general's thinking. At 8:15 P.M. on this Sunday the 14th, from near Halltown, Jackson wrote to Lee that "through God's blessing the advance, which commenced this evening [afternoon] has been successful thus far, and I look to Him for complete success tomorrow. I am thankful that our loss has been small. Your dispatch respecting the movements of the enemy and the importance of concentration has been received. Can you not connect the headquarters of the army, by signal, with

General McLaws?" [61]—a strong implication, in the last sentence, that Lee had expressed to Jackson concern about McLaws.

The hour when Lee received this is not clear, nor is it known when Lee informed Jackson "respecting the movements of the enemy and the importance of concentration." Presumably Jackson received the dispatch from Lee shortly before 8:15 P.M., for normally he replied promptly. But Lee now had word, when the dispatch from Jackson reached him, of the impending completion of the Harper's Ferry operation and of the possibility of his being re-enforced by all the troops engaged in it. This put a different face on his own problems, and he reconsidered returning to Virginia.

Jackson, furthermore, now had formal notice from Lee of the heightened danger from more vigorous Federal movements, the Turner's Gap battle, the decision to retreat to Sharpsburg, and the necessity for his own return to Lee. For the first time since he left Frederick on the 10th, Jackson was under the compulsion of speed. Every move now was directed to that end.

Thus, on Monday, September 15, the stage was completely set, the actors had finished their preliminary exposition, and the climax was at hand. There was even a curtain that would rise; for mist hung over doomed Harper's Ferry this morning, and the gunners on Loudoun could not see their targets, although they had already pinpointed them and could fire through the mist. The great chorus began.

Jackson listed the guns as follows:

Lieutenant-Colonel [Lindsay] Walker opened a rapid enfilade fire from all his batteries at about 1,000 yards range. The batteries on School-House Hill attacked the enemy's lines in front. In a short time the guns of Captains Brown, Garber, Latimer, and Dement, under the direction of Colonel Crutchfield, opened from the rear. The batteries of Poague and Carpenter opened fire upon the enemy's right. The artillery upon the Loudoun Heights, of Brigadier General Walker's command, under Captain [Thomas B.] French, which had silenced the enemy's artillery near the superintendent's house on the preceding afternoon, again opened upon Harper's Ferry, and also some guns of Major General McLaws from the Maryland Heights.[62]

Crutchfield listed also the batteries of Captains Pegram, McIntosh, Davidson, and Braxton. General White, the highest-ranking

Federal officer, estimated the number of guns concentrating on Harper's Ferry this morning at 50.

"Those established at the southern extremity of Bolivar Heights completely enfiladed that part of our line extending from the Charlestown road northward to the Potomac," White reported from inside Harper's Ferry; "those placed on the southwestern slope of Loudoun Heights, and on the west side of Shenandoah nearby, delivered their fire at an acute angle to our line, being half enfilade; those at or near the crest of Loudoun Heights took us in reverse; and still others in the valley beyond Bolivar Heights fired directly at our front." [63]

"We are surrounded by enemy batteries," Lieut. Henry M. Binney, of the Tenth Maine, aide to the commanding officer, wrote in his journal. "They open from Loudoun Mountain and Loudoun Farm, Maryland Heights, Charlestown road, Shepherdstown road. Nothing could stand before such raking cannonade. . . ." [64]

"It was terrific," Col. William H. Trimble of the Sixtieth Ohio, added. "It commanded every foot of it [the ground] around the batteries on the left and along the lines . . . producing a terrible cross-fire . . . there was not a place where you could lay the palm of your hand and say it was safe. . . ." [65]

By 8 A.M. the enemy guns had been silenced, some knocked out, some stripped of ammunition. Hill gave the signal for the storming of the Federal works by stopping the fire of his own guns. Pender went forward on the right flank, near the Shenandoah. Enemy guns began to fire again. But Pegram and Crenshaw ran their batteries up to extremely close range and poured in rapid fire. [66]

Col. Dixon S. Miles, the commanding officer (General White had come in from Martinsburg ahead of Jackson two days before but asked Miles, who was more familiar with the ground, to retain the command), called a council of war. The decision to surrender was virtually unanimous, and a white strip was cut from a tent and hoisted. Awkward moments followed when some batteries were not sure of the white flag, hesitated, then resumed their fire. One of them mortally wounded Miles, and the command went to White. (It was conceivably a blessing of sorts; for a military commission found the dead Miles' defense of Harper's Ferry gravely wanting.) Hill finally sent in one of his officers, Lieut. John H. Chamberlayne, to find out if the Federal forces were surrendering. Jackson sent

Douglas forward for the same purpose. At "near 8 A.M." Jackson–losing no time–was able to write to Lee:

Through God's blessing, Harper's Ferry and its garrison are to be surrendered. As Hill's troops have borne the heaviest part in the engagement, he will be left in command until the prisoners and public property can be disposed of, unless you direct otherwise. The other forces can move off this evening, so soon as they get their rations. To what point shall they move? I write at this time in order that you may be apprised of the condition of things. You may expect to hear from me again today, after I get more information respecting the number of prisoners, etc.[67]

Jackson's awareness that Lee needed the most definite information at the earliest possible moment and his own purpose to join Lee at top speed shine through every word. But the formalities of surrender remained. Jackson had won a notable victory by admirably co-ordinated operations on three different fronts and by a model demonstration of the use of artillery. The terrain was made for such a utilization, it is true. (Had he not shown his understanding of this condition in the first month of the war when, as commanding officer at Harper's Ferry, he had occupied Maryland Heights to the alarm of Lee in Richmond?) Lee had drawn the plan for the three-pronged approach, but the execution was a classroom demonstration.

The number of captured or missing (including the actions on Maryland Heights) was put by Federal authority at 435 officers and 12,085 men–total, 12,520.[68] Jackson reported the number who surrendered on the 15th was "about 11,000." He reported the captured guns at 73. But Maj. H. B. McIlvaine, chief of artillery at Harper's Ferry, reported the number at 47 and said seven of these were spiked.[69] Miles was able to throw into line some 7,000 men along the Bolivar Heights defenses. Jackson had no more than 11,500 in the three divisions he prepared for the assault. Yet of the 1,263 Confederate casualties of the entire operation, 1,189 were incurred at Crampton's Gap and Maryland Heights. The entire force on Bolivar Heights suffered on September 14 and 15 only 74 casualties, and of those only three were killed. The artillery did the work.

The capture did not come as soon as Lee had hoped, but the fact that Walker and McLaws, who were not then under Jackson's control, were unable to arrive at their stations as early as Lee hoped–nor did Jackson–suggests that the difficulties of the operation were not understood in Lee's headquarters. The delay of the 14th has some unexplained aspects.[70] But Jackson was not under any known pressure for speed until the night of the 14th. Then he moved fast. Earlier he had moved with the careful, sure steps of a commander who was making the lay of the ground and the force of his guns do his work for him. In these respects the Harper's Ferry operation was a classic.

Yet there was one striking Federal exploit. Two cavalry officers with the same surname, Col. B. F. Davis of the Eighth New York, and Lieut. Col. Hasbrouck Davis of the Twelfth Illinois, told General White on the 13th that they wanted to run the gantlet of the encircling forces. They knew surrender was inevitable. White approved, and Miles, after hesitation and some sharp words, issued the order. Col. Arno Voss, of the Illinois regiment, was in command, the two Davises at the head, of a column of 1,300 cavalrymen, some from the First Maryland and the Seventh Rhode Island as well as the other two regiments.

On the night of the 14th they crossed the Potomac on a pontoon bridge (the crossing required nearly all night), moved along a road at the base of Maryland Heights, cut across country, and headed north. They made it all the way to Greencastle, Pennsylvania, 60 miles, and captured some 40 wagons of Longstreet's ammunition train en route—all in all a fine feat. Jackson had warned McLaws to watch out for escape attempts across the Potomac,[71] and Stuart had pointed to that particular route [72] (McLaws had all other routes covered), but McLaws was a busy officer during these days.

When Douglas went forward at Jackson's direction, he encountered General White and his staff. Hill joined them, and they all rode back to where Jackson was waiting on the Halltown road. There General White, on a handsome black horse, with bright saber, immaculate gloves, and shining boots, faced the officer whom Douglas called "the worst-dressed, worst mounted, most faded and dingy looking general he had ever seen anyone surrender to." [73]

Jackson told White the surrender must be unconditional, and turned him over to Hill, telling Hill merely that the terms should be liberal. Hill took him at his word. Officers and men were paroled. Officers retained side arms and private baggage. All prisoners kept their blankets and overcoats, took two days' rations (which stripped the post), and received on loan wagons for transport which, both

Jackson and Hill complained later, they were unreasonably slow in returning.[74]

At about 11 A.M. Jackson and some of his staff rode up Bolivar Heights and then down the hill into Harper's Ferry. Federal troops were everywhere, and their curiosity about Jackson was intense. They lined the streets to see him pass, many of them uncovering as he did so, and he returned their salute gravely.

"Boys," said one of them, "he's not much for looks, but if we'd had him we wouldn't have been caught in this trap." [75]

Sometime during the day Jackson found time to write a brief letter to Anna:

It is my grateful privilege to write that our God has given us a brilliant victory at Harper's Ferry today. Probably near eleven thousand prisoners, a great number of small arms, and over sixty pieces of artillery are, through God's blessing, in our possession. The action commenced yesterday, and ended this morning in the capitulation. Our Heavenly Father blesses us exceedingly. I am thankful to say our loss was small, and Joseph [Morrison, Anna's brother] and myself were mercifully protected from harm.[76]

By 3 P.M. Jackson had wrenched his divisions free from the town and the lure of its supplies and had them back in camp west of Bolivar Heights with orders to cook two days' rations. Walker came down from Loudoun and McLaws from Maryland Heights, and some effort was made to equip the ragged and shoeless men from captured stocks. Jackson was restlessly completing necessary duties as fast as possible so that he could unite with Lee. But the rations took time.

Probably it was during this delay that the General's aide, young Lieut. George Junkin, Jr., who was captured at Kernstown but had escaped, told the General that his father was here and wished to see the General. His father was the Rev. Dr. David X. Junkin, brother of Ellie's father and himself as strong a Unionist as the Rev. Dr. George Junkin.

Would the General see him? Certainly, Jackson said. He remembered long and pleasant talks with Mr. Junkin when the latter visited in Lexington. In a war which could be amazingly informal when it was not being amazingly ferocious, he would have no hesitation in talking with a friend from the enemy's country.

So they met under the steep, almost perpendicular cliff of Maryland Heights, the General, the onetime father-in-law's clerical brother, and the young lieutenant. There was no question about Mr. Junkin's purpose. He had come to convince the General of the error of his ways.

Did the General not realize that he was fighting in a rebellion that was without cause? Did he not know that Lincoln sincerely designed to administer the government in a constitutional way, and that "whilst he would discourage the extension of slavery into the Territories, he would not interfere with it, or with any other domestic institution of the South, in the States"? And on, and on, and on, for two solid hours (said Mr. Junkin later).

But if Mr. Junkin thought he could shake his young friend, he did not know his man. Finally, he admitted as much. He summarized the General's reply thus:

As a Christian man, my *first* allegiance is due to my State, the State of Virginia; and every other State has a primal claim to the fealty of her citizens, and may justly control their allegiance. If Virginia adheres to the United States, I must adhere; her determination must control mine.

So they parted. Mr. Junkin described it in these words:

He held his magnificent field-horse by the bridle-rein. His left hand was gauntlet-gloved. He grasped mine with his right. I said "Farewell, General; may we meet under happier circumstances; if not in this troubled world, may we meet in"—My voice failed me,—tears were now upon the cheeks of both,—he raised his gloved hand, pointed upward, and finished my sentence with the words—"in heaven!" [77]

If the General thought it unusual to be the recipient—a few hours after capturing 12,000 Federal troops—of these fervent pleas to desert his cause and his army, which was celebrating an easy victory just up the hill yonder, he did not say so. Mr. Junkin was a friend and almost a kinsman, and, despite the field horse and the gauntlets, the General treated him in the old Lexington spirit.

It was not until 1 A.M. that Jackson's divisions cleared the camps. They strode northward under the stars on an all-night march of 17 miles—"severe," Jackson called it in unusual language for him. It took them to the Potomac at Boteler's Ford, once more into the waters and out on Maryland soil again, and then straight toward Sharpsburg.

Walker overtook Jackson on the march, and the two rode side by side. Walker told the General how he had drawn fire on Loudoun Heights from Harper's Ferry. He was fearful of what the General would say. But after a few moments of silence, the General said: "It was just as well as it was, but I could not believe that the fire you reported [hearing in the east] indicated the advance of McClellan in force."

Then, after a few moments more of silence, the General said, almost as though speaking to himself: "I thought I knew McClellan, but this movement of his puzzles me." [78]

The two found Lee a little after noon at his headquarters in Sharpsburg. Walker thought Lee could not have seemed more composed and confident. Lee told them of his satisfaction with the Harper's Ferry operation. With such re-enforcements, he added, he was confident he could hold his ground until the arrival of the divisions of McLaws, Anderson, and A. P. Hill. The first two had climbed down from Maryland Heights, crossed the Potomac, entered Harper's Ferry, and passed on to the west to follow Jackson's tracks. But they lost time in Harper's Ferry, where narrow streets were jammed with soldiers from both armies, and did not arrive at Sharpsburg until the morning of the 17th. McLaws had some 25 miles to go by this route. Hill was still dealing with prisoners and captured supplies.

The two divisions with Jackson (Lawton's and Jones') marched through Sharpsburg and continued northward about a mile until they approached a white Dunkard church. They halted, stacked arms, fell out in the field, and rested several hours. Late in the afternoon they marched half a mile northward on the Hagerstown road. Federal artillery on the high ground beyond Antietam had been growling all day. Now the shells fell close. Jones' division formed for battle on the left (west) of the road, partly in woods, partly in an open field. Jones placed the Stonewall Brigade under Grigsby on the right, with its right resting on the road, and Bradley Johnson's Second Brigade to its left. Two or three hundred yards to the rear he stationed his second line, Taliaferro's old brigade, now under Col. E. T. H. Warren, and Starke's brigade. Two companies from the front brigades went forward as skirmishers. Poague's battery occupied a knoll near the road in front and opened fire quickly on an annoying battery up ahead and silenced it in twenty minutes.

Lawton's division followed Jones' but remained near the church. Early's brigade broke the pattern. Stuart's cavalry, well supported by artillery, was far out to the left, and Jackson appears to have thought it needed unusual infantry support. He himself directed Early to the left to protect Jones' flank and to stiffen the defenses where much artillery was concentrated. Hays' brigade, stumbling in the dark, ended up behind Early and remained there for the night. The two divisions were facing north, at right angles to Lee's main line.[79]

Grigsby's men, from their right-hand position in the front line, could reach across the Hagerstown road and touch Hood's two brigades. These Lee had shifted from Longstreet when he saw signs that McClellan was building up his right, seemingly with the design of attacking Jackson. Lee had released Hood from arrest, after a quarrel between Evans and Hood, and had restored him to the command of his Texans.

The men did not know it, but they were forming in a region destined to be one of historic trial and bloodshed in a struggle they could sense even now but the magnitude and horror of which no man could imagine. The wood on the east of the road was the East Wood. That in which Jones' division was placed was the West Wood. The cornfield between the two, where the corn was head-high and still green, was to become a slaughterhouse. Even now, on the afternoon and night of the 16th, McClellan was shifting two army corps— his First under Hooker with 13,000 men and his Twelfth under Mansfield with 8,000—to his right and to the north of the battle line in order to sweep down on the flank that Jackson held; and Sumner's Second Corps, 17,000 strong, was being made available and would participate in the onslaught.

Hooker, feeling his way during the late afternoon for this purpose, bumped into Hood's skirmishers just west of the road, and a sharp and indecisive engagement followed until darkness fell. Hood's men had been on short rations, and after this first blooding Hood went to Lee and insisted that he be allowed to pull them out of line so they could get food. Lee had no others to relieve Hood, but he suggested that Hood speak to Jackson. The latter agreed to place two brigades in the position temporarily, with the understanding that Hood would return whenever Jackson thought he was needed there. About 10 P.M. Lawton and J. A. Walker (the latter with Trimble's brigade) took over the position, Walker on the right, where he connected with Ripley's brigade of D. H. Hill's division, and Lawton on the left. The line turned between Ripley and Walker, Ripley facing eastward toward the Antietam, Walker facing northward.[80]

That night a gentle rain began to fall. On both sides the men sought shelter in barns and outhouses in the surrounding farmland, in fence corners and by stone walls, in ravines among the rolling hills, and under blankets and coats if they had any. But the pickets' and skirmishers' guns cracked throughout the night as men peered for shadowy figures they could hardly see but were close enough to hear.

Lee had chosen the region because it was the best available rallying spot for his scattered army and had good, though not spectacular, defensive potentials. If worse blows fell, it was on the route toward Virginia—provided always he could cross the Potomac, which swung backward and forward in great loops a mile to two miles in his rear. He occupied a low ridge between two streams, the Potomac behind him and Antietam Creek in front of him. The ground sloped down to the creek in broken patterns, sometimes smooth, sometimes rolling, and sometimes, as on his right, hilly. The ridge itself was broken, with groves of trees on the left, with outcroppings of rock in many places, and with twisting little hills and slopes. The village of Sharpsburg lay behind the crest, from the view across the Antietam, and was about midpoint in the line Lee was drawing. All around were small, well-cultivated and developed farms. This was a settled, placid country, with a look of solid permanence and of rural comfort and virtue.

Across the creek the ground rose again so that at chosen spots there men with glasses—or even with the naked eye—could sweep the ridge where Lee rested. The creek was fordable to the north (Lee's left) where it twisted out of sight. It had three stone bridges, one of which, on Lee's right, crossed where defenders could line steep banks and hills. There were no fortifications anywhere. Lee reached the position early on September 15 and knew by 2 P.M. that McClellan's advance was near the Antietam. But he had few tools for digging or other defensive works. Though well enough known at this stage of the war, these were developments for fixed positions rather than the instant resort of armies in the field.

The 18,000 men who came in on the 15th lined up on the north

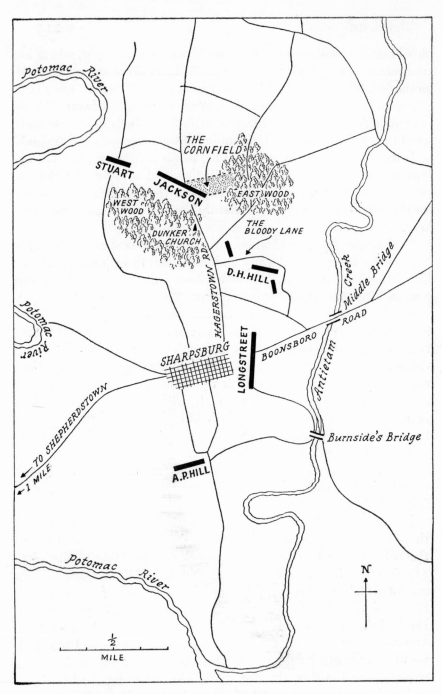

THE PRINCIPAL CONFEDERATE UNITS IN THE BATTLE OF
SHARPSBURG.

and south line along the ridge facing the creek, Longstreet's two divisions (Evans' and D. R. Jones'—his other three were at Harper's Ferry) to the south and east of Sharpsburg, D. H. Hill to the north. Jackson's two divisions extended the line to the north, and Walker's division went to the extreme south. By the afternoon of the 16th after Jackson and Walker had arrived, Lee had nearly 25,000 men, but he was sending couriers for McLaws and Anderson to hurry from Harper's Ferry. When they arrived early on the 17th, his infantry rose to barely 30,000, so extensive was the drainage of the stragglers. He had lost men also at South Mountain, Crampton's Gap, and even Harper's Ferry, and in all the little outpost affairs that carried no names but took their toll. Yet here along the three miles from the great bend of the Potomac on the north to the stone bridge that is still today Burnside's Bridge he was planning to stand up and fight McClellan's 87,000—and another 14,000 half a day away.

McClellan had come through Turner's Gap on the 15th with three corps, the First, Second, and Twelfth, and advanced westward toward the Antietam. Arriving there that afternoon, he found Lee on the low ridge opposite. In his leisurely way McClellan spent the afternoon examining the position, holding back the troops while he and a group of officers (so large that they attracted artillery fire) walked up and down inspecting the Confederate line.[81] At the time McClellan had 33 brigades against Lee's 14, but he was still bemused by his theory that Lee was always stronger than he.

The same kind of contemplative examination continued on the morning of the 16th, while most of his troops merely waited, although by this time the Ninth Corps had arrived. Had McClellan forced his preparations on the 15th and 16th, he would have had a promising opportunity to crush the weak forces opposite him, possibly before the arrival of Jackson and Walker on the 16th, certainly before the arrival of McLaws, Anderson, and A. P. Hill on the 17th. But the initial energy which McClellan had displayed after the finding of Special Orders, No. 191 (never really a show of driving determination), had dwindled away. It was afternoon on the 16th before he determined to make his main effort against Lee's left flank where Jackson had command.

Lee's determination to stand up and fight was, nevertheless, compound audacity or contempt for an army he had handled roughly two and a half weeks earlier at Manassas; and it was probably a

combination of the two. Longstreet, who had disagreed with much
that Lee did during this campaign, thought it a mistake, and by the
strict and technical balance of factors it could be counted one. The
material odds were nearly as large in artillery—now grown in Federal hands into an effective arm—as they were in sheer numbers.
The battlefield was remarkably shallow, and if Lee had to retreat
he might find the Potomac a trap, even though Jackson had sent
Hotchkiss to search and thereby had located two practicable fords
in addition to the one near Shepherdstown.[82] The men's spirit was
good in spite of retreats in Maryland, but they were hungry and
tired. Lee planned a defensive battle and fought one, but he had
more to lose from defeat than he could hope to gain from anything
short of a miraculously large victory.

Yet Lee had small respect for McClellan on the battlefield. He
had appealed only nine days ago to the people of Maryland to rally
to his cause, and he would not go back on the spirit of his own words
now. "I went into Maryland to give battle," Lee exclaimed, almost
in anger, in one of the few moments he permitted himself after the
war to discuss his decisions.[83] He had immense confidence in his
army. But undoubtedly the odds were high.

They seemed so in the dawn of the 17th when the guns went to
work. Jackson shifted Hays early this morning to the east of the
road to support Col. Marcellus Douglass, now in command of Lawton's brigade. The long-range rifles across the Antietam, scarcely
2,000 yards away, could saturate the flank with shells. They smashed
into Lawton's division and enfiladed Jones' with the assurance of
gunners who had the range and could not be reached themselves.
Hooker's batteries added to the drumfire that now beat on both
sides of the road.

Jackson's artillery could not carry effectively to the Federal batteries across the Antietam, but all the guns from Jones' division—
the batteries of Poague, Carpenter, Brockenbrough, Raine, Caskie,
and Wooding—could concentrate on attacking infantry. Stuart on
the far flank, in admirable position for enfilading fire, had not only
his own guns under Pelham but other batteries from Jackson's command. They could lay down a terrible sheet of fire.

They did so when Hooker threw three divisions forward, Ricketts
on the attacking left, Doubleday straddling the road, and Meade between the two and somewhat to the rear—a reserve at first, but

quickly an active participant. Hooker's men looked southward some three-quarters of a mile to the gleaming white Dunkard church on high ground that Hooker planned to seize. Ahead of them, to the east of the road, stood the Miller farm, with houses, outbuildings, fences, an orchard, a garden. The East Wood was farther to the left. Across the road the grove called the West Wood followed the road, but with open ground between the two. Beyond the Miller farm stood the cornfield, some 30 or 40 acres. The ground rose and fell in gentle swells that made it difficult to know what lay ahead.

Ricketts' and Doubleday's brigades stormed into this rural death trap and began to lose men. As they approached the lines of infantry the volleys rang out again and again, crumbling their fronts and staggering their advance. But they moved with a relentless fury, sometimes firing, sometimes running forward. Across the Miller farm they trampled, in and out among trees, and then into the cornfield. The hidden lines there cut them down until Hooker, seeing the glint of Confederate bayonets among the stalks, assembled quickly half a dozen batteries, ordered them to load with canister, and turned them loose with a simultaneous roar.

"In the time that I am writing," he reported, "every stalk of corn in the northern and greater part of the field was cut as closely as could have been done with a knife, and the slain lay in rows. . . . It was never my fortune to witness a more bloody, dismal battle-field." [84]

Two forces, comparable in determination and endurance, though not in numbers, were colliding headlong. The one would not halt, the other would not give in, and neither would waver until broken and crushed beyond ability to stand. The losses on both sides mounted fearfully, but whereas Jackson was sharply limited in reserves, the mass of manpower pressing against him seemed endless. Eventually it forced Warren and Douglass and Hays back through the corn stalks and the East Wood. It fell upon the thin, 1,600-strong Jackson division on the west of the road with irresistible weight and, after bitter fighting, drove it backward through the West Wood.

Jones went out, stunned by an explosion. Starke, who succeeded him, was killed. Douglass, in the very teeth of the storm, was shot to death. Col. Joseph Walker, commanding the brigade next in line, was wounded. Lawton himself went down with a wound. Five out of six regimental commanders in Douglass' brigade were lost, and the brigade itself had 554 killed and wounded out of 1,150. Hays lost 323 of his 550, including every regimental commander. Three of the four regimental commanders were out in Walker's brigade.

The inexorable attack of Ricketts and Doubleday swept over these men and drove them out of the line. On the far west Early was relatively untouched, and D. H. Hill to the southeast and Longstreet's command farther south had suffered only from long-range artillery fire. But by 7 A.M. the northern flank was in collapse.

In this crisis Jackson turned to Hood's two brigades, Hood's own command and Law's, held out since they left the line the previous evening. Jackson summoned Early from the west flank. He called on Hill, and he told Lee that he must have re-enforcements.

The men of Hood and Law, in the process of cooking their rations, were jerked from their fires, still unfed and still hungry. Hardly more than 2,000 strong, they plunged into the mass ahead of them with cold anger and the *élan* which was their pride. They had the advantage of striking at the exact moment when the advance had spent itself and was scattered as well as shocked by its losses. They bored ahead with great spirit, taking heavy losses themselves, but forcing the Federal troops back along a broad front. Early's troops began coming in on the flank, and Hill's left flank brigades hit the Federal forces on the other side. In another hour Hooker's advance had been thrown back across the cornfield and the grove, and the battle hung momentarily in the balance.

Mansfield's Twelfth Corps, following well after Hooker (at no time did McClellan manage to bring united force to bear this day), came up at a fortunate moment for Hooker's badly blunted corps. He had not made as wide a sweep as Hooker, and when he threw forward his two divisions, under Alpheus S. Williams (the opponent of Jackson in the Valley) and George S. Greene, they hit near the junction of Hill and Hood. Mansfield was fatally wounded before the attack began, and Williams succeeded him.

Once more the fury of the assault and defense was renewed. Once more forces equal in determination grappled. Once more the carnage mounted. Once more the fighting broke into innumerable confused clashes, advances, withdrawals. Once more the weight of the Federal assault pressed back the defense gradually, bending it though not breaking it, until Greene had penetrated the West Wood and was all around the Dunkard church. But once more the magnitude of the effort, and the losses Williams and Greene suffered, drained the attack so that, like the defenders, the men lay exhausted, and a lull fell on the field.

Behind Mansfield there was Sumner's big Second Corps, 17,000 strong. Its circling movement fell shorter than Mansfield's, and its line of attack—marking the third major effort on the left flank—did not run southward into the original Jackson position so much as southwestward and westward into the junction but also into Hill's position. Sumner suffered by reason of coming to the field late, with no clear knowledge of what had happened to Hooker (who was wounded in the heel and had gone from the field) except that his corps was out of action. Sumner had not much better understanding of where Mansfield's men were, or, more to the point, where the Confederate lines and centers of resistance were.

Lee was bringing all possible aid to Jackson, stripping his right to do so. Walker was swinging around from the extreme right. A brigade from Longstreet, G. T. Anderson's, came in to support Hill. Hood's brigades were exhausted and without ammunition, and lay wounded and dead in great numbers along the line of their counter-attack and had to be withdrawn. But McLaws and Anderson were coming in from Harper's Ferry now, after marching most of the night, and Lee sent McLaws to take Hood's position. Early was bringing all his strength to bear, and the remnants of Jones' and Lawton's divisions were recovering on the left flank so that Early obtained more freedom to maneuver. Stuart shifted his guns closer and a little more to the rear for a better firing angle.

He needed to do so. For Sumner sent Sedgwick forward and in person accompanied the division in a massive formation that looked beautiful to officers with telescopes in the yard of the Pry house on the other side of the Antietam where McClellan watched and waited. The 6,000 men pierced areas of little resistance with seemingly irresistible force, and the advance had the look of victory about it. But Stuart, Early, McLaws, and Hill gathered unseen on its flanks. In its advance it strode forward into the West Wood until it had blundered into an ambush.

Then the trap was sprung. From the woods to the right, then to the left, then all around, the volleys crackled and the bullets bit. Men fell in droves from an enemy they could not see. "My God, Howard, you must get out of here!" Sumner shouted to a brigade commander (Brig. Gen. O. O. Howard).[85] The division broke from the rear, where the attack had hit heaviest, and it dissolved. It lost 2,210 men, most of them in a few minutes.

McLaws shifted to the offensive, and drove after the fleeing Federal troops. The pattern was duplicating itself, with McLaws taking on Hood's earlier role. He had the psychological advantage of Sedgwick's debacle, and he swept ahead with such force that the whole line bent back with him. It bent across the road, into the cornfield and the East Wood until the whole of Sumner's achievement had been lost.

But McLaws had little support on his flanks, and he faced increasingly formidable fire in front. His division lost heavily as it bent its head to the blast, then stopped, then fought to hold on, and then fell back sullenly. Kershaw's, Semmes', Barksdale's, and Cobb's brigades had losses averaging 39 per cent, but they had done more than carry the battle out of the West Wood: they had carried the battle away from Jackson's front, not to return this day.[86]

It was now 9:30 A.M., and the fighting had been going on for four hours. Hooker's corps, Mansfield's corps, and part of Sumner's corps had battered against this northern flank that with all its re-enforcement did not total 20,000 men. They had hammered it back from the East Wood and the cornfield. They had bled the Confederate regiments white. But Hooker, Mansfield, and Sumner had not broken the line beyond repair, close though they came to doing so. They themselves had lost so largely that Hooker and Williams (in command of Mansfield's corps) withdrew from the field, and Sumner was badly shaken, physically and morally.

These results Jackson's part of the defense line had accomplished by heroic efforts and shattering losses up and down the commands. They had been aided by admirably timed use of re-enforcements. They were aided, in another sense, by McClellan's inability or unwillingness to bring more of his force to bear at the same time. If Hooker, Mansfield, and Sumner had hit simultaneously, the result might have been decisive. As it was, in these successive slugging matches that permitted little maneuver, Lee and Jackson co-operated with remarkable effectiveness in producing, out of desperately slim resources, just the requisite fresh strength to meet the successive crises without complete collapse, and of utilizing it to the fullest extent. But it was a near thing.

It was a near thing on D. H. Hill's front when Sumner's left divisions threw their strength against the worn-down and twisted wagon track that took on the nature of a sunken road and lives in history as the Bloody Lane. Hill's left brigades, Colquitt's, Ripley's, and Garland's (now under D. K. MacRae), had spent their strength aiding Jackson's front and were much demoralized.[87] Hill had two other brigades, Rodes' and G. B. Anderson's, and Lee had sent R. H. Anderson's division to help him. Sumner threw French's division against this formidable line (the same French who eleven years earlier had battled in verbal charge and countercharge with Jackson at Fort Meade), and then Richardson. Greene's remnants from Mansfield's corps joined in. They met fanatical resistance, and the struggle took on an epic quality that moves every person who in the subsequent years has stared at Bloody Lane.

His division battered almost beyond survival, and split apart when orders were misunderstood and some of his men pulled out of the line, Hill himself took part in the fighting. He found a battery (Boyce's) and put it to work anew. He gathered a group of some 200 staff officers, headquarters men, lost soldiers, and stragglers, and led them in counterattack until they could advance no more. Two North Carolina colonels, a captain, an adjutant, and a lieutenant, collecting another group of 200 men mostly from broken regiments, moved over to the right at Hill's direction and launched an attack there as though they were division-strong. They made notable progress before the inevitable happened and they fell back.[88]

To such plights were Hill's men reduced in a crisis of immense possibilities for the Federal command if anyone had taken advantage of it. But though Franklin's corps, some 12,000 strong, had now reached the field, and some elements became involved, Sumner, who was badly upset by his own experiences, ordered Franklin to wait. When McClellan came up to survey the situation, Sumner convinced him of the wisdom of his judgment, and the battle rolled southward to where Burnside was trying to storm the stone bridge that led to Lee's right flank.

Lee knew the weakness of his center so well that he sought anxiously to divert enemy attention from it. He sent word to Jackson, now relieved of immediate pressure on his front, to move to the left with the purpose of turning the Federal right if that was possible. Jackson and Stuart set out to reconnoiter, the cavalry in the lead.

But Jackson found Federal artillery shrewdly placed all around the northern flank, in numbers too great to deal with and extending almost to the great curve of the Potomac. He judged the hazard too high.[89]

The bridge in front of Burnside presented a challenge, and he spent three hours struggling with it against the few regiments— though well placed and determined—that Robert Toombs had to defend it. Eventually Burnside crashed through the fire with the Fifty-first New York and the Fifty-first Pennsylvania Regiments, and all of his four divisions could now follow. They pressed the defense back, aided by crossings above and below the bridge, and the way opened up once more for the Federal command to take advantage of an opportunity of great potentials. But Burnside (like other generals this day) was shaken by his experiences and sought time to reorganize. It was three more hours before he was ready to launch an advance that looked toward Sharpsburg. It almost caught the village in its grip, and it might, with more vigor, have rolled up Lee's right and eventually his whole army.

The crisis of the northern flank (the three crises of the northern flank) and the crisis of the center had now become, as the afternoon wore on, the crisis of the southern flank. Longstreet was beaten back to the point at which he was seeking individual guns and a regiment of a few score men looked like a genuine re-enforcement. "As I rode along the lines with my staff," Longstreet recounted, "I saw two pieces of Washington Artillery (Miller's battery), but there were not enough men to man them. . . . I put my staff officers to the guns while I held their horses. It was easy to see that if the Federals broke through our line, the Confederate army would be cut in two and probably destroyed, for we were already badly whipped and were only holding our ground by sheer force of desperation." [90]

This was the moment, near the setting of the sun on a long, long day, that Isaac Rodman's division on Burnside's extreme left—it had forded the Antietam below the bridge—began to feel the bite of fresh fire from its left. The shells grew in number, and men in blue uniforms, puzzling to Rodman's men, rose over the hills, opened fire, and came forward in one rush after another. Rodman's green regiments wavered and broke. Rodman tried to change front to meet this strange new danger, but he fell with a mortal wound, and the division could stand no more. As it turned back toward the Antietam, it carried all of Burnside's lines with it.

A. P. Hill had arrived!

Hill had remained at Harper's Ferry until the morning of the 17th. Lee's order to hurry to Sharpsburg reached him at 6:30. He left Thomas' brigade to complete the removal of the prisoners and the captured property, and by 7:30 he was on the march. Seventeen hot miles lay ahead of him, and his men were not in good condition to start with. But he drove them relentlessly, pressing on without regard to those who dropped out, pounding through heat and dust, fighting to deliver the greatest possible strength at the earliest possible moment.

By 2:30 P.M. the head of the column had arrived on the battlefield, and Hill, flamboyant in a red shirt this day,[91] offsetting the captured blue Federal uniforms that some of his men wore, was conferring with Lee. Sent to the right flank, he had the advantage of joining the fight when least expected by the enemy. A good third of his division strewed the miles back to Harper's Ferry, but some 2,000 were present and ready to go—the last 2,000 Lee could possibly place his hands on, and, in the dramatic denouement, the decisive 2,000.

With high spirit Archer's brigade drove deep into Rodman's flank, recaptured a battery, and threw the Federal left into confusion. Branch and Gregg blocked Federal advances, smashed the advancing front with repeated volleys, and then pushed their foes backward toward the heights beside the Antietam. Branch was killed, and Gregg wounded. But the attack was decisive. It stopped and turned back Burnside, forced a Federal retreat to the creek, and ended the last of McClellan's threats.

The red sun sank slowly behind the hills overlooking a blood-red battlefield on which 2,108 of McClellan's men lay dead and 9,549 were wounded, beside 753 missing, or 12,410 all told. Lee had almost as many, probably 9,500 to 10,000 of the 13,609 he lost in the entire Maryland campaign.[92] But Lee had lost perhaps one quarter of his whole strength on the field. Not until 1865 did his army shrink as it did on this terrible day.

Yet Lee would not give up the field. That night he called in Longstreet and Jackson, and some division commanders, including the two Hills, D. R. Jones, Hood, and Early, checked with each as to his position and his command, and listened to their reports of staggering losses. But he would not withdraw. To attack in the morning seemed out of the question, though Lee directed one final survey to find out; to defend his ridge between the Antietam and the Potomac seemed to him well within the army's capacity. Lee stood his ground.

Once Lee made that decision, Jackson, who almost certainly agreed,[93] turned back in the darkness of a night made ghastly by the cries of the wounded to the left flank. There he had withstood more, and for a longer period, than had either the center or the right. He had done so without any opportunity to do more than hold on. McClellan made the critical decisions, and made most of them wrong, exercising little control from start to finish, never bringing more than 20,000 men—less than a quarter of his strength—to the attack at one time, and never using at all Porter's corps or most of Franklin's, some 18,000 to 20,000 men. But he had the weight of numbers and of powerful and well-handled guns and much individual and unit heroism, and he could punish the thin Confederate lines to the very limit of their ability to resist.

On the Confederate side the tactical possibilities had been few. Except for quick action in bringing up re-enforcements and the timing of counterattacks, this was a day for endurance, for holding on, for cold nerve, for courage in crisis, and for calm facing-up to the worst odds and the most shattering losses of the year. In these respects Lee was superb. In these respects the manner in which Jackson measured up is inherent in the record of the left flank and in every known action and attitude through the fierce test of Sharpsburg. Significant pictures emerge.

Douglas, sent for by Jackson about dawn, found the General with Lee and received directions to ascertain the position of all the artillery, to refamiliarize himself (this was Douglas' country) with all roads by which ammunition would come up and disabled guns would be drawn off, and to circle throughout the battle among the artillery to see what was needed. Douglas spent his whole day carrying out these directions.[94]

Young Edward Moore of the Rockbridge Artillery saw the General early in the day sitting quietly on his horse and listening intently while his courier, the almost boyish Charles Randolph, reported to him with animation, pointing to various parts of the field.

Jackson was concerned by the straggling that always took place when action was joined. He put his staff and members of the Rock-bridge to work halting and trying to turn back men who streamed to the rear.[95]

Sandie Pendleton, waiting with the General when Hood's men made their heroic counterattack, received orders to follow the Texans to see how they fared and what they needed. Sandie went.

Such a storm of balls I never conceived it possible for men to live through [he wrote home]. Shot and shell shrieking and crashing, canister and bullets whistling and hissing most fiend-like through the air until you could almost see them. In that mile's ride I never expected to come back alive. Out to the front, and then to find General Hood. "Tell General Jackson unless I get re-enforcements I must be forced back, but I am going on while I can." Off, then to General Lee with Hood's message and our appeal for help. . . .[96]

Jackson himself was frequently in the midst of danger, exposing his life, "with his customary imperturbable bravery, riding among his batteries and directing their fire, and communicating his own indomitable spirit to his men. Yet he said to a Christian comrade, that on no day of battle had he ever felt so calm an assurance that he should be preserved from all personal harm, through the protection of his Heavenly Father." [97]

Sometimes the General seemed to think that protection extended to others. After Walker had arrived from the right flank, his Thirty-third North Carolina under Col. Matthew Ransom attacked a battery but failed to take it. Jackson rode up to order a second attempt. Ransom pointed out that much of McClellan's army was over the rise ahead. Jackson doubted it, but he could not be sure. A tall hickory tree gave him an idea. He called for volunteers to climb it, and one of Ransom's men, barefooted William Hood, scrambled up the trunk and the branches. Could he see any Federal troops over the hill?

"Oceans of them," Hood hollered back to the General at the foot of the tree.

"Count the flags, sir!"

Young Hood began shouting back the number of regimental colors. The Federal troops saw him, and their sharpshooters enjoyed the sport of trying to pick him off. Down came the numbers:

"Seven, eight . . . twelve . . . fourteen. . . ." Across the enemy lines came the crack of guns aimed at the man in the treetop. The General, unmoved by his own or anyone else's danger, listened only to the number of regiments.

"Thirty-seven, thirty-eight, thirty-nine," the barefooted target in the lookout shouted.

"That will do. Come down, sir," the General called up. He turned to Ransom with a question as to why he had attacked a battery backed up by 39 regiments. Ransom told him that he had attacked in order to prevent being attacked himself, by a greatly superior force, though he did not know it was that large. Jackson understood and liked the attitude well enough. He left his lookout without a word, but not without a thought. At the next brigade review young Hood, still barefooted, but now horsed and armed with spurs on his naked ankles, was riding a brigade general's mount behind the brigade commander himself—a brigade courier now! [98]

McGuire came to the General about 11 o'clock, almost overwhelmed by the number of wounded men he and the other surgeons were treating. He was disturbed by reports that the battle was going badly, and wondered if the field hospitals should be transferred across the Potomac. In Shepherdstown the wounded men "filled every building and overflowed into the country around, into farmhouses, barns, corn-cribs, cabins; six churches were all full, the Odd Fellows' Hall, the Freemasons', the Town Council room, the school houses." A volunteer nurse looked around her at "men with cloths about their heads, about their feet, men with arms in slings, men without arms, with one leg, with bandaged sides and back; men in ambulances, wagons, carts, wheelbarrows, men on stretchers or leaning on their comrades, men crawling with inflamed wounds, thirsty, bleeding, weak." [99]

McGuire had brought Jackson some peaches. The General welcomed these. Though the situation there in the West Wood seemed desperate to McGuire, Jackson ate the peaches with relish. Then Jackson pointed to the plainly visible Federal troops in the cornfield and said: "Dr. McGuire, they have done their worst." [100]

An hour and a half later Walker came up to the General to report a movement of the enemy. He found Jackson sitting his horse under an apple tree behind Barksdale's brigade of McLaws' division, one leg thrown over the pommel of his saddle while he plucked and ate apples. (It appears to have been a day for fruit for the General.) This was after the storm of attack had rolled farther south.

Jackson listened to what Walker said, but had other thoughts. "Can you spare me a regiment and a battery?" he asked abruptly.

Walker offered the Forty-ninth North Carolina and one of two batteries if ammunition could be found for them. Jackson told Walker that he wished to make up a force of 4,000 to 5,000 men, place them under Stuart's command, and send them around the enemy's right. Walker would have to attack when he heard Stuart's guns, and the whole left wing would advance. The General swung his foot back to his stirrup and said emphatically: "We'll drive McClellan into the Potomac."

Whether this effort resulted from Lee's idea of action on the left to divert the powerful Federal attacks on the center, or whether Jackson and Lee were thinking alike, as they often did, is not clear. The plan proved impracticable. The Forty-ninth North Carolina was already in action. Eventually Jackson told Walker that Stuart had found the enemy right, which swung around so far that it reached the great loop of the Potomac, too strong. Jackson added: "It is a great pity—we should have driven McClellan into the Potomac." [101]

Still later, Douglas saw the General at Lee's headquarters in the afternoon when Burnside was pressing the right wing. Lee asked Jackson for a reliable battery for use at a strategic point he had detected, and Jackson sent for Poague's Rockbridge.[102] Graham's section, with only one gun, came by soon, Private Robert E. Lee, Jr., with it, begrimed by the day's work and unseen by his father until the young man spoke to him.[103]

That night, when he came back from Lee's conference with his generals, Jackson placed his headquarters in front of Capt. David Smith's residence. He had no tent, but there were trees to lie under and grass underneath. Stuart came about midnight, concerned about a hill on the left that would be dangerous if occupied by the enemy. Jackson sent Douglas to Early, then bivouacked near the Dunkard church, for fifty men to occupy that hill immediately. Federal General Franklin did have his eye on the hill and discussed with McClellan the next day placing some guns there, but held off when he found it occupied.[104]

Jackson was up early on the 18th and went quickly to the front.

He found Hood there, and they noted Federal troops still present. Jackson was disappointed. Lee had wondered the night before whether McClellan's right was vulnerable, and this morning he sent Longstreet's artillery chief, Col. Stephen D. Lee, to Jackson to find out. In the unearthly quiet of a day after the bloodiest battle of the war, when no guns spoke, Jackson with one orderly and Colonel Lee rode to a hill (perhaps the one Stuart had been interested in) on the far flank. They climbed it on foot, careful not to display themselves to an enemy within easy sight. Jackson told Lee to examine with glasses the opposing Federal guns and lines. After Lee had looked long and had measured the formidable strength he saw, Jackson said: "I wish you to take fifty pieces of artillery and crush that force, which is the Federal right. Can you do it?"

Lee knew this was impossible, but he hesitated to say so. He asked where the fifty guns would come from. He inquired whether he should collect them. He said (Jackson was pressing him) that he would try. "I can do it if anyone can," he said.

"That is not what I asked you, sir. If I give you fifty guns, can you crush the Federal right?"

Lee parried further, looked again and again, and finally blurted out his conviction: "General, it cannot be done with fifty guns and the troops you have here."

That ended it. Jackson turned back immediately, sent Lee to General Lee with instructions to report what had happened and what he had said, and himself dismissed the matter from his mind. The artillery colonel reported to General Lee, and the General listened and dismissed him. Stuart had thought the Federal right impossible to turn, Jackson had reached the same conclusion, and now an artillery officer as able as the army possessed expressed under pressure the same conviction.[105]

The stragglers were coming in now, and the army picked up strength during the 18th, but Lee could expect no re-enforcements. He knew that McClellan could—Couch's division, which had been left on Maryland Heights, and A. A. Humphreys' division at Frederick, to start with. Proportionately Lee was weaker now than when the battle began, and would grow still weaker. He had scored heavily in morale by holding his ground, but against a steadily growing enemy the position was unwise. By 2 P.M. on the 18th Lee ordered retirement across the Potomac.

This was a difficult and delicate movement. The army used but one ford, Boteler's, below Shepherdstown. The number of guns, caissons, wagons, ambulances, and wounded men was large. The need to carry every man, well or wounded, and every piece of equipment and all supplies, was great. The danger of the enemy's detecting the movement and of launching an attack midway was acute.

Yet by 2 A.M. on the 19th Longstreet's entire wing, moving first after dark fell, had crossed, and part of it was lining the opposite bank to hold off the enemy while the remainder of the army crossed. Jackson followed during the night and continued on the 19th. Two hours after daylight the whole army had crossed, and Fitzhugh Lee's cavalry brigade, covering the rear, had little to do but follow. Gen. Alfred Pleasanton, following up with Federal cavalry, found several hundred badly wounded men in Sharpsburg, and picked up less than two hundred stragglers and negligible supplies. Stuart had crossed earlier, ridden up to Williamsport, and recrossed, carrying some infantry regiments and batteries with him, to hang on McClellan's flank if he pursued.

But the crossing had been a major task. Jackson and Lee took it with deadly seriousness. Jackson sat for hours on his horse in the river [106] as the men splashed through the water and the wagons rocked through the darkness and the dawn. A fearsome traffic jam backed up wagons for long distances until the bank was full and the ford was full and the pressure was pushing wagons into the adjacent canal.[107] Rains had made the roads slick and tempers short. It was another setting for the talents of Jackson's hard-swearing, mule-familiar quartermaster, John A. Harman. Hotchkiss had no doubt that the army crossed safely because Harman "cussed it over," and Douglas was sure that Harman, "big-bodied, big-voiced, untiring, fearless of man or devil, who would have ordered Jackson himself out of the way if necessary to obey Jackson's orders," was "the genius of this retreat." [108] The final picture is Walker's:

Detained in superintending the removal of a number of the wounded of my division, I was among the last to cross the Potomac. As I rode into the river I passed General Lee, sitting on his horse in the stream, watching the crossing of the wagons and artillery. Returning my greeting, he inquired as to what was still behind. There was nothing but the wagons containing my wounded, and a battery of artillery, all of which were near at hand, and I told him so. "Thank God!" I heard him say as I rode on.[109]

But there was a curious postlude. General Pendleton, the army's artillery chief, had lined the Potomac with thirty-three guns of the reserve artillery, and had eleven more waiting, under orders to place them so as to hold off the enemy. The remnants of Lawton's and Armistead's brigades, now commanded by Cols. John H. Lamar and J. H. Hodges, had been assigned to Pendleton's support. Apparently the two had about 650 men all told.[110]

But when Morell's and Sykes' divisions of Porter's corps appeared on the north bank of the river, with artillery and thousands of infantry, Pendleton's guns and their small infantry support could not hold on long.

During the afternoon Pendleton began withdrawing the guns farthest from the river, but before dark came on the infantry could stand no more. It fell back from river-bank positions under attack, and followed the main army. Pendleton ordered all his guns to pull back, but in the darkness he lost track of what was going on. He sought support from Brig. Gen. Roger A. Pryor, who thought he needed higher authority. He looked for Hood but could not find him. He inquired for Longstreet, but in the darkness could not locate him.

Still stumbling through the night, Pendleton arrived at last—it was after midnight now—at Lee's headquarters. He roused the General and poured out a tale of woe.[111] Federal troops, he reported, had stormed across the river and captured all the reserve artillery.

All the reserve artillery! Forty-four guns gone!

The report shocked Lee's staff. It must have shocked Lee himself. But he held his composure, sent Pendleton off for rest, and directed Jackson, early in the morning, to take charge of the situation, whatever it was, in the rear. Jackson may have moved already.[112] McGuire, who usually bivouacked near him, said that the word of Pendleton's staggering report reached Jackson directly and that he leaped into action before hearing from Lee. None knew better than Jackson the value of forty-four guns. It is quite possible that, as Mrs. Jackson wrote later, "the news of this appalling disaster caused Jackson more anxiety than he had ever shown before during the war." [113] Douglas said he was disgusted "beyond words."

Jackson called up A. P. Hill's division and sent it fast toward the Potomac. He directed Early to follow in support. He himself rode back immediately along the track of the army, and when couriers from Lee reached him they found him far out in front examining the ground.[114] The enemy had much artillery on the other side of the river, but Hill and Early would have to face that.

They did, Hill in advance, Early spread out on both sides of the road behind him. Hill's men swept forward into heavy fire from across the Potomac, but they did not hesitate. They caught the One Hundred Eighteenth Pennsylvania Regiment and a few Federal forces on the river bank, smothered them with infantry fire (Hill had not one piece of artillery) and the bayonet, drove them into the river, and cleared the entire side.

When the guns were counted, only four were missing. The remainder had been shepherded back through the woods during the night by battery commanders and by Pendleton's Maj. William Nelson.

There was a curious disparity in Federal casualties in this brief encounter. Hill, who had reported that his men advanced through "the most tremendous fire of artillery I ever saw," also reported that the Federal forces "by their own account . . . lost 3,000 men, killed and drowned." He described "the broad surface of the Potomac" as being "blue with the floating bodies of our foe." [115] Jackson spoke of "an appalling scene of the destruction of human life." [116] But the Federal reports put the casualties, killed, wounded, and missing, at 269.[117] There was no question about the effectiveness of Jackson's actions. He took command instantly and resolutely. He moved with great speed and sureness, and with clear appreciation of the importance of his mission, and he redeemed a potentially bad situation.

Hill and Early held the bank until the covering cavalry took charge. McClellan had no stomach for another crossing until he had licked his wounds. Jackson pulled back on September 21, a Sunday, to the high south bank of Opequon Creek and went into camp. A weary army found rest at last, and the men converted the creek into a vast cleansing pool, washing off the dirt of long marches and hard battles and ugly memories, and soaking their vermin-filled clothes.[118] They lay long in the September sun, relished the cooling nights, and ate ravenously of the food that the wagons were bringing up now. Maryland was behind them, and the stragglers were coming in, and the eternal resilience of youth was lifting them to new strength and hope. The campaign did not pan out, but not because of them. They had fought magnificently, and they knew it.

"Achievements such as these," Lee told them a few days later, when he summed up the August and September operations, "demanded much valor and patriotism. History records few examples of greater fortitude and endurance than this army has exhibited; and I am commissioned by the President to thank you, in the name of the Confederate States, for the undying fame you have won for their arms." But Lee had to add: "Much as you have done, much more remains to be accomplished." [119] Maryland had hurt rather than helped.

# 29 ‖ FREDERICKS-BURG I

*"This is . . . the Second Corps*
*of the Army of Northern Virginia."*

Two months of comparative rest followed Sharpsburg, the longest such period for Jackson during 1862. McClellan sat on his side of the Potomac most of that period regathering strength in his slow, methodical way and fending off Lincoln's appeals for action. Lee's army grew. Stragglers poured in from the back areas. J. R. Jones, sent to Winchester for the purpose, reported forwarding 5,000 to 6,000 by September 27, an "astonishing" number of them officers,[1] he said. Conscripts came up from Richmond, and men came back from field hospitals; and the discipline of the camps kept units intact as they could never be kept on the road or in battle. Jackson's old division, which had gone into Sharpsburg on the 17th with not many more than 1,600 men and lost 700 there, was up to 3,900 by September 30. Lawton's division was up on the same date from 2,500 to 4,450.[2] Secretary Randolph wrote Lee from Richmond on October 8 that "I am happy to observe an increase of over 20,000 in eight days."[3] When Lee left the hills about November 20, the Army of Northern Virginia had 76,427 men,[4] not far from twice as many as he commanded at Sharpsburg.

Arming and equipping these men was a slower and never completed task. As late as November 14 Longstreet reported that 6,648 men in his corps were without shoes[5] (although J. R. Jones thought some stragglers threw away their shoes to keep from being pulled back into the ranks[6]). Jackson reported during the autumn that 3,000 of his men lacked weapons, but apparently that shortage was overcome.[7] Blankets and shoes were more difficult to obtain. In distress for his command, when cold weather hit in November, Jackson appealed to Boteler in Richmond to cut through red tape. Twice in that month he wrote to Anna in appreciation of Boteler's efforts, saying once that Boteler "deserves the lasting gratitude of the country for having done so much toward clothing our men." [8] In physical strength, health, and military effectiveness the army gained fast during the fall days in crisp (though abnormally dry and dusty) upcountry weather. Its confidence grew conspicuously.

Reorganization of the army helped morale. It began near the top, and it lifted Longstreet and Jackson to lieutenant generals in command of newly created army corps. The wing system under which the Army of Northern Virginia had been operating was a makeshift approach to a plan of organization not yet authorized by military law but clearly needed, as Lee knew and as Davis and the Confederate Congress eventually recognized. Davis asked Lee on September 28 for recommendations for lieutenant generals, only a week after the army had settled down in Virginia, and Lee replied on October 2 in these words:

I can confidently recommend Generals Longstreet and Jackson, in this army. My opinion of the merits of General Jackson has been greatly enhanced during this expedition. He is true, honest, and brave; has a single eye to the good of the service, and spares no exertion to accomplish his object. Next to these two officers, I consider General A. P. Hill the best commander with me. He fights his troops well, and takes good care of them. At present I do not think that more than two commanders of the corps are necessary for this army. I need not remind you of the merits of General E. K. Smith, whom I consider one of our best officers. . . .[9]

Lee had already filed with Davis a list of officers who he thought deserved promotion. Davis appointed seven lieutenant generals on October 11, and the Senate promptly confirmed them. Longstreet, with a commission dating from October 9, was the senior, followed by E. Kirby Smith, Leonidas Polk, William J. Hardee, Jackson, whose commission was dated October 10, T. H. Holmes, and John C. Pemberton.

The formal announcement and assignments for Longstreet and Jackson were in Special Orders, No. 234, November 6,[10] which designated Longstreet to command the First Army Corps and Jackson the Second Army Corps. The orders included in the Army of Northern Virginia two new major generals, George E. Pickett (last man in Jackson's class of 1846 at West Point) and Hood, and eleven brigadier generals.

To the First Corps were assigned five divisions: McLaws', Anderson's, Pickett's, Hood's, and Walker's, together with 24 batteries of artillery consisting of 99 guns. The corps strength on November 1 was 34,916.

The organization of the Second Corps on November 1, with four divisions, was as follows:

Ewell's division, commanded then by Brig. Gen. Jubal A. Early while Ewell was recuperating from the loss of his leg. It consisted of the brigades of A. R. Lawton, Early, I. R. Trimble, and H. T. Hays, with J. W. Latimer's artillery battalion; in all 7,716 men, 6 batteries, 26 guns.

D. H. Hill's division, with the brigades of R. E. Rodes, George Doles, A. H. Colquitt, Alfred Iverson, and S. D. Ramseur, and H. P. Jones' battalion of 5 batteries with 22 guns—in all, 6,944 men.

A. P. Hill's division, often called the "Light Division," with the brigades of C. W. Field, Maxcy Gregg, E. L. Thomas, James H. Lane, James J. Archer, and W. D. Pender, and with R. Lindsay Walker's battalion of 7 batteries with 28 guns—in all, 11,554 men.

Taliaferro's division (this was the old Jackson division, commanded in Maryland by J. R. Jones, but now by Taliaferro, recovered from his wound), with the brigades of E. F. Paxton (the Stonewall Brigade), J. R. Jones, E. T. H. Warren, and Edmund Pendleton, and J. B. Brockenbrough's battalion of 5 batteries with 22 guns —in all, 5,478.

The total corps strength was then 31,692. It had 18 brigades and 23 batteries with 98 guns.

Jackson had gone out of his own command to recommend, immediately after Sharpsburg, that Hood be promoted to major general. He knew well what Hood had done at Gaines' Mill back in the Seven Days and at Sharpsburg. Jackson recommended the wounded Trimble for the same promotion, saying as he did so that "it is proper, in this connection, to state that I do not regard him as a good disciplinarian, but his success in battle has induced me to recommend his promotion." He cited Trimble's assault on the Federals at Manassas Junction, after the march around Pope's right flank into his rear, and in remarkable words from Jackson said: "I regard that day's achievement as the most brilliant that has come under my observation during the present war." [11] Lee approved of both Hood and Trimble, but Davis in Richmond would not appoint Trimble until he was physically fit again.

Jackson sought vigorously, and obtained, the promotion to brigadier general, for command of the Stonewall Brigade, of E. F. Paxton, a Lexington lawyer and banker. He had gone into the war with the Twenty-seventh Virginia and rose to major there before losing out in an election. Jackson brought him to headquarters after Dabney left, and then named him for the brigade in which some officers and men disliked the idea. Conspicuous among these was the brigade's senior colonel, A. J. Grigsby, who thought he himself deserved the promotion and was furious at Jackson for passing him by. He was too good a soldier to disrupt discipline, but he swore that when the war ended he would challenge Jackson to a duel.[12]

Jackson appears to have taken his own promotion in stride. There is no evidence that he sought it, as he had his brigadier generalship, or that it stirred him unreasonably. He wrote to Anna on October 13, when he might have known of President Davis' nomination of him on the 11th, without, so far as appears, mentioning the subject.

"I am sitting in my tent, about twelve miles from our 'war-home,' where you and I spent such a happy winter," he told Anna, thinking of the weeks in Winchester when they were much in love. On the day before, he wrote, the Rev. Mr. Graham, in whose home they lived that winter, had invited him to attend communion in the Presbyterian Church in Winchester, but he could not accept. He had attended a religious service in Ewell's division at which the Rev. Dr. Joseph C. Stiles had preached "an excellent sermon," based on I Tim. 2:5-6.

"It was a powerful exposition of the Word of God," Jackson continued, "and when he came to the word '*himself*'—in 'who gave himself a ransom for all'—he placed an emphasis upon it, and gave it a force which I had never felt before, and I realized that, truly, the sinner who does not, under Gospel privileges, turn to God deserves the agonies of perdition." The sermon led Jackson to say that "it is a glorious thing to be a minister of the gospel of the Prince of Peace. There is no equal position in this world." [13] But he said nothing, so far as the record shows, about being a lieutenant general.

Jackson may have had the subject in mind when he wrote to Anna on October 20, but he did not say so specifically. She had read an article about her husband which she did not like, and she suggested having something written for publication. Jackson wrote her:

Don't trouble yourself about representations that are made about your husband. These things are earthly and transitory. There are real and glorious blessings, I trust, in reserve for us beyond this life. It is best for us to keep our eyes fixed upon the throne of God and the realities of a more glorious existence beyond the verge of time. It is gratifying to be beloved and to have our conduct approved by our fellowmen, but this is not worthy to be compared with the glory that is in reservation for us in the presence of our glorified Redeemer. . . . I would not relinquish the slightest diminution of that glory for all this world can give. . . . It appears to me that it would be better for you not to have anything written about me. Let us follow the teaching of inspiration—"Let another man praise thee, and not thine own mouth: a stranger, and not thine own lips." I appreciate the loving interest that prompted such a desire in my precious darling. . . .[14]

The words Lee used about Jackson in recommending him to the President and the absence of any comment on Longstreet have caused debate ever since. Did Lee intend to single out Jackson above Longstreet? Did he think the choice of Jackson had to be justified? What did Lee mean by the words he chose? Truthfulness, honesty, and bravery could be taken for granted in such an officer. "A single eye to the good of the service" would seem only moderate praise unless Lee was trying to assure someone who had a different idea. The reference to Jackson's sparing no exertion to accomplish his object would seem unnecessary in the light of Jackson's almost universal reputation for prompt and energetic action and for persistence, unless Lee thought he was addressing one who might not completely agree.

Since the Seven Days, Lee had entrusted Jackson with a series of semi-independent command responsibilities: Cedar Run; the maneuvers preceding Second Manassas, and the Harper's Ferry operation; and in all of them, he had done well, and in the last two Jackson's record had been brilliant. Jackson had come under criticism at the Seven Days, and Lee knew that still earlier, because of the Romney campaign collision, Davis' opinion of Jackson was not of the highest and Jackson's coolness toward the President was unmistakable.

Longstreet had done well all that was asked of him in the Second Manassas and Maryland campaigns, and had shown admirable battle qualities at Manassas and Sharpsburg. He had come out of the Seven Days in higher regard among general officers than Jackson, though Jackson's popular standing then was probably higher.

There is no positive answer to such uncertainty as Lee's words suggest. The army knew that Longstreet and Jackson had earned their promotions and were pre-eminently the officers to command the two corps. The same opinion might well have agreed with Lee's citation of A. P. Hill as next in line. Yet there is a certain piquancy in the fact that the general officer whom Lee ranked just behind Longstreet and Jackson in command capacity had engaged in such controversies with the other two within the past three months that each of them had put him under arrest and that the suspended controversy between Hill and Jackson was already flaring again.

Hill was determined to have a showdown. On September 22— only two days after the two generals had been working hand in glove to rescue Pendleton's missing guns and only five days after the battle of Sharpsburg—Hill requested a court of inquiry to determine the cause of his arrest. When the request reached Jackson for endorsement, he described the circumstances of Hill's actions on September 4 and the poor march discipline of which Jackson felt Hill was guilty. Thus the document reached Lee.

Lee returned Hill's request to him, pointing out on September 24 that Hill would see from Jackson's endorsement the cause of his arrest and adding:

His [Hill's] attention being now called to what appeared to be neglect of duty by his commander, but which from an officer of his character could not be intentional and I feel sure will never be repeated, I see no advantage to the service in further investigating this matter nor could it without detriment be done at this time.[15]

Far from satisfying Hill, this led that officer to think that Lee had credited the truth of Jackson's charges while refusing the court of inquiry which Hill requested. He directed on September 30 a letter to Lee denying "the truth of every allegation made by Major-General Jackson," and asserting his ability "to prove my denial by any number of honorable men, including members of General Jackson's own staff." Hill continued:

If General Jackson had accorded me the courtesy of asking an explanation of each instance of neglect of duty as it occurred, I think that even he would have been satisfied, and the necessity avoided of keeping a black-list against me . . . these charges made by General Jackson are of a serious nature, involving my reputation and standing as an officer commanding a division of this army, and if true, I should be deprived of the command; if untrue, then censure should be passed upon the officer who abuses his authority to punish, and then sustains his punishment by making loose charges against an officer who has done and is doing his utmost to make his troops efficient.[16]

Hill asked again for a court of inquiry. In a postscript he added an explanation of one of Jackson's charges, about his not being up early enough one morning. Hill denied the charge. At or about this time Hill took the additional step of filing formal charges against Jackson.[17] The text of these charges has been lost.

Jackson, bending over Hill's answer to Lee, attached on September 30 an endorsement saying that since Hill insisted upon having his case investigated, he would forward the charge and specifications "to enable the commanding general to order a general court-martial for the investigation, should the interest of the public service so require." Jackson added that an officer should report his own neglect of duty without waiting to be called in each instance; that no black list had been kept against Hill; that the specifications extended over four weeks, approximately, and that they were of such a character as would not readily escape the memory.[18]

Three days later, October 3, Jackson sent to Lee's assistant adjutant general the charge and specifications, saying that he would have sent them earlier if he had thought a judicial investigation necessary. "As the object in arresting General Hill, which was to secure his stricter compliance with orders, had been effected," he said, "I do not consider further action on my part necessary, and consequently he has not been rearrested nor furnished with a copy of the charge and specifications. Should General Hill be rearrested upon this charge of neglect of duty, I will send a copy of the charge and specifications." [19]

The copy sent to Lee's headquarters covered the criticisms Jackson had already made of Hill's marching, four of the seven specifications relating to the events of September 4 when Hill was arrested. But Lee, busy with many duties, perhaps hopeful that time would solve these problems, and perhaps unable to find a satisfactory way out, laid them aside and waited. That was satisfactory to Jackson. It was not satisfactory to Hill. He would raise the issue again.

Meantime, rest, reorganization, and rehabilitation seemed to the army much more important than the reports drifting in of Lincoln's preliminary emancipation proclamation. The President read a draft to his Cabinet on July 22 (between the Seven Days and the Cedar Run battle), but Seward advised waiting for a military success so that it would not look like an act of desperation, and Lincoln agreed. Sharpsburg was the spark. On September 22 Lincoln read it again to his Cabinet and published it on the 24th. This war measure proclaimed that on January 1, 1863, slaves in states "in rebellion" would be recognized as free.[20]

A wave of bitterness swept the South, and, as some of Lincoln's Cabinet feared, tightened Southern ties. But the Federal writ could not run then to the regions of resistance, and in hard practicality the proclamation had small immediate effect there. More significant was the effect of the moral issue on neutral opinion, especially in the British Isles. The British government might have swung further toward the Confederate side. Now the war by the North was to end slavery as well as to preserve the Union, and that made a difference. This was a transformation in the ideology of the struggle that removed all chance of compromise and assured a fight to the last ditch. It made the position of the moderate McClellan increasingly intolerable.

Little of this broader effect, although more of the South's renewed anger, impressed the Army of Northern Virginia during these weeks while McClellan was making up his mind. Jackson had heavy administrative duties as his ranks swelled again. When Lee placed him in charge of destroying the Baltimore and Ohio Railroad west of Harper's Ferry, and the line that connected Harper's Ferry and Winchester, he moved about frequently. In the two months after Sharpsburg his headquarters changed eleven times, although within a small area in the lower Valley. His longest stay was three weeks (September 27–October 18) near Bunker Hill, north of Winchester, chiefly in tents on the lawn of the Boyd home. The war pressure had eased. Watching, reconnoitering, planning, although important, were quite different from the drive of marching and the strain of battle. Jackson was in the midst of a relaxed army. He too relaxed.

In these weeks the friendship of Jackson and Stuart developed a new depth. Stuart, with an eye to elegance and a fondness (when military work was done) for ease and comfort, had located his headquarters at The Bower, the seat of the Dandridge family and then the home of Mr. and Mrs. A. S. Dandridge. This was a large redbrick mansion on a hill in a grove of oaks, not far from the Opequon and some four miles from Bunker Hill. Stuart's headquarters forces bivouacked on the extensive grounds, and the young officers who surrounded him found the natural beauties attractive. With the Dandridge daughters they made The Bower a center of quickly developing social activity.

Jackson visited The Bower less than his own young staff officers, but Stuart he saw often. The young men might wonder (in Douglas' words) "how could Prince Rupert or Murat be on congenial terms with Cromwell," but they knew, as Douglas also said, that "Jackson was more free and familiar with Stuart than with any other officer in the army," and they thought that "Stuart loved Jackson more than he did any other living man." [21]

Certainly Stuart was more informal with Jackson than was any other officer. It was a common sight, in hours of ease, to see Stuart dancing verbally around the amused Jackson, making fun of him and attributing to him the qualities of a gay blade. No other man dared follow Stuart's example, but Jackson basked under it.

Stuart did more. Early in October, when he was on the point of setting out on his long raid around McClellan, he sent his giant aide, Heros von Borcke, to Jackson with a new uniform coat made by a Richmond tailor, magnificent, in von Borcke's description, "in gilt button and sheeny facings and gold lace"—a striking contrast to the old, weather-stained coat, now buttonless, that Jackson had worn since the start of the war.

The General unpacked his present in "modest confusion," scarcely dared to touch it, and folded it carefully away in his portmanteau. He told von Borcke to thank Stuart, and added: "The coat is much too handsome for me, but I shall take the best care of it, and shall prize it highly as a souvenir. And now let us have some dinner."

Von Borcke protested that Stuart would want to know how it fitted, and the General must put it on. Finally the General donned it. Out of the tent he came now to the table in the open where the staff had gathered and a servant was bringing in a turkey. The staff stared at the General in amazement and broke into grins and congratulations. The General was embarrassed. Then the word spread that Old Jack had dressed up like a prince, and soldiers began reconnoitering to see if this could be true. The period was already a high peak of the army's warm feeling toward the General, and if he was going in for a magnificent uniform, the army wanted to be on hand for that event.[22] Before the evening was over he had a big and enthusiastic audience.

It was an era of presents. Colonel White, of Leesburg, sent the General a handsome sword and gilded spurs. Col. Blanton Duncan, of Kentucky, gave him a pair of imported field glasses. Mrs. Graham, of Lexington, sent him "two excellent sponge cakes . . . and a Mr. Vilwig, of the same place, sent me an excellent arm-chair for camp use. I wish I could keep it until the end of the war, as I think my *esposa* would enjoy it." Miss Osbourn, of Jefferson, sent socks and a "beautiful scarf, which I wish my darling had." [23] There was, said the newest aide, Lieut. James Power Smith,* "no end to the socks and gloves, knit by good and loving women, and there was a great roll of gray cloth for suits to come." [24]

A day or so after Stuart came back from his Maryland–Pennsylvania raid, a long, hazardous, and nerve-racking expedition, he rode into Jackson's headquarters gay and noisy as usual. The General greeted him before he could swing out of his saddle.

"Get off and tell us about your trip," Jackson called to him. "They tell me that from the time you crossed the Potomac into Maryland until you got back again you didn't sing a song or crack a joke, but that as soon as you got on Virginia soil you began to whistle, 'Home, Sweet Home.' " [25]

It was a rare gibe from him, and it would have been made to no other officer. Nor would any other officer in the army have done as Stuart did the night he rode late into Jackson's headquarters, weary from work among the outposts, and flung himself down beside the

---

* Young Smith was the son of a Presbyterian minister whose parents were living in the North when the war began. He was a divinity student at Hampden-Sydney College then, but soon he joined the Rockbridge Artillery. He had seen and been attracted by Jackson before the war, and the General knew something about him. During the Maryland campaign he asked the young man, then a corporal, to be his aide; and with some trepidation, for he had little military background, Smith accepted. After the war he had a long career as a Presbyterian minister, but he found time to record in writing, out of personal knowledge and a good mind, much valuable information about Jackson.

sleeping Jackson without taking off anything but his saber. When the night grew cool, Stuart absorbed more and more of the blankets and ended up with nearly all the bedcover.

In the morning, Jackson was up and out first. When Stuart came out of the tent to join the group around the log fire outside, he bowed with a grin. "Good morning, General Jackson," he said. "How are you?"

Jackson, fully alert to the situation, responded: "General Stuart, I'm always glad to see you here. You might select better hours sometimes, but I'm always glad to have you. But, General"—he reached down and rubbed his legs—"you must not get into my bed with your boots and spurs on and ride me around like a cavalry horse all night." *

There were times to control situations. One of them was when Col. Bradley T. Johnson, who had been assigned to the escort duty, brought three English visitors to see Jackson. They were Col. Garnet Wolseley, later Viscount Wolseley and the ranking officer of the British Army; Francis Charles Lawley, a well-educated British Liberal, a member of the House of Commons in the 1850's, private secretary to William E. Gladstone, and at the time a correspondent of the London *Times;* and Frank Vizetelly (often confused with his brother Henry), who represented the *Illustrated London News* in the United States during the war and drew many sketches of war scenes. Wolseley wrote much about the American Civil War later, including a military analysis of the Virginia campaigns.[26]

Jackson received them with a flourish of awkwardness, taking their hats as he welcomed them and, not finding any other place, piling the hats on his camp desk. The visitors were honorable men, but they had the run of the camps; and Jackson had no intention of

---

* Douglas, 196.

Once von Borcke, whose slips in the use of English were familiar, tried to say of Jackson that "it warms my heart when he talks to me" but actually said, "It makes my heart burn . . ." Stuart leaped on that with delight. When he told it to a headquarters group he had von Borcke saying that "it gave me the heartburn to hear Jackson talk." The table roared.

But Jackson took it seriously. He reached over and shook von Borcke's hand and said (this is the heavily von Borcke version in von Borcke, II, 36–37): "Never mind, Major, for Stuart's jokes; we understand each other, and I am proud of the friendship of so good a soldier and so daring a cavalier as you are." The words are not Jacksonian, but the spirit is. Stuart, only mildly embarrassed, bounded back by slapping his Prussian friend on the back and crying out: "Hurrah for old Von! And now let us be off!"

giving them military information of value—he who rarely told his own chief lieutenants what he was going to do next. But he was not, for that reason, at a loss. These were Englishmen.

The General launched immediately on the conversational gambit of Durham Cathedral, which he had visited on his 1856 trip and about which, with his long memory, he knew much. He talked about the setting, the architecture, and the history of the bishopric. The bishops had been until recently palatines since the Norman Conquest, and their unusual powers interested historians and legal minds. Jackson fired questions, and, when it developed that he knew more about the subject than the visitors, he renewed his questions and his dissertation. The conversation never really left Durham.

Johnson, listening with amazement and amusement, could not restrain himself as he escorted the visitors away. "Gentlemen," he told them, "you have disclosed Jackson in a new character to me. . . . You have made him exhibit *finesse*, for he did all the talking to keep you from asking too curious or embarrassing questions." That did not keep the visitors from recording in their various ways a strong admiration for their host.[27]

Belle Boyd also came out to see the General. By her account, the General greeted her outside his tent, placed his hands gently on her head, and welcomed her. He told her (she continued) that if he withdrew his forces from Martinsburg, she would have to leave that town in order to avoid imprisonment; and he promised (she said) to give her timely notice. When she left, he bade her good-by with "God bless you, my child."[28]

But Smith, Jackson's aide, told a sharply different story. He reported that Belle Boyd came to see the General, well mounted and looking, in Smith's young eyes, like "quite a soldierly figure." But Jackson refused once, and refused again, to see "the young woman, of whose loyalty he was not altogether assured." She exploded in anger, especially against the aide—probably Smith himself—who had denied her admission to the General's tent. A few days later she sent word to the aide that if she ever caught him in Martinsburg she would cut his ears off.*

* S.H.S.P., XXXXIII, 21.
There is no reason to doubt Smith's report. He was generally accurate on information about Jackson during his months as aide, and he was careful and conscientious in all respects. Louis A. Sigaud, author of *Belle Boyd, Confederate Spy,* The Dietz

There is no disagreement in the recollections of men around Jackson about his continued and deep interest in religion. His corps —the whole army, in fact—was beginning to reflect the spirit that led to the great revival of the winter and the following year. Dr. Stiles' sermon which moved Jackson was one of a series that moved many men. Prayer meetings as well as church services began to be held in many regiments. The General attended frequently. He sat among the soldiers, as likely as not in the rear or in a corner of a church. When called upon to pray, as he was many times, he would do so with intense fervor.[29]

Dabney tells of a conversation about redemption that Jackson had with an unidentified officer. The visitor had heard Dr. Stiles and had understood him to say that the fear of wrath did not play a part in repentance, but that repentance was prompted by gratitude and love. Did the General agree?

The General thought that in the newborn believer both fear and love were factors, but as he developed in his new state love counted for more, and in "the most favored saints [as Dabney told it] perfect love cast out fear." As for himself, Jackson continued, he had been for a long time a stranger to fear of wrath because he knew and was assured of the love of Christ, although he was a great sinner.

"I know that heaven is in store for me," Jackson added, "and I should rejoice in the prospect of going there tomorrow." He was not sick or sad, he had been greatly blessed, and life was bright for him. "But, still, I am ready to leave it any day . . . for that heaven which I know awaits me. . . . I would not agree to the slightest diminution of one shade of my glory there, not"—he searched for the phrasing of his thought—"not for all the fame which I have acquired, or shall ever win in this world." [30]

He could turn from such thoughts, on a night when he and Douglas walked home after a prayer meeting. He pointed at the moon and asked his aide, "Are you acquainted with the man in the moon?" When Douglas confessed inability to see him, the General explained at length, though without success. They went on to their tents. Douglas tells what happened then:

Press, Richmond, Virginia, 1944, thought that "Smith's factual and not unfriendly recital requires full acceptance." He thought, because of Belle Boyd's differing account, that there might have been two visits. No original of any letter from Jackson to Belle Boyd has been found.

The hour for tattoo came, and the rolling drums scattered it through the camps. Suddenly out upon the beautiful night there broke forth that wild and joyous yell for which the Stonewall Brigade was famous. Other brigades and divisions took it up and it sprang from camp to camp with increasing vigor, until the bright arch of heaven seemed to resound with the thundering acclaim. The mingled roar was grand, peculiar, impressive in the extreme. When it was at its height I saw the General come out, bareheaded, from his tent, walk to the fence and lean his elbow upon the topmost rail. Resting his chin upon his hand he waited in silence the climax, fall, and conclusion of this strange serenade. The shouts decreased, the noise became fainter and fainter, and when it had almost ceased to be audible, he lifted his head to catch the last note and its last echo. When it was all over he returned slowly to his tent, and said in soliloquy as he entered, "That was the sweetest music I ever heard." *

Through these events the two armies were watching each other intently. McClellan pushed forward a corps to Maryland Heights on September 20 and occupied Harper's Ferry on the 22nd. Lee stationed his left at Bunker Hill, his right near Winchester, and had his own headquarters at Falling Waters. His intention was to recross the Potomac at Williamsport and advance again to Hagerstown, but the army's condition was such that the hazard was great and a reverse would have been disastrous. He gave up the idea.[31]

Perhaps it was about the abandoned plan, perhaps about Stuart's raid, that Lee and Jackson talked when Lee came to Jackson's headquarters on October 7. The two spent a long time poring over maps of Maryland and Pennsylvania spread out before them,[32] and the staff wondered if another offensive was in the making. On October 9 Lee sent Stuart with 1,800 cavalrymen across the Potomac to ascertain the position and designs of the enemy.

Stuart, duplicating the circle around McClellan on the Peninsula, rode all the way to Chambersburg with negligible opposition, swung to the rear of the Federal forces, and ultimately—with a narrow

---

* Douglas, 198.

Of formal music Jackson had meager knowledge. Douglas told the story (Douglas, 120–121) about a young woman playing a piano, in a home near Gordonsville where the previous July the General had been waiting for breakfast. He listened for a while, then asked: "Won't you play a piece of music they call 'Dixie'? I heard it a few days ago and it was, I thought, very beautiful."

The young pianist was embarrassed. "Why, General, I just sang it a few minutes ago," she said. "It is about our oldest war song."

"Ah, indeed, I didn't know it." Yet Douglas thought he must have heard it "a thousand times."

escape at the last—recrossed the Potomac below Harper's Ferry. He destroyed some enemy supplies, picked up 1,200 horses, and could find no evidence of a major eastward move. Better yet, the efforts of the Federal cavalry to catch him, as troopers rushed after false clues over two states, wore out many hundreds of their horses.

The damage to McClellan's prestige was large. "When I was a boy, we used to play a game, three times round and out," Lincoln told a group. "Stuart has been around him twice. If he goes round him once more, gentlemen, McClellan will be out." [33]

That was as much the reflection of Lincoln's impatience with what he called McClellan's "slows" as it was with Stuart's raid. Although Lincoln ordered McClellan early in October to cross the Potomac, McClellan continued to argue about supplies and held his ground.

From the high south bank of the Opequon which he had occupied on September 21 Jackson moved close to Martinsburg on the 24th to escape filth and vermin before going to the Bunker Hill camp on the 27th. On October 18 he moved forward to Martinsburg to tear up the Baltimore and Ohio Railroad track. Without adequate tools this was hard work. The men lifted the rails, pulled up and stacked the ties, dragged the rails on top of them, and set the ties on fire. When the heat rose, the ends of the rails sagged of their own weight. If trees or telegraph poles were handy, the men twisted the hot and pliable rails around them.[34] Thus for many miles to the west of Harper's Ferry, including the burning of the railroad depot and hotel in Martinsburg, in a savage destruction which the General did not like but would see through to the finish.

In these bitter scenes a young railroad section foreman's wife brought one day a touch of beauty that no one present forgot. Pretty and well educated, she delighted in hearing the soldiers talk of Lee, Jackson, and Stuart. When she heard that General Jackson was leaving the neighborhood, she ran into her home, brought out her eighteen-month-old son, raised him up to the General, who was astride Sorrel, and asked him to bless the child.

The General seemed no more surprised, said Charles M. Blackford, "than Queen Elizabeth at being asked to touch for the 'King's Evil.'"

[He took the child in his arms], sitting there on his old sorrel at the end of the wrecked and torn up rail line, the grey section house to one side, and breastworks of logs and iron at the other, while behind were trees, their autumn foliage turning brown. Around-about the soldiers in their worn and patched clothing [stood], in a circle at a respectful distance, while his staff officers sat a little on one side.

Then Jackson, the warrior-saint of another era, with the child in his arms, head bowed until his greying beard touched the fresh young hair of the child, pressed close to the shabby coat that had been so well acquainted with death . . . closed his eyes, and seemed to be, and I doubt not was, occupied for a minute or two with prayer, during which we took off our hats and the young mother leaned her head over the horse's shoulder as if uniting in the prayer.

When he finished, he handed the child back to its mother without a word, who thanked him with streaming eyes while he rode off back down the road.[35]

He moved back on October 22 to Bunker Hill, but on the 25th he shifted to the Charlestown area to work on the line to Winchester —the one Herman Haupt, the Federal railroad operator, called "perhaps the worst in the Union." [36] It ceased to exist when Jackson's wreckers had finished with it. The General was on the Berryville–Summit Point Road, "at Mr. Pendleton's, near Blackburn's," in Clarke County, on the 28th. On November 3 he was camping in a tent under a walnut tree in front of "Carter Hall," at Millwood.[37]

The men had no tents, but they had learned to do with oil or rubber cloths and cotton cloths with buttons and buttonholes, three of which (captured from the enemy) made a comfortable shelter for three men. If the enemy would not supply them, the men resorted to "shebangs," made by thrusting forked sticks into the ground some six feet apart, laying a pole from fork to fork, and inclining bushes from the ground to the pole. With care, Private Worsham noted, shebangs could be made impervious to rain and would provide a night's comfort for three or four men.[38] This was an army that had learned to take care of itself.

McClellan finally gathered up his army for an advance. It began on October 26 with passage of the Potomac (not completed until November 2) and continued on a broad movement east of the Blue Ridge, his right resting on the mountain slopes and sealing off each gap as it passed, his left on the Orange and Alexandria Railroad. The general direction was toward Warrenton.

Lee had sent Walker's division across the Blue Ridge to Upperville on the 22nd and had Stuart operating still farther eastward. The cavalry connected with a small force near Fredericksburg so that the whole front in that direction was under observation. When Mc-Clellan's advance became a certainty by the 28th, Lee split his army. Longstreet's First Corps pulled back comfortably to Culpeper, rolling with the punch—not sharp—of McClellan's advance. Jackson's Second Corps remained in the Valley, most of it along the Charlestown–Berryville road. He hung there on McClellan's flank, threatening it by his presence and watching for opportunities.

McClellan's broad and vague plan included designs against Jackson in the Valley. He hoped—but did not count on the hope—that he might turn westward across Ashby's Gap or another convenient gap in a swift rush through the mountains and fall upon Jackson there. His major purpose was to thrust between the Longstreet and Jackson corps and beat them in detail or force Longstreet back to Gordonsville. Beyond that McClellan held out the possibility of turning eastward to the Fredericksburg route to Richmond or even of returning to the Peninsula,[39] but he hadn't made up his mind. He moved cautiously with cavalry skirmishing ahead of him to the Warrenton neighborhood by November 6.

Lee watched the movements step by step and kept in steady touch with Jackson. He wrote on October 28 that, when the two were not within reach, "I wish you, without referring to me for authority, to regulate the movements of your corps as circumstances may require."[40] By November 6, when McClellan was reaching toward Warrenton, Jackson's advanced force (southward) was in Front Royal, his rear still in Winchester. Lee did not think McClellan would advance far (he wrote Davis in Richmond) while Jackson was in position to threaten his flank. Should McClellan continue to advance, "General Jackson is directed to ascend the Valley and, should they [McClellan's forces] cross the Rappahannock, General Longstreet's corps will retire through Madison . . . and the two corps unite through Swift Run Gap."[41]

To Jackson, Lee wrote on the same day that apparently McClellan desired "either to detain you in the Valley or to get above you, so as to cut you off from a junction with Longstreet, neither of which must you permit. It will be necessary for you to make every arrangement, so that you may move promptly up the Valley, that the two corps can be kept in communication with each other and unite when necessary."[42]

Two days later, on November 8, Lee wrote to Jackson of McClellan's advance to the Rappahannock and added: "You will see it is more necessary than ever that you should move up the Valley, as Swift Run Gap is now the nearest one open to you, unless the road through Fisher's is practicable." He was hurrying Jackson. "You could push your main body, leaving a light corps to observe and follow you." Steuart (the Maryland officer), who was in Jackson's rear, "will have to move at least as high as Strasburg. Give him such directions for his government as you may see fit. Turn off everything for Longstreet's corps through Swift Run Gap." [43]

Jackson's letters to Lee during this watchful and increasingly tense period have been lost. It is apparent, from Jackson's leisurely pace and from later comment by Lee, that while aware of all that Lee was pointing out, he was hopeful of striking a blow at McClellan's flank or rear, and that he outlined these views to Lee.

Jackson moved his headquarters on November 6 from Millwood to "Saratoga," a mile from Nineveh on the Front Royal–Winchester road,[44] and only a few miles from "Carter Hall." In Lee's letter to Jackson on November 9—he was writing every day now—more of Jackson's thinking comes to light. Lee warned him that the enemy seemed to be massing troops along the Manassas Railroad near Piedmont, and wondered if McClellan's object was to seize Strasburg with his main force so as to intercept Jackson's ascent of the Valley—"hence my anxiety for your safety." Then in words that illumine Jackson's ideas Lee wrote:

"If you can prevent such a movement [by McClellan into the Valley], and operate strongly upon his flank and rear through the gaps of the Blue Ridge, you would certainly in my opinion, effect *the object you propose*. A demonstration of crossing into Maryland would serve the same purpose, and might call him back to the Potomac. As my object is to retard and baffle his designs, if it can be accomplished by maneuvering your corps *as you propose*, it will serve my purpose as well as if effected in any other way. With this understanding, you can use your discretion, which I know I can rely upon, in remaining or advancing up the Valley." [45] (Italics are the author's.)

Jackson was looking for the soft spot where he could deliver an unexpected blow or was considering demonstrations to deceive the enemy if, apparently, he had to pretend a thrust across the Potomac to do it. Both conformed to the classic pattern of Jackson's strategical thinking—his restless searching for opportunity, his constant peering under the surface for the hidden weakness at which to aim the blow.

These purposes continued during and after the crisis that now gripped the Army of the Potomac. For the curtain was falling on McClellan. Lincoln, worn out by his commander's "slows" and disappointed by Lee's success in keeping between the Federal army and Richmond, removed McClellan on November 7. Ambrose E. Burnside, with the heavy face and the historic whiskers, succeeded to the command, reluctantly, for he was a modest officer. There was no elevation of army morale. Burnside was well enough liked, but he had proved ineffective in command of the left at Sharpsburg and could present no convincing record earlier. No clear and certain choice appeared in the corps commanders; no rich promise was visible among the generals of divisions. Lincoln knew only that he could put up no longer with McClellan.

On the 9th Burnside took command. He required time to survey the scene from the commanding general's desk and to make his own plans. All movement stopped except the departure of McClellan in emotional farewells from an army that poured out affection on him and from a war in which he played no further part.

Early in November Jackson discovered that Snicker's Gap, east of Berryville, was open. A. P. Hill sent a force across it and pushed pickets down to Snickersville on the eastern side of the Blue Ridge.[46] This was getting into the rear area and was pointing, though distantly, toward the Federal line of supply, the Orange and Alexandria Railroad. On the 10th Jackson directed D. H. Hill, who had been at the forks of the Shenandoah, near Front Royal, to disregard previous orders to move toward Winchester, prepare three days' rations, and destroy the Manassas Gap Railroad as far as he could.[47]

Lee's concern about Jackson's pushing farther down the Valley, thereby widening the distance between the two army corps, was growing, but he recognized the possibilities of what Jackson was doing. He told Jackson on the 12th that whether he remained in the Valley would depend on the advantages he could effect by operating against the communications of the enemy. It would be easier for Jackson to determine that. He himself could not tell whether the enemy would cross the Rappahannock or proceed to Fredericksburg. "You may learn more from the rear than we can in front." [48]

On November 14 Lee told the Secretary of War that these penetrations of Jackson's troops through the Blue Ridge eastward "have served to embarrass and produce hesitation in a forward movement of the enemy." [49] They had also picked up 300 prisoners and inflicted damages without material loss. Yet Lee was still troubled, as he wrote Jackson on the same day, as to how much Jackson was affecting the Federal communication line. He thought bad weather might seriously handicap Jackson's eventual marching to join Longstreet. "Your remaining in the Valley was based upon the supposition that, by operating upon the flank and rear of the enemy, you might prevent his progress southward. . . . As you are the best judge of your ability to operate advantageously against him, I leave you to determine the question whether you will continue in your present position or march at once to join Longstreet." [50] He warned Jackson to be ready to move up and out of the Valley at any moment.

Lee had recognized before McClellan was ousted the possibility of a Federal swing toward Fredericksburg. Now that a new commander had taken hold, he thought a change of plans likely, and he suspected that it would be in that direction. He suggested as much to Jackson on November 12, and to both Randolph and Jackson on the 14th. Simultaneously Lee issued orders for the destruction of the railroad between Fredericksburg and the Aquia landing where supplies would come from Washington by the Potomac; and he had a few guns and a regiment from Richmond sent to bolster the handful of troops already there.

Jackson continued trying to exploit his position in the lower Valley. On November 14 he shifted his headquarters from "Saratoga" to Hogg Run, two and a half miles from Winchester, and on the 19th he moved into Winchester. [51]

The farther north he moved, the more nervous grew the Federal command in this sensitive region and far behind it. Jackson in the lower Valley, Jackson on the prowl, Jackson in Winchester again— all these woke memories of the Romney expedition ten months ago, of the slashing campaign against Banks last May, and of a reputation that had mounted elsewhere. The results now took strange forms.

Col. Jacob M. Campbell, who was guarding the Baltimore and Ohio Railroad at Sir John's Run (where Jackson and Loring had nearly frozen with cold in January), sounded the alarm on November 10 with a telegram to Brig. Gen. B. F. Kelley, in Cumberland, commander of the railroad division, saying that "Jackson, with 40,000 men, re-entered Winchester, and is advancing northward, by way of Romney and Cumberland" [52]—one of which was 35 miles away, the other 55. At the time Jackson was near Nineveh, a dozen miles south of Winchester.

The report set off a flurry of activity. Brig. Gen. George W. Morell, in Hagerstown, who was informed by Kelley, sent the report to Burnside. Maj. Gen. Jacob D. Cox, commanding in Charlestown, who was also informed, asked Kelley for verification but forwarded the report to Maj. Gen. H. G. Wright in Cincinnati. Wright also asked Kelley for verification, but he too notified Burnside. How much verification Kelley attempted is not clear, but he went straight to Halleck in Washington with the report.[53]

"I have reliable information," he telegraphed Halleck on November 13 at 11:30 P.M., "that Jackson, with a large force, has left Winchester and is moving this way [Cumberland] for the purpose, undoubtedly, of carrying out his favorite policy—to destroy the Baltimore and Ohio Railroad, and then recapture Northwestern Virginia. . . . I have not sufficient force to repel him."

A copy went to Burnside. A copy went also to Brig. Gen. Robert H. Milroy in Beverly, with the additional statement that "General Cox has directed me to call on you for re-enforcements. You will, therefore, send me all the force you can spare without delay."

Kelley, who was spreading the news in all directions, informed Governor Francis H. Peirpont in Wheeling, on November 13, that Jackson already had a brigade at Pughtown and another on the Romney pike, near Cacapon Bridge (neither statement had any basis in fact), and he feared the results. "What is the condition of the First Virginia," he asked; "how many men fit for duty?"

Cox broke into this chorus of excitement with a telegram on the 13th from Charlestown to Wright saying that he did not think the report accurate—"it would be giving Burnside a chance to whip Lee, in Jackson's absence." But he ordered Milroy, on a call from Kelley, to send him everything, except small garrisons of observation, and to go himself with his force, if the call was urgent. He added: "Kelley asks if there is any force in Ohio that is available. Some new regiments might be well placed, say, at Marietta, where they would be available for that direction, or any other, if really needed." An unidentified source in Fairview, Maryland, sent to an unlocated "operator" named Charles H. Lounsberry the same day a confirmation of Jackson's presence in Winchester, although, quite sensibly, not all over northwestern Virginia; and Lounsberry notified Maj. Gen. Henry W. Slocum in Harper's Ferry.

Halleck came to life on November 14 with a message to Morell to "assume command of the troops left by General McClellan on the Upper Potomac, and co-operate with General Kelley against Jackson." He added a warning, having been through other campaigns involving Jackson, to "be careful and not get your troops entrapped in Harper's Ferry."

But Morell in Hagerstown came back with a long and fearful message. He pointed out that Halleck was requesting him to enlarge "to an extent which will, I presume, be specified in writing." He could find within reach only 5,018 men, and "I ought not to take a man from this part of the line. . . . Troops are now being organized in this state and Pennsylvania. Why cannot some of them be ordered here, to Chambersburg and to Cumberland?" The safety of Hagerstown, he confessed, "consists chiefly in the absence of inducement to attack it. . . ."

President Garrett of the Baltimore and Ohio Railroad now got into the game. From Baltimore he telegraphed no less a personage than Secretary Stanton on November 14 that "the statements from the Valley of Virginia are hourly becoming more definite and serious." Jackson and A. P. Hill had returned to Winchester with 40,000 men. "A very large force" had been reported at Pughtown. Bridges over South Branch, North Branch, Patterson's Creek, New Creek, and the Potomac River were endangered. Cumberland and Piedmont, with large quantities of machinery, etc., were within reach of Jackson. The forces at Harper's Ferry were believed poorly disciplined, and the enemy seemed to be moving there. He hoped the Secretary would obtain full and reliable information and "take prompt and vigorous action to prevent renewed and grave disasters."

Kelley steadied sufficiently on November 14 to notify Cox that Milroy was on the way to join him and "if he gets here in time, we will take care of the Baltimore and Ohio Railroad and Jackson too." Wright, out in Cincinnati, felt more cheerful that day too: "I cannot believe that Kelley is correct in his conjectures as to Jackson's movements. Still," he was careful to add, "it would be proper to prepare against them." Halleck snapped back at Morell that "you must co-operate with General Kelley . . . this necessity is imperative."

Garrett had a message on November 15 from his railroad agent in Wheeling repeating the now-standard reports, though adding that Jackson forces "did not move yesterday; may be waiting transportation." Garrett pronounced these words "official and reliable." He directed "a general movement of machinery from Back Creek, etc., to points west of the threatened district," and took other steps. He warned Stanton that "Jackson's designs may embrace the destruction of the Pennsylvania, as well as the Baltimore and Ohio Railroad," and he noted gloomily that "the reported extent of his force would indicate serious work." The correspondent of the London *Times* might have been in touch with Garrett when he reported "the universal belief that Stonewall Jackson was ready to pounce upon Washington from the Shenandoah, and to capture President, Secretaries, and all." [54]

All this time Jackson, with no intention whatever of going farther north or west, was south of Winchester until the 19th except perhaps for visits to friends in town. Quite possibly—it would have been like him—he was encouraging, facilitating, and even inventing the reports that were crackling back and forth among generals, officials, railroad agents, and railroad presidents in Charlestown, Beverly, Wheeling, Cincinnati, Cumberland, Harper's Ferry, Hagerstown, Baltimore, and Washington. Had not Lee told him on November 9 that a demonstration of crossing into Maryland might call the enemy back to the Potomac? The power of his name and the memory of his deeds did the rest.

To the credit of Burnside it should be said that none of these alarms appears to have disturbed him or interfered with his thinking. Burnside had never been in the Valley, or on the Baltimore and Ohio's line, or on the mountain roads that led to Romney, in the days which men who had been there did not forget. He went right ahead with his plans.

The flurry died away, though Kelley would not give up easily and insisted as late as December 4 [55] that "Jackson is undoubtedly yet in the Valley" and that "great apprehension is now felt for the safety of Harper's Ferry." * Jackson continued his cheerful conversations with the Rev. Dr. Graham and his household. He loved Winchester, and what could be better than seeing friends again while extraordinary exaggerations of his movements alarmed the enemy from Chesapeake Bay to the Ohio? But he was 50 miles from Culpeper, longer by roads across the mountains, and there was serious work ahead.

Burnside was, in fact, on the move. Although he was now in an excellent position between Lee's separated corps, closer to each of them than they were to each other, a position that would have tempted most generals, he discarded any idea McClellan had entertained of continuing toward Gordonsville. He favored, instead, an abrupt shift to Fredericksburg. That was on the direct line to Richmond, he told Halleck, but he also told Halleck that he would not produce until later his plan for movements beyond Fredericksburg. He had not thought that far ahead.

With unusual speed for one who took command only on November 9, and after prodding Halleck and Lincoln for approval (a new experience for them), Burnside had Sumner's grand division of two corps on the move at dawn on November 15. Franklin and Hooker followed close with two other grand divisions, the new organizational arrangement set up by Burnside for combining corps. Sumner's men reached Falmouth, across the Rappahannock from Fredericksburg, after dark on the 17th. They had covered some 40 to 45 miles in three days, and 31,000 of them could gaze now on a wintry night across the river at two regiments of infantry, two batteries, and a regiment of cavalry, surely not 2,000 men, the only Confederate opposition within nearly 40 miles. When Franklin and Hooker fell in behind Sumner by the end of the 19th, Burnside had 113,000 men,

---

* One of those who was not deceived or excited by reports of Jackson's movements was Brig. Gen. G. P. Cluseret, who commanded Milroy's first brigade in Beverly. He wrote to Kelley in Charlestown on November 19 from New Creek, protesting against being kept there to contain Jackson (*O.R.*, XXI, 779). He argued: "As we told General Kelley, his fears were entirely without foundation. What interest can Jackson have to destroy more of the railroad than he has done, when we reflect on the risk and possible consequences that may arise to him from pushing up into the northwest. The object of destroying a railroad is not so much to capture property as to destroy communication. The latter object Jackson has already attained; further destruction would not advance that object; it would be a piece of folly or deliberate malice, of neither of which Jackson is ever guilty. . . ." The B & O remained inoperable, after Jackson's troops tore it up, until the last rail in its reconstruction was laid on January 5. (*O.R.*, XXI, 947.)

possibly as many as 118,000, within nine miles of the river, and a reserve of another 28,000 men under Sigel at a farther distance.

Burnside had the jump. Lee knew on the 18th that Federal troops were moving eastward, but he did not know how many. He suspected, on the strength of a report from Jackson of re-enforcements at Harper's Ferry (that was Federal excitement over rumors about Jackson), that something was brewing in the Valley. He started one division to the area between the North Anna and the Rappahannock on the 18th. By November 19 he started all of Longstreet's corps hurrying toward Fredericksburg.

After a forced march the first of Longstreet's divisions reached Fredericksburg at 3 P.M. on the 21st. But Sumner had been on the opposite bank of the Rappahannock since the 17th. He had the 18th, 19th, 20th, and half of the 21st for action across the river, opposed only by the meager defensive force already there. The last of Longstreet's divisions did not arrive until the 23rd, and only then did Lee have as many men on his side of the river as Sumner had in his grand division alone, though Sumner did not have a third of Burnside's full force there.

Lack of pontoons for crossing the river held up Burnside at first, a bad logistical mistake that disappointed him greatly. He had hoped to cross before Lee arrived in strength. Now the bridges were down, the weather was threatening, and on the 20th and 21st a storm deluged the area. Sumner was all for finding fords and pushing ahead, but Burnside didn't like the thought of having part of his force cut off by high water. He sat tight, and the opportunity that he had created washed out in the confusions of the lost pontoons and the autumn rains.

Burnside's delay did not relieve the potentially dangerous position of Lee. Nearly 140 miles now separated his two corps. Ten days, and probably more, would pass at best before Jackson could join Longstreet on the Rappahannock. There was no other such widely divided separation of Lee's strength in the face of the enemy during the war.

Yet Lee's aplomb was superb. He wrote Jackson on November 18, when he knew that part of Burnside's army was moving in the Fredericksburg direction but did not know how much, that "unless you think it is advantageous for you to continue longer in the Valley, or can accomplish the retention and division of the enemy's forces by so doing, I think it would be advisable to put some of your divisions in motion across the mountains, and advance them at least as far as Sperryville or Madison Court House." But the discretion was still Jackson's, and the next day Lee wrote him that "you can remain in the Valley as long as you see that your presence there cripples or embarrasses the general movement of the enemy, and yet leaves you free to unite with Longstreet for a battle." [56]

Jackson (in one of his lost letters) had expressed to Lee some views on the disadvantages of major resistance on the Rappahannock, and Lee told him on the 19th that "I do not now anticipate making a determined stand north of the North Anna." [57] Lee changed his view, but Jackson did not.

By November 23 Lee put the case of Jackson's joining him stronger than before. After reviewing the reasons for their separation, he concluded: "If, therefore, you see no way of making an impression on the enemy from where you are, and concur with me in the views I have expressed, I wish you would move east of the Blue Ridge, and take such action as you may find best." [58]

The language presents as impressive evidence of Lee's confidence in Jackson's judgment as the entire record of their relations discloses. Lee had been reporting the situation almost daily for many days. He had constantly reviewed and stressed the nature of Jackson's mission. He had repeatedly urged him to keep in mind always the probable ultimate necessity of joining Longstreet, and the possible difficulty of marching to do so in bad weather over muddy roads. But invariably he left the decision with Jackson, even to the "action" Jackson would undertake after he had crossed the mountains.

Lee thought, at the end of the separation, that Jackson's presence in the Valley had been highly advantageous. He wrote to Davis on November 25 to say that "I have waited to the last moment to draw Jackson's corps to me, as I have seen that his presence on their flank has embarrassed their plans and defeated their first purpose of advancing upon Gordonsville and Charlottesville." [59]

When the move developed, Jackson initiated it—acting on his general authority—before Lee's letter of November 23 had been written. He knew by the 21st that, whatever he had accomplished in the Valley, the issue would be decided not on the Potomac but on the Rappahannock, as it now appeared, or on the North Anna, as he hoped. On that day the men of the old Valley Army marched through the streets of Winchester once more on the way to join Longstreet and Lee—"a melancholy spectacle" [60] to the people of Winchester who knew that Federal troops would march in.

Jackson could hardly tear himself away from Winchester, in particular from the house, perhaps the room, where last February Anna and he had known such great happiness. Anna, at Cottage Home with her family now, or in nearby Charlotte, was about to give birth to a child. Visiting the James R. Grahams at the Presbyterian manse was, in a spiritual sense, a way of visiting Anna. On the 21st, his last day in Winchester, he went there for "tea"—the evening meal; and, Mrs. Graham wrote to Anna that night, "it did seem so much like old times—those good old times of last winter; we are all so cozy in our dining room, and around the table we did wish for you in your seat between us."

The children had obtained permission "to sit up to see 'General Jackson,' and he really seemed overjoyed to see them, played with and fondled them, and they were equally pleased." He seemed, Mrs. Graham thought, "to be living over last winter again, and talked a great deal about the hope of getting back to spend this winter with us, in that old room, which I told him I was keeping for you and him." Mrs. Graham thought him in "perfect health," "far handsomer than I ever saw him," and "in fine spirits." Although "he certainly has had adulation enough to spoil him," she thought it seemed not to affect him. "He is the same humble, dependent Christian, desiring to give God the glory, and looking to Him alone for a blessing, and not thinking of himself."

She prepared a lunch for him for the next day, "and the evening was concluded by bowing before the family altar again, and imploring our Father's blessing upon you and all of us. . . ." [61]

In the morning of November 22 he was off up the Valley, moving fast to catch up with the troops. This was the familiar road, past the hills where he had seen Taylor's Louisiana brigade storm to the top last May, and on to the Kernstown battlefield. There the General reined in his horse. He and his whole cavalcade turned off the road, climbed the slopes, and examined the ground. Jackson, thinking back to that bad day, spoke well of the Rockbridge Artillery.[62] He spent the night at the Old Stone House, on Tumbling Run, south of Strasburg—Strasburg, where Frémont and McDowell had pressed him on both sides, while the Valley Army and the great baggage train and the prisoners had moved up the Valley as they all slid through the trap by the narrowest margin.

November 23, a Sunday, brought another ride up the Valley, beside the Massanuttens now as they rose on the General's left to remind him of many a calculation and many a strategic move. He rode into Woodstock and out again, and pressed on through the deep gorge at Narrow Passage, and across the high bridge at Edenburg and still southward through Mount Jackson—the old scenes were coming back now!—and to a welcoming house near Mill Creek beyond the town.

Monday, the 24th, the General, his staff, and his couriers pressed on southward toward New Market. Ashby and his men—how many gone now!—knew these hills, these turns of the road, these stone walls, these streams. Jackson, riding across the bridge over the North Fork south of Mount Jackson, knew every detail himself. He came into the rich farmland of Meem's Bottom which he had admired earlier in the year, and then to Rude's Hill, every foot of it familiar, and on to New Market.

There the General turned—he had done that before, too!—and climbed to the gap in the Massanuttens that led to Luray and down to the Columbia Bridge. In the distance the high slope of the Blue Ridge loomed before the eyes of the men following. They stopped a mile from Hawksbill on the road to Madison Court House, and a young engineer officer who had joined the staff, Lieut. W. G. Williamson, sketched the General as he sat on a log in the rain, wearing the big black hat that Jed Hotchkiss had bought for him in Martinsburg.[63]

November 25 now, and the road led upward to the high pass of Fisher's Gap. A soldier, standing on a towering rock in the pass and looking back, could see half a dozen units of the army struggling up the winding road; "some seemed to be coming toward us, some going to the right, some to the left, and some going away from us." [64] The weather was bad enough at best, with winter coming in early that year all over Virginia and bringing snow and low temperatures. It was infinitely worse on men without shoes who sought to follow Jackson's advice on making moccasins out of cow hides from their beef ration. The General pushed them to the limit.

The straggling in the Maryland campaign had led him to take drastic steps, and he would take more. The officer who was detailed to command the rear guard as they crossed the Blue Ridge had orders to allow no one to remain behind. "It was one of my most painful experiences of the war," he remembered, "for by noon I gathered up a party of stragglers, a few of whom were stragglers from pure viciousness, but the rest from sheer suffering. The poor fellows were actually barefooted, and their feet were cracked and bleeding on the ice, and these I had to force on, painfully climbing the mountain road." [65]

Yet this same officer thought that no more admirable march was ever made by any body of troops. Notwithstanding the want of shoes and clothing, "Jackson's corps had marched from Winchester to Fredericksburg, in the depth of winter, with the utmost regularity and precision, and took up their position behind the Massaponax hills ready for battle."

On this same November 25 the General told the staff where they were going. When he came out for breakfast, at a table in the open, he was resplendent in his new uniform and was blushing and grinning like a schoolboy. "Young gentleman," he said, "this is no longer the headquarters of the Army of the Valley, but of the Second Corps of the Army of Northern Virginia." [66] His words were the formal announcement—though no one had any doubt—that they were returning to Lee's immediate command. No one could know what was also true: that, here on the height that looked far eastward over the descending hills of Madison and Orange, poised between the land he was leaving and the future he was facing, Jackson was giving his farewell to the Valley of Virginia.

The headquarters horsemen rode down from Fisher's Gap, passed through Criglersville, and moved on to Madison Court House and a mile beyond on the Gordonsville road near Ewell's encampment. Here Jackson stayed for two days, November 26 and 27. Perhaps the men, with five days' marching, much of it up and down mountain roads, needed a rest. Lee, his nerves steady in front of Burnside's nearly three times as many men, had told Jackson to move by easy marches. But Jackson had written to Anna to write to him at Gordonsville.[67] He wanted no telegraphed news from her. He asked for the privacy and intimacy of a letter, and he waited for it.

It came on the 27th or on the 28th when he had ridden on to Orange and a mile beyond it to Haxall's. Anna's sister, Harriet, who had married James P. Irwin, wrote to him from Charlotte

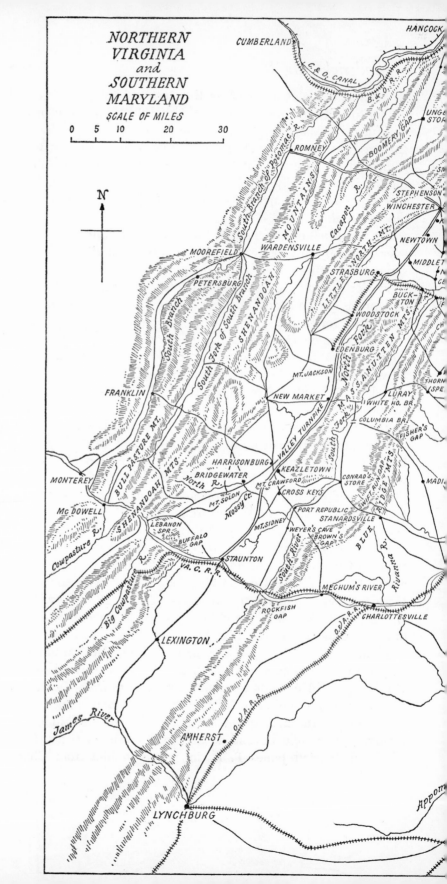

NORTHERN
VIRGINIA
and
SOUTHERN
MARYLAND

SCALE OF MILES

0  5  10  20  30

N

HANCOCK

CUMBERLAND

C & O. CANAL

B. & O. R.R.

BOOMERY GAP

UNGE STOR

ROMNEY

STEPHENSON

WINCHESTER

NEWTOWN

MOOREFIELD

WARDENSVILLE

MIDDLET

STRASBURG

BUCK-TON

PETERSBURG

WOODSTOCK

CH

EDENBURG

MT. JACKSON

THORN SPE

FRANKLIN

NEW MARKET

LURAY

WHITE HO. BR.

COLUMBIA BR.

FISHER'S GAP

VALLEY TURNPIKE

HARRISONBURG

KEAZLETOWN

MONTEREY

BRIDGEWATER

CONRAD'S STORE

MADI

MT. CRAWFORD

CROSS KEYS

McDOWELL

MT. SOLON

Mossy Cr.

PORT REPUBLIC

STANARDSVILLE

LEBANON SPR.

MT. SIDNEY

WEYER'S CAVE

BROWN'S GAP

BUFFALO GAP

STAUNTON

VA. C. R.R.

MECHUM'S RIVER

ROCKFISH GAP

CHARLOTTESVILLE

LEXINGTON

AMHERST

O.& A.R.R.

LYNCHBURG

Appom

James River

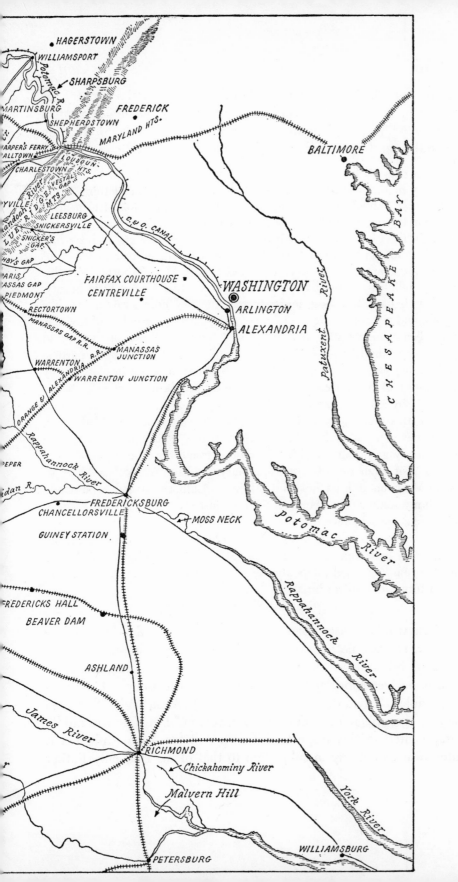

where Anna had gone from the Morrison home in the country for the birth. There in the Irwin home on Sunday, November 23, Anna had given birth to a daughter. Harriet wrote the next day pretending to be the child, her words reflecting the spirit of her times:

My own dear Father,

As my mother's letter has been cut short by my arrival, I think it but justice that I should continue it. I know that you are rejoiced to hear of my coming, and I hope that God has sent me to radiate your pathway through life. I am a very tiny little thing. I weigh only eight and a half pounds, and Aunt Harriet [Mrs. Irwin] says I am the express image of my darling papa, and so does our kind friend, Mrs. Osborne, and this greatly delights my mother. My aunts both say that I am a little beauty. My hair is dark and long, my eyes are blue, my nose straight just like papa's, and my complexion not all red like most young ladies of my age, but a beautiful blending of the lily and the rose. Now, all this would sound very vain if I were older, but I assure you that I have not a particle of feminine vanity, my only desire in life being to nestle in close to my mama, to feel her soft caressing touch, and to drink in the pearly stream provided by a kind Providence for my support. My mother is very comfortable this morning. She is anxious to have my name decided upon, and hopes you will write and give me a name, with your blessing. We look for my grandmother [Mrs. Morrison] tomorrow, and expect before long a visit from my little cousin, Mary Graham Avery [daughter of Susan Morrison and her husband, Alphonso Calhoun Avery], who is one month my senior. I was born on Sunday, just after the morning services at church, but I believe my aunt wrote all about the first day of my life [no such letter is known to exist], and this being only the second, my history may be comprised in a little space. But my friends, who are about me like guardian angels, hope for me a long life of happiness and holiness and a future of endless bliss.

Your dear little wee Daughter.[68]

These words Jackson read—it is impossible to doubt—in complete privacy. He said nothing of his daughter to any man, and some of the staff did not learn the news until a month later; Douglas, for instance, on December 26.[69] But the happiness it brought him is indisputable. He had desired a son, believing (Anna said) "that men had a larger sphere of usefulness than women." But if he was mildly disappointed in this respect, "his own will [as Anna explained it later] was so entirely in subjection to that of his Heavenly Father

that he said he *preferred* having a daughter, since God has so or-
dained it."

To the theological interpretation was added the visible and continuing evidence. An excerpt in his response to Harriet's letter, when
he sought to reassure Anna because the child was not a boy, said:
"Give the baby-daughter a shower of kisses from her father, and
tell her that he loves her better than all the baby-boys in the world,
and more than all the other babies in the world." [70] The date of his
letter is not certain, but on December 4 he wrote to Anna with emotions almost overwhelming him:

Oh! how thankful I am to our Heavenly Father for having spared my
precious wife and given us a little daughter! I cannot tell you how gratified I am, nor how much I wish I could be with you and see my two
darlings. But while this pleasure is denied me, I am thankful it is accorded to you to have the little pet, and I hope it may be a great deal of
company and comfort to its mother. Now don't exert yourself to write to
me, for to know that you were taxing yourself to write would give me
more pain than the letter would pleasure, so you *must not do it*. But you
must love your *esposo* in the meantime. . . .

He came back to his child:

Don't you regard it as the most precious little creature in the world?
Do not spoil it, and don't let anybody tease it. Don't permit it to have a
bad temper. How I would love to see the darling little thing! Give her
many kisses from her father.[71]

This Jackson wrote after he had joined Lee and was in camp a
mile from Guiney's Station on the railroad between Richmond and
Fredericksburg. He was looking forward definitely to Anna's coming
to see him with the child before spring. His eyes were so much better that he could write at night [72]—a far cry from the struggles with
his health during the long 1850's. The improvement he attributed to
"our ever-kind Heavenly Father," who "continually showers blessings upon me; and that *you* should have been spared, and our darling
little daughter given us, fills my heart with overflowing gratitude.
If I know my unworthy self, my desire is to live *entirely and un-
reservedly to God's glory*. Pray, my darling, that I may so live."

He had written Harriet the day before, thanking her for informing him. "I haven't seen my wife since last March, and, never having seen my child, you can imagine with what interest I look to

North Carolina." The separation made him gloomy, and he remarked that "not much comfort is to be expected until this cruel war
terminates." [73]

By December 10 he had decided upon the name of Julia, after
his mother—the memories of the old days at Weston and of the long
journeys to Fayette County would not die. He himself was so happy
with the thought of his wife and daughter that he wrote her, in the
stern thinking he reflected more than once: "Do not set your affections upon her, except as a gift from God. If she absorbs too much of
our hearts, God may remove her from us." [74]

These were thoughts he could keep to himself. No one near him
knew of them when on November 20 he set out, with his aide, Captain Smith, and four or five couriers, on a 40-mile ride to find Lee.
They rode down the plank road by Verdiersville and rested at noon
at the Rev. Melzi Chancellor's home near the Wilderness Church.
This was strange and uninviting country, with a thick forest of small
and tangled trees all around that closed down on travelers and op-
pressed them. They rode on through snow to Salem Church. It was
crowded now by refugees from Fredericksburg. The women and the
old men who could not get in tried to build shelters with blankets
and quilts on the outside, and others were walking on the road
searching shelter where they could. [75]

Night came on before the General, riding the Telegraph Road
and the Mine Road, through pine trees, found in the snow the tents
of Lee's headquarters. Lee came out to welcome him, and there was
(Smith wrote later) quite a stir, now that Jackson had come back
again. This was the land of Muscoe Garnett, whose home was nearby.
Smith went there to ask shelter for the night. Garnett, surrounded
by soldiers and suspicious of them, rebuffed him bluntly. "I have no
room for anyone; my house is full," he said abruptly, and sought to
close the door. But Smith held on and mentioned the General's name.
The effect was electrifying.

"What! General Jackson? Stonewall Jackson? Is he here? Go and
tell him to come at once. All my home is his, sir!"

So the General and his aide, as the young man recalled, "cold, wet,
weary, and hungry, sat before the blazing fire," and "after a good
supper, the General went to sleep in a bed, and the aide rested on
the rug before the fire and thought he was in Paradise." [76]

Next day, while the Second Corps was slogging its way through the snow toward Fredericksburg, the General and his aide rode into that historic and pleasant town. It was Sunday morning, but no church bells rang. The soldiers in the streets were Mississippians of William Barksdale's brigade. Only a few citizens held on, but in the John Scott home the two officers dined. They rode down to the river and looked across its 400 feet to the opposite bank where some 115,000 Federal soldiers waited. Smith's horse drank of its water, and then they rode back toward newly located corps headquarters at "Sunnyside," the French home. There the General and some of his staff accepted Mrs. French's invitation for supper, and before the evening was over—again at her request—he read from the family Bible and, kneeling in the parlor, prayed.[77] It was as natural to him as the great test in battle that lay just ahead.

# 30 | FREDERICKS-BURG II

*"We shall see very soon whether
I shall not frighten them."*

For a commander like Burnside who was planning to attack at Fredericksburg, and had the superior strength to do so, the Rappahannock River was the first consideration. The hills east of the river, where his troops camped from Falmouth along the Stafford Heights to the south, provided an admirable defensive line. Burnside's superior and increasingly professional artillery hidden among these hills commanded the river. His guns could sweep the gently rising and undulating plain on the western side and might even penetrate the lower but appreciable hills that rose a mile to a mile and a half from the stream. The Federal guns could cover any advance. They could protect any retreat. They could smash any assault by Confederates who might seek to cross.

In this formidable Federal position that looked across a stream toward Confederate positions on elevated ground beyond, there were similarities to Sharpsburg. But there were differences too. The stream was much broader than Antietam Creek. The high ground occupied by Lee was higher. It had no obstacle behind it, like the Potomac behind Sharpsburg, and a beaten Lee could pull back. On the other hand, though Lee held a formidable position, he had no prospect of achievement by follow-up if he smashed Burnside's attack. If he followed broken troops, he would come under the fixed guns of the enemy and have a river to cross besides.

Jackson saw that objection from afar. "I am opposed to fighting here," he told D. H. Hill. "We will whip the enemy but gain no fruits of victory. I have advised the line of the North Anna, but have been over-ruled." [1]

Lee had the same thought. But finally Lee thought it unwise to retreat 25 to 30 miles for the sake of a better position for reaping the fruits of victory while giving up much productive and untouched country from which he could draw supplies. The political effect would be bad too. Lee was confident of holding his ground along the Rappahannock, and he decided to stick it out there. He waited for Burnside to move.

Though the river was for Burnside the first problem, it was not an insoluble problem. It was 400 feet broad at the town, and bridging it was easy. Higher up to the north of Fredericksburg, the river was rocky, and pontoon bridges were impracticable. Fords could be found in this rough area, but the hills that ran down to the river created defenses difficult to penetrate. Below the town, where the flow was smooth, the river banks gradually widened, until five miles downstream they were some 1,000 feet apart. The back country on both sides smoothed out, and the ridge on which Burnside knew Lee would place his troops disappeared altogether.

The Richmond, Fredericksburg, and Potomac Railroad track came up from Richmond through this flattened country until it reached to within a mile or a mile and a half of the river. It turned then and ran along the front of the Confederate ridge all the way to Fredericksburg. About halfway between the river and this stretch of the railroad, where they paralleled each other, the River Road, which was also called the Richmond Stage Road, the Port Royal Road, and the Bowling Green Road, paralleled the other two.

For the mile to a mile and a half from the river to the railroad the land was open and cultivated, with ditches and hedges, but the ridge was wooded; and at one point the woods extended across the railroad toward the River Road. A small stream called Hazel Run tumbled out of the Confederate ridge just south of Fredericksburg and flowed into the Rappahannock. A mile farther south Deep Run almost duplicated it. The protruding patch of woods was still another mile to the south, and the ground in it was believed by the Confederates to be wet and boggy. Where the ridge flattened out, and the R.F.&P. curved in from the south, Massaponax Creek, the largest of these minor tributaries, searched wanderingly for the river and found it still farther south.

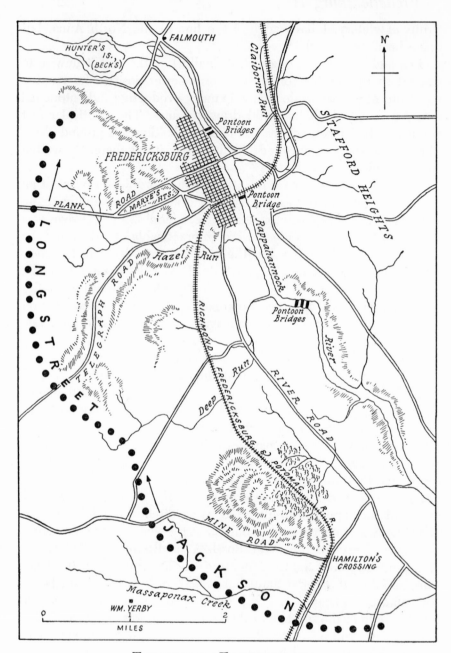

THE LINES AT FREDERICKSBURG.

Burnside liked the look of this low country on his left and studied its possibilities for attack, especially at a point where the river made a horseshoe bend called Skinker's Neck. But Lee had anticipated this possibility. As the Second Corps divisions marched in from the west, Lee directed Jackson to place them to the right of Longstreet's First Corps. They had covered 140 miles, more for some of the divisions, in eleven days of rugged winter weather, two of which were days of rest; but they were in good form. On December 1 they filed into new and widely separated positions.

Early carried Ewell's division to Skinker's Neck, some 15 miles downstream from Fredericksburg; and D. H. Hill dropped farther downstream to Port Royal, 18 to 20 miles distant. A. P. Hill camped at Yerby's, south of the Massaponax and only five miles from Fredericksburg. Taliaferro was south of him at Guiney's Station on the R.F.&P., about 12 miles from Fredericksburg. He could support either D. H. Hill or Early. Jackson found quarters near the Chandler home at Guiney's.

This was a scattered arrangement within the Second Corps and a widely scattered one for the whole army, now spread over a front of more than 20 miles. It reflected Lee's judgment that he could not risk weakening his defenses near Fredericksburg, where he knew Burnside was strong, but that he would have to watch also the lower river, where signs of enemy activity were plentiful. D. H. Hill had two affairs with gunboats near Port Royal. Early detected much Federal reconnaissance opposite him. Lowe and his balloons were there, and his presence alerted Lee. But aerial observations warned Lowe that Jackson was present in strength.

Reluctantly Burnside gave up the lower Rappahannock as an attack point, pondered his problems slowly, and eventually decided to lay his pontoon bridges right at Fredericksburg and a mile below it. The town had possibilities as a strong point for Lee. Men could hide among its houses better than they could defend the river on open banks that were under the Federal guns; and the hills that rose behind it were steeper, and offered more concealment for artillery and riflemen, than other parts of the ridge. But Burnside thought Lee would be more surprised by a crossing there. The Federal preparations moved slowly.

So Jackson waited with the remainder of the army, reconnoitering every day, chiefly along the lower reaches of the Rappahannock. The weather varied sharply. It was pleasant on December 4 when Lee visited Jackson. What the two said is not known and therefore impossible to relate to Jackson's directing Hotchkiss this day to make a map of Caroline County immediately to the south, along the southern border of which the North Anna ran. On the 5th rain, hail, and snow all day made it rough for the troops. (Hotchkiss stayed under cover, and read Lincoln's message to Congress, with what he called "his claptrap argument for emancipation." [2]) The mud was deep and partly frozen the next day. On Sunday the 7th there were no church services. On the 10th, which was pleasant, Jackson and Hotchkiss had a long talk about hats and caps.

When Hotchkiss bought the soft black hat in Martinsburg for the General back in September, he asked if he could take care of the General's cap in his saddlebags—the cap that had come from old Lexington days and perched on the General's nose. Hotchkiss heard now that the General had been asking for it, "so I took it to him and he put it on, remarking that it fitted him better than any other cap he had ever had, but it was no longer fit to wear and he thought of having another made like it. I told him that if he was going to have it cut up I wanted a button from it as a souvenir of what it had seen."

The talk turned to other topics. But when Hotchkiss rose to go, the General said: "I reckon you may have the cap," and Hotchkiss walked off with it to his tent. There S. Howell Brown, of the topographical engineering group, saw it and begged for a button, and Hotchkiss gave him one.[3]

At the opposite pole from these pleasant relations was the problem of Napoleons, much-esteemed smoothbore artillery pieces, for D. H. Hill. Lee wrote to Jackson on December 3 to point out that Jackson's corps had 127 pieces of artillery against 117 in Longstreet's corps. Jackson's were made up of 52 rifles, 18 Napoleons, and 57 standard smoothbores. D. H. Hill had no Napoleons, whereas A. P. Hill had eight, Early had six, Taliaferro (the old Jackson division) had three, and Brown's artillery battalion had one. D. H. Hill was not only anxious to have some but also to have the four which he had captured at Seven Pines back in June. They had been assigned by Lee or Longstreet to the Louisiana battery in Longstreet's corps, but Hill still had his eye on them.

Lee pointed out to Jackson that he would be able "by a proper distribution of Napoleon and rifle guns in your corps, to give General D. H. Hill a fair proportion, and I recommend that this be done." Lee said also that "if it will be more pleasing to General Hill to have those guns [that is, the four captured at Seven Pines, now with a battery in Longstreet's corps], than others, I know of no objection to their being exchanged, provided you send four Napoleons from your corps to replace them."

Jackson hit the ceiling. If there was to be any redistribution of rifles and Napoleons in his corps, he wrote on the same day, "I respectfully request . . . that you will direct your chief of artillery or some other officer to do it"—obviously he himself wouldn't do so unless directly ordered. Jackson hoped that none of the guns that belonged to the Army of the Valley before it became part of the Army of Northern Virginia would be taken away from it. If any artillery had improperly come into his command since the union with the Army of Northern Virginia, he continued, "I trust that it will be taken away," and punishment fall on the officer who had it, if he deserved punishment. He himself had been punctilious at Harper's Ferry with written orders to turn over captured artillery to proper army officers. Finally, "General D. H. Hill's artillery wants existed at the time he was assigned to my command, and it is hoped that artillery which belonged to the Army of the Valley will not be taken to supply his wants." [4]

That ended the matter so far as Jackson was concerned. Lee turned to the War Department with the notification that "I require immediately, for a particular purpose, four 12-pounder Napoleons, and I request that they may be furnished to me without delay." [5] Richmond was the natural place to seek a means of supplying Hill's wants. Something of Jackson's insistence upon what he believed to be his own rights, and much of his fierce pride in the Army of the Valley, permeate this letter to his commander about his brother-in-law. These were matters for which he would take his stand. So far as the records disclose, the exchange had no aftermath of any kind in the Lee-Jackson relationship.

There were other things to think of. Burnside set his attack in motion on the night of December 10. He ordered his engineers to lay two pontoon bridges (one for artillery) at the site of the old pontoon bridge on the upper side of Fredericksburg, "opposite Hawk Street, site of the rope ferry"; [6] one pontoon bridge at the site of the old canal-boat bridge, near the railroad bridge, on the lower side of the town; and two more (one for artillery) a mile lower down, just below the mouth of Deep Run. The engineers hauled in their material during the night of December 10–11 and began unloading about 2 A.M. on the 11th. The night was bitter with a temperature of 24 degrees and a half-inch skim of ice on the river.[7]

The lower bridges went up fast during the 11th. They were under the protection of Federal guns and out of the range of Confederate guns, and small Confederate pickets on shore were dispersed by artillery fire. (A third bridge was built here on the 12th.) But troops did not cross here until the bridges at Fredericksburg could be built, and there the issue was touch and go.

That was because some 1,600 men of Barksdale's brigade of Mississippians from McLaws' division had dug in throughout the town. McLaws had them scoop out rifle pits near the river bank. They threw up shelters of cordwood, established barricades by filling boxes and barrels with earth, and erected continuous defense lines through streets, lanes, and yards as well as connecting cellars. Their own artillery on the hills behind them could not help without endangering the town, and Lee and Longstreet had decided against that.

Before dawn on the 11th the noises in the darkness left no doubt. By 5 o'clock McLaws fired the two artillery shots that announced to the army that the attempt to cross the river had begun. The Mississippians and a Florida contingent that helped them began firing at the sound of work. When the fog that followed the dawn permitted a view, the hidden rifles blazed in fury at engineer troops naked in their defenselessness on the partly constructed bridge. Men on the bridge staggered and fell. They ran back, crawled back, or sometimes lay still. All work stopped. Men rushed forward and jumped to the task again, but again they fell under fire. Nine separate and desperate attempts were made to complete the bridge before 10 A.M.[8] All failed in the face of the biting infantry fire. Out there on the river—while two armies waited—the unfinished bridge led to wounds and death, and nowhere else.

Then Burnside changed tactics. He ordered all workers in, cleared the decks, and directed Brig. Gen. Henry J. Hunt, his artillery chief, to let loose every gun within reach to smash the defenders. Hunt could bring more than 100 guns to bear on the target[9] which, in practice, became the town of Fredericksburg. He ordered fifty rounds per gun. The spectacle that followed remained in the minds of every man, on both sides, who saw it. "It was terrific . . . a cyclone of fiery metal . . . the town caught fire in several places, shells crashed and burst, and solid shot rained like hail," Longstreet wrote later.[10] "It is impossible fitly to describe the effects of this iron hail hurled against the small band of defenders and into the devoted city," [11] McLaws said of it. "The roar of the cannon, the bursting shells, the falling of walls and chimneys, and the flying bricks and other material . . . made a scene of indescribable confusion, enough to appall the stoutest hearts." Men who had lived through Malvern Hill and Antietam said (in Catton's account) that "this was the most thunderous cannonade they had ever heard." [12]

Yet the barrage could not beat down the defenders. As military students had learned before and since (including the most recent wars), determined men can burrow deep. When the engineer troops rushed out for the tenth time to complete the bridge, the rifles spat, bullets crashed among them, and one more attempt failed.

The intelligent Hunt then came up with the answer. At his suggestion the unused pontoons were converted into landing craft, filled with volunteers, and poled across the river in an amphibious operation that disregarded the bridge entirely.

The Mississippians had been thinned out and beaten down more than their good shooting indicated. They fired bullets into open boats and caused losses, but they could not stop the movement. The Seventh Michigan and the Nineteenth and Twentieth Massachusetts rushed ashore at the town and the Eighty-ninth New York lower down. Sharp house-to-house and street-to-street fighting followed in the town. The defense broke. By the end of the day the bridgehead was secure, and work could resume on the bridges without interference.

Barksdale's brigade had held up, nevertheless, the advance of 100,000 troops. The time won was invaluable for Lee. He knew now that the weight of one blow would fall on his left, where the First Corps defended from strong positions. To make the defense even stronger he directed a Second Corps division—A. P. Hill's was the nearest and most logical—to come into line along the railroad on Longstreet's right. Hill moved at dawn on the 12th and took over the line held until then by Hood's division, which shifted to the left to tighten Longstreet's defenses. Hill's right rested at Hamilton's Crossing, his left adjoined Hood's right at Deep Run. The distance he held was a mile and a half. It looked down on open, slightly rolling country, except near the center of the line. There the woods that covered the ridge protruded nearly half a mile toward the River Road that bisected the plain between the river and the ridge.

Simultaneously Taliaferro's division behind Hill's moved toward the line, still supporting Hill, and went into position in the hills behind him. But Early at Skinker's Neck and the distant D. H. Hill at Port Royal held their ground. Lee waited and watched to see whether Burnside meant to hit far down also or whether the whole issue would be fought out along the five miles between Fredericksburg and Hamilton's Crossing.

The 12th came in cold and foggy after a temperature of 26 degrees that made it a night of suffering for the troops. At new headquarters two miles from Hamilton's Crossing and not far from John Ewing's, Jackson had all his staff up for breakfast at 4 o'clock. Some of his officers had slept in the dining tent, and now they all ate outdoors. None of them could see through the opaque gloom of the winter morning, but the murmur of an army in motion rolled up the hill through the mist and the darkness. A small Federal force had crossed Deep Run bridge late on the 11th. Now, by the predawn sounds, more were following.

All during the 12th Burnside's army marched to the bridges, broke step to cross on their swaying planks, and spread out on the opposite shore. They crossed during the morning under the cloak of the fog and always—except occasionally over the Fredericksburg bridges—beyond the reach of Confederate artillery. Lee could not defend the river under the Federal guns. The farther the blue infantry moved away from its long-range artillery, the better for him. The enemy would have enough rolling artillery in any event.

Sumner's right grand division, with the Second Corps of Darius N. Couch and the Ninth Corps of O. B. Willcox, crossed by the upper bridges and occupied Fredericksburg. Franklin's left grand division with the First Corps of John F. Reynolds and the Sixth Corps of W. F. Smith crossed by the Deep Run bridges in front of Hood's sector. Franklin had 42,500 men, plus another 4,000 in W. W. Burns' division of the Ninth Corps of Sumner's grand division, which had been assigned to Franklin. Their purpose, as events soon showed, was to attack farther south. Hooker's center grand division waited on the east side of the river (which here ran nearly north and south), but two of his divisions, David B. Birney's and Daniel E. Sickles', had been assigned to Franklin's corps and were waiting at the bridge. With them Franklin would have about 60,000 men, including 3,500 cavalry under George D. Bayard.[13]

Sumner marched over about 27,000 men on the 12th (and received another 26,000 from Hooker the next day), but he waited for further orders from Burnside. The guns behind them fired spasmodically; the infantry, operating under a leisurely schedule, bivouacked in the flats near the river. If Burnside did not give Lee the 12th, for the nearly 17,000 men of Early's and D. H. Hill's divisions to come up, he aided materially in providing the time for the Army of Northern Virginia to unite.

Jackson was up and down the line all day. He rode to Fredericksburg early in the morning, taking Hotchkiss and Brown of the topographical engineers with him. Late in the afternoon he rode with Hotchkiss close to the river near Hamilton's Crossing, at the other end of the line. There he examined the terrain intently. Like Lee, Jackson had in mind the possibility of a major Federal movement around his right. After that, Hotchkiss recorded, the General rode back whistling—the only time anyone noted his doing so.[14]

Von Borcke of Stuart's staff (whose memory sometimes enlarged events) reported later that Stuart took him along on a tour of the line, starting about 11 A.M. Some time after 2 o'clock Stuart decided to take a closer look at Federal troops digging gun emplacements by the river. He and von Borcke tied their horses in a barn, crawled down a ditch, came to a dismantled gate, and looked at the enemy only a few hundred yards away. What they saw principally was the massive strength of the troops that had crossed. Here was a major striking force.

The two crawled out and rode off, Stuart to confer with A. P. Hill. Von Borcke encountered Lee and Jackson (he said), told them of the reconnaissance, and was told by Lee to take them to the spot. He guided them, then withdrew a short distance while they studied the enemy. Von Borcke felt "extremely nervous about their safety." [15]

Lee determined that Early and D. H. Hill must come up. He could see no evidence of a downstream crossing. The area of the coming conflict would be confined to the Fredericksburg–Hamilton's

Crossing line. The necessity now was to bring the Army of Northern Virginia together on the battlefield.

Couriers went galloping to Skinker's Neck and Port Royal. Later in the day Smith, Jackson's aide, found Jackson growing impatient when he could learn nothing of the approach of his divisions, and he sent other couriers. Then Smith himself rode—rode fast, for he was nervous now. When he reached Skinker's Neck, Early was resting easily. He had received no order.

Smith gave it to him with great urgency and set out for Port Royal. "Riding as fast as I could, I came on General D. H. Hill in camp at Rappahannock Academy and repeated the instructions for the movement to Hamilton's." When Smith heard the drums rolling assembly, he sent word to Jackson and only then relaxed.[16]

The young aide's action was important. D. H. Hill said he did not receive his marching orders until "just before sundown."[17] He faced a march of 15 to 18 miles through a winter night over a route along frozen ground that was certainly not good. Early could not have started much sooner and did not have much less distance to cover. Yet it was of great importance for their 16,000 men to be on the battlefield early on December 13. They reached it near dawn after, in Jackson's words, "a severe night's march from their respective encampments."[18] They could not have been in first-rate condition after such a night, but the Army of Northern Virginia was united at last on the battlefield.

D. H. Hill and Early arrived too late to strengthen their positions. Jackson placed Early on a line with Taliaferro, and on Taliaferro's right, in support of A. P. Hill's front of a mile and a half. D. H. Hill he placed behind Early in a second reserve line. A. P. Hill had organized his defense in two lines. Though it had no fortifications to speak of, the Jackson position, with its four lines, had unusual defense in depth. It reflected great confidence as to where the attack would come and a seeming willingness to sacrifice strength at the front in exchange for impenetrability in distance.

How well Jackson inspected A. P. Hill's plan of defense is difficult to determine. He changed nothing there until, on the morning of the 13th, he shifted three batteries.[19] The strained relations between the two generals would not deter Jackson from reordering anything about such a plan that he did not approve. Apparently he was content to leave the organization of the position, at least until the morning of the 13th, to Hill, for whose battlefield capacities he had shown respect many times.

Yet there was a peculiarity about Hill's front. Hill placed 14 rifles and Napoleon guns under Lindsay Walker on a hill crowning the right of his line. He placed 21 pieces of artillery under Capt. Greenlee Davidson at the left of his line in front of Pender's brigade. Farther to the left was Hood's division of Longstreet's corps. To

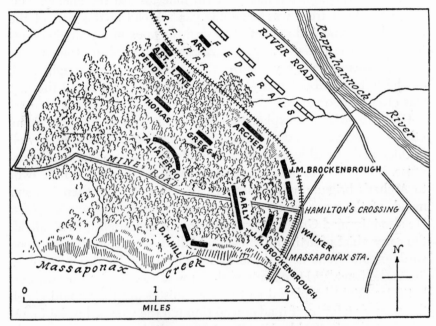

PRINCIPAL UNITS OF THE SECOND CORPS AT FREDERICKSBURG, DECEMBER 13, 1862.

the right of these guns, 200 yards in front and beyond the railroad, were 12 more guns under Capt. J. B. Brockenbrough.

On Pender's right Lane's brigade was 150 yards ahead of the line because the ground favored this position. On Lane's right stood Archer, and still farther to the right were two regiments of Col. J. M. Brockenbrough's brigade earlier commanded by Fields, now out with wounds.

In his second line Hill stationed—along a new road cut along the

top of the ridge a few days earlier by Hood—J. M. Brockenbrough's
other two regiments on his right, then Gregg's brigade behind the
interval between Archer and Lane, and finally Thomas' brigade
behind the interval between Lane and Pender. These were normal
stations, when the ground was favorable, in the organization of such
a defense. But the interval between Archer and Lane was distinctly
abnormal.

There the woods, along the edge of which the front line lay for
the most part, projected nearly a half mile toward the enemy. This
dense tangle of trees was some 200 yards broad at this part of the
Confederate line and narrowed toward the apex of a triangle pointing toward the Federal area. But Archer's left flank on the right of
this gap was some 150 yards from the trees, and Lane's right flank
on the left was about 250 yards from them; so that in all the gap
was close to 600 yards.

Hill left no direct explanation about this gap in his line. Some
other Confederate leaders thought the woods were swampy as well
as thick and probably were impenetrable in any formidable military
sense. Many officers noted the existence of the gap. Lane rode over
to Archer's brigade and informed Col. Peter Turley, then in command, of the open space of 600 yards between the two brigades.
He also informed Gregg, his support, and Hill himself.[20] Crutchfield,
the corps chief of artillery, knew that "there were some 800 or 1,000
yards of our front near the center undefended by direct artillery
fire to the front." [21] He examined the ground to see whether howitzer
batteries might be placed so that by canister fire they could check
the enemy's infantry if it advanced through the woods, but he found
the ground unfavorable. Von Borcke remarked on the gap to Stuart,
suggesting that the trees should be cut down.[22] Stuart thought the
artillery cross fire would prevent advances here. Archer worried
about it until told that Gregg in reserve was close enough to prevent his flank from being turned.[23] Jackson (in Dabney's account)
saw the gap just before 9 A.M. on the 13th and said: "The enemy will
attack here," [24] but there is no record of his doing anything about it.

That morning of December 13, after a night of bitter cold and
great discomfort, the fog lay like a blanket over the river and along
the banks. Burnside's host was concealed beneath it. When the mist
began to thin under a red sun that warmed the whole valley, the
blue uniforms, the bright, proud colors, and the rolling guns spread

far to the left and right. Men watched with fascination the unfold-
ing of the stage and the actors. They never saw a braver display of
Federal martial might. Nearly 90,000 superbly uniformed, equipped,
and drilled soldiers were lining up along the river front, and in the
far distance more than 25,000 more waited their orders to cross.

All the Confederate generals were active this morning. Jackson
dressed himself as if for a feast: his coat was the splendid garment
that Stuart gave him, his trousers a gift in the Valley, his boots a
present from Staunton and his saber and spurs presents from Col.
Elijah White. His cap—grayish blue, with the top falling over in
front, kepi style, adorned with a half-inch gilt braid—had just come
to him from Anna. He thought the braid conspicuous but (said
Smith) feared to hurt Anna's feelings by removing it. Few of the
troops had ever seen him caparisoned thus, and some of them did
not know him at first. But the word spread fast. One of the men
thought it didn't seem right for Old Jack "to be dressed up as fine
as a lieutenant or a quartermaster," and to at least one witness the
General seemed a little ashamed of his unusual finery.[25] But most
of the men roared their approval as he rode by,[26] and roared, too,
at the joking that went on for days. "Boys," called out an Alabama
infantryman when he saw the General later, "come here! Stonewall
has drawed his bounty and bought himself some new clothes." [27]

Thus the General came up to the hill back of Fredericksburg
where the courteous, dignified Lee greeted him cheerily.[28] They
tried to pierce the fog that concealed Fredericksburg. Longstreet
and Stuart joined them, and there was more talk of the hidden
enemy. To Jackson the fog offered an opportunity. They knew where
the Federal infantry was. Why not attack that infantry under cover
of the fog when the Federal artillery would be blinded by it? Later,
when the fog lifted, those guns would have clear targets. Now they
might as well not be present.

Stuart said he liked the idea. But Lee thought the enemy too
strong. He was confident he could defeat an attacking enemy, and
he preferred to avoid the risk of taking the offense.[29]

That decided, the generals grew jocular. The fog was disappearing now, and the massed forces opposite them, obviously organizing
for assault, loomed up with majestic might. Longstreet began to
rib Jackson.

"General," he said, pointing to the blue lines, "don't those multitudes of Federals frighten you?"

Raillery was not Jackson's forte, but he hit back. "We shall see very soon whether I shall not frighten them," he said.

But Longstreet would not let up. "What are you going to do," he asked, "with all those people over there?"

Jackson was mounting Sorrel now, and he was anxious to be off. "Sir," he said, with a touch of bluntness, "we will give them the bayonet"—and he was off to his own corps.[30]

There von Borcke, watching Franklin's force that nearly doubled Jackson's, echoed Longstreet's questions, but seriously. He wondered whether the Second Corps could stand off so many. Jackson turned on him abruptly. "Major," he said, "my men have sometimes failed *to take* a position, but *to defend* one, never! I am glad the Yankees are coming." *

The test was at hand. Burnside's orders had reached his commanders. They were to hit the two ends of Lee's line, Franklin to smash Jackson on Lee's right and Sumner to storm the slopes above Fredericksburg where Longstreet anchored Lee's left. Then, in Burnside's reasoning, they would crush the whole of the five-mile line. The plan made little use of Burnside's superior numbers, directed the attacks where Lee was strongest, and neglected the middle part of his line where he was weakest. It called for two lesser blows instead of one greater one, and, as the movement developed, did not bring the full Federal strength to bear at any one time on Burnside's right and did not utilize much of it at any time on Burnside's left.

In front of Jackson, Franklin had placed Reynolds' corps with Doubleday's division on the extreme left, not directly facing Jackson but bent back in a line from the railroad track to the river so as to face Stuart's cavalry and some additional guns which Jackson had placed in advance of his own extreme right. Meade's division, on Doubleday's right, moved south until, when it right-faced, it looked directly toward the center of A. P. Hill's line. Gibbon's division, to

---

* The words are von Borcke's (II, 117), and they sound more like him than like Jackson, who rarely spoke heroically. Freeman inquired in a footnote (*LL*, II, 349): "Had he [Jackson] forgotten Kernstown?" There was the affair at Falling Waters, too, when Jackson was heavily outnumbered again. But it is doubtful if von Borcke's report of Jackson's words should be held too seriously, in the exact sense, against the General.

the right of Meade, faced Hill's left. Still farther to his own right Franklin had placed W. F. Smith's corps; and there it remained, under fire throughout part of the day and with skirmishers engaged spasmodically but contributing nothing important to Burnside's attack on the Confederate right. One division in Reynolds' corps (Doubleday's) and all three divisions in Smith's corps (William T. H. Brooks', Albion P. Howe's, and John Newton's) played minor roles. The assault was carried by Meade and Gibbon.

When these two began the long climb to the A. P. Hill line, the morning had just turned 10 o'clock and the day was coming out much warmer and more pleasant—almost an Indian summer day, some of the Northern soldiers thought. Meade set his First Brigade in front, his Second Brigade 300 paces to its rear, and his Third Brigade off to his left. As they crossed the River Road, the ditches and hedges had to be cleared for the rolling artillery, and the advance was delayed. At that moment artillery from the far left began to plump shells into the blue lines and, with the advantage of enfilade fire, to drop men through all the ranks.

Young Pelham—Maj. John Pelham of Stuart's horse artillery—was at work. He had seen the chance and begged permission to take advantage, and had been told to take two guns and see what he could do. He was beyond the Federal flank, beyond Jackson's flank too, out in the open, and a sure prey to retaliation as he was a sure and destructive menace to the Federal advance as long as he could fire.

Meade reacted quickly and forcibly. He turned his Third Brigade to the left, thus forming with the First two sides of a square. He opened battery after battery on this annoying fire from the left until he had twelve guns blazing away. Then he sent companies of sharpshooters out to beat down enemy skirmishers and get at the annoyance. His advance, meantime, had come to a halt.

This was Pelham's hour. The young and handsome Alabamian, who had left West Point within a few months of graduation to join the Confederate forces, had risen steadily in Stuart's estimation as an artillery officer. His zest and eagerness, and his blossoming under danger, were building a reputation. Now he was firing with audacity and effectiveness. But when Meade's guns began to get his range, the odds were too much for him. He shifted his pieces rapidly, fired again, shifted and fired, and did this again, almost dodging the shells that fell around him. One of his guns went down, but he kept on shooting until Stuart sent repeated orders for him to withdraw. He finally did so, though not until Lee, watching far away through glasses, inquired who that was, and added a warm compliment. Later Lee called him "the gallant Pelham," and the name stuck.

With Pelham's needling from the southern reaches of the River Road stopped, Meade's artillery turned now against the hill where Lindsay Walker had placed fourteen guns, not one of which had fired. The Federal shells raked the hill backward and forward, and still drew no fire, though the batteries there were taking punishment that strained their capacity to endure. Meade assumed that he had silenced the guns.

The passage of the River Road, the interruption by Pelham, the shelling of the hilltop at the right end of Hill's line, and the re-organization for the advance cost Meade more than an hour. He was close enough to the silent top of the ridge, where no gun spoke, to drench it now with artillery fire. All along the front his shells sprayed among the trees, searching out the unseen shelters, and fell cruelly among the crouching young men—thus for half an hour. Still no guns fired in return. In ominous quiet, well after noon now, Meade's ranks plodded forward closer, closer, closer, until no more than 800 yards separated them from the edge of the wood. Then the furies burst in their ranks.

All forty-seven guns at both ends of Hill's line, plus eight brought in from the army reserve, crashed out of the silence with a stunning roar. Shell and balls smashed into the Federal ranks. Meade's front ranks reeled under the blows. Men fell screaming. Gaps opened up in the lines. Surprised and shocked, the attack wavered, lost mo-mentum, stopped, and even fell back. But Meade and Gibbon were quick to bring their own guns into renewed action. They had certain targets now, and again they swept the ridge.

The Federal artillery, firing while Meade re-formed, was doing more damage than the gunners could see. Meade was receiving help in other ways. Gibbon on his right formed in a column of brigades for the assault. Doubleday on his left and rear pushed forward to engage Stuart's skirmishers and took that weight off the storming troops. Birney's and Sickles' divisions of Hooker's center grand division were crossing the river to add to the Federal force. Far off to the right, where the ground rose above Fredericksburg to Marye's Heights, they could hear the guns working swiftly, could see the lines surging forward in the distance like toy soldiers, and knew that two battles were in progress now. About 1:30 o'clock on an almost cloudless afternoon Meade and Gibbon pushed forward again.

This time they found their goal. Meade's right brigades came into the tongue of the woods that reached down from the center of Hill's line. His left brigade (the Third under C. F. Jackson, no relative of the Confederate), smarting under fire from Stuart's guns, had shrunk over behind Meade's main line of advance, and it too came into the woods. There they all found peace. In the tangle of the trees no enemy faced them, no shells crashed, no Minié balls thudded against bone and muscle. The soldiers could advance untouched. They had a safe and secret pathway to the vitals of Hill's front line, and they burst into the midst of it unseen and unsuspected.

The effect was drastic. Of Lane's five North Carolina regiments that held the ground nearest the left of the wooded gap the Thirty-seventh was closest to the trees, and then, extending to Lane's left, the Twenty-eighth, the Thirty-third, the Eighteenth, and the Seventh stood in line. The first two of these, the Thirty-seventh and the Twenty-eighth, suddenly found themselves surrounded on their right as well as attacked on their front. Their flank was turned, their rear threatened. They fell back. The Thirty-third Regiment, under Col. Clark M. Avery, held the hinge stubbornly, and Avery even ordered a charge, but, without support on his right, he swung back. The other two regiments to his left followed in turn.

Of Archer's five regiments that held the ground nearest the wooded gap on the right of A. P. Hill's line, the Nineteenth Georgia, the Fourteenth, Seventh, and First Tennessee, and the Fifth Alabama stood in that order, extending from left to right. The first three —the Fourteenth Georgia and the Fourteenth and Seventh Tennessee—experienced the same shock as the North Carolinians on the other side of the wood. They looked up to find the unknown enemy surging all around them. Archer sent a warning to Gregg in his support and shifted his own Fifth Alabama from his right to his left to stem the tide. But he too, like Lane, was outflanked and overwhelmed. The First Tennessee stood firm. But when most of his brigade fell back, it opened the second of the swinging doors through which Federal forces could stream by almost untouched.

Some of them did so. The gap was so broad—600 yards to start with and widened now by most of the ground formerly occupied by Lane's and Archer's brigades—that Meade's following regiment pushed straight forward to the supporting line of Gregg and caught it by surprise. They found stacked rifles and lolling troops. One of Gregg's regiments stared open-mouthed and broke. Three hundred prisoners fell into Federal hands here during an advance of nearly a half a mile.

Gibbon on the right had also come to life. He had lost heavily in the early hours of the attack, and his brigades had bogged down. But when Meade forced his way upward through the woods to the railroad line and crossed it, some of Gibbon's men, notably a brigade under Col. Adrian R. Root, rushed ahead, "and as the men recognized the enemy their movement increased in rapidity until, with a shout and a run, the brigade leaped the ditches, charged across the railway, and occupied the wood beyond, driving the enemy from their position, killing a number with the bayonet, and capturing upward of 200 prisoners." [31]

Meade's thrust plus this aid from Gibbon was the peak achievement, the farthest west, of the entire day. The Federal forces had suffered grave losses—Gibbon had a 40 per cent loss before the day was over—before finding the area where Jackson had said the enemy would attack and where officers like Lane had endeavored to prepare for their attacking. Once they found it, these men on the spot exploited it brilliantly. But they did so without any re-enforcing of their success by the corps command behind them or the grand division command behind it. Half of Franklin's force—Smith's three divisions—remained in a purely defensive position. Though Hill erred in leaving the gap no better protected, and Jackson let Hill's mistake stand, the defensive depth of the position as a whole was too much for Meade and Gibbon and probably too much for a much larger attack. The only question was how fast the Second Corps would rally in this critical moment.

Gregg was the first beyond the front line to feel the shock. He paid the penalty. Caught up in the confusion of his surprised brigade, he thought the Federal troops were retreating Confederates and bellowed at his men to stop firing at them. Then he saw the enemy all around. Astonished but courageous, he plunged into the disorder to straighten it out. But a bullet found him on his horse and he fell, mortally wounded.

Thomas with his Georgia regiments was the first to come up from behind Lane, too late to save Lane's line but in time to stiffen men who were catching their second wind. This was desperate going, and the officers looked around for more aid.

It came from Early, and it came with a rush. When an officer galloped up wildly to Jackson with word from Gregg that the enemy had broken Archer's left and he must have help, "the General turned round as quietly as if nothing extraordinary had happened, and ordered up Early's division to support the centre." [32] Early had previously received word from Jackson to be ready for a move to the right where Doubleday was reported—erroneously, as it turned out —to be advancing. Hill himself had sent word to Early to come to his aid—"an awful gulf" had developed in the front line, an excited staff officer told Early.

Early jumped into action. He sent Lawton's brigade, now under Col. E. N. Atkinson, forward on the run. J. A. Walker with Early's own brigade and R. F. Hoke with Trimble's old brigade followed fast. This was the response that Hill thought of with gratitude when he wrote later that "that gallant warrior, General Early . . . came crashing through the woods at the double-quick." His men rushed forward, said Early himself, "with the cheering peculiar to the Confederate soldier . . . which is never mistaken for the studied hurrahs of the Yankees."

The high scream of the rebel yell rose, fell, rose again, over and over, all through this scramble through the trees. It penetrated so many ears so deeply and impressively that officer after officer, reporting later on the day's events, referred to the unearthly sound. But Early's men let loose their emotions in other ways. Lane's men, angry and humiliated at being surprised on the flank by an enemy they had been holding off in front, heard the jests and the reassurances from the men who came running up behind them: "Here comes old Jubal!" "Let old Jubal straighten that fence!" "Jubal's boys are always getting Hill out o' trouble!" [33]

Atkinson drove his brigade into the Federal advance like a knife thrust deep. Walker and Hoke followed on his left and right. Hays with Early's remaining brigade came up shortly. Thomas was getting in blows on Lane's side of the gap. There Taliaferro advanced his division, and the Second Virginia Regiment—one of Jackson's old regiments in the Stonewall Brigade—came up by Lane's side and engaged sharply. The regiments which had held their ground stood out like rallying posts now, and most of Lane's and Archer's men who had fallen back gathered around them. The gap was sealed. Left, right, center, the Confederate forces closed in on Meade's and Gibbon's depleted and exhausted brigades. "The combat in the wood," Jackson said, "was brief and decisive." [34] It was also furious and bloody. The Federal troops, taking severe punishment and finding no re-enforcements, gave ground and in growing disorder trickled back through the trees down the hill.

As they did so the high yells of Hill's and Early's men rose and swelled through the woods. Caught up in an emotion beyond their control as they counterattacked, the men—Atkinson's and Hoke's brigades principally—swept on in hot pursuit, down the slopes, across the tracks, and out into the open. But there they ran into artillery fire and into the fresh troops and solid volleys of Birney's division, which Reynolds brought up from his reserves to the area of the disordered retreat for that purpose. Atkinson fell badly wounded and was captured. The odds turned swiftly, the Confederate losses began to mount, and cooler heads pulled back an excited movement that could never hope to succeed.[35] Some of the men thought otherwise. Hoke's North Carolinians were pulled back with difficulty and even then were bitter. "They don't want the North Carolinians to git anything," one of them muttered, half crying. "They wouldn't have stopped Hood's Texicans—they'd have let them go on." [36]

One picture of Jackson remains. Early in the day, when his artillery had crashed down on the Federal lines, thrown them into disorder, and forced them to retire, he rode off to the right, dismounted, and walked forward to see for himself. Smith, his aide, accompanied him, but no other. A sharpshooter, rising quickly from his cover in high grass 200 yards away, fired. The bullet came close—between the General and the aide, Smith always thought. The General turned to him. "Mr. Smith," he said, "had you not better go to the rear? They may shoot you!" [37]

Jackson suspected further attacks and reorganized his position quickly so as to stiffen the front line. Lane and Pender came back to their positions. Archer went to the rear for ammunition, and Hoke of Early's division took his place. Thomas' brigade (in Hill's words) "was not recalled from the position it had so gallantly won in the front line," [38] and some of Early's brigades were close up—Walker's for one. D. H. Hill took the position Early had held before the attack.

This was a makeshift reorganization with brigades from different divisions intermingled. Jackson reorganized more logically the next day. He was concentrating strength now to make up for casualties and to provide better defense for the area where the gap had been. The casualties were severe. Within A. P. Hill's division they were 2,120, and within Early's division they were 932. Taliaferro suffered only 190 casualties, and D. H. Hill only 173. A. P. Hill's loss was thus two-thirds of the total of 3,415. [39] The Federal losses in all units facing the First Corps were higher at 4,857, [40] and probably were worse in effect than the figures suggest. Many of the wounded men in the Second Corps, it turned out, had minor injuries.

These missing, wounded, and dead soldiers of the Second Corps were primarily the penalty for the gap in Hill's line. Jackson had force in plenty to stand off Meade and Gibbon's division. He did not use D. H. Hill at all. Only one regiment of the eighteen in Taliaferro's division was actually engaged. One brigade of A. P. Hill's division— Pender's, on the left—was not within the path of the Federal attack and participated in it only in slight degree, though suffering from artillery fire. Only about one-half of the Second Corps joined in the major battle. The loss was concentrated, and the reasons are clear.

What would have happened if Franklin had thrown the weight of both his corps, plus two divisions from Hooker's center grand division, is a question which the events of the day do not answer. As the Federal attack did develop it caught Hill by surprise in the center, but there the defense in depth, though giving ground, rebounded with such stunning force that Meade and Gibbon were thrown back quickly and lost heavily. The day's record was marred, but the corps turned back decisively all that a greatly superior force attempted to do.

All this time, from about 11 o'clock in the morning and continuing until late in the afternoon, the other battle of Fredericksburg—less than five miles away, but curiously separate and distinct—was fought out with complete self-possession by the First Corps and with bravery, blood, and futility by the Federal divisions. In the end Longstreet stood off with comparative ease a long succession of

head-on attacks—Alexander counted fourteen of them.[41] Each one
was almost exactly like its predecessor. Most of them reached up to
approximately the same distance short of the goal. None of them
showed imagination or flexibility or ability in the high commands
to learn from failure, and all of them combined into a dull obduracy
which, though lightened by the superb bravery of many officers
and men, demonstrated unbelievably bad judgment and produced
tragic losses.

Longstreet set up a four-division front—actually five-division, because at the point of danger he placed one division behind another,
with two divisions on one side and one on the other. Hood was on
A. P. Hill's left, and Pickett still farther to the left. Then, west of
Fredericksburg, McLaws at the bottom and Robert Ransom at the
top of Willis' Hill, a high point of Marye's Heights, held the area
directly opposite the pontoon bridges above and below the town,
confronting the mass of troops Burnside had concentrated within
Fredericksburg. McLaws had nearly 8,000 men, some of them south
of Willis' Hill, but Ransom had less than 4,000. Farther to the left
was R. H. Anderson's division.

Hood, Pickett, and Anderson were outside the line of direction
of the major Federal attack. Except for a lesser thrust against Hood,
which E. M. Law's brigade turned back without trouble, they stood
their ground, endured annoying but not serious artillery fire, and
(from Pickett and Anderson) supplied minor re-enforcements. Burnside elected to throw his principal attack—with most of three corps,
comprising most of eight divisions (and others lending assistance)
and more than 40,000 men in the assault—at McLaws and Ransom.
This required the passage of an open area of some 600 to 800 yards
that was no more than a mile broad where the troops debouched
from Fredericksburg's shelter and hardly more than a half-mile
wide where McLaws and Ransom held the fortified summit.

Almost immediately they moved out from Fredericksburg the
Federal troops faced the spillway of a canal. They crossed it by
two bridges, one of which had lost its boarding and required walking
on stringers. Huddled together for this crossing, the troops were
an open target for Confederate artillery. Once across, they had brief
protection, for the slope rose sharply at this point. They could deploy
in safety. But when they scrambled over the top, they faced an
open slope and looked upward at a frowning summit. A few scat-

tered houses along the way offered deceptive protection. Slight undulations in the ground could conceal men when they lay flat from
the vision of the enemy on top. About halfway up the slope a slight
depression ran across it, in which men could find thin shelter. Beyond, the ground rose gently, with nothing to cover the nakedness
of an assault.

Longstreet had much longer time to prepare the ground for defense than Jackson had, and he had better natural defenses to start
with. The Telegraph Road approached the town in a generally northeastern direction, ran by the southern side of Marye's Heights,
turned north at that point and stretched along the base of the
heights, and then turned easterly again and dropped into the town.

Where the road extended for half a mile along the base of the
hill it was supported on both sides by stone walls, "shoulder-high,"
in Longstreet's words. The road itself was slightly sunken. Between
walls it was about 25 feet wide. Soldiers could jam into it in great
numbers without stepping on each other, and they could fire from
behind its stone walls with perfect trench protection. McLaws lined
it with Thomas R. R. Cobb's brigade, Phillips' Legion on the left,
the Twenty-fourth Georgia in the center, and the Eighteenth
Georgia on the right. A North Carolina regiment of Ransom's brigade, the Twenty-fourth (part of the division which he also commanded), prolonged the line in a ditch to the left. Cooke's brigade
of the same division occupied the crest of Willis' Hill and fired over
the heads of the men in the sunken road.

Behind the sunken road the ground rose abruptly. Here the guns
of the Washington Artillery under Col. J. B. Walton, partly concealed, in some instances covered with brush, had a clear field of
fire. Ransom's division supported them. Rifle pits and breastworks
of logs, with abatis in front of them, had been constructed. Guns on
hills to the south had the slope along this part of Marye's Heights
within their sights, especially from Telegraph Hill, where Lee set
up headquarters—thereafter called Lee's Hill. Marye's Heights was
such an ideal defensive position that the only real question was
whether Burnside would try to assail it. No high officer on Lee's
side had any doubt that the defense could smash into bits any frontal
assault. Nor did any Federal officer, so far as the record shows, face
the prospect with confidence.

Yet frontal assault is just what Burnside ordered. About 11 A.M.

Longstreet, seeing in the distance that Franklin was beginning to attack Jackson, started artillery fire in the hope of diverting attention to himself. Federal forces came boiling out of Fredericksburg, Couch's corps first, and French's division (Jackson's old company commander at Fort Meade) in the lead, followed by W. S. Hancock's division. French deployed with Nathan Kimball's brigade to go first, followed by John W. Andrews' and Oliver H. Palmer's.

Out tramped Kimball's men from the town with their "Hi! Hi! Hi!" beating time in a steady rhythmical count. The guns caught them at the bridges, and men began to drop. "From the time my column came in sight at the depot building," Kimball reported, "all these movements were executed under a most murderous fire from the enemy's artillery, several shells bursting in the ranks and destroying a company at a time. Yet all the regiments, without an exception, moved steadily forward without confusion, those in the rear quickly closing up the gaps left by their fallen comrades." [42]

So, in iron discipline and cold nerve, the First Delaware and the Eighth and Fourth Ohio marched straight ahead with fixed bayonets and without firing a gun. In constantly dwindling numbers they climbed forward until the almost hidden stone wall ahead of them burst into flame, and the slaughter grew overwhelming. Men could not stand this without firing. But when they fired, they stopped; and when they stopped, they could not start again. And then it was over, and the remnants clung to the ground or dropped down the hill. In twenty minutes Kimball's brigade lost 520 men.

This, with variations, was the pattern. Andrews' brigade came next and lost 342 before it stopped. Palmer followed. His casualties were 291. The division (counting artillery) lost 1,160.

Hancock's turn now, and Samuel K. Zook led his brigade out and up. It marched in bravery, and it lost 527 men before it reached the end of its journey. Thomas F. Meagher's turn came next, a fiery outfit from New York, Massachusetts, and Pennsylvania called the Irish Brigade—it collapsed with a loss of 545. Caldwell brought up the division rear, walked firmly into destruction, and came out with casualties of 942. The division's loss exceeded 2,000 men.

Couch's last division, O. O. Howard's, followed with obstinate intrepidity, and again brigade followed brigade, was slaughtered, lost contact, broke into fragments, hugged the tiny dips in the slope where it could find them, disappeared in the rear, strained in the torment of unattended wounds, or lay still in death—ripped, torn, twisted in the grotesque indignities of canister and musket fire. The corps lost 4,114 men and was through for the day.[43]

Lee and Longstreet, peering through smoke that hung over the field of horror, checked events in their own lines carefully. At some moment during the day, probably early when the scene was brilliant, before the dead and wounded loomed large, Lee turned to Longstreet and said: "It is well that war is so terrible, or we would grow too fond of it." [44]

When the attacks had continued long enough to disclose their severity, Longstreet ordered Kershaw's brigade to join the front line in the sunken road. When Cobb was killed, and almost simultaneously Cooke was wounded, Kershaw was ordered to take charge in the front line, and three of Ransom's regiments came forward. Soldiers stood four deep, in places six deep. Firing, stepping back to load, coming up to fire again, they constituted a strange production line for the mass delivery of bullets. So rapidly did they fire that their principal problem was, not the enemy in front, but their own dwindling ammunition.

That problem grew so large with the batteries that the Washington Artillery, unable to obtain more ammunition, had to be pulled out. The sight of its departure and the movement of other batteries under E. P. Alexander in replacement led Federal officers at a distance to think that Lee's defense was breaking up. About 3 P.M. on some parts of the field, about 4 P.M. on other parts, the terrible march of the brigades up the hill began again.

But it was the same story. Orlando B. Willcox's Ninth Corps, occupying the ground between Couch and Franklin (his left division was Burns', which operated with Franklin), sent S. D. Sturgis' division to support Couch's crumbling left. Edward Ferrero's brigade advanced under heavy fire, broke down, found depressions for shelter, and lay in them the rest of the day, firing intermittently at the stone wall. A second Sturgis brigade under James Nagle met the same fate. Its losses were 500, and Ferrero's were 491.

Amiel W. Whipple's division (Stoneman's corps of Hooker's center grand division) sent forward Samuel S. Carroll's small brigade. It made a brilliant attempt, but it met the common fate. Griffin's division (Butterfield's corps, Hooker's grand center division) sent in a brigade, James Barnes'; it collapsed with 500 casualties.

Two other Griffin brigades stormed up the slopes, Jacob B. Sweitzer's and T. B. W. Stockton's, to no avail.

Toward the end of the day Andrew A. Humphreys' division of Butterfield's corps sent forward Peter H. Allabach's brigade with the standard results and then called, in almost the last gesture of the day, when the dusk was beginning to settle down, on Erastus B. Tyler's brigade.

Tyler's men advanced with a hurrah. Firing not a shot, they strode forward until they reached the lines of men lying where they had halted in depressions. In Humphreys' words:

> They called to our men not to go forward, and some attempted to prevent by force their doing so. The effect upon my men was what I apprehended—the line was somewhat disordered, and, in part, forced to form into a column, but still advanced rapidly. The fire of the enemy's musketry and artillery, furious as it was before, now became still hotter. The stone wall was a sheet of flame, that enveloped the head and flanks of the column. Officers and men were falling rapidly, and the head of the column was at length brought to a stand when close up to the wall. Up to this time not a shot was fired by the column, but now some firing began. It lasted but a minute, when, in spite of all our efforts, the column turned and began to retire slowly . . . the united efforts of General Tyler, myself, our staffs, and the other officers could not arrest the retiring mass. . . .[45]

In the two brigades more than 1,000 men went down.

There were other attacks—one by George W. Getty's division of Willcox's corps, so late that darkness obscured both sides, but the climax had come and passed. The long list of brigades and divisions that rolled forward like waves beating on a shore tells the story of the separated and futile tapping. Here and there, by some miracle, a bold or reckless spirit managed to reach within 25 or 30 yards of the wall, but the lines of the dead were thickest from 100 to 150 yards out. "Every man fought as if the fate of the day depended upon his own individual exertion," Sturgis thought. "The advance in line of battle in the face of the terrific fire from the enemy's batteries and rifle-pits was magnificent," Ferrero recorded.

But individual and unit bravery could not make up for this kind of warfare. "At each attack," Longstreet reported, "the slaughter was so great that by the time the third attack was repulsed, the ground was so thickly strewn with dead that the bodies seriously impeded the approach of the Federals." At the end "the dead were piled sometimes three deep, and when morning broke, the spectacle . . . was one of the most distressing I ever witnessed. The charges had been desperately bloody, but utterly hopeless." If he had been in Burnside's place, Longstreet added, he would have sought to resign rather than attack Lee in his stronghold.[46]

The attacks had cost the Federal right 7,817 casualties. With the 4,857 casualties in front of Jackson and the center, Burnside lost all told 12,674 men against 5,309 in Lee's forces. Within all of Longstreet's corps the casualties were only 1,589.[47] McLaws' division that stood the brunt suffered 616 casualties exclusive of the 242 of Barksdale's brigade earlier in the pontoon fighting. Ransom lost 534. Outside this realm of fire Hood had 251 casualties, Anderson only 66, and Pickett only 47.[48]

A. P. Hill's division of Jackson's corps lost more (2,120) than Longstreet's entire corps, and Early, with 932 casualties, more than McLaws or Ransom.

Jackson—to whom defense was only the start and a leap for his enemy's throat was the goal—had waited impatiently for the ending of Longstreet's battle. He expected Franklin to renew the attack against him, knowing that Federal strength was still large. When no signs of renewal appeared, Jackson turned to the idea of driving Franklin's force into the river. The enemy was still under occasional fire from Jackson's right where Walker's guns and Stuart's horse artillery were stationed. But the enemy still possessed superior artillery of high skill, both in Franklin's division and in guns on Stafford Heights across the river. It would be a risk to dare their worst.

Yet if Jackson's infantry could survive the artillery fire well enough to reach the enemy, the chance of tearing Franklin's division into bits excited Jackson's mind. "Those who saw him in that hour," wrote Cooke, "will never forget the expression of intense but suppressed excitement which his face displayed. The genius of battle seemed to have gained possession" of a leader who was ordinarily calm; "and his countenance glowed as from the glare of a great conflagration." [49]

Stuart played a role at this moment. His cavalry could do little in the circumstances in which the battle was fought, but his mind was not still. From his good, though distant, view of the Federal lines as they gathered below the River Road he thought the enemy was demoralized. He rode over to confer with Jackson. Jackson moved down close to observe personally the effect of Stuart's guns and the conditions ahead of him. He made up his mind: he would attack.

Three other decisions followed swiftly. First, Jackson would attack with his entire force—more than 30,000 men before the battle, nearer 26,000 now. Since the enemy was much more numerous, he would need all possible strength to hit him effectively. Second, the danger of the enemy artillery was so great that Jackson would not commit his full force until he knew definitely the strength of the artillery barrage it would encounter. He would adopt the unusual device of attacking with his artillery in the lead. It would measure the enemy's fire. The infantry would not plunge into it blindly. Third, Jackson would wait until sunset. He was taking a calculated risk, and he had to count the cost if the worst came to the worst. If the attack failed in full daylight, the Federal artillery would slaughter his men in retreat. If it failed after sunset, darkness would throw its protection over his broken lines.

The hour of these decisions was late in the afternoon. "As the sun declined toward the west," Dabney wrote, "he was seen sitting upon his horse a long time, with his watch in his hand, considering the effect of the cannonade with which Stuart was still plying the enemy's left, and counting the minutes until the sun should touch the horizon." [50] The time for organizing a large and complicated maneuver—changing 26,000 men from a tight defensive position into an assault force—was so short that it was not done well. D. H. Hill received his order—"toward sundown," he said [51]—in time to call for volunteer artillery officers for the hazardous duty of leading the assault. A. P. Hill received his order "about dusk." [52] D. H. Hamilton, commanding Gregg's brigade, had his order "at dark"; [53] but when he moved forward to the railroad, he found J. A. Walker's brigade there and learned that Walker had no order at all. Hood, whom Longstreet had directed to co-operate with Jackson if called on, learned of the plan at sunset. [54]

Early saw D. H. Hill moving forward "about sundown" and heard for the first time of the movement from one of his brigadiers. A Jackson aide (Lieutenant Morrison, Anna's brother) arrived shortly with the word that Early should hold himself in readiness to advance. In a few minutes one of his own aides galloped up with the further word that Early was to command the advance on the right, regulating his distance behind the artillery by the effect the artillery was having on the enemy. This order put Early in an embarrassing position.[55] His brigades were scattered, and if he was to command on the right, he would have to give orders to A. P. Hill, a higher-ranking and sensitive general. Early rode to the front, encountered Jackson, and must have mentioned his problem to the General. Learning that Early had Hoke's and Hays' brigades at hand, Jackson directed him to advance with them.

When Taliaferro received his order is not clear. Sandie Pendleton was riding with it when a musket ball (probably from a Federal sharpshooter among skirmishers on both sides who kept up sporadic exchanges during the afternoon) ripped through his overcoat, his undercoat, his trousers, and smashed against a pocketknife that Sandie thought saved his life.[56] The bullet bruised him badly but did not knock him out. It appears to have knocked out the delivery of Taliaferro's order.

To Jackson it did not matter. He was willing to plunge into the assault without waiting for the precise arranging of every detail. If he waited, the opportunity would disappear. It was now or never. In other engagements when it was to his advantage to hit fast he had attacked with the head of his column while the tail stretched far away. He had no doubt now that when this attack was launched the whole corps would swarm into the fight.

The end was anticlimax. Stuart launched the attack, as agreed, from the far right. A signal gun was to unleash him. He thought he heard it and pushed out sharpshooters and Pelham with his horse artillery at a trot. They swung forward, fired, advanced, fired, advanced; then the musket balls began to bite among them and enemy batteries came into action. The guns were in danger.

In the center, batteries rumbled out of the wood, bounced across the railroad track, and rolled down the slope—firing, advancing, firing. The massed infantry waited in the woods. But the guns had gone forward no more than a hundred yards when Jackson had his answer, loud and emphatic.

All across his front, close and far, the Federal artillery blazed in his face. A whirlwind of shells crashed everywhere in the open ground. It "so completely swept our front," Jackson reported, "as to satisfy me that the proposed movement should be abandoned." [57]

He countermanded it immediately. This time the orders went home fast enough. The guns scurried back to shelter. The infantry, never departing from the darkening woods, turned around and went off in search of bivouacs. The unfought counterattack was over.*

On the First Corps's front the last Federal attacks died out in darkness. It would have been well into the night before Longstreet could have regathered his divisions from their scattered defensive positions for counterattack had Lee desired to make one. He had no such thought. Lee's thoughts were on the next day. He expected —and even hoped—that Burnside would attack again. He was confident he could defeat Burnside again even if, as Lee also expected, Burnside would resort to more maneuver and less suicidal assault up the slope of Marye's Heights. When the generals gathered that night they thought, with the exception of Hood, that more fighting was to come.[58] There is no indication that Jackson saw Lee then.

Lee sent out orders to commanders to prepare for further enemy attack. To Jackson he wrote with a sense of urgency: "Will you direct your Ordnance Officer, Major Bier to send to Guinea's Depot *immediately* all the empty ordnance wagons he can, to be replenished with ammunition for which they must remain till loaded? To obtain as many wagons as possible, let him empty all he can in replenishing the ammunition of men and batteries." And in a postscript: "I need not remind you to have the ammunition of your men

---

* McGuire wrote to Henderson about Jackson's more detailed thinking. "He asked me how many yards of bandaging I had," said McGuire, "and when I replied that I did not know the exact number, but that I had enough for another fight, he seemed a little worried at my lack of information and showed his annoyance. I repeated rather shortly, 'I have enough for another battle,' meaning to imply that this was all that it was necessary for him to know. I then asked him: 'Why do you want to know how much bandaging I have?' He said: 'I want a yard of bandaging to put on the arm of every soldier in this night's attack, so that the men may know each other from the enemy.' I told him I had not enough cotton cloth for any such purpose, and that he would have to take a piece of the shirt tail of each soldier to supply the cloth, but, unfortunately, half of them had no shirts! The expedient was never tried. General Lee decided that the attack would be too hazardous" (Henderson, II, 324).

The meaning of the last sentence is not clear. According to Henderson, II, 322, when Jackson determined to attack, "a message was at once sent to Lee, requesting permission for an advance." Henderson does not report any action by Lee. Smith said Lee "came riding down the lines and counseled Jackson against his intended effort to 'drive them into the river.'" But no one else appears to have mentioned this ride, which would have been unusual while the First Corps was still under heavy attack. Lee would have had to ride several miles each way. Lee's reports say nothing about Jackson's counterattack, and there is no official evidence that he approved or disapproved it, or even that it was formally presented to him.

and batteries tonight, everything ready by daylight tomorrow. I am truly grateful to the Giver of all victory for having blessed us thus far in our terrible struggle. I pray He may continue it." [59] Lee wrote to Secretary Seddon at 9 P.M. in a brief report that "I expect the battle to be renewed at daylight." [60]

When Jackson reached his tent and the headquarters wagons (Hotchkiss placed the location at "Darnabus' Pond near Curtis Shop"), he found his friend Boteler there with a group from Richmond, including one of the Volck brothers, Adelbert or Frederick, both of whom had some facility in sketching. Boteler brought a bucket of oysters, and the General's Jim combined this unusual delicacy with normal rations.[61] There was satisfaction over the major events of the day, but the General was thinking of the gravely wounded Gregg. He had already sent Smith to convey his sympathy and good wishes. Smith found Gregg on a bed in a large room surrounded by surgeons and officers, and gave him Jackson's message. "He was much affected," Smith said, "and desired me to thank General Jackson for his thoughtful remembrance." [62]

After supper Volck, having obtained permission, began to sketch the General. Smith had to go out of the tent briefly. It was a night of brilliant auroral display, rare for that latitude, and rarer still for soldiers from farther south; and the army marveled at the northern lights. When Smith returned, he saw Volck working busily with his pencils, the remainder of the company silent and smiling, and the General erect on his campstool sound asleep.[63]

If Dabney's report is correct, it was not a night for sleep for the General, although nights after battle normally were. Jackson invited Boteler to share his tent, but after Boteler lay down for the night, he himself wrote until midnight, slept in his uniform for two or three hours, and then went to work again. His candle shone on Boteler's face, and the General set up a book for a shield.[64]

About 4 o'clock, thinking still of Gregg, he sent for McGuire and asked him to see what Gregg's condition was. Not content with that, he decided to go himself. He had heard that Gregg wished to see him. Arousing Smith, who had just returned after a hard night's search of commanders in the darkness to deliver the order about replenishing ammunition, he set out with him.

They came into the room of a dying man.[65] Gregg thought he had written something that offended Jackson, and he wished to express his regret. This he did in distress of spirit and in mortal pain. Jackson did not recall what he had in mind, but he told Gregg that he was not offended and that Gregg must not worry. Then, sitting close by the bed and taking Gregg's hand in his, he said: "The doctors tell me that you have not long to live. Let me ask you to dismiss this matter from your mind and turn your thoughts to God and to the world to which you go."

They were both much moved. Gregg, with tears in his eyes, said, "I thank you; I thank you very much."

The General walked out into the dawn, with what troubled spirit it is possible only to imagine. It had been a night of torture for many a soldier lying wounded on the slope. One newspaper reporter thought this mid-December night was mild,[66] but Couch was probably nearer right when he recorded that the night "was bitter cold and a fearful one for the front line hugging the hollows in the ground, and for the wounded who could not be reached. Many died of wounds and exposure, and as fast as men died they stiffened in the wintry air, and on the front line were rolled forward for protection to the living." [67]

But a dying comrade and friend was one thing, and the war's duties were another. When McGuire asked the General, back at his headquarters where the staff was still somber, what was the best way of dealing with the greatly superior numbers of the enemy, he answered swiftly and succinctly: "Kill them, sir! Kill every man!" *

Lee put the army to work on the 14th digging trenches, throwing up earthworks, scouring out holes for riflemen, and providing shelter for the guns. Jackson had Early and Taliaferro in the front line now, with D. H. Hill behind them and A. P. Hill in reserve. By night he shifted D. H. Hill to he front, A. P. Hill next, and Taliaferro and Early to the rear. He himself was reconnoitering much of the day, starting early. Lee rode up early too, and he and Hood and Jackson climbed to Prospect Hill where Walker's guns were placed. After the fog lifted, they could see, with their long flank view, the whole of Franklin's force. To these soldiers' eyes it looked powerful: the men

---

* Henderson quotes McGuire to this effect. (Henderson, II, 326.) McGuire told more than once of this incident. In another account of it (*S.H.S.P.*, XIX, 309) he described Jackson as walking away from Gregg's bedside in silence. Then: "When we got to the camp he looked up at the sky for a moment and said: 'How horrible is war!' I said: 'Horrible, yes, but we have been invaded. What can we do?' 'Do?' he said, and his manner was savage and his voice ringing. 'Do? Thrash them!'"

well uniformed, the guns numerous, the lines firm, the appearance of discipline strong. Hood pointed out that no standards were up, and they could not understand why not. But they were all impressed. Jackson asked Hood to estimate the number of soldiers in view. Hood said 50,000. Jackson commented that he had put the number at 55,000.[68] They were both close, but Jackson was nearer the number remaining after the fighting on the 13th.

Aside from an occasional shell and the popping of the sharpshooters as they crept around no-man's land for chance shots, there was no activity. Nor was there any in front of Longstreet where the shelters around the town looked like defenses against expected attacks. Lee could not understand, nor could his generals. What was Burnside waiting for? So sure was Lee that eventually Burnside would resume his attack that he would not give up his own superb defensive position. He waited.

Burnside had indeed been determined to resume the attack and had even thought of launching his entire old corps, the Ninth, with himself in the lead—a strange idea for the commander of an army that still numbered more than 100,000. But the generals who had crossed the river and had lived with yesterday's slaughter had no hope of breaking the lines against which they had battered without success. They let Burnside know, and he bowed to their common judgment.[69]

The day of strange quiet, with the armies not much more than a half-mile apart, ran out, and the wounded on the slope suffered through another long winter night. The 15th came on in the same unearthly calm. Jackson was up by 5 o'clock, lively in the expectation that surely Burnside would attack now. But instead the white flags of truce appeared in the Federal lines, and officers came forward with requests for an agreement for the burial of the dead. Jackson was willing enough for that, but after unsatisfactory earlier experiences he insisted upon having a high officer sign the agreement, not a junior, and he held up the proceedings until he had won. Before Smith went out to meet the Federals, Jackson told him: "If you are asked who is in command of your right, do not tell them I am, and be guarded in your remarks."

While Smith was with the Federal group, a Federal surgeon came up. Smith recognized him as John Junkin, an acquaintance of old days in Lexington, brother of Elinor Junkin, and therefore brother-in-law of Jackson. Junkin had gone north at the start of the war with his father, the Rev. George Junkin. He asked Smith to give his regards to the General and to deliver a message from his father. Smith, with the General's admonition in mind, was wary.

"I will do so with pleasure when I meet General Jackson," he told Junkin. But that officer smiled.

"It is not worth while for you to try to deceive us," he replied. "We know that General Jackson is in front of us." [70]

When Jackson heard from Smith of this meeting, he wrote to Margaret Junkin Preston back in Lexington to give her this glimpse of her brother. Margaret's journal entry for December 19 speaks of Jackson's letter having been "most kindly written amidst the hurry of a day or two succeeding the Fredericksburg battle." In January she wrote in her journal: "I think a great deal about my father and sister, and am about to try to get a letter to them thro' General Jackson." She sent such a letter to Jackson by a chaplain. In March she received a note from Jackson "promising to do all he could to get a letter I sent him for Sister Julia, across the lines." [71]

That night of December 15 a storm came up with rain and a high wind from the southwest, blowing from the Confederate lines toward the Federal bivouacs in the low land between the River Road and the Rappahannock. The next morning the fog hung low again. Soon a Confederate skirmisher came running back in excitement, and far up the line toward Fredericksburg another, and then another. Lee had come over to Jackson's front, and together they rode across D. H. Hill's position in Jackson's first line. Hill was talking to a North Carolina colonel, Bryan Grimes. He blurted out a report from Grimes that the enemy had left that front. Jackson turned immediately to Grimes and ordered him to send skirmishers down and see where the enemy was.

It was true. Between darkness and dawn of the long winter night, nearly fourteen hours and in conditions ideal for the purpose, the entire Federal army had recrossed the river. It had moved silently, carrying all guns and all equipment and pulling back the bridges on which it had crossed. Hours later, when Longstreet's men pressed into empty Fredericksburg, they learned that troops poured through the streets all night, jamming them from side to side, marching through the rain and wind with remarkable quiet, and leaping swiftly

with word or action—"Put out that light! Put out that light!" [72]—on
any man in Fredericksburg who lit a candle.

Even in a maneuver in peacetime this would have been a remarkable exploit. In war, with the Confederate forces only some 800
yards from the advanced Federal troops, with the vast equipage of
the superbly supplied Federal army to move, including all the rolling guns, this was extraordinary.

How Lee's army, how Longstreet's and Jackson's corps, were so
lax in contact with the enemy is difficult to understand even today.
Confederate apologists laid much to the weather, especially the
wind that blew (it was held) all sounds away. The very strength of
the defensive positions exercised a psychological effect, pinning the
troops to them, building up the hope that Burnside would attack
again, and relaxing the aggressive spirit that would have kept in
better touch with the enemy. How much damage Lee could have
done in the darkness is beyond estimation. But he was much cha-
grined. The Army of Northern Virginia had won its most strictly
defensive battle with ease and with heavy casualties for the enemy,
but it had not exploited the victory in any degree. The army's leaders knew that an opportunity had been lost, and some of them wondered whether it would come again.

To the normal thanks and appreciation in reports Lee added unusual words about Longstreet and Jackson. His full comment included not only praise for the disposition and management of their
respective corps, but this: "Besides their services in the field—
which every battle of the campaign from Richmond to Fredericksburg has served to illustrate—I am also indebted to them for valuable counsel, both as regards the general operations of the army
and the execution of the particular measures adopted." [73]

The emphasis upon "valuable counsel" was an emphasis upon the
new status, as corps commanders, of Longstreet and Jackson, and
simultaneously on their new relation to Lee. There was never any
question about his own status, which had risen in brilliance as well
as excellent administration, as none recognized better than his two
corps commanders. But at the same time he was giving fresh recognition to them as his principal counselors.

Jackson's own administrative spirit emerges from the report of
his chief provost marshal, Maj. D. B. Bridgford, who had joined
the staff in July originally as ordnance officer. Before the Fredericks-

burg battle Bridgford received orders (in his own words) "to shoot all stragglers who refused to go forward, or, if caught a second time, upon the evidence of two witnesses to shoot them." This was Jackson's answer to the excessive straggling in the Second Manassas and Maryland campaigns.

Bridgford did not shoot anyone. He placed a line from his command behind the entire corps to arrest soldiers without proper passes for authorized business, and a surgeon was on hand to examine soldiers claiming to be sick. "When a sufficient number were collected together," as Bridgford described the process, "I sent them under charge of cavalry to be delivered to the first major general whose command was going into the fight, to place them in front and most exposed portion of his command. I am happy to state," Bridgford continued, "the number arrested and sent forward were comparatively few in consideration of the size of the army." [74] During the 13th and 14th "the number sent in under guard was only 526," and others were turned back because their passes were not properly made out.

Jackson thought enough of this achievement to give it special mention in his report. It seemed to him "further evidence of the improving discipline and spirit of the army." A. P. Hill thought "the absence of all straggling was remarkable," [75] and Early noted that "the absence of straggling or skulking to any considerable extent was a gratifying fact." [76]

Once Burnside's withdrawal was clear, Lee expected a renewal of his efforts farther down the Rappahannock. He sent one of Stuart's cavalry brigades southward. When word came of a Federal threat at Port Royal, he directed Jackson to follow with the Second Corps. By 1 P.M. on December 16 Early's division was leading the march toward Port Royal.

The corps followed the River Road into the thick woods that pressed hard upon it below the Massaponax, Jackson and his staff in the lead. Later in the afternoon the news reached him that Port Royal was clear—there was no sign of a Federal crossing. Jackson halted the column, ordered it to reverse course to find a better bivouac area, and pondered how he himself could turn back along a narrow road full of soldiers beside whom he did not like his party to push its way and from whose cheers—inevitable these days—he shrank. He considered going back on foot, the better to escape attention; and he inquired about other routes or cross-country cutoffs. There was no choice. He turned his horse and rode carefully back along the narrow road.

So began a tribute to its commander by the Second Corps that was spontaneous, full of good will, and universal. The soldiers looked up to see beside them Old Jack on his horse, close enough to touch— and instinctively they let themselves go. The whoops and cheers rolled along the column, company by company, regiment by regiment, brigade by brigade. They had Old Jack where he could not escape, and he had to face the music.

He was at this time at the very peak of his reputation: an inexplicable figure in the new Fredericksburg uniform, a general about whom the tall tales were wonderful to hear and tell, and perhaps to enlarge; a victor on the battlefields whose methods were rarely conventional and often a surprise; and a leader whom they had learned to trust. He would work them until their bones ached, but he would produce marvelous triumphs, and he was never like anyone else.

Look at Second Manassas! Look at Harper's Ferry and Sharpsburg! Look at the events they had just passed through! Look at a thousand details of what he did and how he did it, what he said, which officers he cracked down on, what new inordinately strict orders he would invent next!

Something of all this, something of the satisfaction of winning another big battle, something of the confidence of an army that had grown to the largest size it had ever known (or would ever know again), and was beginning to think itself invincible—something of such a combination rose with the revelry that greeted, embarrassed, and followed the General as he made his way through their ranks.

For the following staff officers there was another tale to tell. No soldier liked a staff officer. Everybody knew a staff officer trailed in reflected glory and had it infinitely softer in his encampments than the infantry. "Close up! Close up!" the orders rose from the ranks to a hurrying lieutenant or major. "You'll get lost," they told him. "You'll never find him."

Soldiers' cheers for the General, in lesser but impressive volume, had now become almost standard behavior. Nearly every diarist, journal keeper, letter writer, and historian records the common belief that shouts and cries at a distance arose from one of two causes. "It's Jackson or a rabbit," men in the ranks assured each other.

Eventually the General and his staff made their way out of the pine tunnel lined with soldiers and reached clearer ground where the trees were farther apart, the fallen leaves were more abundant, and men could stretch out. Night had come on. The headquarters wagons were lost along the road. No one had any rations. The air was growing sharp and raw. A large and luxurious house was somewhere close, the home of the Corbins at Moss Neck. So much was intimated to the General, but he would have none of that. They would bivouac where they were and as they were, cold and hungry, with a long December night before them.

The couriers rounded up wood and built roaring fires. They discovered a large, hollow tulip-poplar tree and built one fire at its base; and sparks danced upward into the skies while the miserable young men watched. They lay down with their feet to the fire, angry as hornets but keeping their mouths shut. Old Jack! Why not go to Moss Neck? What was the sense—

A crackle, then a cracking and rending sound broke into their consciousness. A great crash shook them. The tree! The tulip-poplar! It collapsed and fell—to the other side, luckily—and its stump of a chimney stood before eyes that were hopelessly wide open now.

The young men looked at the General to see if he was relenting. He could be human. When someone said Hugh McGuire knew this part of the country, the General sent him scouting to see if he could rustle something to eat. Off he went, and back he came with half a ham and some biscuits. They ate voraciously. Still, this was not enough, and the long night was ahead.

The General gave up. In maneuvers so swift that he would have admired their skill at any other time the staff sought and won the invitation, and the General was leading the way to Moss Neck. Presently they stood, marveling in the darkness, where lights were welcoming them from window after window in a long brick house of great frontage. They looked with admiration and delight at its dignity and impressive size sitting quietly on a knoll among the trees and inviting them to enter.

Jackson had found on this knoll his home for the next three months —the happiest time he was to know since Anna had left him in Winchester bearing the daughter whom now perhaps he would have the chance to see.

# THE WINTER
# at MOSS NECK

*"Always mystify, mislead,
and surprise the enemy . . ."*

The house at Moss Neck, only a few years old, measured
more than 250 feet from wing to wing. The two-story brick structure in the center, rising to a pointed roof and a small cupola, with
chimneys on each side, stretched out long many-windowed arms
to identical wings. These were a single story high with a chimney
in each gabled roof. Above a columned doorway a second-story
porch extended across the middle part of the central house. The
depth of the structure was slight, except in the center, and its length
and lack of height made it unusual; but from the front this was an
impressive house, architecturally familiar in its fundamentals, although different in detail and distinctive in spirit. Young Smith
thought it was designed "after the style of an English country residence."[1]

Its interior lived up to its outer promise. The entrance hall was
broad and gracious, and the ceilings were high. The main rooms
had much fine teak and mahogany paneling with intricate carving
and plaster designs for the ceiling. All the large rooms had marble
mantelpieces, and the floors of the south and north porticoes were
laid with marble slabs of different colors. Much of the furniture
was missing at this time, after Federal troops had occupied the
region and local control had deteriorated.[2] The house was lighted
with gas and equipped with coal grates, the fuel being brought by
boats on the Rappahannock to the Moss Neck landing.

The front looked southward, across a yard filled with forest trees;

and the rear, which was much like a second front, gave a view toward the river, nearly two miles away, and to the hills beyond it. A kitchen, icehouse, laundry, and other buildings stood to one side. Out from the left wing, on the front side, about 135 feet from the house, stood a small frame structure a story and a half high, that was—after the custom at many country homes—the owner's office. It became Jackson's home.

There was a small lobby in the front, a closet for wood on the left and a narrow stair on the right to the attic, where young Smith, the aide, slept. Straight ahead, across the room, was a fireplace. The General's cot was on one side and a table and chair on the other. Several stools completed the furniture. On each side of the door were shelves with books of all kinds except (said Douglas) military books. There were legal, medical, scientific, and agricultural books; books in various languages; books for sportsmen and horsemen; ladies' magazines and black letter-books.

The owners showed here their fondness for hunting and fishing and for sports of many kinds. The office housed fishing tackle, traps, skins, antlers, feathers, engravings of race horses, pictures of game-cocks, fine dogs, and cats.[3] The room had its fascinations, but many an officer who thought he knew the General was startled to see him in such surroundings.

James Parke Corbin built Moss Neck when he was a man of wealth. (Jackson heard that it cost $60,000.[4]) Richard Corbin was its master now, but he was away—though in the neighborhood—as a private in the Ninth Virginia Cavalry. His young wife was the mistress of the house, and their five-year-old daughter, Jane Welford Corbin, lived there. Living there, too, was Kate Corbin, Richard's sister, a young woman of charm who would become in this winter of 1862–1863 an exciting personality for more than one young officer on Jackson's staff.

The General received an invitation to stay in the house, but he would not accept it. He had the headquarters tents pitched in the woods about 500 yards from the house. The location was convenient for the scattered units of the Second Corps, and the utilities of Moss Neck were helpful.

"Do you approve of your accommodations, General?" a cavalry-man waiting in front of the house asked him.

"Yes, sir," the General replied. "I have decided to make my quarters here."

"I am very much pleased," the cavalryman told him, and then added, "I am Mr. Corbin, the owner of the property." [5]

But when the weather turned worse in a few days—it was pointing already to a bad winter—Jackson's ear gave him trouble, the only recorded instance when he suffered from physical disability during the war except from fever during the Seven Days. McGuire treated him for several days and then advised the General to get under a roof. [6]

Still the General would not accept the offer of a room in the big house. But the office was there, and he turned to its protecting walls and roof—and to its sportsman's paradise. When the commanding general of the Second Corps had finished with his military duties, the professor of natural and experimental philosophy could study government reports, the owner and operator of the Lexington farm could read the *Farmer's Register,* and Uncle Cummins' jockey could revel in the exploits of "Boston" and other great figures of the race track. Others might smile at Old Jack among the sports prints. He took them in his stride. [7]

In the postbattle realignments Longstreet had extended his sector from above Fredericksburg to Massaponax Creek, taking over the area Jackson had held. Jackson's sector extended now, as it had before the battle, from the Massaponax along the river to Port Royal, nearly 20 miles. [*]

In all Lee was watching the Rappahannock over a 25-mile front. After Burnside's exhibition at Fredericksburg, no one could tell what he would do next. Most of Lee's command went into winter quarters well back from the river, but picketing along the stream was required. Brigades went down to the banks for stated periods. The military duties there were slight, but the weather could be bad, and the men turned back gladly to the huts they had built.

Cavalry raids had begun before the battle, with Wade Hampton leading a 208-man force across the Rappahannock on November 27 and a 520-man force on December 10 toward Occoquan on the Telegraph Road as it ran directly north toward Alexandria. Both

[*] Smith said that D. H. Hill was at Grace Episcopal Church, A. P. Hill at a house halfway between D. H. Hill and Jackson's headquarters, Taliaferro was "near us," and Early was "below, near Carolina Academy." (*S.H.S.P.*, XXXXIII, 37.)

were neat affairs: disruptions of Federal pickets, captures of men
and horses, no losses of importance. After the battle, on December
17, Hampton tried for Occoquan again, and achieved good results
once more. On December 26 Stuart led 1,800 men on a long, involved, and moderately successful sweep far to the north and northwest that lasted until January 1. But nothing of major military importance was happening.

Burnside did initiate a massive movement January 20, under
stimulation from Halleck, and marched up the Rappahannock,
crossed the river above Fredericksburg, and came down on Lee's
left flank. But rain poured down on men, horses, and wheels, and
reduced all roads to quagmires. The army bogged down in what became unofficially the Mud March. It was over in two days, though
mud-covered soldiers were returning to Falmouth over a much
longer period.

Later, in March, the weather improved briefly to the west, and
Federal cavalry pushed across the Rappahannock at Kelly's Ford.
Fitzhugh Lee ripped into them with his own cavalry. Stuart was on
hand. There was a sharp clash of galloping horsemen and sharpshooters behind a stone fence, but with no great military significance.
What mattered most to the Confederates was that young Maj. John
Pelham, "the gallant Pelham" of Lee's praise—whose handling of
guns at Fredericksburg led Lee to tell Jackson he ought to have a
Pelham on each flank [8]—happened to be in the neighborhood. He
had started out to pay a social call in Orange Court House, but he
couldn't resist a fight—and he fell in a moment of high exultation
with a piece of shell in the back of his head, and died within hours.
The loss of no other young officer at that time could have caused
so much mourning in the army.

On January 25 Burnside lost the command of the army—he had
proposed to Lincoln that he remove Hooker along with several division commanders and other officers—and Hooker came in as his
successor. He came in looking a little solemn with the responsibility
of command and with the letter from Lincoln, which he said sounded
like a father talking to his son, telling him that "there are some things
in regard to which I am not quite satisfied with you" and ending
with: "Beware of rashness, but with energy and sleepless vigilance
go forward and give us victories." [9]

But along the Rappahannock the pickets viewed each other more calmly. Winter was taking command, and the rain and the snow and the mud were reducing their work to formalities. They would not shoot unless they had to, and they much preferred to holler across the waters, sometimes gibing, sometimes inquiring, and to listen to each other's bands and to exchange tunes. Presently adventurous spirits were sending tobacco and newspapers across in tiny boats from Lee's side and were receiving in return coffee, sugar, and newspapers from the North. The traffic grew, and the little boats swelled into fleets of small craft.

A strange war it was! In the woods where the Second Corps lay and on the slopes that led up to Marye's Heights the killing had been determined and thorough. But now human nature had taken charge.

Once, when Jackson was inspecting near the river the Confederate pickets who saw him began cheering. The noise carried across the water, and a hail from the other side was followed by a question as to what the cheering was about.

"General Stonewall Jackson," a picket shouted back.

Immediately from the Federal bank came the cry: "Hurrah for Stonewall Jackson!" [10]

Gradually the army settled down into winter quarters. Jackson worried about whether the men could stand the weather without tents, nearly always without adequate winter clothing, and sometimes without shoes.[11] They showed soldiers' ingenuity in constructing huts, crude but effective. Lee put them to fortifying for miles along the Rappahannock. They worked all winter on what became before spring the most elaborate field fortifications that the Army of Northern Virginia had ever seen.

Jackson plunged into military work. His battle reports were far behind. Looking around for an officer to collect material and write drafts (he would do the refining), he called back Lieut. Col. Charles J. Faulkner, originally of Martinsburg, four times a member of Congress, and Minister to France for two years preceding the war. Faulkner was an old friend.[12] Jackson had designated him as an aide in the Romney expedition period [13] and later sent him to Richmond [14] to plead with the government about needs in that part of northwestern Virginia. More recently Faulkner had been on duty with the Adjutant General in Richmond. He had much to learn about Jackson's campaigns, but he was an industrious man. Before the

winter was out he had enabled Jackson to bring the record up to
date, although the report on Sharpsburg was delayed. Jackson
named him his senior assistant adjutant general, and simultaneously
elevated Sandie Pendleton to major and called him junior assistant
adjutant general. In the handling of military operations Pendleton
was in effect the chief of staff.

Faulkner had a difficult assignment. The reports of most sub-
ordinates were on hand, but there were many disputed points, and
some of the principals were dead or absent with wounds. Jackson
was a stern taskmaster. He insisted that reports be kept lean—"severe
Roman simplicity," Faulkner said [15]—and that they contain no statement that could not be verified. He eliminated a reference to
Winder's being missed after his death at Cedar Run because, said
Jackson, it would look like a reflection on Paxton, his successor.[16]
He weighed carefully the amount of emphasis to place on Cross
Keys and Port Republic. He required Hotchkiss to correct a sketch
of troop positions at Cedar Run.[17] He directed Faulkner to eliminate
certain words because they might tell more than the enemy should
know.[18] He strained to give proper credit and, where the claims were
conflicting, to satisfy both parties but adhere to the exact truth.

To write such reports six months after the engagement proved
so annoying and difficult that Jackson turned once to Faulkner and
told him that when the corps went into another battle, though he
hoped it would not, "I want you to get where you can see all that is
going on, paper and pencil in hand, and write it down so we may
not have so much labor and so many conflicting statements, and then
write up the report at once after the battle." *

The administrative work of the corps required, in different ways,
the same exactitude. The General received each morning, for reports and plans, his quartermaster, commissary, ordnance, and medical officers.[19] His adjutant general brought in two arrays of papers,
one from the army and the other, through Lee, from the War Department; and another line of papers was coming up from the di-

---

* Hotchkiss Diary, March 26, 1863.
  Douglas thought (Douglas, 210–211) the reports under Faulkner's efforts were
"very unsatisfactory and do both General Jackson and Colonel Faulkner great injustice," and particularly the staff. He thought Sandie Pendleton would have been
a better choice for this work. Jackson was such a scrupulous editor and rewriter of
Faulkner's reports that if there is any merit in Douglas' complaints, which others
do not appear to have made in like degree, some of the fault at least should rest with
Jackson.

vision commanders. The inspector general must report, the military courts must be checked, the progress of topographical engineers with maps must be checked, and reports on the road building must be made. The General worked fast, but he was exacting. At the end he had many letters to write. Signing a pile of them in the evening sometimes he fell asleep, pen in hand.[20]

Absences from the corps drew his special interest—he who in two years was never absent a day. He wanted to fill his ranks. One of his brigades listed on its rolls 1,200 absentees, men who had disappeared in one way or another. If all these could be brought back, the General wrote to Boteler in Richmond, the army would be so increased that, with divine blessing, one more campaign would sweep the enemy from the soil of the Confederate States.[21] He proposed a detailed plan that would rest on rewards for the apprehension and return of all men reported absent without leave, the money to come from the government with reimbursements to be taken eventually from the pay of the returned soldiers.

When Richmond did not put the plan into effect, Jackson turned to another effort. He directed division commanders to send a detail to the area where each regiment was formed and to gather conscripts and volunteers and bring them to the command without passing them through camps of instruction. For this purpose he laid down suggestions about kind treatment, arguments to prospects, arrangements for letting them choose commands, and assuring conscripts the privileges of volunteers.[22]

When Brig. Gen. Alfred Iverson of D. H. Hill's division greatly desired a furlough but was turned down, and then threatened to resign, Jackson wrote to his division commander on February 10: "No one can tell what day a battle may be fought. Whilst I would regret to see General Iverson resign yet I would rather see him do so than to approve of his furlough under present circumstances." [23]

Deserters got short shrift. Six of them from the Stonewall Brigade were convicted in February by a court-martial, and three of the six were ordered to be executed. Two others were to be flogged, and one was sentenced to six months' hard labor. Paxton, their commander, was shocked. He thought only one, chosen by lot, ought to be shot. But the General turned sharply upon his fellow townsman. "With the exception of this application," he wrote in denial, "General Paxton's management of his Brigade has given me great satisfaction. One great difficulty in the army results from over lenient Courts, and it appears to me that when a Court Martial faithfully discharges its duty that its decisions should be sustained. If this is not done, a lax administration of justice and corresponding disregard for law must be the consequence." [24]

Lee took the same stand, upholding the sentences, and only Davis saved the three from death, though not from flogging.[25] But Hotchkiss recorded in his diary that a deserter from the First (Stonewall) Brigade was shot on February 28. Eight days later he told of three men from the same brigade being "whipped for desertion." [*]

A more embarrassing issue rose over allegations against Brig. Gen. J. R. Jones, who had commanded the Stonewall Brigade at Sharpsburg and more recently the Second Brigade in the same division. The charge was cowardice—an offense with which no general of the Army of Northern Virginia had ever been formally charged.[26] Hotchkiss' diary records the charge on February 27. On March 2 Pendleton wrote [27] to Trimble that information had reached Jackson of a captain's having spoken of Jones as being "deficient in courage" or "as having misbehaved in the presence of the enemy." It was Jackson's opinion, Pendleton wrote, that an officer who made such comment should either prefer charges or publicly retract what he had said. If the captain did neither, Jackson thought charges ought to be preferred against him.

The General thereupon called upon divisional officers not to forward the resignation or application for leave of the captain in question until it was known if judicial action was necessary. If either the captain or General Jones was to be court-martialed for the state-

---

[*] Henderson records the execution of a soldier under Jackson who entered a private home and used insulting language to women there and of a soldier who struck his captain. Both these executions were earlier. In the second instance Henderson reports the Rev. Dr. Graham, of Winchester, who interceded, as saying his friend General Jackson used these words: "It is unquestionably a case of great hardship, but a pardon at this juncture might work a greater hardship. Resistance to lawful authority is a grave offense in a soldier. To pardon this man would be to encourage insubordination throughout the army, and so ruin our cause."

Henderson told also of four soldiers being executed for desertion. According to him, an unidentified chaplain went at the last to the General's tent to plead for them. The General, watch in hand, was pacing up and down. He heard the chaplain out. But at the latter's words: "General, consider your responsibility before the Lord. You are sending these men's souls to hell!" he grabbed the chaplain by the shoulders and told him sternly: "That, sir, is my business. You do yours!" and forced him out of the tent. (Henderson, II, 364, 365, 366.)

ments the captain had made, that officer should remain in the army until the case was disposed of.

General Jones remained in command of his brigade through the next engagement (at Chancellorsville, April 29–May 6), during which, in Colston's words, "owing to the ulcerated condition of one of his legs [he] was compelled to leave the field. . . ."[28] After the Chancellorsville engagement he retired.[29]

In another instance Jackson sent back to a military court for reconsideration the sentence of a convicted soldier in so far as the sentence "forfeits the rights of the accused to his discharge from the army and requires him to continue on duty with his company till the 1st of May, 1863." Jackson characterized this part of the sentence as "in conflict with the legal rights of the accused and unknown to the law and customs of the service . . . and is objectionable in placing the continuance of the accused in the army (which should be regarded as an honorary service) on the footing of a punishment."[30]

But the General could be blunt when he thought the need was great. He wrote Crutchfield to arrest a man and send him to the provost marshal "on charge of disloyalty in aiding the enemy to demoralize our army"—a serious offense—"by selling liquor to the troops after he had been notified not to do so."[31]

The winter was a period for all kinds of military housekeeping. Jackson kept courts at work on the banked-up cases which a corps in the field had not been able to attend to. He had many requests for furlough to consider. The effectiveness of units of his command, and even of junior officers, was much on his mind; and he pointed out to Hoke some defects in the Twenty-first North Carolina Regiment and to Brig. Gen. A. H. Colquitt, of D. H. Hill's division, other weaknesses in the Twenty-eighth Georgia.

Supply deficiencies were a problem always. The correspondence and orders of the winter disclose Lee's concern with scurvy and his directions that men should be sent to the field to gather sassafras buds, wild onions, garlic, lamb's quarter, and poke sprouts.[32] Sandie Pendleton sent out a circular instructing quartermasters and artillery officers "to browse their horses, as much as possible, on the twigs of the poplar, maple, sweet gum, etc., which can be cut in abundance, and also that the animals be allowed to graze in the bottoms of the small streams instead of being tied up all day."[33]

Promotions and changes of command, now a major problem for Lee, involved Jackson as a corps commander. Gregg's death and Cobb's wounding required new brigade commanders in the Second Corps, and others were in prospect. Jackson's own division, now under Taliaferro, a brigadier, needed a major general. Ewell's continued absence because of his wound at Groveton left Early, a brigadier, in command of Ewell's division. Soon the dispatch of D. H. Hill to North Carolina created a vacancy in another division. Promotions created vacancies in turn, and many changes among lower-ranking officers were necessary.

The shift of D. H. Hill drew no comment of a public nature from his brother-in-law. Federal forces in eastern North Carolina were showing more activity, and the Confederate resistance was weak and ineffective. The danger grew that they might cut important rail communications to Richmond. Word reached Lee also that Federal troops were moving toward Hampton Roads by ship down the Potomac and Chesapeake Bay. The whole region to the south and east of Richmond seemed stirring with Federal energy.

Early in January Lee started Ransom's two-brigade division for Richmond. In February, under War Department prodding, he followed with Pickett's division, and then with Hood's. To command these Longstreet set out on an independent operation in the Suffolk area. His presence there would stiffen all Confederate plans to the south and east, it was hoped, and would produce additional benefits in supplies. The loss to the Army of Northern Virginia in manpower was about 18,000 men. It left Lee with approximately 62,000. Burnside opposite him, and later Hooker, had twice as many.

If new major generals were to be commissioned, Jackson wanted for one Edward Johnson, the craggy brigadier who had been out with a wound since McDowell.* Everyone recognized the virtues of Early, and his choice, depending somewhat on Ewell's uncertain return, appears to have been taken for granted. Jackson's recommendation of Trimble in September was still on the record. He had told Trimble on October 30, in reply to that officer's request to continue under him, that "if you were only ready to take the field, I am

---

* "Whilst I highly prize Military education," Jackson had written in the previous May, "yet something more is required to make a general." He specified "judgement, nerve, and force of character," and he said then, as he did at other times, that "Merit should be the only basis of promotion." (William Porcher Miles Papers, Southern Historical Collection, Chapel Hill.)

of the opinion that there would be no difficulty in your being made a Maj. General & put in command of my division." [34]

The Early and Trimble promotions came through in January. The latter brought great disappointment to Taliaferro, then commanding Jackson's old division. He could stand no longer what he regarded as the affront of not being chosen, and he asked for transfer from the Army of Northern Virginia.[35] For the vacancy which his departure created Jackson recommended Brig. Gen. Raleigh E. Colston. Jackson had known him at Virginia Military Institute, where, after graduation, he taught French and later other subjects. After Seven Pines he was ill for months. Most recently he had been in southeastern Virginia, with the troops stationed there under Maj. Gen. Samuel G. French (Department of Southern Virginia), and he was now attached to Pickett's division. Though there was nothing against him, his field record was brief and undistinguished. But Jackson's conviction about him, like his conviction about Edward Johnson, whose record was also brief, was strong enough to convince Lee. Colston came to the Jackson division as a brigadier general, and, as it happened, the senior. That meant, so long as Trimble was still away, that he would command the division.

Trimble was an old Jacksonian, but in Edward Johnson and Colston, Jackson was recommending one officer with a short connection with his command and another who had none at all. This ran counter to his stated policy. Some promotions among artillery officers were necessary at this time after General Pendleton, at Lee's direction, had produced a plan of reorganization by which batteries would be grouped in artillery battalions and the battalions assigned to the corps, not to brigades or divisions. Each battalion would have a lieutenant colonel and a major.

Jackson sent to Lee a report from his own artillery chief, Crutchfield, listing objections to some promotions under contemplation and recommending others. "You will observe," Jackson wrote to Lee, "that I do not recommend the promotion of Captain [J. Gibbes] Barnwell, and the reason of this is, that I do not think it right to pass over officers who belong to my command, or have belonged to it, and are known to be worthy of promotion, and select one who has never been with me, and with whose qualifications I am unacquainted." [36] Jackson wanted promotion for Capt. R. P. Chew, then in the Valley but earlier, during Jackson's own Valley campaign, an artist with the guns.

Lee replied on February 27 that "I regret I do not concur altogether with the principle there laid down regulating claims to promotion. I think the interest of the service, as well as justice to individuals, requires the selection of the best men to fill vacant positions. It is on this principle that I applied for General [Henry] Heth for one of your brigades, and Colonel [E. Porter] Alexander for another. On the same principle many valuable officers have been lost to this army, but I think the general service has gained. I do not think it right, however, at any time to pass over worthy men who have done good service, unless you can get better." [37] Chew's battery, he thought, belonged to the cavalry brigade.

Jackson fired back immediately. "I am well satisfied," he wrote to Lee, "that there is nothing in my letter in opposition to this rule"—that is, to Lee's "selection of the best men to fill vacant positions" statement. "On the contrary," he continued, "my rule has been to recommend such as were, in my opinion, best qualified for filling vacancies. The application of this rule has prevented me from ever recommending for the command of my old brigade one of its own officers, because I did not regard any of them as competent as another, of whose qualifications I had a higher opinion. This rule has led me to recommend Col. Bradley T. Johnson for the command of Taliaferro's brigade."

Jackson added that he approved of promotion for Alexander, "as my indorsement on General Early's recommendation will show." As for Heth, whom Lee had chosen for promotion, "from what you have said . . . I have been desirous that he should report for duty." Then to a deeper statement of his views:

I desire the interest of the service, and no other interest, to determine who shall be selected to fill vacancies. Guided by this principle, I cannot go outside of my command for persons to fill vacancies in it, unless by so doing a more competent officer is secured. This same principle leads me to oppose having officers, who have never served with me, and of whose qualifications I have no knowledge, forced upon me by promoting them to fill vacancies in my command, and advancing them over meritorious officers well qualified for the positions, and of whose qualifications I have had ample opportunity of judging from their having served with me.

In my opinion, the interest of the service would be injured if I should quietly consent to see officers with whose qualifications I am not acquainted promoted into my command to fill vacancies, regardless of the merit of my own officers who are well qualified for the position. The same principle leads me, when selections have to be made outside of my command, to recommend those (if there be such) whose former service with me proved them well qualified for filling the vacancies.

That was why he recommended Chew. "As I hold my chief of artillery responsible for the efficiency of his artillery," he went on, "I feel it my duty to let him select his own officers, so far as I may be able to favor such selections, ever having in view the selection of the best qualified."

Then, finally, these blunt words: "I have had much trouble resulting from incompetent officers having been assigned to duty with me regardless of my wishes. Those who assigned them have never taken the responsibility of incurring the odium which results from such incompetency." [38]

Lee let the exchange end there. Actually the differences between the two appear more in refinements of degree than in principle. Lee had the broader view of the whole army. Jackson was intensely loyal to his own corps, though not so blindly loyal as to seek the promotion of an incompetent Second Corps officer when a qualified officer was available elsewhere. In seeking to have Colonel Alexander of the artillery reserve promoted to brigadier general and assigned to Lawton's old division, he went outside his own command. But he fought hard to obtain promotion for Crutchfield to brigadier general in the artillery. Crutchfield, he wrote to Cooper in Richmond, "took first honors at the V.M.I. and of all its graduates he is one of the most gifted. He has been my Chief of Artillery for more than eleven months. He has discharged his duty with great ability and fidelity." [39] But Jackson could not carry his point. Nor did he succeed in obtaining promotion for his engineer officer, Capt. J. K. Boswell.

Another picture should be set beside these promotion problems. Robert F. Hoke had a major whom he regarded as so inefficient as to be worthless, and he wished to rid himself of the officer. There must have been some conferring between Hoke and the corps headquarters. Finally Jackson wrote on February 11 to Hoke (through Sandie Pendleton) that if he wished the major dropped as an inefficient and worthless officer, Jackson would gladly approve, "but he does not think it would be right to relieve you of a bad officer by imposing him on someone else." [40]

In the midst of such winter activities A. P. Hill returned to his personal war again. His determination to bring Jackson to account for arresting him had been suspended in October—never dropped— after Lee had tried to show that no further action was necessary. Now, once the army was settled in winter quarters, Hill wrote to Lee on January 8 calling attention to the charges preferred against him by Jackson and requesting a trial. Two of his important witnesses had been killed, said Hill (Branch and Gregg), and others were leaving and would not be available. So strongly did he feel that he waived any claim he may have had to "officers my peers in rank," and offered to accept a court composed of officers of any degree. [41]

The charges he referred to dealt under the general charge of "neglect of duty" with marching conduct: on August 8, when Jackson charged that Hill failed to move in obedience to orders "but did continue in the vicinity of Orange until night, thus remaining a day's march in the rear of the position he should have occupied"; on August 19, when he failed to move, as ordered, when the moon rose, and neglected to give orders to his brigade commanders; on August 31, when he marched too fast, and continued to do so after Jackson called his attention to the pace, thus causing straggling; on September 4, when he failed to move his troops as ordered near Drainesville, and three other offenses on the same day, all relating to troop movements.

Since then Hill's conduct in the Harper's Ferry operation after being restored to command, and at Sharpsburg, had been excellent. Some fault might have been found with him at Fredericksburg, but not of a nature to justify formal charges. Hill had remained in command of the Light Division since his restoration before Harper's Ferry. But he was so deeply disturbed that Lee realized he would have to bring all possible persuasion to bear on him. The one thing Lee did not want was a court-martial involving two of the three best generals in his army. On January 12, with care and patience, Lee addressed Hill in one of the finest of all his letters:

Your letter of the 8th instant is received. At the time the charges preferred by General Jackson were first brought to my attention, in September last, I was unable to give them a careful examination, and have no recollection of having made any indorsement indicating an opinion as to their correctness, as intimated in your letter of the 30th September.

I do not think that in every case where an officer is arrested there is a necessity for a trial by a court-martial, and I consider yours as one in which such a proceeding is unnecessary.

A commanding officer has the right to make an arrest, and to release the officer arrested without prosecuting the matter further, when, in his judgment, the exigencies of the service require such a course. An arrest is often resorted to in order to give point and prominence to an expression of disapprobation, even when, in the opinion of the officer making it, the act is not one requiring a judicial investigation.

The exercise of this power may sometimes appear harsh, and in some cases may actually be so. But the power itself is one too important and essential to the maintenance of discipline to be denied because it may be abused. In the present instance, General Jackson exerted this authority for what he thought at the time good and sufficient reasons. He exercised a discretion which you or any other commanding officer must use, and which, I have said above, must be committed to superior officers for the good of the service.

In deciding whether the supposed offense is one which the rights of the person arrested or the good of the service requires to be brought before a court-martial, other considerations than those which induce the arrest must be taken into account.

Upon examining the charges in question, I am of opinion that the interests of the service do not require that they should be tried, and have, therefore, returned them to General Jackson with an indorsement to that effect. I hope you will concur with me that their further prosecution is unnecessary, so far as you are concerned, and will be of no advantage to the service.[42]

This admirable statement made no impression on Hill unless it led him to review all the circumstances of the controversy. It was more than two weeks before he replied to Lee's adjutant on January 29. But he had retreated not one inch. He wrote, after acknowledging Lee's letter:

I beg leave to state that I do not now nor ever have disputed the right of the superior to arrest any officer under him, and to release him whenever he saw fit so to do, or that he might do so and prefer no charges, provided the party arrested consented thereto. Otherwise an engine of tyranny is placed in the hands of commanding officers, to be exercised at their will, to gratify passions or whims, and against which there is no appeal. In my own case, the commanding general having returned the charges preferred against me by General Jackson without trial is a rebuke to him, but not as public as was General Jackson's exercise of power toward me. The general must acknowledge that if the charges preferred against me by General Jackson were true, that I do not deserve to command a division in this army; if they are untrue, then General Jackson deserves a rebuke as notorious as the arrest. I beg leave most distinctly to disclaim any credit which General Jackson may have given me for the good results of his punishment, as to my better behavior thereafter, and that its only effect has been to cause me to preserve every scrap of paper received from corps headquarters, to guard myself against any new eruptions from this slumbering volcano. I respectfully forward again my charges against Lieutenant-General Jackson, and request that he may be tried on them.

As to the indorsement of the commanding general on these charges, I will state that these charges were forwarded by me to General Jackson several days before I had any intimation that General Jackson intended to prefer charges against me, and that, so far as I know, his charges grew out of mine, not mine out of his.[43]

The Hill charges against Jackson, as already noted, have disappeared, and no copy is known to exist. Lee did not answer Hill's letter.

But still the controversy would not end. A difference of opinion had arisen between Lee and Hill which in origin had no relation to Jackson.[44] Hill held that all orders affecting his division, not only orders relating to strictly military matters but also those of the staff, should reach his division through him and by him be handed down to the proper officers. The medical officer of the corps, for instance, could not address directly the medical officer of the division but (Hill held) must go to him first.

Lee disagreed. "Otherwise," he said, "I shall have to give all directions, and the corps and division commanders, &c., have to attend to all the staff operations of their commands in addition to their military operations. . . ."[45] Lee referred the issue to the Adjutant General in Richmond for a ruling.

While he waited for this ruling, a new incident involving this issue came to light. Lee heard that a message copied from a Federal signal line, which under orders should be kept secret while being sent to the proper officer, was being talked about in Lane's headquarters. He directed Jackson to find out who had talked too much and to relieve him of duty. Jackson directed his signal officer, Capt. R. E. Wilbourn, to find out, and Wilbourn reported that Hill's signal officer, Capt. R. H. T. Adams, was the officer in question. Adams was reminded of the requirements, but he replied that he was responsible to Hill and that Hill's orders were different. With that Jackson relieved him of duty and directed that he report to Lee. Hill jumped in to defend his signal officer with an inquiry as to why Adams had been relieved—and the war began all over again.

While considering this situation, Jackson learned of—or for the first time made use of—a letter by Hill of November 13, five months earlier. It placed Hill's policy and actions under it on formal record. A minor controversy was running then about the same question, but on a different application of the Hill doctrine. Hill wrote then in a letter which Jackson now considered intently:

> I have received but one order from Maj. Gen. Jackson, to Capt. Adams, to detail three signal operators to report to Capt. Boswell. This order was received yesterday and obeyed the same day. A copy of this *same order* was received by Capt. Adams direct, not through me, and I directed him to pay no attention to it.

The combination of events now seemed to Jackson too much. He sent forward to Lee Hill's request for information about Captain Adams' being relieved from duty, and in his own endorsement of Hill's inquiry he inserted Hill's earlier statement of the previous November. Then he mounted to his own conclusion so far as the relations of Hill and himself were concerned. To Lee, Jackson wrote:

> When an officer orders in his command such disregard for the orders of his superiors I am of the opinion that he should be relieved from duty with his command, and I respectfully request that Genl Hill be relieved from duty in my Corps. It is very important to have harmony in my command; but to do so, orders must be obeyed. The within letter of yesterday from Genl. H. has not been replied to, as I deem it best not to countenance such an improper correspondence. If Genl. H. had properly asked for the information it would have been given.[46]

This was late in April. Lee set it aside, perhaps to ponder, perhaps to let it simmer, but clearly not to act upon it then. Before a week ran out, other and larger forces had taken hold. When they arrived they found Jackson and Hill acting on the battlefield with a stiff formality in personal relations, no doubt, but with a realization of the responsibility of each, with co-operation, and in the end with an extraordinary climax.

There would even be an anticlimax to all this. For eventually the Secretary of War, to whom the technical question had been referred, handed down his opinion on Lee's statement of the case in these words: "The opinion of General Lee approved." In consequence Lee wrote to Hill on May 8: "I request, therefore, that all orders from the chiefs of staff department may be considered as emanating directly from me, and executed accordingly." [47] But by May 8 these things did not matter to Jackson.

In January there were incidents that suggested the existence of differences between Jackson and Longstreet. Lee went to Richmond on January 16, but when Burnside showed signs of activity he hurried back on the 18th. (The activity was preliminary to the Mud March.) During Lee's absence of three days Longstreet was acting commander of the army, as he had been briefly on other occasions. He and Jackson had some discussion about the exposed position of Jackson's pickets near the Rappahannock, and Jackson wrote a note to Longstreet about it. The note was lost, and its contents are not definitely known.

Longstreet answered at length in a letter [48] which dealt with Longstreet's idea for protecting riflemen with traverses in trenches, spoke of the improbability of an enemy attack before spring, referred to Federal morale, dwelt on Confederate defenses, told of a note from Richmond about the movement of Pender's and Lane's brigades to Richmond, as previously agreed to by Lee, directed Jackson to see that they moved the next day, and instructed him in some detail how to do so. The tone was a little smug.

On the same day, though this letter does not show it, reports about Federal activity reached Longstreet and Jackson. Twenty years later Longstreet wrote that Jackson disagreed with his own view that the Federal advance would be above Fredericksburg and that the Second Corps should move accordingly. He added that Jackson "was not satisfied with the refusal to accept his [Longstreet's] construction of the enemy's purpose, and demurred against authority less than General Lee's, but found that the order must be obeyed." [49]

These words had the flavor, somewhat stronger now, of the attitude Longstreet showed in March when, as ranking officer in Johnston's absence, he was acting commanding general in northern Virginia. Jackson in the Valley was asking for re-enforcements,[50] and Longstreet suggested that he himself accompany re-enforcements and take command of the contemplated operation.[51] When Lee returned, Burnside's plan bogged down, and the incident, such as it was, blew over.

No evidence is known to exist which depicts Jackson's attitude in this minor affair except that of his silence. Longstreet made other critical appraisals of Jackson in the long postwar years. He sought, for instance, to explain the Jackson record in the Seven Days by saying that "Jackson was a very skilled man against such men as Shields, Banks, and Frémont, but when pitted against the best of the Federal commanders he did not appear so well," [52] although the demonstrable facts and the weight of military opinion, British as well as American, both Northern and Southern, held otherwise. Longstreet was critical of Jackson's behavior at Second Manassas, where he "did not respond with spirit to my move." [53] Jackson had been leading the Confederate campaign with such energy, perception, skill, and endurance as to win the admiration of virtually all others in what was probably the most brilliant of his operations. He had engaged in heavy combat, whereas Longstreet was comparatively fresh. There are other examples of a curiously derogatory attitude toward Jackson—as distinct from objective analysis and criticism—in Longstreet's writings.[54]

So it may be that under the surface of 1862 and 1863 Longstreet felt more strongly about Jackson than his outward demeanor indicated. Normal rivalry existed between the two corps—"a generous sort of rivalry," said McGuire [55]—but it does not appear to have gone, in the minds of officers who commented on it, beyond a healthy degree. There is no known instance of Jackson's showing by word or action any personal feeling against Longstreet.

That officers were referred to sometimes as "Jackson men" would be expected, just as others were known as "Longstreet men" or "Lee men." In particular, some of the officers on Jackson's staff—McGuire, Hotchkiss, Douglas, Pendleton, Dabney while he was present, for particular examples—were intensely loyal to him, although they were not blind to mistakes. Stuart was another. The extent to which references to Lee or Jackson factions are justified is difficult to pin down by evidence, but it does not appear that the loyalties that gather

around any notable commander, and certainly gathered around
Lee and Jackson (and Longstreet too), led in this instance to serious
factionalism.

The spirit of Lee's letters to Jackson during the autumn when
they were discussing Jackson's operations, the respect which these
letters expressed for Jackson's judgment, and the value Lee said
he placed on Jackson's counsel leave no room for doubt as to the
nature and depth of Lee's feeling toward Jackson.

As for Jackson's feeling toward Lee, the record shows the proper
respect of a corps commander for his army commander and the
continuing admiration for Lee the leader that Jackson had acknowl-
edged when he said in July that he would follow Lee blindfolded.
No word of criticism or of envy, no lack of co-operation by Jackson,
mars this record. If there was a Jackson faction, it was the natural
grouping of men close to him who were animated by respect, admiration, and affection for their General. No known evidence suggests that such officers sought improperly to influence administrative or military matters.

It was inevitable in such a winter that the thoughts of the men
around Jackson should turn back to their experiences in 1862. It
had been a year of extraordinary, indeed unparalleled, campaigning.
A year ago, on January 1, Jackson had launched his Romney campaign, and before the month was out had encountered the worst
winter weather of his career, had swept the region clean, and had
stood up to the Benjamin-Davis crisis. In February, Banks crossed
the Potomac and Jackson fenced with him north of Winchester.
March saw the retreat up the Valley, the about-face that led to
Kernstown, and the withdrawal after that bitter battle. In April the
Army of the Valley moved slowly backward before Banks' cautious
advance, crouched in its lair in the Elk Run Valley, and then crept
out mysteriously while Ewell moved in.

In May, Jackson reappeared in Staunton, crossed farther to the
west, struck Milroy at McDowell, turned back to the Valley, joined
Ewell, marched swiftly and secretly north, overran Front Royal,
drove Banks headlong toward Winchester, pursued him all night,
broke through his defenses on the hills south of Winchester, entered
that well-loved city in triumph. He pressed on toward Harper's
Ferry, paused in sight of the Potomac, and then turned south again
for the critical marches of the 30th and 31st through surrounding
forces and the safe passage up the Valley again.

Maneuvers at Cross Keys in June and rough fighting at Port Republic marked the end of the Valley campaign. With only a few days of rest in the new summer the Army of the Valley turned eastward, crossed Virginia toward Richmond, and stumbled into the dark uncertainties of the Seven Days.

July brought the climax at bloody Malvern Hill and the final collapse, in spite of that repulse, of McClellan's Peninsula campaign. July brought, too, the shift of Jackson's command to the Gordonsville area, where John Pope presented a new threat.

August began with the Cedar Run operation, followed with the uniting of the Army of Northern Virginia on the Rapidan, and sent Jackson along the upper reaches of the Rappahannock in the search of Pope's right flank. He circled it in the historic marches of the 25th and 26th, and, completely in the enemy's rear now, Jackson struck at Groveton, held off the foe in the desperate fighting at Second Manassas, and swept forward with the whole army the next day, and then on to Chantilly.

By September 6 Jackson was crossing the Potomac, by the 15th he had captured Harper's Ferry, and on the 17th he endured the long agonies of Sharpsburg.

October brought the first real rest of the year, but it was a month of work and watchfulness while the army regathered its scattered strength. Before November was out the Second Corps of the Army of Northern Virginia under Lieutenant General Jackson was climbing the Blue Ridge for the last time, in snow and over iced roads, for the goal at Fredericksburg. And then that strange battle against a greatly superior but blundering foe, and the year ran out in these winter quarters. Here men who had survived these months of marching, fighting, half-starving, great physical effort, and spiritual travail might still bend beneath the rains and shiver in the cold, but they could carry themselves at heart with the pride of a remarkable record.*

In their own way the soldiers knew that. One who looked upon

---

* Jackson had a high opinion of volunteers. Early in the war, at Harper's Ferry, when Johnston was looking at the Second Virginia Regiment as it marched past him, McGuire said to him, "If these men of the Second Virginia will not fight you have no troops that will." Johnston retorted, "I would not give one company of regulars for the whole regiment." But when McGuire related this incident to Jackson, that officer exclaimed, "Did he say that, and of those splendid men?" Then, after a pause, Jackson stated, "The patriot volunteer fighting for country and his rights makes the most reliable soldier on earth." (Couper, IV, 75–76.)

"the tatterdemalion regiments of the South" after Sharpsburg thought it strange to contemplate these men, "so ragged, slovenly, sleeveless, without a superfluous ounce of flesh upon their bones, with wild matted hair, in mendicants' rags, and to think when the battle-flag goes to the front how they can and do fight."

These were strikingly like the thoughts of a Federal officer who, in this approaching spring of 1863, found himself a prisoner.

Their artillery horses [he said of his captors] are poor, starved frames of beasts, tied to their carriages and caissons with odds and ends of rope and strips of raw hide; their supply and ammunition trains look like a congregation of all the crippled California emigrant trains that ever escaped off the desert out of the clutches of the rampaging Comanche Indians. The men are ill-dressed, ill-equipped, and ill-provided—a set of ragamuffins that a man is ashamed to be seen among, even when he is a prisoner, and can't help it. And yet they have beaten us fairly, beaten us all to pieces, beaten us so easily that we are objects of contempt even to their commonest private soldiers with no shirts to hang out the holes of their pantaloons, and cartridge-boxes tied around their waists with strands of rope.[56]

In the Second Corps they had learned, for one thing, the military philosophy of their commanding general. Imboden wrote down, earlier in 1862, two ideas which Jackson expressed to him. Wolseley, the British Adjutant General, called them "those golden sentences of Jackson's which comprise some of the most essential of all the principles of war." [57] They were these:

Always mystify, mislead, and surprise the enemy, if possible; and when you strike and overcome him, never let up in the pursuit so long as your men have strength to follow; for an army routed, if hotly pursued, becomes panic-stricken, and can then be destroyed by half their number. The other rule is, never fight against heavy odds, if by any possible maneuvering you can hurl your own force on only a part, and that the weakest part, of your enemy and crush it. Such tactics will win every time, and a small army may thus destroy a large one in detail, and repeated victory will make it invincible.[58]

These primary principles, well known to every trained soldier, were simpler to state than to exemplify. Yet in the record of the great year instance after instance—from the Valley in May to the march around Pope—illustrates Jackson's ability in the field to mystify, mislead, and surprise the enemy, and the most notable illustration was still to come. Instance after instance—from First Manasses to Fredericksburg itself—illustrates Jackson's desire and effort, when he had struck the enemy and overcome him, never to let up in the pursuit, although sometimes he was overruled. In his own operations he did in fact manage nearly always—from every Valley operation after Kernstown to Cedar Run and Groveton—to strike with greater weight than the enemy could bring to bear at the point of impact, though he might have more just beyond reach.*

The principles were living practices. Jackson's immense energy, his passion for starting early and moving fast ("we must burn no more daylight"), his religious conviction that he must do his duty, beginning right now, gave life to these principles. He endowed the force under his command, from brigade to army corps, with the discipline he insisted upon and the obedience to orders which he enforced with exactness and severity. He added to sound military knowledge a capacity for detail that kept him acquainted intimately with the condition of his commands.

The doing of the deed, the accomplishment of the purpose, was to him so important that he insisted the Confederacy could not afford to keep a man in a responsible position who did not succeed. ("Get rid of the unsuccessful man at once, and trust to Providence for finding a better." [59]) Yet in the bending of all efforts to succeed he managed to impart to his commands something of his own spiritual quality to such an extent that the soldiers under him—indeed, a whole generation around him—were deeply moved by those verses of John Williamson Palmer entitled "Stonewall Jackson's Way":

> Silence! Ground arms! Kneel all! Caps off!
> Old Blue-light's going to pray;
> Strangle the fool that dares to scoff!
> Attention! It's his way!
> Appealing from his native sod
> *In forma pauperis* to God,
> "Lay bare Thine arm—stretch forth Thy rod,
> Amen!" That's Stonewall's way.

* Ewell thought "the secret of Jackson's success as a soldier lay in his emphasis on the maxim, 'Time is everything in war'—more than numbers, preparation, armament, more even than all these and all else." (Robert Stiles in *S.H.S.P.*, XXI, 25 ff.)

The Rev. Dr. Graham pointed out with theological accuracy and a personal knowledge of the General that that *wasn't* Stonewall Jackson's way. "There was never anything that savored in the slightest degree of irreverence, or flourish, or parade, or impropriety, in any act of devotion performed or ordered by him," he said. On the contrary, Dr. Graham continued, "there was always a decent regard for the proprieties of worship and a solemnity in keeping with the veneration due to God." [60] He would pray in a prayer meeting or some other formal religious gathering, but never in public in a way to intrude on others. The many stories from men who saw him lift his hand while riding his horse and were confident that he was praying * never suggest that this personal act extended beyond the General. He prayed much alone in his room or tent, but in the open he went out of his way to do so by himself.

"I find that it greatly helps me in fixing my mind and quickening my devotions to give articulate utterance to my prayers," the General told a friend, "and hence I am in the habit of going off into the woods, where I can be alone and speak audibly to myself the prayers I would pour out to my God. I was at first annoyed that I was compelled to keep my eyes open to avoid running against the trees and stumps; but upon investigating the matter I do not find that the Scriptures require us to close our eyes in prayer, and the exercise has proved to me very delightful and profitable." [61]

But no one would cause men in uniform, or people at war, who built a tradition on the General's name and fame, to doubt the importance of spiritual quality in "Stonewall Jackson's Way."

The Second Corps felt it in this winter below Fredericksburg. Like most Northern Virginia winters it mingled snow and rain, and sharp cold for the region, with bright and even warm days. January

---

* McGuire did not accept this theory held by many soldiers. He wrote in the *Richmond Medical Journal*, February, 1866, that after Jackson was wounded in the hand at First Manassas, "during the treatment, the hand was kept elevated and confined in a sling, and when the use of this was discontinued, and the hand permitted to hang down, there was, of course, gravitation of blood toward it. Under the circumstances you would expect this. In consequence of it, however, the hand was sometimes swollen and painful, and to remedy this, he often held it above his head for some moments. He did this so frequently that it became at length a habit and was continued, especially when he was abstracted, after all necessity for it had ceased. I have seen it stated somewhere that, whenever during a battle his hand was thus raised, he was engaged in prayer; but I think the explanation I have given is the correct one. I believe he was the truest and most consistent Christian I have ever known; but I don't believe he prayed much while he was fighting."

had some rain and cold, especially on the 21st and 22nd when the
Mud March was under way across the river. But it was not until
the 29th that the first real snow—a foot of it—fell. It lingered two
days. In mid-February another fall left a foot or more that remained
for days. March produced more in the middle of that month and at
the end, and still more fell during the first week in April.[62]

This was enough to stir young men and boys with time on their
hands, especially youngsters from Southern States where snow was
a curiosity. The army was not equipped for winter sports, but soldiers were. They went into snow warfare on an unprecedented scale.
Rival armies in brigade strength of 2,500 or more were organized
on military principles, with commanding officers (on horseback),
staffs, formal demands under flags of truce, strategies, tactical
maneuvers, fortifications, large stocks of ammunition (snowballs),
the booty of camp utensils to fight for, and a dash and enthusiasm
that led to long and youthfully ferocious combats. Black eyes, body
bruises, and an occasional broken leg could not restrain the campaigns.[63]

The energy spent thus might even have brought a shade of re-
assurance to Lee in his long efforts this winter to maintain the ration,
increase the volume of clothing, and save horses which were dying
in dangerous numbers for lack of forage.

I am informed by the chief commissary of the army [Lee wrote to
Secretary of War Seddon on April 17] that he has been unable to issue
the sugar ration to the troops for the last ten days. Their ration, consequently, consists of one-fourth pound of bacon, 18 ounces of flour, 10
pounds of rice to each 100 men about every third day, with some few
peas and a small amount of dried fruit occasionally, as they can be obtained. This may give subsistence to the troops while idle, but will certainly cause them to break down when called upon for exertion.[64]

The problem grew steadily worse.

At bright intervals this problem lightened; when boxes from home,
gifts from friends, or unusual supplies for an unusual event poured
in. For Jackson the most notable such occasion was at Christmas. He
invited Generals Lee, Pendleton, and Stuart, and some of their staffs
to join him and his personal staff for Christmas dinner. This brought
Lee's two aides, Cols. Charles S. Venable and Charles Marshall,
Stuart's von Borcke, Pelham, John Esten Cooke, and Cadet W. Q.

Hullihen, and a few others—one of them George Peterkin, later
Bishop of West Virginia.

Jackson's own staff was scattered at this time, some almost surely
attending to duties farther back, or absent for other reasons. His
veterans, Harman and Hawks, were still on the staff, and so were
the younger veterans: McGuire, Crutchfield, and Sandie Pendleton.
Smith and the General's brother-in-law, Lieut. J. G. Morrison, were
aides. G. H. Bier was chief of ordnance, Bridgford was provost marshal, Boswell his engineer with Second Lieut. W. G. Williamson aiding him. Col. Abner Smead was assistant inspector general. Wilbourn
was chief signal officer. Faulkner had not arrived, Douglas had left
the staff for line duty with the Second Virginia Regiment, and
Hotchkiss, a civilian employee still, would have been present but
was on leave, as were Harman and Boswell. Many of the others
were present.

The task of organization for the Christmas dinner fell on young
Smith, then acting as caterer for Jackson's staff (a duty which ro-
tated), but he was fortunate to start with. Friends in the neighborhood gave him two turkeys, and a third came in later. He located a
bucket of oysters. The General had a box of fine food sent (said
Smith) by "some Staunton ladies." There was a ham, and what is
spoken of as *a* bottle of wine. The General's Jim added more from
the regular rations, including "white biscuits," and an unexpected
supply of pickle turned up. A white apron was even found for the
staff servant, John. It was startling. Lee, taking a look at it, and observing the wealth of the banquet, and its setting, remarked that
they were all playing at being soldiers—they should come to his
headquarters and see how soldiers really lived.

The setting of the Corbins' office was for the guests equally startling. Its atmosphere of sportsmen's pleasures led officers brought
up on the tale of "Blue-Light" morality to marvel at this room. Stuart,
full of life as usual and very much on his toes this day, jumped, as
soon as he saw the surroundings, into an attack on the breakdown of
Jackson's standards.[65]

Parading before the pictures (Smith remembered), "he read
aloud what was said about each noted race horse and each splendid
bull. At the hearth he paused to scan with affected astonishment the
horrid picture of a certain terrier that could kill so many rats a minute. He pretended to believe that they were General Jackson's selec-

tions; with great solemnity he looked at the picture and then at the
General. He paused and stepped back, and in solemn tones said he
wished to express his astonishment and grief at the display of General Jackson's low tastes. It would be a sad disappointment to the
old ladies of the country, who thought that Jackson was a good
man."

When Stuart discovered finally a large pat of butter, sent by the
Taylors at Hayfield and bearing a chanticleer imprint on top, he
pointed at what he pronounced to be Jackson's coat-of-arms. "See
there, gentlemen!" His finger pointed at the butter. "If there is not
the crowning evidence of our host's sporting tastes! He even puts
his favorite gamecock upon his butter!" [66]

The General, never a man for repartee, grinned and blushed—
while the company roared.

It was the fashion that winter, for those who knew him well
enough, to tease the General. Lee sometimes rallied younger officers
but rarely let down the bars with seniors—he who always said "General Jackson," and to whom Jackson always said "General Lee." (Gen.
Harry Heth, the West Pointer of 1847 who had been acting quartermaster general of the Virginia forces under Lee's command, and
after other assignments, was coming into A. P. Hill's brigade, has
been called the only officer whom Lee called by his first name.[67])
But at Hayfield once, in a company of guests, Lee took turns in
describing the other officers to the elderly Mrs. W. P. Taylor, a
kinswoman. When he came to Jackson, Lee told her that General
Jackson standing there, who was smiling so pleasantly, was "the most
cruel and inhuman man she had ever seen."

Mrs. Taylor demurred at that. General Jackson she had always
heard spoken of as "a good, Christian man." But Lee would not let
up: "Why, when we had the battle up at Fredericksburg, do you
know, Mrs. Taylor, it was as much as we could do to prevent him
from taking his men, with bayonets on their guns, and driving the
enemy into the river?" [68]

If, in such circumstances, the strict Presbyterian with his tight,
tense ways, seemed an easy mark for men relaxing in good humor,
still Stuart and Lee would not have made fun of Jackson if they had
not felt, in addition to their own affection, the good will of other
officers who knew him less well but were sensing that there was more
to this man than the old tales of the camps. Jackson the general stood

in a place of his own. Jackson the man, long considered a curiosity, was coming into a new understanding and appreciation, and his stature was rising in the estimation of those around him.

Some of the staff noticed a considerable change in him, a new kind of relaxation and a larger indulgence in the social instincts he had always possessed but sometimes could not express easily. On occasion he spent a longer time over his meals, and more often the business of eating, which often had been hurried and silent, became increasingly pleasant.[69]

The differences were neither revolutionary nor invariable. Nor did all the staff think any changes were significant. The General could still arise in the middle of a conversation and stride off to attend to some duty he had thought of. McGuire thought life at headquarters was "decidedly dull" and the meals "often very dreary. The General had no time for light or trivial conversation, and he sometimes felt it his duty to rebuke our thoughtless and perhaps foolish remarks. Nor was it always quite safe to approach him. Sometimes he had a tired look in his eye, and although he never breathed a word to one or another, we knew that he was dissatisfied with what was being done with the army." [70]

Ordinarily he would be speechless when young women swarmed around him at Hayfield, as they sometimes did; for his name was universally known and his personality interested people. When two girls demanded a lock of his hair, he agreed, provided they took no gray hairs. They insisted that he had none. But he met that one head-on. "Why," he said, "the soldiers call me 'Old Jack.'" [71]

The General seemed guilty of levity in another incident of the winter. He wrote to Anna in January that "Mrs. General Longstreet, Mrs. General A. P. Hill, and Mrs. General Rodes have all been to see their husbands . . . it made me wish I had Mrs. Jackson here too. . . ." [72] But their daughter was only three months old and had not been well. General Early, a bachelor, had other views. He wrote to Jackson that the visits of wives, mothers, and sisters were disrupting army work. Shouldn't the General do something to stop all this?

The General—that man of duty—disagreed completely. "I will do no such thing!" he told the staff. "I wish my wife could come to see me."

Shortly afterward an unusual and perhaps suspicious complaint reached him that Early had been using ambulances to carry friends of the neighborhood, including some wives, mothers, and sisters, on social visits around the countryside. Members of the staff pointed out with solemn faces that this utilization of military vehicles for nonmilitary purposes needed investigation. They urged the General to act. Eventually he did. To Early went an inquiry as to how many times, and for what purposes, he had used ambulances? Early, as blunt in such circumstances as on the field of battle, put down the whole list.[73] The records do not show what happened next, nor do they mention the grins on the faces of young staff officers—perhaps even on their General's.

Perhaps there was a grin on the face of General Early, who, next to Stuart, took more liberties with Jackson than did any other officer. Jackson, on the road one day when the corps was marching, didn't like some straggling he saw and directed Pendleton to write a note to Early in these words:

"General Jackson's compliments to General Early, and he would like to be informed why he saw so many stragglers in rear of your division today."

Back came Old Jube's reply immediately:

"General Early's compliments to General Jackson, and he takes pleasure in informing him that he saw so many stragglers in rear of my division today, probably because he rode in rear of my division." [74]

It is doubtful whether even Stuart would have written such a note, but there is no indication that Jackson resented it.

He was entirely at home with the English visitors who were in and out of the camps during much of the winter. Francis Lawley, the London *Times* correspondent who had been a visitor when the army was at Bunker Hill, came in after Christmas and spent a week. Accompanying him were the young Marquis of Hartington (later the Duke of Devonshire) and a member of the House of Commons, Colonel Leslie.* The General must have continued his earlier decision to talk more about Britain than about the war. "His chief delight," Lawley reported to the *Times*, "was in the cathedrals of England, notably in York Minster and Westminster Abbey. He was never

---

* Not identified by men at Jackson's headquarters, but apparently either William Leslie of Aberdeenshire or Charles Powell Leslie of Monaghan, Ireland, Colonel of the Monaghan Militia—probably the latter.

tired of talking about them, or listening to details about the chapels
and cloisters of Oxford." [75]

Col. Garnet Wolseley, who had visited the General near Bunker
Hill, wrote later that "he told me that in all his travels he had seen
nothing so beautiful as the lancet windows in York Minster." Jackson, Wolseley continued, had very little to say about military operations, and it was impossible to make him talk of his own achievements. But "he was intensely proud of his soldiers, and enthusiastic
in his devotion to General Lee." Wolseley thought "his manner,
which was modesty itself, was most attractive. He put you at your
ease at once, listening with marked courtesy and attention to whatever you might say; and when conversation was congenial, he was
a most interesting companion. I quite endorse the statement as to
his love for beautiful things." [76]

Young Hartington spent much of his time with Smith, sharing his
blankets and riding his horse. But Leslie, an older man, saw more
of Jackson. He said afterward that Jackson was the best-informed
military man he had met in America and as perfect a gentleman as
he had ever seen. [77]

When another English officer named Bushby arrived later, and
was brought by von Borcke to call on Jackson, he asked for an autograph. Jackson wrote out his name but spilled ink on the paper and
so threw it aside. Bushby recovered it. The General, a little surprised, told the officer, if he valued "my simple signature so much,
I will give you a number of them with the greatest pleasure," and
he wrote his name many times across a sheet of paper. [78]

Another English officer, who brought a box of goods from England for the General, received an invitation to visit him. The Eng-
lishman set out from Richmond by train, but from Guiney's Station,
some eight or nine miles from Jackson's headquarters, he had to
travel overland (apparently on foot) through snow and in heavy
rain, in the Virginia mud, which he thought "quite as villainous as
that of Balaclava." Jackson received him warmly, took off his
drenched and muddy coat, stirred up the fire, helped the visitor dry
his feet, escorted him to dinner with the staff, talked long with him
afterward, and offered to share his bed for the night.

An aide had provided sleeping quarters, but the General took
him to breakfast ("I noticed that the General said grace before the
meal with the same fervour I had remarked before"), and spent

some time during the morning trying to dry his visitor's greatcoat before the fire and apologized for not doing so completely. "With the care and responsibilities of a vast army on his shoulders he finds time to do little acts of kindness and thoughtfulness, which make him the darling of his men, who never seem to tire talking of him." [79]

The person outside the army who interested him most this winter —always excepting Anna and their daughter Julia—was young Janie Corbin. Janie had a childish curiosity about these military visitors, close to her home, about whom she must have heard much talk; and she had a natural tendency to peek around in the vicinity of the office where the General lived, and men came and went, and a soldier strode up and down in front of the door.

The friendship of Janie and the General ripened during the winter. She visited him frequently late in the afternoon, was always welcomed, generally received a piece of fruit or some small present, and one day received a present that no one forgot. This day Jackson could find nothing to give her until, looking around his quarters, he saw the brilliantly braided cap that Anna had sent him just before the battle of Fredericksburg. He had worn it then because he did not wish to hurt her feelings, but he told her later that "I became so much ashamed of the broad gold lace that was on the cap you sent me, as to induce me to take it off. I like simplicity." (Anna commented that it was "the most modest mark of his rank that a field officer could wear." [80])

The General cut the braid off his cap with a pocketknife, arranged it in circular form, and placed it with ceremony on Janie's head like a coronet, to her delight and his. Everyone around Moss Neck found pleasure in this charming child, with long light brown hair and large and beautiful eyes. She had a manner and expression that delighted older people, the General especially. And then, all of a sudden, she was ill with scarlet fever, as were two of her cousins, Parke and Gardner Dickinson, of about the same age, who were staying at Moss Neck. The General learned of it just when he was preparing to move nearer Hamilton's Crossing. He left his young friend sick, but not, he thought, seriously.

Two days later she was dead. In another day her cousins died. When his aide gave him the news, the General was so moved that he wept. He asked James Power Smith to ride back to Moss Neck that night to express his sympathy and to remain if he could be of any service to the family.[*]

The long months of relative quiet were broken from time to time, when the weather permitted, by reviews of parts of the army. A. P. Hill's division, more than 10,000 strong, paraded on January 6 in a broad meadow on the bottom of the Hayfield estate, a splendid pageant until a cold rain swept over the soldiers. On the 10th Fitz-hugh Lee's cavalry brigade marched in review, and on the 20th W. H. F. Lee's brigade attracted many officers and many women despite the cold, biting wind.

Jackson was too much a soldier to miss events like these, but he was not limited by them. His interest in maps—he would not forget what the lack of them had cost him in the Seven Days—kept him pushing Hotchkiss to more and more work. He ordered a map of the fortifications along the Rappahannock, showing the location of pickets, and another of the region between the Rapidan and the Rappahannock, and other maps for the Faulkner reports, showing troop locations, about which he was precise and sometimes asked Hotchkiss to check further. But principally he set Hotchkiss to work —"wishing the preparation to be kept a profound secret"—on a great map [81] that would extend to Philadelphia and be detailed enough to show individual houses and the names of people who lived in them. Jackson had no occasion to use this map, but Lee did. It was a principal reliance for him in the Gettysburg campaign.

The staff, meantime, ransacked the Corbins' library. Sandie Pendleton had been reading everything he could find: a life of Charles Lamb and a volume of Cowper's poems months ago, and Carlyle's life of Cromwell in October, where he discovered, as he thought, that "General Jackson is the exact counterpart of Oliver in every respect, as Carlisle draws him"—a comparison made later by many others, but lacking accuracy (and spelling). He wrote this to his mother on

[*] Mrs. Jackson, 410.

The surgeons of the nearby brigades did all they could to save these children, and provided as good medical service, probably, as any others could. The military units were much upset by the deaths, for everyone knew Janie; and carpenters from the Stonewall Brigade made her coffin out of the fence that enclosed the lawn. Clement D. Fishburne, in his narrative of personal experiences, wrote later, from a knowledge of life at Moss Neck, where he was stationed, that "altogether it was a sad commentary on the horrors of war. The body was finally laid away in the family burying ground, near the house, in gloomy bad weather, by sympathizing friends, the most of whom a very few months before had never heard of the family."

a rainy November day in a tent in which Douglas was reading a Victor Hugo novel and McGuire *Charles O'Malley.* A little later Pendleton, McGuire, and Crutchfield read Shakespeare together, "McGuire reading excellently and Crutchfield being more conversant with it than anyone I ever saw." These three dipped during the winter into Napier's account of the Peninsula war in Spain, and Sandie was charmed by *Vanity Fair* and learned that Mr. Pickwick offered "unfailing amusement." Hotchkiss read a life of Lorenzo d' Medici and then turned to a Bulwer-Lytton novel.[82] Douglas, a frequent visitor, devoured every book he could get his hands on.[83] The General was reading Henry Hunter's *Moses* and finding it "delightful" and feeling (he told Anna) "more improved in reading it than by an ordinary sermon." [84]

But the General did something else this winter: he talked—often with Hotchkiss. He talked of the year's battles and the horrors he had seen. The plight of the people of bombarded Fredericksburg moved him greatly, as it did the whole corps. The General encouraged a relief fund and gave $100. His headquarters gave $800. A. P. Hill's division raised $10,000, and the Second Corps gave all told some $30,000, or about a dollar for each soldier.[85] "War is the greatest of evils," the General told Hotchkiss when they were talking of Fredericksburg, though a railroad accident that day led him to say that such accidents had been the most horrid sights he had ever seen. But he could not forget the battered town or the bereft people.[86]

Faulkner asked many questions for his reports, and they led to talk of why the General hit first at Shields at Port Republic instead of Frémont, against whom Ewell fought merely a defensive engagement. There were several reasons, said Jackson. First, he was nearer to Shields. Second, Shields had the smaller army. Third, he himself was nearer his base of supplies and had a good route for retreat if beaten. Fourth, Frémont would have had a good route for retreat if Jackson beat him, but Shields, if beaten, had a bad road for withdrawal.[87]

Some talk of the recent fighting near Fredericksburg led the General to say that Federal engineers were better than Confederate in discovering weak spots in defense lines—they had done it at Second Manassas as well as at Fredericksburg. He talked of panic in battle, recalled one battery that had fled at Cedar Run, and remarked that it was no great loss. He couldn't remember what had happened on his left at First Manassas, and he doubted if Kirby Smith joined in the charge there as he was usually credited with doing—though in that respect the weight of evidence runs against the General. He argued with Hotchkiss about whether a long horseback ride he took was at Port Republic or at Frederickshall, agreed that Hotchkiss was right in saying it was at Frederickshall, and remarked that it showed the importance of comparing ideas.[88]

It was a winter for talk of many kinds, and officers of his command may have told each other stories about the relations of the General and his sister Laura—Mrs. Jonathan Arnold—in Beverly. The area where she lived was occupied most of the time during the war by Federal troops. Majority sentiment in Beverly was sympathetic to the Confederate cause, and Jonathan Arnold shared this sentiment. He was arrested in 1863 on a general charge of disloyalty to the Union but was not convicted. But Laura, a woman of independent mind and of strong convictions, as her brother's letters to her in the prewar years indicated many times, supported the Union and worked actively for it. Her attitude excited much attention.

"Lieut. Long, of the Thirty-first Virginia, one of my Valley friends, came to see me today," Hotchkiss wrote in his diary on March 23. The lieutenant told Hotchkiss of having heard that the General's sister, in Beverly, was "a Union woman." He reported for Hotchkiss to record that "she said she could take care of wounded Federals as fast as brother Thomas would wound them."

The language may be uncertain, but her action was not. Laura nursed the sick and wounded Union soldiers (apparently Confederate soldiers too) in her own home and in hospitals. She was called "an angel of mercy among the sick," "a noble woman," and one who, in the words of a Union regimental surgeon, "merits special recognition at the hands of the republic." Laura did receive special recognition at the hands of Union veterans who, at a meeting of the Grand Army of the Ohio in Cincinnati years later, greeted her as a heroine.

The effect on the General of Laura's devotion to the Union does not appear in any known evidence. If he corresponded with Laura during the war years, the letters have not been found. He had written to her from Lexington two weeks before he marched off to war, in a letter of great earnestness (partly quoted above Vol. I, p. 307).

She was troubled then by her husband's religious views, which were less ardent than her own. Anna was to write to Laura September 12, 1864 (the text is in Cook, 172–174), in warmth and friendliness. But such a division of thought and feeling as that between the General, with a name known around the world as a Confederate officer, and Laura, with her intense devotion to the Union cause, may well have been disturbing to them both—certainly to the brother. Laura had been from his boyhood the symbol, as she was the only survivor, of his immediate family. Her brother's devotion to her from before his West Point years to the opening of the war, which he poured out in the long series of letters he wrote to her, had been a sustaining force in his life. He must have been deeply upset by the wartime curtain that fell between brother and sister.*

The staff picked up subjects for the talk of soldiers on long winter nights. Hotchkiss and Faulkner recalled much about the Romney expedition, including the General's extreme reticence about the first movement toward Bath. He had not told Loring, second in command, what his plan was; he had not told Preston, his adjutant general, with whom he shared a tent. If the General had been killed, no one would have known what to do.

Sometimes Harman joined in the reminiscences. He remembered telling the General at Port Republic that the field of battle was littered with arms, and the General told him to pick them up. Harman said, "General, a good many of them look like ours." That, said Harman, threw the General into "a towering passion." He wanted to hear no such talk! Shields had many muskets of the same kind. Harman had no business making such intimations.

At that Harman lost his temper. He would not stand for such talk, he said, and would send in his resignation. Harman did send it in, but the General called him in, told him that he was much annoyed at the time by other things, and refused to accept the resignation.[89]

The staff heard and repeated stories that amused the General this winter. He asked McGuire to inquire of the commissary officer,

* For these and other details see Hu Maxwell's *History of Randolph County, West Virginia,* and Reader's *History of the Fifth West Virginia Cavalry and Battery G, First West Virginia Light Artillery,* and Anna Pierpont Siviter's *Recollections of War and Peace, 1861-68.* The author is indebted to Mrs. E. Randolph Preston, granddaughter of General Jackson, and to Roy Bird Cook, of Charleston, West Virginia, for information on this subject.

Major Hawks, if some chickens could not be sent to headquarters mess—he had heard that some were on hand. Back came McGuire with the report about the chickens. The Hawks, he said, had eaten them. The report delighted Jackson,[90] as, indeed, did a story about Early. That officer was inspecting artillery near the river. One gun, trained to shoot at gunboats, had its muzzle elevated so high that it pointed at the top of a tree. A soldier was sighting it with great care when Early rode up. The soldier turned aside finally, saw Early, and asked him "if there was ary squirrel up that tree." McGuire, who told the story, said the air was blue with Early's comment, all of which he relayed to the General, and "I know General Jackson enjoyed the story very much."[91]

McGuire, who thought that stories had to be "very plain ones for him to see them," thought the General enjoyed the remark, which ran all through the army, of the Confederate soldier during the burying truce after Fredericksburg. The soldier, on duty during the truce, ragged and poorly equipped like most of his comrades, found a new Springfield rifle on the field of battle and took charge of it. A well-dressed Federal major reprimanded him for taking it. The soldier looked him up and down, walked around him for a slow inspection, and finally replied thus: "That's a monstrous fine pa'r of boots you got on—if you don't watch out I'll git 'em befo' night."[92]

The talk might run to nonmilitary subjects. One night the General turned back to his experiences as a teacher. He said he was very fond of teaching. When Hotchkiss asked which language he liked best, the General, without any hesitation at all, said Spanish. He began to explain some peculiarities of Spanish pronunciation and spelling, and that led him to talk about the peculiarities of the English language. Somehow the conversation jumped to the scenery in western Virginia, especially along the New River. He spoke of his mother, buried not far from Hawk's Nest, and he told of other members of his family, long dead, except Laura in Beverly, and perhaps his half-brother (Wirt Woodson), whose whereabouts he did not know.[93]

On another day, when spring was coming in, the conversation turned to food, and an officer who was present remarked that beans were the most nutritious of all substances. "Oh, no," the General said, "rice has 95 per cent and beans only 92 per cent." But he added that hog drivers in western Virginia said their hogs could go farther on honey than on any other food.[94]

This was the talk of men relaxed and at ease, reminiscing about the great year or drawing on incidents, experiences, and thoughts far away. It was the talk of men who had marched through the fires and the storms, and were intimately acquainted with danger, and could afford to be light and casual as they waited for the spring and the certain renewal of their struggle. From the General down they were in a mood that none of them had known before, and not many would know again. It was the hush before the curtain rose, and these were intensely human men.

Not that Jackson thought only of the past. "We must make this campaign an exceedingly active one," he said of the coming spring. "Only thus can a weaker country cope with a stronger. It must make up in activity what it lacks in strength."[95]

The General had talked a few days before with a member of his staff, telling why he thought a great battle would soon be fought, and adding: "My trust is in God." There was a silence; then, rising to his feet, the picture of martial energy, the General exclaimed: "I wish they could come!"[96]

From the beginning he had never despaired of ultimate success.[97] "Duty is ours; consequences are God's," he said many times. But he could also say: "I do not desire to survive the independence of my country."[98] The talk that Hotchkiss remembered from the odd corners of the day was a minor detail in a winter of constant activity dedicated to efforts to present the best possible corps to the enemy.

When the news of the Federal occupation of Winchester reached him, the General thought imaginatively of what could be done to keep the enemy out of the Valley (and perhaps out of the homes of his friends). A force of 20,000, he calculated, could subsist in the lower Valley and could preserve a valuable region while annoying from its flank position any Federal advance into Northern Virginia. He had a commander in mind, one who he thought would be sufficiently active—General Early.[99] But Lee was unwilling to scatter his forces to this extent.

Nor, it seems clear, would Lee have been willing to permit the transfer of Jackson, now or later in the spring, to the Army of Tennessee. This is a question on which the direct evidence is so slight as to be negligible. In the winter evenings at Moss Neck and Hamilton's Crossing, Jackson read of operations in the West, especially Bragg's success at Murfreesboro ("very gratifying intelligence," he called it [100]), and discussed the subject with members of his staff. But that would seem so natural that it is difficult to interpret it as significant preparation for an expected transfer to the West.

A single sentence in a letter from Jackson to Anna has been cited as evidence that he was expecting such a transfer. He wrote to Anna on April 18, in warm anticipation of her coming with Julia. In it he told of a dream in which Anna was on one side of the room and he on the other, and the baby (then not quite five months old) "started from her mother, making her way along under a table, and finally reached her father," whom she climbed upon and kissed. He continued with the statement that "yesterday I received your letter, but you did not say a word about coming to see your *esposo*. . . . There is no time for hesitation if you have not started. *There is increasing probability that I may be elsewhere as the season advances. . . .*" [101]

The italicized words (the emphasis is supplied) have been interpreted [102] as Jackson's telling Anna, in his careful way of guarding information, that he would make a major individual move soon. The more natural interpretation is that he was expecting the movements of the Army of Northern Virginia to take him away from the region of the Rappahannock. He said as much on March 14: "We can't say where we shall be a week hence." [103] It is natural to suppose also that Lee and Jackson, who had many conversations during the winter, discussed another advance into Maryland and Pennsylvania, a subject which was certainly on Lee's mind. Jackson's direction to Hotchkiss to prepare a large, detailed map of Pennsylvania suggests that the subject was also on his mind.

There is no direct evidence to show that Jackson expected soon to be transferred to another command, but the probability that he would have been transferred eventually, if he had lived longer and had continued to display the qualities that had won him confidence in the army and in the country, is so strong that it may be reckoned a certainty. The transfer would probably have been to an army command in the West. Lee would not have liked to lose him, but probably he would have bowed to a reasonable and virtually inevitable attempt to make the most of the Confederacy's command resources.[*]

In many respects Jackson never changed. Lee sent him a note one evening asking him to come to see him. Jackson told Smith to be ready early the next morning. Smith woke to a world of snow with the flakes falling heavily, and he assumed the trip would be postponed. He turned back to sleep. But an orderly brought him word that the General was waiting, and the aide dressed fast and ran out without breakfast. They rode some dozen miles through the storm to Lee's headquarters. There Lee looked at them with amazement. "You know I did not wish you to come in such a storm," he told Jackson. "It was a matter of little importance. I am sorry you have had this ride."

Jackson said: "I received your note, General"[104]—that to him was enough. The cadets who had been at the V.M.I. with him would have understood.

Gifts poured in to Jackson. Early in January citizens of Augusta County gave him "a magnificent horse, with an excellent saddle and bridle . . . the most complete riding equipment I have seen." It included "patent stirrups," constructed so as to open and throw the foot from the stirrup if the rider fell and his foot hung. ("How kind is God to us! Oh, that I were more grateful!")

A month later Col. M. G. Harman (brother of his quartermaster) and William J. Bell, Jr., of Staunton, presented to him "an excellent horse." In the middle of January a pair of gauntlets came from "near the Potomac River" and at the same time another pair from Mrs. Preston Trotter, of Brownsburg. A different, but surely welcome, present was a barrel of "pippins" from "a kind gentleman, Mr. Stephens, of Nelson County."

The interest and good will of English people were unmistakable. An English captain brought in a box of goods from Nassau. Captain Bushby, whom Jackson tried to dry out before his fireplace, gave him a waterproof oilcloth case "in which to sleep on a wet night in summer campaigning." In February W. F. De La Rue, of London,

[*] J. W. Jones said (*S.H.S.P.*, XIX, 156), "I have it from excellent authority that if Jackson had not been killed at Chancellorsville he would have been sent to command the Army of Tennessee." Jones did not identify his "excellent authority." Douglas Southall Freeman pointed out to the writer that sometimes, though not necessarily in this instance, the source of Jones' statements of this kind was President Davis. D. H. Hill was quoted by Maj. Robert Stiles (*S.H.S.P.*, XXI, 25) as predicting during the winter of 1861–1862 that "if the war should last six years, and Jackson should live so long, he would be in supreme command."

sent him "a superb English saddle, bridle, holsters, saddle-cover, blankets, whip, spurs, etc.—the most complete riding equipage that I have seen for many a day."

A week later (on the 14th) he received from John Johnson, of London, a box containing two flannel shirts, two pairs of long woolen stockings extending above the knee, a buckskin shirt, a pair of boots, a pair of leather leggings extending about eight inches above the knees, two pairs of excellently fitting leather gloves, and "a very superior variegated colored blanket." Contemplating these gifts, the General wrote to Anna that "our ever-kind Heavenly Father gives me friends among strangers. He is the source of every blessing, and I desire to be more grateful to Him." [105]

The record of this long winter shows how continually, earnestly, intelligently, and yet modestly, Jackson did indeed show his gratitude to "our ever-kind Heavenly Father." Dabney had no doubt that there was an increase in his "spirituality and Christian activity" and that "his plans of exertion for the Church of God became more bold and comprehensive." His enjoyment of the Sabbath "became higher than ever." [106] His letters to Anna were full of praise of God, and he attributed all happiness to that source.

He wrote, after telling of some presents, that "our ever gracious heavenly Father is exceedingly kind to me, and strikingly manifests it by the kindness with which He disposes people to treat me. . . . And so God, my exceeding great Joy, is continually showering His blessings upon me, an unworthy creature." [107]

On a day set aside for praying for peace Jackson wrote that he would join in prayer too, and he hoped that all Christian people would, "but peace should not be the chief object of prayer in our country. It should aim more specially at imploring God's forgiveness of our sins, and praying that He will make our people a holy people. If we are but his, all things shall work together for the good of our country, and no good thing will He withhold from it." [108]

Yet he came back to the idea of praying for peace. "I do hope, trust, and pray, that our people will religiously observe the 27th day of next month [March] as a day of humiliation, prayer, and fasting, as the President has designated in his proclamation. . . . My Sabbaths are looked forward to with pleasure. I don't know that I have ever enjoyed Sabbaths as I do this winter." [109]

In a letter on March 28 to his father-in-law, Dr. Morrison, he reported that the day of prayer had received in the army "a more general response than I have seen on any similar occasion since the beginning of the war." The chaplains preached twice, once to their own troops and once to other troops. He hoped "that God in His mercy will give us a speedy peace," but he had other ideas in mind too.

"I feel a deep interest," he told Dr. Morrison, "in seeing a Christian daily paper established. I believe there is not a single daily paper in the country but which violates the Sabbath by printing on that holy day for its Monday issue . . . now is a good time to start such a paper whilst our country is in trouble, and is looking to God for assistance." The newspaper he had in mind would be printed on Saturday but not mailed until Monday.[110]

These ideas conformed to long-held beliefs which were much on his mind this winter. He wrote to Anna on January 17 that "I derive an additional pleasure in reading a letter, resulting from a conviction that it has not been travelling on the Sabbath." Just before the fighting at Fredericksburg he wrote to Boteler in Richmond, on December 10, to express his great interest in a report that a congressional committee was recommending repeal of the law that required the mails to be carried on the Sabbath. "I do not see how a nation that thus arrays itself, by such a law, against God's holy day," he told Boteler, "can expect to escape His wrath. The punishment of national sins must be confined to this world," he continued, because "there are no nationalities beyond the grave."

As for himself, "for fifteen years I have refused to mail letters on Sunday, or to take them out of the office on that day, except since I came into the field; and, so far from having to regret my course, it has been a source of true enjoyment." He had never sustained loss thereby. "My rule is, to let the Sabbath mails remain unopened, unless they contain a despatch; but despatches are generally sent by couriers or telegraph, or some special messenger. . . . I am well satisfied that the law should be repealed at the earliest practicable moment," and "if you desire the repeal of the law, I trust you will bring all your influence to bear in its accomplishment. Now is the time, it appears to me, to effect so desirable an object." [111]

To his old friend Preston, in Lexington, teaching at the V.M.I., he wrote to enlist his influence with the General Assembly of the Presbyterian Church in carrying the idea of praying for peace much

further. "Let our Government acknowledge the God of the Bible as
its God," he explained, "and we may soon expect to be a free and
happy people." He elaborated:

It appears to me that extremes are to be avoided; and it also appears
to me that the old United States occupied an extreme position in the
means it took to prevent the union of Church and State. We call ourselves
a Christian people; and it seems to me that our Government may be of
the same character, without connecting itself with an established Church.
It does appear to me that as our President, our Congress, and our people
have thanked God for victories, and prayed to Him for additional ones,
and He has answered such prayers, and gives us a Government, it is
gross ingratitude not to acknowledge Him in the gift. Let the framework
of our Government show that we are not ungrateful to Him.[112]

Most especially Jackson sought to stimulate religious efforts within
the army, particularly within the Second Corps. The times were
propitious. The Confederacy's desperate struggle, the hardships of
army life, the knowledge of deprivations and sacrifices in their
homes, the horrors of many experiences and the certainty of more
to come, the presence of death—these turned the thoughts of many
men in uniform inward with questions they could not answer. Their
search for light and strength was already bringing about those personal changes which, when thousands of Confederate soldiers publicly professed their religious faith a little later, came to be known
as the "Great Revival."

In the Second Corps, Sunday services grew in number and scope.
Rude chapels followed soon after the construction of the huts in
which men lived. The Stonewall Brigade (to Jackson's great satisfaction) led the way with a log-cabin chapel. Many others followed.
When Jackson moved his headquarters close to Hamilton's Crossing
in mid-March, an outdoor meeting place was built there at which
thousands of soldiers could, and did, attend Sunday services. Two
or three regiments stationed close together frequently built chapels,
but when the weather permitted, services were held outdoors in
many parts of the area.

The soldiers thronged to such services. The General attended invariably, and always sought to do so unobtrusively. He turned back
once from the Stonewall Brigade chapel when an aide told him the
chapel was so crowded that it would be difficult to obtain a seat.[113]
Generally he sought a place in a corner or in the rear, and always

in the midst of the soldiers, crowded among them shoulder to shoulder.

Some admirable ministers came to the army to preach at these services, the notable Presbyterian minister Dr. Moses Drury Hoge, of Richmond, among them. (He "was listened to," Hotchkiss said, "with great attention.") The army chaplains included men of capacity and leadership, but there were not, Jackson was sure, enough of them. He set about enlarging and strengthening this corps with the greatest vigor. He did so in individual action, as when he wrote to his old pastor, Dr. White, in Lexington, not a young man, urging him to visit the army and preach at a few services. Or he would urge that the distinguished minister from New Orleans, the Rev. Dr. Benjamin Morgan Palmer, who left that city when the Federal forces captured it, come to the Second Corps as a missionary, and he offered to pay $500 a year from his own funds for the support of Dr. Palmer.[114]

Jackson sought more generally to stimulate the denominations themselves to send more and better chaplains to the army. Half the regiments, he pointed out, had no chaplains, and some others had chaplains who labored without plan or concert with others—inefficiency, the General called it. He knew of others who disappeared when hardships or dangers grew severe. This he would not countenance. The spiritual leader must share the life of the army as much as the military leader.

Dr. White urged Jackson to outline his views in some public way, but the General hesitated. "This I shrink from doing," he wrote to Dr. White, "because it looks like presumption in me, to come before the public and even intimate what course I think should be pursued by the people of God. I have had so little experience in church matters, as to make it very proper, it appears to me, to keep quiet beyond the expression of my views to my friends." [115] Although Dr. White and Preston might use his ideas, if after prayer they thought it wise to do so, they must not attribute the views to Jackson. To Dr. White he outlined what he considered the fundamentals of his proposal. He wrote:

My views are summed up in a few words, which are these: Each Christian branch of the church should send into the army some of its most prominent ministers, who are distinguished for their piety, talents, and zeal: and such ministers should labor to produce concert of action among chaplains and Christians in the army. These ministers should give special attention to preaching to regiments which are without chaplains, and induce them to take steps to get chaplains, to let the regiments name the denomination from which they desire chaplains selected; and then to see that suitable chaplains are secured. A bad selection of a chaplain may prove a curse instead of a blessing. If the few prominent ministers thus connected with each army would cordially co-operate, I believe that glorious fruits would be the result.

Denominational distinctions should be kept out of view, and not touched upon; and as a general rule, I do not think that a chaplain who would preach denominational sermons, should be in the army. His congregation is his regiment, and it is composed of persons of various denominations. I would like to see no question asked in the army, as to what denomination a chaplain belongs; but let the question be, does he preach the Gospel? [116]

Within his own corps Jackson organized weekly meetings of chaplains, on Tuesdays, at which they consulted on common problems, sought to provide religious services in areas which had none, and discussed, on a nondenominational basis, the spiritual needs of the corps. Although Jackson was responsible for this weekly conference, he thought it better not to attend it; but his interest in its findings was strong. "Now come and report," he told his own chaplain after such a meeting.[117]

This was the Rev. B. Tucker Lacy, of a family which sent many members into the Presbyterian ministry. Earlier he was in the Army of the Valley. Now he was commissioned simply as an army chaplain, without assignment to a unit, but in practical effect he was the leader of the chaplains in the Second Corps. He preached with great vigor and learning, and he commanded respect among the soldiers. Jackson listened to him on March 22 (said Hotchkiss) with "all attention." A week later Lacy's sermon left some of the listeners "much affected." He told Hotchkiss that Jackson was the most humble and devoted Christian he ever saw. Jackson—in circumstances that are not clearly indicated—confessed to him that he had almost lost confidence in man, that when he thought he had found a man he needed and was about to rest satisfied, something turned out to be lacking— "I suppose it is to teach me to put my trust only in God." [118]

Jackson sought not only to obtain more chaplains but to strengthen their position. They lacked statutory standing. He appealed to the military committee of the Confederate Congress to provide for chaplains tents, fuel, and forage for their horses just as the army did for officers. Eventually Congress did. Jackson, meantime, had already given "his finest horse" to Lacy (said Pendleton) and was sharing his own quarters with him.[119]

These were the actions of a man of religion who encouraged prayer meetings on Wednesday and Saturday nights, at which he frequently led in prayer, held brief prayer services each morning at his headquarters, and joined with members of the staff in the singing of hymns on Sunday afternoons. He could act ingeniously and thoughtfully in other ways. Months before, during a lull in the Valley campaign, he had learned that among the privates in the Rockbridge Artillery were two nineteen-year-old ministerial students from the Presbyterian seminary at Hampden-Sydney who had almost finished their theological course before they enlisted. One of them was William S. Lacy, son of the Rev. Dr. Drury Lacy who had performed the ceremony when Jackson and Mary Anna Morrison were married; the other was George H. Gilmer, son of Virginia's Governor in the early 1840's, Thomas W. Gilmer.

The General called in the two young men, to their great astonishment. He knew they needed only licensing by their presbyteries to enable them (as the General said) to do some service, though privates in the ranks, as ministers of the gospel.[120] He asked when and how their licenses could be obtained and gave them eighteen day's leave to obtain them. The young men went away, won their licenses, and returned to the army.

All these religious activities were no substitute for other responsibilities. The record of the General's respect for military duty, and of the energy, persistence, and the dedication with which he performed it, is overwhelming. The relations between himself and his God did not interfere with his obligations to defeat the enemy or to plan and prepare with continuing and searching effort to do so.

Nor did the composition of Jackson's staff or the atmosphere of his headquarters suggest an undue fondness on his part for theologians or Presbyterians or, in fact, for any others than competent military officers. Dabney is the unusual example of a staff officer plucked from a chair of theology. But he was with Jackson less than four months, from April into July. James Power Smith was a theological student when he enlisted in the army and was a Presbyterian minister after the war, but he had become an aide too recently

(September) and was too young to exercise influence of importance or to affect materially the atmosphere of the headquarters.

The more than forty other officers who were members of Jackson's staff at different periods included men of religious feeling, for this was an age of religion, though there is no man like Dabney among them. This large group included primarily proficient, even hard-bitten men of war who had learned through long training or under rugged experience—such officers, for instance, as Harman, Hawks, Pendleton, Boswell, Crutchfield, Wilbourn, Douglas, and Hotchkiss, and others. The professional skill and the general intelligence among such men was high. They could display a full share of lively youthfulness, romantic spirit, and personal attractiveness in the eyes of women as well as men.

A nice balance of maturity and broad experience in varied activities is also evident in the presence for brief periods of men like Preston, Boteler, Faulkner, S. Bassett French, who had been Governor Letcher's military aide, and William L. Jackson, a cousin of the General who had been a judge in western Virginia and lieutenant governor of the State. They had limited experience in the field, but they were men of affairs with a knowledge of public life and politics; and they had special duties rather than the military functions of the regulars. Among the officers who remained long with Jackson and carried on the daily duties of the staff the chief characteristics were hard work and professional competence. Without these no one remained long.

Jackson—in the view of the Rev. Dr. Joseph C. Stiles, the unofficial chaplain general of the Confederacy—"came nearer putting God in God's place than any other human soul I ever met," [121] but he also had a war to win, and he never forgot or slighted that duty for a moment.

The General was, at the same time, the father of an unseen daughter and the husband of a woman he loved. "I was made very happy," he wrote to Anna on December 16, three days after the fighting at Fredericksburg, "at hearing through my baby daughter's last letter that she had entirely recovered from a minor set-back. [The home headquarters continued writing in the baby's name.] I was much gratified to learn that she was beginning to notice and smile when caressed. I tell you, I would love to caress her and see her smile. Kiss the little darling for her father. . . ." [122] On the 18th: "It does her father's heart good" to hear about her. On Christmas Day: "Yesterday I received the baby's letter with its beautiful lock of hair. How I do want to see that precious baby!"

The Dabneys at Hampden-Sydney had invited the General and his family to meet there, but "whilst it would be a great comfort to see you and our darling little daughter, and others in whom I take a special interest, yet duty appears to require me to remain with my command. It is important that those at headquarters set an example by remaining at the post of duty." On the 29th: "May every needful blessing rest upon you and our darling child. . . ."

This spirit carried into the new year. On January 5 Jackson wrote to his wife: "How much I do want to see you and our darling baby!" The next day: "I am very thankful to our kind Heavenly Father for good tidings from you and baby—specially that she is restored again to health, and I trust that we all three may so live as most to glorify His holy name."

This may have been after the time when the General, hearing that his daughter was not well, described her symptoms to McGuire, obtained suggestions for treatment from him, and wrote them down carefully for Anna. His own health was "essentially good, but I do not think I shall be able in future to stand what I have already stood, although, with the exception of the increased sensitiveness of my ears, my health has improved."

By January 17 Jackson struck a new note: "I am gratified," he wrote to Anna, "at hearing that you have commenced disciplining the baby [then about seven weeks old]. Now be careful, and don't let her conquer *you*. She must not be permitted to have that will of her own, of which you speak. How I would love to see the little darling, whom I love so tenderly, though I have never seen her; and if the war were only over, I tell you, I would hurry down to North Carolina to see my wife and baby."

This letter of the 17th suggested much variation in the General's mood. "I am still thinking and thinking about that baby, and do want to see her," he wrote. "Can't you send her to me by express? There is an express line all the way to Guiney's." Then the tone shifted. For though he was glad to hear that Julia slept better, "it would be better not to call her *cherub;* no earthly being is such." Some other remark of Anna's brought a quick, perhaps sharp reply. "Don't you accuse my baby of not being *brave*. I do hope she will get over her fear of strangers." He had a suggestion for this problem: "If, before strangers take her, you would give them something to please her, and thus make her have pleasant association with them, and seeing them frequently, I trust she would lose her timidity."

An old Calvinistic fear came back at the end: "I am sometimes afraid that you will make such an idol of that baby that God will take her from us. Are *you* not afraid of it? Kiss her for her father."

On February 7 the General was thinking that "our baby is nearly three months old. Does she notice and laugh much? You have never told me how much she looks like her mother. I tell you, I want to know how she looks. If you could hear me talking to my *esposa* in the mornings and evenings, it would make you laugh, I'm sure. It is funny the way I talk to her when she is hundreds of miles away."

Young Joseph Morrison, the General's aide, had a leave of absence, partly because of the illness of his and Anna's mother. The General sent his letter by him, and he sent a silk handkerchief to Julia because "I have thought that as it is brightly colored, it might attract her attention. Remember, it is her first present from her father, and let me know if she notices it."

Julia did notice it, and laughed and was, Anna wrote, much pleased. When the General had this word, it was mid-February, and he was thinking more and more about the possibility of Anna's and Julia's coming to see him. At the moment he was looking far ahead. "If peace is not concluded before next winter," he wrote, "I do hope you can bring her and spend the winter with me." Anna wondered why he could not visit them now, and he had to deal with that issue again. "You say you don't see any use of my not taking a furlough. I think the army would be much more efficient if all belonging to it were present. . . ."

By mid-March Anna may have had more to say on this subject. The General moved from Moss Neck on the 17th to a tent near Hamilton's Crossing, on the railroad about five miles from Fredericksburg. "It is rather a relief," he told Anna, "to get where there will be less comfort in a room, as I hope thereby persons will be prevented from encroaching so much upon my time." He was still far behind in his reports and was trying to complete them before another campaign began, which he expected would be soon—a second, and perhaps the most important, reason for his move. He had to tell Anna that "I do not know of any house near by where you could be accommodated should you come; and, moreover, I might not be here when you would arrive, as the season for campaigning has come . . . we can't say where we will be a week hence."

By April these difficulties cleared. The weather precluded campaigning. The Federal army remained quiet. Jackson found quarters at the nearby home of William Yerby. Could Anna come? And then he was anxious to know why she didn't hurry.

Anna, with Julia and her servant Hetty, was hurrying as fast as depleted railroads and the family preference against travel on Sundays permitted. She left Cottage Home in North Carolina in time to arrive at Richmond for Sunday, April 19. The peach trees were in full bloom, and a few wild flowers were showing themselves. A week earlier variable April had produced such a wonderful spring day, with the grass and grain brightening, and birds enlivening the scene, that Hotchkiss marveled at it in his diary. On Monday, April 20, the rain was heavy, but Anna set out early by train. Julia had a long sleep en route, to her mother's satisfaction. She and Hetty were anxious to have the baby present her best appearance for her father's first sight of her, and she could not, said Anna, have better realized their wishes.

As the train stopped, in strode the General through the rain, his rubber coat dripping, "but his face was all sunshine and gladness; and, after greeting his wife, it was a picture, indeed, to see his look of perfect delight and admiration as his eyes fell upon that baby!" Julia did her manners with (in Anna's words) "her brightest and sweetest smiles." The General, unwilling to take his daughter in his arms because of his wet coat, led the way to a carriage. The soldiers at Guiney's and along the road, seeing the General and his daughter together, greeted them with cheers.

At the Yerby house the new father shook off his coat quickly enough and for the first time held his daughter in his arms. It was the beginning of a genuine love affair. He held her in his arms upon every possible occasion, walked up and down with her, asked after close inspection, "Isn't she a little gem?", lifted her up before a mirror ("Now, Miss Jackson, look at yourself"), and knelt over her cradle while she slept. Anna said that Julia looked like him, but he would have none of that. "No," he said, "she is too pretty to look like me."

She must be baptized, the General and Anna decided. April 23 would be five months to the day from her birth. That would be the time, and Mr. Lacy, the chaplain, would be the minister. The place would be right here in Mr. Yerby's parlor. The chaplain thought the Jacksons wished the ceremony to be private, but young Smith appealed the issue to higher authority. "Certainly, Mr. Smith, you can go; ask the others to go with you," the General said. So a cavalcade of staff officers rode to William Yerby's, and the room was full of young men in uniform who had seen many babies before—and many other sights across the Virginia and Maryland slopes—but never a father like the General there as he held his child in his arms for Mr. Lacy's ministerial words and the laying-on of his hand.

There had been a slight delay, when the group had all assembled, before Julia herself appeared. When the hour came and nothing happened, the General, taking precedence over the father, went into action. Out he strode, and in a moment back he came, Julia in his arms. (When he said the troops would march at early dawn, he meant it.)

There had been, earlier, a test of another kind. Julia, wishing on another day to be taken up from the bed where she lay, raised her voice and almost raised the roof. When the father picked her up she stopped crying. He put her down, and she started crying again. "This will never do," the General said, and they settled down to a long, loud, and (to Anna) disturbing test of wills. "He stood over her," said Anna, "with as much coolness and determination as if he were directing a battle; and he was true to the name of *Stonewall*, even in disciplining a baby!"

General Lee called on another day with some of his staff, and when the word went up to Anna in her room she was nervous at the prospect. She walked down the stairs to a cordial greeting from a gentleman with a kind, fatherly face. The formidable staff consisted of two or three courteous, pleasant-looking gentlemen, and she was reassured and put at ease, and enjoyed herself thoroughly.

On Sunday, April 26, a congregation of 1,500 to 2,000 soldiers heard the chaplain preach from the text of Lazarus and the rich young man. Anna thought the attention and behavior of the soldiers remarkable, and she was greatly impressed by their singing—"one grand volume of song," she called it. It was a fine day, with a sparkling breeze, and spring was breaking out all over the countryside. Lee, Early, and a long line of officers were present, Lee seeming handsome to Anna and impressive with "his splendid figure and faultless military attire." Anna drew all eyes. "She is slightly built and tolerably good looking, and was somewhat gaily though modestly dressed," Hotchkiss wrote for his diary.

That was a Sunday to remember. The General remained all afternoon with Anna in the large room of the Yerby house, "hospitably furnished with *three* beds," as Anna recorded. (General Lee had stayed there a few weeks before when he had been ill, and he told Anna that he had written to Mrs. Lee and their daughters that if they would come to see him, he would entertain them all in this one room.) The General seemed, she thought, to be "giving utterance to those religious meditations in which he so much delighted," but she did not fail to note that he had never seemed so handsome or so noble.

Anna's visit stimulated a flurry of social activity—slight though it had to be. Many officers called on the Jacksons. Troops marched near for parade and review, and Julia was lifted up whenever possible so that the Second Corps could see her. Douglas thought that "Mrs. Jackson's attractive looks, manners, and good sense did much to make these visits to her popular and pleasant, and the General was the model of a quiet, well-behaved first father. He was much in evidence," but, Douglas continued, although unnecessarily, he did not seem to neglect any of his official duties.[123]

Underneath the surface, and in private, emotions must have been given free rein. Jackson had just passed his thirty-ninth birthday (on January 21), and Anna was thirty-one years old. They had not seen each other since they parted in Winchester in March of 1862— thirteen months before. That winter when Julia had been conceived was unforgettable for them both. This spring they were together almost in the presence of the enemy and with the certainty that fighting lay ahead. She would have to leave any day. Beyond that no one could tell.

They had now "the additional charm and the attraction of the lovely child that God had given us" (Anna wrote), but first of all they had each other. They had waited long for this renewing. Now they were face to face. It is small wonder that in retrospect Anna said this visit exceeded even the Winchester days in happiness.[124]

She remembered long a day when Jackson rode from his head-

quarters on his big bay horse, "Superior," in order to show this fine
animal to her. After he had done so, he mounted again and in sheer
exuberance rode off at a furious gallop. His cap swept off, but he
did not stop. He was flying like the wind (said Anna). Watching
him in admiration, she thought him "the impersonation of fearless-
ness and manly vigor." [125]

Anna persuaded him during this visit to permit a photographer
from the studio of Minnis and Cowell in Richmond to take a picture
of him. She thought he had never presented a finer appearance of
health, and she liked the uniform coat which Stuart had given him
—"the handsome suit," she called it. Anna arranged his hair herself,
noting that it was unusually long and curled in large ringlets. The
chair was in the hall of the Yerby house, before an open door, and
the strong breeze in his face caused him to frown a little, "giving a
sternness to his countenance that was not natural" (she thought),
though "some fine copies have been made from the original."

This was the three-quarter view, the second of the only two photo-
graphs made during the war. It was the favorite picture of his old
soldiers because they thought it was the more soldierly-looking.
Anna liked the Winchester picture, "which has more of the beaming
sunlight of his *home-look*." [126]

The days passed in a rush. The long and wonderful Sunday was
behind them now. Anna walked abroad in a spring that was steeped
in beauty. The grass was fresh and green, the peach and cherry
trees were in full bloom, the anemone, the houstonia, and the san-
guinaria dotted the fields,[127] and the whole plain of the Rappahannock, washed clean by winter of the blood that lay upon it,
sang in its new loveliness. Jackson let nothing—neither wife nor
daughter—interfere with his duty, but now he had a home to come
back to, and Anna in the great room at Mr. Yerby's with the three
beds had a reason for waiting for the evening to come.

They were very much in love, but the days were passing fast, and
the signs of enemy activity were rising all along the river. Lee was
confident Hooker was about to move. He thought Hooker had
started on the 24th only to be deterred by a heavy rain. Balloons
had been rising on the far shore. Cavalry were discovered up the
Rappahannock. Federal troops in the rear were reported moving up
nearer the front. A Federal force launched an attack on Port Royal
and then withdrew before defenders could get at them. Lee advised

Jackson not to send more troops to the far right of the line because of that affair, suggestive though it was of something in the making, because "I think that if a real attempt is made to cross the river it will be above Fredericksburg." [128]

Through Monday the 27th and Tuesday the 28th Anna and Julia remained at the Yerby house and roamed outside in the capricious April days. The General did his duty in the almost certain knowledge that the enemy would strike any day. The family united in the evenings.

Then on Wednesday the 29th, so early in the morning that the General was not up, a messenger knocked on the Jacksons' door. "General Early's adjutant wishes to see General Jackson," he said.

The General turned to Anna and said: "That looks as if Hooker were crossing." Early was on the left of the Second Corps, near the position the corps occupied in the battle of Fredericksburg.

Jackson drew some clothes on and hurried downstairs for the message from Maj. Samuel Hale. Back he came, still in a hurry. Hooker was crossing. He must go forward immediately. Anna must prepare to leave at a moment's notice. He would try to get back, but he could not tell. If he could not return, he would send her brother Joseph (his aide) to help her catch the train at Guiney's.

He finished dressing. There was no time for breakfast. He looked around, checking fast on his possessions and his needs in battle—for he had no doubt about that. He looked at Anna standing there. He looked at Julia in her bed. He looked at Anna again. He must go. This was the end of the visit—nine days—nine wonderful days—Anna—Julia—Anna. He took her in his arms. Then he was gone.

He had scarcely left before the crash of cannon shook the house.[129] Anna, knowing it had to come but stirred to her depths now, went mechanically about the business of attending to Julia, packing their possessions, preparing for departure. Nine wonderful, wonderful days!

A knock at the door, and word that someone had come to see her. It was the chaplain, Mr. Lacy, with a note from the General. The General—Mr. Lacy was sorry to have to say it—could not come back. He had directed Lieutenant Morrison to join Anna, but young Morrison, a soldier as well as a brother, suggested to the General that if a battle was coming on, he might be needed. Couldn't the chaplain go to Anna? The General nodded at that. Now the chaplain asked Anna what he could do to help her.

They left to the rattle of musketry amid growing excitement. Anna looked back at soldiers she had never seen—wounded coming in from somewhere, brought to nearby houses. The war! She turned back to the chaplain, and they drove the rough miles over a newly cut road, over roots and among stumps, to Guiney's Station and an almost empty train. She looked at a pretty young Creole mother and a little boy from New Orleans, who were riding South too, and she thought, "She came to see her husband as I did." [130]

The train moved out slowly toward Richmond. Nine wonderful days!

# 32 | CHANCELLORS-VILLE

*"My God, here they come!"*

Jackson hurried on April 29 from William Yerby's great room to his headquarters tents a mile away. He sent Smith to the army headquarters to give Lee the news. Smith found one of the aides, Venable, and at his suggestion entered Lee's tent and awoke the commander. Lee swung his feet out of his cot, sat up, and looked intently at Smith's face for his report. He showed no surprise and was even a little jocular.

"Well, I thought I heard firing," he told Smith, "and I was beginning to think it was time some of you young fellows were coming to tell me what it was all about. Tell your good general that I am sure he knows what to do. I will meet him at the front very soon." [1]

Sedgwick's Sixth Corps was crossing in heavy fog by a pontoon bridge thrown near the mouth of Deep Run almost at the spot where Franklin's grand division had crossed on December 11 and 12. Jackson had already sent word to his four divisions to be on the alert. Now through the fog he was trying to examine the Federal movement. He could not contest it without coming under the superior enemy guns on the opposite bank. Lee had decided, if the enemy crossed the Rappahannock in his face, to fight it out on the lines he had used against Burnside, but he doubted that Hooker, even with his 133,000 men and 404 guns to Lee's own 62,000 men and 228 guns, would butt his head against that wall.

The greatest concern of both Lee and Jackson was to penetrate Hooker's mind and to determine where he meant to throw the major part of his weight. Sedgwick, they soon discovered, was fortifying wherever his troops spread out and showed no disposition now to assail Early's division in the old A. P. Hill defense line, including the protruding patch of woods that was well occupied this time. The main blow seemed likely to fall somewhere else.

Sedgwick commanded one of the seven corps with which, plus a cavalry division under George Stoneman, Hooker had replaced Burnside's grand-division scheme of organization. Reynolds had the First, Couch the Second, Daniel E. Sickles the Third, Meade the Fifth, Sedgwick the Sixth, O. O. Howard the Eleventh, and Henry W. Slocum the Twelfth. This reversion to standard organization was one of the moves Hooker made when he inherited from Burnside an army that was depressed in spirit, bitter when it thought of its frustrations and losses, dissatisfied with its food, deficient in medical treatment, and anxious to go home. Soldiers were deserting at the rate of two hundred a day.[2] Altogether Hooker faced a problem in morale that demanded exceptional command ability.

Hooker—his name "Fighting Joe Hooker," which he did not like, came from a newspaper man's love of a headline more than from his own slam-bang characteristics in the field [3]—proved himself an excellent organizer. He provided leaves of absence in large numbers, improved the rations, cleaned up the muddy camps, reorganized the hospitals, drilled the commands with ardor, held large and polished reviews, and sought in many ways to stimulate *esprit de corps.*\*

The response was remarkable. Aided by the resilience of youth and by shifts in corps and division commanders, Hooker whipped the downcast army which he took over in January into a well-drilled, eager, and formidable fighting force by April. He called it the finest army on the planet and discussed future successes in a "when I get to Richmond" vein. The attitude disturbed Lincoln. He ended a talk with Hooker and Couch by saying, "I want to impress upon you gentlemen in your next fight *put in all your men.*" [4] Hooker was a handsome officer with a strong physique and a manner that made soldiers like him as they had not liked any other general except McClellan.

---

\* One of the devices Hooker put into effect was shoulder badges of different designs for each corps, with different colors to indicate divisions (they were worn either on the slanting front of the forage caps or on the breast of the uniform by officers), somewhat of the type that American units used at the shoulder in the world wars of 1917–1918 and 1941–1945.

He produced, moreover, a bold plan of unusual possibilities (although with one serious defect), and he set about putting it into effect with energy that brought excellent initial results. Hooker had planned to lead with his cavalry on a broad, sweeping march around Lee's left that would destroy supplies and communications but primarily would place 10,000 men on horseback on Lee's flank or rear when, as Hooker confidently assumed, the main Federal army would wrench him out of the carefully built fortifications along the Rappahannock.

Stoneman set out on this mission in mid-April but ran immediately into another deluge. The high waters and the mud forced him to halt and then withdraw before crossing the river. Hooker was disappointed but not deterred from trying again. This time Stoneman broke free, turned Lee's left flank (though at a far distance from it), and swept eventually to the west, south, and east behind Lee's army, with annoying damages in many areas and a scare for Richmond. Lee lacked the cavalry to contest this move and would not have done so if he had much larger resources. Stuart sent two regiments to hang on Stoneman's flank in observance, but the main body of the Confederate horse Lee kept at hand for the major movements. If Hooker could force Lee to retreat, Stoneman's cavalry might rip into a beaten army. But for the test to come, Hooker had disposed of most of the eyes of his army.

On April 27 Meade's Fifth Corps, Howard's Eleventh, and Slocum's Twelfth moved in secrecy up the river on a long march to Kelly's Ford, 27 miles from Fredericksburg. They marched with few wagons but with eight days' rations, including cattle in herds. At Kelly's Ford they brushed aside minor opposition and crossed by pontoon bridge on the night of the 28th.

On the morning of the 29th—the morning that Jackson was awakened by the news that separated him from Anna—Meade moved southward toward Ely's Ford on the Rapidan, and Slocum, followed by Howard, swung out wider toward the south on a route that carried them toward Germanna Ford, about 13 miles for Meade and a little less for Slocum and Howard, to the second crossing.

Stuart picked up the movement this day. He sent word to Lee on the morning of April 29 that 14,000 infantry, with guns and cavalry, had crossed the Rappahannock at Kelly's Ford, but were heading in a southwest direction toward Gordonsville—away from

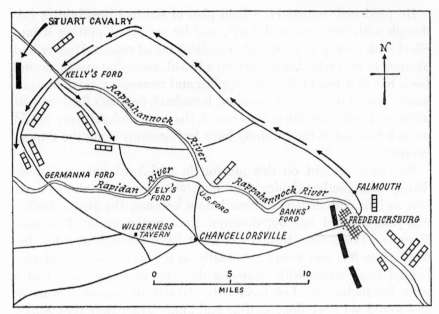

HOOKER'S ENVELOPMENT OF LEE'S LEFT FLANK IN THE
CHANCELLORSVILLE CAMPAIGN.

Lee's army. A few hours later Stuart corrected that information. He
knew now that the Fifth, Eleventh, and Twelfth Corps were on the
south side of the Rappahannock, moving in a southeast direction
toward Ely's Ford on the Rapidan. This meant some 40,000 men
aiming straight at Lee's left and rear. In front of Lee part of Hooker's
army was threatening to storm his lines on the heights above Fredericksburg. In his rear Hooker was completing a pincer movement
that threatened to grind him to pieces.

The Rapidan was high from recent rains, and the ford at Germanna
was waist-deep. Men with heavy packs waded into danger. Many
of them slipped and floundered in the water. Some of them were
swept off their feet and drowned before Slocum and Meade lined
cavalrymen on horses downstream to set them on their feet again.
But the Confederate resistance at the fords consisted only of pickets,
and Hooker's massive movement pressed farther to the southeast on
the morning of the 30th.

The farther the three corps advanced, the more they opened up—

merely by being in its rear—the United States Ford about halfway between Fredericksburg and Kelly's Ford and just below the junction of the Rappahannock and the Rapidan. If they kept pressing on, they would uncover Banks' Ford, hardly five miles above Fredericksburg. Uncovering these two was important. Hooker had lined up at each more troops to cross and join Meade, Slocum, and Howard without taking their long route.

These three followed roads that would come together at a large brick residence, formerly an inn, with a few outhouses, called Chancellorsville. It sat a mile or so within the Wilderness. There the original forest had been cut long ago for charcoal, and a thick, tangled second growth, shutting off sunlight and creating gloom, stretched twelve to fourteen miles along the Rapidan with a depth of eight to ten miles. Intermittent farms and small homes could be discovered here and there, and a few roads ran between the trees.

Two principal roads led out of Chancellorsville, both looking to Fredericksburg, the Old Turnpike from Orange Court House straight east to Fredericksburg, and the Plank Road, dipping toward the south and then rejoining the Turnpike five miles farther, near Tabernacle Church. To the north a river road followed the convolutions of the Rappahannock, which the Rapidan had now joined. The thick woods made this bad country for fighting, especially for artillery, but Hooker did not plan to fight here. He planned to dislodge Lee by maneuver, force him out of the lines along the Rappahannock and toward the more open country to the south (where Stoneman's 10,000 sabers were supposed to be waiting for him), or force him to attack superior numbers under disadvantageous conditions.

Some of this Lee could discern before the 29th ran out, some of it he could not. He knew that Hooker had divided his army and had carried through a large-scale turning movement around Lee's left. The direction was no surprise, but Lee does not appear to have foreseen that Hooker, who he expected would attack above Fredericksburg, would make the turning movement cover such a broad arc or would cross two rivers by choice. Hooker's concept was admirable, his secrecy was good enough, and the large operation had moved without material delay. He had an impressive achievement to his credit, and his position was now excellent—so excellent, indeed, that it forced Lee to act.

Lee began shifting to the left to meet this ominous threat. Anderson's division began moving on the night of the 29th toward Chancellorsville, and Anderson himself arrived there at midnight and set about organizing against the Federal advance. For that purpose only three brigades were at hand: Ambrose R. Wright's, which was hurrying up during the night from near Fredericksburg, and Carnot Posey's and William Mahone's, both from their earlier positions opposite the United States Ford.

The Second Corps had also shifted to the west during the 29th, but to a much less extent. Early held his position in the front lines which A. P. Hill had occupied during the battle of Fredericksburg. Hill came up closer behind him and dug in on the military road that topped the ridge to his rear. Colston moved from the Moss Neck and Skinker's Neck area to Hamilton's Crossing. He had the old Jackson division which Trimble would command when he was able to return to field duty. To the same area Rodes (in command while waiting for Edward Johnson) brought the old D. H. Hill division up from Grace Church, placing it on the extreme right of the line and, since he guarded the flank, in a position perpendicular to the railroad. The corps was better concentrated to meet a direct attack of the Burnside style but also to move farther west if that proved to be where the battle would be fought.

Jackson directed these movements with an energy and decisiveness that communicated themselves to all around him. He was up and down the lines much of the day, and everywhere he went the men cheered him; but that was now normal. The change that seemed to have come over him—marked by many who knew him and the more conspicuous because of his relative calm and ease during the long winter—was that of new confidence, new sureness, new animation, and even greater sense of will power. In manner and bearing he seemed to be rising to an emergency.[5]

"Who said that?" he demanded when a suggestion that the army might have to retreat reached him. "No, sir! We shall not fall back! We shall attack them!" [6]

Morning and afternoon on this day Jackson and Lee were in consultation, at first in Lee's tent and later, during the afternoon, in a long examination of the enemy in front of them. About that threat they needed much more information.

On April 30, a cool and foggy Thursday with a touch of drizzle that did not clear until noon, Jackson could detect no change in the Federal troops that lay beside the river below him. They were not active, and their numbers had not increased. They showed no sign of preparations for attack. To him they were an opportunity. He had not forgotten the abortive attack of December 13 when he discovered the weight of Federal guns just in time. But with Hooker's army divided, the natural move—indeed, the necessary move short of a retreat—was to hit at one of its parts while the other was too far away to come to its aid. Why not at Sedgwick here?

Jackson pressed this view so strongly that Lee gave new consideration to it. "It will be hard to get at the enemy, and harder still to get away, if we succeed in driving him to the river," Lee pointed out. "But, General, if you think you can effect anything, I will give orders for the attack." [7]

With the responsibility placed on his shoulders, Jackson began an intensive study that lasted most of the day. In the end he gave up. The move could not be made. He reported his changed view to Lee, and there the issue ended—except to disclose once more the relations between these two officers.

At Chancellorsville before dawn on the 30th Anderson decided that his line of defense should not be drawn there. The ground, the woods, the roads, the fields of fire were not good. He withdrew about three and a half miles, fighting off cavalry stabs as he did so, to a position between Zion Church and Tabernacle Church that extended across both the Turnpike and the Plank Road.

Wright came into place by 8 A.M. between the Plank Road and an unfinished railroad line still farther to the south. Posey and Mahone were in position by 9 A.M., Mahone on the Turnpike and Posey between the Turnpike and the Plank Road. They were in the open where they could see what they were doing, and the ground they occupied was higher. Lee sent some engineers to help Anderson in fortifying, and the three brigades began digging furiously—as Lee specifically had directed. [8]

Meade's Fifth Corps began arriving at Chancellorsville about 11 A.M. Slocum's Twelfth swung in near 2 o'clock, and Howard's Eleventh was showing up at Dowdall's Tavern, about two miles west of Chancellorsville, by 4 o'clock. All of them were enthusiastic. They had been through no fighting to speak of, and they knew that their long and hard swing around Lee's left was a success.

"We are on Lee's flank and he does not know it," Meade burst out to Slocum. But Slocum had a sobering message from Hooker. It directed that "no advance be made from Chancellorsville until the columns"—that is, Couch's Second and Sickles' Third Corps, which were scheduled to cross at United States and Banks' Fords, as well as the three corps on the ground—"are concentrated." [9] He himself would be at Chancellorsville that night.

This was discouraging to men who could see no resistance against them. They felt the tingle of achievement and were eager to press on. Now, for reasons they could not discern, they had to wait. Slocum, senior officer on the ground, placed Meade in position just east of Chancellorsville. He formed his own corps a little to the south and west of it. Howard's Eleventh Corps he placed still farther west, at the rear of these three corps; and Howard placed Charles Devens, Jr.'s, division on the extreme west. Part of the division faced south and part west. The Eleventh partook of the nature of a flank detachment set up to secure Hooker's entire right wing from attack from the west.

Two divisions of Couch's Second Corps, crossing at the United States Ford, reached Chandler's, half a mile north of Chancellorsville, at 10 P.M.; and Hooker, having arrived between 5 and 6 P.M., ordered Sickles' Third Corps to come in at 7 A.M. on May 1. It had been shifted to the United States Ford for crossing.

Hooker, fairly bubbling with confidence, issued this day a congratulatory proclamation to the army. "It is with heartfelt satisfaction," he said, that "the commanding general announces to the army that the operations of the last three days have determined that our enemy must either ingloriously fly or come out from behind his entrenchments and give us battle on our own ground, where certain destruction awaits him." [10] Yet the energy of these three days was even now giving way in Hooker to caution or uncertainty or inability to decide. Simultaneously events were spurring Lee to action.

Before the end of the day Lee had made his first major decisions. The Federal effort would be on his left. He would meet it there. He would leave a deterring force in front of Sedgwick. The greater part of his army must move fast to the Chancellorsville region. These decisions Lee embodied in new orders.

He ordered McLaws, minus one brigade, to march at midnight to Chancellorsville to join Anderson. He ordered Jackson, minus one division, to march at dawn to the same region, there to "make arrangements to repulse the enemy." [11] The division left was Early's and the brigade left was Barksdale's, less than 10,000 men between them, but well served by artillery. They guarded the five-mile sweep from Fredericksburg to Hamilton's Crossing which Lee had held with 70,000 men on December 13.

The figures are the evidence of the risk Lee was taking, but the one thing he was not going to do was, in Hooker's phrase, flee ingloriously. He would do more for Hooker's other supposition: attack Hooker on his own ground. In this determination McLaws, hurrying out at midnight for the Chancellorsville area, and Jackson, straining at the leash to follow, were the living symbols.

The night of April 30–May 1, a brilliant moonlight night, was full of Confederate activity. Semmes' brigade of McLaws' division, already on the move from its separated position near Fredericksburg, took position at 1 A.M. on the right of Mahone, whose left rested on the Turnpike. Wofford's and Kershaw's brigades arrived at daylight and lengthened the line on Semmes' right.

Jackson, directed by Lee to proceed "at daylight" to Tabernacle Church, had Hill, Rodes, and Colston (Early being left at Fredericksburg) on the move at 3 A.M., even earlier than his customary "early dawn." He himself, under Lee's directions to "make arrangements to repulse the enemy," hurried ahead of his divisions and arrived at Anderson's line at 8 A.M. and took command there. He had no orders to go beyond Tabernacle Church, but he had no orders to remain there. The best arrangement he knew of to repulse the enemy was to attack. He pulled Anderson's and McLaws' divisions out of the trenches immediately and converted them from a digging defensive force into an assault force.

It would be a two-pronged attack. Mahone went into the lead on the Turnpike with his 2,000 men. McLaws' brigades backed him up: Wofford and Semmes with 4,000 between them, and Kershaw with 2,700—all told, 8,700 in this prong, with 24 guns, under McLaws' command. Wilcox's brigade from Banks' Ford and Perry's from opposite Falmouth, both of Anderson's division, were coming in to follow.

Posey and Wright with 14 guns of Alexander's battalion led the left prong down the Plank Road, 3,000 infantry and 260 artillerymen. Behind them, two miles or more distant, the Second Corps was com-

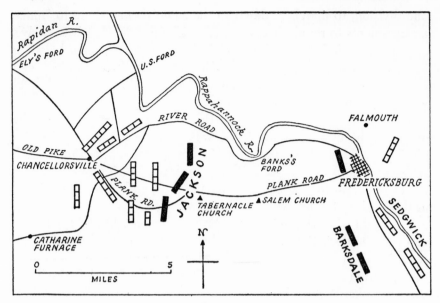

JACKSON ATTACKS HOOKER'S FLANKING MOVEMENT,
MAY 1, 1863.

ing up from Fredericksburg, but Jackson did not wait for it. He
was thrusting 13,000 men (they would be nearer 40,000 when his
corps was up) at four full corps and most of a fifth—upwards of
70,000 men.

The shift from a defensive line to advancing columns took time,
and it was not until 10:30 or 11 A.M. that Jackson's attack moved
ahead on the two roads. After early fog it was a May day of full
beauty, bright and warm, with a fine breeze.[12] The columns had
skirmishers thrown well out, and cavalry units scouted far to the
flanks and ahead. They looked straight into the thick woods and
narrow roadways to Chancellorsville and the Federal mass waiting
there—not only waiting but moving now straight toward them.

Hooker began this May Friday with talk that seemed full of confidence. "The rebel army is now the legitimate property of the Army
of the Potomac," he told a group at headquarters.[13] Sickles was
crossing the United States Ford at 7:30 A.M., and by 11 o'clock his
leading units were coming to the junction of the road from the ford

and the road from Ely's Ford where it was to concentrate. When he came in, Hooker would have the full strength of his right wing at hand. But it was not until that hour that Hooker sent out formal orders for the day, though he may have issued them by word of mouth earlier. In either event, the late start suggested uncertainty.

The Fifth Corps (Meade) was to advance on both the river road and the Turnpike, an awkward assignment because the roads diverged widely and the leading units would be marching away from each other. Griffin's and Humphreys' divisions took the river road, Sykes' the Turnpike. Hooker ordered the first two to reach a point between Mott's and Colin Runs at 2 P.M. He did not say what to do thereafter.

The Twelfth Corps (Slocum) was to "be massed below the Plank Road," the head near Tabernacle Church, by noon in order to clear the way for the Eleventh to follow at a mile's distance. The Eleventh was to be in this position by 2 P.M.

Hooker said later of his action this morning that "I went out to attack the enemy." [14] The wording of his 11 A.M. order suggests an intent to take a different defensive position. It would be on the line from Tabernacle Church on Hooker's right to the vicinity of Banks' Ford on his left. This was the line to which Anderson had withdrawn the day before and along which he had organized field fortifications. Hooker must have assumed that he would have to dislodge Anderson. Whether he knew that McLaws had arrived is not certain. He did not know that Jackson's Second Corps was arriving. The three corps he sent forward had about 40,000 men, or almost exactly the same number Jackson would have when his full strength was up; and the difference in guns was only 16, in Jackson's favor.

Almost simultaneously Hooker directed his chief of staff, Maj. Gen. Daniel Butterfield, who had remained at army headquarters near Falmouth, to tell Sedgwick "to threaten an attack in full force at 1 o'clock, and to continue in that attitude until further orders. Let the demonstration be as severe as can be, but not an attack."

This obviously was a belated attempt to keep Lee from doing what he had already done—from moving out of the defense lines at Fredericksburg the large proportion of his army which was already on its way. Hooker had scored first in the preliminary maneuvers

when he circled Lee's left and came up in his rear. Lee had scored
now by shifting, without Hooker's knowledge, the major part of his
army from Fredericksburg to the region east of Chancellorsville
toward which Hooker was now advancing.*

The collision of the advancing forces marching through the
Wilderness directly toward each other came quickly. Cavalry and
skirmishers preceding Sykes along the Turnpike encountered Mahone's skirmishers in front of the McLaws' column. Men dodged
from tree to tree, rifles cracked, artillery came up the road, and then
the weight of Sykes' regulars forced the skirmishers back. As the
sound of the artillery reached a Federal captain in Slocum's corps
to the south he looked at his watch. "Twenty minutes past eleven,"
he said, "the first gun of the battle of Chancellorsville." [15]

McLaws notified Jackson, then with Posey and Wright on the
Plank Road, that the enemy was in force in front of him and was
advancing. Farther off, a mile ahead, he had noted even larger
enemy forces. The situation seemed to him to invite a flank attack
from Jackson. Could the General manage that?

Jackson replied quickly with orders for McLaws to hold his
ground. Artillery was coming up, and if this was not enough, he
would try for the enemy's rear. McLaws swung Wilcox's and Perry's
brigades, which had now joined him, out to his right, extending his
front and protecting his flank. His main force went into a defensive
position and held its ground, but the skirmishers multiplied their
activity with remarkably effective results.

Sykes interpreted the skirmishers that swarmed on his flank as
evidence of superior numbers in front of him. The advance of Griffin
and Humphreys on the river road carried them away from him on
one side, and the advance of Slocum's corps on the Plank Road
carried it away from him on the other side. He felt isolated. With
a strongly resisting enemy in front and the woods full of gray rifle-

* Butterfield sent to Hooker at 5:30 A.M. on this day the following: "From deserter just in, learn that Jackson's whole corps is opposite Franklin's Crossing [below
Fredericksburg]. Camp rumor that Longstreet had gone to Culpeper; that Lee said
it was the only time he should fight equal numbers; that we had about 80,000. Some
of Trimble's division told him they had to march to Culpeper tomorrow. They all knew
we had crossed 40,000 men above." (*O.R.*, XXV, pt. 2, 322.) Longstreet was still near
Suffolk. Trimble's division, now under Colston, was hotfooting it toward Tabernacle
Church. But if the deserter had been sent by Jackson, as some students of the campaign have suggested, notably Bigelow, the most important impression he would
have tried to leave was that Jackson was still staring across the Rappahannock at
Sedgwick below Fredericksburg, as Butterfield seemed to think he was.

men to the right and to the left, he feared that his rear was in danger of a movement through the forest and that his whole position was critical. He said as much to Hooker's chief engineer, Brig. Gen. G. K. Warren, who rode back and told Hooker. Hooker ordered Sykes to retire toward Chancellorsville. The time was between 1 and 1:30 P.M.,[16] and the decision was historic.

Jackson had joined Anderson's column as it pushed out along the Plank Road straight toward Slocum, now coming from the opposite direction. He heard from Stuart about this time, probably from Welford's Furnace, more generally called the Catharine Furnace. This meant that Stuart was off to his left, and Stuart informed him that Fitzhugh Lee was still farther to the left, "and extends scouts to Plank Road (Orange), and has Turnpike watched beyond to see if any large movement takes place that way. I will close in on the flank and help all I can when the ball opens. . . . May God grant us victory."

Jackson replied with an "I trust that God will grant us a great victory." He added, in a clear indication of what he was thinking about: "Keep closed on Chancellorsville." [17]

This was about 12:30 P.M. Almost immediately afterward Lee, who had been far to the east inspecting Early's position, below Fredericksburg, rode up, and Jackson joined him with a report on operations. Lee made no change. The soldiers of the Second Corps, now coming up for action, were all around them, and the sight of the two generals brought the loud whoops and the high, shrill yells of men of the ranks. Lee rode off to the right to look at the situation nearer the Rapidan. Jackson turned back to the Plank Road.

Word came that Posey and Wright had run into skirmishers and seemed to be facing formidable forces. Jackson pulled Ramseur's brigade out of Rodes' division and sent it forward. It went into action in the center, with Posey on the right and Wright on the left, all deployed through the woods on both sides of the Plank Road. Slocum deployed his main body with two divisions straddling the road and prepared, though the shift in the thick woods took a long time, to advance. Artillery on both sides began to blast through the trees, and the preparations pointed to a major engagement.

But about 1:30 P.M. Slocum received word from Hooker to pull back the Twelfth Corps toward Chancellorsville [18]—another historic decision. Farther to the rear the Eleventh Corps had hardly moved

out before its order to advance was countermanded, and it returned
to its encampment west of Chancellorsville. Whether Hooker sent
these orders before or after his order to Sykes to retire (apparently,
after) is not important. The decisions came from the shock to which
Hooker had been subjected and the mood that had now taken
possession of him.

The same mood reflected itself in Hooker's orders about the same
hour for Meade's divisions on the river road, which had met no
opposition, to pull back, and for Couch, who was trying to help
Sykes, to retire to his position of the previous night near Chancellorsville.*

These withdrawals all along the Federal front were neither hasty
nor disorderly. All the Federal commanders had control of their
troops. But Jackson's advance continued right along. Jackson encouraged it in person. "Press on, Colonel," he urged many times.
At 2:30 P.M. he sent a message to McLaws that he was "pressing on
up the Plank Road; also that you will press on up the Turnpike, as
the enemy is falling back. Keep your skirmishers and flank parties
well out, to guard against ambuscade." [19] A short time afterward
Heth was detached with the three brigades from Hill's division and
pushed across to the Turnpike to see if he could find a way to Chancellorsville. Heth moved with eagerness and actually reached the
Turnpike ahead of McLaws' advance.

At about the same time Wright moved with his small brigade
out to the left, reached the right of way of the unfinished railroad
to the south, and advanced fast. He was trying to reach around
Slocum's right and threaten his rear. Slocum, pressed from his front
as well as his right, continued his withdrawal.

---

* Hooker's orders for retirement occasioned surprise and met outright resistance
from some commanders. Couch opposed the withdrawal of Sykes and sent an aide to
Hooker to express the view that the situation on the Turnpike was not serious, only
to be told that the order would stand (*B. & L.*, III, 159). Meade, who had advanced
on the river road toward slightly higher ground, burst out: "If he thinks he can't hold
the top of the hill, how does he expect to hold the bottom of it?" (Bigelow, 254.)
Hooker changed his mind to some extent later in the afternoon and sent a message to
Couch, received at 4:30 P.M., telling him to remain on the Turnpike, where he was
acting as rear guard, until 5 P.M., and saying that Slocum would hold a position on
the Plank Road equally advanced. But Couch thought that impossible now. He told
the bearer of Hooker's message: "Tell General Hooker he is too late. The enemy are on
my right and rear. I am in full retreat." (Bigelow, 254.) Hooker's own explanation of
his withdrawal orders was that "I was being rapidly outflanked upon my right, the
enemy having open ground on which to operate." (*B. & L.*, III, 218.)

As Wright advanced far out on the left, he came up to Stuart at the Catharine Furnace, where six guns of Stuart's artillery under Maj. R. F. Beckham were stationed. When Wright collided with the fringe of the Federal line he asked Stuart for help. Beckham went forward with four of his guns, opened fire on Federal regiments in the woods, and forced them back, but brought in return a blast of artillery shells that led Beckham to say later: "I do not think that men have been often under a hotter fire than that to which we were exposed." [20]

It was still in progress when Jackson rode up, joined Stuart, and, while trying to determine what was happening, came under this fire. Stuart turned to him sharply: "General Jackson, we must move from here." [21] They did, but not before Stuart's adjutant general, Maj. Channing Price, who accompanied them, was mortally wounded.

Growing evidence all along the front indicated that the Federal forces, now forced back to positions half a mile to three-quarters of a mile on the west and south sides of Chancellorsville, were retreating no farther and presented there a powerful defensive line. But there were mysteries about this day's operations. Why had troops which had marched out from these positions in midmorning under orders to construct a new line nearly five miles ahead halted under the first pressure and retreated with suspiciously little resistance?

What did Hooker mean when he telegraphed his chief of staff, Butterfield, at 2 o'clock: "From character of information have suspended attack. The enemy may attack me—I will try it. Tell Sedgwick to keep a sharp lookout, and attack if [he] can succeed"? [22]

What did he mean when he wrote about the same hour: "Hope the enemy will be emboldened to attack me. I *did* feel certain of success [italics are the author's]. If his communications are cut [by Stoneman] he must attack me . . ."? [23]

Why did the general who had thrown three army corps around Lee's left flank and deep into his rear, and then had brought up most of two other corps, or above 70,000 men in all, in a remarkably successful maneuver which demanded, of all things, continued swift pressure, retire after attacks from hardly 25,000 men?

The "information" Hooker had received was of many kinds, positive and negative. At his post of command at Chancellorsville, he was too far from Butterfield at the Falmouth headquarters, and still farther from Sedgwick at Fredericksburg, to have any direct or effective control of the whole battlefield. The telegraph system operated badly much of the time (Hooker's order to Sedgwick to demonstrate, sent at 1 P.M., did not reach him until after 5 P.M.), and the distances were long for couriers. It was 20 miles from Hooker to Sedgwick by the route couriers had to take through the United States Ford. Hooker was suffering from the loneliness of command. He was puzzled by reports that Longstreet had returned, that re-enforcements had reached Lee from Richmond, that Lee had as many men as he had. He did not know whether Sedgwick still faced a formidable force or whether much of it had shifted toward Chancellorsville. He seemed to hold all the high cards, and yet Lee was behaving as though he held the high cards.

There was an old army story about Hooker to the effect that he "could play the best game of poker . . . until it came to the point where he should go a thousand better, and then he would flunk." [24] There was also a theory, quite seriously advanced, that Hooker suffered at Chancellorsville from lack of liquor. He had the name of a steady drinker, and he drank with regularity without being visibly hurt; but in this first operation as commanding general he forswore his daily drinks. He may have paid a cruel penalty for abstinence in loss of nerve.[25]

But about one fact there is no room for debate. Hooker faced the aggressiveness of Jackson and he recoiled before it. It caught him by surprise. It came when, by all available information, no important parts of Lee's army should have been in the way of Hooker's movements. It showed a cool confidence that might mean a major force was attacking him. It was vigorous, persistent, energetic, and businesslike.

It was also, on the known record, wholly Jackson's doing. When Lee sent him from the hill beyond Fredericksburg to Tabernacle Church at dawn (for Jackson 3 A.M.) on May 1, it was to "make arrangements to repulse the enemy." The generality of the words is the evidence of Lee's confidence. Lee was too good a soldier to assume that repulsing the enemy would exclude attacking the enemy. He made no objection when he learned that Jackson was repulsing by attacking. But an officer under the same orders might have thought himself justified in building up the defensive line along which Anderson had his men constructing field fortifications (at Lee's orders) and fighting it out there.

Such an officer would not have been Jackson. The first thing Jackson decided when he assumed command at Tabernacle Church was to attack. The consequence was that instead of Jackson's fighting a defensive battle along the Tabernacle Church line, Hooker fell back to a defensive line at Chancellorsville. The ultimate effect is beyond measurement. It is possible only to say that Jackson's aggressive attack on the morning of May 1 altered the whole nature of the campaign.

Lee was not satisfied with the long-range prospects. He had not identified the units opposite Jackson's advance. Prisoners from Meade's corps were in hand, but he did not know that the Federal troops on the Plank Road were Slocum's Twelfth Corps, and no Confederate unit had established contact with Howard's Eleventh Corps. At 4 P.M. Lee sent a message to Stuart to find out what had become of these two corps which, as Stuart had reported earlier, had crossed the rivers.[26]

Aside from this uncertainty, Lee was searching for a point of entry. What about the right? He took two companies out of Wilcox's brigade and parts of the Third and Fourth Virginia Cavalry and sent them to the right to reconnoiter. But they could find no inviting avenue for attack against Federal forces which stretched, though sometimes thinly, all the way from Chancellorsville to the Rappahannock. Yet Lee could not wait. He was taking a risk already by leaving Early with 10,000 men at Fredericksburg against a far stronger force. He might rule out the right, but he knew little about the strength of the enemy directly in his front, and he was almost completely in the dark about the situation on the left.

In the midst of these uncertainties Lee rode in from the right and Jackson came in from the left. They met about 7 P.M. on the Plank Road near where the road to the Catharine Furnace cut across it. A Federal sharpshooter in a tree began firing in their direction, and they pulled back out of his way. In the twilight they found a log and sat down together.[27]

Calmly, patiently, thoroughly, Lee reviewed the situation with Jackson. What did Jackson know about the Federal position directly in front and on the left? Jackson's report on the left was necessarily sketchy. He told about the quick and heavy Federal counter battery

fire when Beckham had opened fire for Wright. Obviously there
was some strength out there. He told of Wright's advance, although
it does not appear that he realized the full effect of Wright's movement on the minds of the Federal commanders, especially Hooker,
who (as we have seen) thought the ground there permitted flanking
operations and thus presented a reason why he had better withdraw
before an aggressive enemy. But neither Wright nor the Confederate
cavalry had yet discovered the location of the Federal right.²⁸

Jackson told Lee that the Federal withdrawal directly in their
front was suspicious. Lee thought so too. The Federal forces had
fallen back before the pressure was really severe. There had been
no major battle. Since the attackers had stopped and then withdrawn under moderate pressure, Jackson believed they would keep
on withdrawing. "By tomorrow morning there will not be any of
them on this side of the river," he said.²⁹

But that Lee would not accept. He had been confident—he still
was—that Hooker was making his major effort right *here*, strange
though the withdrawal had been. He was sure Hooker would renew
his effort. In any event, he continued, we must get ready to attack
the enemy if we should find him here tomorrow. How strong was his
position at Chancellorsville? Maybe they could find out by a reconnaissance now. Talcott could go.³⁰ Jackson said his engineer officer,
Boswell, could also go. The moon was high. Its rays penetrated the
woods, which were not too thick here. Let the two officers go immediately, Lee said.

Lee and Jackson continued to examine the possibilities, exchanging ideas, pondering their practicalities, revising, estimating, specu-
lating about Federal lines and strengths and purposes. Then Stuart
rode up through the moonlight to them. He had something to report.
Fitzhugh Lee had been reconnoitering to the west and was now satisfied that he had identified Hooker's right flank. It was wide open—
in the air—unprotected by natural obstacle, fortification, or troop
arrangement.

Hooker's right flank in the air!

From this moment Lee and Jackson gave scant thought to their
right or center. When Talcott and Boswell came back an hour or so
later, their report was anticlimactic. It was definite enough. The
Federal defenses in front were strong. They included trenches and
earthworks. Abatis extended all along the line. Guns commanded

the roads. The woods were too thick for effective passage by large bodies of troops. The possibilities were bad.

This report Lee set aside. The real issue was on his left. An open flank! Could it be reached? Stuart assured them that the Federal cavalry presented no problem. Stoneman's 10,000 horsemen, ranging far to the west and south across the Virginia countryside, now took on by their very absence an importance in reverse far greater than they had seemed to possess.

Were there any roads? Could troops in large numbers move to Hooker's open, exposed flank without being seen?

Stuart didn't know, but he would try to find out. He rode off into the moonlight, undoubtedly excited by the idea that now possessed all three of them. From now on they would consider nothing else.

On maps before them, Lee and Jackson looked hard at their left. Nothing they had gave them the information Stuart was seeking. But if there was a way to get there, what should they do? Half to himself, half to Jackson, Lee asked: "How can we get at those people?"

Talcott understood Jackson to reply ("in effect," he said): "You know best; show me what to do, and we will try to do it." *

They continued to look at the map. Presently Lee pointed along it, indicating a wide circling march to the left and around to the west, flanking the open right of Hooker's lines and extending into his rear. That was the movement, he said. Then Lee told Jackson that he should lead it. Stuart would cover his march.

This was all Jackson needed to know. He rose immediately, saluted, and said: "My troops will move at 4 o'clock."

Lee continued. If there was any doubt in the morning as to whether the enemy was in the same position he occupied today, Jackson could send guns to a position nearby (perhaps where Beckham had begun to fire that afternoon and drawn swift and smashing replies) and test the response.

Jackson turned away. Lee had given him no more to go on than when he sent him hurrying forward to Anderson's line at Tabernacle Church to make arrangements for repulsing the enemy. Everything

---

* This is the testimony of Talcott, who overheard part of the Lee-Jackson conference. (*S.H.S.P.*, XXXIV, 34.) No contrary evidence is known to exist, and there is no reason to doubt the sincerity of Talcott's testimony. But both the words and the spirit seem unlike Jackson. Ordinarily he did not talk like this. He did not often shrink from presenting his ideas when asked to, and generally he had ideas to present.

was now left to him: the strength of his force, the nature of the advance, the route he would take, the exact destination, the decisions as to where, how, and when to attack, all the possibilities that would emerge from complete or moderate success or failure, and every arrangement that would have to be made or kept in mind for an operation that involved the unorthodox and fearful hazard of splitting into three parts a numerically inferior army that was already split into two parts. If an aggressive enemy knew what they were doing, he could not ask for a more inviting opportunity to fall upon one of the separated segments of Lee's army and crush it with the overwhelming pressure he could bring to bear.

Jackson had yet to find out whether terrain and roads permitted any plan of moving fast around Hooker's right flank—which would involve the classic danger of marching across the front of Hooker's corps—without being discovered. His mind must have been racing with innumerable issues, problems, and possibilities. But with Stuart at work he could wait. It was somewhere near midnight, probably earlier. Dawn would come about 5 o'clock. He would be up early. Now he would sleep.

He looked around, remembering he had brought nothing with him, and prepared to stretch out under a tree. He unbuckled his sword and placed it, leaning, against a tree. The night was cold. So Sandie Pendleton, watching the General, thought. He came forward with his overcoat. No, the General said, he wouldn't take it. Sandie retreated, rallied his forces, and came forward again. Well, why not take the cape of the overcoat? He unbuttoned it and held it out. The General accepted that, lay down under his tree, and—despite ten thousand uncertainties—slept.[31]

Lee was still up. Lacy, the chaplain, appeared. He told Lee that he knew something of the country about Chancellorsville and the Wilderness. He had had a church nearby. Lee asked him about roads. The two talked long enough for Lee to feel encouraged about the possibilities of the movement around Hooker's right. Then they both found beds on the pine needles within sight, almost within the heat, of the quietly flickering fire.

Jackson woke first, in the darkness long before dawn of this Saturday, May 2, stiff and uncomfortable, shivering from the chill May night and from the beginnings of a cold.[32] He shook out Sandie's cape and, looking around for that young officer, placed it on him as he continued to sleep. Then he turned to the small fire made of twigs, hovered over it to absorb some of its warmth, held out his hands almost in its flames. He saw a cracker box that had carried Federal rations, left here in the wake of Slocum's withdrawal before Posey, Ramseur, and Wright's advance. He pulled it up to the fire and sat down.

Lacy, the chaplain, woke up, cold like everyone else this morning. He saw the fire and the figure beside it, and he came forward and spoke to the General. Jackson looked up, and a flash of new interest swept across his face. Lacy ought to know. He invited the chaplain to sit down. When Lacy hesitated, the General moved over on his cracker box and urged him again. Lacy joined him. Now, the General asked him, tell me about roads to the south and west.[33] Lacy complied with a detailed description. Jackson pulled out a map. Show them to me on this map, he said. As Lacy did so Jackson watched intently.

This is too close to the Federals, he said, pointing. Their pickets can see anyone passing by. What about other roads? Farther to the south and out of sight? Lacy didn't know. But Col. Charles C. Wellford, proprietor of the Catharine Furnace, would know. His house was just below the furnace—about two miles or so from where they were. He had a son who might make a good guide.

Jackson decided instantly. Get Jed Hotchkiss, he said, and the two of you go to see Wellford immediately. Ask him about roads. They must be the shortest roads that will provide cover and circle around to the south and west. Hotchkiss was sleeping nearby. Lacy woke him, and the two rode off to look for Wellford. Jackson turned back to the fire.

Lee's aide, Col. A. L. Long, waking up a few minutes later, saw General Jackson thus and knew that he was cold. He spoke to the General and then went into action. Scouting around the neighborhood, he found a campfire. Presently he came back to the General with a tin cup full of steaming coffee. Ah! This was better.

As Long moved about he heard a clatter. He turned to the sound of the noise and saw that Jackson's sword, which had been leaning against the tree, had fallen to the ground. The soothsayers used to say that was bad luck. Long thought of the old tales as he walked over to pick up the sword and take it to the General. The General thanked him and buckled on his sword.[34]

Lee woke up. He shook off the night and regained quickly his characteristic dignity and command presence. He joined Jackson at the fire. The two sat on their cracker boxes, leaning toward the warmth. It was still before dawn. They took up their talk of the night. It dominated their minds, and each in his own way turned it over again and again, searching for weaknesses, building on strength. Jackson told of seeing Lacy and of sending him to the Wellford house with Hotchkiss. No word had come in from Stuart. Lee knew about Lacy, but Wellford ought to be useful.

A sound of horses reached them. Hotchkiss rode up fast, swung off, and came to them quickly. He was full of information. Lacy and he had found the Wellford house, had waked the Colonel, had asked him about roads. The Colonel had told them. Now he had it.

Hotchkiss looked around, saw another cracker box, and pulled it between the generals.[35] He spread a map on it. With the light of the fire playing on the intent faces, he traced the Plank Road and the road to the furnace. Then he explained, talking calmly, his finger running over the map, darting, stopping while he made a point, going on again, stopping again.

He traced the route along the Furnace Road to the Catharine Furnace and then straight south away from the enemy. Eventually the road turned a little southwest and then west and thus ran into the north-and-south Brock Road. But Hotchkiss' finger did not turn north on the Brock Road, the natural choice. It turned south, still farther away from the enemy. If they kept south for three-quarters of a mile or so, he said, they would come to a lesser road, branching out of the Brock Road and running north roughly parallel to it but on the western side—that is, away from Federal eyes. This lesser road led eventually, after making a loop, back into the Brock Road just a mile below the Plank Road.

The important steps were to turn south at the furnace, and get away from the enemy; and to turn south when they first reached the Brock Road, and get away from the enemy a second time.

The distance was 11 to 12 miles, a little more for others farther back. The surface was good enough for artillery and wagons. Most of the way the cover was excellent. The route was roundabout, but wasn't that what they were looking for?

It was. Hotchkiss searched the grave faces. The generals kept on looking at the map. Then Lee turned to Jackson.

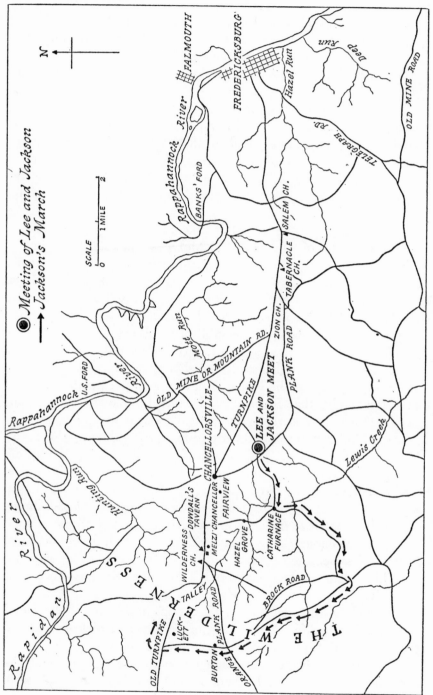

The Chancellorsville campaign area and Jackson's march of May 2, 1863.

"General Jackson, what do you propose to do?"

"Go around here," Jackson replied, redrawing with his finger the route Hotchkiss had drawn on the map.

"What do you propose to make this movement with?" Lee asked him—quiet, solemn, intent.

"With my whole corps," Jackson answered.

He did not hesitate. He had thought it out. If the flanking movement was worth making—and about that, like Lee, he had no doubt—it was worth making in full force. He would hit like a great hammer; he would go for the top prize of a staggering and completely destructive blow. Twenty-eight thousand men were hardly enough for this purpose.

"What will you leave me?" Lee asked.

"The divisions of Anderson and McLaws," Jackson told him.

Two divisions—13,000 to 14,000 men—against an enemy who could throw 50,000 in his face if Hooker would go all-out to do so! Even Lee hesitated. But if he hesitated ever so slightly, to the credit of a great general must go the fact that he examined, accepted, decided in a moment, and did so in the spirit of greatness.

"Well, go on," Lee said and turned to details and instructions.

Jackson said he would leave immediately, although he could not make the 4 A.M. start he had spoken of last night. Lee told him, as he had already, that Stuart would cover his movement with his cavalry. Speed and secrecy were critical needs now.

Lee's mind was turning already to his own problems—alone with McLaws and Anderson. Jackson would not only become the hitting force: he would become the major force of the army. Lee had no doubt of him. But holding the hinge with McLaws and Anderson was the essential and indispensable prerequisite. It was also an assignment of extreme delicacy in which every detail of just enough pretense, just enough show of strength, just enough deception, must keep Hooker bemused right where he was, waiting, for all his numbers, like a lamb to be slaughtered. This was Lee's duty. He met it superbly.

It was close to daylight now. The troops in the woods all around were coming to life. The shifting of units that had been ordered yesterday, with no thought of movements today, was getting under way. Iverson's brigade was going up to relieve Ramseur's at the front on the Plank Road where it had led Anderson's advance.

Thomas' brigade was getting ready to relieve Posey. Posey and Wright were preparing for the shift of their brigades on the left of the Plank Road. Jackson's three divisions were scattered, separated, already in motion for other purposes, or were scrambling for breakfast. The General had to reorganize them for the road under difficulties and at a late hour for him—and later than even he knew.

Smith, the aide, chose this morning, of all mornings, to sleep until broad daylight. He came to life only when someone shouted, "Get up, Smith, the General wants you!" He found the General sitting his horse by the road as the troops began their march. Smith never forgot that moment: "His cap was pulled low over his eye, and, looking up from under the visor, with lips compressed, indicating the firm purpose within, he nodded at me, and in brief and rapid utterance, without a superfluous word, as though all were distinctly formed in his mind and beyond question, he gave me orders for our wagon and ambulance trains." [36] Those wagons not with the troops were to move by roads farther south so as not to clog the movement.

It was between 7 and 8 o'clock [37] when Rodes' division moved out of its bivouac near Aldrich on the Plank Road. Colquitt's Georgia Brigade was in the lead—the Sixth, Nineteenth, Twenty-third, Twenty-seventh and Twenty-eighth Georgia Regiments. Colston's division followed. Hill would come last. Each division had its artillery, ambulances, and ammunition wagons behind it. The column when stretched out on a single road, as it would be, measured ten miles, of which the infantry took up six. Hill did not clear the Plank Road–Furnace Road crossing until nearly 11 A.M.

Elements of Fitzhugh Lee's cavalry brigade were out in front with Stuart accompanying them. The Second Virginia Cavalry was ahead, and the First and Fifth and part of the Third were on the right. Jackson made special efforts to prevent straggling on a march he knew would be severe. He placed colonels at the rear of their regiments with strong men, bayonets on their rifles, guarding the units. Hotchkiss had the mission of sending couriers back to Lee periodically.

Jackson and his staff followed the leading regiments as they reached the crossroads where Lee and Jackson had conferred the night before. Lee was waiting there. Jackson joined him, and they pulled off to the side, out of hearing, for a brief talk. Men watching their faces saw earnestness written there. Suddenly Jackson raised his arm and pointed down the Furnace Road. Lee nodded. Jackson turned and rode straight ahead into the forest. They never saw each other again.

The day was crystal-clear, with not a cloud in the sky, and the sun was growing warmer. The road was narrow. Trees crowded in on it so that the column seemed to be moving through a green tunnel. The footing was damp and soft enough for ease. In the cool of the morning when the marching was good the men were full of zest. Young Smith, coming back from his errands, started behind them, and to reach the General up near the front he had to ride for a great distance, along narrow roads, through these ragged irreverents. They let him have it.

"Say," one of them cried out at the sight of the aide, "here's one of Old Jack's little boys. Let him by, boys!"

"Have a good breakfast this morning, sonny?" asked a gaunt Georgian who, like as not, had had none at all.

"Better hurry or you'll catch it for gettin' behind."

"Tell Old Jack we're all a-comin'. Don't let him begin the fuss till we get thar!" [38]

Old Jacksonians in the Second Corps had no illusion. They could sense a flank march in the making, and this had all the marks of one. The intensity and eagerness on the General's face no less than the sudden rush of orders that had brought them out this morning in a hurry meant that something was in the air.

"Press forward, press forward!" the General said again and again to unit commanders. McGuire thought he leaned over the neck of Little Sorrel more than usual, as if in this way he could hurry the march along. "Press on! Press on!" rose from every officer today.

Shortly after 8 o'clock the head of the column came out into high and open ground just before the road ran downward to Lewis' Creek (also called Scott's Run). A mile to the north the clear ground led to an eminence called Hazel Grove, itself more than a mile southwest of Chancellorsville. Birney's division of Sickles' Third Corps, which was now occupying the area between Slocum's Twelfth Corps and Howard's Eleventh, had men on Hazel Grove. Some of them had climbed tall trees to scout the country. Looking southward, they could see plainly the column of infantry that rose to the high ground near Lewis' Creek and then dropped out of sight at the creek and the furnace. Birney himself stared at the sight.[39]

These Federal soldiers and officers were men who believed, almost to a man, that Hooker's successful concentration at Chancellorsville meant (in Hooker's own words) that Lee must ingloriously flee or attack him on his own ground; and most of them were confident that he must flee. This moving column was not moving toward them —that seemed plain enough to them. It must be retreating, probably toward Gordonsville. With Stoneman's cavalry farther south Lee would find retreat that way uncomfortable. There was no concern, but Birney ordered a battery to open up.

The shells (with a range of about 1,600 yards) began to fall close. Jackson ordered the troops to double-quick across the open space. The artillery and trains presented more difficulties, but hasty reconnaissance disclosed luckily a road by which they could detour to the south, under cover. Colquitt was directed to drop off the Twenty-third Georgia to stand guard at the furnace against the possibility that the Federals would try more seriously to cut the road. Jackson pressed right on.

The sight of the flowing troops, double-quicking and disappearing, aroused more Federal effort. Sickles climbed Hazel Grove and took a long look at the column. Birney's reports had already gone to Hooker, now just back from an inspection tour of his right flank. Sickles proposed a major attack on the column with his full corps, which would need the support, he thought, of Slocum on his left and Howard on his right.

Hooker, now that his attention was called to the moving column, could see it from his headquarters. By noon he directed Sickles to advance, but cautiously. Birney's division was followed by Whipple's division and eventually by Williams' division from the Twelfth Corps, and still later—between 4 and 5 P.M.—by Barlow's brigade, 3,000 strong, which was the Eleventh Corps's reserve. Before the day was out Sickles had sucked 20,000 men into this southward advance.[40]

Birney's advance overran part of the Twenty-third Georgia and took 40 prisoners. But the remainder of the regiment fought with spirit. Thomas' brigade of Hill's division, which now was on the march, heard the firing, and turned back. So eventually did Archer's brigade. Lee, much concerned because of the possibility that Federal troops would wreck Jackson's trains, or even cut his column in two, sent Posey and later Wright. The resistance held up Sickles, who did not know at any time what he was getting into and was under Hooker's adjuration to move cautiously. Birney first, and Sickles later, halted for further reconnaissance and re-enforcement. But Birney surrounded the remainder of the Twenty-third Georgia and captured most of it.

Even from talkative prisoners the Federal commanders would learn nothing this day. Some rough gibing met the Georgians as they were herded by their captors. When a Federal trooper said he and his outfit would capture them all before they could get away, a prisoner gave him fair warning: "You think you've done a big thing just now," he said, "but you wait until Jackson gets around on your right." [41] But the assumption that Lee (and Jackson) was on the run was too fixed for the tall talk of prisoners to jar it.

The moving column kept on moving. When the last train of Hill's division had cleared the danger by detouring south, Thomas and Archer themselves took up the pursuit of the remainder of the Second Corps. It was late in the afternoon now, and these two brigades did not catch up with the main body until long after nightfall. The whole affair had slowed up the tail of the column materially.

Nothing stopped Jackson. As the day advanced, the sun grew hotter, the tight tunnels through the brilliant green of spring grew more repressive, and the men grew more weary. Jackson did not drive them relentlessly. They had three breaks during the march, probably of about twenty minutes each [42]—a variation from the standard ten-minute break after every fifty minutes which, the General calculated, would cover two miles. The column stretched out— lost distance—in spite of all that was done to keep it closed up; and men dropped out, primarily because of exhaustion from hunger. Deliberate straggling was under good control.

The main movement kept right ahead, down the Furnace Road, across to the Brock Road, southward there instead of northward, until the column hit the new road that doubled back to the north. Then, their faces once more to the enemy, Colquitt's Georgians led the way through this heavily wooded, remote-seeming country, on and on, ever northward.

Noon came and passed, and the narrow road swung back to the Brock Road. The Plank Road could not be far now. They were com-

ing closer with every step to Federal-held country, yet not a soldier
had they seen. Far off to the right the cavalrymen had run across an
occasional horseman who took off after a quick look.

There was no sign, other than the affair near the furnace, that
Hooker's army understood what was happening; no evidence that
the controlling commands realized that Stonewall Jackson was leading 70 regiments of infantry, 28,000 strong, and 112 guns with 2,240
artillerymen to serve them, screened by 1,450 cavalrymen—in all,
some 31,700 men—across the face of five army corps, around their
flank, and into their rear, throughout a bright May day, with the
deadly purpose of hurling the whole force like a thunderbolt into
their vitals.

Up front there was a flurry. Fitzhugh Lee rode in from the screen
far ahead, looked around for Jackson, and went straight to his side.
"General," he said, "if you will ride with me, halting your column
here, I will show you the enemy's right." He suggested that the
General bring only a courier—they would be in danger of detection.

Jackson followed Lee's guidance toward the Plank Road and across
it. They continued well beyond, turned off the road to the right, and
moved forward diagonally through trees and brush. A hill loomed
up ahead on the Burton property. They made for it and, cautiously
now, ascended it. Parting the boughs of trees, walking their horses
with extreme care, they reached the summit, and peered below and
across the open country. In Fitzhugh Lee's words about his own
first view a short while before:

What a sight presented itself before me! Below, and but a few hundred yards distant, ran the Federal line of battle. . . . There were the
line of defense, with abatis in front, and long lines of stacked arms in
the rear. Two cannon were visible in the part of the line seen. The soldiers were in groups in the rear, laughing, smoking, probably engaged,
here and there, in games of cards, and other amusements indulged in
while feeling safe and comfortable, awaiting orders. In rear of them were
other parties driving up and butchering beeves.

Jackson gazed at Howard's troops. Fitzhugh Lee, who did not
know Jackson well but was aware of the meaning of this moment,
thought as he watched him intently that "his eyes burned with a
brilliant glow, lighting up a sad face. His expression was one of intense interest, his face was colored slightly with the paint of the

approaching battle, and radiant in the success of his flank movement."

For five minutes Jackson said nothing. But his lips were moving,
and Lee thought he knew what the General was doing. "Oh, beware
of rashness, General Hooker! Stonewall Jackson is praying in full
view of your right flank." [43]

The General was calculating as well as praying. He was at the
point of a great success—this anyone could tell. But the new information before his eyes was disconcerting. He had counted on advancing eastward on the Plank Road and plowing straight into
Hooker's undefended flank. But the Plank Road would lead to an
attack on the front, or the right front, of the Federal line. Instead
of hitting the enemy from the rear, he would have to storm his defenses. If he could reach farther to the rear, he could hit where it
would hurt, though that would require more marching time.

The General whirled his horse toward his courier. "Tell General
Rodes to move across the Old Plank Road," he said. "Halt when he
gets to the old turnpike, and I will join him there."

He looked once more at the open Federal lines below and in front
of him, and then "he rode rapidly down the hill," as Lee described
the scene, "his arms flapping to the motion of his horse, over whose
head it seemed, good rider as he was, he would certainly go."

The General was seeking now to wring every ounce of advantage
out of his achievement. He would press on past the Plank Road and
go to the Turnpike, and launch his attack here. It meant another
mile and a half to the Turnpike, and a deeper and more dangerous
thrust into a region which the enemy ought to be swarming over
even if he wasn't. But it would provide a jump-off line from which
he could hit from the right rear instead of the right front, and that
might make a decisive difference.

He had already forgotten Fitzhugh Lee. That officer had expected a pat on the back for a valuable personal reconnaissance
which might save many lives, but the General had leaped far ahead
of his present surroundings in preparation for what was to come. He
sent Paxton's brigade—the old Stonewall—down the Plank Road for
a short distance with two batteries and some cavalry, all under Fitzhugh Lee, to prevent interruptions from that quarter. The main
body followed Rodes farther northward on the Brock Road, crossing
the Plank Road at right angles and the Germanna Plank Road at

an acute angle, and coming into the Turnpike between Wilderness Tavern and Luckett. On the Turnpike the troops turned eastward and moved to the Luckett vicinity, an additional three to four miles. They were then about six miles from their start this morning, but they had marched 12 miles, and more for some of them, to get there. The time was about 3 o'clock.

The General swung off Sorrel, found a stump by the road to sit on, and wrote with a pencil this note for Lee:

Near 3 P.M.
May 2d, 1863

General,

The enemy has made a stand at Chancellor's which is about 2 miles from Chancellorsville. I hope as soon as practicable to attack.

I trust that an ever kind Providence will bless us with success.

Respectfully,
T. J. Jackson
Lt. Genl.

Genl. R. E. Lee

The leading division is up and the other two appear to be well closed.

T. J. J.[44]

Chancellor's was the farm of the Rev. Melzi Chancellor, about two miles west of Chancellorsville. It was also known as Dowdall's Tavern.

Looking to his left, Jackson turned to Munford, commanding the Second Virginia Cavalry, and directed him to guard the approach from that direction and, as the Confederate advance proceeded, to try to seize the Ely's Ford Road. Munford had been with Jackson frequently during the day. Now, looking around, he could see Rodes, Colston, and Stapleton Crutchfield, as well as Jackson—all four professors at the Virginia Military Institute when Munford was adjutant of the corps of cadets. Other former V.M.I. cadets were in sight. Munford remarked on the fact. The General replied: "Yes, the Institute will be heard from today." *

---

* William Couper, in *One Hundred Years at V.M.I.*, listed sixteen former cadets or teachers from V.M.I. in high command in the Second Corps, seven of them generals, six colonels, and three lieutenant colonels. In Fitzhugh Lee's cavalry brigade the first four regiments were commanded by V.M.I. men. In Munford's Second Virginia Cavalry twenty-three officers had V.M.I. backgrounds. Numerous others were in other units. Most of them had studied artillery tactics under Jackson.

Back of them the long, narrow column of men kept winding out of the trees and pushing to the Turnpike and eastward on it. Time was now precious beyond counting. It would be long before this thin stream of Rodes' division and then Colston's arrived and could be organized for assault. It would be longer before Hill would arrive. Jackson did not know it, but two of Hill's brigades, Thomas' and Archer's, had not yet left the furnace.

The sun, which would not sink fast enough at Second Manassas and at Sharpsburg, was racing to the horizon now. The assault could not possibly be launched before late in the afternoon. Meantime, they were in danger of discovery.

Federal outposts, pickets, and small-unit commanders did discover the presence of Confederate soldiers many times during the afternoon. They did warn division, corps, and army headquarters again and again, but neither Howard and his staff nor Hooker and his accepted the reports as serious or acted upon them more than perfunctorily.

Hooker had ridden early in the morning to his right flank, had looked at the defenses, had ejaculated: "How strong! How strong!" [45] and had ridden back to his headquarters. The defenses he had looked at faced southward, not westward. He found at his headquarters Birney's report about seeing a column moving westward across the high ground near the furnace. Hooker turned to a map and looked at it carefully. Then talking to himself, he said: "It can't be retreat; retreat without a fight? That is not Lee. If not retreat, what is it? Lee is trying to flank me." [46]

Hooker touched the truth, but he did not grasp it. He sent a message to Howard at 9:30 A.M. saying that the corps's defenses looked to a frontal attack. Howard should consider his defenses against an attack from the western flank. Because "we have good reason to suppose that the enemy is moving to our right," Howard should advance his pickets in order to observe and give timely information.

At 10:50 A.M. Howard sent word back to Hooker that at the headquarters of Brig. Gen. Charles Devens, Jr., who commanded the most westerly of his divisions, an enemy column going west could be seen. "I am taking measures to resist an attack from the west," he said. But his actions were minor, and his mind did not accept any thesis of danger. He continued to look straight ahead to the south.

A signal station set up at the extreme western end of the line, under Capt. D. E. Castle, saw the Confederate column and reported the fact to Howard.[47] A small body of Union cavalry from Brig. Gen. Nathaniel C. McLean's brigade skirmished between 11 and 12 o'clock with a body of enemy cavalry and sent a report to higher command. Pickets from Devens' division captured two Confederate soldiers who said they were part of a force of great strength that was moving around the Federal right. Still neither Howard nor Hooker regarded any of these reports as important.

In the early afternoon Federal cavalry attached to Devens' division reported encounters with enemy cavalry. Brig. Gen. Alexander Schimmelfennig of Schurz's Second Division sent reconnoitering forces into woods to the south, ran into skirmishers, and reported his findings. At 1 P.M. and again at 2 P.M. Lieut. Col. J. C. Lee of Devens' division reported to Devens that the enemy was moving across the front of the division to its right flank. Devens was skeptical. He said headquarters had not told him anything about it. Lieut. Col. C. W. Friend, Devens' officer of the day, informed him that a large force of the enemy was passing to the rear. Devens didn't believe it, and Friend went to corps headquarters. There he was told not to bring on a panic.

Similar reports continued during the afternoon, including a frantic appeal from Maj. Owen Rice to Col. Leopold von Gilsa, commanding Devens' First Brigade: "A large body of the enemy is massing on my front. For God's sake, make disposition to receive him." This cry of woe went to Howard, but he dismissed it.

Maj. Gustav Schleiter carried the Seventy-fourth Pennsylvania westward for reconnaissance on the Plank Road and returned with word that the enemy was massed for attack. Howard's staff laughed at him. When Capt. Hubert Dilger, an artillery officer, rode west on a personal reconnaissance, he ran into Jackson's column and was pursued and almost caught by Jackson's cavalry. He fled far north and made a wide circle to Hooker's headquarters and told his story. He was advised to go back to Howard and tell him. Nobody did anything.

Even without this long series of reports the attitude of the Federal command was unmistakable. Hooker wished to believe that Lee was fleeing ingloriously, and so he believed it. Howard took his tune from Hooker, and so he believed it. Sickles, who had brought his

Third Corps into line between Howard's Eleventh Corps and Slocum's Twelfth, thought he had *seen* Lee fleeing, and so he believed it.

Sickles had gone in pursuit of a column crossing the southern front, and he had convinced Hooker that, down south somewhere in the Wilderness, he was tearing Lee's trains to pieces. When he asked for re-enforcements, he got them, although when 20,000 troops went south with him they left a huge gap in the Federal line. His last appeal won for him Howard's reserve: Barlow's brigade, 3,000 strong. It marched out and left an open mile to the east of Howard's corps. If Howard had to fall back, he would fall back on open space—rather like sitting in a chair that wasn't there. If he needed re-enforcements, they would have to tramp a long way to reach him.

The indispensable arm—and Hooker did not have it—was a proper cavalry force. Stoneman's 10,000 cavalrymen, if they had not been dispatched fruitlessly into regions far to the west and south, would have provided sufficient forces to patrol even the thick woods to the west where Jackson had to concentrate, and should have discovered and located him. They could have patrolled the Brock Road far to the south and thus should have known that Jackson's column meant to use it for a surprise flank movement. They could have patrolled down the opening between the trees which enabled Birney's men to see from Hazel Grove to the furnace and should have learned the nature of the movements Birney and Sickles could see but could not understand.

Federal cavalry would have had to deal with Confederate cavalry in all such respects, and Stuart might have given them a rough time. But they outnumbered him heavily, and always, if cavalrymen want seriously enough to find out what is going on, some of them will get through to see and to report. As it was, Stuart's thin screen protected Jackson so competently that the Federals who did break through—enough, as has been suggested, to put Howard and Hooker on guard—could not make any impression on generals and staffs who had determined upon their formula and would not, on the evidence before them, give it up. Lee and Jackson, it is true, counted on the absence of Federal cavalry as a factor that went far toward justifying the extraordinary risk they were taking. But if Hooker had not thrown away his eyes, Chancellorsville would have been a different affair.

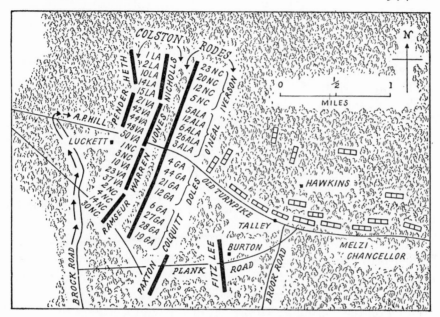

THE SECOND CORPS AS JACKSON LINED IT UP FOR THE
ASSAULT OF MAY 2, 1863.

Sickles accomplished nothing beyond Birney's capture of most of
the Twenty-third Georgia, left on guard at the furnace. His foray,
with Hooker's blessing, made it certain that if a hard blow from the
west should jar Howard back slightly, it would be devastating. Jackson, waiting restlessly and sending back messages to his column to
press on, was preparing that kind of blow.

He was lining up the brigades now for assault. On the reverse
slope of a slight ridge Rodes' division was going into the first wave
with a four-brigade front, two brigades on each side of the Turnpike,
each regiment in two lines. Colquitt's four Georgia regiments (his
fifth was the Twenty-third Georgia) were filing to the right. George
Doles' four Georgia regiments followed, taking position on Colquitt's left, with their own left resting on the road.

On the left side of the road, to the north, Rodes' brigade, now
under Col. E. A. O'Neal, extended the line to the north with his five
Alabama regiments. Still farther to the north, on the extreme left,

Iverson's four North Carolina regiments stretched out. Ramseur's brigade dropped back into the second wave and took position on the right about 150 yards behind Colquitt, extending beyond him by one regiment.

The four-brigade front ran north and south nearly two miles, one mile on either side of the Turnpike—the guide. Two artillery pieces from Capt. James Breathed's battery of Stuart's horse artillery were hauled up the road ready to advance side by side, or, when the road proved too narrow, one leapfrogged the other. Four more guns from M. N. Moorman's battery lined up to follow. Most of the Second Corps artillery was in an open field in the right rear. The front was long and thin, 17 regiments from flank to flank, but behind it to give support, depth, and driving power came the second wave.

Ramseur of Rodes' division on the right of this wave wheeled his four North Carolina regiments into place. The old Colston brigade under Col. E. T. H. Warren, with two North Carolina and three Virginia regiments, came up beside him, a little to his rear, its left resting on the Turnpike. To the left of the road Colston's two other brigades lined up: first, J. R. Jones' five Virginia regiments behind O'Neal of the first wave, their right on the Turnpike, and then F. T. Nicholls' five Louisiana regiments farther to the left (north) behind Iverson. Nicholls had difficulty finding his position and fell in somewhat to the rear of the Jones-O'Neal line. The second wave was not neat and trim to look at, but that did not matter. This was rough country.

Paxton's brigade of this division had been left to guard the Plank Road. If the main hitting force broke through the Federal crust and kept on, it would clear the way for Paxton to advance as part of the right. Without him the second wave consisted of 19 regiments of approximately the same length of front as the first wave. The two together had 36 regiments. They numbered about 15,000 men as they stood, slightly more in the first wave than in the second. In distance the second ranged from 100 to 200 yards in the thick undergrowth behind the first.

This was the primary assault force, augmented as fast as possible by the arriving brigades of Hill. Pender's was the first to arrive. Jackson pushed it quickly toward the waiting lines and held them up so that Pender could form. A precious half-hour of daylight burned up while Pender tried to lengthen the lines already in position, as Jackson probably intended. He didn't succeed, but he managed to fall in 200 yards behind Jones, with his right resting on the Turnpike.

When Heth came up next he was under orders to extend Colston's second wave to the left. Jackson wanted more weight on his left so as to hit harder at the enemy's rear. Before Heth could do so, Colston was up and off, and Heth joined Pender's line to the left in an extension of the third wave. Lane was back in column formation, McGowan still farther to the rear, and Archer and Thomas miles down the Brock Road.

With Pender and Heth the assault force rose to 45 regiments and about 18,500 men. It lacked at the start five of Jackson's 15 brigades (Paxton on the Plank Road, and Lane, McGowan, Archer, and Thomas), which would have lifted the ground attack to nearly 28,000. A third of the infantry was missing. But Jackson could not wait longer.

This had been, for all its movement, a day of frustration: a late start, a longer march than expected, a stretched-out column on the road, and a difficult and slow deployment in thick woods under the compulsion of silence. All these had eaten away the hours. The sun would sink at 6:48 P.M. The time left was only a remnant of daylight, and the battle this day could not possibly be long.

The men were physically tired, and most of them needed food. But they had come out of the winter high in morale, old horrors forgotten in their resilient youth, new adventure calling through the matted trees. They knew they were on the brink of battle, and they knew Old Jack had another surprise. No matter how calm and professional their young faces seemed, they were on fire with excitement as they peered out at life and death.

Jackson's orders, built to the scheme of headlong attack, were simple and direct. The entire assault force was to go ahead with the greatest possible energy. It was to carry the Talley's house position three-quarters of a mile ahead at all costs. That position was believed to overlook the next assumed Federal position at Melzi Chancellor's (Dowdall's Tavern). If the Federals held hard at Chancellor's, the infantry was to stop until the artillery could come up and clear the way. Under no other circumstances was the attack to stop. If any brigade commander needed re-enforcements, he was to call on the wave behind him with authority and without going to a division commander. Each brigade commander received these orders. Each knew the emphasis on speed, drive, pressure.

On the right flank Ramseur in the second wave was to watch for enemies coming in from the right, and Colquitt in the first wave was to go straight ahead. On the left flank Iverson was to detach one regiment (Twenty-third North Carolina) to advance in column in order to guard against surprise from outside. In front Rodes' skirmishers under Maj. Eugene Blackford of the Fifth Alabama were to burrow out 400 yards and lead all.

By 5 o'clock the long delays were over.[48] The two-mile lines stretched through forest, underbrush, and farm land—quiet, tense, waiting. The skirmishers were out in front, the flankers on the sides. The brigades of Hill's division not yet in line were coming up from the rear as reserves. The headquarters staff, its deployment duties over, was watching the General with the utmost intentness. Rodes of the assault wave and Blackford of the skirmishers sat their horses beside him wherever he turned. The sun was beginning to sink low.

The General, his watch in hand, turned to Rodes: "Are you ready, General Rodes?"

"Yes, sir."

"You can go forward then." He spoke quietly, almost matter-of-factly.[49]

Rodes nodded to Blackford and signaled to his own division. Blackford shot out his orders for the skirmishing units far out in front and was off in an instant to command their operations. The commands rang along the first wave of the battle lines, broke out from the Turnpike north and south, were picked up and repeated in brigade after brigade, regiment after regiment, for a mile in either direction. Men leaped to their feet and grasped their rifles tighter. All up! Here we go!

Colquitt, Doles, O'Neal, and Iverson plunged into the trees and bushes straight ahead. Ramseur, Warren, Jones, and Nicholls strode behind them. Pender and Heth in the still-forming third line followed after.

Almost immediately the first wave crowded in on skirmishers on the left who had not caught the order. The battle line slowed up, halted in jerks, and flared in irritation and uncertainty.[50] But only for moments. For now the skirmishers, released and hurled forward, turned with a rush, shouldering their way through the trees and twisting free when the thick growth snagged them and slashed their shirts from their bodies. They burst into open country surrounding Talley's farm, all concealment behind them. The sight of Federal pickets brought guns to their shoulders, and the skirmish line crackled with fire up and down its twisting length.

The sound of the guns was a signal to the assault waves in the forest to break all silences. A bugle rang out in the afternoon sunlight with the rich, clear tones of the "Advance." Bugles everywhere echoed it, up and down the line, and again and again. As the waves rolled forward, the high defiance of the rebel yell pierced the forest cover and swept over the farm land where Howard's right flank hung wide open to him who could take it. Breathed's two guns raced down the Turnpike, wheeled around in orderly haste, and crashed solid shot straight down the road.

The roar of the advance as it rolled through the trees brought the very forest to life. Leopold von Gilsa's brigade of German-Americans who sat and smoked their pipes in the calm of the afternoon on the edge of Hooker's army were startled to see young deer leaping out of the woods [51]—impenetrable for any army, the professionals said— and running straight toward them and on through the camps. Rabbits and foxes were fleeing the holocaust. A forest was on fire, and the roar of the flames was swelling insanely, but the fire was human, and the flames were Jackson's assault waves in the full rush of excitement that the old tradition and the new opportunity were creating.

They beat down on the two regiments of von Gilsa's brigade and the two guns of Devens' division that had been turned to the west. The two regiments fired bravely enough in the few startled minutes at their disposal. But they had only a thin line of rifle pits and a slashing of trees in front of them. Doles sent one regiment to their left, one to their right, and two in their teeth; and they collapsed.

It was symptomatic. The long, thin lines into which Jackson had deployed three divisions were designed to attack end-on the long thin lines of the Eleventh Corps as it stretched along the Turnpike looking south while he enveloped it from the west. In naval terms Jackson had crossed Howard's T. He kept boring in with all guns blazing in an overwhelming demonstration of enfilade.

When the local commanders had time to wheel out of their fixed defenses and establish new, hard knots of defense looking in a new direction, as some of them did, Jackson had the answer. His long lines surged around the enemy and overlapped them to the right and to the left; and many times, as the Federal reports of the day describe, some of Jackson's men were firing into the rear at the same time that others were crashing headlong into the front of the new defenses.

Caught in the surprise, the power, and the width of this attack, Devens' whole division melted away. All of his regiments facing south gave way before this yelling assault on their flank and rear. Four of his guns at the Taylor house near Talley's farm fell to Jackson's men before they could fire a shot. The first of the day's panics seized his units.

"The officers had hardly had time to give a command," Carl Schurz wrote ten days later of his adjoining Third Division, "when almost the whole of General McLean's brigade, mixed up with a number of Colonel von Gilsa's men, came rushing down the road from General Devens' headquarters in wild confusion, and, worse than that, the battery of the First Division broke in upon the right at a full run. This confused mass of guns, caissons, horses, and men broke lengthwise through the ranks of my regiments deployed on the road." [52]

Jackson swept over the first objective of Talley's farm within the first half-hour and was surging against Schurz's regiments in the Hawkins' farm area. He was striving to keep the momentum rolling toward Dowdall's Tavern—where he himself had stayed in the home of the Rev. Melzi Chancellor. There was no halt, but the situation on the right had deteriorated. [53]

Colquitt on the right of the first wave had advanced but a few hundred yards in the original rush before his skirmishers reported Federal infantry and cavalry in the woods on his right. He halted immediately, pulled back his left regiment as it was keeping pace with Doles' right, and ordered his right regiment to change front to the right and prepare to resist.

When word of these moves reached Ramseur, behind him, that officer fumed and sputtered. He had heard brisk firing ahead and to the left. He sent word that Doles appeared to be engaged. His impression was, he said, that Colquitt's support was needed there. His own brigade would guard the flank as planned and ordered. But Colquitt sent out a regiment several hundred yards to investigate.

Ramseur, following his battle orders, made an even more thorough investigation, though fretting at the delay. A picket of some 40 men was captured. The horsemen have never been accurately identified. Paxton was on the Plank Road to the right, and Stuart had cavalry out in that direction (some of them may have been the Federal threat). It would have been difficult, if not impossible, for any formidable Federal force to slip into the area.

Eventually Colquitt resumed his advance, but he did not catch up until long after nightfall.[54] Since Ramseur could not pass him, the brigades available for the critical afternoon assault shrank by two. Thereby Jackson lost nearly 4,000 men—possibly more, since swift advance on the right might have freed Paxton to join the attack. Six brigades in the first two waves—Doles', O'Neal's, and Iverson's in the first, and Warren's, Jones', and Nicholls' in the second—had carried the assault to this point, with Pender's and Heth's brigades close behind them.

The same six plunged straight ahead toward the Melzi Chancellor–Dowdall's Tavern position. The advance carried them through the Third Division's line and camps.

Schurz had shown during the day more concern than any other general officer about a threat from the west. Before Jackson's men came tearing out of the forest, he had warned his regiments to be on the alert against a thrust from that direction—nobody estimated the full weight of it—and had begun to shift regiments. When the roar of the advance told him the thrust was upon him, he ordered all his regiments within reach to pivot around toward the west.

The judgment was good, but it went into effect too late. It did not reckon on the length of Jackson's lines. It could not compensate for the swift collapse of the Devens units or the panic of the Devens men as they streamed back into the Schurz regiments. The combination was too much. Schurz's whole first position crumbled and broke. He fell back after sharp fighting in which individual units fought bitterly—the Twenty-sixth Wisconsin, for one, and Dilger and his guns for another—but helplessly against an attack of great driving power and constantly flanking lines.

Howard came up in the midst of this movement and caught the full impact of its confusion and dismay. He had ridden south, with von Steinwehr of the Second Division, to accompany Barlow's brigade (his last reserve) as it joined Sickles in the imaginary destruc-

tion of Lee's trains. Howard saw quickly that no real fighting was
going on there. But he knew nothing of any fighting anywhere else.
He was back at his headquarters at Dowdall's Tavern when, close
to 6 o'clock, he heard firing to the west and rode out with his staff
to investigate. He rode straight into the whirlwind.

"It was a terrible gale," he wrote later. "The rush, the rattle, the
quick lightning from a hundred points at once; the roar redoubled
by echoes through the forest; the panic, the dead and dying in
sight, and the wounded straggling along; the frantic efforts of the
brave and patriotic to stay the angry storm." [55]

A Pennsylvania cavalryman saw Howard in this moment, "in the
middle of the road and mounted, his maimed arm embracing a
standard of colors that some regiment had deserted, while with
his sound arm he was gesticulating to the men to make a stand by
their flag. With bared head he was pleading with his soldiers, literally weeping as he entreated the unheeding horde. . . . At last the
seething, surging sea of humanity broke over the feeble barrier, and
General Howard and his officers were carried away by main force
with the tide." [56]

The farther Rodes' and Colston's waves advanced, the more they
became one wave. Every barrier at the front that caused Rodes'
brigades to slow down or halt brought Colston's men nearer to them.
The attack grew stronger in sheer impetus but more difficult to
control. It surged forward now to a line in front of the Wilderness
Church. Here a brigade of von Steinwehr's untouched Second Division, with a battery, formed a rallying point for parts of Schurz's
division and fragments from Devens', 3,000 to 5,000 men, with some
corps artillery farther to the east aiding with long-range fire.

Rodes saw the strength and called on Warren's brigade for support. Jones' brigade was as close at hand, and both stormed forward.
The fighting sharpened, spread out, and continued for twenty minutes. Then the headlong pressure of the attack, beating relentlessly
on an uncertain and demoralized defense, and feeling always for its
flanks, broke down much desperate individual effort.

The blue lines streamed backward once more. The gray waves,
almost out of control now but still going forward, looked ahead to
Dowdall's Tavern. It was nearing 6:30, and the shades of night were
falling. Ahead of the open farm land they could see the dark wall
of the forest that hid Chancellorsville.

Had the gray waves been able to pierce far ahead, they would have seen strange sights at Chancellorsville. There Hooker and two aides rested on the porch during the warm May afternoon. They heard late in the day cannon shot in the distance, assumed they were from Sickles' guns, and discussed in ease and with professional skill the damage he was doing to a Lee in flight.

By some strange acoustical effect neither the direction of Jackson's assault nor more than a hint of the sound of it (which to men in its path sounded like a roar) reached their ears. One of the aides, Capt. Harry Russell, stepped down into the yard and turned his glass toward Dowdall's Tavern. He peered, then turned and shouted: "My God, here they come!" [57]

Hooker and his staff mounted swiftly, rode hard to the west, and encountered in the flesh what Russell had seen through the glass: a division in retreat, broken and panic-stricken, rushing as heedless of a general's orders as they were of their own sense of control. Scattered officers, men, fragments, even whole units were striving desperately for a footing, and sometimes were succeeding. But now Hooker was paying the penalty for letting Sickles go blindly into the woods to the south where he did not yet know what was happening to his right rear. Behind Howard's Eleventh Corps was only open space. Troops that could be counted on to retain their sanity and stem this tide were far to the rear. The crust was broken, and beneath it was nothing.

Yet the broken bits of the crust and the newly arriving or still holding regiments and batteries contained brave men. Jackson's intermingled regiments, weary now and for the most part out of control, pressed ahead in the twilight toward a new and narrow line of defense—known later as the "Buschbeck line." They ran immediately into thick, concentrated rifle fire and effective but unaided shells from a single artillery piece—Captain Dilger again, fighting his lone battle with undaunted persistence.

Quick reconnaissance up and down this strong point disclosed only a shallow shelter trench but a formidable force within and behind it. Buschbeck's four-regiment brigade with three regiments from Schurz's division, other scatterings, and some of the fugitives from the western collapse added up to some 4,000 men. They were holding their ground.

Then the mingled Rodes and Colston lines—one wave now—discovered that the Buschbeck line ran north and south no more than 1,000 yards.[58] Jackson's long lines were made for such a defense, tough and determined though it was. Like long whips on the left and on the right the extended flanks of the attacking lines cracked around the flanks of the defense, encircling the soft spots all the way to the rear. Then with a wild shout from the front the whole force bore down irresistibly. The lines broke under the pressure, still fighting, and in the gathering darkness drifted steadily back to the walls of the forest.

It was past 7 o'clock now, and the night was coming in like a black fog. Exhausted men from the Rodes-Colston line, so hopelessly intermingled that no officer knew whom he commanded, stumbled ahead behind the retreating enemy. They were moving now more by instinct than by command.

When Col. Samuel B. Pickens of the Twelfth Alabama (O'Neal's brigade) ordered his regiment to halt, he found that only thirty men obeyed his orders. The others kept moving ahead. He left the thirty under another officer and followed the larger part of his command for half a mile or more. When he caught up with this advance, he found that it included men from all regiments of the brigade. They had passed over log breastworks, about three-quarters of a mile west of the Fairview hill, that marked the beginning of Slocum's Twelfth Corps defenses, captured three guns, and taken 150 prisoners or more. Men of the Sixth Alabama advanced beyond the works. Pickens was the senior officer present. He marched the whole crowd back to where the brigade had been ordered to halt, and the log works were abandoned to the night.[59]

Something of these events came to the attention of Maj. N. Cobb of the Forty-fourth Virginia. Part of that regiment kept going through the darkness, passed over enemy fortifications (apparently the same), took some prisoners, but later withdrew—for reasons that are not clear. Major Cobb carried back word to Jackson,[60] and the news excited the General. He directed Cobb to "find General Rodes and tell him to occupy that barricade at once." Either the message did not go through, or Rodes considered it impossible to advance or thought the plan was superseded by Jackson's other orders.

Rodes saw no possibility of maintaining his advance. Units had disintegrated and no longer existed as organizations, ammunition was low and in some regiments entirely gone, and night had taken possession. He sent word to Jackson that he needed time to re-form and urged him to send the reserve division—Hill's—to the front. Lane's and McGowan's brigades of that division had joined Pender and Heth, although Thomas and Archer were still far to the rear.

Jackson had no thought of stopping. He ordered Hill to move to the front and take up the pursuit. This took time. Men stood panting in the night as a full moon rose over the trees. Men slumped to the ground and stretched out, let down nervously as well as physically. Men remembered so vaguely what they had been through that in no other of Jackson's major engagements were the subsequent reports so generalized, so differing in detail, so lacking in precise outlines of the actions during the long, mad rush into the assault and into the darkness.

Officers who used words carefully spoke in strong phrases, like Lee's "the impetuous rush of our troops" and Hill's "the attack of Rodes was made with great energy." Every report tells of the thickness of the trees and the difficulties of advancing through them. Rodes remembered "the wild shout" of his division as it went forward against the Federal position in front of Melzi Chancellor's and "the inextricable confusion" of the mingled waves at the last. O'Neal counted off three breastworks, two of earth and one of logs, and two abatis, that his men carried.

Doles set down in poetic spirit how the enemy "made a stubborn resistance from behind a wattling fence, on a hill covered thickly with pine." Iverson's men found food—"hungry men seized provisions as they passed camps of the enemy and rushed forward, eating, shouting, and firing." Col. Daniel L. Christie of the Twenty-third North Carolina, in the first wave, thought it "unfortunate that the supporting line was so close, or not better managed . . . this line rushed forward and mingled with the first before there was the least necessity for their assistance." But Colston thought that Rodes had called on Warren for assistance before they had advanced more than ten or fifteen minutes—"the troops had pressed on so ardently that they were only a few steps behind." Lieut. Oscar Hinrichs, Colston's engineer, noted that "the men, now mixed up with those of General Rodes, pushed forward at a double-quick, which was only checked into a quick-step by the enemy and the natural difficulties of the ground." [61]

Private Casler recalled:

We ran through the enemy's camps where they were cooking supper. Tents were standing and camp-kettles were on the fire full of meat. I saw a big Newfoundland dog lying in one tent as quietly as if nothing had happened. We had a nice chance to plunder their camps and search the dead; but the men were afraid to stop, as they had to keep with the artillery and were near a good many officers, who might whack them over the head with their swords if they saw them plundering. . . .[62]

Jackson was all calmness before the attack began. Troopers brought in a Federal officer while the General was waiting on the Turnpike for the deployment, and Fitzhugh Lee asked what Hooker would think if Jackson should fall upon his rear. The prisoner, not recognizing the dust-covered figure with the cap pulled down over his eyes standing near by, answered in scorn: "Hooker has both Jackson and your great Lee in the hollow of his hand and it is only a matter of a very short time when your whole army will be bagged." Jackson smiled, but he said nothing.[63]

When he sent Paxton down the Plank Road to guard that point of entry while the main body went on to the Turnpike, Jackson sat on a log by the road, a brown figure in its dust, not gray, his arms folded, explaining in detail precisely what he wanted Paxton to do.[64] He stretched out on the grass near a big oak tree a little later, talking with Stuart and some staff officers.[65] He knew well enough that time was running out on him, but he also knew that there was nothing he could do about that now beyond sending couriers down the Brock Road with the commands to "Press on! Press on!" Captain Randolph, the chief of his couriers, saw him at prayer off the road, late in the afternoon. In all outward manifestations he was steady and in complete control.

Once the assault tore out of the forest into the open ground the General threw off the mask of his control. He followed the guns down the road when Stuart's horse artillery had orders to keep up with the infantry advance and was doing so. His face glowed with battle spirit. He leaned over Sorrel's neck. He seemed personally to be pushing the attack. Every forward lunge of the assault waves seemed to stir his emotion deeper. Captain Wilbourn, who rode with him all afternoon, saw him stop many times and raise his hand, and "I have never seen him seem so well pleased with the progress and results of a fight." But the General had never seemed, in one respect, so concerned about the men who went down: "On several occasions, during this fight, as he passed the bodies of some of our veterans, he halted, raised his hand as if to ask a blessing upon them, and to pray God to save their souls." [66]

Yet he did not lose his balance of military and spiritual duty. A young officer, explosive in his excitement, cried out to the General: "They are running too fast for us. We can't keep up with them."

"They never run too fast for me, sir!" the General shot back.[67]

The central purpose of pursuit to the utmost limit of possibility dominated his thinking, and the direction—this appears to have become more clear as the afternoon wore on—must be toward the road to the United States Ford. That was on the left. Jackson knew the importance of uniting his corps with Lee's force on his right. Lee had launched his own attack with Anderson and McLaws as soon as the sound of Jackson's assault came down the wind. Previously, all during May 2, Lee had kept Hooker and his commanders impressed by deceptive demonstrations—a masterly performance—which they took to be feeling-out maneuvers preliminary to a major offensive on that front.

But Jackson's purpose now, once the rollback of Hooker's wing was clearly in progress, was to wring the last advantage out of it. That would be by cutting off Hooker's escape route to the United States Ford and by an envelopment in that northerly direction which, with Lee pressing Hooker from the south, would tend to encircle his whole wing. There would be difficulties aplenty, including Jackson's numerical inferiority (and Lee's) and the probability that he would encounter formidable, if not overwhelming, resistance from Meade's Fifth Corps, Reynolds' First, and possibly Couch's Second, none of which had been drawn into the battle. But for a general who looked forward to overwhelming victory, this was the direction in which to look. A moon-filled night was a poor substitute for daylight, and the corps had endured heavy strains during a long day, and two divisions were deeply tangled and organizationally in disorder, but the chief requisite now was to keep going.

The General, pressing on toward the front, took a personal hand in straightening out confused commands. "Men, get into line! get into line!" he called out many times. "Whose regiment is this?" he inquired; and, when he found out, "Colonel, get your men instantly into line." He caught hold of an officer: "I need your help for a time; this disorder must be corrected. As you go along the line, tell the troops, from me, to get into line, and preserve order." [68]

Rodes went on a personal reconnaissance along the road toward Fairview and Chancellorsville. When he returned he was confident that no Federal troops occupied the area up to Fairview. When Stapleton Crutchfield, of the artillery, brought some guns up to replace the horse artillery that had kept pace with the infantry, he began firing with three of them. But that woke up the Federal guns that had been rolling into position on the Fairview height. They returned the fire with smashing force.

The fire caught Lane as he was leading his brigade along the road to spearhead Hill's division in the night attack Jackson was calling for. The Federal guns immediately drove his men off the road into cover on each side. Lane appealed to Hill to have Crutchfield stop firing in order to induce the enemy to stop, and quiet fell on the night.

Lane deployed. He sent forward the entire Thirty-third North Carolina, under Col. Clark M. Avery, as skirmishers, extending 200 to 300 yards out and along both sides of the road. He placed the Thirty-seventh North Carolina on the right of the road, with its left resting on it, and the Seventh North Carolina farther out. On the immediate left of the road he stationed the Eighteenth North Carolina (Col. Thomas J. Purdie), and beyond it the Twenty-eighth North Carolina. [69]

The deployment placed Lane's brigade within a short distance of the log works. The front had narrowed down from its original two miles to hardly more than half a mile. Lane warned all regimental commanders to look sharp. They had advanced since the afternoon assault nearly three miles into the Federal area. Nobody was between them and the enemy, and the enemy was expected to attack. Lane turned and rode back to see Hill for final instructions. It was about 9 o'clock. Where the trees were thick the night was black. In thinned-out spots the moonlight came through.

Lane saw a figure on horseback and thought it might be Hill. He called out. The figure was that of Jackson, alone then except for a courier or so. He called to Lane to come to him.

Jackson, full of ideas, had picked his way forward slowly. He sent officer after officer scurrying away to deliver orders or to investigate.

A courier named David J. Kyle found him with a message from Stuart, who had ridden out to the left to try to gain possession of the Ely's Ford road. Stuart, like Jackson, knew the value of the Federal lines of communication to the Rappahannock and the Rapidan. Jackson must have known that Kyle lived nearby. He asked him if he knew the region, and when Kyle said he did, the General told him: "Keep along with me." [70]

They reached a school building by the road, stopped briefly while the General checked with officers he found there, and then continued slowly. He was near the point at which a road came in from Hazel Grove when Lane came up. Lane told him he was looking for Hill to get final orders. Could the General give him any instructions?

"Push right ahead, Lane." The words snapped out, the right arm rose thrust forward in a vigorous gesture as Jackson urged him on.[71] Lane understood. He turned and was gone.

Jackson's staff officers began to show up again. Wilbourn rejoined him. Young Morrison—Anna's brother, who had thought three days ago that he might be needed—was here now. Boswell was nearby. Couriers and signalmen added to the group of horsemen. Hill came up with a group of his own. Jackson gave Hill a final—and illuminating—order: "Press them! Cut them off from the United States Ford, Hill. Press them!" [72]

Lane was to go straight ahead, guided by the Plank Road, toward Chancellorsville. But to cut the Federal army off from the United States Ford, Hill would have to strike with other parts of his division in a northeasterly instead of easterly direction. He told Jackson that he did not know that country. Jackson looked around, saw Boswell, who did know it, and told Hill that Boswell would guide him.

They came to a road that took off to the left. Jackson, thinking constantly of possibilities in that direction, asked Kyle about it and learned that the road split a short distance ahead. One fork, called the Bullock Road, led diagonally to a farm north of Chancellorsville. The other was an old track, called the Mountain Road, that paralleled the Plank Road for some 1,200 yards, 60 to 80 yards distant from it, and rejoined it about a half-mile west of Chancellorsville. It was sheltered in the trees, and it was not within the sights of the Federal artillery ahead. Jackson decided to ride along it for a personal reconnaissance to the left and ahead [73] where—he did not know how far—there must be enemy troops. He directed Kyle to lead the way, but he was himself at the front of his party.

The horsemen moved slowly in a diagonal direction behind Lane's regiments until they came up to the Eighteenth North Carolina. They passed through its line quietly, without attracting attention far beyond the men immediately adjacent. They continued along the Mountain Road for several hundred yards but not up to the line of the skirmishers of the Thirty-third North Carolina.[74]

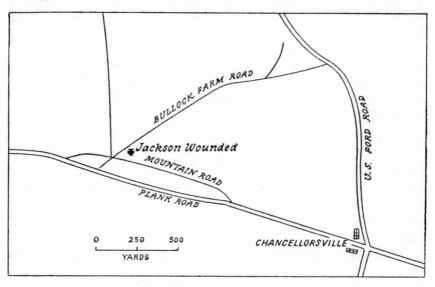

Area where Jackson was wounded, May 2, 1863.

Colonel Purdie of the Eighteenth Regiment had ridden forward along the Plank Road, with his adjutant, to check with skirmishers in that direction. Lieut. Col. Forney George was the second-ranking officer of this regiment, and Maj. John D. Barry, a battalion commander stationed on the left part of the Eighteenth's line, or away from the Plank Road and therefore near the point where the Mountain Road veered off, was the third-ranking officer. None of these knew of the advance of the General and his party through the ranks of the Eighteenth and out toward the picket line. One officer within the party thought the advance dangerous. "General, don't you think this is the wrong place for you?" he asked.

"The danger is all over—the enemy is routed!—go back and tell
A. P. Hill to press right on!" the General replied.[75]

Presently he halted his horse and listened in the night. The guns
were silent. Ahead he could hear the commands of the Federal
officers and the ring of axes biting into wood. Fortifications were
going up. The General listened attentively. His mind must have
been racing. But he showed no sign of changing the plans for sending
Lane straight ahead and for giving Hill the United States Ford road
as the direction of his further attack. He was quiet and seemed
thoughtful. Then he turned and rode slowly back along the track
by which he had come.

Once more he stopped, turned Sorrel's head toward the front
again, and looked toward the enemy, peering into the night and
listening intently. He was sitting thus when a single rifle shot, clear
and startling in the lull between battles, rang out far to the south.
A scattering of other shots followed immediately, then a solid volley,
and then a rolling fire along the front, coming nearer and nearer.

Five or six hundred yards to the south, Lane, riding forward after
he had left Jackson, had gone for a final inspection of his brigade
before he gave it the command to advance. There Lieut. Col. Junius
L. Hill of the Seventh North Carolina urged him not to advance
until he learned whether troops whose movements the Seventh could
hear to the right and ahead were friends or enemies. The right flank
was alert to the possibility that Lee's advance would connect with
it. While they were talking, a Federal officer—Lieut. Col. Levi H.
Smith of the One Hundred Twenty-eighth Pennsylvania—came out
of the trees waving a white handkerchief. He asked whether these
were Federal or Confederate troops.

Lane thought that was an illegitimate use of the white flag.[76] He
ordered the officer held, against Smith's protest, and sent a staff
officer to General Hill to find out what to do with him. Then he directed Lieutenant Colonel Hill to send an officer and a squad to
scout on the right. Their flank was open in that direction. Hill sent
Lieut. J. W. Emack and four men. They came back, later, with most
of the One Hundred Twenty-eighth Pennsylvania, which thought
in the darkness that it was surrounded.

Lane and Hill were still listening to the sounds from their right
when they heard a horseman moving in the distance and an authori-

tative voice call out, "General Williams! General Williams!"—commanding general of the Twelfth Corps's First Division, then trying to find its old place in the corps defense line after coming back from adventures in the south with Sickles. The officer was probably Brig. Gen. Joseph F. Knipe, of Williams' First Brigade.[77]

The call brought the skirmishers of the Thirty-third North Carolina to life. Lieut. Col. Robert V. Cowan [78] ordered them to fire at that officer. One of his men was ready and fired instantly—his was the shot that Jackson and his group heard as they stood on the Mountain Road and listened. Others followed quickly. Federal skirmishers replied. The Seventh joined in the action with a volley that frightened the Thirty-third in front and sent its skirmishers scurrying forward for safety. The entire front—nervous in the night, knowing the enemy was close at hand, seeing movements and imagining others in the shadows—picked up the fire and carried it on in hurried, excited shots.

Purdie of the Eighteenth and his adjutant, up near the Thirty-third in the Plank Road area, hearing this fire, turned their horses and rode fast back to their posts with the Eighteenth, coming in with a clatter and exciting the right companies of the regiment near the Plank Road. Men there began to fire into the trees, singly and spasmodically, at first on the right, less on the left. It was on the left that Jackson was now leading his group back toward the Eighteenth —a group that had grown with A. P. Hill and some of his staff to nearly a score of horsemen. In the night they may well have sounded like more. They may well have seemed to nervous troops and a nervous commander like the arrival of a Federal attacking wave.

General A. P. Hill shouted loudly: "Cease firing, cease firing!" The occasional shots frightened Sorrel. He swerved so that the General, to protect himself from the overhanging boughs of the scrubby oaks, held his reins with his left hand and raised his right in front of his face. He regained control of his horse and rode back along the track.

Morrison leaped out ahead of him, riding fast directly toward the unseen kneeling Eighteenth. He shouted: "Cease firing! You are firing into your own men!"

Instantly Major Barry's voice rang out to his battalion: "Who gave that order? It's a lie! Pour it into them, boys!" [79]

The line flashed and crashed with a full volley in their faces, scarcely twenty paces away.[80] Jackson's group went down in a turmoil of pitching horses, gasps of surprise, shock, and pain, and the rush of death itself. Jackson's two arms fell to his side. The left was completely helpless, smashed badly below the shoulder joint and hit with less effect below the elbow by a bullet that entered the forearm and came out on the opposite side above the wrist. The right hand was hit in the palm by a bullet that penetrated but hung on the outer surface of the back of the hand.

Sorrel, mad with fright from the volley, whirled and galloped furiously in the opposite direction. An oak limb caught Jackson full in the face, tore off his cap and swept him back until his body almost touched the horse behind the saddle. The left hand was hopeless, but the right might do something. The instinct of a horseman did more. With almost the last possible strength he headed Sorrel back toward his own line.

Wilbourn, alive by a miracle after the volley, grasped the reins of the horse, caught the General in his arms and held him in the saddle.[81] Lieutenant Wynn, a signal officer, rode up and braced him on the other side. The General seemed dazed. He stared in the direction from which the fire had come as if he could not understand what had happened. "Wild fire, that, sir; wild fire," he exclaimed.[82]

"They certainly must be our troops," Wilbourn said to Jackson's unspoken question. The General continued to stare as if in disbelief.

"How do you feel, General," Wilbourn asked him. "Can you move your fingers?" Jackson tried with poor success. Wilbourn, seeking to determine the nature and extent of the wounds, took hold of the left arm. He was careful, but the pain was too much.

"You had better take me down," the General said. "My arm is broken."

He was bleeding freely from the left arm and was so weak that he could not move his feet out of his stirrups. Wynn did that for him. The two young officers, on the ground now, lowered him with difficulty from his horse and held him limp and almost helpless between them. Partly carrying, partly walking him, they moved a few yards to a tree and laid him under it. Wilbourn sat down beside him, and the General's head fell against his breast.

"Captain, I wish you would get me a skilled surgeon," the General said.

Wilbourn told Wynn to go for McGuire or some other skilled

surgeon, but not to tell others that the General was wounded. In the gloom of night Wilbourn saw another figure. He did not know who it was, but he told the man to find out which Confederate regiment was in the direction the volley had come from. The figure disappeared in the darkness and has never been identified.[83] Wilbourn took off the General's field glasses and his haversack. He unloosed the gummed coat Jackson wore, freed his uniform coat and the inner shirts, and began cutting the sleeves. The two were alone.[84]

The volley from the Eighteenth was devastating. Of Jackson's staff group Wilbourn and Wynn survived whole and on horseback. Morrison, hearing the command to fire as he rode forward, threw himself from his horse and, except for a heavy fall, escaped miraculously. Boswell was mortally wounded. Several couriers and signalmen were killed outright. A. P. Hill, a little distance away, escaped, but his group lost heavily in deaths and wounds, and others lost their horses or were carried far—in one instance, into enemy lines—by maddened animals. In the area the bodies of fourteen horses were counted later.[85]

Hill was the first to reach the two men at the foot of the pine tree, followed quickly by Capt. Benjamin Watkins Leigh, who had come up to Hill shortly after the fusillade. With tenderness Hill knelt beside the General and asked if the wound was painful.

"Very painful," said Jackson. "The arm is broken."

Hill tried to make him comfortable. He saw that Jackson still wore gauntlets, and he began to take them off. They were full of blood. James Smith came up. He had been stationed by Jackson far in the rear to see that oncoming regiments continued to advance in the right direction, and had remained there until all the corps had reached the battle area, then had ridden forward, had learned that the General was wounded, and had rushed ahead at top speed. He joined Hill and Leigh, deeply moved by the figure of the General; and he tried to make him more comfortable, removing his saber and his belt and hovering over him anxiously.

Hill sent Leigh for a surgeon and an ambulance. Leigh went back, encountered Pender's brigade, and told him of the need. Pender had an assistant surgeon in his brigade, Dr. Barr, and sent for him. Barr reported that no ambulance was nearer than a mile at best, but he went forward to see Jackson. Leigh returned with him, and soldiers with a litter accompanied them.[86]

The General lay quiet and did not complain. The bleeding disturbed the others, and they sought with handkerchiefs to check it. Their efforts or the clotting of the blood lessened the flow, and they rigged up a sling for the arm, now swelling fast. The General seemed weak, and someone produced a flask with whiskey or brandy. Jackson swallowed a little—repugnantly, Leigh thought—and then drank heavily of water from a canteen. He appeared to rest easier.

Wilbourn asked him about the wound in his right hand. "Never mind that," the General said. "It is a mere trifle." When Barr came up, the General whispered to Hill, "Is he a skilled surgeon?" Barr examined him briefly, but did little [87]—almost surely because he saw at once that nothing could be done, beyond trying to make the General comfortable, until they carried him to a field hospital.

Captain Adams, of Hill's staff, joined the group. Suspicious noises ahead, seemingly of soldiers' movements, led him to investigate. He was only ten or fifteen yards forward when his voice rose sharply: "Halt! Surrender! Fire on them if they don't surrender!"

Hill jumped up, mounted his horse, drew his pistol and rode forward. Two Federal soldiers, surprised to find any Confederates about, surrendered willingly enough. But Morrison, finding his way to the stricken General, reported that the enemy was advancing. They must move.

Morrison proposed taking the General in their arms, but Jackson said, "No—if you can help me, I can walk."

They stood him up, pale, weak, uncertain, and he tried to walk. The motion started the blood again, and it flowed over the uniform of Leigh, one of the officers supporting him. Federal artillery had begun again with heavy fire (thirty-four guns were now posted on Fairview hill).[88] Canister crashed down the road and struck fire from its stones, but in the woods they could still move feebly forward. Soldiers seeing them noted unusual efforts with a wounded man and looked hard to find out what was going on. They came over to look closer. "Who is that? Who've you got there?" they asked.

"Oh, it is only a friend of ours who is wounded," the reply came back. Jackson's mind was working well enough to join in the concealment. "When asked, just say it is a Confederate officer," he advised. But soldiers are curious of unusual efforts. They crowded around. One of them leaned forward close enough to see. "Great God!" he exclaimed. "That is General Jackson!" [89]

The struggling group conceded nothing and continued to move a little in the darkness. It seemed a long time, but they advanced hardly more than twenty steps, so great was the effort required to move at all. The General was at the end of his strength. Then a litter came up, and they laid him on it. Leigh, Smith, and two ambulance men carried it. The others walked beside and behind, leading horses.

This was good fortune, but the Federal guns offset it immediately. They raised the fury of their fire. The road was their target, but the shells scattered enough to drench the nearby trees. Part of a shell hit Hill's foot. Pender, whose brigade was on Lane's left, was wounded. Crutchfield was hit hard in the leg and went down in extreme pain. The group around Jackson scattered, horses rearing, men seeking cover. Grapeshot ripped through both arms of one of the ambulance men carrying the litter. He dropped his end, but Leigh reached out quickly and caught it and kept the litter from falling. In the crashing noise they stumbled forward almost blindly, into the road itself— the worst spot for collapse.

They did what they could to protect the General. The litter lay with his feet toward the guns. Smith, Morrison, and Leigh stretched close on each side and in front, shielding him with their bodies. The heavy bombardment had cut up units, scattered men, driven horses in all directions, and left a grisly wreckage of human flesh. The shells were still crashing around them. Jackson raised himself on his right elbow, but Smith laid his arm across his body. "Sir," he said, "you must lie still. It will cost you your life if you rise." [90]

When the artillery shifted aim, they started again, bringing the General to his feet with an effort, Smith and Morrison supporting him now, with Leigh carrying the litter behind them. The soldiers around them were coming to life, and Morrison and Smith led the way into the woods again to avoid their inquiries along the clogged roadway. They ran squarely into the slightly wounded Pender. He too looked at the slowly moving group with curiosity, stepped forward, and, when a ray of moonlight came through the trees, recognized the General. He burst out: "Oh, General, I am sorry to see you have been wounded."

Then, thinking perhaps of his own wound as well as the General's, and of the terrible fire which had poured down on them, and of what it had done to his brigade, he burst out with: "The lines here are so much broken that I fear we will have to fall back."

The old instinct gripped the General—the old instinct and the reasoning that remained in spite of the confusion and weakness and uncertainty, and the pain that flowed through his body. In a low voice, but clearly and firmly, he spoke to Pender: "You must hold your ground, General Pender! You must hold your ground, sir!" [91]

The effort seemed to exhaust him. He asked if he could lie on the ground, but the young officers would not consent. Leigh brought up the litter again, and they placed him on it. He asked for spirits again, but they had none. For half a mile they moved slowly through the woods. The undergrowth was tangled and dense, and movement with a burden was extremely difficult. They struggled on. Then one of the bearers caught his foot in a vine. He stumbled, lost balance, and let go of the litter. It pitched to the ground with the General's crushed shoulder hitting it first and the weight of his body hammering it hard—a fall of terrific pain.

A groan broke from Jackson's lips. He thought he was going to die, perhaps because the exquisite agony caused him almost to faint. Yet the very suggestion of death gave him—such was his conviction about the Christian's joy at entering Heaven—a fresh sustaining power. When Smith, himself sorely distressed at the thought of the General's suffering, asked him impulsively, "General, are you much hurt?" the General replied, "No, Mr. Smith; don't trouble yourself about me." [92]

The risk of a further fall was too great. Even though shells were still falling, they turned back to the road. There, with more soldiers helping as carriers, they made better progress. They reached a minor road running southward and followed it in search of the ambulance they had called for. Then, for almost the first relief of this terrible night, they found it. Dr. William R. Whitehead was in charge. Crutchfield, in severe pain from his leg wound, was lying in it, and another officer, Major Rogers. Crutchfield could not be moved, but Rogers, with a lesser wound, gave up his place, and the weary young officers carefully lifted the litter with the General and slid it forward beside his artillery officer.*

* None of the accounts of the night identifies the officer who gave Jackson his place other than as "Major Rogers," and no such officer is known to have been wounded on that day, Freeman—*LL*, II, 576, suggests the possibility that the officer was Capt. H. A. Rogers, of the Thirteenth North Carolina, in Pender's brigade.

The distance to the corps's field hospital was still nearly four miles. Morrison squeezed in the ambulance to hold the General's left arm carefully during a journey that was certain to be rough despite the utmost care. The others followed on horse and on foot. (The ambulance was no better than a wagon, or at best a lighter vehicle, with a high covered top, probably of canvas or other fabric, metal-rimmed wheels, and inadequate springs at best, into which wounded men were stretched out on platforms, sometimes on the floor, generally two to a vehicle.) They turned northwestward and came back into the Plank Road on the Melzi Chancellor land, and then lurched and rocked directly westward over the area of the afternoon's whirlwind advance. The General's pain was intense. He asked again for spirits. They could find none immediately, but eventually a bottle was located,[93] and the General drank.

Laboriously, foot by foot, they bumped along the rutted road—and suddenly there was Melzi Chancellor's house, and McGuire stepped forward. They could have found no one whom they had rather see. The doctor has described that moment:

I knelt down by him and said, "I hope you are not badly hurt, General." He replied, very calmly, but feebly, "I am badly injured, Doctor; I fear I am dying." After a pause, he continued, "I am glad you have come. I think the wound in my shoulder is still bleeding."

His clothes were saturated with blood, and haemorrhage was still going on from the wound. Compression of the artery with the finger arrested it, until lights being procured from the ambulance, the handkerchief which had slipped a little, was readjusted. His calmness amid the dangers which surrounded him, and at the supposed presence of death, and his uniform politeness, which did not forsake him, even under these, the most trying circumstances, were remarkable. His complete control, too, over his mind, enfeebled as it was, by loss of blood, pain, etc., was wonderful.

His suffering at this time was intense; his hands were cold, his skin clammy, his face pale, and his lips compressed and bloodless; not a groan escaped him—not a sign of suffering, except the slight corrugation of his brow, the fixed rigid face, and the thin lips, so tightly compressed, that the impression of the teeth could be seen through them. Except these, he controlled by his iron will, all evidence of emotion, and more difficult than this even, he controlled that disposition to restlessness, which many of us have observed upon the field of battle, attending great loss of blood.[94]

Some whiskey and morphia were procured and given to the General. The field hospital of the Second Corps, Dr. Harvey Black in charge, was still nearly four miles to the west, a little north of the Turnpike near the intersection of the Germanna Plank Road. But the worst was over. The party was now beyond the range of enemy artillery. The road, though rough, could be lighted by torches so that the driver of the ambulance could avoid some of the holes and ruts. The General was in competent professional hands. McGuire's narrative continues:

The General expressed, very feelingly, his sympathy for Crutchfield, and once, when the latter groaned aloud, he directed the ambulance to stop, and requested me to see if something could be done for his relief. . . .

I sat in the front part of the ambulance, with my finger resting upon the artery, above the wound, to arrest bleeding if it should occur. When I was recognized by acquaintances, and asked who was wounded, the General would tell me to say, "a Confederate officer." At one time, he put his right hand upon my head, and pulling me down to him, asked if Crutchfield was dangerously wounded. When answered, "No, only painfully hurt," he replied, "I am glad it is no worse." In a few moments after, Crutchfield did the same thing, and when he was told that the General was very seriously wounded, he groaned and cried out, "Oh, my God." It was for this, that the General directed the ambulance to be halted, and requested that something should be done for Crutchfield's relief.

When the ambulance turned finally into the open field where Dr. Black had his hospital, not far from the Old Wilderness Tavern, they found that word had preceded them. Black had prepared and warmed a tent for the General. McGuire placed him there, gave him another drink of whiskey and water and bundled him up with blankets. It was then perhaps 11:30 P.M., more than two hours since Jackson had been hit. McGuire wished the General to show more recovery from shock before he made a thorough examination of the wounds, and, as he suspected he would have to, undertake the amputation. He and Smith watched the patient carefully. His narrative continues:

Two and a half hours elapsed before sufficient reaction took place to warrant an examination. At two o'clock Sunday morning [May 3], Surgeons Black, Walls and [R. T.] Coleman being present, I informed him that amputation would probably be required, and asked if it were found necessary, whether it should be done at once. He replied promptly, "Yes, certainly; Dr. McGuire, do for me whatever you think best."

Chloroform was then administered, and as he began to feel its effects and its relief to the pain he was suffering, he exclaimed, "What an infinite blessing," and continued to repeat the word, "blessing" until he became insensible. The round ball—such as is used for the smooth-bore Spring-field musket—which had lodged under the skin upon the back of his right hand, was extracted first, it had entered the palm about the middle of the hand, and had fractured two of the bones. The left arm was then amputated, about two inches below the shoulder, very rapidly, and with slight loss of blood, the ordinary circular operation having been made.

There were two wounds in his arm, the first and most serious was about three inches below the shoulder joint, the ball dividing the main artery, and fracturing the bone. The second was several inches in length; a ball having entered the outside of the forearm, an inch below the elbow, came out upon the opposite side, just above the wrist.

Throughout the whole of the operation, and until all the dressings were applied, he continued insensible.[95] Two or three abrasions of the skin of his face, received from the branches of the trees, when his horse dashed through the woods, were dressed simply with isinglass plaster.

Of the operating team, Dr. Coleman administered the chloroform, Dr. Black watched the action of the heart, and Dr. Walls [96] tied the arteries. Smith was brought in to hold the lights. McGuire per-formed the operation, making the incision and sawing the bone. Amputation was then the approved resort, primarily to prevent gangrene, when the damage to an arm was as extensive as in this instance. The decision and the form of the operation were standard. McGuire's emphasis on the round ball which he extracted from the General's right hand was probably because it was evidence of where the shots had come from. Federal troops did not then use smooth-bore muskets as did some Confederate units.

Half an hour after the operation was completed Smith was di-rected to give a cup of coffee to the General. About 3:30 o'clock, about an hour after the operation, when the General was lying quietly asleep, there was another interruption. McGuire's narrative describes it:

About half-past three o'clock Colonel (then Major) Pendleton, the Assistant Adjutant General, arrived at the hospital, and asked to see the General. He stated that General Hill had been wounded, and that the troops were in great disorder. General Stuart was in command, and had sent him to see the General.

At first, I declined to permit an interview, but the Colonel [Major] urged that the safety of the army and success of the cause depended upon his seeing him. When he entered the tent, the General said, "Well, Major, I am glad to see you, I thought you were killed." Pendleton briefly explained the condition of affairs, gave Stuart's messages, and asked what should be done.

General Jackson was at once interested, and asked in his quick, rapid way several questions. When they were answered, he remained silent for a moment, evidently trying to think; he contracted his brow, set his mouth, and for some moments was obviously endeavoring to concentrate his thoughts. For a moment it was believed he had succeeded, for his nostrils dilated, and his eye flashed its old fire, but it was only for a moment; his face relaxed again, and presently he said very feebly and sadly: "I don't know—I can't tell; say to General Stuart he must do what he thinks best."

Either now or when Smith had given him the cup of coffee earlier, Jackson turned his head to look at the stump of his left arm and then asked Smith, "Were you here?" When his aide told him yes, the General was quiet for a few moments and then asked whether he had said anything while under the influence of chloroform. Smith reassured him. Then he said: "I have always thought it wrong to administer chloroform in cases where there is a probability of immediate death." But it was, he continued, "the most delightful physical sensation I ever experienced." He thought he had had enough consciousness to know what was going on. He seemed to remember "the most delightful music that ever greeted my ears"—the sawing of the bone, he supposed now it was. "But I should dislike above all things to enter eternity in such a condition." [97]

Smith told him not to talk. He must conserve his strength. Could he go to sleep? The General closed his eyes and slept until 9 o'clock on Sunday, May 3. He woke to the guns of a furious and terrible struggle all across the wooded front to the east that led to the Federal field works against which he had been trying to hurl Hill's division the night before.

# 33 || THE LAST MARCH

*". . . the great and good
Jackson is no more."*

Sandie Pendleton's visit to Jackson at 3:30 o'clock on
the morning of Sunday, May 3, was on behalf of the acting commanding general of the Second Corps, General Stuart. When Jackson went down with wounds, incapable of command, the senior general was A. P. Hill. When Hill was disabled a few minutes later, the
command descended to Rodes. Rodes had made a record this day
that led Jackson to advocate his immediate promotion and the War
Department to date his promotion, when it acted, from May 2. But
he was only a brigadier general, temporarily commanding a division
for the first time, and was almost a stranger to the Second Corps.

Precisely what happened about the command is not clear. But
eventually Pendleton sent Captain R. H. T. Adams of Hill's staff
on a gallop to Stuart, then four or five miles away in the direction of
the Ely's Ford road, to ask him to return immediately and take command of the Second Corps.

This was an irregular proceeding. Stuart was senior to Rodes, but
there was no provision in the army procedure for the corps command to go to a cavalry officer. Lee's report merely said that Stuart
"was sent for to take the command." Stuart is not more enlightening
in his report: "Captain Adams, of Gen. A. P. Hill's staff, reached me
posthaste, and informed me of the urgent demand for me to come
and take command as quickly as possible." [1] Rodes' report tells more
but not all.

"I was informed," Rodes said, after hearing that Jackson was wounded and then that Hill was disabled, "that the command of the corps devolved on me." He got in touch with Heth, now commanding Hill's division, and with Colston, and made arrangements for "a renewal of the attack in the morning, it being agreed that the troops were not in condition to resume operations that night." About midnight "the enemy made an attack on our right, but being feeble in its character, and promptly met, it lasted but a short time. Very soon after, Maj. Gen. J. E. B. Stuart, who had been sent for by Maj. A. S. Pendleton, assistant adjutant-general of Lieutenant-General Jackson, arrived on the ground and assumed command."

Rodes explained this unusual development thus:

I yielded the command to General Stuart not because I thought him entitled to it, belonging as he does to a different arm of the service, nor because I was unwilling to assume the responsibility of carrying on the attack, as I had already made the necessary arrangements, and they remained unchanged, but because, from the manner in which I was informed that he had been sent for, I inferred that General Jackson or General Hill had instructed Major Pendleton to place him in command, and for the still stronger reason that I feared that the information that the command had devolved on me, unknown except to my own immediate troops, would in their shaken condition, be likely to increase the demoralization of the corps. General Stuart's name was well and very favorably known to the army, and would tend, I hoped, to re-establish confidence. I yielded because I was satisfied the good of the service demanded it.[2]

Jackson had no part in these events. Rodes' report indicates that Hill originally expected Rodes to assume command, as his seniority entitled him to do. It seems likely that Pendleton, who in operations was closer to Jackson than any other officer of his staff and therefore might be expected to reflect his views, conferred with Hill, since Pendleton would hardly have sent one of Hill's staff officers to Stuart without Hill's approval. At that point the decision almost surely had to be made by Hill. Whether Pendleton originated the suggestion of Stuart's being called in, and presented the idea to Hill, it is impossible to say, though that theory would fit the known facts better than any other. In any event, the decision appears to have been made between Hill and Pendleton.

The command placed an extraordinary responsibility on Stuart. He had never commanded an infantry brigade, not to speak of a division or a corps. He had to take charge between midnight and daylight during a lull in a terrible conflict that would certainly be renewed with the dawn. He had no clear idea of its progress thus far. He did not know Jackson's plans. He was not familiar with the ground. At the moment he could not locate any of Jackson's staff except Pendleton. Yet he pitched into this complex task with energy and enthusiasm. One of his first steps was to send Pendleton to Jackson for information or advice.

Almost simultaneously Wilbourn, having seen Jackson placed under McGuire's care, was riding through the night to Lee's headquarters. He reached the commander about 3 A.M., and with an aide waked him. At Lee's invitation he sat on the General's blankets under a pine tree and told the story of Jackson's great day. When he came to the wounding of Jackson, Lee moaned and, Wilbourn thought, almost wept.

"Ah, captain," he said, "any victory is dearly bought which deprives us of the services of General Jackson, even for a short time!" [3]

When Wilbourn gave more details of the painful and distressing night, Lee stopped him. "Ah, don't talk about it," he said. "Thank God it is no worse." He was deeply moved.

Wilbourn explained the shift of command from Jackson to Hill to Rodes and now to Stuart, to which Lee acquiesced, then added that Stuart and Rodes hoped Lee would come to the Second Corps sector. He ventured the opinion that Jackson, to judge by his words, had planned to cut the road to the United States Ford and to block that line of enemy movement.

Lee responded immediately by exclaiming: "Those people must be pressed today." He wrote a note to Stuart, starting thus: "It is necessary that the glorious victory thus far achieved be prosecuted with the utmost vigor, and the enemy given no time to rally." [4] Three times Lee stressed uniting the two wings of the army. He said nothing to Stuart about Jackson's purpose to drive to the north of Chancellorsville in the direction of the roads to the Rapidan and the Rappahannock.

About 3:30 A.M. Hotchkiss arrived at Lee's headquarters with more details. Lee would not talk about Jackson's wounding. "I know

all about it and do not wish to hear any more—it is too painful a subject," he said.[5] Lee sent a second note to Stuart. It emphasized twice,
and even more strongly—"all-important," said Lee—that Stuart must
continue pressing to the right so as to unite the two wings of the
army. Again Lee said nothing about striking for the United States
Ford road or other line of communication.[6]

Meantime Stuart, riding with great energy along the Second
Corps's lines for the remainder of the night, brought the tired divisions into position, A. P. Hill's brigade still in the lead. Early on
Sunday, May 3, he launched a headlong attack against strong field
fortifications. A bitter struggle followed, with heavy losses, much
confusion in the attacks, but much persistence too. Stuart stirred
the assaulting waves with his own presence and his gay spirit. Desperate though he knew the fighting was, he sang in the old gay
manner, "Old Joe Hooker, won't you come out of the wilderness?"
and made sure that the lines charged with "Remember Jackson!"
on their lips and in their hearts.[7] They drove straight toward the
Fairview height that was crowned with scores of guns and girdled
all across the front with entrenched lines of infantry behind the protruding rows of tree trunks and boughs. Men who lived through the
morning said afterward that nothing they had experienced was
worse.

Hooker's order to abandon Hazel Grove's high ground enabled
the corps's artillery officer, E. P. Alexander, to line up on that enfilading position the guns that pounded the Federal forces on Fairview. Before the day was out, Lee, fighting up from the right with
Anderson's and McLaws' divisions, joined hands again with the
Second Corps. They forced their way forward to the burning house
at Chancellorsville and to one of the warmest personal ovations Lee
received from troops in the field.

As Lee sat his horse there about 11:30 A.M., surrounded by weary,
dirty, and often bloody men cheering him unrestrainedly, a message
reached his hands. It was from Jackson. The note has been lost, but
the circumstances and Lee's reply indicate that Jackson informed
Lee that he had been wounded, that the command had devolved on
Hill, and probably that the attack had smashed the enemy right and
carried to within a mile of Chancellorsville. Turning to Marshall, his
aide, Lee dictated or directed the reply that reads as follows:

Headquarters,
May 3, 1863

General Thomas J. Jackson,
  Commanding Corps:

General: I have just received your note, informing me that you were
wounded. I cannot express my regret at the occurrence. Could I have directed events, I should have chosen for the good of the country to be
disabled in your stead.

  I congratulate you upon the victory, which is due to your skill and
energy.

Very respectfully, your obedient servant,
R. E. Lee,
General.[8]

When Smith read this to Jackson later in the day the General
turned his face away and said: "General Lee is very kind, but he
should give the praise to God." [9]

Jackson had waked this morning of Sunday, May 3, at 9 o'clock.
He was free from pain and cheerful and, for a man whose arm had
been amputated six hours before, he seemed to be doing well. He
took a little nourishment. Then, his mind working quickly, he went
into action. He told Smith to stay with him. Morrison, he said,
should go to Richmond and inform Mrs. Jackson of his being
wounded. She would want to come at once, and Morrison could
accompany her. The others of his staff and his headquarters should
return to their duties with the corps in the battle which they could
hear plainly enough. He himself would inform Lee, and he dictated
to Smith the note that reached Lee in sight of the flames of the
Chancellor house.

About 10 o'clock that morning Jackson's right side began to pain
him, and he asked McGuire to look at it. "He said," McGuire's narrative tells, "he had injured it in falling from the litter the night before, and believed that he had struck it against a stone or the stump
of a sapling. No evidence of injury could be discovered by the examination; the skin was not broken or bruised, and the lung performed, as far as I could tell, its proper functions. Some simple application was recommended, in the belief that the pain would soon
disappear." By 8 o'clock that night the pain had disappeared, "and
in all respects," McGuire thought, "he seemed to be doing well."

Lacy, the Second Corps's chaplain, came in during the morning. As he took his first look at the stump of the General's left arm, he could not restrain himself. "Oh, General, what a calamity!" he exclaimed.

But the General would have none of that. He wanted to talk, and he wanted especially to rationalize the loss of his arm in terms of his understanding the relations of a true believer to his God.[10] He insisted that he was not depressed and not unhappy. He was certain that his Heavenly Father had designed the affliction of the loss of his arm for his own good. In time, in this world or in the life to come, he felt sure he would discover that what seemed like a calamity now was actually a blessing; and he could wait for the coming of that knowledge. So strongly did he feel thus, he said to Lacy, that if he had the power to replace his arm, he would not dare to do so unless he could know that it was the will of God.

"You never saw me more perfectly contented than I am today," the General told Lacy.

Lacy asked him about what had happened, and Jackson told him, quietly and freely. He spoke of the fall when the litter bearer went down with tangled feet. That moment, with its exquisite pain, seemed to him a moment of death, and he knew perfect peace in the thought that he was approaching his Heavenly Father and could do so without fear.

"It has been a precious experience to me," he told Lacy, "that I was brought face to face with death, and found all was well."

He doubted whether a person who had not (in Lacy's words) made his peace with God would have the same experience. The thought interested him, and he expressed it in various ways to Lacy until McGuire and Smith put an end to the conversation so that the General could rest.

Douglas came to the field hospital a little later, fresh from the morning's desperate fighting.[11] He gave news of the battle to Smith, and later Smith told the General. Douglas had much information about the Stonewall Brigade. At each note of bravery the General brightened, and "his head gave the peculiar shake from side to side, and he uttered his usual, 'Good, good,' with unwonted energy. . . . The men of that brigade he told McGuire at his cot, "will be, some day proud to say to their children, 'I was one of the Stonewall Brigade.'"

Smith told him, in answer to a question about losses, of the death of Paxton.

"Paxton? Paxton?" he said as if in disbelief.

"Yes, sir, he has fallen," Smith told him.

The General turned his face to the wall, closed his eyes, and lay long in silence. Then he spoke seriously and tenderly of Paxton's virtues. Smith had additional news. Paxton had a strong conviction that he would be killed. He gave minute instructions for such an event, and read calmly and devoutly from his New Testament just before advancing with the brigade under the Federal guns.

Jackson listened intently, and then said, of his friend's preparations in event of death, "That's good; that's good." [12]

In the afternoon a message came in from Lee directing McGuire to move Jackson to Guiney's Station as soon as his condition allowed. There was some danger, said Lee, that Federal troops would swoop around from Ely's Ford on the Rapidan. He had sent troops to that spot to stop the movement.

McGuire told Jackson of the message, but the General objected to being moved if, in McGuire's opinion, it would do him any harm. He had no objection to remaining in a tent, and would prefer it, provided his wife could find quarters in a nearby house. "If the enemy does come," he added, "I am not afraid of them. I have always been kind to their wounded, and I am sure they will be kind to me."

If he did move to Guiney's, the General continued, he did not wish McGuire to go with him. Complaints had run through army ranks about generals who, when they were wounded, took surgeons off with them. Jackson wanted nothing of the kind now.

Guiney's itself suited Jackson well enough as a temporary haven. He knew the Thomas Coleman Chandlers there. But he hoped, after resting for a day or two, to move southward on the railroad to Ashland, 12 miles from Richmond, and ultimately to go to Lexington. He didn't like the thought of the capital's bustle, and he longed for the quiet of his home and the air of the Valley, which, he thought, would help in healing his wounds and restoring his strength. [13]

Lee sent a second message, this time with greater urgency. McGuire must move in the morning; and, specifically, McGuire must accompany Jackson. His duties as medical director of the corps would be turned over to the surgeon next in rank. This McGuire told to Jackson. The General said: "General Lee has always been very kind to me, and I thank him."

Lee's orders to move Jackson resulted almost certainly from a startling change in the battle. Lee received Jackson's note on the morning of May 3rd while near the burning Chancellor house, and at about the same time he received word that Sedgwick had stormed Marye's Heights and was now advancing on Lee's rear.

The news altered drastically the whole nature of Lee's plan. He detached McLaws' division, and later Anderson's, from the force that had pushed Hooker's right wing out of Chancellorsville, and sent them to strengthen Early. The Second Corps would have to handle the Federal right wing. Stuart, though still much inferior in numbers, would have to hold steady with his 30,000 men against Hooker's 75,000 instead of pushing even harder with all of the 46,000 men that the united army on the left could continue to hurl against Hooker.

To balance these enforced realignments, a Confederate cannon ball had crashed during the morning into the porch of the Chancellor house, striking the pillar against which Hooker was leaning. The blow knocked him unconscious, left him in severe pain, and deprived his army of control for several hours while neither the surgeons nor Hooker could make up their minds whether he was capable of exercising command. But this Lee did not know. He did know that Sedgwick's advance created new dangers, and he did not wish Jackson to fall into the hands of Federal troopers who might now be active in his rear.

Early on Monday morning, May 4, McGuire had Jackson lifted with care and placed on a mattress laid out in an ambulance. Stapleton Crutchfield was again his ambulance companion. They had twenty-seven miles ahead of them, and the road could not possibly be anything but rough. Special efforts were made to smooth it. Hotchkiss and a party of pioneers went ahead to clear away obstructions.

They had a tougher time with ammunition and quartermaster wagons crowding the principal line of communication from the railhead at Guiney's. Teamsters were an unyielding crew who ruled the roads and took orders only from high command and not always then. If they were in ruts to their liking, they would rarely go through the strain of jerking their wagons out merely because of an ambu-

lance. But when word reached them that this was the General—
Old Jack himself—going back with bad wounds, that was different.
The great whips lashed, the teams strained, the wheels creaked to
the side of the roads, and the drivers came down to stand bareheaded
and solemn-faced as the ambulance went by.[14]

The road was the route by which many walking wounded were
going to the rear or coming up, like the wagons, from the stations
behind the lines. They looked up at an ambulance of obvious importance, with more than the usual officers and men accompanying
it. Then the news broke through.

"Old Jack!" "It's the General!" "Clear the road!"

So they stood, hats off, as the General passed, men who ordinarily
would greet him with whoops and high yells, silent now, following
the ambulance with their eyes and wondering what this meant in
terms of command and survival.

The route, chosen by Hotchkiss, ran southwestward to Todd's
Tavern and on to Spotsylvania Court House. From there it continued in a southeasterly direction to the crossing of the Mattaponi
and on to the Richmond, Fredericksburg and Potomac Railroad at
Guiney's. Word of the General's coming had run ahead of him to
Spotsylvania Court House, and men and women lined the road
there. Many of them presented delicacies. They stood—as people
did at many points along the road—hushed and solemn.

Inside the ambulance the General was feeling good. He wanted
to talk. McGuire, who rode with him, was always within reach, and
sometimes Smith and Lacy were nearby on horses. The military
operations were uppermost in the minds of all. What did the General
think of Hooker's plan?

"It was, in the main, a good conception, sir, an excellent plan," he
answered. "But he should not have sent away his cavalry; that was
his great blunder. It was that which enabled me to turn him, without
his being aware of it, and to take him by the rear. Had he kept his
cavalry with him, his plan would have been a very good one." [15]

Of his own part in the operation he said that it was "a great success." He thought it "the most successful movement of my life. But
I have received far more credit for it than I deserve. Most men will
think that I had planned it all from the first; but it was not so. I
simply took advantage of circumstances as they were presented to
me in the providence of God. I feel that His hand led me." [16]

He had intended, the General continued, to try to cut off the Federal forces from the United States Ford and, by taking a position between them and the Rappahannock, to compel them to attack him. "My men sometimes fail to drive the enemy from a position," he added with a smile, "but they always fail to drive us away." [17]

He spoke again of the Stonewall Brigade, then popularly, but not officially, bearing that name. It had applied to the War Department for official sanction for the name. The General said "the government ought certainly to accede to their request and authorize them to assume this title; for it was fairly earned." He called them "a noble body of patriots." The thought led him back to the early days. "The name 'Stonewall' ought to be attached wholly to the men of the brigade, and not to me," he said; "for it was their steadfast heroism which had earned it at First Manassas." *

The General spoke of Rodes with warmth and admiration. He should be promoted immediately, he said, for the manner in which he led the assault of May 2. Gallantry on the field ought to be rewarded quickly. In that way the incentive effect was greater. He spoke well of Colston, for his part in the attack of the 2nd (after Jackson was wounded Colston came under criticism); and of Col. Edward Willis of the Twelfth Georgia, who had taken a leading part in the advance of Doles' brigade. The death of Paxton and of Boswell † lingered in his mind, and he spoke of them again as officers of great merit and promise. [18]

---

* Dabney, 712, 713.

So far as the record shows, Jackson never used the term "Stonewall" in reference to himself. Most other people did in popular usage, though not in formal correspondence or official papers; and by this time the name was almost universally known and widely used in the civilian Confederacy. Jackson's words quoted above have been cited sometimes as a reason for saying that the brigade but not the commander—or the brigade more than the commander—was in Bee's mind at First Manassas when he said, "There is Jackson standing like a stonewall." This is needless hairsplitting. The contemporary custom of calling brigades and other units by the names of their commanders might create confusion in the rare instances in which a commander did one thing and his unit another. But the context and the circumstances make it clear in words like "Jackson advanced on the right, Longstreet on the left," that the reference is to both the units and the commanders. The units would not advance without the commanders, or unless ordered by commanders; and the commanders would not set out by themselves. At First Manassas, Bee was speaking of Jackson in his role as brigade commander and therefore of both the commander and the brigade.

† Hotchkiss' diary contains a moving account of his burial of Boswell, an intimate friend. On Sunday, May 3, after delivering to Stuart the message from Lee to press on, Hotchkiss searched the area where Jackson had been shot. There he found Boswell's body. It had been rifled of hat, field glasses, pistol, a daguerreotype, and other articles. Much upset, Hotchkiss himself buried his friend "in a grave which I dug in the family burying ground at Elwood, the home of Major J. Horace Lacy, by the side of General Jackson's arm which had been amputated and buried there."

The long day rolled on. It was hot, and although those with him found the General bright and cheerful (full of hope and vivacity, said Dabney), the ride must have been wearing on him. In the afternoon he had slight nausea. He suggested to McGuire—turning back to his experiences with therapies involving water—that a wet cloth be placed on his abdomen. McGuire agreed, and the ambulance stopped at a spring so that a towel could be wet and placed as the General requested. He said the relief was distinct and welcome. But he had a return of the pain in his side.

About 8 o'clock, when night was falling, they arrived at Guiney's. Lacy had ridden ahead to the Chandlers', and preparations were made there to place the General in one of the parlors. But the Chandler house had wounded officers in it already, and much coming and going raised a question as to whether the General would be sufficiently quiet. When McGuire arrived, he learned that a case of erysipelas had developed there, and he looked around for other quarters.

The Chandlers had, close by, a small office-type building somewhat like that which the General had stayed in at Moss Neck. Two big oaks stood in front of a porch on this small, low frame structure. A small room in front led to two larger rooms in the rear, with low ceilings, and two half-story rooms were above. This was quieter. It would leave the General by himself, and it would provide space for those with him. In a violent thunderstorm McGuire moved him in immediately. The General ate a little bread and drank some tea, and then he went to sleep and slept long and quietly.

He woke on Tuesday, May 5, much refreshed. The thunderstorm had broken the heat. There was a flurry of excitement at Guiney's because of a report that Federal troops were near. Some wagon trains moved, and some ambulatory wounded left. But McGuire and Smith, determined to stick it out, kept all this from the General.

McGuire thought the General's wounds were doing well.

Union by the first intention, had taken place, to some extent in the stump [his narrative reports], and the rest of the surface of the wound exposed was covered with healthy granulations. The wound in his hand gave him little pain, and the discharge was healthy. Simple lint and water dressings were used, both for the stump and the hand, and upon the palm of the latter, a light short splint was applied, to assist in keeping at rest, the fragments of the second and third metacarpal bones. He expressed great satisfaction when told that his wounds were healing, and asked if I could tell from their appearance, how long he would probably be kept from the field. Conversing with Captain Smith, a few moments afterwards, he alluded to his injuries and said, "Many would regard them as a great misfortune, I regard them as one of the blessings of my life." Captain S. [Smith] replied, "All things work together for good to those that love God." "Yes," he answered, "that's it, that's it." [19] . . . He ate heartily for one in his condition, and was uniformly cheerful.

Two days of suspense followed, Tuesday the 5th and Wednesday the 6th, with no marked changes. The weather was cool for May, and Tuesday ended with another rain and a raw feel to the air. Jackson sent for Lacy Tuesday morning about 10 o'clock and asked him to read from the Bible and pray by the bed. He told the chaplain he would like him to come every morning at 10 o'clock. They talked about religious matters. The General told Lacy that he was perfectly willing to die, but that he believed his time had not yet come, that his Heavenly Father still had work for him to do in defense of his country, and that he would be spared until that was completed.

These talks continued several days, and Lacy's reports [20] leave some uncertainty as to what was said on a particular day. Perhaps it was this Tuesday that the General spoke of how Christianity made a man better in any lawful calling. For a cobbler or a tailor, he thought, religion would result in more care in doing work, more punctuality, more fidelity. He had no doubt that religion helped to make a better general. So did prayer. At a critical hour of battle, religion calmed a general's perplexities, moderated his anxieties, steadied his judgment, and preserved him from exaggerated and rash conclusions. Religious thought, he continued, could extend to every act; and he liked to think of religious relationships when he washed himself, when he dressed, when he ate. The Bible, indeed, furnished rules for everything.

Turning to Smith (this morning or another), he asked the young student of theology: "Can you tell me where the Bible gives generals a model for their official reports of battles?" Smith smiled and said he had never thought of turning to the Bible for that. "Nevertheless," the General said, "there are such, and excellent models, too. Look, for instance, at the narrative of Joshua's battle with the Amalekites [Exod. 17:8–16]. There you have one. It has clearness, brevity, fair-

ness, modesty; and it traces the victory to its right source, the blessing of God."

It was probably when McGuire was dressing his wounds this day
that he turned upon the doctor with a question as to whether people
whose bodily afflictions had been healed by Jesus would ever suffer
again from the same affliction. McGuire did not try to answer. But
the General felt strongly that once such a person was healed, he
would never again suffer in the same way. He thought about it
quietly for a time and then exclaimed: "Oh, for infinite power!" [21]

Hotchkiss left on the 5th to rejoin the Second Corps's headquarters. When he came in to say good-by, the General requested him
especially to present his regards to General Lee.

Far to the north, before this day ran out, Hooker had given up
hope of further fighting south of the Rappahannock. Lee had contained Sedgwick with the additions of McLaws and Anderson to
Early's division, then forced him back across the river. Turning then
on Hooker's right flank as it had entrenched itself in a great semicircle based on the United States Ford, Lee prepared to assail it
headlong—an idea of great boldness, since Hooker had some 75,000
men behind strong fortifications and Lee no more than 35,000 for
attacking, although everything Lee had done in this campaign had
seemed hazardous.

Hooker removed the possibility of further battle by withdrawing
in a drenching rain during the night of May 5–6 and the morning
of the 6th, without Lee's knowledge, in good order and with virtually
all of the army's equipment. At the finish, as at the start, Hooker
maneuvered well. But when the armies came to grips, his control
faded, his purpose weakened, and his moral strength proved inadequate.

Jackson, in his bed in the Chandler office—it looked out toward the
railroad tracks where he had boarded the coach sixteen days ago
in his rain-drenched rubber coat to welcome Anna and young Julia—
knew nothing of these events. Wednesday the 6th was, to outward
view, an uneventful day. Jackson seemed to be holding his own.
Lacy came in at 10 o'clock, and there was more religious talk, with
Smith participating. Possibly it was this day that he asked Smith:
"What were the headquarters of Christianity after the crucifixion?"
Smith replied that at first Jerusalem was the chief seat, but when
persecution drove the disciples out there was a lapse until Antioch,

Iconium, Rome, and Alexandria were established as "centers of influence." That phrase caused the General to interrupt him.

"Why do you say 'centers of influence'? Is not 'headquarters' a better term?"

Smith, uncertain as to whether this kind of talk would tire the General, looked inquiringly at McGuire, but the doctor nodded. The young theologian explained that the apostles were directed, seemingly by divine Providence, to plant churches in these cities. Because of their political, commercial, and ethnical relations, they were "headquarters" of influence for the known world.

The General listened carefully. Then he said: "Mr. Smith, I wish you would get the map and show me precisely where Iconium was."

Smith protested that no map was available. But the General caught him up on that. "Yes, sir," he said. "You will find it in the atlas which is in my old trunk."

The trunk was searched, but no atlas could be found. Smith suggested that probably the General had left it in his portable desk.

"Yes, you are right," the General conceded. "I left it in my desk," and he said it was on a certain shelf of the desk. He mused for a little while and then said: "Mr. Smith, I wish you would examine into the matter, and report to me." [22]

McGuire was by this time physically exhausted. He had been up nearly all of the night of the 2nd, when he had operated on the General, and as a nurse on the subsequent nights. To provide relief for him, and to bring another doctor in for consultation, Lacy rode to army headquarters this day to see Lee and request that Dr. S. B. Morrison, chief surgeon of Early's division, be sent to Guiney's. Morrison was a kinsman of Anna's, and Jackson knew him well. Lee readily assented.

After listening carefully to the chaplain's report on Jackson's condition, the General gave Lacy this message for Jackson: "Give him my affectionate regards, and tell him to make haste and get well, and come back to me as soon as he can. He has lost his left arm; but I have lost my right arm." [23]

If there was any marked change as daylight faded on the 6th, McGuire did not record it in his narrative. Dabney, whose source on this period was principally Lacy, included in the biography he wrote at the request of Anna that "after Monday [May 4] the bright promise of his recovery began to be overcast; pain and restlessness gradually increased, and he was necessarily limited in conversation. It became necessary again to resort to his favorite remedy, the wet napkins, and to employ anodynes to soothe his nerves." But none of this comes from the physician in charge so far as the period before the night of May 6–7 is concerned.

During this night of May 6–7, however, a striking change took place. Jackson woke up about 1 A.M. with an attack of nausea. McGuire, very tired, had decided it was safe for him to sleep this night on a cot in the General's room. Jim, the servant, was sitting awake, on guard. The General knew of McGuire's exhaustion, and he would not wake him. To Jim he whispered instructions for a wet towel to be placed on his abdomen. Jim obeyed orders.

It did no good. The nausea continued, and pain in the right side added to it. Still the General would not wake McGuire. He braced himself to endure until morning. Through the long hours he held on tightly, but at early dawn—did he, on a bed of pain, think how many times he had gone into action at early dawn?—he called McGuire. The physician's narrative reports his finding:

About daylight I was aroused and found him suffering with great pain. An examination disclosed pleuro-pneumonia of the right side. I believed, and the consulting physician concurred in the opinion, that it was attributable to the fall from the litter, the night he was wounded. The General, himself, referred it to this accident. I think the disease came on too soon after the application of the wet cloths, to admit of the supposition, once believed, that it was induced by them. The nausea, for which the cloths were applied that night, may have been the result of inflammation already begun. Contusion of the lung, with extravasation of blood in his chest, was probably produced by the fall referred to, and shock and loss of blood, prevented any ill effects until reaction had been well established, and then inflammation ensued.

Pneumonia, developing so soon after an amputation, impelled McGuire, and subsequently other physicians, to regroup their forces for attacking a new enemy. The standard treatment called for cupping—drawing blood to any part by creating a vacuum at that point, and doing so by applying to the skin a cupping glass within which the air had been rarefied, usually by heat. Cupping required opiates. In McGuire's words, "Cups were applied, and mercury, with antimony and opium, administered."

This was the bad news of Thursday the 7th. The good news was the arrival of Anna and Julia, now five and a half months old, accompanied by Hetty, the nurse.

After Anna left the Yerby house on April 29 for Richmond, she visited Mrs. John Letcher in the Governor's Mansion. Later she went to the Moses D. Hoge home as the guest of Mrs. Hoge and of Mrs. William Brown, who lived there. The Rev. Dr. Hoge was in Europe on a governmental mission trying to obtain a large quantity of Bibles for soldiers. Anna knew—all her world knew—when Hooker struck. She knew that a battle was developing. This was familiar experience, though not the less nerve-racking on that account. But it was no preparation for ill-tidings she was to receive.

On Sunday, May 3, Dr. Brown came to her with the news: the General had been wounded—seriously, but, it was thought, not dangerously.[24]

She bowed beneath the blow. This was what she had feared ever since his wound in the hand at First Manassas. But she rose instantly to the challenge. When could she go to her husband? She must take Julia. She could take Hetty. When did the train leave? She must go.

Stoneman's raiders were loose all over the country between Richmond and Fredericksburg. The R.F.&P. had ceased to operate. Travel by carriage was too dangerous. There was nothing she could do except endure.

On Tuesday, May 5, Joseph Morrison reached Richmond, sent by the General to escort Anna to him. He had needed two days, and Anna could not duplicate his journey on horseback. In anxiety and restlessness, in terrible concern and helplessness, she had to wait.

On Thursday the 7th the blockade lifted and Anna left on the first train, taking Julia and Hetty with her. It was slow going on the 45-mile trip, and even slower to Anna that May morning. She was torn between the memories of those nine wonderful days in April and the anxieties of these days of crisis. A member of the staff, probably James Smith, met her. She inquired anxiously. He said the General was doing "pretty well," and Anna's heart "sank like lead . . . from his tone and manner I knew something was wrong. . . ."

Dr. McGuire was dressing the General's wounds, and she could not go in immediately. The Chandlers received her warmly and assured her that, although the General was not in their own home, as they wished him to be (there was still erysipelas there), he was well looked after in the office. Anna paced the piazza. It did not help when she realized that the soldiers digging within a stone's throw of the house were exhuming a coffin. It was far worse when she was told that it was the coffin of General Paxton. She had known him well in Lexington. His wife was a neighbor and a friend, and Anna thought first of her. But it was worst of all when finally she went into the room where her husband lay.

Eight days ago when she had left him, "he was in the full flush of vigorous manhood, and during that last, blessed visit, I never saw him look so handsome, so happy, and so noble. Now, his fearful wounds, his mutilated arm, the scratches upon his face, and, above all, the desperate pneumonia, which was flushing his cheeks, oppressing his breathing, and benumbing his senses, wrung my soul with such grief and anguish as it had never before experienced."

Under the influence of the opiates the General did not realize that Anna was standing by his bed. "He had to be aroused to speak to me," she said later, "and although he expressed much joy and thankfulness at seeing me, he was too much affected by morphia to resist stupor, and soon seemed to lose the consciousness of my presence, except when I spoke or ministered to him." His condition had changed rapidly and was now approaching crisis.

He had changed in other ways. While Anna was waiting, someone thought it would help her to make the lemonade which was to be given to the General. James Smith took it to him, but when the General tasted it, he said immediately: "You did not mix this. It is too sweet. Take it back." Normally he accepted the food before him almost indifferent to its quality. But in a few minutes he roused himself sufficiently to note the anxiety Anna could not conceal. More gently he reproached her: "My darling, you must cheer up, and not wear a long face. I love cheerfulness and brightness in the sickroom." Whenever he waked from stupor and saw Anna, he spoke to her tenderly: "My darling, you are very much loved. . . . You are one of the most precious little wives in the world."

Once he told her—and it was the mark of his mood—"I know you would give your life for me, but I am perfectly resigned. Do not be sad; I hope I may recover. Pray for me, but always remember in your prayers to use the petition, 'Thy will be done!'"

Anna proposed to bring the baby in, but he put her off. "Not yet. Wait till I feel better," he told her. But from now on, as Anna wrote in complete honesty, "from the time I reached him, he was too ill to notice or talk much, and he lay most of the time in a semi-conscious state; but when aroused, he recognized those about him and consciousness would return."

When Dr. Morrison came at 2 o'clock, he went into Jackson's room immediately. As he leaned over the bed, the General looked up in recognition. "That's an old, familiar face," he said. A little later Morrison and McGuire decided that someone must aid Mrs. Jackson if she was to be of greatest help, especially since her daughter had not been weaned. She agreed, and they determined to ask Mrs. Hoge to come from Richmond. The doctors wished at the same time the best professional advice in the capital, and they decided to ask Dr. David Tucker, who had much experience with pneumonia, to come too. James Smith, they decided, must go to Richmond to escort Mrs. Hoge.

"Towards the evening" of this Thursday, McGuire records in his narrative, "he became better, and hopes were again entertained of his recovery." It was the first time that he had recorded formally the danger which must have been in many minds. The old Jacksonian spirit could flare. Dr. Morrison sat by his bed this night and, following a schedule, aroused him once for medication. "Will you take this, General?" he said.

The General looked steadily at him. "Do your duty," he said. Then, to emphasize the doctor's responsibility, he said again, and with firmness, "Do your duty." [25]

Friday the 8th came in cool. McGuire dressed his wounds again, this time with two other surgeons, Drs. Breckinridge and Smith,[26] whom he had called in for consultation. "Although the quantity of discharge from them"—that is, from the wounds—"had diminished, the process of healing was still going on," McGuire recorded in his narrative. "The pain in his side had disappeared, but"—here was the ominous finding—"he breathed with difficulty and complained of a feeling of great exhaustion." Breckinridge said that he hoped the blister which had been applied would afford him relief, and the General expressed his own confidence in it and in his final recovery.

The day dragged on. To Anna's eyes, his fever and restlessness increased, and he was growing perceptibly weaker. When he roused himself from his stupor, his disjointed words reflected other moments, other scenes, other strains. "Tell Major Hawks to send for-

ward provisions to the men," he would say in delirium. "Order A. P.
Hill to prepare for action!" "Pass the infantry to the front!" [27]

Sandie Pendleton came back in his irrational expressions again
and again: "Major Pendleton, send in and see if there is higher
ground back of Chancellorsville. . . . I must find out if there is
high ground between Chancellorsville and the river. . . . Push the
columns! Hasten the columns! Pendleton, you take charge of that.
. . . Where is Pendleton? Tell him to push up the columns." [28]

Then silence, and the quick breathing, and the lapse into coma.
Anna knew that everything possible was being done for his relief
and benefit, but she knew the desperate nature of his condition. Dr.
Morrison went much further. During the day he suggested to the
General his fear that he would not recover. But the General dis-
sented positively. He said (Dabney added: "precisely in these
words") that "I am not afraid to die. I am willing to abide by the
will of my Heavenly Father. But I do not believe I shall die at this
time. I am persuaded the Almighty has yet a work for me to perform."

Saturday the 9th marked the steady deterioration of his strength.
Anna stayed by his bed so much that Julia suffered from hunger.
Mrs. Hoge had come in from Richmond and aided Hetty in caring
for the baby and helping Anna. Dr. Tucker arrived and examined the
General, but there was nothing he could do. Perhaps now, or after
Drs. Breckinridge and Smith had attended him, the General said
to McGuire: "I see from the number of physicians that you think
my condition serious, but I thank God, if it is his will, that I am ready
to go." [29]

In the afternoon the General roused himself and asked for Lacy.
His breathing was so labored that the others thought he should not
try to talk. They sought to dissuade him, but he insisted. When Lacy
came in, the General asked if he was trying to carry out the plans
for Sabbath observance about which they had talked. Lacy assured
him, and the General expressed gratification. He told Lacy that he
must not stay with him Sunday but must return to the corps and
conduct his regular Sunday services. "He suffered no pain today, and
his breathing was less difficult," McGuire noted, "but he was evidently hourly growing weaker."

Anna, in the hope of soothing him, suggested that she read some
of the Psalms. He told her, contrary to McGuire's view, that he was

suffering too much to listen, but then he caught himself. "Yes," he said, "we must never refuse that. Get the Bible and read them." She read with all the control she could manage, and he lay quietly.

As night came on and he grew more tired, he asked Anna to sing to him. She must sing the most spiritual songs, he said. She strove desperately to control herself. Her brother Joseph joined her, and the two sang a few hymns quietly.*

The General asked in a whisper for "Shew pity, Lord"—Isaac Watts' hymn based on the Fifty-first Psalm. It makes verses of the Psalmist's "Have mercy upon me, O God, according to thy loving kindness: according to the multitude of thy tender mercies blot out my transgressions . . . Purge me with hyssop, and I shall be clean; wash me, and I shall be whiter than snow . . . Create in me a clean heart, O God; and renew a right spirit within me. . . ."

Two years before, Anna and he had sat in their Lexington home on the April day he marched off to war, reading together the fifth chapter of Second Corinthians: "For we know that if our earthly house of this tabernacle were dissolved, we have a building of God, an house not made with hands, eternal in the heavens." Now Anna and Joseph sang Watts' words:

> Shew pity, Lord; O Lord, forgive;
> Let a repenting rebel live;
> Are not thy mercies large and free?
> May not a sinner trust in thee?

Anna thought the song had a quieting effect. To her "he seemed to rest in perfect peace." But the night was bad. He tossed feverishly and could not sleep. A moist cloth pressed across his brow seemed to bring him a little relief, and when those at the bedside stopped momentarily he indicated with a gesture that he wished it to continue. He was growing weaker visibly. In his delirium he would still whisper disjointed words, mention this officer or that one, live in the twilight of half-memories, or submerge into unconsciousness.

The weather was more like May now, and the morning of Sunday,

---

* If they sang from his favorite hymns, they chose from among "How happy are they Who the Savior obey"; "Come, humble sinner, in whose breast a thousand thoughts revolve"; " 'Tis my happiness below not to live without the cross"; "When gathering clouds around I view and days are dark and friends are few"; and "Glorious things of thee are spoken, Zion, city of our Lord." This was the list prepared May 8, 1920, by Superintendent E. W. Nichols, of V.M.I. His letter to Dr. Arthur V. Hargetts of New York telling of this list is in the Institute files.

May 10, was pleasantly warm and gave promise of a fine spring day. Shortly after daylight Dr. Morrison took Anna aside. He must tell her, he said, that the doctors, who had done everything they could, had lost all hope. Her husband could not live. He thought the General's strength was draining away fast, and he was afraid he had only a few more hours. She should know, he said.

Anna must have known, but this had finality. Yet again she rose to duty. She told Dr. Morrison that her husband should be informed. She had heard him say that, although he was ready whenever God might call him, he would prefer a few hours' knowledge of his dying so that he might prepare. It was her duty, she said, to tell him now. Dr. Morrison assented.

Early in the morning Anna went to his bedside and looked at his quiet face, now almost lost in unconsciousness. She began to talk to him. Presently her voice reached him. Did he know, she was saying, that he must be very soon in heaven? She repeated it several times. He seemed aware that she was speaking to him.

"Do you not feel willing to acquiesce in God's allotment if He will you to go today?" she asked him.

His eyes opened, and he looked her full in the face. With great difficulty but distinctly he said, "I prefer it."

Anna continued: "Well, before this day closes, you will be with the blessed Saviour in his glory."

"I will be an infinite gainer to be translated." *

He lay in virtual unconsciousness all morning. To the north where the army rested after bitter fighting and heavy losses, Lee had formally urged officers and men to gather at religious services today and to give thanks for the victory of Chancellorsville. Lacy came back, as his commanding officer had directed, and Lee found him early in the morning. Lacy gave him the critical news. Lee refused to believe it.

"Surely General Jackson must recover," he said. "God will not take him from us, now that we need him so much. Surely he will be spared to us, in answer to the many prayers which are offered for him."

When Lacy had completed the service, Lee sought him out again.

---

* These are direct quotations in Dabney, 722–723, probably recited to him by Lacy. It is impossible to say whether the language is exact, although speech, on such subjects, was different in the 1860's from that of more recent times. There is no reason to doubt the substance of the conversation. McGuire quotes the General as saying: "It will be an infinite gain to be translated to heaven."

"When you return," he said, "I trust you will find him better. When a suitable occasion offers, give him my love, and tell him that I wrestled in prayer for him last night, as I never prayed, I believe, for myself."

The tears were gathering in his eyes, his voice was shaking, and he left Lacy abruptly.[30]

About 11 o'clock Anna, weaker now herself, worn by the strain, spoke to her husband again. His exhaustion had increased rapidly. She wished to make sure that he understood. Kneeling by his bed, she asked him if he realized that before sunset he would be with his Saviour.

He roused himself at her words and replied to her with clarity. "Oh, no! You are frightened, my child," he told her. "Death is not so near. I may yet get well." [31]

Before his voice and these words Anna gave way. She fell across the bed and wept bitterly. But she held to her hard duty enough to rouse herself once more. She told him again that the doctors said there was no hope.

He pondered a moment, then asked her to call McGuire.

"Doctor," he said, "Anna informs me that you have told her, that I am to die today. Is it so?"

McGuire said it was so.[32] The General looked at the ceiling, as if in intense thought. Finally he said: "Very good, very good; it is all right."

He turned to Anna and tried to comfort her, fumbling in his weakness. He had much to say, he managed to tell her, but he could not tell her now. Anna recovered enough to speak to him again. Did he wish that she should return with Julia to her father's home in North Carolina? [33]

"Yes, you have a good, kind father," he said, and then he added, "But no one is so kind and good as your Heavenly Father."

Anna asked him then about the place of his burial. What was his wish about that? His mind was growing cloudy again, and she thought he said, "Charlotte"—probably because he was still thinking of her father's home near Charlotte. He spoke again, and this time she thought he was trying to say "Charlottesville." The two places puzzled her, for neither had any intimate relation to him or to her.

She asked him then if he did not wish to be buried in Lexington, and that question he understood. He answered at once: "Yes, in

Lexington, and in my own plot"—the one he had bought when their first daughter, Mary Graham Jackson, had died.

These words he wrenched out of a body that had almost completed its journey. Anna thought he must see their daughter. Mrs. Hoge came in with Julia, and Hetty followed. The father responded immediately. He had almost ceased to notice anything, but his face lit up for a moment, and a suggestion of a smile crossed it. The baby was placed on his bed. He greeted her with "Little darling . . . sweet one." She smiled at his weary, sunken face; and then he fell back into unconsciousness again.

About 1 o'clock Sandie Pendleton arrived and was taken into the bedroom—Sandie, who could not stay away when he knew of the General's condition, who must come once more, and for the last time, to his General's side. That was his place in battle, and he thought it his place now in the final crisis. Jackson showed interest in his young assistant and in what he might have to report.

"Who was preaching at headquarters today?" he asked.

Sandie told him, and then told him more: "The whole army was praying for you, General," he said.

"Thank God—they are very kind," the General replied. Then with almost the last of his strength he said: "It is the Lord's day; my wish is fulfilled. I have always desired to die on Sunday." [34]

At 1:30 o'clock, McGuire noting a moment of consciousness, thought he should speak to the General again. He told him that he had but two hours to live.

"Very good, it is all right," the whisper came back. [35]

McGuire offered him some brandy and water, but the General declined it. "It will only delay my departure, and do no good," he said. "I want to preserve my mind, if possible, to the last." But that he could not do. In McGuire's words:

His mind began to fail and wander, and he frequently talked as if in command upon the field, giving orders in his old way; then the scene shifted, and he was at the mess-table, in conversation with members of his staff; now with his wife and child; now at prayers with his military family. . . .

A few moments before he died, he cried out in his delirium, "Order A. P. Hill to prepare for action! Pass the infantry to the front rapidly! Tell Major Hawks"—then stopped, leaving the sentence unfinished. Presently, a smile of ineffable sweetness spread itself over his pale face, and he said quietly, and with an expression, as if of relief, "Let us cross over the river, and rest under the shade of the trees"; and then, without pain, or the least struggle, his spirit passed from the earth to the God who gave it.[36]

❀      ❀      ❀

The official grief poured out. "It becomes my melancholy duty," Lee telegraphed to the Secretary of War on the 10th, "to announce to you the death of General Jackson. He expired at 3:15 P.M. today. His body will be conveyed to Richmond in the train tomorrow, under charge of Major Pendleton, assistant adjutant-general. Please direct an escort of honor to meet it at the depot, and that suitable arrangement be made for its disposition." [37]

"A great national calamity has befallen us," President Davis telegraphed in reply to Lee, "and I sympathize with the sorrow you feel and the embarrassment you must experience. The announcement of the death of General Jackson followed frequent assurances that he was doing very well, and though the loss was one which would have been deeply felt under any circumstances, the shock was increased by its suddenness. There is sincere mourning here, and it will extend throughout the land as the intelligence is received." [38]

To Stuart, Lee was more personal: "I regret to inform you that the great and good Jackson is no more. He died yesterday at 3:15 P.M. of pneumonia, calm, serene, and happy. May his spirit pervade our whole army; our country will then be secure." [39]

The proclamation to the army—General Orders, No. 61, Headquarters of the Army of Northern Virginia, May 11, 1863—had a notable dignity:

With deep grief the commanding general announces to the army the death of Lieut. Gen. T. J. Jackson, who expired on the 10th instant, at 3:15 P.M. The daring, skill, and energy of this great and good soldier, by the decree of an all-wise Providence, are now lost to us. But while we mourn his death, we feel that his spirit still lives, and will inspire the whole army with its indomitable courage and unshaken confidence in God as our hope and our strength. Let his name be a watchword to his corps, who have followed him to victory on so many fields. Let officers and soldiers emulate his invincible determination to do everything in the defense of our beloved country.[40]

In Lee's own report of the campaign he was, though still formal, slightly more personal:

The movement by which the enemy's position was turned and the fortune of the day decided was conducted by the lamented Lieutenant-General Jackson. . . . I do not propose here to speak of the character of this illustrious man, since removed from the scene of his eminent usefulness by the hand of an inscrutable but all-wise Providence. I nevertheless desire to pay the tribute of my admiration to the matchless energy and skill that marked this last act of his life, forming, as it did, a worthy conclusion of that long series of splendid achievements which won for him the lasting love and gratitude of his country.[41]

The President wrote later a higher tribute than in his first response to the news:

Too devoted to the cause he served to have any personal motive, he shared the toils, privations, and dangers of his troops when in chief command; and in subordinate position his aim was to understand the purpose of his commander and faithfully to promote his success. He was the complement of Lee. . . . To us his place was never filled.[42]

The Secretary of War, James A. Seddon, went further:

It may be safely said he has become, in the estimation of the Confederacy, emphatically "the hero of the war." Around him clustered with peculiar warmth their gratitude, their affections, and their hopes. His deeds had approved him a warrior of the highest order, as the whole tendency of his life, in peace and war, had shown him the very type and model of the Christian and hero . . . his loss is felt to be . . . irreparable . . .[43]

In less formal utterances Lee went much further. "It is a terrible loss," he told his son Custis.[44] "I am grateful to Almighty God for having given us such a man," he said to his brother, Charles Carter Lee.[45] When he spoke to the elder Pendleton about Jackson, Lee wept openly.[46] To Hood he attempted to explain: "We must all do more than formerly. We must endeavor to follow the unselfish, devoted, intrepid course he pursued." [47] When he spoke of Jackson, he used again and again the words "great and good." "Such an executive officer the sun never shone on," he told Francis Lawley, of the London *Times*.[48] The same thought was in his mind when he said to an officer that "I never troubled myself to give him detailed instructions. . . . The most general suggestions were all that he needed." [49]

But it was shock and numbness and something of fear and almost of despair that swept out to the people in Virginia and all across the Confederate States. "Oh, the havoc death is making!" Margaret Junkin Preston wrote in her journal in Lexington. Just after she had prepared an invitation to her old friend to recuperate in the home of her husband and herself, she received the news of his death. "The beautiful sky and the rich, perfumed spring air seemed darkened by oppressive sorrow. Who thinks or speaks of victory? The word is scarcely ever heard. Alas! Alas! When is the end to be?" [50]

Lee's strength of character, his capacity for command, and his remarkable military skills were growing in the public consciousness and would grow more. But at this stage of the war Jackson, with his unique combination of qualities, and his long succession of achievements in the field, had caught the popular mind more than any other officer. People at a distance warmed at the thought of him. He was the spirit of a cause that seemed to them capable of winning. When he was dying, something more precious even than the life of Stonewall Jackson was slipping out of their hands. While Jackson was alive, there was no Lost Cause. With Jackson dead, who could tell? Freeman's conclusion seventy years later that "the death of Jackson was the turning point in the history of the Army of Northern Virginia," [51] reflected a judgment which at the time many people feared.

In this mood of incomprehension, in the half-hidden alarm that gripped the land, and would presently settle down to deep and possessive grief, Anna and the men about the General prepared his body for the last march. His uniform had been ripped by bullets and cut by those caring for him before the amputation, and was unwearable. They clothed him in civilian garments and a blue military overcoat. Late in the evening Anna went into the Chandlers' parlor, where the body lay. She thought all traces of suffering had disappeared from his face. Although it seemed somewhat thin, the expression was "serene and elevated." [52]

Early next morning, Monday, May 11, Anna went into the parlor again. The body was now in a wooden coffin, covered with spring flowers, with sprays of lily of the valley around the face. She looked

long. Then she turned to join those who were riding with her to
Richmond. A special car had been set aside for them: Anna and Julia,
and the nurse; Mrs. Hoge, who had come from Richmond, and Mrs.
Chandler, who was accompanying Anna now. Sandie Pendleton,
McGuire, the two aides, James Morrison and James Smith, and
Douglas, and the chaplain, Tucker Lacy, were with them. Maj. W. J.
Hawks, the commissary officer, and Maj. D. B. Bridgford, provost
marshal, were present also. Dr. David Tucker, who had come from
Richmond, was returning now. With him was Dr. Smith, who had
participated in the consultations.[53]

Among those who wished greatly to go to Richmond were officers
and men of the Stonewall Brigade. The officers asked Douglas to
request Lee to grant them that privilege or at least allow them to
escort the General's body to the train. "The brigade rigged up in
the best they had, cleaned their arms, and were anxious to go, and
kept waiting impatiently. . . ." Private Casler remembered.[54]

But Lee told Douglas that "those people over the river are again
showing signs of movement and I cannot leave my headquarters
long enough to ride to the depot and pay my dear friend the poor
tribute of seeing his body placed upon the cars. His friends of the
Stonewall Brigade may be assured their General will receive all the
honor practicable. He never neglected a duty while living and he
would not rest the easier in his grave if his old brigade had left the
presence of the enemy to see him buried." *

Forty-five miles to Richmond this steaming day required hours.
In Ashland a group of women boarded the train with fresh flowers

---

\* Douglas, 228.

The designation of Jackson's old brigade as the Jackson Brigade, indicated here by
Lee's reply to Douglas, was made formal three weeks later. Special Orders, No. 129,
Adjutant and Inspector General's Office, Richmond, dated May 30, 1863, took note of
the submission to the Secretary of War of a resolution from "the officers and soldiers
of the brigade formerly commanded by Lieut. Gen. Thomas J. Jackson," which read:
"Resolved, that in accordance with General Jackson's wish, and the desire of this
brigade to honor its first great commander, the Secretary of War be requested to order
that it be known and designated as the 'Stonewall Brigade,' and that, in thus formally
adopting a title which is inseparably connected with his name and fame, we will
strive to render ourselves more worthy of it by emulating his virtues, and, like him,
devote all our energies to the great work before us of securing to our beloved country
the blessings of peace and independence."

The Secretary of War "cheerfully" acquiesced and directed "that the brigade referred to be hereafter designated as the 'Stonewall Brigade,'" trusting that "the zeal
and devotion, the patience and courage of the fallen hero . . . may attend and ani-
mate" all brigades and soldiers. (O.R., XXV, pt. 2, 840.)

for the coffin. It was nearly 4 o'clock when the train stopped on the outskirts of the city so that Anna could avoid facing the immense throng that choked Broad Street nearer in. Mrs. Letcher met her there with carriages, and they drove along unfrequented streets, through the heat of the afternoon, to the Governor's Mansion. The train went on to Fourth and Broad Streets for the solemn greeting of a capital in full mourning.

The Mayor had requested all business to suspend. State and national authorities had closed their offices. Flags were at half-staff. Though the streets were full of people, the silence was deep. A crowd of 5,000 persons waited quietly at the station. The train had been announced as arriving at noon, but the time was put back four hours, and some of the mourners drifted away. By 4 o'clock they were all back, and others swelled the crowd to greater size.

General Arnold Elzey, who led Kirby Smith's brigade into action on Jackson's left at First Manassas, commanded the Department of Richmond and superintended arrangements now. When the coffin was lifted from the train and placed in a hearse surmounted by raven plumes and drawn by two white horses, Elzey and his staff took their places in the lead, two of the Governor's aides with them. Behind them a detachment of the Public Guard and the Forty-fourth North Carolina Regiment, with reversed arms, fell into line. Pendleton, Morrison, Smith, McGuire, Hawks, Bridgford, and Douglas followed immediately behind. Then came the City Council, walking two abreast, and "an immense host of citizens and strangers." [55]

With the Armory Band playing dirges, they moved thus through the silent streets and the solemn people with bowed heads on the sidewalks, along Broad to Ninth Street, and thence to Capitol Square, entering it through the gate on Grace Street. There the soldiers formed lines through the Square and past the Washington monument. The coffin moved slowly along their front and into the Mansion. It was placed in the center of the large reception room. A new Confederate flag enveloped it, the first model of a white, blue, and red flag which was to have been raised over the Capitol but was sent by the President to Anna as the gift of the country. Evergreens and flowers were placed on the coffin.

Outside the bells tolled until sundown, "till which time," the *Dispatch* reported, "hundreds of people remained on the Square. We have never before seen such an exhibition of heartfelt and general sorrow in reference to any event as has been evinced by all since the announcement of the death of Stonewall Jackson."

That night Anna, clad now in full mourning clothes,* came into the reception room for her last look. She found the lid sealed, and had to look at her husband through glass. It was unsatisfactory and disappointing. But she thought that "no change had taken place." [56]

A few government officials, a few officers in Richmond, a few friends visited the Mansion that night and looked at the General's face. Brig. Gen. Richard Garnett, just up from Suffolk with Longstreet, was one of them—Garnett, the officer at Kernstown who had aroused Jackson's wrath, had faced charges, and had remained for more than a year at odds with him. Pendleton and Douglas met him at the door and took him to the coffin. He was profoundly moved. Turning to the others, he reminded them of "the unfortunate breach" which "I can never forget" or "cease to regret. But I wish here to assure you that no man can lament his death more sincerely than I do. I believe he did me great injustice, but I believe also he acted from the purest motives. He is dead. Who can fill his place?" [57] Pendleton invited him to be one of the guard of honor, or pallbearers, and he accepted.

During the night Frederick Volck made a death mask of Jackson, and the body was placed in a metal coffin.

Tuesday, May 12, was another day of intense heat. Richmond had now given itself entirely over to the tribute to Jackson. Business and offices were closed. The signs of mourning were everywhere. People walked slowly and spoke quietly, their faces marked by the sense of loss that permeated the city. The bells tolled again, and the slow guns sounded their salute to a soldier. The streets filled with the solemn throngs. The capital of the Confederacy, acquainted though it was with grief, had never known anything like this.

About 11 o'clock the body of the General was placed again in the plume-draped hearse, drawn now by four white horses. Elements of Pickett's division, just in from Longstreet's Suffolk operation, led the military escort, followed by the Public Guard and then the Camp Guard from Camp Lee. Six pieces from Dearing's battery

---

*Margaret Junkin Preston recorded in her journal (June 1), in connection with other information about the rise of costs, that "the perfectly plain crepe bonnet which Mrs. Jackson got in Richmond cost $75 and a bombazine dress, as plain as could be made, cost about $180."

(Captain Blunt) and the Twenty-first Battalion, Virginia Cavalry (Major Wrenn), followed.

Beside the hearse rode the generals, from Longstreet's First Corps or the Richmond Department, who were acting as pallbearers. Four of them had served under Jackson: Elzey, Garnett, George H. Steuart, the Marylander, and Ewell, now well on his way to mobility after the loss of his leg at Groveton. Kemper and Corse were here from Longstreet's command, John H. Winder from the Richmond area, and Commodore French Forrest from the Navy.* General George W. Randolph was chief marshal.

Behind the hearse came one of Jackson's horses,† led by his body servant. Members of Jackson's staff who were in Richmond formed next, and behind them strode—or sometimes hobbled—wounded or recuperating veterans of the Stonewall Brigade. The officers wore insignia or badges of mourning, their swords draped at the hilt. All banners were draped with crape, and all drums were muffled.

Behind the military came the civilians. The President and the Vice President rode together in a carriage, the President looking thin and frail.⁵⁸ They led a large contingent of governmental officials headed by the cabinet, walking two by two, with Benjamin, now Secretary of State, and Seddon of the War Department in the lead. Governor Letcher was in the forefront of the Virginia group, including judges and the city officials, with a long line of "citizens and good people generally" ⁵⁹ coming after them—in all, a procession nearly a mile long.

When a signal gun was fired from near the equestrian statue of Washington in Capitol Square, and a military band began to play the Dead March from *Saul*, the procession moved out slowly from near the Governor's Mansion by Governor Street to Main Street,

---

* The information on the pallbearers is curiously confusing. The Richmond *Dispatch*, the Richmond *Sentinel*, Douglas (who was present), and Cooke and Richardson among the early writers on Jackson, all recorded lists, and no two agree. Douglas said Pickett was present, and Dabney mentioned Longstreet. The names used are those of officers clearly established as being present or most frequently listed in reports. There may have been others.

† The horse was not Sorrel, which, after the wounded Jackson had been lifted from its back, fled in fright and ended up in Federal hands. Sorrel remained a prisoner of war until recaptured months later and recognized. The horse was sent to Lincoln County, North Carolina, where Anna and Julia were living. Sorrel was a family pet for years, attracted much attention as a hero of the war, and lived until 1886, more than thirty years of age, dying then at the home for old soldiers in Richmond. The body was mounted and is now at the V.M.I. in Lexington. The groom leading the horse was, presumably, the General's Jim.

then along Main to Second Street, northward to Grace Street, and by Grace Street back to Capitol Square. The loop carried the General's body through long lines of bareheaded men, and bowed and often sobbing women, and many children. There was "no vain ostentation" to the procession, a war-office clerk thought as he watched. To him it seemed "very solemn and imposing because the mourning was sincere and heartfelt." The grief, he thought, was universal, and "the victory involving such a loss is regarded as a calamity." [60]

The *Enquirer's* chief reporter, who spoke of the "tumultuous outburst of mourning," thought that in no public ceremony, not even "the grand display which attended the inauguration of the monument to Washington some years ago," had Richmond been "rendered more memorable." Words like "sympathy," "love," and "admiration" run through these accounts. But "words," the *Dispatch* wrote, "have no power to express the emotions which the death of Jackson has aroused in the public mind."

Back at Capitol Square, the hearse wheeled up to the Capitol itself. The pallbearers lifted the coffin out and carried it through lines of soldiers standing at present-arms into the Confederate House of Representatives (historically the House of Delegates of the Virginia General Assembly) and placed it on a catafalque covered with white linen in front of the Speaker's chair. The hall itself was draped in mourning and Confederate flags. Here the Virginia Convention had commissioned the unknown Major Jackson from V.M.I. as a colonel; here the doors were thrown open now for the people to pay their tribute to their most beloved General as he lay in state.

The people streamed in all afternoon—20,000 before the doors closed. The ones most openly affected were the recuperating soldiers or the men who could fight no more. They knew war and they worshiped the General. Many persons along the waiting lines brought flowers, so many that flowers overflowed the coffin, covered all the legislative furniture, and spread out to the floor. Still the men, women, and children came, and still the little bouquets mounted. Even when the doors were closed, a fiery voice demanded admittance, and a veteran whose arm had been amputated pointed to the stump, the tears heavy in his eyes, and cried out, "By this arm which I lost for my country I demand the privilege of seeing my General once more." [61] Governor Letcher called him in.

Anna sat through all these tributes in a darkened room in the Governor's Mansion. Her eldest brother, Maj. W. W. Morrison, had arrived from North Carolina. Mrs. William N. Page—"my motherly friend"—was with her much of the time. A minister whom she had never seen before but instantly liked, the Rev. Dr. T. V. Moore, read to her from the fourteenth chapter of John: "Let not your heart be troubled . . ." [62] Hetty, when Julia became worried at the attention of the throngs, took the baby into the back yard, and they sat beneath Anna's window. [63]

On Wednesday, May 13, early in the morning, the coffin was moved from the Capitol back to the Governor's Mansion. At about 7 o'clock it was carried once more to the railroad station, escorted by the Public Guard, and placed in a Virginia Central coach for the trip to Gordonsville. Anna and Julia, with Hetty the nurse, and Anna's two brothers, members of the General's staff, General Ewell, Governor Letcher and his military aide, Col. S. Bassett French, and a number of others boarded the train. In Gordonsville they changed to an Orange and Alexandria train for the run to Lynchburg.

The funeral party did not stop in Lynchburg any longer than the change from the train to the canal packet *Marshall* required. But Lynchburg met the mourners with a full tribute to the dead. The bells tolled, minute guns fired, and a throng of citizens led by Mayor W. B. Branch escorted the coffin; and some of them went on to Lexington. Silent people brought spring flowers, here as everywhere else, and offered them mutely. The baby Julia was the object of much interest. On several occasions she was handed out the window of the railroad coach to be kissed.

The long, slim packet moved slowly through the canal toward Lexington, and it was not until the evening of the 14th that they arrived at the General's home. That village had just buried its native son, Brig. Gen. Frank Paxton. A little earlier, on May 5, Margaret Junkin Preston had written in her journal that "today brings news of a terrible battle. . . . Of the mothers in this town, almost all . . . have sons in the battle: not one lays her head on her pillow this night, sure that her sons are alive." On Sunday, May 10, Dr. White of the Presbyterian Church had attempted to hold service. But just as he was beginning, the mail arrived, and so intense was the desire for news, that he was obliged to dismiss the congregation. [64]

On May 12 the blow fell. In the morning word came that the

General was dead. Later news from Richmond said nothing about him and led to doubts, but confirmation followed in the afternoon. "The grief in this community is intense," Margaret Junkin Preston wrote, "everybody is in tears . . ." °

"It is the painful duty of the Superintendent," General Smith wrote in the Institute's General Orders, No. 30, on May 13, "to announce to the officers and cadets of this institution the death of their late associate and professor, Lieut. Gen. Thomas J. Jackson."

Associate and professor! The Superintendent could call the roll of military achievements, and did, but the heart of his message was that "our loss is distinctive. He was peculiarly our own." He could the better adjure the cadets to "reverence the memory of such a man as General Jackson. . . . Let the Cadet Battery, which he so long commanded, honor his memory by half-hour guns tomorrow, from sunrise to sunset. . . . Let his lecture room be draped in mourning for the period of six months. Let the officers and cadets of the Institute wear the usual badge of mourning for the period of thirty days. . . ." 65

Anna stepped off the canal boat on the 14th to face the people of Lexington and the battalion of cadets, all of whom shared the grief with her. They carried his body up the hill to the classroom where the Professor of Natural and Experimental Philosophy had struggled ten years with the young men before him and with his own ineptness. It lay now before his old chair, still covered with the new Confederate flag and with fresh spring flowers. Cadets, straight as bayonets, stood guard at his head and feet, an hour at a time, through the night, and counted it a distinction the rest of their lives. Dr. White had been waiting for Anna, along with friends and neighbors; and she did not go to the house in which she and her husband had lived. She faced now on Friday, May 15, the final chapter.

The funeral service was held in the Presbyterian Church of which the General had been a deacon. The cadets placed his coffin on one of the caissons of the cadet battery which he had commanded. Four horses—not the cadets themselves—drew it now, and servants of the Institute acted as grooms. Eight companies of cadets made up most

° The sister of Elinor Junkin continued in her journal for May 12: "All his [Jackson's] letters to Mr. P [reston] and me since the war began, have breathed the spirit of a saint. In his last letter to me he spoke of our precious Ellie, and of the blessedness of being with her in heaven. And now he has rejoined her, and together they are united in ascribing praises to Him who has redeemed them by His blood. . . ."

of a regiment of escort, and veterans of the Stonewall Brigade in the neighborhood, marching under the flag of the Liberty Hall Boys (of Washington College) which the General's old Fourth Regiment had carried at First Manassas, joined the cadets. By chance two companies of cavalry, passing through Lexington from the West (Sweeney's Battalion, Jenkins' command), arrived just before the funeral and, borrowing badges of mourning, joined the procession.

Immediately behind the caisson the Lexington that Jackson knew paid tribute to a neighbor and friend with honorary pallbearers representing the Presbyterian Church of Lexington, the Virginia Military Institute, Washington College, the Franklin Society, the Bible Society of Rockbridge County, the town council, the county magistrates, and the district court. Sandie Pendleton, Hunter McGuire, and James Power Smith walked on foot behind the family carriage, and Governor Letcher and a Confederate Senator G. A. Henry, of Tennessee, with other governmental officials, and teachers, students, elders, deacons, and citizens followed in the long procession.

In the crowded church, with a great throng outside, the General's pastor, Dr. White, stood in the pulpit while "a touching voluntary was sung with subdued, sobbing voices"—the hymn, "How blest the righteous when he dies!"

A friend of the General, the Rev. James B. Ramsey, of Lynchburg, prayed with the "most melting tenderness." Dr. White read the fifteenth chapter of First Corinthians and made, Margaret thought, "very true and discriminating remarks." They were intensely personal, for this was a group of friends. Dr. White read to them— though it must have been a wrench to him—the letter which the General had written to him after the death at Second Manassas of his son, Capt. Hugh A. White: "The death of your noble son and my much esteemed friend, Hugh, must have been a severe blow to you, yet we have the sweet assurance that, whilst we mourn his loss to the country, to the church, and to ourselves, all has been gain for him. . . . That inconceivable glory to which we are looking forward is already his. . . ." There was a "beautiful prayer" from the Rev. William F. Junkin,[66] and the simple service was over.

The funeral procession moved, "amid the flowing tears of a vast concourse of people," [67] to the cemetery at the top of the hill. There, in the sunshine of a warm spring day, the cadets laid the General— his coffin still wrapped in the flag President Davis had given to

Anna—by the side of his daughter and his first wife; and they heaped
flowers over the grave while people stood and looked, and sorrow
and depression possessed them.

(A year later, on the anniversary of the burial, a flag from England
was raised over the grave, sent by men who admired the General.
A few days afterward, in June, 1864, a Federal officer quartered in
Lexington, talking to Margaret Junkin Preston, "took from his
pocket-book some leaves which he had gathered from Jackson's
grave, which he said he would keep as sacred mementoes. One of
the guard which he sent us asked me for some trifle that belonged
to Jackson, saying, 'We think as much of him as you do.' I gave them
each an autograph." [68]

In the shock of the death the press of the Confederate States wrote
as it had never written of a man before. "Words have no power to
express the emotions which the death of Jackson has aroused in the
public mind," said the Richmond *Dispatch* of May 12. "There was
such an entire absence of pretension, vanity, ambition, and self in
every shape about General Jackson that he had become a popular
idol. The affections of every household in the nation were twined
about this great and unselfish warrior, who, two years ago, was an
unknown man!"

"Everyone feels," said the Charleston *Courier*, "as though he had
sustained a personal bereavement. . . . In the agony of this overwhelming sorrow we exclaim, 'Would God I had died for thee.' " The
Knoxville *Register* thought that "for the first time since the war
began this whole nation weeps as one man. . . . There lives not a
leader whose memory shall be cherished more sacredly than that of
Stonewall Jackson and not one whose loss we could have borne with
less fortitude."

"He occupied a place in the heart of every friend of his country,"
the Raleigh *State Journal* was sure. It called him "the inspirer of
energy and courage in his followers—the man who saw no obstacles
in his path so therefore rarely found them." To this another Raleigh
newspaper, the *Standard*, added that "the death of no other citizen
of the Confederate States would have caused as deep grief. The
loss which the cause has suffered by his removal from the world
cannot be overstated . . . he was absolutely invaluable to the
cause. . . ." [69]

Something of this spirit appeared in the London press. Jackson, said the London *Times* (May 26), "will carry with him to his early grave the regrets of all who can admire greatness and genius. . . . That mixture of daring and judgment, which is the mark of 'Heaven-born' generals, distinguished him beyond any man of his time. Although the young Confederacy has been illustrated by a number of eminent soldiers, yet the applause and devotion of his countrymen, confirmed by the judgment of European nations, have given the first place to General Jackson. . . ." In the opinion of the London *Telegraph* (May 27), "Assuredly the most fatal shot of the war to the Confederates, whether fired by friend or foe, was that which struck down the life of 'Stonewall' Jackson—a soldier, every inch of him, for whatever cause he contended."

In Washington one of John W. Forney's assistant editors wrote in the *Daily Chronicle* (May 13) that "while we are only too glad to be rid, in any way, of so terrible a foe, our sense of relief is not unmingled with emotions of sorrow and sympathy at the death of so brave a man." The article spoke of "the qualities for which Stonewall Jackson was celebrated—his heroism . . . his sublime devotion, his purity of character." It called him "a genuine fanatic" as well as "a great general," but added that "we do not less admire the great and wonderful powers he possessed." His death, it concluded, takes from the "accursed cause" of secession "its bravest, noblest, and purest defender."

President Lincoln read this article and wrote immediately to the editor of the *Chronicle* to thank him "for the excellent and manly article in the *Chronicle* on 'Stonewall Jackson.' " [70]

These words had hardly been written before men in the North as well as in the South were beginning the biographies. The first of them were finished before the war had run its course. Men of the Stonewall Brigade were meeting in formal session to raise money in the camps for a monument to the General's memory. They did not reach their goal that year (too many of them died), but Douglas, who was elected treasurer, had $5,688 on hand by May 21.[71] A group of "English gentlemen" who admired from a distance—part of a long procession of British people who have done much for the General's fame—began almost as quickly to arrange for the statue *

---

* This statue, by J. H. Foley, R.A., carries on one side the inscription: "Presented by English Gentlemen as a Tribute of Admiration for the Soldier and Patriot, Thomas J. Jackson. . . ."

that was unveiled eleven years after the war in the Capitol grounds in Richmond, the first of many statues of the General.

These words, these deeds, these hopes were touched by emotion. But even in the grief of this May there was understanding too. People as well as soldiers knew that the war had produced in Jackson an officer who united exceptional personal character and exceptional military qualities in ways that are rare in any war and were unmatched in this war. With the public he was, until the hour of his death, such a stimulant, such a force for the morale of the Confederacy, that the sense of loss now was universal and profound. Within the army he had risen by the common judgment of soldiers and of officers of all ranks to a unique position.

At Chancellorsville Jackson's relations with Lee were on a higher level of mutual confidence and trust, and of intimacy, than they had ever attained before. He was still rising. His technical status as a corps commander below Longstreet, who was slightly senior to him, does not require any detailed comparison of these two. Longstreet had admirable capacity, and Lee fully appreciated it. But Jackson had a combination of qualities which no other general officer had. He could rise to military genius.

What these qualities would have led to if Jackson had survived in full strength is beyond estimation. But because the increasing exigencies of Confederate military leadership led to separate commands for Longstreet and Hood, as well as J. E. Johnston and Beauregard (and others), the normal assumption is that the government would have given separate command to Jackson. It could hardly have avoided doing so.

In that event the Confederacy would have produced a test of the judgment sometimes heard that strategically Jackson was capable of being a great army commander but administratively he was not. Administratively he had much trouble with officers under him, more frequently those close to him in rank, though never—save with French at Fort Meade and perhaps in a certain sense with Davis and Benjamin in the Romney campaign, where he was clearly right —with his superiors. He never repeated the mistakes of the French affair. He made no mistakes in his relations with officers above him unless it was during the Seven Days, where every high Confederate officer, including Lee, contributed to the confusions of the operations.

Virtually all Confederate commanders, starting with Lee, had troubles with officers under them. Lee handled these inevitable problems with quiet skill. Some other commanding generals created clashes and turmoil. Jackson angered many good officers, but under him the brigade, the division, and the corps did not seem to suffer thereby. In separate army command he would have had, almost surely, to lessen his secrecy in planning, but he had grown in other respects, and he might have realized, in a large force, that the commanding general would have to rely more on other officers and must keep them informed. Though he came into the war prepared psychologically and soundly trained as an officer, he had learned in every engagement from Harper's Ferry in May of 1861 to Chancellorsville in May of 1863. It does not seem impossible for him to have kept on learning.

Lee found out two months after Jackson's death what the loss of Jackson meant to him. In the calm of the postwar period, when the strains of the conflict had eased and he could reflect in relative comfort, Lee told his brother Cassius that if Jackson had been with him at Gettysburg (two months after Chancellorsville, almost to the day), that battle would have been a Confederate victory. "Jackson," Lee said, "would have held the heights which Ewell took on the first day." [72] In the same conversation Lee spoke less favorably of Jackson in the early part of the Seven Days. The Gettysburg judgment was discriminating. It did not try to foretell the effect on the war, and it could not remove the weight of Federal numbers and resources which in the end were decisive. It did record the estimate of Lee.

Partly because of the declining strength of the Army of Northern Virginia, but definitely because there was no other Jackson, Lee attempted no more after Chancellorsville the spectacular dividing of his army which he felt free to risk five times in Jackson's prime while confronting superior foes. The Army of Northern Virginia was never again what it had been.

In their grief in this May the people sensed as much. Today the truths are unmistakable. The actions which men thought peculiar, the rigidity of much of the General's outward behavior, the sternness with associates who relaxed and with enemies who didn't, the elevation of duty to the fundamental force of his daily, almost his hourly, life, the intimacy with his Saviour which set him apart even in that age of religion as an exceptional child of God—these marked, though they did not delimit, the man even more vividly after two years of war. But they could not conceal the soldier. Indeed they heightened and colored the view of that energy and artistry, that comprehension and speed, that directness and subtlety, which in combination set him apart and marked his greatness. The cadets who buried him buried more than the General. They buried their symbol of victory.

The American heritage now—the world's heritage—is the record of the General and the spirit of the man. They remain forever to light up the human story with the antique virtues and the military genius of Stonewall Jackson.

# ACKNOWLEDGMENTS

In the autumn of 1947, Frances Phillips, then editor-in-chief of William Morrow and Company, Publishers, of New York, came to me with the idea that I write a book about Stonewall Jackson.

The very name of Stonewall Jackson evoked a figure and a personality almost universally recognized and almost universally puzzling. His military achievements—on a hilltop beside Bull Run, in the parry and thrust of the Valley of Virginia campaign, in the marching and onslaughts at Second Manassas and Chancellorsville—had excited generations of people and had stimulated, abroad as well as in the United States, the close study of professional soldiers. In the background was the picture of a deeply religious man, strait-laced and much given to prayer, sometimes stern, sometimes tender, but a leader to stir the imagination. His death at the height of his fame, from the gunfire of his own troops, was one of the most grievous memories of a region that cherished its heroes.

What kind of man was Stonewall Jackson? And whence the source of his capacity?

I had a boyhood recollection of a great lady in Charlotte, invariably clad in black, with a widow's cap and veil. It was said that Presidents of the United States, on their occasional visits to North Carolina, were expected to pay their respects to her, and did. Everyone knew Mrs. Jackson and the pinnacle on which she stood.

I had also the portrait of a Calvinist man of God that hung in my boyhood home and hangs over the fireplace in my home today. It is a portrait of my great-grandfather, the Rev. Dr. Drury Lacy. He was the Presbyterian minister before whom Mary Anna Morrison and Thomas Jonathan Jackson stood in 1857 when they were married.

I turned from Miss Phillips' suggestion and read the sketch of Jackson by Dr. Douglas Southall Freeman in the *Dictionary of American Biography,* the sketch by Maj. Gen. Sir Frederick Barton Maurice, K.C.M.G., in the *Encyclopedia Britannica,* and the sketch by the Rev. Dr. J. William Jones in the *Encyclopedia Americana*. I read Lieut. Col. G. F. R. Henderson's two volumes, *Stonewall Jackson and the American Civil War*. Then I went to work.

The result is these two volumes. They are certainly not what Frances Phillips had in mind when she gave me, at the end of our first talk, seven lines from Stephen Vincent Benet's *John Brown's Body*. They read:

> Awkward, rugged and dour, the belated Ironside
> With the curious, brilliant streak of the cavalier
> That made him quote Mercutio in staff instructions,
> Love lancet windows, the color of passion-flowers,
> Mexican sun and all fierce, taut-looking fine creatures;
> Stonewall Jackson, wrapped in his beard and his silence. . . .

"Let us cross the river," he said, "and rest under the shade of the trees."

There was need of a new study of this man. No thorough examination of Jackson had been made since Henderson's great work in 1898. Modern historical scholars had discovered rich mines of information about the Civil War and about Jackson's life and his part in the war.

Among them, Roy Bird Cook, of Charleston, West Virginia, had dug deeply in the western Virginia and family backgrounds. The late Thomas Jackson Arnold, nephew of the General, had brought together the largest collection of Jackson letters, even though some of them as published were unhappily edited. Mary Anna Jackson, his widow, had opened whole chapters of his domestic life and brought many letters to light. Col. William Couper of the Virginia Military Institute had found much new material (and corrected some erroneous assumptions) relating to Jackson's ten years at the Institute. Dr. Freeman had examined with characteristic detail and thoroughness Jackson's military operations and had made easier, with his bibliographical outlines and his studies of the Army of Northern Virginia, the tasks of everyone who followed him.

University, library, and historical society collections of memoirs, letters, and other documents had grown immensely. The National Archives and the Manuscript Division of the Library of Congress could aid all researchers more effectively and had more material for study. Virtually all of Jackson's major associates and opponents in the 1860's had come under the fresh analysis of historians. The war itself, in all its aspects, was a subject of increasingly broad and deep American interest. Almost it could be said that everything of importance about Jackson could be examined in the 1950's in the light of new information and new ideas.

In the pages that follow I have tried to make it clear why I thought this remarkable man deserved careful study. In doing so I have received far more help than I could ever acknowledge.

# Acknowledgments

I give my gratitude to Frances Phillips for starting me on this adventure, and for her intellectual precision and her faith. She has been patient beyond description, stimulating, and strengthening.

I give appreciation also to Helen Brinkley King, an editor whose professional knowledge, judgment, and encouragement have helped me at every point.

I am indebted to General Jackson's granddaughter, Mrs. Edmund Randolph Preston, and to her late husband, Edmund Randolph Preston (whose family was also intimately associated with General Jackson), for their gracious aid and encouragement, and their ideas, suggestions, and information, and to Mrs. Preston for her special assistance at one point.

Men with much knowledge of Jackson—especially Cook, Couper, and the late Dr. Freeman—responded to my numerous inquiries in the most courteous and generous spirit; and they gave me, in many letters and conversations, at much cost of time to them, valuable advice and guidance. Out of his familiarity with the region, the period, and its personalities, my college teacher, Dr. J. G. de R. Hamilton, father of the University of North Carolina's Southern Historical Collection, pointed the way to me many times. Gerald W. Johnson, of Baltimore, alternately cheered me and spurred me. Phillips Russell and Louis Graves, both of Chapel Hill, did much in starting me on my way.

The help of librarians has been unending. Members of the staff of the Norfolk Public Library, especially its librarian, Arthur M. Kirkby, and Mary C. Brown of its Sargeant Room; members of the staff of the Virginia State Library in Richmond under its librarian, Randolph W. Church; Drs. C. Percy Powell and Elizabeth McPherson of the Manuscript Division, Library of Congress; Dr. James W. Patton of the Southern Historical Collection in Chapel Hill and his staff; Lieut. Col. W. J. Morton, librarian at the United States Military Academy, West Point; members of the library staff at Duke University and at Washington and Lee University; Chalmers G. Davidson, librarian at Davidson College; H. M. Brimm, librarian at the Union Theological Seminary, Richmond, Virginia; members of library staffs in Clarksburg and Weston in West Virginia; and a long list of librarians from New Hampshire to New Orleans to California—all these intelligent and eager men and women have searched, listed, checked, corrected, pointed out, and done many fine things for me. I thank them all.

The Catholic University of America came to my aid through the courtesy of the Rev. A. K. Ziegler, head of the Department of History, and the Rev. Antonine Tibeshar, O.F.M., specialist in Ibero-American history.

The Florida Historical Society in Gainesville provided me with useful material.

I have made use of facilities and collections at the Virginia Historical Society, the Confederate Museum, Battle Abbey (Confederate Memorial Institute), all in Richmond, Virginia, and of the North Carolina State Department of Archives and History in Raleigh; and I am indebted to their officials and staffs for kindnesses.

To the Library of Congress and to the National Archives I am indebted for permission to use the pictures of the young Jackson and the last portrait of the General, respectively.

I am grateful to the late H. J. Eckenrode of Richmond; Dr. A. J. Hanna, of Rollins College, Winter Park, Florida; Gen. Lemuel C. Shepherd, Jr., United States Marine Corps, retired; Vice Adm. Ralph O. Davis, United States Navy, retired; Miss Ellen G. Anderson and the late Dr. E. P. Tompkins, of Lexington, Virginia; Miss Anna Barringer, Charlottesville; Mrs. S. D. Blackford, Charlottesville; John Scott Walker, Orange, Virginia; Archibald K. Davis, Winston-Salem, North Carolina; Monroe F. Cockrell, Chicago; my sister, Mrs. Elisabeth Chambers Holt, of Charlotte, North Carolina, and my daughter, Elisabeth Lacy Chambers; and to many friends, old and new.

Above all, and beyond any counting, I am indebted to my wife, Roberta Strudwick Chambers.

L. C.

Norfolk,
May, 1959.

# THE EARLY
# JACKSON FAMILY

The Jacksons came to Ireland from Scotland. They settled along the Bann River on the Antrim-Londonderry border in Northern Ireland, especially around Coleraine. From that region John Jackson joined in the migration that carried the Scotch-Irish deep into the life and character of the new land. He was born about 1715. (Cook, 7 ff.) When he was perhaps ten years old, his family moved to London, and he worked at the trade of a builder. In 1748, when he was 33 years old, he sailed to America and settled in Cecil County in northeastern Maryland where the Susquehanna flows into Chesapeake Bay, and where Delaware on one side and Pennsylvania on the other form the background. Seven years later, in July, 1755, John Jackson took the step that helps explain much about all later Jacksons. He married Elizabeth Cummins. (Mrs. Jackson, 2.)

Born on January 8, 1723, and grown to six feet tall, with vivid blond hair, great physical strength and energy, a powerful will and high courage, she was a veritable Viking, and the dominant woman of the family for three generations. About her legends multiplied.

One account is that she came to America on the ship that brought John Jackson, and that a romance began then. (Mrs. Jackson, 3.) Another traces Elizabeth Cummins to a father of property who operated a public house in London called "The Bold Dragoon." After he died (legend runs) her mother married again, and Elizabeth could not establish happy relations with her stepfather. When they quarreled (the legend continues), the Viking hurled a silver tankard at his head and fled as an indentured servant to America (Mrs. Jackson, 2), picking up John Jackson en route, though he was no man to be treated casually even by such a woman as Elizabeth Cummins.

The more likely account (Cook, 10) is that she and a sister were orphans who were raised by an aunt; that her sister married and moved across the Atlantic while Elizabeth, on a promise of a thousand pounds at her aunt's death, stayed at home; and that, having received the money, she came to America in search of her sister, who had died. Elizabeth went to Maryland to shelter with friends and there married John Jackson. She still had some of her thousand pounds, and that was in character.

Their first child was George, born January 9, 1757, the most notable of eight children. When Edward, the second child (father of Jonathan who in turn was the father of Thomas) was born, the elder Jacksons had left Maryland, crossed the Blue Ridge, and turned south along the South Branch of the Potomac near Moorefield. Edward was born in this rugged country on May 1, 1759, and a succession of children followed.

The Jacksons moved on, ultimately in 1770 to lands where Turkey Run flows into the Buckhannon. Elizabeth Cummins Jackson patented 3,000 acres here, paying the fees in English gold from her London inheritance. Some of these acres became the site of present Buckhannon. (Cook, 10.)

John Jackson became a militia captain during the Revolution. Gov. Henry Lee commissioned him to engage in certain spying activities against Indians. He was a justice of the peace, member of the county court, and commissioner of revenue for Randolph County. (Cook, 12.) After he died in Clarksburg, September 25, 1801, at the age of 86, his grandson, Judge John G. Jackson, wrote to his sister-in-law, Dolly Madison, wife of President Madison, that his grandfather enjoyed "all his mental faculties and great corporeal strength, until a few days before his death. I saw him breathe his last in the arms of my aged grandmother, and can truly add, that to live and die as he did would be the excess of happiness." (Cook, 178.)

The redoubtable Elizabeth held on to life with characteristic tenacity. She lived to be 101 years old, and by some accounts to 105. (Cook, 178.) In the latter event she would have been living, and in Clarksburg too, when her great-grandson, Thomas Jackson, was born.

George, the first son, had a notable career and a notable family. He fought Indians, organized a military company to join George Rogers Clark on the expedition to attack Detroit, and rose to militia colonel. Besides holding many local offices, he was a member for six years of the Virginia General Assembly, of the Virginia convention that approved the Constitution, and of three early Congresses. Eventually he moved to Ohio and was a member of the State Legislature there. (Cook, 13.)

The fourteen children of George included judges, generals, legislators, congressmen, and a governor. One of them, John G. Jackson (the judge), after his first marriage to Mary Payne, sister of Dolly Madison, later married Mary Meigs, daughter of Gov. Return Jonathan Meigs of Ohio, who was also Postmaster General under Madison and Monroe. (Cook, 14 ff.) It was of such men that Thomas was thinking years later when

he said, "I have some hopes that our ancient reputation may be revived."
(Arnold, 171, 172.)

Edward, the second son of John the First and Elizabeth, was much
the same type as his brother George. He fought Indians, too, and rose
to colonel. Trained as a surveyor, he traveled widely, held offices such as
that of sheriff and revenue commissioner, ran county lines, laid out the
streets of Weston when it was young, and traded in land, holding at
one time more than 10,000 acres. Although he was several times a Virginia legislator, his primary interest was in local activities such as mill
construction, lumber sawing, and surveying. He even acquired a reputation for medical knowledge. He had nine slaves, most of them engaged
in farm, lumber, and mill work. (Cook, 16, 31.)

# APPENDIX II | THE EARLY NEALE FAMILY

The first of the Neales to reach America was Daniel, who came from Limerick County in Ireland; and the date is between 1640 and 1660, probably 1649. (Arnold, 45; Cook, 23.) The name then was O'Neal or O'Neill, but it changed in the next generation. Daniel reached Northumberland County in Virginia, at the tip of the peninsula that juts into Chesapeake Bay between the Potomac and Rappahannock Rivers.

Thereafter a succession of Neales—Christopher, a second Daniel, Presley, Richard, and Thomas—married in turn and produced progeny, shifting gradually westward to neighboring Westmoreland, and thence to Fairfax, and on to Loudoun County. Thomas Neale, with his parents, Richard and Frances Underwood Neale, made this last move after 1774, the year of Thomas Neale's birth in Westmoreland. Richard was a private in the Second Virginia Regiment during the Revolutionary War. (Cook, 25.) Thomas, father of Julia, grew up in Loudoun County.

# HOW THE NAME "STONEWALL" ORIGINATED

Although some persons said later that they heard Bee's words to his troops: "Look! There is Jackson standing like a stone wall!" there is no agreement among them as to what was said or as to details of time and place. The report that received public attention was by the correspondent of the Charleston *Mercury,* whose brief account in that newspaper on July 25, 1861, was reprinted in the Richmond *Whig* and *Daily Dispatch* of July 29. In the Richmond *Whig* and *Public Advertiser* of July 31, under the heading of "General Jackson," these words appear:

In the following merited notice of the heroism of Gen. Bee by the correspondent of the Charleston Mercury, is incidental mention of one, of whom little has been said, though, in fact, he was one of the main instruments in the achievement of the great victory. For three solid hours, he stood unflinching the most violent assaults of the enemy, and was the *stone wall* to which his overpowered forces constantly rallied, and whose invincible bearing infused into them renewed ardour. Gen. Bee was not the only gallant officer in that well-stricken field, who cheered his overtasked troops by pointing to Jackson as the exemplar of patriotic and indomitable courage.

There follows immediately, in more solidly set type, this report "from the correspondent of the Mercury":

The remains of Gen. Barnard E. Bee leave here tomorrow for Charleston. The name of this officer deserves a place in the highest niche of fame. He displayed a gallantry that scarcely has a parallel in history. The brunt of the morning's battle was sustained by his command until past two o'clock. Overwhelmed by superior numbers, and compelled to yield before a fire that swept everything before it, Gen. Bee rode up and down his lines, encouraging his troops, by everything that was dear to them, to stand up and repel the tide that threatened them with destruction. At last his own brigade dwindled to a mere handful, with every field officer killed or disabled. He rode up to Gen. Jackson and said:—"General, they are beating us back."

The reply was: "Sir, we'll give them the bayonet."

Gen. Bee immediately rallied the remnant of his brigade, and his last words to them were: "There is Jackson standing like a stone-wall. Let us determine to die here and we will conquer. Follow me!"

His men obeyed the call; and at the head of his column, the very moment when the battle was turning in our favor, he fell mortally wounded. Gen. Beauregard was heard to say he had never seen such gallantry. He never murmured at his suffering, but seemed to be consoled by the reflection that he was doing his duty.

It is impossible to determine now how accurate are the words attributed to Bee. But there is abundant evidence to show that in succeeding days the "stonewall" reference had reached the attention of many people. For one instance, Mary Boykin Chesnut wrote in her diary (subsequently published as *A Diary from Dixie*) on July 24, three days after the battle, of what she had heard. Her husband, Col. James Chesnut, a voluntary aide-de-camp to Beauregard, just arrived at Richmond from Manassas, said that he had taken orders to "Col [*sic*] Jackson, whose regiment stood so stock still under fire that they were called a 'Stone-Wall.'"

The designation of General Jackson as Stonewall Jackson does not appear to have been widespread in succeeding weeks or even months, probably because he was not thereafter in the public eye until the Romney campaign the following January and the Valley campaign shortly afterward.

# APPENDIX IV

# THE UNIDENTIFIED HORSEMAN AT CHANCELLORSVILLE

One claimant emerged to assert that he was the mysterious figure in the background at Chancellorsville after Jackson had been wounded. Brig. Gen. Joseph W. Revere, a grandson of Paul Revere, the New England silversmith celebrated in Longfellow's poem, wrote in his autobiography, *Keel and Saddle* (1872), that he met Jackson in 1852, established a common interest in astrology, learned from a horoscope that their paths would recross in early May, 1863, in a moment of danger, and that he, Revere, was the figure on horseback who saw Jackson lying wounded on the ground.

The first meeting between the two men, said Revere, occurred when he returned from Mexico in 1852. He arrived at New Orleans, boarded a river steamboat, and traveled by the Mississippi and Ohio rivers to Pittsburgh. A fellow passenger, Revere said, was Lieut. Thomas J. Jackson, "a remarkably quiet, reserved, although very intelligent officer . . . with whom I became acquainted." They discussed astrology, "to which Jackson led the way," showing, said Revere, "some belief in astrology as a science."

In Revere's words: "I had given the necessary data for calculating a horoscope; and in a few months I received from him a letter, which I preserved, inclosing a scheme of my nativity." The "destinies" of the two seemed to run "in parallel lines," and the two men were shown by this finding to be marked for exposure to a common danger "during the first days of May, 1863."

At Chancellorsville, Revere, then a brigadier general in command of the Second Brigade of the Second Division (Maj. Gen. Hiram G. Berry) of the Third Corps (Maj. Gen. Daniel E. Sickles), said he rode ahead of his troops on the moonlit night of May 2. He heard galloping, volleys, and human cries, and saw a riderless horse dashing in his direction. Proceeding cautiously, he came upon "a group of several persons gathered around a man lying upon the ground apparently badly wounded." Revere

473

realized that these were Confederates and sat still to avoid capture. One of them, seeing him, "and speaking in a tone of authority," ordered him "to ride up there and see what troops those were," indicating the Confederate position.

Revere, by his own account, rode forward slowly in the night, then circled and returned to his own lines. A week later he read in a Richmond newspaper of Jackson's wounding and concluded that he had seen the General. Thus "Jackson's death happened in strange coincidence with his horoscopic prediction made years before."

The story has discrepancies. Jackson returned from Mexico to New Orleans in 1848, not 1852. He traveled from New Orleans to New York by ship through the Gulf of Mexico, around the Florida peninsula, and northward along the Atlantic Coast, not up the Mississippi and Ohio Rivers to Pittsburgh. There is no record that Jackson was ever in New Orleans except in 1846 when he was en route to Mexico and in 1848 when he returned from Mexico. Nor is there any record that he sailed up the Mississippi and Ohio rivers to Pittsburgh at any time. (He sailed down them in 1846.)

After the war, when Gen. Jubal A. Early inquired about these matters at the Virginia Military Institute, Gen. Francis H. Smith, Superintendent, and close associate of Jackson, replied, after investigation, that Jackson could not have been in New Orleans in 1852 or on a steamboat traveling up the two rivers in that year. (*S.H.S.P.*, VI, 261 ff.) Abundant evidence from other Lexington sources, which permits an almost day-by-day knowledge of Jackson's whereabouts, established that Revere was mistaken in time and place.

No known evidence exists of any Jackson interest in astrology or horoscopes. General Smith informed Early, after investigation on this point, that after the war he was unable to find any Lexington associate of Jackson who had ever heard of such interest. Jackson's religious convictions (which, however, developed to their highest level after 1852) would seem to preclude any serious possibility of the thinking Revere ascribed to him.

Early suggested that Revere may have encountered another lieutenant in the United States Army, Thomas K. Jackson, whose name was close enough to Thomas J. Jackson to give them trouble about mail at West Point.

The Revere account of the night of May 2 was sharply challenged by Early, principally for two reasons: first, that Revere described the scene inaccurately, Wilbourn and Wynn being the only persons with the wounded Jackson when Wilbourn saw the unidentified figure on horseback—not "several" persons as Revere said; and, second, that Revere could not have ridden toward the Confederate lines, as Wilbourn directed the figure to do and as Revere said he did, and then have circled and returned to Federal-occupied ground, without encountering, almost certainly, Confederate troops.

Early suggested that the unknown on horseback may have been a Federal courier lost in the night's confusions, and that Revere may have seen another group, wounded officers being no novelty. In the *Dictionary of American Biography*, Allan Westcott writes in his sketch of Revere that *Keel and Saddle* "is largely autobiographical but contains also a number of romantic stories, both of fact and fiction, entertainingly written and reflecting the author's restless, adventure-loving spirit."

| APPENDIX<br>V | REMNANTS OF<br>JACKSON'S<br>LIBRARY |

Jackson's earlier reading appears to have had more range than depth. Anna said that in his Lexington home he had a library "which, though small, was select, composed chiefly of scientific, historical, and religious books, with some of a lighter character, and some in Spanish and French." Nearly all of these, she said, "were full of his pencil marks, made with a view to future reference." (Mrs. Jackson, 111.)

The chief remnant of this library consists of some 90-odd volumes in Battle Abbey in Richmond. A score or more other books, some of them Anna's, some of them originally Dr. Morrison's, though possibly given to Anna or to Jackson, are also there. They are in a simple wooden bookcase with glass doors, believed to have been constructed by Jackson.

The original Jackson library was larger, but after the war Anna gave some of his books to friends and former soldiers who wanted souvenirs of the General, and other books were scattered.

Though the remnant is small, it reflects in a remarkable manner the man who collected these books. They divide definitely into six groups: school and textbooks, about twenty volumes; military books, six volumes; religious books, twenty-one volumes; travel guides and aids, five volumes; history and general literature, about thirty-four volumes; and a miscellaneous group of six volumes.

These volumes represent the chief interests of Jackson's mind and the chief activities of his life. Nothing is included that does not relate to these interests and activities. Here also, as Anna said, are heavily marked books, some of them worn with use, many of them with marginal markings and notes and underlined words, phrases, and sentences. They dispel any doubt that Jackson was a close reader.

The list of books is as follows:

SCHOOL AND TEXTBOOKS:

An elementary geology, 1843, by Edward Hitchcock, used at West Point, with Jackson's name inscribed and with marginal markings; Davies and Legendre's *Geometry*, inscribed with Jackson's name; Roger's French Dictionary, 1841, inscribed with Jackson's name; *Elements of Logic*, 1845, by Richard Whateley, also with Jackson's name inscribed; Peter Bullions' *Principles of English Grammar*, with marginal markings; J. G. Spurzheim's *Education: Elementary Principles*, 1847; an elementary treatise on astronomy, 1842, by John Gummere, heavily used and marked; a handbook of natural philosophy and astronomy, 1857, by Lardner; *A Treatise on Lights and Shadows and Linear Perspective*, second edition, 1840, by Charles Davis, with Jackson's inscription and markings; *A Manual of Magnetism*, 1842, by Daniel Davis, Jr., with Jackson's name and the date, "April 14, 1845," and a second and larger edition, published in 1855; *An Elementary Treaty on Optics*, 1839, for West Point cadets, by Jackson's teacher, W. H. C. Bartlett, with Jackson's name inscribed, and an *Acoustics and Optics*, 1856, and an *Analytical Mechanics*, 1853, both by the same author, with markings; an *Elementary Course in Civil Engineering*, 1846, for use at West Point, by D. H. Mahan, another of Jackson's teachers, inscribed with Jackson's name and the date, "February 20, 1846"; *Elements of Political Economy*, 1837, by Francis Wayland, President of Brown University, inscribed with Jackson's name and containing a bookplate marked "Chaplain's Library, Fort Columbus, New York"; G. P. Quackenbos' *Natural Philosophy;* a much used and marked Spanish grammar, 1836, by Mariano Cubi I Soler, with a flyleaf notation, "Thomas J. Jackson, $3.50"; a Spanish grammar in Latin, published in Mexico, 1840; and an *Ancient Geography*, 1849, by S. Augustus Mitchell.

MILITARY BOOKS:

*Heavy Artillery*, 1851, prepared by a board of officers for the use of the United States Army, with many markings; *Instruction for Field Artillery*, 1850, also prepared by a board of officers for army use, heavily marked and showing signs of much use; *Instruction d'Artillerie*, 1842, Paris, used by students at Saint-Cyr; *A Course of Instruction in Ordnance and Gunnery*, 1861, for the use of West Point cadets, by Capt. J. G. Benton, also heavily marked and with numerous marginal notes; *The Artillerist's Manual*, 1860, by First Lieut. John Gibbon, apparently given to Jackson while he was at the V.M.I.; and *United States Army Regulations*, 1861 (a book which appears to have been acquired after the outbreak of hostilities), given to Jackson by Maj. Elijah V. White, as a note by Jackson states, with a date, "Nov. 15th, 1862," appended.

RELIGIOUS BOOKS:

*History of the Bible,* two volumes, by Thomas Stackhouse, with Jackson's name inscribed; a New Testament in Spanish, 1851, bound in red and gold leather, marked on the flyleaf, "T. J. Jackson from his affectionate sister, M. J. [Margaret Junkin], Christmas, 1853"; a New Testament in French, 1837, Paris, with Jackson's name inscribed; *The Bible and Men of Learning,* 1855, by J. M. Matthews, D.D., with this handwritten notation, "For Major T. J. Jackson, V.M.I. from some friends of the V.M.I. in New York," followed by initials which are difficult to decipher; a *Constitution of the Presbyterian Church,* well marked; Ashbel Green's *Lectures on the Shorter Catechism* of the Presbyterian Church, well marked, Vols. 1 and 2; *Psalms and Hymns* of the Presbyterian Church, also well marked; a group of studies by Albert Barnes on different parts of the Bible, including *Questions on the Historical Books of the New Testament, Notes on the Gospels,* well marked, and *Notes on First Corinthians* and on *Hebrews;* a publication of the American Sunday-School Union, Philadelphia, called *Questions on Selected Portions of the Scripture,* Vol. 1, with Jackson's signature and the date, "November, 1853," heavily marked; the Presbyterian Board of Publication's *Seventy Times Seven, or The Law of Kindness—The Fifth Petition of the Lord's Prayer,* 1857; Thomas Chalmers' *Institutes of Theology,* 1847, Vol. I; the *Works* of the Rev. John Newton, 1831; *Invitations to True Happiness,* 1844, by Joel Parker, D.D.; *Morning Exercises for Every Day in the Year,* by the Rev. William Jay, published by the American Tract Society, New York, and inscribed, "T. J. Jackson from his estimable friend Mrs. Kelly"; the *Works* of Jeremy Taylor, 1835, Vols. 2 and 3; *The African Preacher,* by the Rev. W. S. White; and *The Principles of Courtesy,* by George Winfred Hervey, 1856, heavily marked.

TRAVEL GUIDES AND AIDS:

Calignani's *Paris Guide,* 1856; H. C. Wilson's *A New Guide to Florence and Its Vicinity* (A. Bettini, Bookseller and Editor), with frequent markings, underlinings, and notes besides descriptions of specific pictures and pieces of sculpture; Menzie's *Scottish Tourist's Pocket Guide,* published in Edinburgh, 1855; *The French Guide,* a grammar and textbook, with some front and back pages missing, apparently well used; and *Illustrated Handbook for Travellers through the United States,* 1846, by Sherman and Smith.

HISTORY AND GENERAL LITERATURE:

A broken series of volumes from *The Family Library,* including volumes on *Apostles and Early Martyrs, History of the Jews, Lives of Ancient*

*Philosophers,* a *Life of Mohammed,* and *British Painters and Sculptors;* a group of historical studies by the brothers Jacob and John S. C. Abbott, including lives of Cyrus the Great, Xerxes, Julius Caesar, Cleopatra, William the Conqueror, Queen Elizabeth, Charles I and II, and Madame Roland; four volumes of Charles Rollins' *Ancient History,* translated from the French; Plutarch's *Lives,* 1851, Vols. 2, 3, and 4; Grimshaw's *History of France,* 1849; Macaulay's *History of England,* 1850, two volumes, inscribed with Jackson's name and well marked; Hallam's *Middle Ages,* 1856, three volumes; Egbert Guernsey's *History of the United States,* 1851, well marked; George Bancroft's *History of the United States,* 1853, five volumes, with many markings; G. P. R. James' *Dark Scenes of History,* 1851; *Obituary Addresses on Henry Clay in Congress and Funeral Sermon,* 1852, inscribed with Jackson's name; a life of Andrew Jackson, 1845, by Lindsay and Blakiston; a volume of Shakespeare's plays with the notation, "Sold at Devaux's—English Circulating Library, Mexico"; a well-bound six-volume set of Shakespeare's work, inscribed with Jackson's name; the third of a three-volume set of Milton's works; *Don Quixote,* 1850; Bunyan's *Pilgrim's Progress,* 1846; *Pedro,* a Spanish story; Thomas Campbell's *Poetical Works,* 1832; *Rationale of Crime,* a treatise on criminal jurisprudence, 1846, by M. B. Sampson; *My Schools and Schoolmasters,* 1854, by Hugh Miller; and a bound volume of *Harper's New Monthly Magazine,* 1852.

HEALTH AND MISCELLANEOUS:

*The New Hydropathic Day Book, with Recipes for Cooking on Hygienic Principles,* 1853, by R. T. Troll, inscribed "T. J. Jackson, September, 1860"; *The Principles of Physiology Applied to the Preservation of Health,* seventh edition, 1855, by Andrew Combe, M.D., "Physician Extraordinary to the Queen in Scotland and Consulting Physician to the King and Queen of the Belgians"; *Physiology, Animal and Mental,* 1851, by O. S. Fowler; *Fowler on Memory,* 1850, the author of which is identified on the title page as a "practical phrenologist"; *The Family Kitchen Gardener,* 1858, by Robert Buist, with markings beside sections dealing with cabbage, carrots, beans, and asparagus; and Robert Mason's *Farrier and Stud Book,* 1858.

Also in this collection are three books of Anna's which have some special interest: *The Hydropathic Family Physician,* 1857, by Joel Shew, inscribed "Mrs. Mary Anna Jackson, Cottage Home, N. C." in handwriting that looks like Jackson's; Longfellow's *The Golden Legend,* inscribed "To Miss Anna, December, 1854," in what appears to be Jackson's handwriting; and Comstock's *Physiology.*

# REFERENCES

## CHAPTER 1

1. Dabney H. Maury in *Southern Historical Society Papers*, XXV, 313. Hereafter *S.H.S.P.*     2. Margaret Junkin Preston, *Century Magazine*, Vol. XXXII (New Series X), October, 1886, 927–936.     3. *S.H.S.P.*, XIX, 302.     4. *Ibid.*, XXXV, 90.

## CHAPTER 2

1. Roy Bird Cook, *The Family and Early Life of Stonewall Jackson*, 37. Hereafter Cook.     2. Cook, 37.     3. *Ibid.*, 28 ff.     4. *Ibid.*, 36.     5. *Ibid.*, 38.     6. *Ibid.*, 10.     7. Thomas Jackson Arnold (Jackson's nephew), *Early Life and Letters of General Thomas J. Jackson ("Stonewall" Jackson)*, 54. Hereafter Arnold.     8. Cook, 18–19.     9. *Ibid.*, 42.     10. *Ibid.*, 19.     11. *Ibid.*, 43.     12. Henry Haymond, *History of Harrison County, West Virginia*, and Edward Conrad Smith, *A History of Lewis County, West Virginia*, provide many details of the region and times.     13. Cook, 17.     14. *Ibid.*, 19.     15. Arnold, 26.     16. Mrs. Mary Anna Jackson (Jackson's widow), *Life and Letters of General Thomas J. Jackson (Stonewall Jackson)*, 14. Hereafter Mrs. Jackson.     17. Cook, 26.     18. Mrs. Jackson, 14; Cook, 31.     19. Cook, 31.     20. R. L. Dabney, D.D., *Life and Campaigns of Lieut.-Gen. Thomas J. Jackson*, 9. Hereafter Dabney.     21. Cook, 26.     22. Mrs. Jackson, 10.     23. *Ibid.*, 14.     24. *Ibid.*, 40.     25. Cook, 138.     26. *Ibid.*, 26.     27. *Ibid.*, 45.     28. Mrs. Jackson, 15.     29. Cook, 26.     30. *Ibid.*, 21.     31. It may have been Cummins. See Cook, 47.     32. Arnold, 28.     33. *Ibid.*     34. Mrs. Jackson. 16.     35. Arnold, 28; Mrs. Jackson, 17.     36. Mrs. Jackson, 17.     37. Cook, 21.     38. *Ibid.*, 29, 36.     39. *Ibid.*, 37.     40. *Ibid.*, 38.     41. Arnold, 53 ff.; Dabney, 13 ff.     42. Dabney, 14.     43. Arnold, 59.     44. Cook, 50.     45. *Ibid.*, 53.     46. Cook, 52; Mrs. Jackson, 22.     47. Cook, 55.     48. *Ibid.*, 53.     49. *Ibid.*, 50.     50. Mrs. Jackson, 26.     51. Cook, 51.     52. *Ibid.*, 50.     53. Cook, 56; Dabney, 17. Some evidence suggests this may have been a grandson of Joseph Rhea, 1715–1777, a scholarly clergyman who came from Ireland in 1769 and lived in Holston County in what was to be Ten-

481

nessee. His sons and grandsons include many well-known men. See Alfred Mynders in the Chattanooga, Tenn., *Times,* April 22, 1950. 54. Cook, 58. 55. *Ibid.* 56. *Ibid.,* 59. 57. *Ibid.,* 66. 58. In Cook, 56, it is stated that the slave supplied Tom with pine knots in exchange for instruction. 59. Cook, 60. 60. *Ibid.,* 64. 61. Dabney, 23, 24. 62. This subject is reviewed at length in Arnold, 47–51, and Cook, 61–63. 63. Cook, 63. 64. *Ibid.,* 48. 65. Cook, 48. Mrs. Jackson thought this incident involved Warren, not Tom. She wrote that Tom remained at Jackson's Mill after his step-grandmother's death. Mrs. Jackson, 19, 20. 66. Arnold, 32; Cook, 54. 67. Cook, 54. 68. Mrs. Jackson, 24. 69. Arnold, 35. 70. Cook, 65. 71. *Ibid.,* 54. 72. *Ibid.,* 67. 73. Mrs. Jackson, 28; Cook, 70. 74. Arnold, 37. 75. Cook, 71, 72. 76. Cook, 73. The journal was printed in the *Clarksburg Telegram,* Clarksburg, W. Va., of January 20, 1924.

### CHAPTER 3

1. Cook, 93. 2. Army Section, War Records Branch, National Archives; Cook, 85–86. 3. Cook, 84. 4. *Ibid.,* 84–85. 5. *Ibid.,* 85. 6. *Ibid.,* 86. 7. *Ibid.* 8. *Ibid.,* 87. 9. *Ibid.,* 88. 10. *Ibid.* 11. *Ibid.,* 89. 12. *Ibid.* 13. *Ibid.,* 90. 14. *Ibid.* 15. Mrs. Jackson, 32. 16. Cook, 60. 17. Arnold, 68. 18. D. H. Maury in *S.H.S.P.,* XXV, 309. 19. *Ibid.,* 310. 20. G. F. R. Henderson, *Stonewall Jackson and the American Civil War,* I, 15. Hereafter Henderson; Arnold, 75. 21. *Cadet Life Before the Mexican War,* 12. 22. Lloyd Lewis, *Captain Sam Grant,* 70. Hereafter Lewis. 23. D. H. Maury, *Recollections of a Virginian,* 125. Hereafter Maury. 24. *Centennial of the United States Military Academy,* II, contains much information about teachers and classes. 25. Lewis, 89. 26. Mrs. Jackson, 35. 27. Henderson, I, 15. 28. Arnold, 66. 29. Dabney, 34. 30. Lewis, 89. 31. *Ibid.,* 90. 32. Henderson, I, 21. 33. Mrs. Jackson, 35 ff., where many other such precepts are listed. 34. These details kindly supplied by Lieut. Col. W. J. Morton, U.S.A., Librarian at the United States Military Academy. 35. Mrs. Jackson said that he received some demerits for acts of others but chose to bear the blame silently rather than expose others. Mrs. Jackson, 35. 36. Arnold, 62 ff. 37. *Ibid.,* 71. 38. *Ibid.,* 62. 39. *Ibid.,* 65. 40. *Ibid.,* 67. 41. *Ibid.* 42. Maury, 25. 43. The details kindly supplied by Lieut. Col. W. J. Morton, U.S.A. 44. Henderson, I, 19. 45. *Ibid.,* 20. 46. Dabney, 38. 47. *Ibid.,* 39. 48. Maury in *S.H.S.P.,* XXV, 315. 49. Dr. Hunter McGuire in *S.H.S.P.,* XIX, 313. 50. Mrs. Jackson, 35. 51. Dabney, 37. 52. Arnold, 72. 53. *Ibid.,* 68. 54. *Ibid.,* 69. 55. *Ibid.* 56. *Ibid.,* 73. 57. Margaret Junkin Preston, *Century Magazine,* XXXII (New Series X), October, 1886, 927–936. 58. Arnold, 70. 59. *Ibid.,* 74. 60. Dabney, 36. 61. Mrs. Jackson, 33. 62. Dabney, 35. 63. Mrs. Jackson, 33–34. 64. Maury in *S.H.S.P.,* XXV, 311.

### CHAPTER 4

1. Holman Hamilton, *Zachary Taylor, Soldier of the Republic,* 177. Hereafter Hamilton. 2. Justin H. Smith, *The War with Mexico,* I, 143. Hereafter

Smith—*Mexico*.  3. Smith—*Mexico*, I, 166, 169.  4. Cook, 98.  5. Cook, 98; Arnold, 79.  6. Cook, 98.  7. Records Office of the Adjutant General, National Archives.  8. Arnold, 80.  9. Cook, 99.  10. *Ibid.*, 10. 11. *Ibid.*, 99.  12. Army Section, War Records Branch, National Archives. 13. Arnold, 79.  14. *Ibid.*, 80.  15. Smith—*Mexico*, I, 202, 203.  16. *Ibid.*, 218.  17. Maury, 28.  18. Lewis, 182, 183.  19. Smith—*Mexico*, I, 211. 20. Arnold, 88.  21. *Ibid.*, 89.  22. Smith—*Mexico*, I, 356.  23. Army Section, War Records Branch, National Archives.  24. Daniel Harvey Hill, "The Real Stonewall Jackson," *Century Magazine*, February, 1894, 623–681. Hereafter Hill—*Century*.  25. Army Section, War Records Branch, National Archives.  26. Smith—*Mexico*, I, 349.  27. *Ibid.*, II, 25.  28. This account follows in many details Smith—*Mexico*, II, 25 ff.  29. Edward D. Mansfield, *The Mexican War*, 178. Hereafter Mansfield.  30. Arnold, 84. 31. Smith—*Mexico*, II, 343.  32. Arnold, 85.  33. *Ibid.*  34. *Ibid.* 35. Cook, 100; Army Section, War Records Branch, National Archives. 36. Army Section, War Records Branch, National Archives.  37. Arnold, 84. 38. *Ibid.*  39. *Ibid.*, 86.  40. Cook, 101.  41. Smith—*Mexico*, II, 48. 42. The moves at Cerro Gordo, here greatly condensed, follow Smith—*Mexico*, II, 45–56.  43. Arnold, 89.  44. *Mexican Reports*, U.S. Senate, Executive Document, first session, 30th Congress, Vol. I, 278, in National Archives. Hereafter *Mexican Reports*.  45. Arnold, 90.  46. Jackson to Laura, May 1, 1847, in Library of Congress, Manuscript Division.  47. Lewis, 210. 48. Arnold, 92; Lewis, 211.  49. Winfield Scott, *Memoirs of Lieut. Gen. Winfield Scott*, 466. Hereafter Scott.  50. The day advance American troops reached Jalapa.  51. Arnold, 90.  52. Both quotations in a letter of Jackson to Laura, May 1, 1847. Original in Library of Congress, Manuscript Division.  53. Arnold, 91.  54. Jackson to Laura, *op. cit.*  55. *Ibid.* 56. Arnold, 92.  57. Jackson to Laura, *op. cit.*  58. The writing is blurred. 59. The writing is blurred.  60. Smith—*Mexico*, II, 366.  61. Lewis, 129. 62. Dabney, 44; Mrs. Jackson, 40, 41.  63. Arnold, 134.  64. *Ibid.*, 129.

CHAPTER 5

1. Clyde H. Metcalf, *A History of the United States Marine Corps*, I, 127. Hereafter Metcalf.  2. Smith—*Mexico*, II, 93.  3. Scott, 465.  4. *Mexican Reports*, I, 350.  5. Magruder's reports say 29. Some others, including Scott, put the figure at 22.  6. *Mexican Reports*, Appendix, 104.  7. *Ibid.*, 101. 8. *Ibid.*, 102.  9. *Ibid.*, 104.  10. *Ibid.*, 102.  11. Both of these tributes are in *Mexican Reports*, I, 322, 337.  12. Smith—*Mexico*, II, 109.  13. *Ibid.*, 114.  14. *Ibid.*, 118.  15. *Ibid.*, 403.  16. *Ibid.*, 149.  17. *Mexican Reports*, Appendix, 192 ff.  18. *Ibid.*, 194.  19. The events here are based on the far more detailed narrative in Smith—*Mexico*, II, 154 ff.  20. *Mexican Reports*, Appendix, 219.  21. Margaret Junkin Preston, *Century Magazine*, Vol. XXXII (New Series X), September, 1886, 927–936; Henderson, I, 41. 22. *Mexican Reports*, Appendix, 194.  23. Magruder, *ibid.*  24. Smith— *Mexico*, II, 159.  25. Henderson, I, 43.  26. *Mexican Reports*, Appendix, 195.  27. Magruder, *ibid.*  28. Arnold, 177; Margaret Junkin Preston,

*op. cit.* This incident may have taken place earlier near the northeast corner of Chapultepec.    29. Smith—*Mexico*, II, 162.    30. Arnold, 130.    31. *Mexican Reports*, Appendix, 196.    32. *Mexican Reports*, I, 391.    33. *Ibid.*, 403. 34. *Ibid.*, 380.    35. Dabney, 52.    36. Margaret Junkin Preston, *op. cit.* 37. Dabney, 52.    38. Arnold, 77.    39. *Ibid.*, 128.    40. Lewis, 266. 41. Smith—*Mexico*, II, 163.    42. Scott, 535.

CHAPTER 6

1. Smith—*Mexico*, II, 167.    2. G. W. Kendall's letters in Littell's *Living Age*, No. 183, November 13, 1847, 331. Hereafter Kendall.    3. Smith—*Mexico*, II, 227.    4. *Ibid.*    5. Kendall, 333.    6. Lewis, 272.    7. *Ibid.*, 265. 8. Arnold, 128.    9. Henderson, I, 47.    10. Cook, 102.    11. *Ibid.*, 103. 12. *Ibid.*, 104.    13. *Ibid.*, 105.    14. Arnold, 131.    15. *Ibid.*, 129. 16. *Ibid.*, 132.    17. *Ibid.*, 136.    18. Smith—*Mexico*, I, 23 ff.; Susan Hale, *The Story of Mexico*, 291 ff.; Mme. Calderon de la Barca, *Life in Mexico*, 106 ff. Hereafter Calderon.    19. Arnold, 125.    20. Cook, 182.    21. Arnold, 136.    22. Arnold, 138.    23. Dabney, 54.    24. Mrs. Jackson, 46. 25. *Ibid.*, 47.    26. Elizabeth Preston Allan, *The Life and Letters of Margaret Junkin Preston*, 75 ff. Hereafter E. P. Allan.    27. Arnold, 134. 28. *Ibid.*, 129.    29. Dabney, 54, 55.    30. Henderson, I, 52.    31. Mrs. Jackson, 47.    32. Arnold, 132.    33. *Ibid.*, 136.    34. Calderon, 212, 225, 349; Smith—*Mexico*, I, 44.    35. Arnold, 134, 135.    36. These events are summarized in Smith—*Mexico*, II, 185–188.    37. Arnold, 132.    38. Lewis, 276.    39. Roy Frank Nichols, *Franklin Pierce—Young Hickory of the Granite Hills*, 167.    40. Hill—*Century*, 624.    41. Col. William Couper, *One Hundred Years at V.M.I.*, I, 175. Hereafter Couper.    42. Maury in *S.H.S.P.*, XXV, 312. 43. From publications of the patriotic society of the same name, F. Stirling Wilson, Secretary, 2721 Blaine Drive, Chevy Chase, Md.    44. Arnold, 137. 45. *Ibid.*, 135.    46. *Ibid.*, 134.    47. Arnold, 138.    48. *S.H.S.P.*, X, 190. 49. Mrs. Jackson, 48.    50. Arnold, 131.    51. Margaret Junkin Preston, *Century Magazine*, Vol. XXXII (New Series X), October, 1886, 927 ff. 52. Mrs. Jackson, 48.    53. I am indebted for this information to the Catholic University of America, especially to the Rev. A. K. Ziegler, head of the Department of History, and the Rev. Antonine Tibeshar, O.F.M., a specialist on Ibero-American history in the department.    54. Dabney, 56.    55. McGuire in Couper, IV, 80.    56. Dabney, 56, 57.    57. Hill—*Century*, 624. 58. Arnold, 138, 139.

CHAPTER 7

1. Army Section, War Records Branch, National Archives; New Orleans, La., *Daily Delta*, July 18, 1848, through the courtesy of the New Orleans Public Library.    2. Army Section, War Records Branch, National Archives. 3. Arnold, 140.    4. *Ibid.*, 141.    5. *Ibid.*, 142.    6. Douglas Southall Freeman, *R. E. Lee*, I, 201, 202. Hereafter Freeman—*Lee*.    7. Mrs. Bleecker Bangs, *Reminiscences of Old New Utrecht and Gowanus*, 77 ff., through the courtesy of the New York Public Library. Hereafter Mrs. Bangs.    8. Adjutant

General's Records, Thomas J. Jackson Personal Service File, National Archives.
9. *Dictionary of American Biography.* Hereafter D.A.B.    10. Cook, 107, 108.
11. Arnold, 144.    12. *Ibid.*, 145, 146.    13. *Ibid.*, 144.    14. *Ibid.*, 147.
15. *Ibid.*, 149.    16. *Ibid.*, 150.    17. *Ibid.*, 152.    18. Cook, 100.
19. Arnold, 154.    20. *Ibid.*, 157.    21. *Ibid.*, 158.    22. *Ibid.*, 159.
23. *Ibid.*, 160, 161.    24. *Ibid.*, 164.    25. *Ibid.*, 165.    26. Maury, 71.
27. Arnold, 147, 148.    28. Cook, 108.    29. Arnold, 257.    30. *Ibid.*, 147.
31. *Ibid.*, 149.    32. *Ibid.*, 151, 152.    33. *Ibid.*, 147.    34. *Ibid.*, 162, 163.
35. *Ibid.*, 149.    36. *Ibid.*, 150.    37. *Ibid.*, 165.    38. Mrs. Bangs, 111,
169.    39. *Ibid.*, 155.    40. *Ibid.*    41. *Ibid.*, 169.    42. Cook, 110;
Arnold, 162.    43. Arnold, 162.    44. *Ibid.*, 186.    45. Mrs. Jackson, 49.
46. *Ibid.*, 48.    47. *Ibid.*, 49.    48. Mrs. Bangs, 169 ff.    49. Dabney, 60;
Margaret Junkin Preston, *Century Magazine*, Vol. XXXII (New Series X),
October, 1886, 927 ff.    50. Mrs. Bangs, 111.    51. Arnold, 158–160, has
part of this letter; the original is in the University of Virginia Library.

CHAPTER 8

1. Cook, 111.    2. Arnold, 166.    3. Kathryn Trimmer Abbey, *Florida, Land
of Change*, 215–267. Hereafter Abbey.    4. Abbey, 267.    5. *Florida Historical Quarterly*, April, 1951, 264–267.    6. Arnold, 169, 170.    7. *Ibid.*,
170.    8. Abbey, 215.    9. *Ibid.*, 216.    10. Army Section, War Records
Branch, National Archives.    11. This and all subsequent reports and documents from Fort Meade are from the War Department Records, U.S. Army
Commands, Department of Florida, National Archives, unless otherwise designated.    12. Arnold, 170.    13. *Ibid.*, 169.    14. *Ibid.*, 170, 171.    15. *Ibid.*,
169.    16. Mrs. Jackson, 51.    17. Couper, I, 251, 252.    18. *Ibid.*, 252.
19. *Ibid.*, 253.    20. Arnold, 172.    21. War Department Records, U.S.
Army Commands, Department of Florida, National Archives.    22. The writing in this letter is blurred.    23. The writing in this letter is blurred.
24. Hill—*Century*, 624.

CHAPTER 9

1. Couper, I, 5.    2. *Ibid.*, 9.    3. *Ibid.*, 2.    4. *Ibid.*, 236.    5. E. P. Allan,
36.    6. Couper, I, 15.    7. *Ibid.*, 17.    8. *Ibid.*, 43, 44.    9. *Ibid.*, 20.
10. *Ibid.*, 247.    11. *Ibid.*, 250.    12. *Ibid.*, 249.    13. *Ibid.*, 250.    14. Hill—
*Century*, 624.    15. Couper, I, 251.    16. *Ibid.*, 253.    17. Arnold, 172,
173.    18. Couper, I, 252.    19. *Ibid.*, 253.    20. The original letter is
among the Jackson Papers in the personal records of the V.M.I. files.
21. Arnold, 175.    22. *Ibid.*, 176.    23. Cook, 117.    24. *Ibid.*, 113–115.
25. *Ibid.*, 114, 115.    26. *Ibid.*, 118.    27. *Ibid.*, 117.    28. Couper, I,
253, 254.    29. From the Munford Papers, Duke University.    30. Couper,
I, 244.    31. *Ibid.*, 245.    32. Arnold, 179.    33. *Ibid.*, 188.    34. *Ibid.*,
179.    35. Couper, I, 187.    36. *Ibid.*, 230.    37. *Ibid.*, 246. The following
year Jackson moved to No. 91, later to No. 401, on the fourth stoop, where he
roomed with Lieut. Thomas A. Harris. *Ibid.*, 178.    38. *Ibid.*, 232.    39. *Ibid.*,
233.

CHAPTER 10

1. War Department Records, U.S. Army Commands, Department of Florida, National Archives. 2. *Ibid.;* Cook, 123. 3. *Ibid.,* 128. 4. Arnold, 179. 5. *Ibid.,* 186. 6. Cook, 190. 7. Arnold, 181. 8. *Ibid.,* 185. 9. *Ibid.,* 186. 10. *Ibid.,* 187, 188. 11. *Ibid.,* 195. 12. *Ibid.,* 192. 13. *Ibid.,* 220. 14. *Ibid.,* 223. 15. *Ibid.,* 185. 16. *Ibid.,* 185, 186. 17. Cook, 130–132. 18. Arnold, 194. 19. Mrs. Jackson, 96. 20. S.H.S.P., XXXVIII, 270; S.H.S.P., XIX, 309. 21. E. P. Allan, 75 ff.; Dabney, 78. 22. Couper, IV, 77, 78. 23. S.H.S.P., IX, 41. 24. Mrs. Jackson, 96. 25. Henderson, I, 64. 26. Dabney, 79. 27. S.H.S.P., IX, 41. 28. *Ibid.,* XX, 309. 29. Richard Taylor, *Destruction and Reconstruction,* 50. Hereafter Taylor. 30. The Clement D. Fishburne Manuscript, for which I am indebted to Miss Anna Barringer, Charlottesville, Va. Hereafter Fishburne Manuscript. 31. Margaret Junkin Preston, *Century Magazine,* Vol. XXXII (New Series X), October, 1886, 927–936. 32. E. P. Allan, 82. 33. Hill–*Century,* 623–681. 34. Mrs. Jackson, 57. 35. Margaret Junkin Preston, *op. cit.* 36. *Ibid.;* Mrs. Jackson, 109, 110. 37. S.H.S.P., XX, 307; XVI, 36. 38. *Ibid.,* XX, 307; XVI, 36. 39. *Ibid.,* XVI, 45. 40. Couper, I, 313. 41. *Ibid.,* III, 179. 42. *Ibid.* 43. Hill–*Century,* 625 ff. 44. *Ibid.* 45. S.H.S.P., XX, 307. 46. *Ibid.,* XVI, 36; Dabney, 65. 47. S.H.S.P., XIX, 307. 48. Couper, III, 184. 49. *Ibid.,* 183. 50. *Ibid.,* I, 263. 51. *Ibid.* 52. *Ibid.,* III, 183, 184. 53. *Ibid.,* I, 313, 314. 54. *Ibid.,* 314. 55. *Ibid.* 56. The Fulkerson and Penn incidents are told by J. C. Hiden in S.H.S.P., XX, 309. 57. James H. Lane in S.H.S.P., XX, 309 ff. 58. Couper, III, 186, 198. 59. *Ibid.,* I, 168. 60. *Ibid.,* III, 183. 61. Thomas S. Doyle in Richmond, Va., *Times-Dispatch,* October 2, 1910. 62. S.H.S.P., XXXVIII, 270. 63. *Ibid.,* XVI, 44. 64. *Ibid.,* XX, 309. 65. Doyle, *op. cit.* 66. S.H.S.P., X, 424. 67. Margaret Junkin Preston, *op. cit.* 68. Couper, III, 178. 69. S.H.S.P., XVI, 44. 70. *Ibid.,* IX, 41. 71. *Ibid.,* XXXVIII, 270. 72. Couper, III, 187. 73. Dabney, 82.

CHAPTER 11

1. Fishburne Manuscript; Mrs. Jackson, 79; *William S. White and His Times,* an autobiography, edited by his son, Rev. H. M. White, D.D., 139. Hereafter White. 2. White, 139. 3. Couper, I, 134 ff. 4. Hill–*Century,* 625. 5. Dabney, 84. 6. *Ibid.,* 85. 7. Jackson's copy of George Winfred Hervey, *The Principles of Courtesy,* is in the remnants of his library now stored in Battle Abbey (Confederate Memorial Institute), Richmond, Va. Hereafter Hervey. 8. Hervey, 118, 119. 9. *Ibid.,* 194. 10. *Ibid.,* 243. 11. In part in Arnold, 180. The full letter is in the University of Virginia Library, Charlottesville, Va. 12. Arnold, 201, 202; the full letter is in the University of Virginia Library. 13. Details about the Junkin family, unless otherwise indicated, are from E. P. Allan. 14. Hill–*Century,* 625. 15. *Ibid.,* 16. The Dabney Papers; Library of Union Theological Seminary, Richmond, Va. 17. Arnold, 204. 18. Mrs. Jackson, 95, 96. 19. *Ibid.,* 97.

20. Arnold, 199, 200.    21. *Ibid.*, 201, 202.    22. *Ibid.*, 203.    23. Mrs. Jackson, 98, 99.    24. Cook, 129, 130.    25. Arnold, 205, 206.    26. Margaret Junkin Preston, *Century Magazine*, Vol. XXXII (New Series X), October, 1886, 931.    27. E. P. Allan, 62.    28. *Ibid.*, 73 ff.    29. Hill–*Century*, 625 ff. 30. So described to the author in the early 1950's by occupants of the house, Professor and Mrs. L. J. Desha.    31. Arnold, 205.    32. *Ibid.*, 206.    33. *Ibid.*, 208.    34. Philip Alexander Bruce, *History of the University of Virginia*, III, 4.    35. Dabney, 69, 70.    36. Couper, I, 282.    37. Cook, 134. 38. Cook, 133, where it is pointed out that some doubt exists as to the words "determination of purpose" and "not having previous." The original is in the Virginia Historical Society, Richmond, Va.    39. University of Virginia Library. 40. Arnold, 212.    41. *Ibid.*, 209, 210.    42. *Ibid.*, 217.    43. *Ibid.*, 219. 44. Dabney, 115.    45. Hill–*Century*, 625 ff.    46. Arnold, 219.    47. *Ibid.*, 220.    48. *Ibid.*, 224.    49. *Ibid.*, 225.    50. *Ibid.*, 224.    51. *Ibid.*, 234. 52. *Ibid.*, 221.    53. E. P. Allan, 72.    54. *Ibid.*, 73.    55. Mrs. Jackson, 84. 56. E. P. Allan, 75 ff.    57. Hill–*Century*, 625.    58. Margaret Junkin Preston Papers, Southern Historical Collection, University of North Carolina, Chapel Hill, N. C.    59. Mrs. Jackson, 85.    60. Cook, 138.    61. Arnold, 234.    62. *Ibid.*, 223, 231.    63. *Ibid.*, 233.    64. *Ibid.*, 232.    65. *Ibid.*, 233.    66. *Ibid.*, 232.    67. *Ibid.*, 233.    68. *Ibid.*, 244.    69. *Ibid.* 70. *Ibid.*, 247.    71. *Ibid.*, 246.    72. *Ibid.*, 247.    73. *Ibid.*, 248, 249. 74. In Battle Abbey (Confederate Memorial Institute), Richmond, Va. 75. Mrs. Jackson, 87.    76. Arnold, 25.    77. Mrs. Jackson, 86.    78. *Ibid.* 79. H. C. Wilson, *A New Guide to Florence and Its Vicinity* (A. Bettini, Bookseller and Editor).    80. Mrs. Jackson, 86.    81. Dabney, 82.    82. *S.H.S.P.*, XIX, 310.    83. Mrs. Jackson, 88.

CHAPTER 12

1. Mrs. Jackson, 77; Dabney, 76.    2. Mrs. Jackson, 74.    3. *Ibid.*, 63. 4. Dabney, 92, 93.    5. White, 156 ff.    6. The date is uncertain. In Mrs. Jackson and Dabney it is 1855, in White it is 1856. The records of the sessions of the church for 1854, 1855, and 1856 do not mention the subject. Details are to be found in White, 156 ff.; Dabney, 93 ff.; Mrs. Jackson, 77 ff. 7. *S.H.S.P.*, IX, 44, 45.    8. Mrs. Jackson, 59.    9. *Ibid.*, 61.    10. The records of The Franklin do not include Jackson's name as a member, but his wife (Mrs. Jackson, 62) and his close friend, D. H. Hill (Hill–*Century*, 625 ff.), say he was a member, and Dabney agrees (Dabney, 72).    11. Dabney, 94.    12. Mrs. Jackson, 73.    13. *Ibid.*, 59.    14. *Ibid.*, 78.    15. Mrs. Jackson, 72. In Margaret Junkin Preston, *Century Magazine*, Vol. XXXII (New Series X), October, 1886, 935, it is "I could go without my hat."    16. Mrs. Jackson, 74.    17. E. P. Allan, 73 ff.    18. *Ibid.*    19. Margaret Junkin Preston, *op. cit.*, 927 ff.    20. Mrs. Jackson, 89 ff.; Laura Morrison Brown, in her *Historical Sketch of the Morrison Family* records many details.    21. Mrs. Jackson, 99.    22. *Ibid.*    23. *Ibid.*, 100.    24. *Ibid.*    25. Mary Johnston Avery in *Holland's, The Magazine of the South*, October, 1933, in an article entitled "When Stonewall Jackson Went a-Wooing."    26. Mrs. Jackson, 102,

103. 27. *Ibid.*, 101. 28. *Ibid.*, 101, 102. 29. *Ibid.*, 102. 30. *Ibid.*, 103. 31. Arnold, 254, 255. 32. Details of the wedding plans, and of the wedding, are (where not otherwise indicated) from the Fishburne Manuscript. 33. Mrs. B. G. Clifford to Miss Cornelia Shaw (Librarian at Davidson College), July, 1920, from a Ms. in Davidson College Library, Davidson, N. C. 34. Mrs. Jackson, 104. 35. *Ibid.*, 103, 104. 36. Arnold, 256, 257. 37. Mrs. Jackson, 104, 105. 38. *Ibid.*, 105. 39. Cook, 146. 40. Mrs. Jackson, 105. 41. *Ibid.*, 106. 42 Arnold, 43 43. *Ibid.* 44. *Ibid.*, 260. 45. *Ibid.*, 261. 46. *Ibid.*, 264. 47. *Ibid.*, 265. For further details on Carnochan, see *D.A.B.* 48. Arnold, 265, 266. 49. Couper, I, 338. 50. Mrs. Jackson, 111. 51. Arnold, 262. 52. *Ibid.*, 263. 53. Mrs. Jackson, 111. 54. *Ibid.*, 112. 55. *Ibid.*, 113. 56. These details are in Mrs. Jackson, 113. 57. Arnold, 265. 58. *Ibid.*, 298. 59. *Ibid.*, 300. 60. *Ibid.*, 302. 61. *Ibid.*, 303. 62. *Ibid.*, 305. 63. *Ibid.*, 237. 64. *Ibid.*, 280. 65. *Ibid.*, 276. 66. *Ibid.*, 266. 67. *Ibid.*, 267, 268. 68. *Ibid.*, 261. 69. *Ibid.*, 271. 70. *Ibid.*, 269. 71. *Ibid.*, 271, 272. 72. *Ibid.*, 270. 73. Couper, I, 23. 74. Mrs. Jackson, 106. 75. Couper, I, 23. 76. Mrs. Jackson, 108. 77. *Ibid.*, 107. 78. *Ibid.* 79. The description of Jackson's day is in Mrs. Jackson, 109, 110. 80. Arnold, 272. 81. Cook, 147, 148; Mrs. Jackson, 108, 109; William Couper in the Rockbridge County *News*, January 28, 1943. 82. Mrs. Jackson, 47. 83. *Ibid.*, 114. 84. *Ibid.*, 115, 116. 85. Mrs. Jackson, 119. 86. *Ibid.*, 116, 117, 118. 87. Margaret Junkin Preston, *op. cit.* 88. Mrs. Jackson, 142, 143. 89. Cook, 148, 149; Couper, III, 181. 90. Couper, I, 321. 91. Cook, 144. 92. *Ibid.*, 144, 145.

### CHAPTER 13

1. Couper, I, 319. 2. *Ibid.* 3. Oswald Garrison Villard, *John Brown, A Biography after Fifty Years*, 354. Hereafter Villard. 4. Couper, II, 6, 8. 5. *Ibid.*, 10, 11. 6. *Ibid.*, 12. 7. Mrs. Jackson, 129, 130. 8. Couper, II, 14. 9. *Ibid.*, 16. 10. Avery Craven, *Edmund Ruffin, Southerner*, 176. 11. Villard, 555. 12. Mrs. Jackson, 130, 131, 132. 13. Couper, II, 23. 14. Arnold, 277. 15. Mrs. Jackson, 121, 122. 16. *Ibid.*, 122. 17. *Ibid.*, 123. 18. *Ibid.*, 128. 19. *Ibid.*, 129. 20. Cook, 153. 21. Couper, II, 41, 42. 22. *Ibid.*, 43. 23. *Ibid.*, 44. 24. *Ibid.* 25. *Ibid.*, 45. 26. Arnold, 281. 27. *Ibid.*, 282. 28. *Ibid.*, 284, 286. 29. *Ibid.*, 285, 286. 30. Mrs. Jackson, 133. 31. *Ibid.*, 135. 32. *Ibid.*, 133, 134. 33. *Ibid.*, 139. 34. *S.H.S.P.*, IX, 41. 35. Couper, II, 62. 36. Arnold, 291, 292. 37. *Ibid.*, 291. 38. *Ibid.*, 293, 294. 39. Cook, 154. 40. Mrs. Jackson, 141. 41. Mrs. Jackson, 142. The friend was the Rev. Dr. J. B. Ramsey of Lynchburg, Va. 42. Couper, II, 79. 43. The account here is based largely on Couper, II, 79 ff. This includes Colonel Smith's account. 44. Arnold, 296. 45. *War of the Rebellion: Official Records of the Union and Confederate Armies*, Series 3, I, 76. Hereafter *O.R.* This is the 128-volume collection which is the main basis (though some important documents are missing from its pages)

of official information about Civil War operations. Published over a period of eleven years (1880–1891), it is organized in four "Series," within each of which a designated volume number may refer to a single volume or may include more than one volume, or "part." Thus a reference may be to Series 1, Volume I, Part 1, page 1, or to Series 1, Volume I, Part 2, page 1, which is another volume. The references that follow are in Series 1 unless otherwise indicated. Accordingly, *O.R.*, XXV, 100, means page 100 of Volume 25; and *O.R.*, XXV, pt. 2, 100, means page 100 of the second volume, or part, of Volume 25.    46. Couper, II, 88.    47. White, 170.    48. Couper, II, 92. 49. *Ibid.*, 94.    50. Mrs. Jackson, 144.    51. Couper, II, 95.    52. *Ibid.*, 97. 53. *Ibid.*, 96.    54. Mrs. Jackson, 145, 146.    55. Couper, II, 96, 97. 56. Mrs. Jackson, 145.    57. *S.H.S.P.*, IX, 44.    58. One paragraph of Major Preston's order, referring to the cadets, read: "At 12½ o'clock they will be formed to march. Dinner at 12 o'clock." It may be that the words indicate the moment of departure. Mrs. Jackson said twice that Jackson set the time of departure at one o'clock.    59. *S.H.S.P.*, IX, 44.    60. Couper, II, 98. 61. *Ibid.*, 99.    62. Mrs. Jackson, 148.    63. *Ibid.*    64. *Ibid.*, 150.

## CHAPTER 14

1. Couper, II, 102.    2. Mrs. Jackson, 148.    3. Cook, 157.    4. Mrs. Jackson, 151.    5. *Ibid.*    6. *O.R.*, II, 784.    7. *Ibid.*    8. *Battles and Leaders of the Civil War*, I, III. Hereafter *B. & L.*    9. *B. & L.*, I, 118.    10. *Ibid.* 11. *Ibid.*, 121.    12. *Ibid.*    13. *Ibid.*    14. *Ibid.*, 122.    15. *Ibid.* 16. Mrs. Jackson, 156.    17. *B. & L.*, II, 122.    18. *O.R.*, II, 122.    19. *Ibid.*, 806.    20. *Ibid.*, 809.    21. *Ibid.*, 814.    22. *Ibid.*, 822.    23. *Ibid.*, 823. 24. *Ibid.*, 824.    25. *Ibid.*, 825.    26. *Ibid.*, 832.    27. *Ibid.*, 836. 28. *Ibid.*, 840.    29. *Ibid.*, 848.    30. *Ibid.*, 860.    31. *Ibid.*, 863. 32. *Ibid.*, 861.    33. *Ibid.*, 867.    34. *B. & L.*, I, 124.    35. Hotchkiss Papers, Box 14, Library of Congress, Manuscript Division.    36. Jackson's Letter Book in Box 8 of the Hotchkiss Papers. Hereafter Jackson's Letter Book. Additional information about Hawks is in the V.M.I. file of material about his son, Arthur Wells Hawks.    37. *S.H.S.P.*, XIX, 298.    38. *Ibid.*, 298 ff. 39. There is much about him in Susan P. Lee, *Memoirs of William Nelson Pendleton* (hereafter *Pendleton*), and more in the Pendleton Papers at the University of North Carolina. In 1959, W. G. Bean brought together much new personal material relating to the family and the marriage of Sandie in a biography of this young officer entitled *Stonewall's Man—Sandie Pendleton*.

## CHAPTER 15

1. *B. & L.*, I, 122.    2. *Ibid.*    3. G. E. Turner, *Victory Rode the Rails—The Strategic Place of the Railroads in the Civil War*, 75. Hereafter Turner. 4. Mrs. Jackson, 171.    5. Henry Kyd Douglas, *I Rode with Stonewall*, 206, 207. Hereafter Douglas.    6. Mrs. Jackson, 151.    7. *Ibid.*    8. *Ibid.*, 152. 9. *Ibid.*    10. *Ibid.*    11. *Ibid.*, 146.    12. *Ibid.*, 152.    13. *Ibid.*, 161. 14. *Ibid.*, 152.    15. *B. & L.*, I, 241.    16. *O.R.*, II, 871.    17. Dr. Hunter McGuire in *S.H.S.P.*, XIX, 302.    18. *O.R.*, II, 877.    19. Mrs. Jackson, 157.

20. *Ibid.*, 158.    21. *Ibid.*    22. *Ibid.*, 159.    23. Register of Former Cadets, V.M.I.; John O. Casler, *Four Years in the Stonewall Brigade*, 16. Hereafter Casler.    24. Dabney, 200.    25. *O.R.*, II, 881.    26. *Ibid.*, 883.    27. *Ibid.*, 889.    28. *Ibid.*, 890.    29. *Ibid.*, 896.    30. *Ibid.*, 897.    31. *Ibid.*, 898. 32. *Ibid.*, 908.    33. *Ibid.*, 898.    34. *Ibid.*, 908.    35. *Ibid.*, 910. 36. *Ibid.*, 922.    37. *Ibid.*, 923.    38. *Ibid.*, 925.    39. Mrs. Jackson, 160. 40. *O.R.*, II, 689.    41. *Ibid.*, 671.    42. *Ibid.*, 696.    43. Edward Hungerford, *The Story of the Baltimore and Ohio Railroad*, II, 10 ff. Hereafter Hungerford.    44. Hungerford, 9.    45. *Ibid.*, 10.    46. *Ibid.*, 10 ff.    47. Mrs. Jackson, 163.    48. *Ibid.*    49. *Ibid.*    50. *Ibid.*    51. *O.R.*, II, 704. 52. *Ibid.*, 725.    53. *Ibid.*, 185.    54. Mrs. Jackson, 135.    55. *O.R.*, II, 186. 56. *Ibid.*    57. *Ibid.*, 185.    58. *Ibid.*    59. Mrs. Jackson, 166.    60. *Ibid.*, 167.    61. Cook, 158.    62. *Ibid.*    63. *Ibid.*    64. *Ibid.*    65. *Ibid.* 66. The Clement D. Fishburne Narrative, in the possession of Mrs. Staige Blackford, Charlottesville, Va., mentions the white cotton stripes. Hereafter Fishburne Narrative.    67. *O.R.*, II, 967.    68. *Ibid.*, 969.    69. *Ibid.*, 162. 70. *Ibid.*, 160.    71. *Ibid.*, 478.    72. *Ibid.*, 167.    73. *Ibid.*, 108.    74. *Ibid.* 75. *Ibid.*    76. *Ibid.*, 171.    77. *Ibid.*, 172. The figure is more than three times as large as Johnston's strength of about 11,000. Beauregard said Johnston brought 8,334 men to the battlefield.    78. *B. & L.*, I, 229.    79. *O.R.*, II, 982.    80. *Ibid.*, 773.    81. Mrs. Jackson, 175.    82. *Ibid.*    83. D. B. Conrad in *S.H.S.P.*, XIX, 82 ff.    84. *Ibid.*    85. Mrs. Jackson, 175. 86. Casler, 22.    87. *B. & L.*, I, 200.    88. Jefferson Davis, *The Rise and Fall of the Confederate Government*, I, 372. Hereafter Davis.

CHAPTER 16

1. *O.R.*, II, 985.    2. *Ibid.*, 473.    3. *Ibid.*    4. *Ibid.*, 474.    5. *Ibid.*, 486. 6. *Ibid.*    7. *Ibid.*    8. *Ibid.*, 474.    9. *B. & L.*, I, 184.    10. *Ibid.* 11. *O.R.*, II, 505.    12. *Ibid.*, 486, 487.    13. *O.R.*, II, 395; *B. & L.*, I, 184. 14. *O.R.*, II, 348; but Evans put the time at 5:15 A.M. *Ibid.*, 558.    15. *Ibid.*, 560.    16. *Ibid.*, 559.    17. *Ibid.*, 487.    18. *Ibid.*    19. A detailed account of these confusions appears in Douglas Southall Freeman, *Lee's Lieutenants*, I, 53–60. Hereafter Freeman—*LL*.    20. E. P. Alexander, *Military Memoirs of a Confederate*, 30. Hereafter Alexander.    21. Alexander, 30.    22. Ibid., 31.    23. Freeman—*LL*, I, 63.    24. *B. & L.*, I, 232.    25. *Ibid.* 26. *Ibid.*, 233.    27. *O.R.*, II, 567.    28. *B. & L.*, I, 234.    29. *Ibid.* 30. *Ibid.*    31. *Ibid.*, 235.    32. Casler, 22.    33. *O.R.*, II, 481.    34. Casler, 25, cites a four-mile march up the run, and then back.    35. Dabney, 217. 36. Fishburne Narrative, 97.    37. *Ibid.*, 98.    38. Conrad in *S.H.S.P.*, XIX, 82 ff. There are other versions and it is difficult, probably impossible, to determine with confidence the precise timing, sequence, and details of these events.    39. There is no satisfactory authority for this conversation or for the following quotation attributed to Bee which is generally accepted as the origin of the name "Stonewall" for Jackson and his brigade. Jackson made no record of either incident and Bee was mortally wounded before the battle was over. For further details of the origin of the name "Stonewall," see Ap-

pendix III. The designation became fixed and, in popular usage, almost universal in the period of the Romney and Valley campaigns. Freeman—*LL*, I, Appendix V, 733, discusses R. M. Johnston's rejection, in his *Bull Run, Its Strategy and Tactics,* of the report of Bee's apostrophe (though Johnston believed that "something was said by somebody, during or immediately after the battle that likened Jackson or his men or both to a stone wall"). The same Appendix quotes from the *Reminiscences of Col. J. C. Haskell* the belief that Bee's remarks were derogatory and meant Jackson was blocking, like a stone wall, Bee's advance. 40. Alexander, 36. 41. *Ibid.,* 34. 42. Fishburne Narrative, 100. 43. *O.R.,* II, 494. 44. *B. & L.,* I, 236. 45. Casler, 36. 46. *Ibid.* 47. *Ibid.,* 42. 48. Freeman—*LL*, I, 68. 49. Casler, 38. 50. *O.R.,* II, 481. 51. Conrad in *S.H.S.P.,* XIX, 90 ff. 52. *O.R.,* II, 495. 53. It is difficult to tell from varying and contradictory accounts when Bee was shot. It may have been earlier. 54. McHenry Howard, *Recollections of a Maryland Confederate Soldier and Staff Officer under Johnston, Jackson and Lee,* 38. Hereafter Howard. 55. *B. & L.,* I, 215. 56. The companies were from the Second, Third, and Eighth U.S. Infantry. Sykes had been assigned to the Fourteenth, but had not joined it. (For this information I am indebted to Maj. Arthur P. Wade, U.S. Army.) 57. *O.R.,* II, 317 ff. 58. *Ibid.,* 404. 59. London *Times,* August 6, 1861. 60. *B. & L.,* I, 193. 61. Carl Sandburg, *Abraham Lincoln, the War Years,* I, 301, 302. Hereafter Sandburg. 62. *O.R.,* II, 483. 63. *O.R.,* II, 532–533; Alexander, 45; Joseph Mills Hanson, *Bull Run Remembers: The History, Traditions, and Landmarks of the Manassas (Bull Run) Campaigns before Washington, 1861–1862,* 7. Hereafter Hanson. 64. *O.R.,* II, 478. 65. W. W. Blackford, *War Years with "Jeb" Stuart,* 27. Hereafter Blackford. 66. Mrs. Jackson, 178. 67. *S.H.S.P.,* XIX, 304 ff. 68. *Ibid.,* 303. 69. McGuire in Couper, IV, 66; Alexander, 42. 70. *O.R.,* II, 470 ff. 71. *Ibid.,* 484 ff. 72. Mrs. Jackson, 177–178. 73. *O.R.,* II, 481 ff. 74. Cook, 162. 75. Mrs. Jackson, 179 ff. 76. *O.R.,* II, 570. 77. Mrs. Jackson, 182.

CHAPTER 17

1. Casler, 47. 2. Mrs. Jackson, 179. 3. *Ibid.,* 185. 4. G. Moxley Sorrel, *Recollections of a Confederate Staff Officer,* 28 ff. Hereafter Sorrel. 5. Casler, 5. 6. Henderson, I, 175. 7. *Ibid.,* I, 176 ff. 8. Mrs. Jackson, 184. 9. *Ibid.,* 186. 10. *Ibid.,* 188. 11. *Ibid.,* 190, 191. 12. *Ibid.,* 193. 13. *Ibid.,* 197. 14. *Ibid.,* 199. 15. *B. & L.,* I, 238. 16. Mrs. Jackson, 194. 17. *Ibid.,* 179. 18. *Ibid.,* 182. 19. *Ibid.,* 183. 20. *Ibid.,* 195. 21. *Ibid.,* 197. 22. *O.R.,* V, 906. 23. *Ibid.,* 909. 24. Mrs. Jackson, 199. 25. Mrs. Jackson, 200. The spelling of "Sandy" is Jackson's. The Pendleton family spelled it "Sandie." 26. *O.R.,* V, 889, 898. 27. *Ibid.,* 92. 28. Casler, 59. 29. *O.R.,* V, 938. 30. *Ibid.,* 939. 31. Fishburne Narrative. 32. *O.R.,* V, 940. 33. *Ibid.* 34. *Ibid.,* 944. 35. *Ibid.* 36. *Ibid.,* 945. 37. *Ibid.,* 937. 38. *Ibid.,* 942. 39. *Ibid.,* 937. 40. *Ibid.,* 942. 41. *Ibid.,* 965. 42. *Ibid.,* 966. 43. *Ibid.,* 968. 44. *Ibid.,* 983. 45. *Ibid.,* 988. 46. *S.H.S.P.,* XXXXIII (New Series V), 120. 47. *O.R.,* V, 976.

48. *Ibid.*, 390.      49. *Ibid.*, 395.      50. *Ibid.*, 399.      51. Mrs. Jackson, 222.
52. *O.R.*, V, 399.      53. Mrs. Jackson, 206, 209.      54. *Ibid.*, 207.      55. *Ibid.*,
209.      56. *Ibid.*, 210, 211.      57. *Ibid.*, 212.      58. *Ibid.*      59. *Ibid.*, 213.
60. *Ibid.*, 214–215.      61. *Ibid.*      62. *Ibid.*      63. John H. Worsham, *One
of Jackson's Foot Cavalry*, 53. Hereafter Worsham.      64. Worsham, 54.

CHAPTER 18

1. *O.R.*, V, 390.      2. *Ibid.*, 1005.      3. *Ibid.*, 644.      4. *Ibid.*, 601.
5. Casler, 62.      6. *Ibid.*      7. Henderson, I, 190.      8. *O.R.*, V, 390.      9. *Ibid.*
10. *Ibid.*      11. *Ibid.*      12. *Ibid.*, 391.      13. *Ibid.*      14. *Ibid.*      15. *Ibid.*
16. *Ibid.*      17. Douglas, 23.      18. Richmond, Va., *Daily Dispatch*, January
15, 1862.      19. *O.R.*, V, 392.      20. Dabney, 268.      21. *O.R.*, V, 392.
22. *Ibid.*      23. *Ibid.*      24. Worsham, 59.      25. Casler, 62.      26. Worsham,
59.      27. *S.H.S.P.*, XXXVIII, 274.      28. "C.D.F." (Clement D. Fishburne)
in *S.H.S.P.*, XXIII, 128.      29. Richmond, Va., *Daily Dispatch*, January 15,
1862.      30. Allan in *S.H.S.P.*, XXXXIII, 131.      31. *O.R.*, V, 392.      32. *Ibid.*
33. *Ibid.*, 1033.      34. *Ibid.*, 1034.      35. Casler, 63.      36. *O.R.*, V, 1036.
37. Worsham, 61.      38. *O.R.*, V, 1033.      39. *Ibid.*, 1039.      40. *Ibid.*
41. Worsham, 63.      42. Dabney, 272.      43. *O.R.*, V, 1039.      44. Mrs.
Jackson, 237.      45. *O.R.*, V, 694.      46. *Ibid.*, 1043.      47. *Ibid.*, 1044.
48. *Ibid.*, 1040.      49. *O.R.*, 1042.      50. *O.R.*, 1046. Taliaferro said it was
written by Fulkerson. Taliaferro Papers.      51. *Ibid.*, 1048. Taliaferro said he
carried the document to Richmond and personally gave it to President Davis
"and explained personally at the request of Mr. Davis the true conditions of
affairs and the exact location of the troops on a map which he handed me.
He did not hesitate to say at once that Jackson had made a mistake." Letter of
Taliaferro to "Conrad," July 11, 1867, in Taliaferro Papers, pointed out to the
author by William B. Taliaferro of Norfolk, Va.      52. Dabney, 274, 275.
53. *O.R.*, V, 1049.      54. *Ibid.*, 1050.      55. *Ibid.*, 1051.      56. *Ibid.*, 1054.
57. *Ibid.*, 1059.      58. *Ibid.*, 1050.      59. *Ibid.*, 1053.      60. *Ibid.*      61. Richmond, Va., *Whig*, April 26, 1873.      62. *O.R.*, V, 1056.      63. *Ibid.*, 1059.
64. *Ibid.*, 1062.      65. *Ibid.*, 1060.      66. *Ibid.*, 1059; Robert D. Meade,
*Judah P. Benjamin—Confederate Statesman*, 217.      67. Douglas, 25.      68.
Mrs. Jackson—*Memoirs*, 496.      69. Mrs. Jackson, 233.      70. *O.R.*, V, 1062.
71. *Ibid.*, 1059.      72. *Ibid.*, 1064.      73. *Ibid.*, 1065.      74. *Ibid.*, 1070.
75. *Ibid.*, 1067, 1068.      76. *Ibid.*, 1076.      77. *Ibid.*      78. *Ibid.*, 1079.
79. *Ibid.*, 1071.      80. *Ibid.*, 1080; *Journal of Congress*, V, 13, 36.      81. *O.R.*,
V, 1080.      82. *Journal of Congress*, V, 36, 37.      83. *O.R.*, LI, pt. 1, 461.
84. *O.R.*, V, 1076.      85. *Ibid.*, 1079.      86. *Ibid.*, 966.      87. Allan in *S.H.S.P.*,
XXXXIII, 140.      88. *Ibid.*, 145.      89. Dabney, 250.      90. Henderson,
I, 183.      91. Mrs. Jackson, 170.      92. *Ibid.*      93. Douglas, 27.      94.
*Ibid.*, 28.

CHAPTER 19

1. *O.R.*, V, 41.      2. *Ibid.*, 45.      3. *Ibid.*, 50.      4. *Ibid.*, 56.      5. *Ibid.*
6. *Ibid.*, 57.      7. *Ibid.*, 56.      8. Dabney, 307.      9. *O.R.*, V, 1095.      10. *Ibid.*

11. Henderson, I, 219.    12. *Ibid.*, 228.    13. Mrs. Jackson, 240.    14. Mrs. Mary Anna Jackson (widow of Jackson), *Memoirs of Stonewall Jackson* (1895) 499 ff.; similar to *Life and Letters of General Thomas J. Jackson (Stonewall Jackson)* published in 1892, except that one chapter is omitted and sketches of contacts with Jackson and tributes by 15 Confederate officers and friends and two Englishmen are added at the end of the text. Hereafter Mrs. Jackson—*Memoirs*.    15. Henderson, I, 230.    16. Mrs. Jackson—*Memoirs*, 501. 17. Henderson, I, 230.    18. *Confederate Military History*, III, 216. Hereafter *C.M.H.*    19. *O.R.*, LI, pt. 2, 534.    20. *O.R.*, V, 1087.    21. *Ibid.*, 1092. 22. *Ibid.*, 56.    23. Allan in *S.H.S.P.*, XXXXIII, 146.    24. *O.R.*, XII, 380. 25. Worsham, 66.    26. Dabney, 312.    27. Allan in *S.H.S.P.*, XXXXIII, 156. 28. "C.D.F." (Clement D. Fishburne) in *S.H.S.P.*, XXIII, 130.    29. *O.R.*, XII, pt. 1, 383.    30. Worsham, 68.    31. *O.R.*, XII, pt. 1, 393. 32. "C.D.F.," *op. cit.*, 130 ff.    33. *O.R.*, XII, pt. 1, 398.    34. *Ibid.*, 376. 35. *Ibid.*, 374.    36. Worsham, 68.    37. Henderson, I, 244.    38. Casler, 67.    39. Mrs. Jackson, 246.    40. Henderson, I, 247.    41. Dabney, 324. 42. *O.R.*, XII, pt. 1, 340.    43. *Ibid.*, 341.    44. *Ibid.*, 342.    45. *Ibid.*, 231. 46. *B. & L.*, II, 168.    47. *O.R.*, XII, pt. 1, 5.    48. *Ibid.*, 234.    49. Henderson, I, 219.    50. *O.R.*, XII, pt. 1, 383.    51. *Ibid.*, 384.    52. *Ibid.*, 382. 53. The charges are in the R. B. Garnett Papers in the Confederate Museum, Richmond, Va.    54. Jackson's Letter Book, April 29, 1862.    55. Dabney, 320.    56. *Ibid.*, 321.    57. Mrs. Jackson, 247.    58. *Ibid.*    59. *Ibid.*, 248–249.    60. *Ibid.*, 249.

## CHAPTER 20

1. E. A. Moore, *The Story of a Cannoneer Under Stonewall Jackson*, 35. Hereafter Moore.    2. *O.R.*, XII, pt. 1, 336.    3. Allan in *S.H.S.P.*, XXXXIII, 168. 4. Howard, 84.    5. W. N. McDonald, *A History of the Laurel Brigade*, 50. Hereafter McDonald.    6. *O.R.*, XII, pt. 3, 843.    7. *Ibid.*, 844.    8. James Longstreet, *From Manassas to Appomattox*, 65. Hereafter Longstreet. 9. *O.R.*, XII, pt. 3, 835.    10. Dabney, 354.    11. *O.R.*, XII, pt. 3, 842. 12. *Ibid.*, 844–845.    13. Casler, 70.    14. Howard, 83.    15. Casler, 73. 16. Jackson's Letter Book, April 1, 1862.    17. Thomas C. Johnson, *Life and Letters of Robert Lewis Dabney*, 198 ff. Hereafter Johnson.    18. Johnson, 260.    19. *Ibid.*, 261–263.    20. *S.H.S.P.*, XII, 128 ff.    21. Johnson, 264. 22. *Ibid.*, 270.    23. *Ibid.*, 264.    24. Jackson said, *O.R.*, XII, pt. 3, 880, that they "sent in their resignations." Howard, 90, said Ashby "consented to Winder's retaining the resignation in his own hands at present."    25. Howard, 90.    26. *O.R.*, XII, pt. 3, 880.    27. Harman letters, Hotchkiss Papers, Box 14.    28. *O.R.*, XII, pt. 3, 853.    29. Douglas, 42, 47.    30. Douglas' account of this experience covers five pages in *I Rode with Stonewall*, 42–46, and is full of detail. It is not clear whether he carried one of the messages recorded in *O.R.*, XII, pt. 3, 883.    31. *O.R.*, XII, pt. 3, 94.    32. *Ibid.*, 99.    33. *Ibid.*, 106.    34. *Ibid.*    35. *Ibid.*, 112.    36. *Ibid.*, 107. 37. *Ibid.*, 111.    38. *Ibid.*, 118.    39. *Ibid.*, 122.    40. *Ibid.*, 125. 41. *Ibid.*, 859.    42. *Ibid.*, 862.    43. *Ibid.*, 863.    44. *Ibid.*    45.

*Ibid.*, 870.      46. *Ibid.*, 872.      47. *Ibid.*, 875.      48. *Ibid.*, 878.      49.
Allan in *S.H.S.P.*, XXXXIII, 181–182.      50. Moore, 45.      51. Howard,
91.      52. *O.R.*, XII, pt. 3, 119.      53. *Ibid.*, 126.      54. *Ibid.*, 135.      55.
*Ibid.*, 134.      56. *Ibid.*, 136.      57. *Ibid.*, 142.      58. *Ibid.*, 150.      59.
Dabney, 339.      60. Henderson, I, 287; Dabney, 340.      61. Couper, II,
146 ff., which contains correspondence between Jackson and Smith.      62.
*Ibid.*, 154.      63. Moore, 48.      64. *O.R.*, XII, pt. 1, 471.      65. Howard,
94.      66. *O.R.*, XII, pt. 1, 462.      67. Allan in *S.H.S.P.*, XXXXIII, 184.
68. *O.R.*, XII, pt. 1, 472.      69. *Ibid.*, 465, 467.      70. *Ibid.*, 466, 471.
71. *Ibid.*, 466.      72. Casler, 74.      73. *B. & L.*, II, 287.      74. Dabney, 352.
75. Howard, 98.      76. *Ibid.*, 100.      77. *Ibid.*      78. Allan in *S.H.S.P.*,
XXXXIII, 192.      79. Couper, II, 156–159.      80. Howard, 98.      81. Moore,
51.

CHAPTER 21

1. *O.R.*, XII, pt. 3, 844.      2. *Ibid.*, 201.      3. Percy Gatling Hamlin, *"Old
Bald Head" (General R. S. Ewell)*, 84, 85, 86. Hereafter Hamlin–*Ewell*.
4. R. S. Ewell, *The Making of a Soldier*, 108. Hereafter Ewell.      5. Dabney,
359.      6. *O.R.*, XII, pt. 3, 897.      7. *Ibid.*, 892–893.      8. Mrs. Jackson, 257–
258.      9. Taylor, 36, 47–48.      10. Confederate Records, Vol. 7, Chapter II,
9–11, National Archives.      11. *O.R.*, XII, pt. 3, 898.      12. *Ibid.*, 897.
13. *Ibid.*, 898.      14. Freeman–*LL*, I, 371.      15. *Ibid.*      16. *B. & L.*, II,
371.      17. Douglas, 51–52, Louis A. Sigaud in *Belle Boyd, Confederate Spy*
(hereafter Sigaud), and Belle Boyd in *Belle Boyd in Camp and Prison* (hereafter Boyd) vary in details.      18. Dabney, 366.      19. Taylor, 53.
20. *S.H.S.P.*, XXIV, 131.      21. *O.R.*, XII, pt. 1, 702.      22. Dabney, 368.
23. *O.R.*, XII, pt. 1, 557.      24. Allan in *S.H.S.P.*, XXXXIII, 211.      25. *O.R.*,
XII, pt. 1, 703.      26. Taylor, 54.      27. This account of Banks' action is based
principally on F. H. Harrington, *Fighting Politician–Major General N. P. Banks*,
70 ff. Hereafter *Banks*.      28. *O.R.*, XII, pt. 1, 703.      29. Dabney, 370, 371.
30. *O.R.*, XII, pt. 1, 590.      31. Dabney, 371.      32. *O.R.*, XII, pt. 3, 703.
33. *Ibid.*, pt. 1, 899.      34. *Ibid.*, pt. 3, 573.      35. *Ibid.*, pt. 1, 899.      36. *Ibid.*,
pt. 3, 704.      37. Douglas, 55.      38. Worsham, 84.      39. *O.R.*, XII, pt. 3,
704.      40. Dabney, 373.      41. *O.R.*, XII, pt. 3, 595.      42. *Ibid.*, 754.
43. Moore, 55.      44. Taylor, 56.      45. Douglas, 57.      46. Taylor, 56.
47. Dabney, 375.      48. *O.R.*, XII, pt. 1, 726.      49. Allan in *S.H.S.P.*,
XXXXIII, 225–227.      50. *O.R.*, XII, pt. 1, 735.      51. Dabney, 377.
52. Dabney, 378; *O.R.*, XII, pt. 1, 755.      53. Taylor, 57.      54. Allan in
*S.H.S.P.*, XXXXIII, 228.      55. Taylor, 57.      56. Worsham, 87.      57. Taylor,
59.      58. Douglas, 59.      59. *O.R.*, XII, pt. 3, 617.      60. Dabney, 380.
61. *O.R.*, XII, pt. 3, 706.      62. Worsham, 88.      63. *O.R.*, XII, pt. 3, 617.
64. *Ibid.*, pt. 1, 238.      65. Dabney, 380.      66. Taylor, 59.      67. *Banks*, 77.
68. *Ibid.*, 78.      69. Mrs. Jackson, 265.      70. Dabney, 384.      71. *S.H.S.P.*,
XXX, 230 ff.      72. Allan in *S.H.S.P.*, XXXXIII, 235.      73. *Ibid.*, 234.

CHAPTER 22

1. *O.R.*, XII, pt. 1, 281.　2. *Ibid.*, 282.　3. *Ibid.*, pt. 3, 219.　4. *Ibid.*, pt. 1, 10.　5. *Ibid.*, pt. 3, 219.　6. *Ibid.*, 220.　7. *Ibid.*, 221.　8. *Ibid.*, 222. 9. *Ibid.*, 844.　10. *Ibid.*, 892–893.　11. *Ibid.*, 222.　12. *Ibid.*, 231. 13. *Ibid.*, 241.　14. *Ibid.*, 235.　15. *Ibid.*, 243.　16. *Ibid.*, 248. 17. *Ibid.*, 267.　18. *Ibid.*, pt. 1, 11.　19. Howard, 114.　20. A. R. Boteler in *S.H.S.P.*, XXXX, 165. Hereafter Boteler.　21. Allan in *S.H.S.P.*, XXXXIII, 249.　22. Douglas, 66.　23. Hotchkiss Diary, May 31, 1862. 24. Taylor, 61.　25. Harman letters in Hotchkiss Papers, Box 14.　26. *Ibid.*　27. *Ibid.*　28. Allan, 252.　29. Taylor, 61, 63.　30. *Ibid.*, 61. 31. *Ibid.*, 65.　32. *O.R.*, XII, pt. 3, 293.　33. *Ibid.*, 290.　34. Allan in *S.H.S.P.*, XXXXIII, 254, 255.　35. Casler, 80.　36. *Ibid.*, 80, 81. 37. Howard, 116.　38. Mrs. Jackson, 268.　39. *O.R.*, XII, pt. 1, 14; *Ibid.*, 730.　40. *Ibid.*, 731; *Ibid.*, 15.　41. *Ibid.*, 731.　42. Douglas, 73. 43. *Ibid.*, 71.　44. *O.R.*, XII, pt. 3, 316.　45. *Ibid.*, pt. 1, 14. 46. Douglas, 75.　47. The details of this relationship are found in Harman's letters to his brother, copies of which are in the Hotchkiss Papers, Box 14, Library of Congress.　48. Worsham, 96.　49. Douglas, 81.　50. *O.R.*, XII, pt. 1, 712.　51. Allan in *S.H.S.P.*, XXXXIII, 264.　52. Dabney, 402. 53. Henderson, I, 362.　54. *O.R.*, XII, pt. 3, 710.　55. *Ibid.*, 905. 56. *Ibid.*, 907.　57. *Ibid.*　58. *Ibid.*　59. *Ibid.*, 908.

CHAPTER 23

1. *O.R.*, XII, pt. 1, 781, 782.　2. The hour was reported variously, from 7 to 10 A.M. by Douglas, Howard, Winder, Hotchkiss.　3. *O.R.*, XII, pt. 3, 335. 4. Allan in *S.H.S.P.*, XXXXIII, 271.　5. *O.R.*, XII, pt. 1, 19.　6. The best description is in Trimble's report, *O.R.*, XII, pt. 1, 795.　7. *Ibid.*, 797. 8. *Ibid.*, 798.　9. Hamlin–*Ewell*, 104.　10. Dabney, 418.　11. Taylor, 73. 12. Kenneth P. Williams, *Lincoln Finds a General*, I, 202. Hereafter Williams. 13. Freeman–*LL*, I, 446.　14. Williams, I, 202.　15. Hamlin–*Ewell*, 104. 16. Howard, 123 ff.　17. Freeman–*LL*, I, 447.　18. *O.R.*, XII, pt. 1, 714. 19. Dabney, 415.　20. *Ibid.*　21. Dabney, 420.　22. *Ibid.*, 421. 23. *Ibid.*, 419.　24. *B. & L.*, II, 293.　25. *O.R.*, XII, pt. 1, 740.　26. Allan in *S.H.S.P.*, XXXXIII, 281, counted 1,138.　27. *O.R.*, XV, 690.　28. Taylor, 75, 76.　29. *Ibid.*, 75.　30. *Ibid.*, 76.　31. *Ibid.*　32. *O.R.*, XII, pt. 1, 687.　33. *Ibid.*, 23.　34. Douglas, 91.　35. Alexander, 107.　36. *O.R.*, XII, pt. 3, 354.　37. *Ibid.*　38. Henderson, I, 392.　39. Dabney, 429, 430. 40. Mrs. Jackson, 283–284.　41. *O.R.*, XII, pt. 1, 24.　42. *Ibid.*, 685. 43. *Ibid.*, pt. 3, 372.　44. *Ibid.*, 377.　45. *Ibid.*, 382.　46. *Ibid.*, 391. 47. *Ibid.*, 395.　48. *Ibid.*, 396.　49. *Ibid.*, 379.　50. *Ibid.*, 392.　51. *Ibid.*, pt. 1, 288.　52. *Ibid.*, pt. 3, 910.　53. Hamlin–*Ewell*, 104.

CHAPTER 24

1. *B. & L.*, II, 170.　2. *O.R.*, XI, 51.　3. *B. & L.*, II, 175.　4. *Ibid.*, 173. 5. *Lee's Dispatches*, edited by D. S. Freeman, 5, 6. Hereafter *Lee's Dispatches*.

6. *O.R.*, XII, pt. 3, 906.     7. *Ibid.*     8. *Ibid.*     9. *Ibid.*, 910.     10. *Ibid.*, 908.     11. Lee's Papers in Duke University Library, Durham, N. C. 12. Boteler, 150 ff.     13. *Ibid.*, 162 ff.     14. *Ibid.*, 173–174.     15. Lee's Papers, *op. cit.*     16. *O.R.*, XII, pt. 3, 913.     17. *Ibid.*     18. *O.R.*, XI, pt. 3, 590.     19. Dabney, 433.     20. *O.R.*, XII, pt. 3, 912.     21. *Ibid.*, 914. 22. *Ibid.*     23. *B. & L.*, II, 297.     24. Dabney, 435.     25. *B. & L.*, II, 348. In Dabney, 434, this talk is reported by Dabney to have taken place in Charlottesville; but Boteler's description of Jackson's passage through Charlottesville on a train (*S.H.S.P.*, XXXX, 150 ff.) makes the Charlottesville location unlikely.     26. Douglas, 97.     27. *Ibid.*, 98.     28. *B. & L.*, II, 348. 29. Dabney, 435.     30. Douglas, 98.     31. Howard, 133.     32. The quoted passages and the descriptive adjectives are all from Douglas, 98.     33. Boteler, 174 ff.     34. *B. & L.*, II, 349.     35. Henderson, I, 395.     36. *Ibid.*, 396. 37. This is the report of Harman to Hotchkiss who recorded it in his diary, April 15, 1863. Dabney said (Dabney, 435) that only one courier went with the General.     38. *B. & L.*, II, 347.     39. Longstreet, 121.     40. Freeman—*LL*, I, 497.     41. *B. & L.*, II, 347.     42. *Ibid.*     43. In a period about which the evidence is scant, a useful source is the memorandum prepared by Dabney after the war and now included among the Hotchkiss Papers, Box 13. Hereafter Dabney Memorandum.     44. Dabney Memorandum.     45. Douglas, 99. 46. Freeman's examination, *LL*, I, 500, led him to conclude that this was prepared during the Dabb house conference or was written later by Jackson for his own use.     47. Freeman—*LL*, I, 498.     48. Douglas, 101.     49. *O.R.*, XI, pt. 2, 499.     50. Freeman—*LL*, 500, traces events of June 24 to show the probability that the order did not reach Jackson until midnight or 1 A.M. 51. Dabney Memorandum.     52. Douglas, 100.     53. Dabney, 440. 54. J. W. Thomason, *"Jeb" Stuart*, 172. Hereafter Thomason.     55. Richmond *Whig*, June 16, 1862.     56. *O.R.*, XI, pt. 2, 514.     57. Dabney, 439. 58. *O.R.*, XI, pt. 1, 48.     59. *Ibid.*     60. *Ibid.*, 49.     61. *Ibid.*, 51. 62. Dabney, 440.     63. Dabney Memorandum.     64. Douglas, 101. 65. *O.R.*, XI, pt. 2, 562.     66. Freeman—*LL*, I, 508.     67. *O.R.*, XI, pt. 3, 620.     68. Douglas, 100.     69. Blackford, 71.     70. *Ibid.*     71. *O.R.*, XI, pt. 2, 562, 514.     72. Dabney Memorandum.     73. *O.R.*, XI, pt. 2, 553. 74. *Ibid.*, 562.     75. *Ibid.*, 614.     76. *Ibid.*, 835.     77. *Ibid.*     78. Henderson, II, 16.     79. *O.R.*, XI, pt. 2, 623.     80. Porter's figures are given by him in *B. & L.*, II, 331. The figure of 1,350 is from Alexander, 121, and Porter is authority for "nearly 2,000." Confederate reports generally show casualties for the entire Seven Days rather than individual engagements.     81. Freeman— *Lee*, II, 123.     82. *Ibid.*, 566 ff. This is an analysis of unusual perspicacity and importance. Freeman gave special credit to Col. H. O. Landers, U.S. Army, for his interpretation of Jackson's reasoning.     83. *B. & L.*, II, 331.     84. *O.R.*, XI, pt. 2, 552, 553.     85. *Ibid.*, 560, 622.     86. Boteler, 179.     87. *O.R.*, XI, pt. 2, 835.

## CHAPTER 25

1. Alexander, 129.  2. *B. & L.*, II, 353.  3. Dabney, 443.  4. *B. & L.*, II, 337; Henderson, II, 27, puts the figure at 36,000.  5. *O.R.*, XI, pt. 2, 836. 6. *Ibid.*, 492.  7. Dabney, 443.  8. *O.R.*, XI, pt. 2, 554.  9. Henderson, II, 30.  10. *O.R.*, XI, pt. 2, 757.  11. Douglas, 102.  12. *O.R.*, XI, pt. 2, 615.  13. Henderson, II, 33.  14. *Ibid.*, 34.  15. *O.R.*, XI, pt. 2, 563. 16. *Ibid.*, 595.  17. Dabney, 484.  18. John Esten Cooke, *Life of General Robert E. Lee*, 84. Hereafter Cooke—*Lee*.  19. *S.H.S.P.*, X, 150.  20. Dabney, 455.  21. *O.R.*, XI, pt. 2, 626.  22. *B. & L.*, II, 340.  23. John B. Hood, *Advance and Retreat*, 25. Hereafter Hood.  24. Dabney, 454. 25. *B. & L.*, II, 359.  26. Williams, I, 233.  27. *Ibid.*, 230.  28. *O.R.*, XI, pt. 2, 230.  29. Sorrel, 82.  30. *O.R.*, XI, pt. 2, 274.  31. *Ibid.*, 494. 32. Dabney Memorandum.  33. *Ibid.*  34. *Ibid.*  35. J. W. Jones in *S.H.S.P.*, IX, 564; Freeman—*LL*, I, 561; Henderson, II, 47.  36. *O.R.*, II, 627.  37. Casler, 92.  38. *O.R.*, XI, pt. 2, 663.  39. *Ibid.*, 675.  40. *Ibid.* 41. *Ibid.*, 571, 591.  42. *O.R.*, XI, pt. 2, 518.  43. *Ibid.*, 517.  44. Dabney, 459.  45. *Ibid.*, 461.  46. *Ibid.*, 665.  47. Henderson, II, 49–50. 48. Worsham, 103.  49. *S.H.S.P.*, XXI, 22.  50. Mrs. Jackson, 298. 51. *Ibid.*, 297.  52. *B. & L.*, II, 387.  53. Crutchfield reported 23 guns; Jackson, 28; D. H. Hill, 31, all in their battle reports.  54. *O.R.*, XI, pt. 2, 55. 55. *B. & L.*, II, 388.  56. *Ibid.*, 389.  57. *O.R.*, XI, pt. 2, 566.  58. Henderson, II, 53.  59. Alexander, 149.  60. Henderson, II, 51.  61. *O.R.*, XI, pt. 2, 811.  62. *B. & L.*, II, 378, 381.  63. Alexander, 151.  64. *O.R.*, XI, pt. 2, 557.  65. Howard, 148.  66. Freeman—*Lee*, II, 580.  67. Dabney, 467.  68. Henderson, II, 57.  69. McGuire in Henderson, II, 57. 70. Freeman—*Lee*, II, 574.  71. Freeman—*LL*, II, 574.  72. See Freeman—*Lee*, II, 572, for detailed description of those theories.  73. Freeman—*LL*, I, 500, 501.  74. Dabney, 466.  75. Freeman—*Lee*, II, 580. 76. Mrs. Jackson, 301.  77. Freeman—*Lee*, II, 200, 201.  78. *O.R.*, XI, pt. 2, 667.  79. *B. & L.*, II, 391.  80. *Ibid.*, 390.  81. *O.R.*, XI, pt. 2, 536.  82. Longstreet, 144.  83. *O.R.*, XI, pt. 2, 677.  84. Alexander, 159.  85. *B. & L.*, II, 393.  86. *Ibid.*, 394.  87. *Ibid.*  88. *O.R.*, XI, pt. 2, 557.  89. *Ibid.*, 628.  90. Douglas, 108; *O.R.*, XI, pt. 2, 597. 91. *B. & L.*, II, 392.  92. Dabney, 471.  93. W. C. Oakes, *The War Between the Union and the Confederacy*, 143.  94. Douglas, 109.  95. Blackford, 78.  96. *Ibid.*, 76.  97. Dabney, 473.  98. Blackford, 80–82. 99. McGuire in *S.H.S.P.*, XIX, 304.  100. Davis, II, 150.  101. Dabney as quoted in Henderson, II, 71.  102. Alexander, 71.  103. *O.R.*, XI, pt. 2, 37.  104. *Ibid.*, 497.  105. *Ibid.*, 559.

## CHAPTER 26

1. Worsham, 104.  2. *Ibid.*, 105.  3. Moore, 94.  4. All details and the quoted language of the Jackson-Boteler interview and reconnaissance are based on *S.H.S.P.*, XXXX, 180 ff., and the quoted language is Boteler's.  5. *B. & L.*, II, 449.  6. *O.R.*, XII, pt. 3, 473.  7. *Ibid.*, pt. 2, 50.  8. *Ibid.*, 51.

9. *Ibid.*, 52.    10. Douglas, 113.    11. *Ibid.*, 114.    12. *Ibid.*, 115.
13. *Ibid.*, 116.    14. *B. & L.*, II, 368.    15. Douglas, 119.    16. Mrs. Jackson, 302; Dabney, 489; Peyton Harrison Hoge, *Moses Drury Hoge: Life and Letters*, 165. Hereafter Hoge.    17. Douglas, 119.    18. *S.H.S.P.*, XIX, 313.
19. Mrs. Jackson, 302.    20. Hoge, 166.    21. Ewell, 116.    22. Mrs. Jackson, 302.    23. Henderson, II, 82.    24. Hotchkiss Diary, July 18, 1862 (inserted in the diary by Sandie Pendleton).    25. Mrs. Jackson, 322.
26. *Ibid.*, 323.    27. *Ibid.*, 324.    28. *O.R.*, XII, pt. 3, 919.    29. *Ibid.*
30. *Ibid.*    31. *Ibid.*, 918.    32. Worsham, 108.    33. All these details are from the Hotchkiss Diary, August 3, 1862.    34. *O.R.*, XII, pt. 3, 926.
35. Hotchkiss Papers, Box 8.    36. *Ibid.*    37. Pendleton Papers. Southern Historical Collection, University of North Carolina.    38. R. B. Garnett Papers.
39. *O.R.*, XII, pt. 3, 924.    40. Howard, 163.    41. Hotchkiss Diary, August 7, 1862.    42. *O.R.*, XII, pt. 2, 214.    43. Letter of McGuire, June 27, 1896, in Hotchkiss Papers, Box 12.    44. *O.R.*, XII, pt. 2, 215.    45. *Ibid.*, 200.
46. *Ibid.*, 205.    47. Freeman—*Lee*, II, 264.    48. Banks said later that Brig. Gen. B. S. Roberts, a staff officer sent up by Pope, goaded him. Roberts, said Banks, disliked "political generals" and told Banks, "There must be no backing out this day." *Banks*, 81.    49. Moore, 98.    50. *O.R.*, XII, pt. 2, 200.
51. *Ibid.*    52. *Ibid.*, 227.    53. *S.H.S.P.*, XIX, 314.    54. *O.R.*, XII, pt. 2, 201.    55. *Ibid.*    56. *Ibid.*, 206.    57. *Ibid.*, 202.    58. Worsham, 113.
59. Early, 99.    60. Dabney, 501.    61. Henderson, II, 95.    62. *O.R.*, XII, pt. 2, 198.    63. Lieut. Col. Louis H. D. Crane, Third Wisconsin, as reported in Casler, 104.    64. *O.R.*, XII, pt. 2, 197.    65. Douglas, 124.    66. *B. & L.*, II, 459.    67. *O.R.*, XII, pt. 2, 141.    68. *Ibid.*, 232.    69. *Ibid.*, 184.
70. *Ibid.*, 206.    71. Mrs. Jackson, 326.    72. *O.R.*, XII, pt. 2, 184.
73. *Ibid.*, 183.    74. Casler, 148.    75. *O.R.*, XII, pt. 3, 564.    76. Hotchkiss Diary, August 12, 13, 1862.    77. Mrs. Jackson, 326.    78. Hotchkiss Diary, August 10, 1862.    79. *O.R.*, XII, pt. 2, 185.    80. *Ibid.*, 133–135.
81. *Ibid.*, 185.    82. *O.R.*, XII, pt. 3, 653.    83. These reports are in *O.R.*, XII, pt. 2.    84. *O.R.*, XII, pt. 3, 928.    85. *O.R.*, XI, pt. 3, 674.    86. *Ibid.*, XII, pt. 2, 77.    87. *Ibid.*, XI, pt. 3, 675.    88. *Ibid.*, 674.    89. *Ibid.*, 677.

CHAPTER 27

1. *O.R.*, XII, pt. 3, 940.    2. White, 177.    3. *O.R.*, XII, pt. 2, 726; Heros von Borcke, *Memoirs of the Confederate War for Independence*. Hereafter von Borcke.    4. *O.R.*, XII, pt. 2, 580.    5. Hotchkiss Diary, August 17, 1862.
6. Moore, 103; Hotchkiss in his diary, August 19, 1862, said the execution was on August 19.    7. Ewell, 123.    8. Hotchkiss Diary, August 20, 1862.
9. *O.R.*, XII, pt. 2, 552 ff.    10. *Ibid.*, 605, 719.    11. *Ibid.*, 795.    12. *Ibid.*, 642.    13. Douglas, 130.    14. *S.H.S.P.*, XIV, 183.    15. Hotchkiss Diary, August 24, 1862.    16. *O.R.*, XII, pt. 2, 731.    17. *Ibid.*, pt. 3, 603.
18. *Ibid.*, pt. 2, 553.    19. Henderson, II, 124.    20. Douglas, 132.
21. *O.R.*, XII, pt. 2, 553.    22. *Ibid.*, 642.    23. William Allan, *The Army of Northern Virginia in 1862*, 200.    24. *O.R.*, XII, pt. 2, 650.    25. Henderson, II, 125. The cattle are a mystery. The accounts of the march do not men-

tion them.    26. Worsham, 118; *B. & L.*, II, 532.    27. Mrs. Jackson, 331.
28. Taliaferro in *B. & L.*, II, 502. But in Ewell, 123, it is said there was "a
poor but adequate bridge."    29. Dabney, 517.    30. *O.R.*, XII, pt. 3, 653–
655; Williams, 290 ff.    31. Williams, 292.    32. *O.R.*, XII, pt. 3, 669, 671,
672.    33. *Ibid.*, 675.    34. In later times called The Plains.    35. Allen C.
Redwood, *Scribner's Magazine*, Vol. 18 (May and October, 1879), 228 ff.
Hereafter Redwood.    36. Redwood, 228.    37. Blackford, 108 ff.    38. *O.R.*,
XII, pt. 2, 734.    39. Blackford, 111.    40. Douglas, 135.    41. *Ibid.*, 129.
42. *O.R.*, XII, pt. 2, 720.    43. *Ibid.*, 643.    44. *Ibid.*    45. *Ibid.*, 644.
46. Worsham, 120.    47. *Ibid.*, 121.    48. Casler, 107.    49. *Ibid.*, 108.
50. *B. & L.*, II, 529.    51. All these are mentioned in various reports of the
day.    52. *O.R.*, XII, pt. 2, 644.    53. Dabney, 520.    54. Hotchkiss Diary,
April 15, 1863.    55. *B. & L.*, II, 505.    56. *Ibid.*, 506.    57. Ewell, 125 ff.
58. *Ibid.*, 125, 126.    59. *O.R.*, XII, pt. 2, 35–36, 71–72.    60. Alexander,
196.    61. *O.R.*, XII, pt. 1, 328.    62. *Ibid.*, pt. 2, 360.    63. *Ibid.*, 670.
64. *Ibid.*, pt. 3, 645.    65. This description and the episode following are
based on Blackford, 116, 118–119.    66. *O.R.*, XII, pt. 2, 380.    67. The
quotation and the whole scene are from Blackford, 120.    68. There is an
excellent account of this battle in Bruce Catton, *Mr. Lincoln's Army*, 17 ff.
Hereafter Catton–*Lincoln*.    69. Hanson, 112.    70. *O.R.*, XII, pt. 2, 657.
71. *Ibid.*, 667. Alexander estimated Jackson's total loss at 1,200.    72. *Ibid.*,
645.    73. *Ibid.*, 671.    74. von Borcke, I, 148.    75. *O.R.*, XII, pt. 2, 439.
76. *S.H.S.P.*, XIX, 307.    77. Freeman–*Lee*, II, 319; *B. & L.*, II, 518, 527.
78. *B. & L.*, II, 534, 536; *O.R.*, XII, pt. 2, 669, 701; Worsham, 132.
79. Douglas, 137–138.    80. *Ibid.*    81. *Ibid.*    82. *O.R.*, XII, pt. 2, 687.
83. *Ibid.*, 687–688.    84. Alexander, 203.    85. McGuire in Couper, IV,
78–79.    86. *O.R.*, XVIII, 741.    87. Freeman–*Lee*, II, 330.    88. *B. & L.*,
II, 500.    89. Alexander, 211.    90. *Ibid.*    91. *O.R.*, XII, pt. 2, 658, 663.
92. Moore, 120.    93. *Ibid.*, 121.    94. Hanson, 120.    95. *Ibid.*, 119–120.
96. *O.R.*, XII, pt. 2, 647.    97. *Ibid.*, 666.    98. Casler, 112.    99. Hanson,
129.    100. *B. & L.*, II, 521.    101. *O.R.*, XII, pt. 2, 566.    102. Douglas,
142.    103. Hotchkiss Diary, September 1, 1862.    104. The story is told
by McGuire, Worsham, and others, and McGuire said the officer was A. P.
Hill. *S.H.S.P.*, XIX, 311.    105. Douglas, 144.    106. Sandburg, I, 533.
107. Alexander, 219; Hanson, 149, lists 109 Confederates missing.    108. Mrs.
Jackson, 341.    109. *O.R.*, XII, pt. 2, 648.

CHAPTER 28

1. *B. & L.*, II, 605.    2. Worsham, 137; Bradley Johnson in *S.H.S.P.*, XII,
507.    3. *B. & L.*, II, 621.    4. [John Esten Cooke.] *The Life of Stonewall
Jackson*, by a Virginian, 195. Hereafter *"Virginian's"–Jackson*.    5. Freeman–*LL*, II, 720.    6. Hotchkiss Diary, September 3, 1862.    7. Ellsworth
Eliot, Jr., *West Point in the Confederacy*, 244.    8. Hotchkiss Papers, Box 8.
9. *S.H.S.P.*, XII, 503.    10. Dabney, 545.    11. Hotchkiss Diary, September
5, 1862.    12. Freeman–*LL*, II, 154; *"Virginian's"–Jackson*, 196.    13. *B. & L.*,
I, 238.    14. Hotchkiss Diary, September 5, 1862.    15. Alexander Hunter

in *S.H.S.P.*, XII, 507.     16. *S.H.S.P.*, X, 508.     17. *Ibid.*, 510.     18. Hotchkiss Diary, September 6, 1862.     19. Freeman—*LL*, II, 159.     20. Dabney,
149.     21. Douglas, 150.     22. Mrs. Jackson, 346.     23. *Ibid.*     24. *B. & L.*,
II, 621.     25. Alexander Hunter in *S.H.S.P.*, X, 508.     26. Sandburg, I, 544.
27. *B. & L.*, II, 663.     28. Dabney, in Dabney, 549, said Jackson favored
leaving Harper's Ferry alone for the present, concentrating the army in a
good position and fighting McClellan as he advanced. But Longstreet (*B. & L.*,
II, 663) said flatly that Jackson approved the Harper's Ferry operation, and
Walker (*Ibid.*, 606) intimated as much.     29. *B. & L.*, II, 663.     30. *O.R.*,
XIX, pt. 2, 603–604.     31. This copy is in the possession of the North Carolina
Historical Commission, Raleigh, N. C.     32. *S.H.S.P.*, VII, 435.     33. *Ibid.*,
II, 514.     34. *O.R.*, XIX, pt. 1, 219.     35. *Ibid.*, 233.     36. *Ibid.*, 785.
37. Douglas, 152.     38. *Ibid.*     39. *Ibid.*     40. *B. & L.*, II, 595; Henderson,
II, 243.     41. Hotchkiss Diary, September 11, 1862.     42. *S.H.S.P.*, X, 531.
43. Freeman—*Lee*, II, 366.     44. Douglas, 156.     45. *Ibid.*, 157. Other details from the same source, from Hotchkiss Diary, September 12, 1862, and
Dabney, 551.     46. Hotchkiss Diary, September 12, 1862.     47. The defense
was badly handled, and Col. Thomas H. Ford was pronounced later by a
military commission to be unqualified for command.     48. *B. & L.*, II, 665.
49. *Ibid.*, 603.     50. Catton—*Lincoln*, 223. The quotation is from Brig. Gen.
John Gibbon, *Personal Recollections of the Civil War*.     51. Freeman—*LL*,
II, Appendix I.     52. *O.R.*, XIX, pt. 2, 607.     53. Walker stated, *B. & L.*, II,
609, that Jackson signaled him that he would give 24 hours for removal of non-
combatants, but Johnson and Douglas argue (*Ibid.*, 615, 617) that he had no
such idea.     54. *O.R.*, XIX, pt. 1, 958.     55. *Ibid.*, 953.     56. *B. & L.*, II,
609.     57. *O.R.*, XIX, pt. 1, 954.     58. *B. & L.*, II, 559 ff.     59. *O.R.*, XIX,
pt. 1, 374 ff.     60. *Ibid.*, LI, pt. 2, 618.     61. *Ibid.*, XIX, pt. 1, 951.
62. *Ibid.*, 954.     63. *B. & L.*, II, 613.     64. *O.R.*, XIX, pt. 1, 539.     65. *Ibid.*,
743.     66. *Ibid.*, 955.     67. *Ibid.*, 951.     68. *Ibid.*, 549.     69. *Ibid.*, 548.
70. Hotchkiss wrote of that day: "Jackson intended to advance and storm the
place today, after demanding surrender, but he did not advance; why, I know
not." Hotchkiss Diary, September 14, 1862.     71. *O.R.*, XIX, pt. 1, 954.
72. *Ibid.*, 818.     73. Douglas, 162.     74. *O.R.*, XIX, pt. 1, 958, 980.
75. *B. & L.*, II, 627.     76. Mrs. Jackson, 352.     77. D. X. Junkin, D.D., *The
Reverend George Junkin, D.D., LL.D.*, 552, 554–555.     78. *B. & L.*, II, 611.
79. *O.R.*, XIX, pt. 1, 955.     80. *Ibid.*, 923, 955.     81. *B. & L.*, II, 631.
82. Henderson, II, 241.     83. Freeman—*LL*, II, 717.     84. *O.R.*, XIX, pt.
1, 218.     85. Catton—*Lincoln*, 291.     86. Alexander, 259.     87. *O.R.*, XII,
pt. 1, 1023.     88. *Ibid.*, 1024.     89. *Ibid.*, 956.     90. *B. & L.*, II, 669.
91. *Ibid.*, 629.     92. The number has to be estimated from reports covering
the whole campaign.     93. S. D. Lee reported (Henderson, II, 262) that on
the night of the 17th Jackson favored retreat across the Potomac immediately.
But the S. D. Lee account is open to some doubt as Freeman has shown
(Freeman—*Lee*, II, 404). It would have been strikingly out of character, as
pointed out in Douglas, 179, for Jackson to have advocated retreat then.
94. Douglas, 169.     95. Moore, 151.     96. *Pendleton*, 216.     97. Dabney,

565. 98. *Histories of the Several Regiments and Battalions from North Carolina in the Great War, 1861–65,* II, 604. Hereafter N. C. Regiments. 99. This is a direct quotation from Sandburg, I, 551. 100. Henderson, II, 256. 101. *Ibid.,* 259. 102. Douglas, 173. 103. *Ibid.* 104. *Ibid.,* 174, 176. 105. Freeman concluded that in the account the memory of S. D. Lee had become somewhat confused (Freeman–*LL,* II, 221). But S. D. Lee's account is so detailed and precise, and is not contradicted by known evidence, that in substance it does not seem impossible. Henderson, Alexander and others accept it. 106. Douglas, 180. 107. Hotchkiss Diary, September 18, 1862. 108. Douglas, 180. 109. *B. & L.,* II, 682. 110. *O.R.,* XIX, pt. 1, 982. 111. *Ibid.,* 831 ff. 112. Mrs. Jackson, 358; Henderson, II, 269; Freeman–*LL,* II, 233. 113. Mrs. Jackson, 358. 114. Douglas, 184; Henderson, II, 269. 115. *O.R.,* XIX, pt. 1, 982. 116. *Ibid.,* 957. 117. *Ibid.,* 204. 118. Hotchkiss Diary, September 21, 1862. 119. General Orders, No. 116, dated October 2, 1862; *"Virginian's"–Jackson,* 217.

CHAPTER 29

1. *O.R.,* XIX, pt. 2, 629. 2. Henderson, II, 275. 3. *O.R.,* XIX, pt. 2, 656. 4. Alexander, 280. Henderson's calculation for November 1 is 71,809. 5. *O.R.,* XIX, pt. 2, 718. 6. *Ibid.,* 630. 7. Freeman–*Lee,* II, 416. 8. Mrs. Jackson, 365. 9. *O.R.,* XIX, pt. 2, 643. 10. *Ibid.,* 698. 11. Jackson's Letter Book, Hotchkiss Papers, Box 8. 12. Howard, 180. 13. Mrs. Jackson, 362. 14. *Ibid.,* 363. 15. Jackson Papers, September 24, 1862. 16. *O.R.,* XIX, pt. 2, 731. 17. *Ibid.,* 733. 18. *Ibid.,* 730. 19. *Ibid.,* 731. 20. Sandburg, I, 582 ff. 21. Douglas, 193. 22. von Borcke, II, 295. 23. Mrs. Jackson, 361. 24. *S.H.S.P.,* XXXX, 22. 25. Douglas, 192. 26. Published in *The North American Review,* May–September (exclusive of June), 1889. 27. Henderson, II, 280. 28. Sigaud, 104. 29. Dabney, 584. 30. *Ibid.,* 588. 31. *O.R.,* XIX, pt. 2, 626, 627. 32. Hotchkiss Diary, October 7, 1862. 33. Sandburg, I, 599. 34. Worsham, 149. 35. Charles M. Blackford, *Letters from Lee's Army,* 130. Hereafter Blackford–*Lee.* 36. *O.R.,* XIX, pt. 2, 412. 37. Hotchkiss Diary, November 3, 1862. 38. Worsham, 149. 39. *O.R.,* XIX, pt. 1, 87. 40. *Ibid.,* pt. 2, 685. 41. *Ibid.,* 697. 42. *Ibid.,* 696. 43. *Ibid.,* 704. 44. Hotchkiss Diary, November 6, 1862. 45. *O.R.,* XIX, pt. 2, 705. 46. *Ibid.,* pt. 1, 983. 47. *Ibid.,* 712. 48. *Ibid.,* pt. 2, 715. 49. *Ibid.,* 717. 50. *Ibid.,* 720. 51. Hotchkiss Diary, November 19, 1862. 52. *O.R.,* XIX, pt. 2, 572. 53. *Ibid.,* 577–586 for messages on this episode. 54. Henderson, II, 302. 55. *O.R.,* XXI, 830. 56. *Ibid.,* 1018. 57. *Ibid.,* 1021. 58. *Ibid.,* 1027. 59. *Ibid.,* 1029. 60. Mrs. Jackson, 372. 61. This whole account is taken from Mrs. Jackson, 372–373. 62. *S.H.S.P.,* XXXX, 24. 63. Hotchkiss Diary, November 24, 1862. 64. Worsham, 151. 65. *S.H.S.P.,* XIV, 206. 66. *Ibid.,* XXXX, 206. 67. Mrs. Jackson, 366. 68. *Ibid.,* 374. 69. Douglas, 203. 70. Mrs. Jackson, 377. 71. *Ibid.,* 375. 72. *Ibid.,* 376. 73. *Ibid.,* 377. 74. *Ibid.* 75. *S.H.S.P.,* XXXX, 25. 76. *Ibid.* 77. *Ibid.,* 26.

CHAPTER 30

1. Dabney, 595.        2. Hotchkiss Diary, December 5, 1862.        3. *Ibid.*, December 10, 1862.        4. *O.R.*, XXI, 1043–1044.        5. *Ibid.*, 1047.        6. Freeman—*LL*, II, 333.        7. Alexander, 289.        8. *B. & L.*, III, 87.        9. Bruce Catton, *Glory Road*, 48. Hereafter Catton—*G.R.*        10. *B. & L.*, III, 75.  11. *Ibid.*, 87.        12. Catton—*G.R.*, 49.        13. *O.R.*, XXI, 90.        14. Details of Jackson's moves are from Hotchkiss Diary, December 12, 1862.  15. von Borcke, II, 109, 110.        16. *S.H.S.P.*, XXXX, 28.        17. *O.R.*, XXI, 643.        18. *Ibid.*, 630.        19. *Ibid.*, 645.        20. *Ibid.*, 653–654.  21. *Ibid.*, 636–637.        22. von Borcke, II, 106.        23. *O.R.*, XXI, 657.  24. Dabney, 610.        25. R. K. Charles in *Confederate Veteran*, XIV, 66.  26. J. P. Smith, *W. S. Lacy, A Memorial*, 29. Hereafter Smith—*Lacy*.  27. Douglas, 205.        28. Smith—*Lacy*, 29.        29. von Borcke, II, 114; Freeman—*LL*, II, 454.        30. Dabney, 611.        31. *O.R.*, XXI, 487.        32. Mrs. Jackson, 383.        33. *B. & L.*, III, 140.        34. *O.R.*, XXI, 632.        35. *Ibid.*, 633.        36. Henderson, II, 353.        37. Dabney, 613.        38. *O.R.*, XXI, 647.        39. *Ibid.*, 635.        40. *Ibid.*, 142, including casualties in the divisions of Birney, Sickles, and Burns in addition to those of the Left Grand Division.  41. Alexander, 309.        42. *O.R.*, XXI, 290.        43. The casualties are to be found in *O.R.*, XXI, 129–142 for Federal forces, 558–562 for Confederate forces.        44. Cooke—*Lee*, 184.        45. *O.R.*, XXI, 290.        46. *B. & L.*, III, 85.        47. Alexander, 313.        48. All casualty figures are from reports in *O.R.*, XXI, 558–562 and 129–142.        49. Cooke—*Lee*, 232.        50. Dabney, 620.        51. *O.R.*, XXI, 643.        52. *Ibid.*, 647.        53. *Ibid.*, 652.  54. Hood, 49.        55. *O.R.*, XXI, 666.        56. *Pendleton*, 246.        57. *O.R.*, XXI, 634.        58. Freeman—*Lee*, II, 466.        59. *S.H.S.P.*, XXXX, 32.  60. *O.R.*, XXI, 544.        61. *S.H.S.P.*, XXXX, 32.        62. *Ibid.*        63. *Ibid.*  64. Dabney, 623.        65. The account that follows is from Smith, *S.H.S.P.*, XXXX, 34, who probably was present and certainly near by.        66. Freeman—*LL*, II, 374.        67. *B. & L.*, III, 116.        68. Hood, 50.        69. *B. &L.*, III, 127.        70. Henderson, II, 327.        71. Margaret Junkin Preston, *Century Magazine*, Vol. XXXII (New Series X), October 1886, 157, 159.        72. Dabney, 626.        73. *O.R.*, XXI, 556.        74. *Ibid.*, 641.        75. *Ibid.*, 647.  76. *Ibid.*, 667.

CHAPTER 31

1. *S.H.S.P.*, XXXXIII, 37.        2. Fishburne Narrative.        3. *S.H.S.P.*, XXXXIII, 38; Douglas, 208.        4. Mrs. Jackson, 386.        5. W. B. Taliaferro in Mrs. Jackson—*Memoirs*, 526.        6. *S.H.S.P.*, XXXXIII, 38.        7. *Ibid.*        8. H. A. White, *Robert E. Lee and the Southern Confederacy*, 244. Hereafter White—*Lee*.        9. *O.R.*, XXV, pt. 2, 4.        10. Henderson, II, 381.        11. Hotchkiss Diary, December 21, 1862.        12. Mrs. Jackson, 412.        13. Allan in *S.H.S.P.*, XXXXIII, 123.        14. Hotchkiss Papers, Box 9. Report on Romney Campaign, January 10, 1862.        15. Hotchkiss Diary, March 29, 1863.        16. *Ibid.*, April 4, 1863.        17. *Ibid.*, April 4, 11, 15, 1863.        18. *Ibid.*, April 6, 1863.  19. *S.H.S.P.*, XXXXIII, 39.        20. *Ibid.*, 40.        21. Dabney, 634.        22. Jack-

son's Letter Book, January 14, 1863.    23. *Ibid.*, February 10, 1863.
24. Douglas, 213.    25. *Ibid.*    26. Freeman—*LL*, II, 500.    27. Jackson's
Letter Book, March 2, 1863.    28. *O.R.*, XXV, pt. 2, 1005.    29. Freeman—
*LL*, II, 701.    30. Jackson's Letter Book, February 16, 1863.    31. *Ibid.*,
March 6, 1863.    32. *O.R.*, XXV, pt. 2, 687.    33. Jackson's Letter Book,
March 30, 1863.    34. *Ibid.*, October 30, 1862.    35. Hotchkiss Diary,
January 23, 1863.    36. *O.R.*, XXV, pt. 2, 633.    37. *Ibid.*, 644.    38. *Ibid.*,
645–646.    39. Jackson's Letter Book, April 14, 1863.    40. *Ibid.*, February
11, 1863.    41. *O.R.*, XIX, pt. 2, 731.    42. *Ibid.*, 732.    43. *Ibid.*
44. Other details of this part of the Jackson-Hill controversy are to be found
in Freeman—*LL*, II, 512 ff.    45. *O.R.*, XXV, pt. 2, 786.    46. Jackson
Papers, April 24, 1863; Freeman—*LL*, II, 514.    47. *O.R.*, XXV, pt. 2, 786.
48. *Ibid.*, XXI, 1095.    49. Longstreet, 323.    50. *Ibid.*, 65; see Chapter 20,
Valley II, at Reference 9.    51. Freeman—*LL*, II, 468.    52. *B. & L.*, II,
405.    53. *Ibid.*, 524.    54. *S.H.S.P.*, XXXIX, 104.    55. McGuire to
Hotchkiss, June 27, 1896, Hotchkiss Papers, Box 12.    56. *S.H.S.P.*, XIV, 213,
214.    57. Viscount Wolseley, "An English View of the Civil War," *North
American Review*, July, 1889, 39. Hereafter Wolseley—*N.A. Review*.
58. *B. & L.*, II, 299; Wolseley—*N.A. Review*, 39.    59. Henderson, II, 342.
60. Mrs. Jackson—*Memoirs*, 504.    61. J. William Jones, *Christ in the Camp*, 89.
62. Hotchkiss in his diary recorded the weather systematically.    63. Worsham, 156; Moore, 172.    64. *O.R.*, II, 130.    65. *S.H.S.P.*, XXXXIII, 37 ff.;
Douglas, 209.    66. Mrs. Jackson, 393; J. P. Smith, *Stonewall Jackson and
Chancellorsville*, 5. Hereafter Smith—*Jackson*.    67. Freeman—*LL*, II, 507.
68. Mrs. Jackson, 394.    69. Dabney, 637.    70. Henderson, II, 390.
71. Hotchkiss Diary, April 14, 1863.    72. Mrs. Jackson, 411.    73. Smith—
*Jackson*, 5 ff.    74. Robert Stiles, *Four Years under Marse Robert*, 190.
75. London *Times*, June 11, 1863.    76. Henderson, II, 390.    77. Smith in
*S.H.S.P.*, XXXX, 41.    78. von Borcke, II, 178.    79. Mrs. Jackson, 405.
80. Mrs. Jackson, 410. Jackson requested Anna at the same time not to have
much gold braid about any pantaloons she might have made for him. Mrs.
Jackson, 422.    81. Hotchkiss Diary, February 23, 1863.    82. *Ibid.*, various
dates in January and February.    83. Douglas, 209.    84. Mrs. Jackson, 415.
85. Hotchkiss Diary, January 3, 7, 1863.    86. *Ibid.*, December 21, 1862.
87. *Ibid.*, April 4, 1863.    88. *Ibid.*, April 15, 1863.    89. *Ibid.*, April 14,
1863.    90. Smith—*Jackson*, 5 ff.    91. *S.H.S.P.*, XIX, 312.    92. *Ibid.*, 313.
93. Hotchkiss Diary, April 14, 1863.    94. *Ibid.*, April 18, 1863.    95. Dabney, 660.    96. *"Virginian's"—Jackson*, 394.    97. Henderson, II, 398.
98. *Ibid.*, 346.    99. Dabney, 636.    100. Hotchkiss Diary, January 2, 1863.
101. Mrs. Jackson, 421–422.    102. Especially in Henderson, II, 396.
103. Mrs. Jackson, 419.    104. Smith in *S.H.S.P.*, XXXX, 42.    105. All
reports on presents are from Jackson's letters to Anna. Mrs. Jackson, 405, 412,
414, 415, 417.    106. Dabney, 640.    107. *Ibid.*, 641.    108. *Ibid.*
109. *Ibid.*, 642.    110. Mrs. Jackson, 401.    111. Dabney, 643.    112. *Ibid.*,
644.    113. Douglas, 212.    114. Dabney, 645.    115. *Ibid.*, 646.
116. Mrs. Jackson, 398.    117. Dabney, 651.    118. Hotchkiss Diary, March

29, 1863.      119. *Pendleton*, 254.      120. Smith—*Lacy*, 45.      121. *S.H.S.P.*,
XXI, 26.      122. This quotation, and the following passages, are from letters
in Mrs. Jackson, 386, 387, 389, 411.      123. Douglas, 217.      124. Mrs.
Jackson, 429.      125. *Ibid.*, 427.      126. *Ibid.*, 427–428.      127. Hotchkiss
Diary, April 29, 1863.      128. *B. & L.*, III, 233.      129. Mrs. Jackson, 430.
130. *Ibid.*

CHAPTER 32

1. *S.H.S.P.*, XXXX, 44.      2. John Bigelow, Jr., *The Campaign of Chancellorsville,* 36. Hereafter Bigelow.      3. Bigelow, 6.      4. Sandburg, 82, 92.
5. Mrs. Jackson, 432; Dabney, 666.      6. Dabney, 663.      7. Fitzhugh Lee in
*S.H.S.P.*, VII, 562; Henderson, II, 416.      8. *O.R.*, XXV, pt. 1, 850; Freeman—
*Lee*, II, 514.      9. Bigelow, 221.      10. *O.R.*, XXV, pt. 1, 171.      11. *Ibid.*,
pt. 2, 762.      12. Hotchkiss Diary, May 1, 1863.      13. Bigelow, 236–237.
14. *Ibid.*      15. Bigelow, 245.      16. *Ibid.*, 247.      17. *S.H.S.P.*, XI, 137.
18. *O.R.*, XXV, pt. 1, 670.      19. *Ibid.*, pt. 2, 764.      20. *Ibid.*, pt. 1, 1049.
21. Bigelow, 253.      22. *O.R.*, XXV, pt. 2, 326.      23. *Ibid.*, 328.      24. Alexander K. McClure, *Recollections of Half a Century*, 348.      25. Bigelow, 255.
26. *O.R.*, XXV, pt. 2, 764.      27. Reports of the talk between Lee and Jackson rest on Col. Charles Marshall of Lee's staff and Maj. T. M. R. Talcott,
Lee's aide, as set forth in the latter's "General Lee's Strategy at the Battle of
Chancellorsville" in *S.H.S.P.*, XXXIV, 13. It includes statements by Marshall.
Both were present during part of the conference.      28. *O.R.*, XXV, pt. 1, 866.
29. Talcott, *op. cit.*      30. Maj. T. M. R. Talcott, Lee's aide.      31. Freeman—
*LL*, II, 542.      32. John Esten Cooke, *Stonewall Jackson, A Military Biography*
(1866 edition), 411. Hereafter Cooke—*Jackson.*      33. Dabney, 676.
34. A. L. Long, *Memoirs of Robert E. Lee*, 258.      35. Hotchkiss described
the setting and conversation that followed in detail in a letter to Henderson
that appears in Henderson, II, 432.      36. *S.H.S.P.*, XXXXIII, 47.      37. *O.R.*,
XXV, pt. 1, 940. This is the report of Rodes ("about 8 o'clock"), whose
division led the advance. Most reports say "early in the morning" or words to
that effect. Henderson indicates (Henderson, II, 433) 4:30 A.M., but that
seems too early.      38. *S.H.S.P.*, XXXXIII, 47.      39. *O.R.*, XXV, pt. 1, 408.
Bigelow has many details.      40. *Ibid.*, 386.      41. *B. & L.*, III, 183.
42. Henderson, II, 436 n.      43. Fitzhugh Lee in *S.H.S.P.*, VII, 511.
44. Freeman in *LL*, II, 555, noted that it was an old tradition at the Virginia
State Library, where the original dispatch was on display many years, that
Jackson wrote the dispatch on the pommel of his saddle. Smith wrote (*B. & L.*,
III, 206), "I found the General seated on a stump by the Brock Road writing
this dispatch. . . ."      45. *B. & L.*, III, 195.      46. Bigelow, 276.      47. These
reports are listed in detail in Bigelow, 287 ff., and A. C. Hamlin, *The Battle of
Chancellorsville*, Chapter 6. Hereafter Hamlin.      48. The time is uncertain,
ranging in formal reports from 3 P.M. to beyond 6 P.M. The most frequent
choices are 5:15 and a little before 6 P.M. See Bigelow, 295.      49. *B. & L.*,
III, 208.      50. Hamlin, 64; Bigelow, 295.      51. Hamlin, 64; Henderson, II,
442; Bigelow, 297.      52. *O.R.*, XXV, pt. 1, 654.      53. *Ibid.*, 975, 995.

54. *Ibid.*, 974.        55. Oliver Otis Howard, *Autobiography*, I, 368.
56. *B. & L.*, III, 184.        57. Hamlin, 148.        58. Bigelow, 304.        59. *O.R.*,
XXV, pt. 1, 960.        60. Dabney, 683.        61. All these quotations are from
battle reports in *O.R.*, XXV, pt. 1, 798, 885, 941, 951, 966, 985, 992,
1004, 1009.        62. Casler, 144.        63. *S.H.S.P.*, XXIX, 330.        64. *Ibid.*,
XXXVIII, 284.        65. von Borcke, II, 225.        66. Cooke–*Jackson*, 416.
67. *S.H.S.P.*, XXIX, 331.        68. Mrs. Jackson, 440.        69. *O.R.*, XXV, pt. 1,
916.        70. Kyle in *Confederate Veteran*, IV, 308.        71. *S.H.S.P.*, VIII,
494.        72. *C.M.H.*, III, 385.        73. Hamlin, 107, 108.        74. Bigelow, 317;
Hamlin, 109.        75. Cooke–*Jackson*, 419.        76. *O.R.*, XXV, pt. 1, 916.
77. Hamlin, 106.        78. Hamlin says "Sergeant Corvan" commanded that
part of the skirmish line (Hamlin, 106). Lieutenant Colonel Cowan commanded that part of it, was present, and seems more likely to have given the
order (*O.R.*, XXV, pt. 1, 922).        79. Morrison in *The Land We Love*, I,
181. Freeman argues convincingly (Freeman–*LL*, II, 564) that this unsigned
account must have been written by Morrison. Major Barry does not appear
to have been severely criticized or held back in military advancement for
giving the order to fire. Before the war was over he was promoted to lieutenant
colonel and colonel, and temporarily to brigadier general (*N. C. Regiments*,
II, 41, 63).        80. Bigelow, 317. But Hamlin, 110, says eighty yards. Morrison
and Capt. W. F. Randolph indicate the distance was much shorter than that.
See Randolph's pamphlet, "With Stonewall Jackson at Chancellorsville."
81. Wilbourn in *S.H.S.P.*, VI, 266.        82. Randolph in *S.H.S.P.*, XXIX, 335.
83. It may have been Kyle.        84. Wilbourn was therefore the only witness
to many of these events. His account in *S.H.S.P.*, VI, 266, is detailed.
85. Cooke–*Jackson*, 421.        86. Leigh wrote an account of these experiences,
published in *S.H.S.P.*, VI, 230, from which details have been used.        87. None
of those present told later of Barr's examination, nor is any report by him
known to exist.        88. Bigelow, 318.        89. Wilbourn in *S.H.S.P.*, VI, 270.
90. Dabney, 689.        91. Cooke–*Jackson*, 427. This was Jackson's last order
in the field.        92. Dabney, 691.        93. Cooke–*Jackson*, 429.        94. McGuire's
narrative of these events is in the *Richmond Medical Journal*, May, 1866.
Hereafter McGuire's Narrative.        95. In Dabney, 695, Jackson is reported
as saying during the operation, "Dr. McGuire, I am lying very comfortably."
Dabney obtained much of his information on this period from Smith, who,
however, did not himself report any words from Jackson during the operation.
96. He has not been identified. He may have been Dr. J. William Walls of
the Winchester Medical College faculty before the war. See Wyndham B.
Blanton, *Medicine in Virginia in the 19th Century*, 18.        97. Dabney, 696.

CHAPTER 33

1. *O.R.*, XXV, pt. 1, 887.        2. *Ibid.*, 942.        3. Cooke–*Jackson*, 238.        4. *O.R.*,
XXV, pt. 2, 769.        5. *S.H.S.P.*, VIII, 230 ff.        6. *O.R.*, XXV, pt. 2, 769.
7. Dabney, 703; Freeman–*LL*, 597; Henderson, II, 459.        8. *O.R.*, XXV, pt.
2, 769.        9. *B. & L.*, III, 214.        10. What follows is based on Lacy's report
of Jackson's views as told to Dabney and recorded in Dabney, 707.

11. Douglas said he spent an hour with Jackson. Douglas, 226.     12. Dabney, 709.     13. *Ibid.*, 711.     14. *Ibid.;* Hotchkiss Diary, May 4, 1863.     15. Dabney, 713.     16. *Ibid.*, 710.     17. McGuire's Narrative.     18. *Ibid.;* Freeman—*LL*, II, 660.     19. McGuire's Narrative.     20. They are incorporated in Dabney, 707, 724.     21. Mrs. Jackson, 461.     22. Dabney, 720–721. 23. *Ibid.*, 716.     24. The following narrative is based on Mrs. Jackson, 462–467, unless otherwise stated.     25. Dabney, 718.     26. Neither has been positively identified. McGuire knew Dr. J. P. Smith, who had joined the Second Virginia Infantry of Jackson's First Brigade as surgeon in July of 1861. There was also an assistant surgeon, Dr. John Smith, in the regiment. 27. Mrs. Jackson, 466.     28. *Pendleton*, 271.     29. McGuire's Narrative. 30. Mrs. Jackson, 467.     31. McGuire's Narrative.     32. McGuire's language after saying the General asked him, "Is it so?" is merely, "When he was answered," etc. But there seems no doubt that McGuire was frank with him. 33. The following conversation and the description of Julia's visit to the bedside are from Mrs. Jackson, 470.     34. Mrs. Jackson, 467; McGuire's Narrative. 35. McGuire's Narrative.     36. *Ibid.*     37. *O.R.*, XXV, pt. 2, 791.     38. *Ibid.* 39. *Ibid.*, 792.     40. *Ibid.*, 793.     41. *Ibid.*, pt. 1, 803.     42. Davis, II, 365. 43. *O.R.*, IV, pt. 2, 994.     44. J. William Jones, *Life and Letters of Robert Edward Lee*, 242.     45. May 24, 1863; *Confederate Veteran*, XXXI, 287. 46. Freeman—*Lee*, III, 1.     47. Hood, 52.     48. London *Times*, June 16, 1863.     49. R. E. Lee, Jr., *Recollections and Letters of General Robert E. Lee*, 94.     50. Margaret Junkin Preston's Journal, May 12, 1863, 164.     51. Freeman—*Lee*, III, 153.     52. Mrs. Jackson, 472.     53. Douglas, 229. 54. Casler, 155.     55. Richmond, Va., *Dispatch*, May 12, 1863.     56. Mrs. Jackson, 474.     57. Douglas, 38.     58. J. B. Jones, *A Rebel War Clerk's Diary*, 321. Hereafter *R.W.C.D.*     59. Richmond, Va., *Dispatch*, May 13, 1863.     60. *R.W.C.D.*, 321.     61. Mrs. Jackson, 475.     62. *Ibid.*, 476. 63. *Ibid.*, 477.     64. Margaret Junkin Preston's Journal, May 10, 1863, 164. 65. Couper, II, 188.     66. A description of Dr. White reading Jackson's letter of condolence to him about his son is found in a memorial sermon delivered in June, 1863, by Dr. Ramsey and published in pamphlet form under the title of "True Eminence Founded on Holiness," for a copy of which the author is indebted to Robert C. de Rosset of Lynchburg.     67. Margaret Junkin Preston's Journal, May 15, 1863, 165.     68. *Ibid.*     69. Quotations from these newspapers were published by the Richmond, Va., *Dispatch* on May 15, 1863.     70. Cook, 170–172; Sandburg, II, 464.     71. Douglas, 239. 72. Freeman—*Lee*, IV, 475.

# PRINCIPAL MANUSCRIPT SOURCES

The principal manuscript sources and the principal printed works used in the preparation of these volumes are listed below. Newspaper sources are identified in the text, the footnotes, or the list of references.

The Roy Bird Cook Collection, Charleston, West Virginia. Letters, documents, souvenirs, books, and material of many kinds relating to the Jackson family and connected families and friends, including much material relating to Thomas Jonathan Jackson, especially his early years.

The United States Military Academy records and library, including material relating to cadet life in the 1840's and to Jackson's own career as a cadet.

The Arnold Papers, chiefly letters written by Jackson to his sister, Laura Jackson, later Mrs. Jonathan Arnold, from the time he went to West Point in 1842 until the time he went to war in 1861. Many letters (with some excisions) are in *Early Life and Letters of General Thomas J. Jackson ("Stonewall" Jackson)*, by his nephew, Thomas Jackson Arnold. Others are in the University of Virginia (Alderman) Library. Photostats of many are in the Library of Congress, Manuscript Division.

The Jackson Papers. These are widely scattered. Some are in the Arnold Papers. The largest collection of Jackson's war papers is in the Jedediah Hotchkiss Collection, Library of Congress, Manuscript Division, including Hotchkiss' copying of Jackson's Letter Book.

The Jackson-French Papers. The entire collection of letters and documents relating to the controversy at Fort Meade, with only a few exceptions, is in the National Archives.

The Margaret Junkin Preston Papers. In the Southern Historical Collection, University of North Carolina (Wilson) Library, Chapel Hill.

The Virginia Military Institute files and library. Voluminous material relating to cadets, faculty members, administrative officials, and the life of the Institute and of Lexington, including much about Jackson.

The Couper Collection. Col. William Couper, of Lexington, for many years an administrative official at the Institute, who has done much to add to, and to clarify, knowledge about Jackson, especially the ten years in Lexington, has a large amount of material relating to Jackson's life in Lexington and to many men connected with him then and later.

The Washington and Lee University Library. Letters and documents relating to Lexington history and personalities, as well as the history of the university.

The Virginia Historical Society. Documents and letters, by and to Jackson, and relating to him and to the war.

The Davidson College Library. Letters relating to Jackson's visit to the college in July, 1857.

The University of Virginia (Alderman) Library. Letters, documents, and pertinent books related to, or connected with, persons and incidents of Jackson's life, including his application for membership in the university faculty.

The University of North Carolina (Wilson) Library, Southern Historical Collection. Included are many copies of Jackson's wartime papers and documents; the large Pendleton Collection, including many letters to and from William Nelson Pendleton, his wife, Anzolette E. Page Pendleton, and their son, Alexander S. Pendleton; the large Henry Kyd Douglas Collection; the James A. Walker Memoirs; the William Allan Papers; the Dabney Papers, and others.

The Duke University Library. Many letters and documents, including the Boteler Papers, the Munford Papers, some R. E. Lee letters, some Jackson letters, some Douglas letters, and many military documents of organizations commanded by Jackson or associated with him.

The R. B. Garnett Papers in the Confederate Museum, Richmond, Virginia.

The Jedediah Hotchkiss Collection in the Library of Congress, Manuscript Division. This is an immense collection, including Hotchkiss' wartime diary, his copies of Jackson's orders and letters, and his long correspondence after the war with Hunter McGuire, R. L. Dabney, G. F. R. Henderson, and others regarding facts, figures, conditions, disputed points in operations and events, and personalities.

The Library of Congress, Manuscript Division, contains, in addition, letters and documents relating to Jackson.

The Union Theological Seminary, Richmond, Virginia, contains letters and documents relating to Jackson, his activities and the times.

The William B. Taliaferro Papers, at the family home in Gloucester County, Virginia, and in the library of the College of William and Mary in Williamsburg, Virginia.

The Clement D. Fishburne Manuscript, in the possession of Miss Anna Barringer, Charlottesville, Virginia.

The Clement D. Fishburne Narrative, in the possession of Mrs. Staige Blackford, Charlottesville, Virginia.

Battle Abbey (Confederate Memorial Institute), Richmond, Virginia. Documents, drawings, portraits, and also the remnants of Jackson's library.

The Henry E. Huntington Library, San Marino, California, has in its J. E. B. Stuart Collection important letters relating to Jackson.

# SHORT-TITLE INDEX

### (Cumulative for Volumes I and II)

*Cadet Life.* Cadet Life Before the Mexican War. Foreword by Lieut. Col. William J. Morton, United States Army.

*Calderon.* Mme. Calderon de la Barca. Life in Mexico.

*Casler.* John O. Casler. Four Years in the Stonewall Brigade.

*Catton—G. R.* Bruce Catton. Glory Road.

*Catton—Lincoln.* Bruce Catton. Mr. Lincoln's Army.

*Chesnut.* Mrs. Mary Boykin Chesnut. A Diary from Dixie.

*C.M.H.* Confederate Military History. Clement A. Evans, editor.

*Commager.* H. S. Commager. The Blue and the Gray.

*Cook.* Roy Bird Cook. The Family and Early Life of Stonewall Jackson.

*Cooke—Jackson.* John Esten Cooke. Stonewall Jackson, A Military Biography (1866 Edition).

*Cooke—Lee.* John Esten Cooke. Life of General Robert E. Lee.

*Cooke—Stonewall Brigade.* Stonewall Jackson and the Old Stonewall Brigade.

*Couper.* Col. William Couper. One Hundred Years at V.M.I.

*Craven.* Avery Craven. Edmund Ruffin, Southerner.

*D.A.B.* Dictionary of American Biography.

*Dabney.* Robert L. Dabney. Life and Campaigns of Lieut.-Gen. Thomas J. Jackson.

*Davis.* Jefferson Davis. The Rise and Fall of the Confederate Government.

*Davis—Stonewall.* Burke Davis. They Called Him Stonewall.

*de Fontaine.* Felix Gregory de Fontaine ("Personne"). Marginalia or Gleanings from an Army Notebook.

*Douglas.* Henry Kyd Douglas. I Rode with Stonewall.

*Dowdey.* Clifford Dowdey. Experiment in Rebellion.

*Early.* Jubal A. Early. Operations on the Line of Bull Run.

*Eckenrode.* H. J. Eckenrode and Bryan Conrad. James Longstreet, Lee's War Horse.

*Eliot.* Ellsworth Eliot, Jr. West Point in the Confederacy.

*Ewell.* R. S. Ewell. The Making of a Soldier.

*Fairbanks.* George R. Fairbanks. History of Florida.

*Freeman—Lee.* Douglas Southall Freeman. R. E. Lee.

*Freeman—LL.* Douglas Southall Freeman. Lee's Lieutenants.

*Fremantle.* James Arthur Lyon Fremantle. The Fremantle Story.

*Gordon.* John B. Gordon. Personal Recollections of the Civil War.

*Graham.* Henry Tucker Graham. An Old Manse.

*MacRae.* David MacRae. The Americans at Home.

*Mansfield.* Edward D. Mansfield. The Mexican War.

*Maury.* Dabney H. Maury. Recollections of a Virginian.

*Mayer.* Brantz Mayer. Mexico as It Was and as It Is.

*McCarthy.* Carlton McCarthy. Detailed Minutiae of Soldier Life in the
   Army of Northern Virginia, 1861–1865.

*McClellan.* G. B. McClellan. McClellan's Own Story.

*McClellan.* H. B. McClellan. The Life and Campaigns of Maj. Gen.
   J. E. B. Stuart.

*McClure.* Alexander K. McClure. Recollections of Half a Century.

*McDonald.* W. N. McDonald. A History of the Laurel Brigade.

*Meade.* Robert D. Meade. Judah P. Benjamin, Confederate Statesman.

*Metcalf.* Clyde H. Metcalf. A History of the United States Marine Corps.

*Mexican Reports.* United States Senate Executive Document, first session,
   30th Congress.

*Moore.* E. A. Moore. The Story of a Cannoneer under Stonewall Jackson.

*N. C. Regiments.* Histories of the Several Regiments and Battalions from
   North Carolina in the Great War, 1861–65. Edited by Walter Clark.

*Nevins.* Allan Nevins. The Ordeal of the Union.

*Nichols.* Roy Frank Nichols. Franklin Pierce—Young Hickory of the
   Granite Hills.

*Niles.* Blair Niles. Passengers to Mexico.

*Noll.* Arthur Howard Noll. General Kirby Smith.

*Oakes.* W. C. Oakes. The War Between the Union and the Confederacy.

*O.R.* War of the Rebellion: Official Records of the Union and Confederate Armies.

*Pendleton.* Susan P. Lee. Memoirs of William Nelson Pendleton.

*Poague.* William Thomas Poague. Gunner with Stonewall, edited by
   Monroe F. Cockrell.

*Randolph.* Sarah Nicholas Randolph. The Life of General Thomas J.
   Jackson.

*Rice.* Harvey M. Rice. The Life of Jonathan M. Bennett.

*Richardson.* Charles B. Richardson. Southern Generals.

*R.O.C.* The Register of Officers and Cadets of the United States Military
   Academy.

*R.W.C.D.* J. B. Jones. A Rebel War Clerk's Diary.

*Sandburg.* Carl Sandburg. Abraham Lincoln, the War Years.

*Schenck.* Martin Schenck. Up Came Hill: The Story of the Light Division and Its Leaders.

# INDEX

517